Murderous Elite

The Waffen-SS and its record of atrocities

James Pontolillo

For the SS man, one principle must apply absolutely:
we must be honest, decent, loyal, and comradely
to members of our own blood, and to no one else.

Speech by Reichsführer-SS Heinrich Himmler before SS leaders at Posen
[4 October 1943, U.S. National Archives document 242.256, audio recording]

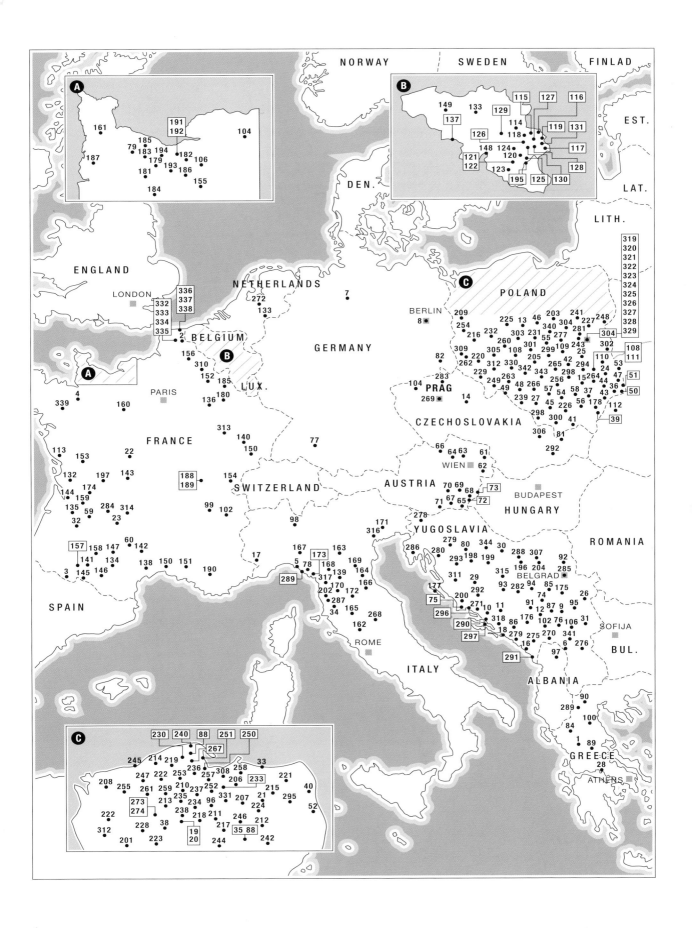

Atrocities Master List Map West

1 Agios Georgios [Greece]
2 Ascq [France]
3 Bagneres-de-Bigorre [France]
4 Bais [France]
5 Bardine de San Terenzo [Italy]
6 Bela Crkva [Yugoslavia]
7 Bergen-Belsen [Germany]
8 Berlin [Germany]
9 Biserske Livada [Yugoslavia] see Goc
10 Bisko [Yugoslavia] see Split
11 Blazevici [Yugoslavia]
12 Blazevo [Yugoslavia]
13 Blonie [Poland]
14 Bohmen-Mahren [Czechoslovakia]
15 Bor Kunowski [Poland]
16 Boronjina [Yugoslavia] see Blazevo
17 Boves [Italy]
18 Bozominu [Yugoslavia] see Blazevo
19 Bydgoszcz 1 [Poland]
20 Bydgoszcz 2 [Poland]
21 Bzura [Poland]
22 Carsac-de-Carlux [France]
23 Chateau Valencay [France]
24 Chelm [Poland]
25 Ciepielow [Poland]
26 Crvenka [Yugoslavia]
27 Czestochowa [Poland]
28 Dhistomon [Greece]
29 Dola [Yugoslavia]
30 Dolac Donji [Yugoslavia] see Otok Cornji
31 Domisevina [Yugoslavia] see Blazevo
32 Dunes [France]
33 East Prussia [Germany]
34 Farneta Monastery [Italy]
35 Farnocchia [Italy]

14. Waffen-Grenadier-
Division-der-SS (ukrainische
Nr. 1) Crimes in Poland Borow
36 Chodaczkow Wielki
37 Goscieradow
38 Gozdow
39 Huta Pieniacka
40 Jaminy
41 Jamna
42 Kaszow
43 Majdan Nowy
44 Majdan Stary
45 Minoga/Barbarka
46 Mlynow
47 Obrowiec
48 Palikrowy
49 Podkamien
50 Poturzyn
51 Prehoryle
52 Siemianowka
53 Smoligow
54 Szczecyn
55 Wicyn
56 Wolka Szczecka
57 Zagaje
58 Zaklikow

59 Fraysinnet-le-Gelat [France]
60 Gabaudet [France]
61 Gau Niederdonau [Austria]
62 Eisenstadt
63 Leiben
64 Lunz am See Thenneberg
65 Nikolsburg
66 Persenbeug
67 Gau Steiermark [Austria]

68 Deutsch-Schützen
69 Egelsdorf
70 Gratkorn
71 Nestelbach
72 Prebensdorf
73 Rechnitz
74 Goc [Yugoslavia]
75 Gornji-Dolac [Yugoslavia] see Split
76 Gradac [Yugoslavia] see Blazevo
77 Grafeneck Castle [Germany]
78 Gragnola [Italy] see Vinca di Fivizzano
79 Graignes [France]
80 Grubisnjici [Yugoslavia]
81 Hnevosice [Czechoslovakia]
82 Horka [Germany]
83 Ilinci [Yugoslavia] see Blazevo
84 Ioannina [Greece]
85 Ivanjica [Yugoslavia] see Goc
86 Jablanica [Yugoslavia]
87 Jablanica-Prozor Railline [Yugoslavia]
88 Jaroszew [Poland]
89 Karpenisi [Greece]
90 Klisoura [Greece]
91 Kopaonik [Yugoslavia]
92 Kosutica [Yugoslavia]
93 Krivodol [Yugoslavia]
94 Kriva Reka [Yugoslavia]
95 Krusevca [Yugoslavia] see Liga
96 Ksiazki [Poland]
97 Kukes [Albania]
98 Lago Maggiore [Italy]
99 L'Arbresle [France]
100 Larisa [Greece]
101 Legatori [Yugoslavia]
102 Lentilly [France]
103 Le Paradis [France]
104 Lidice [Czechoslovakia]
105 Liga [Yugoslavia]
106 Livarot [France]
107 Lodz [Poland]
108 Lublin [Poland]
109 Lublin District [Poland]
110 Lublin/Majdanek [Poland]
111 Lublin - Aktion Erntefest [Poland]
112 Lvov [Poland]
113 Maille [France]
114 Malmedy [Belgium]
115 Baugnez Crossroads
116 Büllingen
117 Butai
118 Cheneux
119 Honsfeld
120 La Gleize
121 Ligneuville
122 Ligneuville-Stavelot Road
123 Lutre Bois
124 Parfondruy
125 Petit Thier
126 Rahier
127 Stavelot
128 Stoumont
129 Trois Ponts
130 Wanne
131 Wereth

Miscellaneous Atrocities
132 Angouleme [France]
133 Arnhem [Netherlands]
134 Aussone [France]
135 Bazens [France]
136 Flavigny [France]
137 Franco-Belgian border

138 Gard [France]
139 Guardistallo [Italy]
140 Jussey [France]
141 Justiniac [France]
142 Leshoguen [France]
143 Limoges [France]
144 Lussac [France]
145 Marsoulas [France]
146 Miremont [France]
147 Montauban [France]
148 Navaugle [France]
149 Nerstal [France]
150 Nimes [France]
151 Permez [France]
152 Plomion [France]
153 Poitiers [France]
154 St. Denis [France]
155 St. Martin [France]
156 St. Venant [France]
157 Tarbes [France]
158 Toulouse [France]
159 Vergt de Biron [France]
160 des Verrieres [France]
161 Yuret [France]
162 Monte Sol [Italy]
163 Caprara
164 Casaglia
165 Casoni di Bavellino
166 Casoni di Riomoneta
167 Cerpiano
168 Creda
169 Marzabotto
170 Pioppe di Salvaro
171 San Giovanni di Sopra & di Sotto
172 Sperticano
173 Monzone [Italy] see Vinca di Fivizzano
174 Mussidan [France]
175 Niksic [Yugoslavia]
176 Niksic-Avtovac Railroad
177 Line [Yugoslavia]
178 Nisko [Poland]
179 Normandy [France]
180 Ancienne Abbaye Ardenne
181 Argentan
182 Authie/Buron
183 Bretteville l'Orgueilleuse
184 Chateau d'Audrieu
185 Fontenay-le-Pesnel
186 Galmanche
187 Le Haut du Bosq
188 Le Mesnil-Patry 1
189 Le Mesnil-Patry 2
190 Les Fains
191 Les Saullets 1
192 Les Saullets 2
193 Mouen
194 St. Sulpice
195 Noville-lez-Bastogne [Belgium]
196 Novi Sad [Yugoslavia]
197 Oradour-sur-Glane [France]
198 Osekovo [Yugoslavia]
199 Otok Cornji [Yugoslavia]
200 Ovrlje [Yugoslavia]
201 Owinsk [Poland]
202 Padule di Fucecchio [Italy]
203 Palmiry [Poland]
204 Pancevo [Yugoslavia]

Poland Miscellaneous Atrocities
205 Aleksandrow
206 Bialochowo
207 Bialuty
208 Biesiekierz
209 Bolewice
210 Bralewnica
211 Buk-Goralski
212 Bursz
213 Bydgoszcz
214 Chojnice
215 Dabrowka
216 Debienko Forest
217 Dzialdowo
218 Grupa
219 Jaroszewy
220 Jedlec
221 Karolewo
222 Kcynia
223 Klecko
224 Komorniki
225 Konin
226 Koscielec
227 Kowalewice
228 Ksiaza
229 Lelazne
230 Lesno
231 Leszno
232 Lopatki
233 Lubichowo
234 Luszkowko
235 Malki
236 Nowy Wiec
237 Olek
238 Oscislowo
239 Panewnik
240 Piasnica
241 Pultusk Pultusk Poplawy
242 Roznowo Mlyn
243 Rozopole
244 Rumoka
245 Rusinowo
246 Rypin
247 Sadki
248 Sewerynowo
249 Siewierz
250 Skarszew
251 Skarszewy
252 Skorcz
253 Sliwice

254 Srem
255 Starogard
256 Swietokrzyz
257 Szpegawsk
258 Tczew
259 Tuchola
260 Turek
261 Wiecbork
262 Wypalanki
263 Wyszanow
264 Zajeziorze
265 Zdunska Wola
266 Zgierz
267 Polish Corridor [Poland]
268 Ponte Santa Lucia [Italy]
        see Vinca di Fivizzano
269 Prague [Czechoslovakia]
270 Pristina [Yugoslavia]
271 Putisic [Yugoslavia] see Split
272 Putten [Netherlands]
273 Radom [Poland]
274 Radom 2 [Poland]
275 Raskoj [Yugoslavia] see Goc
276 Ravniste [Yugoslavia] see Blazevo
277 Rawa Mazowiecka [Poland]
278 Razori [Yugoslavia]
279 Ripac [Yugoslavia]
280 Rodici [Yugoslavia] see Blazevo
281 Rozan [Poland]
282 Ruda [Yugoslavia] see Otok Cornji
283 Ruzyn [Czechoslovakia]
284 Saint Germain-du-Belair [France]
285 Sajmiste Camp, Belgrade [Yugoslavia]
286 Sancaku [Yugoslavia]
287 Sant'Anna di Stazzema [Italy]
288 Sava River / Brcko
289 Siatista [Greece]
290 Sinj [Yugoslavia]
291 Sladovil [Yugoslavia]
292 Slovak National Uprising [Slovakia]
293 Smilici [Yugoslavia]
294 Soltysy-Zabuce [Poland]
295 Sosnowiec [Poland]
296 Split-Sinj Region [Yugoslavia]
297 Srijane [Yugoslavia] see Split

SS-Kavallerie Operations
and Atrocities in Poland
298 Chelm-Sokal
299 Kamiena

300 Krakau
301 Kutno
302 Otwock
303 Ruda
304 Warsaw
305 Zgierz Prison
306 Stara Cernova [Czechoslovakia]
307 Stari Becej [Yugoslavia]
308 Szpegawsk [Poland]
309 Tarnow [Poland]
310 Tavaux-et-Pontsericourt [France]
311 Topoli [Yugoslavia]
312 Torzeniec [Poland]
313 Troyes [France]
314 Tulle [France]
315 Tuzla [Yugoslavia]
316 Valla [Italy]
317 Vinca di Fivizzano [Italy]
318 Vostane [Yugoslavia]
319 Warsaw Ghetto Uprising [Poland]
320 Warsaw Uprising [Poland]
321 Dluga Street Field Hospital
322 Grojecka Street
323 Maria Kazimiera Street
324 Marie Curie-Sklodowska Radium Institute
325 Opera House
326 Wawelberg Apartments
327 Wola District
328 Wola Hospital
329 Wolska Street
330 Warta River [Poland]
331 Wloclawek [Poland]
332 Wormhoudt [France]
333 East of Wormhoudt
334 Southwest of Wormhoudt
335 Town Square
336 Road to Dunkirk
337 British Dressing Station
338 Evacuation
339 La Plaine au Bois
340 Zakroczym [Poland]
341 Zapadne Morave [Yugoslavia] see Sancaku
342 Zborow [Poland]
343 Zdunska Wola [Poland]
344 Zhescin [Yugoslavia] see Goc

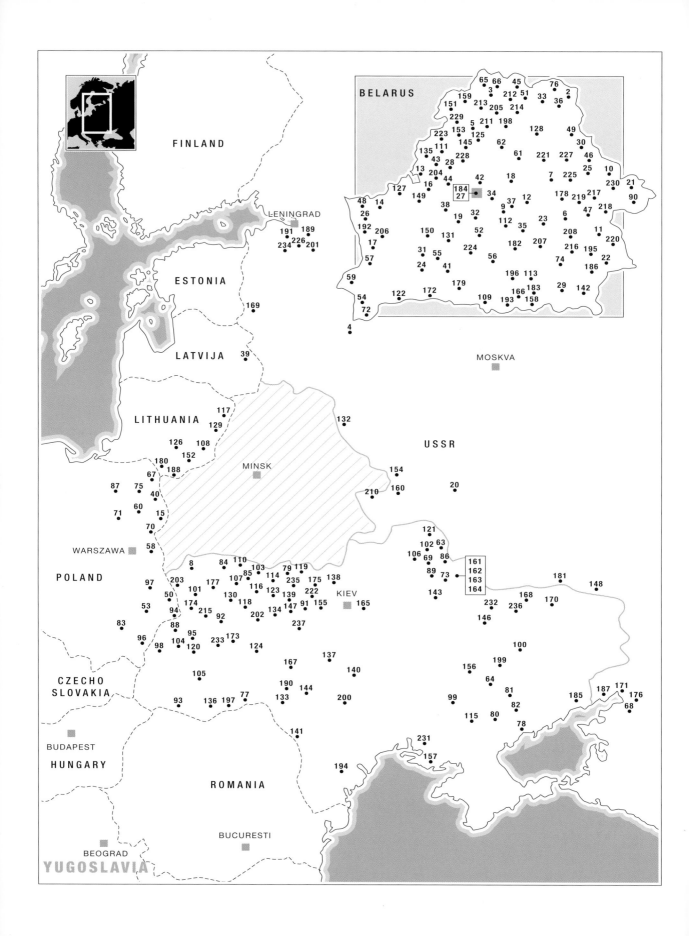

Atrocities Master List Map East

1   Babi Yar [USSR]

Dirlewanger Brigade
Operations & Atrocities
in the USSR
2   Antonopol
3   Belynici
4   Berezino
5   Besyady
6   Bobruisk
7   Bogushevichi
8   Bykhov
9   Cerven
10   Dobraya
11   Dobre Strazn
12   Drut River region
13   Dubniki
14   Dubrovo
15   Grodek
16   Ivenets
17   Jaswenski
18   Khutor
19   Kopyl
20   Kossino
21   Krugloye
22   Lugojsk
23   Ljada
24   Makawczyce
25   Manyly
26   Milevichi
27   Minsk
28   Molodecno
29   Moroc
30   Moshkovo
31   Nagornoye
32   Niemen River region
33   Novaya Niva
34   Novyye Lyady
35   Omgovichi
36   Orsa-Vitebsk road
37   Osipovici
38   Osovo
39   Petrovka
40   Plescenicy
41   Povarchitsky
42   Prilepy
43   Radoshkovichi
44   Rakov
45   Ratkovo
46   Rekota
47   Rogacov
48   Rudnia
49   Ryabki
50   Sakowschtschina-Makon road
51   Sloboda
52   Sluck
53   Smolevici
54   Starinski
55   Starobin
56   Staryye Velichkovichi
57   Svisloc
58   Wejna
59   Wieliczkowicze
60   Wieliczkowicze Nowe
61   Zabashevichi
62   Zembin
63   Zhodino
64   Dnepropetrovsk [USSR]
65   Dolhynov [USSR]

1. SS-Infanterie
(mot.)-Brigade Operations
& Atrocities in the USSR
66   Dolginovo
67   Augustow [Poland]
68   Badichany
69   Baturin
70   Bialokurowicze
71   Biehun
72   Blagowscht
73   Bobrik
74   Bol'Shiye Gorodyatichi
75   Boloschizy
76   Brashinka
77   Buda
78   Chernigovka
79   Chernobyl'
80   Dnjepr Bend
81   Dnjepr Islands
82   Dnjepropetrowsk
83   Duchanowka
84   Dvorishche
85   Yemil'chino
86   Fesovka
87   Fl. Ubortj
88   Fw. Bobruty
89   Gayvoron
90   Gorodets
91   Goroschki
92   Goryn' Valley
93   Goshcha
94   Gremjatheka
95   Hf. Krasnoje
96   Hrycow
97   Jeze [Poland]
98   Kaja
99   Kirovograd
100 Kolkhoz Boljark
101 Kolkhoz Federowka
102 Konotop
103 Korosten
104 Krasnoje
105 Krasuesselka
106 Krolevets
107 Kuliki
108 Kuniow
109 Lel'chitsy
110 Listvin
111 Lyuban'
112 Makarichi
113 Mal
114 Melini
115 Nikopol'
116 Norinsk
117 Novo Niropol
118 Ostrog
119 Ovruch
120 Petrikov
121 Putivl'
122 Radogoshch Ml.
123 Rudnia Czerwonka
124 Rudnia Worowskaja
125 Ryshanskaja
126 Rzepowszczyzna
127 Sch. Janow
128 Shadki
129 Skurowka
130 Slavuta
131 Sluch' Valley
132 Smolensk
133 Soblewka
134 Sokolov

135 Sorchi
136 Sselez
137 Ssilisowks
138 Stayki
139 Szepetowka
140 Terinzy
141 Tonorischtsche
142 Ubortj
143 Ubybaczki
144 Uman'
145 Urech'ye
146 Uschenskoje
147 Vil'sk
148 Vitebsk
149 Volozhyn
150 Weleniki
151 Woroff
152 Wydybor
153 Yuntseviche
154 Zaslavl'
155 Zhitomir
156 Zwiahel
157 Gejgowa/Kherson [USSR]
158 Gorych [USSR]
159 Hauptkommissariat Baranowicze [USSR]
160 Kamenets-Podol'skiy [USSR]
161 Kharkov 1 [USSR]
162 Kharkov 2 [USSR]
163 Kharkov 3 [USSR]
164 Kharkov 4 [USSR]
165 Kiev Region [USSR]
166 Lotoschinsk Psychiatric Clinic [USSR]
167 Brno [USSR]
168 Kharkov [USSR]
169 Pskov [USSR]
170 Smyev [USSR]
171 Taganrog[USSR]
172 Pinsk [USSR]
173 Podvolochisk [USSR]
174 Pripet Marshes [USSR]
175 Radomyshl' [USSR]
176 Rostov-na-Donu [USSR]

2. SS-Infanterie
(mot.)-Brigade Operations
and Atrocities in the USSR
177 Baranowice
178 Imla
179 Kalja
180 Lazdijai
181 Livenskaya
182 Lyuban'
183 Medes
184 Minsk
185 Novgorod
186 Petersburg
187 Rozhdestvenskiy
188 Seirijai
189 Tosno
190 Vilna
191 Wyriza

SS-Kavallerie-Brigade
Operations and Atrocities
in the USSR
192 Baranovichi
193 Berjosawthal
194 Bobrik
195 Bobruysk
196 Bol'Shiye Gorodyatichi
197 Buda
198 Budenichi

Table of Contents

Introduction

A visit to any well-stocked bookstore should quickly convince the average reader that there is certainly no shortage of books about the Second World War, particularly National Socialism and the Third Reich. More than five decades have passed since the war's end and its massive historiography continues to grow and evolve with seemingly no end in sight. It is probably foolish to think that the examination of and reflection on the 20th century's seminal event will ever reach completion. Despite an endless flood of titles, however, our knowledge of the Second World War is still imperfect and full of surprisingly large gaps. For example, there is a curious lack of published information concerning the numerous wartime atrocities (*i.e.*, violations of international law such as killing non-combatant civilians, surrendering opponents, and prisoners of war) committed by Nazi Germany's military elite, the Waffen-SS. In fact, there are very few books currently in print that examine the nature and commission of war crimes perpetrated by any of the armed forces participating in the Second World War. Thus, it appears that the nearly forty divisions of the Waffen-SS have not been accorded any special treatment by military historians, but rather have benefited from an insidious and apparently universal form of ethical tunnel-vision. None of us is immune to the social forces that shape our collective memories and we often feel the need to accept a self-serving national mythos with its concomitant requirement that criminal acts on behalf of the state be ignored or denied. Examining an enemy's wartime behavior holds many potential dangers since our own conduct might then also be scrutinized with the goal of uncovering similar transgressions.

If the number of books published on any topic is a reliable indicator of public interest, then there continues to be a sustained interest in the Waffen-SS. New titles appear regularly. In examining those books specifically addressing the wartime activities of the Waffen-SS it is apparent that each falls into one of three broad categories: 1) academic studies assuming the war crimes guilt of the Waffen-SS but offering only limited supporting evidence; 2) amateur historical studies focusing solely on the military aspects of Waffen-SS wartime involvement; and 3) apologetic studies by former Waffen-SS personnel and a multi-national group of admirers portraying the Waffen-SS as "soldiers like any other" who have been unfairly associated with the crimes of the Third Reich. By far, the majority of books published about the Waffen-SS fall into the latter two categories. As Wegner trenchantly observed,

> If one surveys the literature on the history of the SS and the Waffen-SS, it becomes quite obvious how immense the discrepancy is between the veritable avalanche of titles and the quite modest yield of credible and scholarly insights. The reason for this discrepancy is clear: more than a generation after the collapse of the Third Reich, the SS as a historical phenomenon has exercised a powerful emotional attraction. At the same time it demands that we come to terms with it morally... the demarcation line between scholarly and non-scholarly literature about the SS is less visible than is usual for historical themes. [1]

While much has been published regarding their military prowess, no single publication has devoted itself to fairly examining the subject of Waffen-SS criminality. In fact, the only publication strictly addressing Waffen-SS criminality that I found was a poorly-researched, apologetic thesis defending the Waffen-SS.[2] Numerous apologetic works are available that celebrate Waffen-SS military achievements free of any Nazi-era taint. Unfortunately, there are very few substantial publications available to stem this growing tide of Waffen-SS revisionism. Surely, I thought, there must be at least one publication that conducts an impartial, in-depth examination of Waffen-SS criminality. After all, the post-war International Military Tribunal (IMT) at Nuremberg had branded the Waffen-SS as a criminal organization in the clearest and most strenuous of terms. Despite several years of searching, I was unable to find any such publication either in English or any of the western European languages. The standard academic treatments of the Waffen-SS such as Reitlinger's *The SS: Alibi of a Nation* (1957), Stein's *The Waffen SS* (1966), and Höhne's *The Order of the Death's Head* (1971) are of little help in this regard. For the most part they simply assume Waffen-SS criminality and offer only scraps of supporting documentation. Often their focus is on a handful of events and lacks the breadth of the evidence considered by the International Military Tribunal (IMT) at Nuremberg in reaching their criminality judgment against the Waffen-SS. While Sydnor's *Soldiers of Destruction* (1977) and Weingartner's *Hitler's Guard* (1974) are fine divisional-level studies, their self-imposed boundaries are of limited usefulness in combating the revisionism common in publications about the Waffen-SS. Considering the sweeping criminality that academics have attributed to the Waffen-SS, it seems odd that only limited evidence has been offered in support of their conclusions. If historians' assessments are accurate, however, then many authors have either inadvertently or deliberately ignored a record of widescale criminal activities perpetrated by the Waffen-SS. Even less helpful, the few overtly critical books that have been published consist of a thin, insubstantial item of limited value[3] and a monograph by an author whose barely-disguised hostility toward Germans in general completely undermines his ability to fairly assess Waffen-SS criminality.[4] Fueled by dismay at this situation coupled with my own desire that such information be readily available, I began a research project focusing on the Waffen-SS, their war crimes, and the IMT charge of organizational criminality. The book that I first searched for over a decade ago is now in your hands.

In the course of assembling the present publication, it was apparent that the true extent of Waffen-SS criminality far exceeded the initial impression I received from readily available sources. As the following pages demonstrate, the Waffen-SS undoubtedly has the worst war crimes record of any professional military organization fielded by a modern industrial state. That more of these horrible incidents have not been cited by historians to support their sweeping condemnation of the Waffen-SS is somewhat puzzling, to say the least. I can only speculate that academics have un-

wisely assumed their audience to possess a universal conviction that the Third Reich and all of its constituent organizations were criminal in theory, nature, and practice. In a community where such acceptance is prevalent, any detailed demonstration of Waffen-SS criminality would be an essentially pointless exercise. It is my observation, however, that we are not faced with such a benign situation at all. On the contrary, the public in the United States is historically illiterate to a shocking degree. As noted earlier, we are also faced with the phenomenon that most publications about the Waffen-SS either ignore, deny, or attempt to explain away their crimes. It is abundantly clear that as time passes, the amount of revisionist material on the Waffen-SS grows at an increasing rate. The average reader may consult such works and reach the erroneous conclusion that the wartime conduct of the Waffen-SS really was no different from that of their opponents. I hope my work can serve as a much-needed corrective to the many misleading popular works that strive to recast the Waffen-SS solely in a glorious light.

In addition to expanding upon and clarifying the historical record, there are other pressing reasons for exploring the subject of Waffen-SS criminality. Atrocities have always been a part of warfare and the technologically-enhanced lethality of modern arsenals (*e.g.,* push-button, fire-and-forget weapons) makes it more imperative than ever that we acknowledge and grapple with this often ignored dark corner of human conduct. Since WWI, armed conflicts have increasingly been characterized by industrial killing: "the mechanized, impersonal and sustained mass destruction of human beings" organized by states and legitimized by a variety of social institutions.[5] Modern military operations, even those limited to the use of conventional weapons, are seemingly no longer possible without the wholesale slaughter of civilians -- an unsavory reality that is masked by euphemisms such as "collateral damage." Clearly, an unbridgeable gulf lies between our ethical and moral proclamations and the reality of our behavior during wartime. We have renounced honor, shame, mercy and compassion becoming unscrupulous beyond measure merely to survive on the modern battlefield. As Chittister observed,

> All of us meet and wrestle with authority. The only question is to what authority have I surrendered and   how do I myself use authority when I have it. Authority and self-determination are two of the major problems of the spiritual life. [6]

The price of adhering to our moral and ethical beliefs is usually judged to be too high in the short run; expediency invariably serves as the yardstick by which all our decisions are measured.

The atrocities described herein are not simply historical moments frozen in time for our dissection, classification, and dispassionate study. They are timeless examples of the horrific consequences resulting when men freely give themselves over as servile functionaries to power structures that employ them as instruments in the service of an evil, immoral end. War criminals ignore well-defined legal, ethical and moral boundaries, deny their social responsibility, and act in a reprehensible manner that irrevocably alters the lives of their victims. War does not obviate the need for basic human decency; morality and ethics are not rescinded on the field of battle. There can never be a defense, an excuse, an extenuating circumstance, or a technicality for killing defenceless civilians and prisoners of war. Such an uncompromisingly strict standard of behavior will hopefully lead to self-examination and dialogue addressing the most important question of all: What do war crimes, especially those committed by our own military forces, tell us about human nature?

We are currently living in the most violent century in human history. Of an estimated 149 million total deaths due to warfare since the 1st century, 111 million (74.5%) of these deaths have occurred in the 20th century. Despite these facts, the problem of wartime atrocities (with the exception of genocidal events such as the Holocaust) continues to receive scant attention from both academics and the public. Yet we ignore atrocities at our peril. Lifton and Markusen have noted the interconnections and similarities among state-sponsored genocide, total war, and nuclear omnicide.[8] The threat to the survival of the human species is such

that we can neither permit ourselves to be seduced by the trappings of power and atrocity, nor can we afford to retreat behind our repulsion for such acts in the hope that they will simply go away. While time can certainly blur and erase memories, forgetting and healing are not the same. If we gain no insight into the psychology of war crimes and fail to modify our institutions and group behavior accordingly, then the unspeakable suffering of those already victimized will undoubtedly be visited upon future generations. We must actively work to forestall such evils if there is to be any hope of a positive transformation of the human condition.

This book was not intended to be read from cover to cover as a continuous narrative. Rather it was arranged into well-defined sections to have maximum utility as a reference work. The three main sections -- *Atrocities*, *Unit Histories*, and *Individuals* -- were adopted to guide readers along the most natural paths of inquiry:

- **What happened at [place-name]?**
- **What was [unit]'s record of atrocities?**
- **What was [individual]'s involvement in atrocities?**

It should be noted that throughout the Atrocities section divisional references invariably employ the final designation that the unit received; intermediate titles are noted in the Unit Histories. For brevity's sake, only the last known rank has been indicated for personnel listed in the Individuals section. While an initial draft of the Individuals and Unit Histories sections included source citations, these references were subsequently removed as being of dubious informational value while rendering those sections unreadable. Readers unfamiliar with Waffen-SS ranks and German military terminology should consult Appendices A and B respectively.

It is an additional goal of this volume to demonstrate that wartime atrocities are not spontaneously generated within the realm of individual psychopathlogy. On the contrary, they are intimately related to organizational structures and mythic beliefs imparted in a group setting. With respect to the type of atrocities documented, I have for the most part excluded crimes committed by lone perpetrators and those resulting in the deaths of only a few victims. Had these "minor" crimes been included (many examples of which can be found in the CROWCASS series of volumes [1946 - 1948]), the manuscript would have been unwieldy as well as skewed in focus. The best organization can have bad individuals in it and the worst organization can have honorable individuals. Neither circumstance is a reliable indicator of an organization's overall moral and ethical orientation.

It will be immediately apparent that this book is lacking in background information regarding the history and military campaigns of the Waffen-SS. Since a number of fine publications have already covered this ground, I felt that an abbreviated overview could only be derivative or repetitious at best, and incomplete, flawed or misleading at worst. For those unfamiliar with the Waffen-SS or needing additional historical details not included herein, a number of reliable publications are available.[9] Readers desiring in-depth examinations of Waffen-SS military operations are directed to the representative selection of unit histories listed in the *Sources* section. It should be noted that most of these publications, written by former Waffen-SS personnel or their latter-day admirers, are naturally biased and of especially dubious reliability with regards to the war crimes issue.

Throughout this book the reader will come across three terms that are used to categorize some authors of works on the Waffen-SS: *apologist*, *revisionist*, and *propagandist*. In my usage these terms represent a sliding scale of increasing intellectual dishonesty. All such authors engage to varying degress in the generation of pseudohistory or the "rewriting of the past for present personal or political purposes."[10] One objective of such works is to lessen or remove the stigma of Nazi crimes and thus make a resurgent National Socialism palatable again. For clarity's sake, a brief delineation of these categories and their boundaries is necessary with the recognition, however, that authors frequently employ more than one of these approaches. The term *apologist* is used throughout with the connotation of one who would make unfounded excuses for the activities of the Waffen-SS. They typically invoke such concepts as superior orders and the fear of retribution, immoral equivalence, war is hell, *etc.* in order to "explain" why atrocities occurred. My use of the term *apologist* should not be confused with the

acts of apology, forgiveness, and reconciliation. Nor should it be mistaken for the field of apologetics which strives "to clarify fundamental problems so that Christian theology might better understand itself".[11] Recognizing the weight of evidence against the Waffen-SS, *apologists* are concerned with excuses and little else.

I employ the term *revisionist* for those who actively revise history in a biased manner to serve specific personal or political ends. Such authors deny and obfuscate evidence, often claiming that the victims of crimes legally deserved the treatment they received. Rather than explain how the atrocities could have occurred, the *revisionist* constructs a rationale for why the atrocities should have occurred. As has been previously noted by many embroiled in the "Holocaust Revision" controversy, revisionism is a valid methodological approach to investigation that occurs in any healthy discipline. Historical revision is simply the modification of existing history on the basis of new facts, analysis and/or interpretation. Many historians reject the use of the term *revisionist* in connection with fraudulent changes to the historical record since they are accomplished through a reversal of the accepted methodology of history: facts are revised in accordance with preconceived conclusions. Unfortunately, there is no suitable substitute for the term. The suggested use of revisionist in quotes ("revisionist") to emphasize the methodological dishonesty involved is clumsy at best. While some historians are championing use of the term *denier*[12], such a practice may mischaracterize an author's methodology since outright denial of basic facts is only one of the fraudulent methods usually employed. While false revisionism and denial inevitably overlap at times, by definition they cannot be perfectly congruent. For lack of a better term, I will employ *revisionist* with the understanding that it denotes an illegitimate revision of historical events.

The term *propagandist* is used for those authors who simply deny outright that the atrocities occurred. Such denials are usually accompanied by counterclaims that the Allies were really the major criminals of the war. While "denier" would be a more obvious label, it is a problematic term at best, carrying with it the modernistic cultural meaning of a psychological mindset driven by fear and disfunction.

Additionally, I have chosen the path of brevity with regard to several issues in the discussions that round out this book (see *Examining the Issues*). The international laws of war, for instance, have their own vast body of literature that forms a separate discipline. Rather than repeat the numerous long-standing controversies of the field, I offer some observations regarding the legality of war crimes legislation and post-war tribunals. Those interested in the legal and philosophical arguments that have been debated concerning German atrocities committed during the Second World War may pursue their own inquiry. Since my primary goal is to present an initial survey of Waffen-SS criminality, the many auxiliary issues involved (*e.g.*, ideological training and other psychosocial influences) have received sufficient, but by no means exhaustive, treatment. Observation and interpretation are unavoidable, but the difficulty of satisfactorily explaining the nature of evil and its expression in human behavior remains.

Finally, I am under no illusion that this work is a definitive accounting of Waffen-SS war crimes. Evidence of many more crimes may await discovery in archives throughout the world. The single most important untapped reservoir of Waffen-SS documentation is undoubtedly the collection of the Czech Republic Military Archives (Zasmuky/Prague) which is estimated to possess approximately 90% of the original Waffen-SS archives. Countless original documents detailing German prosecution of the Second World War are also housed at the Institut für Zeitgeschichte (München), the United Nations War Crimes Commission Archives (New York), the YIVO Institute (New York), the Hoover Institution Library (Stanford), the Wiener Library (London), the Bundesarchiv (Koblenz), the Bundesarchiv-Militärarchiv (Freiburg), the Yad Vashem (Jerusalem), the Centre de Documentation Juive Contemporaine (Paris), as well as numerous other institutions. Other recently opened archives of Eastern European nations in particular promise treasures of historical documentation. I sincerely hope that this volume will inspire others to expand upon my examination of the subject.

Notes:

1. Wegner, 1990, pp. 1-8.
2. Wiggers, 1990.
3. Sauer, 1977.
4. Madeja, 1992.
5. Bartov, 1997.
6. Chittister, 1991, p. 134.
7. Merton, 1968, p. 54.
8. Lifton and Markusen, 1990.
9. The following publications are recommended for background information on the SS and Waffen-SS:

Höhne, 1971: a general treatment of SS history

Koehl, 1983: an excellent general history of the SS with a special focus on the Waffen-SS and its place in the scheme of German fascism

Krausnick, 1968: a classic review of SS development with attention given to leadership dynamics

Reitlinger, 1957: the first comprehensive history of the SS and its subsidiary organizations; somewhat dated though still useful

Stein, 1966: a landmark history of the Waffen-SS; somewhat dated though still useful

Wegner, 1990: a critical examination of the pre-war organizational history and wartime structural crises of the Waffen-SS; provides an especially good study of the connection between National Socialism and the legitimization of Waffen-SS military power

Ziegler, 1990: a statistical examination of the social origins of the pre-war SS leadership corp and the internal social and ideological forces that influenced it

10. Shermer, 1994, p. 32.
11. Rahner and Vorgrimler, 1985, p. 183.
12. See Lipstadt, 1993 for an extended defense of the use of the term *denier*.

Acknowledgments

I would first like to thank my publishers, Andreas Leandoer and Hans Ekholm, for having enough faith in my work to bring it into print. Thanks to any editor and other personnel who help to prepare the book.

I am greatly indebted to numerous librarians and archivists who have assisted my research efforts. A number of close friends and loved ones have also given assistance over the last decade. None of these persons or organizations, however, bear responsibility for any factual errors or interpretive failings which is the author's alone.

The Inter-Library Loan staff, Central Branch, Arlington County (Virginia) Library for their timely and unstinting efforts at obtaining even the most obscure published references.

The staffs of the Main Reading Room, Microform Reading Room, Periodicals Reading Room, and Law Library at the U.S. Library of Congress (Washington, DC) for their assistance in locating and viewing a wide variety of research materials.

The Research Library staff of the U.S. Memorial Holocaust Museum (Washington, DC) for their assistance in locating and reviewing archival documents.

The staffs of the Textual Records, Microfilm, and Berlin Document Center collections at the U.S. National Archives and Records Administration (Archives II - College Park, MD) for their assistance in locating and reviewing archival documents.

My wife, Julia Jo, whose love and boundless enthusiasm for this project have bouyed up my flagging spirits on many an occasion. Her research assistance, manuscript reviews, and willingness to share capuccinos on Capitol Hill was simply invaluable. I am indebted to her for having unselfishly tolerated the omnipresence of this project in our life for the last 8 years.

James W. Theisen for his much-appreciated editorial advice, encouragement, and friendship through the years. To meet and work with him in this lifetime has truly been a privilege.

Donald L. Britton, Gregory Embree and L. Paul Heisel for their reviews of an earlier draft of this manuscript.

Their insightful commentary and critiques have greatly strengthened this final work.

Raymond D. Manners for his friendship, enthusiasm, and early support of this project. His untimely passing has left us all considerably poorer.

Raphael Rues for providing hard-to-find references on the Lago Maggiore atrocity.

For obvious reasons, researching and writing this book has often been an arduous task. I am indebted to the Cistercian Order of the Strict Observance at Our Lady of the Holy Cross Monastery (Berryville, Virginia). Through their devotion and gracious hospitality, these monks have created a tranquil place of retreat where burdens can be relieved, perspectives adjusted, and optimism regained.

Atrocities

Atrocities Master List

Agios Georgios [Greece]

Albania

Ascq [France]

Babi Yar [USSR]

Bagneres-de-Bigorre [France]

Bais [France]

Bardine de San Terenzo [Italy]

Bela Crkva [Yugoslavia]

Bergen-Belsen [Germany]

Berlin [Germany]

Biserske Livada [Yugoslavia] ---- see Goc

Bisko [Yugoslavia] ---- see Split

Blazevici [Yugoslavia]

Blazevo [Yugoslavia]

Blonie [Poland]

Bohmen-Mahren [Czechoslovakia]

Bor Kunowski [Poland]

Boronjina [Yugoslavia] ---- see Blazevo

Boskina [USSR]

Boves [Italy]

Bozominu [Yugoslavia] ---- see Blazevo

Bydgoszcz 1 [Poland]

Bydgoszcz 2 [Poland]

Brusilov [USSR]

Bzura [Poland]

Carsac-de-Carlux [France]

Chateau Valencay [France]

Chelm [Poland]

Ciepielow [Poland]

Crvenka [Yugoslavia]

Czestochowa [Poland]

Dhistomon [Greece]

**[Dirlewanger Brigade Operations
& Atrocities in the USSR**

Antonopol

Belynici

Berezino

Besyady

Bobruisk

Bogushevichi

Bykhov

Cerven

Dobraya

Dobre Strazn

Drut River region

Dubniki

Dubrovo

Grodek

Ivenets

Jaswenski

Khutor

Kopyl

Kossino

Krugloye

Lugojsk

Ljada

Makawczyce

Manyly

Milevichi

Minsk

Molodecno

Moroc

Moshkovo

Nagornoye

Niemen River region

Novaya Niva

Novyye Lyady

Omgovichi

Orsa-Vitebsk road

Osipovici

Osovo

Petrovka

Plescenicy

Povarchitsky

Prilepy

Radoshkovichi

Rakov

Ratkovo

Rekota

Rogacov

Rudnia

Ryabki

Sakowschtschina-Makon road

Sloboda

Sluck

Smolevici

Starinski

Starobin
Staryye Velichkovichi
Svisloc
Wejna
Wieliczkowicze
Wieliczkowicze Nowe
Zabashevichi
Zembin
Zhodino]
Dnepropetrovsk [USSR]
Dola [Yugoslavia]
Dolac Donji [Yugoslavia] ---- see Otok Cornji
Dolhynov [USSR]
Domisevina [Yugoslavia] ---- see Blazevo
Dunes [France]
East Prussia [Germany]
Farneta Monastery [Italy]
Farnocchia [Italy]

[1. SS-Infanterie (mot.)-Brigade Operations & Atrocities in the USSR

Altynovka
Augustow [Poland]
Badichany
Baturin
Bialokurowicze
Biehun
Blagowscht
Bobrik
Bol'Shiye Gorodyatichi
Boloschizy
Brashinka
Buda
Chernigovka
Chernobyl'
Dnjepr Bend
Dnjepr Islands
Dnjepropetrowsk
Duchanowka
Dvorishche
Yemil'chino
Fesovka
Fl. Ubortj
Fw. Bobruty
Gayvoron
Gorodets
Goroschki

Goryn' Valley
Goshcha
Gremjatheka
Hf. Krasnoje
Hrycow
Jeze [Poland]
Kaja
Kirovograd
Kolkhoz Boljarka
Kolkhoz Federowka
Konotop
Korosten
Krasnoje
Krasuesselka
Krolevets
Kuliki
Kuniow
Lel'chitsy
Listvin
Lyuban'
Makarichi
Mal
Melini
Nikopol'
Norinsk
Novo Niropol
Ostrog
Ovruch
Petrikov
Putivl'
Radogoshch Ml.
Rudnia Czerwonka
Rudnia Worowskaja
Ryshanskaja
Rzepowszczyzna
Sch. Janow
Shadki
Skurowka
Slavuta
Sluch' Valley
Smolensk
Soblewka
Sokolov
Sorchi
Sselez
Ssilisowks
Stayki

Szepetowka
Terinzy
Tonorischtsche
Ubortj
Ubybaczki
Uman'
Urech'ye
Uschenskoje
Vil'sk
Vitebsk
Volozhyn
Weleniki
Woroff
Wydybor
Yuntseviche
Zaslavl'
Zhitomir
Zwiahel]

[14. **Waffen-Grenadier-Division-der-SS**
    (ukrainische Nr. 1)
    Crimes in Poland

Borow
Chodaczkow Wielki
Goscieradow
Gozdow
Huta Pieniacka
Jaminy
Jamna
Kaszow
Majdan Nowy
Majdan Stary
Minoga/Barbarka
Mlynow
Obrowiec
Palikrowy
Podkamien
Poturzyn
Prehoryle
Siemianowka
Smoligow
Szczecyn
Wicyn
Wolka Szczecka
Zagaje
Zaklikow]

Fraysinnet-le-Gelat [France]
Gabaudet [France]

[Gau Niederdonau [Austria]
Eisenstadt
Leiben
Lunz am See Thenneberg
Nikolsburg
Persenbeug]

[Gau Steiermark [Austria]
Deutsch-Schützen
Egelsdorf
Gratkorn
Nestelbach
Prebensdorf
Rechnitz]
Gejgowa/Kherson [USSR]
Goc [Yugoslavia]
Gornji-Dolac [Yugoslavia] ---- see Split
Gorych [USSR]
Gradac [Yugoslavia] ---- see Blazevo
Grafeneck Castle [Germany]
Gragnola [Italy] ---- see Vinca di Fivizzano
Graignes [France]
Grubisnjici [Yugoslavia]
Hauptkommissariat Baranowicze [USSR]
Hnevosice [Czechoslovakia]
Horka [Germany]
Hungary
Ilinci [Yugoslavia] ---- see Blazevo
Ioannina [Greece]
Ivanjica [Yugoslavia] ---- see Goc
Jablanica [Yugoslavia]
Jablanica-Prozor Railline [Yugoslavia]
Jaroszew [Poland]
Kamenets-Podol'skiy [USSR]
Karpenisi [Greece]
Kharkov 1 [USSR]
Kharkov 2 [USSR]
Kharkov 3 [USSR]
Kharkov 4 [USSR]
Kiev Region [USSR]
Klisoura [Greece]
Kopaonik [Yugoslavia]
Kosutica [Yugoslavia]
Krivodol [Yugoslavia]

Kriva Reka [Yugoslavia]

Krusevca [Yugoslavia] ---- see Liga

Ksiazki [Poland]

Kukes [Albania]

Lago Maggiore [Italy]

Lahoysk [USSR]

L'Arbresle [France]

Larisa [Greece]

Legatori [Yugoslavia]

Lentilly [France]

Le Paradis [France]

Lidice [Czechoslovakia]

Liga [Yugoslavia]

Lithuania

Livarot [France]

Lodz [Poland]

Lotoschinsk Psychiatric Clinic [USSR]

Lublin [Poland]

Lublin District [Poland]

Lublin/Majdanek [Poland]

Lublin - Aktion Erntefest [Poland]

Lvov [Poland]

Maille [France]

[Malmedy [Belgium]

Baugnez Crossroads

Büllingen

Butai

Cheneux

Honsfeld

La Gleize

Ligneuville

Ligneuville-Stavelot Road

Lutre Bois

Parfondruy

Petit Thier

Rahier

Stavelot

Stoumont

Trois Ponts

Wanne

Wereth]

[Miscellaneous Atrocities

Angouleme [France]

Arnhem [Netherlands]

Aussone [France]

Bazens [France]

Brno [USSR]

Flavigny [France]

France

Franco-Belgian border

Gard [France]

Guardistallo [Italy]

Hungary

Jussey [France]

Justiniac [France]

Kharkov [USSR]

Leshoguen [France]

Limoges [France]

Lussac [France]

Marsoulas [France]

Miremont [France]

Montauban [France]

Navaugle [France]

Nerstal [France]

Nimes [France]

Permez [France]

Plomion [France]

Poitiers [France]

Pskov [USSR]

St. Denis [France]

St. Martin [France]

St. Venant [France]

Smyev [USSR]

Taganrog [USSR]

Tarbes [France]

Toulouse [France]

Vergt de Biron [France]

des Verrieres [France]

Yuret [France]]

[Monte Sol [Italy]

Caprara

Casaglia

Casoni di Bavellino

Casoni di Riomoneta

Cerpiano

Creda

Marzabotto

Pioppe di Salvaro

San Giovanni di Sopra & di Sotto

Sperticano]

Monzone [Italy] ---- see Vinca di Fivizzano

Mussidan [France]

Netherlands

Niksic [Yugoslavia]

Niksic-Avtovac Railroad Line [Yugoslavia]

Nisko [Poland]

[Normandy [France]

Ancienne Abbaye Ardenne

Argentan

Authie/Buron

Bretteville l'Orgueilleuse

Chateau d'Audrieu

Fontenay-le-Pesnel

Galmanche

Le Haut du Bosq

Le Mesnil-Patry 1

Le Mesnil-Patry 2

Les Fains

Les Saullets 1

Les Saullets 2

Mouen

St. Sulpice]

Norway

Noville-lez-Bastogne [Belgium]

Novi Sad [Yugoslavia]

Oradour-sur-Glane [France]

Osekovo [Yugoslavia]

Otok Cornji [Yugoslavia]

Ovrlje [Yugoslavia]

Owinsk [Poland]

Padule di Fucecchio [Italy]

Palmiry [Poland]

Pancevo [Yugoslavia]

Pinsk [USSR]

Podvolochisk [USSR]

Poland

[Poland -- Miscellaneous Atrocities

Aleksandrow

Bialochowo

Bialuty

Biesiekierz

Bolewice

Bralewnica

Buk-Goralski

Bursz

Bydgoszcz

Chojnice

Dabrowka

Debienko Forest

Dzialdowo

Grupa

Jaroszewy

Jedlec

Karolewo

Kcynia

Klecko

Komorniki

Konin

Koscielec

Kowalewice

Ksiaza

Lelazne

Lesno

Leszno

Lopatki

Lubichowo

Luszkowko

Malki

Nowy Wiec

Olek

Oscislowo

Panewnik

Piasnica

Pultusk Poplawy

Roznowo Mlyn

Rozopole

Rumoka

Rusinowo

Rypin

Sadki

Sewerynowo

Siewierz

Skarszew

Skarszewy

Skorcz

Sliwice

Srem

Starogard

Swietokrzyz

Szpegawsk

Tczew

Tuchola

Turek
Wiecbork
Wypalanki
Wyszanow
Zajeziorze
Zdunska Wola
Zgierz]

Polish Corridor [Poland]
Ponte Santa Lucia [Italy]
---- see Vinca di Fivizzano
Prague [Czechoslovakia]
Pripet Marshes [USSR]
Pristina [Yugoslavia]
Putisic [Yugoslavia] ---- see Split
Putten [Netherlands]
Radom [Poland]
Radom 2 [Poland]
Radomyshl' [USSR]
Raskoj [Yugoslavia] ---- see Goc
Ravniste [Yugoslavia] ---- see Blazevo
Rawa Mazowiecka [Poland]
Razori [Yugoslavia]
Ripac [Yugoslavia]
Rodici [Yugoslavia] ---- see Blazevo
Rostov-na-Donu [USSR]
Rozan [Poland]
Ruda [Yugoslavia] ---- see Otok Cornji
Ruzyn [Czechoslovakia]
Saint Germain-du-Belair [France]
Sajmiste Camp, Belgrade [Yugoslavia]
Sancaku [Yugoslavia]
Sant'Anna di Stazzema [Italy]
Sava River / Brcko [Yugoslavia]

[2. SS-Infanterie (mot.)-Brigade Operations and Atrocities in the USSR
Baranowice
Imla
Kalja
Lazdijai
Livenskaya
Lyuban'
Medes
Minsk
Novgorod
Petersburg

Rozhdestvenskiy
Seirijai
Tosno
Vilna
Wyriza
Siatista [Greece]
Sinj [Yugoslavia]
Sladovil [Yugoslavia]
Slovak National Uprising [Slovakia]
Smilici [Yugoslavia]
Soltysy-Zabuce [Poland]
Sosnowiec [Poland]
Split-Sinj Region [Yugoslavia]
Srijane [Yugoslavia] ---- see Split]

[SS-Kavallerie Operations and Atrocities in Poland
Chelm-Sokal
Kamiena
Krakau
Kutno
Otwock
Ruda
Warsaw
Zgierz Prison]

[SS-Kavallerie-Brigade Operations and Atrocities in the USSR
Baranovichi
Berjosawthal
Bobrik
Bobruysk
Bol'Shiye Gorodyatichi
Buda
Budenichi
Dnjepr region
Dorohi Stare
Dubrovo
Glussk
Grodno
Krassny Ostroff
Lyakhovichi
Lyaskovichi
Lyuban'
Makarichi
Mokawicze
Novo Andrevskaya

Agios Georgios (Greece)

During August 1944, Waffen-SS troops razed the village of Agios Georgios as part of anti-guerilla operations in the mountains of central Greece. They burned down every house, polluted the village wells with the bodies of dead mules, and destroyed standing crops in surrounding fields. Luckily, the inhabitants had abandoned the town earlier in the day and were able to avoid any personal repercussions. The only Waffen-SS unit in Greece at this time was the 4. SS-Polizei-Panzergrenadier-Division.

Source
(Mazower, 1993, pp. 184-185)

Albania

Between 28 May and 5 July 1944, the 21. Waffen-Grenadier-Division der SS *Skanderbeg* [albanische Nr. 1] (CO: SS-Brigadeführer Josef Fitzhum; after 6/44, SS-Oberführer August Schmidhuber) rounded up "510 Jews, Communists, partisans, and suspicious persons" in Albania. Of this group, 249 were deported to concentration camps. The fate of the remaining civilians is unknown.

Source
(Report XXI Mountain Corps [Chief of Staff von Klocke], 13 July 1944; Nuremberg Documents Collection, NOKW-838, International Law Library, Columbia University, New York City)

Ascq (France)

The 12. SS-Panzer-Division *Hitlerjugend* had been forming and training in Belgium since July 1943. Most of it's officers and NCOs were veterans with combat experience on the eastern front where the rules of war had long since ceased to apply. While the bulk of the division's foot soldiers were 17 year-old former Hitler Youth members, its reconnaissance battalion included a large contingent (10-15%) of Osttruppen (Russian and Ukrainian volunteers). Following its training, *Hitlerjugend* was ordered to take up defensive positions in Normandy in anticipation of an Allied offensive. The division's rail transports began leaving their Belgian encampments

on 1 April 1944. The composition of the reconnaissance battalion at this time was as follows:

SS-Panzeraufklärungs-Abteilung 1
(CO: SS-Sturmbannführer Gerhard Bremer)

1. (Pz. Späh.) Kompanie (CO: SS-Untersturmführer Kudoke)
2. (Pz. Späh.) Kompanie (CO: SS-Obersturmführer Walter Hauck)
3. (Aufkl.) Kompanie (CO: SS-Untersturmführer Hauer)
4. (Aufkl.) Kompanie (CO: SS-Untersturmführer Beiersdor)
5. (schw.) Kompanie (CO: SS-Hauptsturmführer Gerd von Reitzenstein)

Train number 649355 comprising 24 railcars was transporting the first three companies of the battalion (totalling 460 personnel plus vehicles) with SS-Obersturmführer Walter Hauck in overall command of the convoy. As their train passed through Tournai (Belgium) on the night of 1 April, the SS troopers were seen enjoying themselves in drinking and song.

A group of resistance members in the small northern French town of Ascq also went into action on the night of 1 April. By 9:00 pm they had placed explosive charges with contact detonators on the rail line a few hundred yards from Ascq station. As the *Hitlerjugend* reconnaissance convoy approached Ascq station at 10:45 pm, the charges detonated ripping up a section of rail line and causing two flatbed carriers used for vehicle transport to derail. The whole convoy ground to a halt. Initially there did not appear to be much of a reaction among the SS troops as the damage was negligible. The convoy commander SS-Obersturmführer Hauck, however, was in a foul mood and at 11:15 pm ordered several teams to conduct a house-to-house sweep of Ascq centered on the area surrounding the train station. All men between the ages of 17 - 50 were to be forcibly detained as potential suspects.

A kommando under SS-Hauptscharführer Gustav Büss searched the areas immediately adjacent to the halted convoy. A kommando under SS-Unterscharführer Leopold Stun searched rue Marceau, rue Faidherbe, and rue Courbet. Along the way they beat a priest senseless and then riddled his prone body with gunfire. A kommando under SS-Untersturmführer Hauer searched the rue du Marechal Foch, rue Massena, rue Kleber, and rue Mangin. A kommando under SS-Untersturmführer Kudoke, accompanied by SS-Obersturmführer Hauck, searched rue de la Gare and the train station itself. A kommando under SS-Oberscharführer Karl Jura searched rue Marceau. A kommando under SS-Oberscharführer Wetzlmayer searched rue Gallieni, rue Pasteur, and the church square. All along the way, the SS troopers broke doors down and smashed windows.

The hostages were taken from their homes at gunpoint and marched down the rail line to a point close to where the sabotage had occurred. At 12:30 am on 2 April the Ascq residents were gunned down en masse. SS troopers then passed amongst the fallen bodies with flashlights delivering coup-de-grace shots to those who had only been wounded. Following this first mass execution, three more sweeps were made through the town (primarily along rue de la Gare and rue Marceau) with additional hostages being gathered up and brought to the rail line for execution. The final group of civilians taken was saved at the last minute by the German Feldgendarmerie in Lille who intervened after several frantic telephone calls from a French railway worker who was witnessing the ongoing massacre. As abruptly as they had started, the killings ceased. The SS troopers uncoupled the damaged flatbed carriers, reboarded their train, and headed back for Baisieux station to await repairs to the destroyed tracks.

At 2:00 am, elements of the Feldgendarmerie Lille and French collaborationist security forces (Groupes Mobiles de Reserve - GMR) moved into Ascq to secure the town and begin cleaning up from the night's carnage. Altogether 70 inhabitants had been executed beside the rail line and another 16 were found dead scattered throughout the village itself. Several men had lived to tell the tale either by fleeing their captors under cover of confusion and darkness, or by playing dead at the execution site

By midday of 2 April, the minor damage to the rail line was repaired. In the early afternoon the *Hitlerjugend* reconnaissance convoy returned to Ascq, rehitched the two derailed flatbed cars, and continued on to Normandy.

On 5 April a mass funeral which attracted 25,000 mourners was held at Ascq for the slain. The official German reaction to this atrocity was that it was a regrettable, but necessary, action. The SS troopers had been attacked by "terrorists" as they searched Ascq for the railway bombers. They were forced to fire in self-defense and had killed only partisans. Additionally, a search of the town had produced numerous hidden caches of weapons, ammunition and radios. Even if the SS had executed any unarmed civilians, such reprisals had previously been approved by the German high command. In February 1944 the head of Oberkommando West, Generalfeldmarschal Hugo Sperrle, had issued a general order for the suppression of partisan activities. Among the measures sanctioned was the execution of hostages. Similar orders had previously been issued to all fronts under the imprimatur of Generalfeldmarschal Wilhelm Keitel, chief of the OKW, on 16 September 1941. Of course, the wording of these orders and their mode of application in the field were in violation of the Geneva Conventions. After an investigation by the Gestapo, 6 men and 1 woman were arrested on 21 April and charged with planting the bomb. They were found guilty of all charges by the Feldkommandantur Lille. On 7 June the men were executed by firing squad at Fort de Seclin; the lone female resistance member remained imprisoned until liberation by Allied forces. From 1947-1949 various remembrances were held and memorials erected to honor those massacred by the Waffen-SS at Ascq.

French post-war investigations initially focused on determining who had been present at the Ascq massacre and tracking down the perpetrators. This proved relatively easy given the German's excellent recordkeeping and the fact that most surviving Waffen-SS members were already in Allied custody. The problems began when investigators had to decide who was responsible for the massacre. Eyewitness testimony even disagreed as to who had given the actual execution orders: Walter Hauck, Leopold Stun, or both. Did higher authorities such as Generalfeldmarschal Sperrle and battalion commander Gerhard Bremer bear any responsibility for the massacre by creating an atmosphere conducive to such activities? The usual arguments about responsibility vs. superior orders were carefully considered. In the end, all responsibility for the massacre was attributed to the SS personnel on the ground at Ascq. The French investigator's considerations on the issue of culpability, however, led to a series of puzzling decisions. Several of the higher-ranking *Hitlerjugend* officers present at Ascq (Hauer, Krappf, Kudoke, Leideck, Strohfahrt, Stun, Wetzlmayer and Wohlgemuth) were not tried as their involvement was ruled "uncertain" or "debatable." This despite the fact that four of them had directed kommandos which rounded up hostages for execution. The case of Kudoke was a moot point since he had died during the fighting around Caen in June 1944. Leopold Stun, on the other hand, had gone on to commit further war crimes during the fierce fighting in Normandy. Ironically, many of the adjutants of these unindicted officers were themselves tried and convicted for participation in the Ascq mass killings.

The trial of *Hitlerjugend* personnel thought responsible for the massacre was held from 2-6 August 1949 at the Palace of Justice in Lille under the aegis of the Metz Military Tribunal. Survivors of the massacre and other residents of Ascq gave compelling testimony. The defendant's countered that they had been attacked and had merely conducted a lawful reprisal action. The court deliberated quickly and its sentences were unsurprising. Walter Hauck, Werner Fürst, Walter Jung, Günther Baensch, Reinhardt Onken, Johannes Rasmussen, August Zinssmeister, and Werner Voigt were sentenced to death. Fritz Wronna was sentenced to life imprisonment. A number of additional personnel who could not be located were sentenced to death in absentia: Karl Jura (KIA in Normandy, 8 June 1944), Gustav Büss, Hans Painsi, Heinz Munter, Heinz Frakowiak, Theo Flanderka, Horst Loehr, and Hans Vogt. The condemned were sent to Loos Prison to await execution.

From 1950-1955 there were increasing pleas for clemency in German press and religious circles. The government in Bonn also made it clear that any post-war French/German rapproachement was explicitly tied to "solving the war crimes problem." The defendant's French lawyers made particularly strenuous efforts on their behalf criticizing the Metz Military Tribunal's unusual and confusing rulings regarding the culpability of senior and junior personnel. All of these efforts culminated in a high pressure letter-writing campaign to French President Rene Coty requesting mercy for the condemned. On 14 July 1955 Walter Hauck's sentence was reduced to life imprisonment at hard labor and all the other defendant's sentences were reduced to 10 years' hard labor minus time served. Despite these re-

ductions, the calls for clemency continued unabated. By 1956 all of the condemned had been released from Loos Prison with the exception of Walter Hauck. He was finally paroled in July 1957.

Revisionist attempts to explain away this atrocity have an all-too-familiar unbelievable ring about them. Meyer (1982) has claimed that one of the Ascq hostages tried to escape and was fired upon. This caused the crowd to panic and in the ensuing confusion the SS troopers opened fire to protect themselves. When the dust settled, 86 townspeople were dead and 8 wounded. Meyer's account conflicts with the official German explanation of the massacre. Though neither account is factual, they undoubtedly serve their purpose of misleading the unwary.

Sources
(Mocq, 1984) (Mocq, 1994)
(Luther, 1987, pp. 81-84) (Meyer, 1982, vol. 2, pp. 556-557)

Babi Yar (USSR)

On 22 June 1941, the Nazi invasion of the Soviet Union began. The capital city of the Ukrainian Republic, Kiev, was captured by the German 6th Army on 19 September 1941. By this time an estimated 100,000 of the city's population of 160,000 Jews had managed to flee to safety further eastwards in the Soviet Union. Shortly after the German occupation of Kiev, from 20 September to 28 September, a large number of buildings in the city center being used by the German military administration were bombed and destroyed by an NKVD (Soviet secret police, precursor of KGB) sabotage detachment that had remained behind in the city. Many Germans and local Ukrainians were killed. An official German report described the situation prevailing in Kiev :

On September 20, the citadel blew up and the Artillery Commander and his chief of staff were killed. On September 24, violent explosions in the quarters of the Feldkommandatur; the ensuing fire has not yet been extinguished. Fire in the center of the town. Very valuable buildings destroyed. Blasts continuing. Also, fire breaking out. Up to now, 670 mines detected in buildings, according to a mine-laying plan which was discovered: all public buildings and squares are mined. In the Lenin Museum, eight thousand pounds of dynamite discovered which were to be touched off by wireless. It was repeatedly observed that fires broke out the moment buildings were taken over.... A large number of NKVD officials, political commissars, partisan leaders and partisans arrested. According to reliable information, demolition battalion of the NKVD and considerable number of NKVD men in Kiev.

Ereignismeldung UdSSR Nr. 97 (see Sources)

On 26 September at a meeting of the German command in Kiev it was decided to execute all Kiev Jews as a reprisal measure. The officers presiding were: Major-General Friedrich Georg Eberhardt (Military Governor of Kiev), SS-Obergruppenführer Friedrich Jeckeln (HSSPf Süd), SS-Brigadeführer Dr. Otto Rasch (CO Einsatzgruppe C), and SS-Standartenführer Paul Blobel (CO Sonderkommando 4a). The killings were to be carried out by Sonderkommando 4a which was composed of SD and SIPO personnel, 3. Kompanie/ Waffen-SS-Bataillon-zbV, an unidentified platoon of Polizei-Bataillon 9, Polizei-Bataillonen 45 and 305, and miscellaneous units of the Ukrainian auxiliary police. On 28 September notices were posted in the city ordering all Jews to assemble by 8:00 am the following morning at the corner of Melnik and Dekhtyarev streets for "resettlement." The Jews were brought to a ravine named Babi Yar in the northwestern part of Kiev. They were forced to hand over all of their valuables, made to strip naked, and then driven to the ravine's edge in groups of ten. There, they were gunned down with automatic weapons fire by members of Sonderkommando 4a. Not all of the victims died immediately. Several survivors were able to escape from the ravine under the cover of darkness and made their way to a nearby hospital. According to the official reports of Einsatzgruppe C, in two days of shooting (29 and 30 September 1941), a total of 33,771 Jews were murdered. In an odd display of compassion, SS-Standartenführer Blobel spared a small blonde girl from the firing squads, although her ultimate fate is unknown. This massacre yielded 137 train cars full of clothing and personal belongings which were disinfected and distributed to local ethnic Germans and to Waffen-SS military hospitals.

In the years of German occupation that followed, many more thousands of Jews were killed at Babi Yar, as well as Gypsies and Soviet POWs. According to

the official Soviet research committee on Nazi crimes, approximately 100,000 persons were murdered and buried at Babi Yar. In July 1943, SS-Standartenführer Paul Blobel, former commander of Sonderkommando 4a, dispatched to Kiev two units --- Sonderkommando 1005-A (CO SS-Obersturmführer Baumann, 10 SD Lvov personnel, 30 members of 23. Polizei-Brigade, and 327 inmates from Syretzk concentration camp) and Sonderkommando 1005-B (CO SS-Hauptsturmführer Fritz Zietlow, 5 SD Lvov personnel, 50 members of 23. Polizei-Brigade, 50 inmates from Syretzk concentration camp) --- to erase all evidence of the murders. The mass graves were opened with bulldozers; the bodies were then dragged out and incinerated. The resulting ashes were sifted for valuables, such as gold fillings, and then spread out on neighboring fields. This "clean-up action" lasted from 18 August until 29 September 1943. No trace was left of the extensive mass graves. Similar actions were undertaken by these sonderkommandos at numerous locales throughout eastern Poland and European Russia (see *Sonderkommando 1005*).

Sources

(*Ereignismeldung UdSSR Nr. 97 / Berlin, 28 Sept. 1941 / Einsatzgruppe C in Arad et al., 1989, pp. 164-165*)
(*Ereignismeldung UdSSR Nr. 101 / Berlin, 2 October 1941 in Arad et al., 1989, p. 168*)
(*Gutman, 1990, pp. 133- 136*)
(*Krausnick and Wilhelm, 1981, p. 15*)
(*Lozowick,1987, pp. 224-225*)
(*Spector, 199, pp. 17-13*)

Bagneres-de-Bigorre (France)

"Declaration made (by) Mme. Ricard-Pomarede of 4 rue de l' Horlage at Bagneres-de-Bigorre [Department Hautes Pyrenees, 18 km southeast of Tarbes along the Spanish border] -- About 1000 German Waffen-SS [2. SS-Panzer-Division *Das Reich* (CO: SS-Brigadeführer Heinz Lammerding)] arrived in Bagneres from the Tarbes direction in the late afternoon on June 11th. They had been heard arriving as they were firing machine-guns and mortars of 155 mm. They were shooting at all the civilians they saw on the streets and at the doors and windows of the houses. They entered many of the houses, killing some of the inhabitants and pillaging the homes. They also lined up men and women in the streets, sometimes shooting them haphazard, sometimes only threatening them with their weapons and letting them go. In one such instance, the last, the Sous Prefet of Bagneres, M. Haugade, walked out of the Sous Prefecture, alone and in full uniform, asked for the senior German officer and asked him to spare those innocent persons, offering himself as a hostage for them. He asked the officer whether he admitted that not one of the inhabitants had fired a single shot. The Germans admitted they had not, and agreed he would not claim or take away any hostages for this reason. No further atrocities were committed in consequence. The total killed included eighteen men and seven women, twenty-five in all. The wounded totalled seventeen, of which nine were women. The names of the forgoing are registered at the Mairie of Bagneres de Bigorre. Mme. Ricard-Pomarede was tending the wounded throughout these circumstances. Doctor Ricard-Pomarede, Surgeon at Bagneres Hospital and Doctor Decoste of the same hospital certified that the above account is true and accurate. They saw all the victims, dead and wounded and tended the latter from 1700 hours on the 11th of July until early in the morning of the following day.

Declaration made by M. Joseph Cruchou, of 6 Place des Vignaux, Bagneres de Bigorre -- On June 11th, when he heard the Germans arriving, he left his house with his wife and child to go to his mother, as the latter lives alone, his brother being a prisoner of war in Germany. His wife and child remained there upstairs, he and his mother went to the grocer's on the ground floor where the latter, an Italian, and his wife, another Italian and a Spaniard were in the dining room. The Germans came in and ordered the four men out of the house. They were taken, their hands above their heads to the end of the Promenade des Courtous. There they were questioned and their respective nationalities established, their papers being in order. Furthermore no weapons had been found in the house or on them. Then they were marched down again. Opposite the Hostillerie de la Bigorre, the Germans behind, without warning, began firing with one or two automatic rifles. M.D. Malfatto, an Italian, who was walking in front of M. Cruchou, fell. M. Cruchou was not hit, but feigned and fell as though wounded. A German came up to him and with presumably a revolver, shot him

at eighteen inches range through the head, the bullet entered two inches below and to the right of his right eye and came out on the left side of the center of his nose, under his left eye. He never lost consciousness and had the presence of mind and the will-power to keep still. At about this time, the Sous-Prefet intervened, but it was an hour before he dared move. He was taken to the hospital and tended by Dr. Ricard-Pomarede. Doctor Ricard-Pomarede has confirmed to me the exactitude, from a medical point of view of the cause of the wounds, and I have personally seen the marks on the victim's face."

Source
(U.S. National Archives, Records of the Office of the Judge Advocate General [Army], French War Crime Cases RG-153, 151 / File Number 000-11-144, Case Summary)

Bais (France)

"In the region of Bais [Department of Mayenne, 19 km east of Mayenne] the Germans had encountered considerable resistance from F.F.I. units [Forces Francaises de l'Interieur, i.e. French partisans]. To forestall further attacks, and to intimidate the residents of the town they seized hostages and killed them. Their explanation was solely that the men were terrorists.

On the 6th of August 1944 Rene Chancerel was seized by the Germans at his home. He was led to a place where four other hostages were being held. Here the men with the exception of Chancerel were questioned and beaten. Chancerel was questioned for some time and then told that he was free. He returned to his home where he remained for the rest of the night. During the night he heard the cries of the other hostages who were being beaten violently (his home was about 40 yards from the scene of the atrocity). At about one o'clock he heard the sound of automatic rifle fire. Five days later the bodies of the four men were exhumed from the shallow grave into which they had been placed.

The murdered men were identified as the following: M. Vetillard of Bais, Georges Gautier, Rene Guimont, and Marcel Deslandes of Caen who were refugees. No explanation of this act was given. The atrocity was committed by troops of the Das Reich

Division [2. SS-Panzer-Division Das Reich (CO: SS-Standartenführer Otto Baum)]."

Source
(U.S. National Archives, Records of the Office of the Judge Advocate General [Army],
French War Crime Cases RG-153, 151 / File Number 000-11-154, Case Summary)

Bardine de San Terenzo (Italy)

On 19 August 1944, at this northern Italian town in the vicinity of Bologna, elements of SS-Panzeraufklärungs-Abteilung 16 / 16. SS-Panzergrenadier-Division Reichsführer-SS (abteilung CO : SS-Sturmbannführer Walter Reder) executed 53 civilians by pistol-shot in retaliation for a fire-fight with partisans in the area two days earlier. This atrocity occurred during a large anti-partisan sweep that resulted in the deaths of many civilians. After the war, SS-Sturmbannführer Reder was tried before an Italian Military Tribunal for this and numerous other atrocities committed in the Bologna area. The court ruled that Reder ordered the reprisal and found him guilty of murder and wanton destruction of property. For a full accounting of SS-Sturmbannführer Reder's operations in northern Italy and his subsequent post-war trial see the entry for Monte Sol.

Source
(Kunz, 1967)

Bela Crkva (Yugoslavia)

On 12 March 1944, during the course of Unternehmen Wegweiser -- an anti-partisan operation aimed at clearing out the Bosut Forest in northeastern Bosnia, Spearhead F of Kampfgruppe Regiment 27 / 13. Waffen-Gebirgs-Division der SS Handschar [kroatisches Nr. 1] (CO: SS-Brigadeführer Karl-Gustav Sauberzweig) entered the Serbian Orthodox village of Bela Crkva and found all of the town's inhabitants murdered. Initially the massacre was attributed to the partisans. It was subsequently learned, however, that two days earlier other elements of Handschar (Spearhead J / Task Force Regiment 27 and Kampfgruppe Aufklärungs-Abteilung 13) had been ordered

to reconnoiter and seize the village. Given divisional commander Sauberzweig's operational orders stating that since the Bosut was "not inhabited by Muslims, [restraint] was only necessary in dealing with the local ethnic German population," partisan claims that the atrocity was carried out by members of Handschar appear well-founded.

Sources
(Lepre, 1997, pp. 143-150)
(J.J. Peric, "13. SS 'Handzar' divizija i njen slom u is tocna Bosni",
Istocna Bosna u NOB-u 1941-45, vol. 2, p. 587)

Bergen-Belsen (Germany)

Shortly before 15 April 1945 several German officers approached advancing British Army forces to negotiate a truce for the Bergen-Belsen concentration camp. Brigadier-General Hugh Llewelyn Glyn-Hughes (Deputy Director of Medical Services, 2nd Army, British 8th Corps) went to tour the camp which was still under control of its infamous commandant, Josef Kramer. During the course of his visit and over the next several days, Glyn-Hughes witnessed guards indiscriminately shooting prisoners out of hand. The guards in question were Hungarian Volksdeutsche Waffen-SS troopers on loan from SS-Truppenübungsplatz Bergen bei Celle where they were undergoing basic training.

Source
(Phillips, 1949, pp. 32-38)

Berlin (Germany)

As part of the Nazi program to exterminate European Jewry, a series of ongoing deportation actions to the concentration camps had been conducted in Berlin since the beginning of the war. Among the last Jews left in the city, not including those in hiding, were those with industrial skills that were useful to the war-related industries. On the night of 27 February 1943, the SS conducted a major roundup of Jewish workers employed in Wehrmacht munitions factories. The scope of the operations required larger forces than usual. The factories were surrounded by elements of VII. Bataillon (Wach) / 1. SS-Panzer-Division Leibstandarte Adolf Hitler (bataillon CO : SS-Sturmbannführer Ernst Meyer) stationed at Berlin-Lichterfelde for ceremonial duties at the Reichskanzlerei and other state buildings in the capital city. The LAH Wach-Bataillon was composed of four rifle companies:

1. Kompanie (CO: SS-Untersturmführer Deistung)
2. Kompanie (CO: SS-Obersturmführer Knösel)
3. Kompanie (CO: SS-Obersturmführer Blunck)
4. Kompanie (CO: SS-Obersturmführer Drescher)

Trucks of the battalion were then moved into the plants themselves and the Jews bustled aboard. At the same time, smaller groups of LAH personnel raided apartment houses in the Jewish Ghetto and rounded up anyone found at home. All of the Jews were then transported to a satellite labor camp, and from there to Auschwitz concentration camp.

Sources
(Hilberg, 1985, vol. 2, p. 404)
(Reitlinger, 1961, p. 404) *(Lehmann, 1977-1987)*

Blazevici (Yugoslavia)

On 28 March 1944 elements of the 7. SS-Freiwilligen-Gebirgs-Division Prinz Eugen (CO: SS-Brigadeführer Otto Kumm) with the help of the 369. Infanterie Division (CO: Generalleutnant Fritz Neidholdt) fired the town of Blazevici (west of Mostar near Grude, Bosnia/Herzegovina) and shot 80 civilians as part of a larger *säuberungsaktion* ("cleansing action") in the region.

Sources
(Zöller & Leszczynski, 1965, p. 62) *(Kumm, 1978)*

Blazevo (Yugoslavia)

During Winter 1942, 7. SS-Freiwilligen-Gebirgs-Division *Prinz Eugen* (CO: SS-Obergruppenführer Artur Phleps) conducted a series of anti-partisan actions in Serbia that included the mass murder of innocent civilians. In the beginning of December elements of this division blockaded the villages of Blazevo (32 km northeast of Novi Pazar), Gradac (near Brus, 30 km southwest of Krusevac), Bozominu, and Domisevina (near Brus, 30 km southwest of Krusevac). Having heard of the previous SS massacre at Kriva Reka, many of the villagers fled as the troops approached. However, the SS suceeded in detaining 29 villagers who were then executed without any trial or proof of guilt. The SS then fired the villages and destroyed 40 homes, schools, churches, and other public buildings. *Prinz Eugen* then moved on and carried out similar actions against the villages of Boronjina (22 km southeast of Niksic, Crna Gora), Ravniste (15 km south of Krusevac, Serbia), Rodici (near Jablanica, Bosnia/Herzegovina), and Ilinci (27 km south-southeast of Vukovar, Serbia APV).

Sources
(Glisich, 1970, pp. 128-131) *(Kumm, 1978)*

Blonie (Poland)

On the night of 18/19 September 1939 at Burzeum near the town of Blonie, elements of the *Leibstandarte Adolf Hitler* Regiment Musikzug (regimental band), commanded by SS-Hauptsturmführer Hermann Müller-John, rounded up and shot 50 Polish civilians that were judged to be "Jewish criminals." SS-Hauptsturmführer Müller-John was later arrested by Wehrmacht officials. It appears that any charges against him were dropped since he continued on in his capacity as *LAH* Obermusikmeister. The *LAH* Regiment later became the 1. SS-Panzer-Division *Leibstandarte Adolf Hitler*.

Sources
(Krausnick and Wilhelm, 1981, p. 81)
(Weingartner, 1974, p. 42) *(Lehmann, 1977-1987)*
(SS-Hauptsturmführer Müller-John to SS-Obergruppenführer Dietrich, undated, U.S. National Archives Microfilm series T-354, roll 609, frames 000937-38)

Böhmen-Mähren (Czechoslovakia)

A memo dated 14 October 1941 from an unidentified SS-Gruppenführer of the SS-Führungshauptamt / Kommandoamt der Waffen-SS to Reichsführer-SS Heinrich Himmler (*Bericht des SS-Führungshauptamtes über Exekution in der CSR, 1941*) details the following repressive measures taken by Waffen-SS battalions against the Czechoslovak populace : Prague -- 99 shot, 21 hung; Brünn -- 54 shot, 17 hung. The units responsible for these killings were the SS-Wach-Bataillon 2 *Prag* and SS-Wach-Bataillon *Böhmen-Mähren*.

Sources
(Komitee der Antifaschistischen....., 1960, p. 537)
(Schröder, 1979, pp. 84-85)

Bor Kunowski (Poland)

According to one source, on 3/4 July 1943 elements of 17. SS-Infanterie-Regiment executed 42 civilians in the town of Bor Kunowski (south of Radom, south-central Poland). However, there is no documentary evidence that a unit designated "17. SS-Infanterie-Regiment" ever existed. The closest designations of any known SS units are as follows: 17. SS-Polizei-Regiment (a Schutzpolizei, not Waffen-SS, unit that was formed in July 1942 and stationed in northern Russia) and SS-Kavallerie-Regiment 17 (a sub-unit of the 8. SS-Kavallerie-Division *Florian Geyer* detached and serving as a part of SS-Kampfgruppe Gille in the Reschitza-Mostir area in the Soviet Union). While the atrocity claim may be real, the perpetrator's actual identity (and whether they were Waffen-SS personnel or not) remains unknown.

Source
(Röhr et al., 1989)

Boskina (USSR)

"An exchange of fire took place on August 15, [19]41, between partisans and two sub-units of the Waffen-SS platoon attached to the Einsatzgruppe A near Boskina near the H.Q. of the Einsatzgruppe A [i.e., Novoselye]. Thirteen partisans were killed, one has probably escaped." [The unit involved was 1. Kompanie / Waffen-SS Bataillon zbV commanded by SS-Obersturmführer Friedrich Störtz. While this is not an example of an atrocity, the incident does serve to further demonstrate that Waffen-SS units served as part of the murderous Einsatzgruppe operating in the USSR.]

Source
(Ereignismeldung UdSSR Nr. 58 / dated: Berlin, 20 August 1941 in Arad et al., 1989, pp. 94-95)

Boves (Italy)

Following the collapse of the Italian Fascist government in July 1943, Adolf Hitler dispatched German military forces to regain control of his wayward ally. Among the units sent to Italy was the 1. SS-Panzer-Division *Leibstandarte Adolf Hitler* (CO: SS-Brigadeführer Theodor Wisch) which was deployed into the Piedmont of northwestern Italy with the goal of disarming unreliable Italian Army units. In the course of the division's security operations, an atrocity occurred on 19 September 1943 at the town of Boves (8 km south of Cuneo in the Po Valley) which has resulted in a decades-long argument over the exact nature of the events.

There are two basic versions of what transpired in Boves on that fateful day. According to the eyewitness accounts of the town's residents, on 19 September 1943 two SS-Unterführer of the III. Panzerkompanie / SS-Panzer-Regiment 2 (CO: SS-Sturmbannführer Joachim "Jochen" Peiper) were captured by Italian partisans in the town of Boves. SS-Sturmbannführer Peiper immediately had two of the village elders seized as hostages and demanded the release of his men. He threatened to wipe out the entire population of 4,000 if there was any delay in responding to his demands. Less than an hour later the two SS-Unterführer were released unharmed. SS-Sturmbannführer Peiper, however, was not satisfied and ordered that a reprisal should be carried out anyway. The towns of Boves and Castellar were fired and every building burned to the ground; fifty-seven civilians --- including many women and children --- perished in the flames. This version of the incident is in accord with Wehrmacht memoranda concerning the event. The OKW disapproved of the action which they described thusly : "Following the capture of two of his men by Communist guerillas in the Piedmontese town of Boves, Peiper attacked the town, destroying numerous buildings and killing 33 inhabitants." While the OKW may have looked dimly on such activities (and erred in its body count), Hitler approved of them.

Unsurprisingly, the Waffen-SS version of what occurred at Boves is considerably different from the judgements of the Italian and German military authorities. Rudolf Lehmann, a former commander of the 1. SS-Panzer-Division *Leibstandarte Adolf Hitler*, has devoted a considerable amount of space to the incident in his massive five-volume tribute to the division (see Lehmann, 1977-87). He relates the following chronology of events :

9/18/43 -- To the commander of the III. (gep.)/2, Sturmbannführer Peiper, there appeared in Cuneo an Italian Oberstleutnant as the official representative of the 4th Italian Army who demanded of him that within 24 hours his battalion must leave the province of Cuneo, otherwise it would be wiped out to the last man. Sturmbannführer Peiper took the following measures: 1. Appealed to the populace, for them not to aid the troops of the 4th Italian Army in hostilities against the German Army; 2. Printed up pamphlets, in which the soldiers of the 4th Italian Army are called upon to lay down their weapons. The pamphlets were dropped over the mountain valleys southwest and south of Cuneo; 3. Travelled to Boves and warned the Bürgermeisters of the consequences to the civil populace, if it joined forces with the Italian soldiers.

9/19/43 -- At midday the Italian Police Station at Boves reported that two junior officers of the 14. (s)/2 had been captured and taken away by soldiers of the 4th Italian Army in Boves. Here follows the opinion of Sturmbannführer Peiper on the Operation Boves :

"The company chief of the 14. (s)/2, Obersturmführer [Otto] Dinse, received orders that both personnel were to be promptly retrieved. With that, Dinse set out to Boves with an SPW column in order to free the men. They were subsequently ambushed and became engaged with the enemy. Through radio contact he made a report, that they were engaged against superior forces and could not withdraw without assistance; he feared that the whole column would be destroyed, one man was already dead. I immediately alerted the forces at my disposal [13. Schützenpanzerwagenkompanie commanded by SS-Untersturmführer Erhard Gührs] and took the point of my heavily-armed Schützenpanzers advancing towards Boves. Here we received heavy weapon and MG fire from houses and from the surrounding mountainside; particularly dangerous for our very open SPWs were hand grenades thrown down from the slopes. The unit suffered losses; in my own SPW hit from above by a MG-burst, which killed a radioman, another was wounded, my combat jacket was shot through and my radioset smashed. Since we could not see the enemy in the houses and confusing terrain, I ordered my unit to pull back to the village entrance, especially for the SPW the battleplan in the village was unsuitable. To prepare a speedy breakthrough into the village to my trapped comrades I deployed the "cricket" (sIG 15 cm) and brought the front of the village under fire. Through the shelling various houses caught fire. Under cover of the developing smoke clouds, the enemy in uniform and in civilian dress began to pull back from the village, through a narrow mountain cleft and by our positions unseen. The surrounded troops were able to hold on and were freed and linked back up to my unit. Meanwhile the fire... quickly ate its way up the mountain; we continued the battle through visibility that obstructed the valley cleft from outside. The enemy resistance was broken through the use of heavy weapons; behind the earlier described narrow valley our thrust came upon abandoned artillery in firing positions and saw Italian soldiers and civilians disappearing into the mountains.

On our return to Cuneo the Italian prefect, General Salvi, expressed the deepest sympathy of the government about the incident in Boves and distanced the government from the incident, blaming it all on the Communists.

On the following day I sent one of my companies to Peveragno, a village in a region where similar ambushes were occurring. To my satisfaction the Bürgermeister of these villages still had enough influence over his as yet mostly unarmed populace; he decided against the influence of Allied agents in his district and desired a reconciliation and the prevention of additional incidents.

I am of the opinion, that through our intervention in the freeing of our trapped comrades in Boves the embryonic hostile intentions of the Italian Army were choked off, for the Army broke apart and the attack on Cuneo and Turin did not happen. There were unfortunate consequences of our actions in Boves for the affected civilians, which on the other hand could not be forseen. As a result of our single intervention further immeasurable bloodshed in connection with constant Italian actions --- and admittedly on both sides --- was avoided."

Lehmann also notes that the two captured SS-Unterführer were recovered by the unit which had thrust into the narrow valley. During the fighting, they were able to exploit the general confusion and escape from their guards. Thus, in the Waffen-SS view of things there was no mass killing of innocent civilians. Peiper's units were fired on from Boves and had to fight their way into the town.

At the insistence of the Italian Government, West German officials announced in June 1964 that Joachim Peiper (who had already been condemned to death, but later paroled, for his role in the massacre of American POWs during the Battle of the Bulge --- see *Malmedy*) was under investigation on the charge that he played a leading role in the atrocity at Boves. On 11 December 1968, Italian authorities and nine plaintiffs brought charges of murder against Joachim Peiper, Otto Dinse and Erhard Gührs before the Landgericht Stuttgart. The Landgericht ruled that no evidence of the defendants' criminal intent could be found and dismissed the case in February 1969. It was appealed to the West German Supreme Court which upheld the lower court's ruling. The Supreme Court in its decision stated that :

"In spite of evidence with regard to the events in Boves on 19.9.43 none of the accused is sufficiently suspected to be charged (with murder). There remains, in spite of extensive eyewitness statements, no grounds at all for concluding that any of the accused gave an order for the firing of the town or the shooting of civilians or that such events happened with their approval. Despite the fact that Peiper was commander of the group and Dinse and Gührs were company commanders, there were still no reasonable grounds for them alone to be found legally responsible.... Also, that Peiper had previously appealed to the civil populace, who supported the resistance groups, lest retaliatory measures be taken. On 19.9.43 [Boves] was made an example of. It is notable that none of the 127 former battalion personnel, in connection with the proceedings, accused the defendants of issuing criminal orders, although some admitted that fire-setting had taken place. It is significant, that these witnesses from the outset were not biased in favor of the defendants; it appears out of the question that so many witnesses could have agreed on how to testify with regard to such complex actions. It is possible that these connections not previously foreseen provide a sufficient resolution of the circumstances surrounding the events in Boves over 25 years ago."

It is clear from the Court's opinion that the justices di-not accept the Waffen-SS version of events, but merely felt that the three defendants were not legally responsible for the retaliatory measures visited upon the people of Boves. Considering the notorious leniency shown by West German courts where war crimes are concerned, the rulings of the Provincial and Supreme courts in this case are hardly surprising. The late date of the case (1964-69) undoubtedly added to the desire of officials to dismiss it and put to rest things best forgotten. The Supreme Court's positive opinion on the credibility of the 127 former Waffen-SS witnesses exhibits a degree of naivetee that is hard to overstate. A potentially more biased group of witnesses would be hard to find. In no instance on record has a member of the Waffen-SS freely given damning testimony against a comrade. Only individuals who were physically abused (as in the *Malmedy* series of atrocities) or had no emotional commitment to the Waffen-SS (such as the Polish conscript in the *Abbaye Ardenne* case) have given testimony against other Waffen-SS men. Peiper's account of the Boves atrocity is instructive; Waffen-SS officers have claimed on numerous occasions --- despite all evidence --- that the unarmed civilians they killed were, in fact, armed partisans. It is perhaps the most universal excuse given for their murderous excesses. Besides, as Peiper assures us, the unfortunate *incident* undoubtedly prevented "further immeasurable bloodshed." This is yet another common Waffen-SS after-the-fact rationalization of their actions.

Sources
(Stein, 1966, pp. 275-276) (Lehmann, 1977-1987, vol. 3)
(Schreiber, 1996, pp. 130-133)
(Bundesverband der....., 1985, pp. 27-28) (Infield, 1990, p. 4)
(Reynolds, 1995)
(Heeres Gruppe B, Anlage zum Tätigkeitsbericht der Abt.
 Ic, Abschluss bericht der Entwaffnungsaktion
 in Nord Italien, 19 Sept 1943, U.S. National Archives Mi
crofilm, Records of the
 German Field Commands, Army Groups, T-311
/276/000065-67)
(Stellungsnahme des Einheitsführer, no date, op. cit.,
 T-354/624/0000363)
(Besonderes Feindnachrichtenblatt, 22 Sept 1943, op. cit.,
 T-311/276/000084-86)

Brusilov [USSR]

"With the help of a platoon of the Waffen-SS, 29 Communists, five agents of the NKVD were arrested in Brusilov [southwest of Kiev, Ukraine] and liquidated on the spot." [The unit referred to is the 3. Kompanie / Waffen-SS Bataillon zbV (CO unknown). This incident again demonstrates that Waffen-SS units served as part of the murderous Einsatzgruppe operating in the USSR, in this case as part of Einsatzgruppe C.]

Source
(Ereignismeldung UdSSR Nr. 58 / dated: Berlin, 20 August 1941 in Arad et al., 1989, p. 96)

Bydgoszcz (Poland)

On 11 September 1939, five hundred Polish civilians were executed at the town of Bydgoszcz by elements of Einsatzgruppe IV (CO: SS-Brigadeführer Lothar Beutel) as retaliation for the murders of local ethnic Germans. In the official German report of the atrocity (*Berichte der Einsatzgruppen der deutschen Sicherheitspolizei von Sept. - Okt. 1939*, Hauptamt der Sicherheitspolizei [Berlin], Sonderreferat Unternehmen Tannenberg) it was claimed that the reprisals were occasioned by attacks on German troop transports, installations, and patrols in the Bydgoszcz region.

Sources
(Krausnick and Wilhelm, 1981, pp. 51-55) (Aschenauer, 1982, p. 174)

Bydgoszcz 2 (Poland)

SS-Totenkopfstandarte II *Brandenburg* (CO SS-Standartenführer Paul Nostitz) as part of Einsatzgruppe III (CO SS-Obersturmbannführer Dr. Herbert Fischer) advanced into Poland on 13 September 1939 to begin "cleansing and security measures" in the operational zone of the 8th Army. This zone included large areas of Poznan and the entire west-central portion of Poland. On 24 September, two sturmbanne (battalions) of *Brandenburg* arrived in the town of Bydgoszcz having been detached from an ongoing *Judenaktion* (Jewish action) at Wloclawek under the direction of SS-Standartenführer Nostitz. The sturmbanne spent two days pursuing an "intelligentsia action" in Bydgoszcz. As a result, approximately 800 Polish civilians were hunted down, rounded up, and shot. The victims' names appeared on special death lists prepared ahead of time by the SIPO and SD which targeted intellectuals and possible resistance leaders. Photographs of the mass killings during this action can be found in Poznanski.

On 1 November 1939, *Brandenburg* was designated as cadre for the newly-forming 3. SS-Panzer-Division *Totenkopf*. As of July 1944, SS-Standartenführer Nostitz still held the same rank and was attached to SS-Panzergrenadier-Ersatz-Bataillon 1. His fate is uncertain.

Sources
(Sydnor, 1977, pp. 38-40) (Poznanski, 1963)

Bzura (Poland)

The massacre of 50 Jews in the town of Bzura (west of Warsaw) in September 1939 during the German campaign against Poland has been attributed to elements of the 1. SS-Panzer-Division *Leibstandarte Adolf Hitler*. The author making the accusation states that the evidence for this event is shaky at best. In combination with the fact that the author's work is littered with numerous egregious factual errors, this particular atrocity should be treated as an unsubstantiated rumor.

Source
(Wykes, 1974)

Carsac-de-Carlux (France)

On 8 June 1944 while relocating towards the fighting at the Normandy beaches, the 1. Bataillon / SS-Panzergrenadier-Regiment 4 *Der Führer* / 2. SS-Panzer-Division *Das Reich* (bataillon CO: SS-Sturmbannführer Adolf Diekmann) took a wrong turn and moved through the village of Carsac-de-Carlux in southwest France (Department of the Dordogne, 5 km southeast of Sarlat), firing as they went. Thirteen people were killed, including a Jewish refugee doctor, an 80-year old blacksmith named Pierre Trefail, and a farmer driving oxen in some neighboring fields. Several houses were also set on fire by the SS troopers.

Source
(Hastings, 1981, p. 87)

Chateau Valencay (France)

After its arrival in Normandy in early June 1944, elements of the 2. SS-Panzer-Division Das Reich (CO: SS-Brigadeführer Heinz Lammerding) raided Chateau Valencay where the great Louvre Museum sculptures had been stored for safe-keeping. The SS troopers were searching for partisans who had attacked a German armored column in the area several days before. The Louvre staff in residence was rounded up by the troopers and held at gunpoint. After aimlessly shooting up the chateau, the SS released their hostages in order to let them extinguish a fire that had broken out. As they went off to fight the fire, the SS troopers opened fire again killing a member of the museum staff.

Sources
(Nicholas, 1994, p. 288) (Valland, 1961, p. 195)

Chelm (Poland)

On 12 January 1940 six hundred Jews from Lublin were executed at Chelm (east of Lublin in eastern Poland) by members of the 5. Schwadron / 1. SS-Totenkopf-Reiterstandarte (regimental CO : SS-Standartenführer Hermann Fegelein) as an element of Polizeigruppe 3 under the overall command of Oberstleutnant der Polizei Hermann Franz. The executions were conducted in the operational area of the 8. Armee Korps as part of the ongoing Intelligenz Aktion (Fall 1939 through Spring 1940) which targeted Polish intellectuals and potential resistance figures for elimination. On 2 August 1941 this unit was incorporated into the newly-forming 8. SS-Kavallerie-Division Florian Geyer.

Sources
(Röhr et al., 1989) (Zentrales Staatsarchiv der DDR - Potsdam, Microfilm #41345)

Ciepielow (Poland)

In September 1939 unidentified Waffen-SS units tortured and murdered numerous Jews, political and religious leaders, and Polish POWs in the region around Ciepielow. These actions were carried out by either SS-Totenkopfstandarte I "Oberbayern" (CO: SS-Sturmbannführer Max Simon) or SS-Totenkopf-standarte III "Thüringen" (CO: ?), both of which were detailed to "cleansing and security" measures as part of Einsatzgruppe II (CO: SS-Obersturmbannführer Dr. Emanuel Schäfer) in the operational zone of the 10th Army (south-central Poland, Kielce region). Photographs of some of the victims are reproduced in Poznanski. On 1 November 1940, both units served as cadre for the newly-forming 3. SS-Panzer-Division Totenkopf.

Sources
(Sydnor, 1977, p. 41) (Poznanski, 1963)

Crvenka (Yugoslavia)

In the middle of September 1944 as Soviet forces made threatening advances into eastern and central Europe, German occupation authorities began evacuating Jewish slave laborers from the Bor copper mines (200 km southeast of Belgrade, Yugoslavia). An initial group of 3,600 prisoners left on 17 September with an escort of 100 Hungarian guards. They were marched under brutal conditions through Belgrade, Novi Sad, and Sombor to Mohacs. A few lucky individuals escaped along the way. From there they were deported to several concentration camps in Germany (Flossenburg, Sachsenhausen, and Oranienburg). Only a handful survived at war's end.

A second group of 2,500 prisoners left the mines on 19 September also under Hungarian guard. They faced a similarly brutal march through Zagubica, Petrovac, and Smederevo to Belgrade arriving there on 26 September. The march then continued on to Pancevo and Crvenka. Along the way 450 prisoners were shot for a variety of reasons (inability to walk, escape attempts, begging for food and water). The survivors reached the town of Crvenka on 6 October and were quartered in the Glaeser Welker Rauch brickyards. The next day elements of the 31. SS-Freiwilligen-Grenadier-Division (CO: SS-Brigadeführer Gustav Lombard) took over custody of the prisoners from the Hungarian authorities. The SS decided to execute the remaining prisoners in order to free up local roads for retreating Axis forces. On 7 October the prisoners were purposefully exhausted by their Waffen-SS guards by making them run from place to place all day. At 11:00 pm that night, the Waffen-SS troopers began segregating the prisoners into groups of 20-30 individuals. Each group was then marched into a huge claypit on the brickyard grounds and executed with machine-gun fire. Further selections followed and the killing lasted until four in the morning. Approximately 700 - 1,000 prisoners were executed that night; miraculously, two survived and lay undetected among the corpses. At five in the morning on 8 October the remaining prisoners (1,050 - 1,350) were started on a march for Sombor. Executions continued along the way. Waffen-SS troopers killed those who left their rows to drink water, or do their necessities, as well as those who were too weak to keep up with the march pace. Numerous guards also killed prisoners without any pretext; they simply selected small groups, took them away and killed them. The march route (Crvenka - Sombor - Gjakovo - Baja) was soon littered with corpses. When the column finally reached the town of Baja, less than 1,000 persons were still alive. The survivors were deported to concentration camps in Germany (Buchenwald and Flossenburg); few were still alive at war's end.

Sources
(Löwenthal, 1957, pp. 34-37) (Birn, 1991, pp. 351-372)
(Braham, 1977, pp. 50-58)

Czestochowa (Poland)

Following the campaign against Poland in September 1939, elements of II. Bataillon / *Leibstandarte Adolf Hitler* Regiment under the command of SS-Obersturmbannführer Carl Ritter von Oberkamp murdered an unknown number of civilians in the town of Czestochowa. In all likelihood, the massacre occurred on 1/2 October 1939 while the regiment was relocating to security duties in Böhmen-Mähren. The structure of the battalion at this time was as follows:

5. Kompanie SS-Hauptsturmführer Wilhelm Mohnke
6. Kompanie SS-Hauptsturmführer Otto Baum
7. Kompanie SS-Hauptsturmführer Artur Klingemeier
8. Kompanie SS-Hauptsturmführer August Dieterichs

There is no evidence that legal proceedings were ever instigated with respect to these crimes. Carl Ritter von Oberkamp was executed in 1947 by the Yugoslavian authorities for numerous atrocities committed against Balkan civilians.

Sources
(Sayer & Botting, 1989, p. 20) (United Nations War Crimes Commission file number 284/P/G/29)

Dhistomon (Greece)

On 10 June 1944 elements of the 4. SS-Polizei-Panzergrenadier-Division were ambushed by Greek partisans several miles outside of the village of Dhistomon (northwest of Athens, near Delphi) following a routine patrol through the town. After dispersing the partisans, the division's 2 Kompanie / 7. Regiment (kompanie CO: SS-Hauptsturmführer Fritz Lautenbach) drove back into Dhistomon and killed all the inhabitants that they could find. The unit methodically massacred 296 unarmed civilians in their homes; some bodies were strung up on trees that lined the road into the village. Numerous rapes and widespread looting also occurred. Lappas lists 223 of the murdered individuals by name, age, and occupation. In the unit's official after-action report, SS-Hauptsturmführer Lautenbach claimed that his men were attacked by the partisans and villagers *as they first entered Dhistomon*. His statement was contradicted by the report of Georg Koch, a Geheime Feldpolizei officer who accompanied the unit on that day's operations. A Wehrmacht military tribunal ruled that the excesses of the SS troopers were justified and deferred any punishment to the commander of 7. Regiment, SS-Standartenführer Karl Schümers. No punishments were meted out in this affair. SS-Hauptsturmführer Lautenbach and SS-Standartenführer Schümers were both later killed in action (October 1944 and 16 August 1944, respectively).

Sources
(Mazower, 1993, pp. 180 & 212-215)
(Hondros, 1983, p. 158)
(Lappas, 1945, pp. 61-67) (Husemann, 1971-1977)

Dirlewanger Brigade Operations

&

Atrocities in the USSR

Due to its atrocious behavior while conducting various guard duty assignments in occupied Poland, the SS-Sonderkommando Dirlewanger (CO: SS-Oberführer Dr. Oskar Dirlewanger) was transferred to the USSR in February 1942. It was placed under the command of HSSPf Russland Mitte und Weissruthenien SS-Obergruppenführer Erich von dem Bach-Zelewski in order to assist with anti-partisan operations in the region. Many of these anti-partisan campaigns were little more than extermination operations which resulted in widespread civilian deaths with only moderate losses to actual Soviet partisan units. It is estimated that the brigade killed between 100,000 - 150,000 civilians during its operations in the USSR. The unit's field activities were characterized by criminally ruthless tactics which only inspired the civil populace's hatred of the German invaders. Innocent civilians and "suspicious" individuals rounded up by raiding parties were usually executed out of hand. Entire villages were looted and burned after their inhabitants had been shot. Women and children were often rounded up and marched through suspected minefields. Any Jews captured were killed immediately. It was not uncommon for the brigade to "cleanse" entire operational areas in this manner. Prisoners were rarely taken since, by the logic that often governed German policies in the East, "neutral" villagers did not exist. Throughout the war, the sonderkommando was increased in size until it became the 36. Waffen-Grenadier-Division der SS.

Operation	Dates	Location
Adler	7/1/42 - 8/12/42	Bobruisk, Rogacov, Osipovici, Berezino, Bykhov, Belynici, Svisloc
Klette	7/26/42 - 7/29/42	Smolensk region; included participationof the 1. SS-Infanterie (mot.) -Brigade
Greif	8/19/42 - 8/23/42	east and west of the Orsa-Vitebsk roads
Nordsee	9/2/42 - 9/5/42	Drut River region
Regatta	10/4/42 - 10/8/42	Rekota, Moshkovo, Dobraya, Ryabki
Karlsbad	10/14/42 - 10/24/42	north of the Beresino-Cerven highway; included participation of the 1. SSInfanterie (mot.) -Brigade
Frieda	11/6/42 - 11/8/42	north of the Sakowschtschina-Makonroad; included participation of the 1. SSInfanterie (mot.) -Brigade

Operation	Dates	Location
Franz	12/28/42 - 1/14/43	Berezino, Cerven, Khutor, Novaya Niva, Novyye Lyady, Petrovka, Bogushevichi; civilians in the Jaswenski area were rounded up and sent as slave labor to Germany
Erntefest I	1/19/43 - 1/26/43	Minsk, Ivenets, Nagornoye, Krugloye, Osipovici, Sluck, Rakov, Osovo, Omgovichi, Kopyl
Erntefest II	1/30/43 - 2/4/43	Makawczyce, Rudnia("cleansed"),Kopyl
Hornung	2/11/43 - 2/26/43	Pripjet Marshes: Ratkovo, Povarchitsky, Milevichi, Moroc, Staryye Velichkovichi, Starobin; reports that the villages of DobreStrazn,Wejna,Wieliczkow-icze Nowe and Wieliczkow icz-e were "cleansed"; 3,300 Jews killed
unnamed	3/13/43 - 3/22/43	Prilepy, Ljada, Dubrovo and Kossino were "cleansed"
Lenz Süd	3/31/43 - 4/3/43	Borisov, Cerven, Sloboda, Smolevici,Dubniki, Zhodino, Zabashevichi
Lenz Nord	4/8/43 - 4/13/43	Borisov, Molodecno, Smolevici, Lugojsk, Antonopol, Zembin
Zauberflöte	4/17/43 - 4/22/43	city of Minsk
Draufgänger I	4/28/43 - 4/30/43	Molodecno, Plescenicy, Lugojsk
Draufgänger II	5/1/43 - 5/10/43	Molodecno, Borisov, Starinski
Günther	6/28/43 - 7/6/43	Molodecno, Besyady, Rudnia, Manyly

Operation	Dates	Location
Hermann	7/7/43 - 8/7/43?	Rakov, Radoshkovichi, Zaslavl, Grodek, Ivenec, Volozhyn, Niemen River region; included participation of the 1. SSInfanterie (mot.) -Brigade
Kottbus	???? - ????	information not available
Frühlingsfest	4/11/44 - 5/10/44	Lepel-Usaci region; included participation of the RONA Brigade (see 29. Waffen-Grenadier-Division der SS [russische Nr. 1])

Sources
(MacLean, 1998)
(Majewski, 1977, p. 141)

Dnepropetrovsk (USSR)

On 13 October 1941 staff elements of HSSPf Ukraine SS-Obergruppenführer Friedrich Jeckeln with the assistance of the 1. SS-Infanterie (mot.)-Brigade (CO: SS-Brigadeführer Richard Hermann) and Polizei-Regiment Süd murdered approximately 10,000 Jews in the city of Dnepropetrovsk. Later actions by these units in Kamenetz-Podolsk and Dnepropetrovsk resulted in the deaths of an additional 22,600 Jewish inhabitants. The 1. SS-Infanterie (mot.)-Brigade supplied replacement personnel to the main-line Waffen-SS divisions (Leibstandarte, Das Reich, and Totenkopf) in late 1941 - 1942 and provided cadre elements to the newly-forming 20. Waffen-Grenadier-Division der SS [estnische Nr. 1] (5 May 1943) and 18. SS-Freiwilligen-Panzergrenadier-Division Horst Wessel (March 1944).

Sources
(Arad et al., 1989, p. xi)
(Ereignismeldung UdSSR Nr. 135 / Berlin, 19 November 1941 in Arad et al., 1989, p. 242)

Dola (Yugoslavia)

On 7 June 1943 unidentified elements of the 7. SS-Freiwilligen-Gebirgs-Division *Prinz Eugen* (CO: SS-Obergruppenführer Artur Phleps) murdered approximately 500 women, children, and elderly near the village of Dola on the Oiva plateau (15 kilometers south of Foca, Bosnia-Herzegovina). This massacre took place during the final days of *Unternehmen Schwarz II* --- an anti-partisan operation directed against Tito's partisan forces in the mountains of southern Bosnia-Herzegovina and northern Montenegro. German sources have denied that this event ever happened. Kumm provides excerpts from SS-Obergruppenführer Phleps unpublished diaries to demonstrate that *Prinz Eugen* was involved in heavy combat at the time against strong partisan forces that included numerous women members. He also notes that ".... All war is horrible and requires each fighter to be extremely fierce against the enemy. In this theater of war, the fierceness was escalated by the combat methods employed by the partisans. They could not always be recognized as soldiers.... they conscripted women...." Kumm concludes that the division handled all prisoners properly and implies that any women killed were armed combatants. However, the cited diary entries merely prove that *Prinz Eugen* was the only Axis unit in the area at the time of the alleged killings. Considering this unit's record of executing ostensibly innocent civilians, it is difficult to take Kumm's explanations and rationalizations seriously.

Sources
(Kumm, 1978, pp. 271-272)
(Politika [Yugoslav newspaper], 11 July 1977, p. 6)

Dunes (France)

"Direct evidence obtained from M. Edmond Demonchy, confirmed by Pierre Andre Delpech, Jean Batiste Marcadet, Antoine Lacouture, Jean Boy, Ernest Gauran, Ernest Loirat, Pierre Guillemard, Pierre Auricanne, who were all present at the time, the first, one of the intended victims. Declaration made at Dunes [Department of Tarn-et-Garonne, 16 km southeast of Agen]:
On Friday, June 23rd 1944, at 1030 hours, six German soldiers of the SS Division entered his office at the Mairie [in Dunes], and ordered him at revolver point to come out under the arcade in the square. There a lieutenant ordered him to assemble the male population. Out of a total of about 200, only about 60 were available. The officer produced a typed list and called out about forty-two names. Only ten were present, and of these one was exempted at the urgent request, on his knees, of the Cure, on the grounds that this man, M. Pierre Andre Delpech, had been wounded and was a "Grand Mutile" of the last war. But to replace him, two other men were picked, these were M. Paul Masson and M. Roger Dublin. Later M. Gaston Martin was also taken. The names of the men on the original list, who were available, were (apart from P.A. Delpech above-mentioned): Yvon Duburc, Louis Dufour, Gaston Sieurac, Marcel Tonnele, Frank Saint-Martin, Martial Martin, Andre Pelleran, Maurice Mauquie.The Germans then hung ropes from the balcony of the Post Office, placed chairs upon a table on the ground beneath, and hung these eight men and the three picked at random, side by side. After this the Germans, who were already partly intoxicated on ar-

rival, pillaged the Cafe and drank on the square. The officers did not appear drunk. They then left. It was subsequently learnt that two men, also of this commune, had been shot and killed in the field previously that morning.

Note: Of the ten original names, one other, besides P.A. Delpech was not hung, as he attempted to escape when hoisted on the table. He ran about 200 yards but was shot by automatic rifles, and riddled with bullets. The total hung, therefore, was eleven men and three men shot."

[The only Waffen-SS unit in the area at this time was the 2. SS-Panzer-Division *Das Reich* (CO: SS-Brigadeführer Heinz Lammerding). On 10 June 1944 the division began a long northwards march to counterattack the Allied forces invading Normandy. While the bulk of the division was far from Dunes at the time of the atrocity, unspecified sub-units had remained behind to repair and forward AFVs that had broken down on the march north.]

Source

(U.S. National Archives, Records of the Office of the Judge Advocate General [Army], French War Crime Cases RG-153, 151/ File Number 000-11-143, Case Summary)

East Prussia (Germany)

From 21 May through 8 June 1940 a special SS unit known as Sonderkommando Lange murdered 1,900 psychiatric patients from clinics in the towns of Allenberg, Kortau, Tapiau, and Zichenau. The unit was under the command of SS-Sturmbannführer Herbert Lange and operated out of Soldau. Patients were loaded onto specially modified buses and then killed with toxic gas from a hidden cylinder in the cab. One of the buses even bore the name of a fictitious business --- Kaisers-Kaffee-Geschäft. These murders were carried out under the direction of HSSPf Wehrkreis XXI SS-Gruppenführer Wilhelm Koppe and at the request of HSSPf Wehrkreis I SS-Obersturmbannführer Wilhelm Rediess in order to free up the clinics for conversion to military barracks. In correspondence related to Sonderkommando Lange's operations, these killings are referred to as "evacuations". After similar duties in the Berlin area, Sonderkommando Lange was moved

in December 1941 to Chelmno (Kulmhof) in order to operate the first mass extermination center used in the "Final Solution." In 1943, Sonderkommando Lange was temporarily incorporated into the 7. SS-Freiwilligen-Gebirgs-Division Prinz Eugen.

Sources

(Zentral Stelle der Landesjustizverwaltungen, "Euthanasie", Re - Rz, p. 7)
(Zentral Stelle der Landesjustizverwaltungen, 203, AR-Z 69, 1959, vol. 8, pp. 15-17 [Lange biography])
(Burleigh, 1994, p. 132) (Breitman, 1991, p. 102)
(U.S. National Archives, BDC files, Herbert Lange SS file, correspondence: Koppe to Sporrenberg, 18 October 1940)

Farneta Monastery (Italy)

In late August 1944 an abteilung commander of 16. SS-Panzergrenadier-Division Reichsführer-SS, SS-Obersturmführer Hermann Langer, received intelligence that partisans were hiding at the venerable Carthusian charterhouse (monastery) of Farneta near the town of Lucca in Tuscany. Local German authorities had observed for some time that the monks were sheltering refugees, in violation of their ages-old Rule of Enclosure that separated them from the outside world. Prior Dom Martin Binz had asked his 34 fellow monks, "If it were Jesus himself knocking at the door, what would we tell him? Would we have the courage to send him off to die?" In conjunction with the local Gestapo head, SS-Obersturmbannführer Loos, Langer informed his divisional commander SS-Gruppenführer Max Simon of this intelligence. Simon ordered them to "cleanse" the monastery of any partisans and their supporters. Since a subordinate officer (SS-Untersturmführer Eduard Florin) had previously befriended several of the monks, he was employed to get them to open their doors on the night of 1 September. Florin told the nightporter that he had a package for the prior from his commander since the Germans were soon withdrawing from the area. When the doors were opened, 2-3 dozen Reichsführer-SS personnel led by Langer and Loos burst into the charterhouse and began rounding everyone up at gunpoint. This was a fairly easy task as most of the monks and refugees were gathered in the chapel at the Office of Matins, immersed in Gregorian

Chant, when the SS began their raid. Due to the extent of the charterhouse complex, however, 15 refugees were able to escape the Germans and flee across the surrounding fields to safety.

The monks were forced to put on civilian clothing and then all of the prisoners were transported by truck to Nocchi near Camaiore. They were locked up in abandoned warehouse and suffered four long days of interrogation and torture. According to surviving eyewitnesses, the Carthusians ability to calmly, silently, and at times even happily, endure the torture alternately baffled and enraged their SS captors. Some of the monks met an especially grisly end when they were strung up by the neck with wire and beaten to death. On 6 September several of the monks were sent to Forte Malaspina di Massa. They were later executed by SS troopers along with 30 assorted civilians from nearby towns, including several seminarians and Little Carmelite Fathers. The SS troopers dumped all of the bodies into a hastily-dug mass grave.

On 10 September those monks and civilians from Farneta that were still alive at Nocchi were sent to various internment camps in Italy and Germany where a number later died. On 16 September unknown elements of Reichsführer-SS evacuated the last 146 prisoners from Forte Malaspina di Massa. They forced the prisoners into a large bomb crater near the small church of San Leonardo a Taberna and shot them to death. No partisans had been found and advancing Allied forces liberated Farneta charterhouse a few days later. In all, the Carthusians lost 12 brothers including Prior Dom Martin Binz and former Venezuelan bishop Bernardo Montes de Oca (a Carthusian novice). From December 1944 – January 1945, the surviving monks were released by the retreating Germans and returned back to the charterhouse where they resumed their life of prayer and contemplation that continues to this day. Although originally buried in unmarked mass graves, the bodies of the martyred Carthusians were later located, exhumed, identified, and reinterred with proper rites in the confines of the cloister cemetery. The German 14th Army Headquarters naturally had it own version of these events: "the Prior of the Carthusian monastery northwest of Lucca was taken into custody because of arms smuggling, and aiding deserters and partisans. A search of the monastery grounds on the night of 1-2 September netted over 50 bandits and 35 monks as their helpers."

In 1948 Eduard Florin was tried by an Italian military court in Bologna and found not guilty on the grounds that he was unaware that a "cleansing action" had been ordered by his divisional commander. Florin died in 2004 during the trial of his immediate superior Hermann Langer (see below). Max Simon, for his part, was condemned to death by a British military tribunal at Padua for numerous other war crimes during his command of Reichsführer-SS in Italy. His sentence was later commuted to life imprisonment. Despite the serious nature of his crimes, Simon was paroled in 1954 and returned to West Germany. In 1955 West German authorities unsuccessfully tried him for his role in establishing Standgerichte that carried out summary field executions. Max Simon died on 1 February 1961 with a third trial pending. Langer lived in post-war Germany unsuspected and unmolested for nearly six decades due to a simple misunderstanding. Italian authorities had been looking for a "Hermann Gartner" since 1948, when Eduard Florin identified him as the officer in charge of the operation. In his testimony Florin had given Langer's name and profession (gardener, German "Gartner") and the Italians conflated the two leading them on a lengthy fruitless search. The mistake was finally caught in 2002 and Langer was quickly located in Germany. German authorities refused to extradite the 85-year old Langer for trial due to his poor health. Thus, he was tried in absentia by an Italian military court at La Spezia from 8 July - 10 December 2004. It was largely thought to be an open and shut case against Langer due to the detailed military records provided by German archives. After twelve hours of deliberation, the judges acquitted Langer of all charges on grounds that the exact responsibility for ordering the massacre could no longer be determined. The reaction in Italy to this turn of events was one of stunned disbelief.

Sources

(Baglioni, 1975) (Bender & Taylor, 1969-1982, vol. 4, p. 114-115)

(Schreiber, 1996, pp. 200-201)

(Giuseppina Sciascia, 2005, "The 'Silent' Summer of '44", L'Osservatore Romano, February 2, pp. 4-5)

("Prozess gegen früheren SS-Offizier in Italien eröffnet",

Agence France Press, 7/8/04)
("Strage di Farneta, cosa emerge dal processo", Toscana oggi, 7/15/04)
("Assolto il nazista Langer accusato dell'eccidio di Farneta", la Repubblica, 12/10/04)

Farnocchia (Italy)

On 12 August 1944 this northern Italian town in the vicinity of Bologna was set on fire by elements of SS-Panzeraufklärungs-Abteilung 16 / 16. SS-Panzergrenadier-Division Reichsführer-SS (abteilung CO : SS-Sturmbannführer Walter Reder) during a large anti-partisan sweep that resulted in the deaths of many civilians. After the war, SS-Sturmbannführer Reder was tried before an Italian Military Tribunal for this and numerous other atrocities committed in the Bologna area. The court found that while Reder's unit had fired Farnocchia, there was no clear evidence that he had ordered the action. For a full accounting of SS-Sturmbannführer Reder's operations in northern Italy and his subsequent post-war trial see the entry for Monte Sol.

Source
(Bender & Taylor, 1969-1982, vol. 4, p. 114)

1. SS-Infanterie (mot.)-Brigade

Operations & Atrocities in the USSR

All entries are from Baade et. al. (see below), unless otherwise noted, and are annotated either K for Kriegstagebuch Kommandostab RF-SS, T for Tatigkeitsberichte 1. SS-Infanterie-Brigade, or given a fuller attribution. Operations are sometimes cited for specific sub-units of the brigade: SS-Infanterie-Regiment 8 (SS-I.R. 8) and SS-Infanterie-Regiment 10 (SS-I.R. 10). It should be pointed out that "security operations" and "anti-partisan operations" were ofte n synonymous with the murderous "cleansing" operations; any such designations cast suspicion on an operation. For unit details see 1. SS-Infanterie (mot.)-Brigade.

6/20/41 As of 6/21/41, the 1. SS-Brigade (mot) is under Kdo.Stb. RF-SS control. [K]
6/24/41 Cleansing and security operations in the border region from Jeze to Augustow including keeping the Grajewo-Augustow road clear. [K]

7/22/41 Brigade put under temporary control of HSSPf Lemberg. [K]

7/27-30/41 Cleansing action in the Zwiahel-Goshcha region. [K]

On 28 July at 7:00 began a cleansing action in the Zwiahel, Sluch'-Tal, Novo Niropol, Szepetowka, Zaslavl', Ostrog, Goryn'-Tal, Goshcha region. Eliminated elements of the 124th Rifle Division, armed bands, armed insurgents, and communist functionaries. Action was under the command of HSSPf Russland-Süd SS-Obergruppenführer Friedrich Jeckeln. Nine Soviet soldiers were shot as insurgents. Eight hundred Jews and Jewesses, aged 16-60, were shot. Five Soviet Kolkhoz functionaries were shot. [T, 27.7.41/12:00 Uhr - 30.7.41/12:00 Uhr]

8/4/41 SS-I.R. 10 cleansing action in the towns of Ostrog (957 civilians killed), Hrycow (268 civilians killed),and Kuniow-Radogoshch Ml. (160 civilians killed). Action begins at 4:45 am and ends at 8:00 pm. [T, 3.8.41/12:00 Uhr - 6.8.41/12:00 Uhr]

8/6/41 SS-I.R. 10 cleansing action in the Chernigovka-Fesovka-Badichany-Kaja -Dvorishche region. [K]

SS-I.R. 10 cleansing action in the Chernigovka-Fesovka-Buda-Ryshanskaja-Dvorishche region.[T, 3.8.41/12:00 Uhr - 6.8.41/12:00 Uhr]

8/6-10/41 Cleansing action in the Zhitomir-Fesovka-Yemil'chino-Zwiahel region. The following operations were attributed to SS-I.R. 10:

1) Cleansing action in the Tonorischtsche-Terinzy-Dvorishche-Chernigovka region. In Goroschki all Jews and Bolshevists were shot.

2) Clearing action in the Tonorischtsche-Woroff-Rudnja Worowskaja-Brashinka-Wydybor-Shadki-Sselez region. Area declared free of Jews, bolshevists, and functionaries.

3) Cleansing action at Kolkhoz Federowka (15 km NW

Chernigovka). Five "bolshevist agitators" shot.

4) Cleansing action in the Tonorischtsche-Terinzy-Dvorishche-Chernigovka region. Area declared Jew and bolshevist free; nine Jews shot in Mal-Goroschki.

5) Cleansing action in the Chernigovka-Zhitomir-Kolkhoz Boljarka-Vil'sk region. 59 Jews shot.

6) Clearing action in the western Goroschki area. 36 Jews shot in a number of small villages.
[T, 6.8.41/12:00 - 10.8.41/12:00 Uhr]

8/10/41 Several Jews are hung in Zhitomir. [U.S. Holocaust Memorial Museum microfilm RG-48.004M, *Selected Documents from the Military Historical Institute (Prague)*, Reel 1, records of the Kommandostab RF-SS, Karton 19, 1941-42, 1. SS-Infanterie-Brigade Ia report, FN 102469]

8/13/41 SS-I.R. 10 cleansing action in the Melini-Soblewka-Boloschizy-Strasse Korosten-Fesovka-Strassengabel 2 km SW Punkt 186-Waldstück 8 km W Melini. [K]

8/17/41 SS-I.R. 10 cleansing action in eastern Zwiahel region. SS-I.R. 8 cleansing action in the Pripet Sümpfe (Makarichi-Bobrik-Bol'Shiye Gorodyatichi-Ubybaczki- Yuntseviche-Lyuban'-Urech'ye-Sorchi). [K]

8/19/41 SS-I.R. 10 executes an unspecified number of Jews and Communist functionaries during a cleansing action in Sokolov. [T, 17.8.41/12:00 Uhr - 20.8.41/12:00 Uhr]

8/19/41 SS-I.R. 8 executes an unspecified number of Jews at Slavuta (southeast of Staro Konstantinov). [U.S. Holocaust Memorial Museum microfilm RG-48 .004M, *Selected Documents from the Military Historical Institute (Prague)*, Reel 1, records of the Kommandostab RF-SS, Karton 1, 15 June 1941 - 31 August 1941, 1. SS-Infanterie-Brigade report, FN 100377, 100385]

8/23/41 SS-I.R. 10 clearing action in the area of Bialokurowicze (north of StrasseKorosten). 65 Jews executed.
[T, 20.8.41/12:00 Uhr - 24.8.41/12:00 Uhr]

8/24/41 SS-I.R. 10 continues clearing action to the north and northwest. 283 Jews shot. [T. 20.8.41/12:00 Uhr- 24.8.41/12:00 Uhr]. Additional cleansing operations north of the Rosten-Bialokorowice road results in 1018 Jews and 13 "partisans" killed [Zentrale Stelle CSSR I, Teil, Bild 52-4].

8/25-28/41 Brigade cleansing operations in Korosten area at behest of HSSPf Russland-Süd. A total of 187 Jews shot. [T, 24.8.41/12:00 Uhr - 29.8.41/12:00 Uhr]

8/27/41 Security operations along the Strasse Korosten-Ovruch-Biehun. [K]

8/29/41 Cleansing action and establishment of the line Ovruch-Norinsk-Weleniki-Listwin-Kuliki-Rudnia Czerwonka. [K]

8/29-9/12/41 Under the orders of HSSPf Russland-Süd, the brigade continues previous cleansing actions up to the new borders of the Army rear area. The brigade shot 276 Jews in the operational area. In addition, the following actions occurred:

1) On 8/30/41, SS-I.R. 8 shot 33 Jews in Gorodets.

2) On 9/2/41, SS-I.R. 8 shot 26 Jews in the Ssilisowks-Krasnoje-Krasuesselka area.

3) On 9/3/41, SS-I.R. 8 shot 37 Jews in the area south of Ubortj.

4) On 9/4/41, SS-I.R. 10 shot 7 Jews in Petrikov.

5) On 9/3-4/41, SS-I.R. 10 shot 681 Jews in Lel'chitsy.

6) On 9/6/41, SS-I.R. 10 shot 721 Jews in Lel'chitsy.

7) On 9/7/41, the brigade shot 18 Jews in Ovruch.

8) On 9/12/41, SS-I.R. 10 shot 7 Jews in the Ovruch-Sch. Janow area.
[T, 29.8.41/12:00 Uhr - 5.9.41/12:00 Uhr and 1. SS Bde/Abt Ic Eck./Schu./T, 29.8.41/12:00 Uhr - 5.9.41/12:00 Uhr]

9/11/41 Cleansing and security operations along Armeenachschubstrasse Ovruch-Chernobyl' [K]. By

9/14/41, the brigade had shot 437 Jews. [T, 12.9.41/12:00 Uhr - 19.9.41/12:00 Uhr]

9/20/41 Cleansing action in the Nikopol' region. [K]

9/22/41 Security operation along Rollbahn Uman-Kirovograd-Dnjepropetrovsk. Part of SS-I.R. 10 conducting security operation in Nikopol'. [K]

9/25/41 Security operation in the Dnjepr-Bogen. [K]

9/29/41 Security operation in the Dnjepr region and cleansing of the Dnjepr islands. [K]

10/1-6/41 Anti-partisan operations in the Dnjepr-Bogen and islands. [K]

10/7/41 Ten partisans executed in the Blagowscht-Uschenskoje region. [K]

10/31/41 Cleansing action in Duchanowka. 9 bolshevist functionaries shot. [T, 31.10.41/12:00 Uhr - 7.11.41/12:00 Uhr]

11/4/41 SS-I.R. 8 shot 5 "bolshevist plunderers" in the Putivl' area. [T, 31.10.41/12:00 Uhr - 7/11/41/12:00 Uhr]

11/6/41 Cleansing action in the Putivl'-SE Gremjatheka area: 32 partisans and 12 escaped POWs executed. [K]

11/7/41 Four partisans and four "vagabond Mongols" shot by SS-I.R. 8 along the rail-line Konotop-Altynovka. [T, 7.11.41/12:00 Uhr - 14.11.41/12:00 Uhr]

11/8/41 Cleansing action by SS-I.R. 8 in the Gayvoron-Krolewets area: 42 partisans and 5 asiatics killed, 14 prisoners taken. [K and T, 7.11.41/12:00 - 14.11.41/12:00 Uhr]

11/9/41 Cleansing action in Baturin by SS-I.R. 8: 53 partisans and 29 communists killed. [K and T, 7.11.41/12:00 Uhr - 14.11.41/12:00 Uhr]

11/10/41 Execution of 25 POWs by SS-I.R. 10 at camp south of Skurowka. [K and T, 7.11.41/12:00 Uhr - 14.11.41/12:00 Uhr]

11/11/41 Shooting of 51 POWs during an escape attempt at camp south of Skurowka. [K]

11/12/41 Execution of 50 POWs by SS-I.R. 10 at camp south of Skurowka [K and T, 7.11.41/12:00 Uhr - 14.11.41/12:00 Uhr]

12/1/41 Execution of 95 Jews at Konotop. [U.S. Holocaust Memorial Museum microfilm RG-48.004M, *Selected Documents from the Military Historical Institute (Prague)*, Reel 1, records of the Kommandostab RF-SS, Karton 6, 1941-42, 1. SS-Infanterie-Brigade report, FN 101842]

7/26-29/42 Participated in Operation Klette along with SS-Sonderbataillon *Dirlewanger* in the Smolensk region. Executed 511 civilians and rounded up 1454 civilians for deportation to concentration camps. [Report from Himmler to Hitler dated 1 August 1942, cited in Majewski].

8/42 Pacification action in the Vitebsk area. [Report from Himmler to Hitler dated 25 September 1942, cited in Majewski].

Extracts from *1. SS-Brigade Bericht über das Unternehmen 'Nürnberg' vom 22 - 26.11.1942*:

1) On 11/22/42, the brigade subjected 4 men, 4 women, and 7 children suspected of being partisans to "special treatment".

2) On 11/23/42, SS-I.R. 10 shot the entire populations of Fw. Bobruty, Stayki, and Rzepowszczyzna. The operation took place in a wooded area north of Postany.

3) German fatalities: 4 Enemy fatalities: 60 bandits, 10 Jews, 7 Gypsies, 638 "received special treatment."

Sources
(Baade et al., 1965)
(Majewski, 1977, p. 141)

14. Waffen-Grenadier-Division der SS (ukrainische Nr. 1) Crimes in Poland

At the outset it should be noted that several of the units used to form the 14. Waffen-Grenadier-Division der SS (ukrainische Nr. 1) -- Polizei-Bataillon 201, 31st SD Punitive Detachment, and the Ukrainische Schützmannschaft Bataillon 204 -- had a long prior history of participation in extermination operations. Operating in the rear-areas of Poland and the Ukraine, these units collectively murdered thousands of innocent civilians at Lvov, Tarnopol, Lutsk, Kremianets, Voldymyr, Odessa, Izmail, Mikolaiv, Brailov, Vinnitsia, Luminets, Pidhaitsi, and Ustalych.

Soon after the division's recruiting and formation had begun in late April 1943, unidentified elements took part in several anti-partisan operations in Poland which resulted in the wholesale murder of innocent civilians. Its commander at the time was SS-Brigadeführer Walter Schimana. Röhr et al. (1989) reported the following atrocities specifically attributed to the division:

Date	Location	District	Victims
6/24/43	Majdan Nowy	(Zamosc area)	28
7/1/43	Kaszow	Krakow	26
7/3/43	Majdan Stary	(Zamosc area)	65
8/15/43	Zagaje	(S of Kielce)	68

Later that year, divisional elements assisted in the deportation of Polish Jews to KL Auschwitz for extermination. On 20 November 1943, SS-Brigadeführer Fritz Freitag took over as divisional commander and would remain so until his suicide (4/27/45). By early February 1944, the division had completed most of its general training but was still not ready for action. Nonetheless, HSSPf General Government SS-Obergruppenführer Wilhelm Koppe ordered the partial mobilization of the division to assist with rear-area security duties in southeastern Poland following the Soviet siege of Tarnopol and the resecue of German units entrapped in the Kamenets-Podolsk pocket. The resulting unit, SS-Kampfgruppe Beyersdorff under the command of SS-Obersturmbannführer Friedrich Beyersdorff, was composed of Waffen-Grenadier-Regiment der SS 29, Waffen-Grenadier-Regiment der SS 30

and miscellaneous anti-tank, artillery and engineer support elements. Under the guise of anti-partisan operations this kampfgruppe destroyed 20 villages in Poland, killed in excess of 5,000 innocent civilians, and shipped another 20,000 civilians off to Germany as slave laborers. Röhr et al. (1989) has summarized a number of these atrocities:

Date	Location	District	Victims
2/1-2/44	Borow	Lublin	~300
"	Goscieradow	"	143
"	Szczecyn	(SW of Lublin)	~200
"	Wolka Szczecka	(E of Kielce)	~200
"	Zaklikow	(S of Lublin)	217
3/27/44	Gozdow	Lublin	30
4/1/44	Obrowiec	(Zamosc area)	34

The following crimes of SS-Kampfgruppe Beyersdorff are summarized from more substantial accounts in Korman (1990).

Chodaczkow Wielki

On 16 April 1944 elements of SS-Kampfgruppe Beyersdorff entered the town of Chodaczkow Wielki (Tarnopol area) with the apparent intention of exterminating the entire populace. They systematically moved street by street, firing buildings and shooting all civilians they came across. Several small children were caught by SS troopers and hurled into burning buildings to perish in the flames. The conflagration and smoke inevitably drew the attention of the unit's German command staff which dispatched a motorcycle messenger ordering the men to cease their depredations. By the time the Ukrainian SS troopers had been reined in, 862 innocent civilians lay dead amidst the town's smoking rubble.

Huta Pieniacka

At the beginning of February 1944 units of the Polish resistance, as well as 400 Soviet partisan cavalrymen under General M. Naumov, established themselves in the area of Huta Pieniacka near Brody with the dual purpose of disrupting German forces and protecting the local inhabitants. The previous months had seen local Ukrainian nationalist militia forcibly evacuate villagers from Huta Brodzka, Huta Nowa, Litowosko,

Hucisko Litowiskie, Hucisko Pieniackie and Gleboka Bobutycha concentrating them at Huta Pieniacka presumably for no good purpose. The town's population had swelled to approximately 1,300 individuals as a result of these transfers. Following this influx of resistance forces, several skirmishes occurred with reinforced patrols from SS-Kampfgruppe Beyersdorff. Outnumbered by German security forces, the partisans withdrew from the area.

On 27 February, German military authorities received erroneous intelligence from Ukrainian sources that arms and ammunition were secretly cached at Huta Pieniacka. A search and secure action was initially authorized, but this was quickly transformed into a "cleansing" action in order to teach the Polish population a lesson. The next morning elements of SS-Kampfgruppe Beyersdorff surrounded the village and attacked in unison on seeing the launch of signal flares. Resistance was practically non-existent: only a few scattered defensive shots were heard initially. Waves of Ukrainian SS-troopers, followed by Ukrainian nationalist militia, swept through the town. Buildings were carefully searched and their occupants driven at gunpoint toward the town's centrally-located Roman Catholic church. Many civilians were randomly executed along the way and left lying by the side of the road. Buildings were looted of valuables and livestock before being grenaded or fired. Some SS men remained behind lying in wait for anyone hiding in the burning buildings. When desperate civilians emerged, they were mercilessly gunned down.

The whole town was soon a confused mass of burning buildings, screaming women, crying children, and the ever-present staccatto of gunfire. Breathing became more and more difficult as the air filled with smoke and the reek of burning bodies.At the town center, the women and children were separated out and driven into the church where they were shot to death by their captors. SS troopers then looted and desecrated the church. Meanwhile, the men outside in the town square met a similar fate before the guns of the SS. An unlucky few were horribly tortured before they were executed. With the town destroyed and its inhabitants dead, the men of SS-Kampfgruppe Beyersdorff passed liquor around and, raucously singing, performed a victory march out of town. When the fires died down the next morning, all that remained

of Huta Pieniacka was a mass of smoking rubble with an occasional chimney sticking up. More than 1,000 of its residents had been murdered. A lucky few had escaped into the surrounding countryside putting as much distance between themselves and the Ukrainian SS as possible. Today all that exists of Huta Pieniacka is a small memorial and sign that mark the town's former location.

Apologists for the Ukrainian Waffen-SS, such as Logusz (1997), have simultaneously discredited and rationalized the massacre at Huta Pieniacka. In their view, the atrocity probably never occured and is simply Polish Communist propaganda. If the massacre actually occurred, however, then it was undoubtedly justified since (according to Ukrainian sources) Huta Pieniacka was a Communist guerilla stronghold that employed women and children in the manufacture of munitions. Revisionists would have us believe that the inhabitants of Huta Pieniacka were legitimate military targets.

Mlynow

On an unspecified date elements of SS-Kampfgruppe Beyersdorff executed upwards of 1,000 innocent civilians from this town and it neighboring villages (Luck area).

Palikrowy

On 12 March 1944 company-strength elements of SS-Kampfgruppe Beyersdorff, with the assistance of Ukrainian nationalist militia, swept through this town in the Tarnopol area murdering approximately 300 defenceless civilians. After plundering Palikrowy, they fired numerous buildings and then returned to Podkamien where cleansing operations were ongoing. Along the way, they murdered 20 civilians at Maliniskach and another 16 civilians at Czernicy.

Podkamien

In late February 1944, elements of SS-Kampfgruppe Beyersdorff entered the town of Podkamien near Brody and conducted a search for hidden weapon and ammunition caches. They found nothing. In the ensuing weeks the town was searched several more times by Ukrainian nationalist militiamen who only found two old, rusty carbines for all their effort. The atmosphere was tense and many residents felt that the Ukrainians were looking for the slightest pretext to justify repressive actions. Some took these security measures as a warning, fleeing to Podhorce and other nearby areas. Many other residents took refuge in a Dominican monastery outside of town.

On 10 March 1944 elements of SS-Kampfgruppe Beyersdorff returned to Podkamien accompanied by Ukrainian nationalist leaders and militiamen. The following day the Ukrainian militia surrounded the Dominican monastery and demanded entrance so that they could perform security checks. They were rebuffed by the monks. Throughout the day the militiamen alternately tried to persuade and then threaten the monks to allow their entrance into the monastery grounds. All their efforts were fruitless.

On the morning of 12 March, Waffen-SS trooopers and Ukrainian militia carefully surrounded the monastery. Any civilians travelling to or from the monastery that day were waylaid, taken aside and executed. At the monastery itself, handgrenades were tossed into the grounds. Those careless enough to show themselves at the monastery's windows and doorways were fired upon and killed. From within the monastery a handful of local forest rangers retaliated with brisk rifle fire and a few handgrenades that killed and wounded several of the attackers. The remaining Waffen-SS and militia took cover, calling off their abortive attempt to force the monastery gate. Inside the monastery, however, the situation was dire. The forest rangers had used up their scanty supply of ammunition and the only other available weapons were a handful of sickles. The monastery's abbot, Father Josef Burda, readied everyone for death with the sacraments of Confession and Holy Communion. Unexpectedly, the attackers temporarily withdrew leaving sentries behind (left to conduct the massacre at nearby Palkrowy, see above). By 1:00 pm, however, the Waffen-SS and militia had returned to continue their siege of the monastery.

The German commander resumed the siege by sending an ultimatum to those inside the monastery summoning them to surrender immediately. If they did not, heavy artillery would open fire on the monastery building and its grounds. Some civilians complied with the order, exited the monastery and fled toward the nearby town of Budki hoping to find refuge there. Along the way, however, they were intercepted by Ukrainian nationalist militia and gunned down. A handful of those in the monastery made it into sewers that ran beneath the monastery grounds and past Podkamien. In this manner they were able to pass out of the immediate danger zone and flee to safety. The majority of the people, however, remained inside the monastery. When the time for compliance had run out, the Waffen-SS and militiamen forced their way into the monastery killing everyone in sight. The resulting massacre was bestial in nature as civilians were not merely shot: many were killed or mutilated with blows from sickles, pitchforks and shears. Some individuals were even chased up into the chorus balcony and then thrown down to their deaths on the chapel floor below. When it was all over some 300 dead lay scattered about the monastery grounds.

While this bloody assault on the monastery was taking place, events in Podkamien itself were unfolding in a similar manner. Waffen-SS troopers assisted by Ukrainian Police units conducted a careful building by building sweep through the town. When an individual was stopped, he had to present his identity card. All residents of Polish nationality were taken aside and immediately executed. Inhabitants of Ukrainian origin were left unmolested and allowed to remain in their homes.

By the early morning hours of 13 March, the killing had for the most part ceased. Later that morning the serious organized looting of Podkamien and its monastery began. The SS-troopers and Ukrainian militiamen were assisted in their task by 200 teamsters and a fleet of trucks. The plundering lasted for two days, during which time additional Polish civilians that were flushed out of hiding places were executed. On 15 March another search of identity papers was performed on those civilians remaining in Podkamien. The next day further executions of detained Polish civilians took place at scattered locations in and around the sacked town. On 17 March SS-Kampfgruppe Beyersdorff and its accomplices withdrew from Podkamien since the frontlines were drawing nearer. They left behind approximately 500 dead civilians in the ruined town. Within days Podkamien would be in Soviet hands. On 20 March 1944 Father Burda held a funeral mass for the murdered civilians who were all buried together in a common grave at the town's Roman Catholic cemetary.

Poturzyn

On 1 April 1944 elements of SS-Kampfgruppe Beyersdorff, with the assistance of Ukrainian nationalist militia, entered this village in the Lublin area and murdered 162 civilians. Many of the victims came from the parishes of Dolhobyczowa and Krylowa which had previously been devastated by German cleansing operations.

Prehoryle

On 8 March 1944 elements of SS-Kampfgruppe Beyersdorff, with the assistance of Ukrainian Police and nationalist militia, encircled this village near Lublin and murdered 38 inhabitants. The next day they returned for another round of killing, followed by the looting and burning of residences.

Smoligow

On 27 March 1944 elements of SS-Kampfgruppe Beyersdorff, with the assistance of unidentified Wehrmacht units and Ukrainian nationalist militia, conducted an extermination action at this village in the area of Lublin. They surrounded the town and moved through it systematically killing inhabitants, looting buildings and then firing them. When ammunition ran short, civilians were simply beaten to death. Many women were raped prior to being killed.

Wicyn

On the morning of 25 April 1944 elements of SS-Kampfgruppe Beyersdorff, supported by armored cars and with the assistance of Ukrainian nationalist militia, attacked this village in the Zloczow area. Dozens of unarmed civilians, primarily the elderly, were killed as the town's populace was rounded up at gunpoint. For several days homes and businesses were looted, livestock confiscated and shipped off, and buildings set on fire. Approximately two-thirds of the town was destroyed; some 200 men were seized and turned over to the Gestapo for interrogation.

Following its participation in these security operations, SS-Kampfgruppe Beyersdorff resumed its training with the rest of the division. Röhr et al. (1989) has reported a number of later crimes committed by unidentified elements of the 14. Waffen-Grenadier-Division der SS (ukrainische Nr. 1):

Date	Location	District	Victims
6/22/44	Jaminy	Gumbinnen	24
8/15/44	Minoga/Barbarka	Krakau	51
9/24/44	Jamna	Krakau	57

Korman (1990) similarly provides an account of the division's depredations for this time period:

Siemianowka

On the morning of 26 July 1944 two unidentified motorized companies from 14. Waffen-Grenadier-Division der SS (ukrainische Nr. 1) stopped at the village of Siemianowka in the Lvov region. Initially, the inhabitants thought that the SS troopers had halted to gather provisions and ready their weapons before continuing on to the main battle front which was rapidly approaching due to recent German reverses. The Ukrainian SS troopers had other plans. They drove the villagers from their homes, killing many in the process, and gathered the survivors together *en masse*. They then looted and fired the town. At this time some of the Poles tried to flee but were gunned down by the SS. Many Poles who had hidden in their homes or barns were either consumed by the fires or gunned down by the SS as they fled from their burning refuges. The survivors were taken away as hostages by the SS troopers and eventually impressed into compulsory labor battalions at the front. All told, several hundred innocent civilians lost their lives.

Frayssinet-le-Gelat (France)

"Direct evidence obtained from M. Antoine Peyrichou and M. Jean Garraud: On the 21st May at 1900 hours about 1000 Germans of an SS Division with "Fur Fuhrer" inscribed on the sleeve [SS-Panzergrenadier-Regiment 4 Der Führer / 2. SS-Panzer-Division Das Reich (divisional CO: SS-Brigadeführer Heinz Lammerding) --- sleeve brassards bore the legend "Der Führer"], arrived in the center of the village [Fraysinnet-le-Gelat is located in the Department Lot, 25 km northwest of Cahors]. They ordered all men to assemble on the square. Whilst they were arriving a shot was heard near a house called "Lugan." It was not established that it was fired from this house. A German fell killed. Immediately the Germans ordered the remainder of the population, women and children, to assemble also. The Germans meanwhile rushed into the "Lugan" house, and dragged out two of the three women living there, two sisters, Mlle. Agathe Paille, 77 years old and very deaf; Madame Badoures, 62 years old and blind. The third woman, a niece of the other two, Madame Ballet, 42 years old, had run away, frightened, but was caught and brought to the square also.

Everybody was asked who had fired the shot. Obtaining no reply Mlle. Paille was taken under an electric cable support, a rope was placed around her neck, and for twenty minutes she was left there whilst the same question was put over and over again. Then she was hung. She was left hanging for fifteen minutes whilst the village was pillaged and the house above mentioned was set on fire with two incendiary bombs. The children who had witnessed all this, were locked in the church with the Cure. Then Mlle. Paille was taken down, carried to M. Perichou's house, mutilated and thrown into the burning house. Then Mme. Ballet was hung in the same fashion. Lastly Mme. Badoures was hung. Again the remainder were asked who had fired the shot and if no reply was forthcoming all the village would be shot. The Germans then picked seventeen men, mostly strong and young, and lined them up. They took the first ten, one of whom tried to escape, but he was shot and wounded and brained with rifle butts. They then replaced him with an eleventh man. These remaining ten were shot in two groups of five. All the population, including some children, were compelled to file past the corpses and look at them.

The remaining fifty-three men were made to dig a common grave in the dark night, in the cemetary, carry the bodies, bury them and cover the grave with earth. The names of the men murdered are as follows: Ernest Gaston Mourges, George Eugene Verlhac, Guy Christian Mourges, Edouard Delmas, Gaston Marmier, George Leon Lafon, Gabriel Joseph Soulie, Edmond Emile Coudray, Mendes de Signa, Elisee Musqui, and Henri Paul Lemaitre. The body of Mme. Yvonne Vidilles was subsequently found, shot in the brain, the next morning. The whole village continued to be pillaged until 10:00 hours the next day. M. Garraud was designated and held responsible for the quiet behaviour of

the whole village; his family and himself to be considered as hostages in case of any further incident." [The bodies of Mlle. Paille, Mme. Badoures, and Mme. Ballet were thrown into the flames of their burning house after it had been fired. Among the eleven hostages executed were a father and son, Ernest and Guy Mourges. One of the main officers responsible for the atrocity, SS-Hauptsturmführer Otto Kahn (CO: 3. Kompanie / 1. Bataillon / SS-Panzergrenadier-Regiment 4 *Der Führer*), shot them together as they stood in each other's arms. Kahn disappeared at war's end (rumored to be living in Sweden post-war under an assumed identity) and was never tried for this war crime. He apparently died in the early 1980s.]

Sources
(Hastings, 1981, p. 221)
(U.S. National Archives RG-153, 151 -- Records of the Office of the Judge Advocate General [Army], French War Crimes Cases, File Number 000-11-142, Case Summary)

Gabaudet (France)

On 8 June 1944 an unknown unit from the right flank march column of the 2. SS-Panzer-Division Das Reich (divisional CO: SS-Brigadeführer Heinz Lammerding) while patrolling up a side road stumbled upon a large party of young men gathered at a farm in the little hamlet of Gabaudet (Department Lot, 6 km south of Gramat). The young men were preparing to march off and join the resistance. Ten young boys and men, as well as one girl, were shot on the spot by the SS troopers. Eighty other inhabitants of Gabaudet were seized for deportation to Germany and the town was set ablaze. The detainees were later released by their SS captors on the road to Tulle during their post-invasion march towards the Normandy beaches in northwest France.

Source
(Hastings, 1981, p. 88)

Gau Niederdonau (Austria)

As the war drew to it's predictably bloody end and the boundaries of the Third Reich shrank, the increased interactions between battle-hardened Waffen-SS troops and the remaining concentration camp inmates resulted in a series of little known atrocities within the Reich itself.

On 23 March 1945 unidentified elements of the Waffen-SS executed 18 Hungarian Jews in the town of Eisenstadt. A week later unidentified elements of the Waffen-SS executed another 40 Hungarian Jews. In April a company of 2. SS-Panzer-Division Das Reich under the command of SS-? Paul Anton Reiter executed 6 Hungarian Jews and 1 POW in the woods outside of Leiben. On 10 April 1945 an unidentified SS-Feldgendarmerie unit with the assistance of local Schutzpolizei executed 21 Hungarian Jews in the town of Nikolsburg. On 13 April 1945 members of an unidentified Waffen-SS Werfeneinheit set a concentration camp barracks building on fire resulting in the deaths of 76 Jewish prisoners at Lunz am See.

On 18 April 1945, SS-Feldgendarmerie personnel from the 12. SS-Panzer-Division Hitlerjugend (CO: SS-Brigadeführer Hugo Kraas) rounded up 40 Hungarian Jews in the town of Thenneberg "for transport to the West". After marching them out of town, the SS troopers executed them and had an auxilliary unit of Ostarbeiter bury the corpses.. During the night of 2/3 May 1945 elements of SS-Kommando Gutenbrunn rounded up 229 Hungarian Jews in the town of Persenbeug. Those too infirm or too young to travel were shot in their barracks. The survivors were marched out of town to a field in Hoftamt-Priehl, executed, and their bodies set on fire.

Source
(Lappin, 2004, vol. 4, pp. 106-111)

Gau Steiermark (Austria)

As the war drew to it's predictably bloody end and the boundaries of the Third Reich shrank, the increased interactions between battle-hardened Waffen-SS troops and the remaining concentration camp inmates resulted in a series of little known atrocities within the Reich itself. From early November 1944 - 21 March 1945, 2. SS-Baubataillon Kama was based in Jennersdorf. As part of their regular operations, battalion personnel performed guard duties over Hungarian Jews at work camps in Jennersdorf, Neuhaus, and St. Anna am Aigen. They beat and summarily executed individual Jews for a variety of infractions. On 22 March the unit was transferred to Hungary to strengthen German defenses against the advancing Soviets.

On 24-25 March 1945 unidentified elements of 13. Waffen-Gebirgs-Division der SS Handschar [kroatische Nr. 1] (CO: SS-Brigadeführer Desiderius Hampel) massacred approximately 200 Jews they were guarding at Rechnitz.On 28 March 1945 unidentified elements of 5. SS-Panzer-Division Wiking (CO SS-Oberführer Karl Ullrich) massacred upwards of 500 Jews on 28 March 1945 at Deutsch-Schützen.

On 4 April 1945 unidentified elements of 5. SS-Panzer-Division Wiking (CO SS-Oberführer Karl Ullrich) killed 20 Jews near Gratkorn and 18 Jews at Nestelbach.Sometime between 7-11 April 1945 unidentified elements of 5. SS-Panzer-Division Wiking (CO SS-Oberführer Karl Ullrich) killed 32 Jews at Egelsdorf and 21 Jews at Prebensdorf. On 26 April 1945 unidentified elements of 14. Waffen-Grenadier-Division der SS [ukrainische Nr. 1] (CO: SS-Brigadeführer Fritz Freitag) provided guard personnel for several columns of Jews being force marched out of Austria ahead of the advancing Soviets. The Jews were beaten and shot out of hand.

Source
(Lappin, 2004, vol. 4, pp. 86-104)

Gejgowa/Kherson (USSR)

In his memoirs of the German campaign on the Eastern Front Erich Kern, a former member of the 1. SS-Panzer-Division Leibstandarte Adolf Hitler, recounted the division's drive on the city of Kherson in August 1941. At the end of one day's fighting -- the exact date is uncertain since Kern gives erroneous dates for the LAH drive on Kherson -- two companies from the 16. Infanterie-(mot.)-Division (divisional CO: Generalleutnant Ernst Haeckel) were reported as missing. Kern's battalion was dispatched to locate the missing units; at midnight it halted at the village of Gejgowa, five miles east of Nowo Danzig. The next morning Kern's battalion found the missing men --- 103 officers and men were strung up in a nearby cherry orchard. Later that day in Nowo Danzig, they also found the bodies of six German soldiers who had clearly been shot after surrendering. Kern claims that the next day "an order was received from Division" that all Russian POWs taken for the next three days were to be shot. He then describes executions of POWs occuring in groups of eight in an anti-tank ditch; approximately 4,000 men were supposedly killed in this manner. However, there is no evidence that an execution order ever existed. Additionally, the Landesjustizverwaltungen Ludwigsburg (State Justice Administrative Department; group responsible for investigating German war crimes) conducted a post-war investigation and concluded that no such executions took place between 16-18 August 1941. Kern may have either invented the incident out of whole cloth, or taken another incident and woven it into his story. Until evidence of some sort is produced, the Gejgowa/Kherson affair should be treated as an unverified rumor.

Despite this lack of evidence, historians have latched onto Kern's account as a verified Waffen-SS atrocity. They have also misinterpreted it and added spurious elements that have confused the account with other events. Reitlinger was the first to reference Kern's work in a less than accurate manner. He claims that the execution order was given by SS-Obergruppenführer Josef "Sepp" Dietrich, even though it is unclear what Kern meant by his phrase "an order received from Division." This could mean an order from LAH (Dietrich and his staff) or from 16. Infanterie-(mot.)-Division (Haeckel and his staff). Stein followed Reitlinger's lead, but garbled the account even more. He claimed that this execution of Russian POWs was a reprisal for the murder of six captured members of 3. Kompanie / LAH found in March 1942 in a well-shaft at the GPU (Soviet Secret Service) headquarters in Taganrog. Stein does not bother to explain how the SS troopers could have performed a reprisal in August 1941 for murders that would not take place for another six months or so. Additionally, Stein's account follows Reitlinger's wording so closely that it appears that he did not even bother to consult Kern's account firsthand, but merely copied Reitlinger's account and then added further erroneous elements. It is disheartening, to say the least, that two well-regarded historians were unable to accurately report Kern's account of this affair.

Sources
(Reitlinger, 1957, pp. 170-171)
(Stein, 1966, pp. 272-273)
(Höhne, 1971, p. 530)

(Report of the Leibstandarte War Graves Officer, 29 March 1942, U.S. National Archives,
Microfilm series T-175, Records of the Reichsführer-SS, Microfilm roll 108)
(Messenger, 1988, pp. 100-101)
(Madeja, 1985, p. 19) (Kern, 1948)

Goc (Yugoslavia)

In Fall 1942 SS-Obergruppenführer Artur Phleps, commander of the 7. SS-Freiwilligen-Gebirgs-Division Prinz Eugen, began planning a series of offensive actions to disarm Chetnik partisans under Major Keserovic in the Kopaonik Mountains around Kriva Reka in Serbia. In his divisional orders dated 5 October, SS-Obergruppenführer Phleps stressed to his officers that ".... the entire population of this area must be considered rebel sympathizers." The first action took place in the mountainous region of Goc and Zhescin against the Gordichevikh Chetnik detachments. The action began on 8 October when Zhescin was occupied by elements of Prinz Eugen without encountering any resistance. Then in Goc (12 km east of Kraljevo) and the mountains around Biserske Livada elements of II. Bataillon / SS-Gebirgsjäger-Regiment 1 (CO: SS-Sturmbannführer von Steuben) executed 15 men, women, and children. They also looted and burned down 18 homes (as detailed in a report by Phleps dated 9 October). Yugoslav authorities complained about the activities of Prinz Eugen through 19 October citing massacres at Raskoj, Goc, Ivanjica (37 km southwest of Kraljevo), and Goc again (this time resulting in 250 murdered civilians).

Sources
(Glisich, 1970, pp. 128-131)
(Kumm, 1978)

Gorych (USSR)

It has been alleged that in July 1941 a company from SS-Panzeraufklärungs-Abteilung 1 / 1. SS-Panzer-Division Leibstandarte Adolf Hitler, under the command of (SS-rank?) Gottlob Zipfel, was ordered to carry out reprisals in Gorych by their battalion commander SS-Sturmbannführer Kurt "Panzer" Meyer. During earlier fighting, a group of German cavalrymen were cut off from their unit and forced to surrender. They were then decapitated by their Russian guards and their heads impaled on the iron spikes of the Gorych citadel. Zipfel responded by rounding up 200 civilians from the town and herding them all into a gasoline-soaked cottage. The windows and door were barred and then a hand grenade was dropped down the chimney. Zipfel is reported to have said that the explosion was "spectacular and the stink of roasting Russian flesh very satisfying." Wykes gives no documentation for this incident. In view of the fact that this author's work is littered with numerous egregious errors of fact, this particular atrocity should be treated as unsubstantiated rumor.

Source
(Wykes, 1974)

Grafeneck Castle (Germany)

In November 1939 a trainload of personnel from SS-Totenkopfstandarte II (CO: SS-Standartenführer Paul Nostitz), in civilian clothes but armed and bearing their SS paybooks, arrived at Grafeneck Castle in the Swabian Alb near Munsingen. With the aid of local craftsmen, they converted a former home for invalids into an extermination center that was euphemistically designated a "psychiatric asylum." New offices were installed, wooden and barbed-wire perimeter fences erected and posted with signs warning of the danger of infectious diseases, and a gas chamber and crematoria constructed nearby. The retrofitted castle was the first killing site prepared for the extermination of psychiatric patients, the handicapped, and troublesome foreign workers under the "Aktion T-4" and children's euthanasia campaigns run out of the Kanzlei des Führers (Chancellory of the Führer) under Reichsleiter Philipp Bouhler and Oberdienstleiter Viktor Brack. Between January and December 1940, 9839 individuals were murdered at Grafeneck Castle under the auspices of these programs. On 1 November 1939 Brandenburg was designated as cadre for the newly forming 3. SS-Panzer-Division Totenkopf.

Source
(Burleigh, 1994, pp. 120-121)

Graignes (France)

In November 1943 a new division designated 17. SS-Panzergrenadier-Division Götz von Berlichingen (CO: SS-Brigadeführer Werner Ostendorff) began formation and training in the countryside west-southwest of Tours. The D-Day landings by Anglo-American forces on 6 June found the division still at only 66% of its authorized strength, lacking required armored vehicles and motor transport, and with only limited supplies of heavy ammunition. Nevertheless, by 10 June most of the understrength division had reached the American inland defensive positions south of Carentan. Along with Luftwaffe Fallschirmjäger-Regiment 6 (CO: Oberst Friedrich August Freiherr von der Heydte), the 17. SS was ordered to counterattack and retake the city of Carentan preparatory to attacking the Allied beachheads. In the way of this divisional-strength German force stood the U.S. 82nd Airborne, 101st Airborne, and 2nd Armored divisions in nearly impregnable defensive positions. The countryside around Carentan was very marshy and most of the German advance routes consisted of exposed, causeway roads onto which the Americans could pre-register defensive fire from the elevated stone villages that they occupied. For nearly two weeks the SS troopers and paratroopers bravely, but vainly, attacked the American positions around Carentan. They suffered severe losses in the process, but gained very little ground before being forced back by the numerically superior American forces.

One such stronghold was at the village of Graignes, southeast of Carentan. A company of the U.S. 3rd Battalion / 507th Parachute Infantry Regiment / 82nd Airborne Division had landed approximately 17 miles south of its target zone and had taken up positions in and around the village's hilltop church. They were joined by scattered elements of the U.S. 101st Airborne Division. The residents of Graignes fed the 180 Americans and helped them find their scattered heavy weapons and ammunition that were still recoverable from the surrounding marshes. Several days of nervous inactivity passed and then on the afternoon of 10 June a patrol from the 17. SS stumbled upon their position. The Germans attacked the next day in force with 1,000 men of II. Bataillon / SS-Panzergrenadier-Regiment 38 (SS-Sturmbannführer Nieschlag) and 180 men of 2. Kompanie / Heeres-Pionier-Bataillon "Angers" (CO: Hauptmann Neumann). The fighting carried over into 12 June before the Germans were able to bring up two 88mm anti-aircraft guns to shell the village church. The Americans retreated back through the countryside leaving behind 9 dead and 25 wounded in the church under the care of two parish priests and two nurses. Most of the survivors were able to make their way back to American positions closer to Carentan; one group of 20+ paratroopers hid out in the Giroud sisters' barn until the area was retaken on 16 June by elements of the 101st Airborne.

By all accounts, SS-Sturmbannführer Nieschlag's force had taken severe casualties in the two day battle for Graignes. American estimates of 1,200 killed (greater than the number of attackers) are clearly erroneous; French civilian estimates placed the number of dead at nearly 500. This also appears to be an overestimate since 17. SS divisional records report approximately 1,200 killed and wounded for all of their operations around Carentan. In any event, SS-Sturmbannführer Nieschlag's men were in a foul mood when they entered Graignes. They shot the priests and nurses caring for the American wounded out of hand. The 25 wounded paratroopers were taken to a farm outside of town, executed, and thrown into a ditch. To repay the locals for their assistance to the Americans, the SS troopers executed 30 villagers and then burned down most of the houses in Graignes. The German advance toward Carentan in this area ground to a halt two days later several kilometers north of the village.

The fate of SS-Sturmbannführer Nieschlag is uncertain. He was later badly wounded in the continuing Normandy fighting, but remained in command of his battalion due to the division's acute shortage of officers and NCOs. Nieschlag appears to have been either killed or captured in the Roncey Pocket fighting (~ 28 July) that developed following the American breakout from the city of St. Lo. He ceases to be mentioned in divisional histories after this date. Most of the remainder of the 17. SS division was also captured or destroyed at this time. No one was ever tried for the killings at Graignes.

This atrocity was virtually unknown until 2004 when a major U.S. cable television channel (The History Channel) aired a documentary entitled D-Day: The Secret Massacre. Unfortunately, the film was typical of the distortion and exaggeration that characterizes much of American reporting on the fighting in Normandy. The documentary claimed to reveal "how under two hundred soldiers and the citizens [of Graignes] banded together to face an entire SS-Panzer regiment of some 2,000 troops, holding off the German force for nearly a week." Of course, the fighting lasted two days and the main attacking force was one understrength panzergrenadier battalion without its usual complement of armored fighting vehicles (i.e., one understrength infantry battalion).

Sources
(Bender & Taylor, 1969-1982, vol. 4, pp. 128-138)
(Madeja, 1992, p. 86)
(Perrigault & Meister, 2004, vol. 1, pp. 259-262)
("On D-Day: The 507th at Graignes", www.habitablezone.com/OffTopic/messages/330075.html)
("Normandy: A Glider Pilot's Story", www.71stsos.com/normandygeobuckley.html)
(Normandy Sightseeing Tours Newsletter, May 2004, www.normandywebguide.com/newsletter)

Grubisnjici (Yugoslavia)

On 28 March 1944 elements of the 7. SS-Freiwilligen-Gebirgs-Division Prinz Eugen (CO: SS-Brigadeführer Otto Kumm) with the help of the 369. Infanterie Division (CO: Generalleutnant Fritz Neidholdt) fired the town of Grubisnjici and shot 65 civilians as part of a larger säuberungsaktion ("cleansing action") in the region. See also Blazevici, Otok Cornji and Split.

Sources
(Zöller & Leszczynski, 1965, p. 62)
(Kumm, 1978)

Hauptkommissariat Baranowicze

(USSR)

From February 1942 on, numerous "actions" (killings and reprisals carried out under the guise of anti-partisan operations) were performed by unidentified Waffen-SS units in the five Kreis that comprised the Hauptkommissariat Baranowicze : Lida, Novogrodek, Slonim, Baranowicze, and Hansewicze. The area, southwest of Minsk in Belorussia, was well behind the front and none of the main series Waffen-SS divisions or brigades were in the area at this time. In all likelihood, the atrocities were committed by elements of Einsatzgruppe B (commander SS-Oberführer Erich Naumann) acting under the direction of HSSPf Russland-Mitte SS-Obergruppenführer Erich von dem Bach-Zelewski.

Source
(Krausnick, 1981, p. 601)

Hnevosice (Czechoslovakia)

At the end of January 1945 approximately 10,000 political prisoners were matched through the village of Hnevosice (Opava district) accompanied by Waffen-SS guards. Any prisoners who fell down due to hunger or exhaustion were immediately shot in the nape of the neck by one of the Waffen-SS troopers. Some 23 prisoners were killed in this manner in the village. On 18 February another transport passed through during which some 90 prisoners were shot or beaten to death. Several more transports passed through the area as late as April 1945. The scenes were always the same; the dead were buried along the roadsides where they fell. The identity of the Waffen-SS unit involved is unknown.

Source
(IMT, 1948/1971, vol. 36, pp. 86-93, document D-959 [exhibit GB-571])

Horka (Germany)

The atrocity at Horka has been touched on by a number of historians, but the most complete account to date has been given by Rostkowski. He felt that the massacre was a natural outgrowth of desperate German end-of-the-war "take no prisoners" / "annihilate the enemy" propagandizing.

The Polish Second Army (8th and 9th Polish Infantry Divisions, 1st Polish Armored Corps) and elements of the 52nd Soviet Army were in position near Kohlfurt in the area of Bautzen-Dresden during the leadup to the Soviet's Berlin offensive. By 19 April 1945 they were attached to the 1st Ukrainian Front and facing Heeresgruppe Mitte in the Görlitz area. On 23 April, two German divisions and 100 tanks from 48. Korps broke through the lines of the 52nd Soviet Army and took the Polish Second Army in the rear. The Polish defenders found themselves in a desperate situation and took heavy casualties. That same day the Polish commander, General K. Swierczewski, ordered a retreat of the Polish Second Army from the Bautzen area. On 23/24 April, the 9th Polish Infantry Division took heavy casualties but held the line Kamenez-Mittelbach-Leppersdorf-Grossröhrsdorf. A Red-Cross marked convoy was organized to evacuate the unit's wounded; approximately 300 personnel were loaded into a number of light trucks. Aside from the wounded, the convoy was made up of doctors, nurses, and a few officers bearing sidearms. It planned to travel the route Pulsnitz-Elstra-Panschwitz-Kuckau-Horka-Königswartha.

On the afternoon of 26 April, the column stopped in Horka, a small town located 12 kilometers east-northeast of Kamenz in Silesia) to give the wounded some rest and treatment. Between 17 and 1800 hours, elements of the "1. SS-Panzergrenadier-Division *Brandenburg*" overtook the column and wiped it out. On the morning of 27 April, the SS men impressed local residents to dig a large mass grave and two smaller ones and the murdered were buried in them.

In early May 1945, Horka was retaken by the Soviets and Poles and they discovered the mass graves. A staff group from the Polish Second Army investigated the site on May 8th. Nineteen officers were identifiable by name among the dead. Witnesses from the town named the perpetrators as members of the

"Brandenburg Division SS." The Poles made the remaining townspeople exhume and clean the bodies. The bodies were then re-interred with ceremony in three new mass graves. According to a staff report of the Polish Second Army, the bodies of the dead were heavily mutilated (i.e., cut tongues, poked-out eyes, beaten with gun-butts, broken ribs, organs cut-up). A veteran of the unit, S.L. Wadecka, claimed in a letter to Rostkowski that the bodies showed knife and bayonet damage. Many had been shot once or twice in the back of the head. The Red Cross doctors and nurses were also found in the mass graves. The exact number killed at Horka remains speculative due to conflicting claims: 300 (S.L. Wadecka), 200 (Horka town records), 165 - 200 (Kaczmarek; Kmiecik).

The problem with all of the accounts, however, is assigning guilt for this crime to the "1. SS-Panzergrenadier-Division *Brandenburg*". No such unit ever existed in the German Order of Battle. A Panzergrenadier-Division *Brandenburg* did exist and was on the very stretch of front opposing the Polish units. It was a Wehrmacht (German Army) unit commanded by Generalmajor Schulte-Heuthaus and located in the Bautzen area (Heeresgruppe Mitte, 4. Panzer Armee) from 10 February 1945 - 30 April 1945. According to Cyz-Ziesche, the *Brandenburg* division was known for its bloodthirsty tendencies and policy of taking no prisoners while in the USSR and Yugoslavia. They are known to have murdered hundreds of Polish and Soviet POWs and wounded in other incidents. On 22 April 1945 in the school at Guttau they murdered a group of Polish wounded. On 25 April 1945 at Salzenforst they murdered 14 Soviet and Polish wounded. It is possible that eyewitnesses to the Horka massacre honestly mistook *Brandenburg* to be a Waffen-SS unit due to uniform similarities (i.e., identical Wehrmacht tunic and trouser styles, use of camouflage jackets, tunic cuffbands with divisional names).

The only Waffen-SS units attached to 4. Panzer Armee were Kampfgruppe 35. SS-Polizeigrenadier-Division and Kampfgruppe 36. SS-Waffengrenadier-Division, neither of which saw action anywhere near the Polish positions. Interestingly enough, the closest SS unit to the action was the 10. SS-Panzergrenadier-Division *Frundsberg* (CO: SS-Brigadeführer Heinz Harmel) which was being held in reserve near Spremberg, south of Cottbus. It would only take two minor mistakes (substituting a 1 for a 10 and *Brandenburg* for *Frundsberg*) to arrive at the Polish claim. Additionally, the staff report by the Polish Second Army mentions that the SS were accompanied by members of the Vlassov Division, designated by the Germans as 600. sowjetisches Infanterie Division (Wlassow) [CO: Gen.Maj. Bunjachenko]. This is especially significant since the 600. Infanterie Division was also part of the same OKH Reserve as the 10. SS-Panzergrenadier-Division *Frundsberg*. Unfortunately, the staff report has several minor errors which might cast some doubt on its reliability. Short of some new original information, we are left to ponder which unit committed the massacre of the Polish wounded --- *Brandenburg* or *Frundsberg*.

Sources
(Tutorow, 1986)
(Gac, 1962)
(Kmiecik, 1972, p. 30)
(Kaczmarek, 1978, p. 513)
(Cyz-Ziesche, 1970, p. 73)
(Rostkowski, 1980)
(Protokol komisji sztabu 2 armii WP w sprawie bestialstw niemieckich na terenie
wsi Horka, pow. Kamenz in Gac, 1962, pp. 146-148)
(Madeja, 1985)

Hungary

To prosecute the Final Solution in Hungary, an Einsatzkommando of approximately 800 effectives was secretly organized under the command of SS-Oberführer Dr. Hans Geschke. The personnel were overwhelmingly members of the Sicherheitspolizei (Security Police), although about 60 men were from the Waffen-SS. Shortly after the unit's arrival in Budapest it was further reinforced with an unidentified Waffen-SS battalion. The group operated in Hungary from March - June 1944 and was responsible for the roundup and deportation to Auschwitz of an estimated 458,000 Jews.

Source
(Testimony of SS-Hauptsturmführer Dieter Wisliceny at Nuremberg Trials in Zeiger, 1960, pp. 155-156)

Ioannina (Greece)

On 25 March 1944 an unidentified Waffen-SS unit supplied guards and drivers for motor transports taking Jews from Ioannina (northwestern Greece) to a concentration camp at Larisa. The Jews were then sent by train from Larisa to Auschwitz. The only Waffen-SS unit in Greece at this time was the 4. SS-Polizei-Panzergrenadier-Division (CO: SS-Brigadeführer Fritz Schmedes).

Source
(Mazower, 1993, p. 253)

Jablanica (Yugoslavia)

It has been alleged that on or about 9 October 1944 elements of 9. Kompanie / Waffen-Gebirgs-Jäger Regiment der SS 28 / 13. Waffen-Gebirgs-Division der SS Handschar [kroatisches Nr. 1] under the command of SS-Obersturmführer Hans König executed a group of partisan POWs from the Fourth Battalion / XVII Majevica Brigade at the town of Jablanica in northeastern Bosnia. After the war Yugoslavian authorities requested that König be extradited by the British in order to face war crimes charges. Before they could comply with the request, he committed suicide (sometime in 1947).

Sources
(Lepre, 1997, pp. 263-264)
(J.J. Peric, "13. SS 'Handzar' divizija i njen slom u istocna Bosni", Istocna Bosna u NOB-u 1941-45, vol. 2, p. 587)

Jablanica-Prozor Rail line

(Yugoslavia)

At the Nuremberg Trials of Major German War Criminals the prosecution cited the testimony of Leander Holtzer, a Volksdeutsche Waffen-SS man, contained in the Report of the Yugoslav War Crimes Commission, (Document D-944 / exhibit GB-566): "In August 1943 the 23rd Company [7. SS-Freiwilligen-Gebirgs-Division Prinz Eugen] under the command of the company leader SS-Untersturmbannführer Schuh set fire to a village on the railway line Jablanica-Prozor [north of Mostar, Bosnia-Herzegovina] by order of the battalion commander, SS-Obersturmbannführer Wagner. The inhabitants of the village were shot in the meantime."

When asked to respond to this allegation, former SS-Obergruppenführer Paul Hausser defended the Waffen-SS by objecting that it did not use a numbering scheme that would have included a "23rd Company." He went on to say, however, that he was not familiar with this division and if the atrocities did occur, then it was the result of having too many Volksdeutsche personnel in the unit. Hausser was incorrect; Prinz Eugen division did possess a 23rd Company as part of its IV. Bataillon / SS-Gebirgsjäger-Regiment 1. However, the battalion commander at this time was SS-Sturmbannführer Horst Strathmann. The former battalion commander, SS-Obersturmbannführer Jürgen Wagner, had already been assigned to command the 23. SS-Freiwilligen-Panzergrenadier-Division Nederland which had recently been deployed to Yugoslavia for working up and training.

Sources
(IMT, 1948/1971, vol. 20, p. 398)
(IMT, 1948/1971, vol. 36, pp. 69-70)
(Kumm, 1978)

Jaroszew (Poland)

On 25 October 1939 elements of SS-Wachsturmbann Eimann (CO: SS-Sturmbannführer Kurt Eimann) executed 46 Polish civilians at the town of Jaroszew in Gemeinde Schöneck, Danzig-Westpreussen Province.

In January 1940 the unit was disbanded and its personnel distributed to various SS-Totenkopfverbände serving as replacement/training elements for the Totenkopf Division (3. SS-Panzer-Division Totenkopf). SS-Sturmbannführer Eimann later served with the II. SS-Panzerkorps in Normandy and the Ardennes. After the war, he was briefly detained but then released. He was finally brought to trial in 1962 and in 1968 sentenced to four years imprisonment for his role in killing an estimated 1,200 psychiatric patients.

Sources

(Jansen and Weckbecker, 1992, p. 213)
(Burleigh, 1994)

Kamenets-Podol'skiy (USSR)

In the course of three days in early September 1941, a Kommando of the HSSPf Russland-Süd with the help of elements from the 1. SS-Infanterie (mot.)-Brigade (CO: SS-Brigadeführer Richard Hermann) and Polizei-Regiment Süd murdered 23,600 Jews in a mass shooting action at Kamenets-Podol'skiy. This atrocity was part of a larger "cleansing action" ordered by HSSPf Russland-Süd SS-Obergruppenführer Friedrich Jeckeln that took place in the region from 29 August - 12 September 1941.

Sources
(Arad et al., 1989, p. xi)
(Ereignismeldung UdSSR Nr.80 / Berlin, 11 September 1941 in Arad et al., 1989, p. 129)

Karpenisi (Greece)

During August 1944, elements of II. Kompanie / 7. SS-Panzergrenadier-Regiment / 4. SS-Polizei-Panzergrenadier-Division (kompanie CO: SS-? Werner Schlätel) reduced the small market town of Karpenisi to a pile of rubble as part of an anti-guerilla operation in the mountains of central Greece. The post-war fate of Werner Schlätel is unknown.

Sources
(Mazower, 1993, pp. 184-185)
(Husemann, 1971-1977, pp. 343-347)

Kharkov 1 (USSR)

In Summer 1941, the bulk of Kharkov's Jewish population fled as the Germans advanced into the Ukraine. The city was captured by the Germans on 23 October 1941 and became headquarters of the Sixth Army. Jews were daily taken as hostages and shot by representatives of the military government. On 26 November, Sonderkommando 4a (CO: SS-Standartenführer Paul Blobel) arrived for operations in Kharkov. The killing of Jews accelerated. They were seized in groups, taken to the Hotel International for torture, and then murdered with the use of carbon monoxide gas vans.

On 14 December 1941, the city's remaining Jews were ordered to assemble at the site of a tractor plant in two days. In the intervening time, Sonderkommando 4a murdered 305 Jews on the pretence that they had been rumour mongering. The detained Jews were kept in this make-shift ghetto under intolerable conditions. After three weeks, the planned liquidation began. Volunteers were taken away on the pretext that they were going out for day work at Poltava and Lubny. Instead they were taken to the nearby Drobitski Yar (ravine) and murdered in pre-dug pits. Some of the Jews were killed in gas vans. The extermination was performed by Sonderkommando 4a (SD and SIPO personnel, 3. Kompanie / Waffen-SS-Bataillon-zbV, a platoon of Polizei-Bataillon 9, etc.) with the help of Polizei-Bataillon 314 and an unidentified Waffen-SS unit. Kharkov was liberated on 15 February 1943, recaptured by the Germans the following month, and liberated again by the Russians on 23 August 1943. Following the city's final liberation and the discovery of mass graves of murdered civilians, the Soviets held the first war-crimes trial of the war. Soviet estimates have placed the total number of victims as high as 30,000. However, a Sixth Army intelligence officer testified at the Nuremberg Einsatzgruppen trial that SS-Standartenführer Blobel had told him that Sonderkommando 4a had killed 21,685 Jews. This figure covered all Jews killed from the beginning of German occupation until January 1942 when the liquidation was complete. For these crimes the Soviet Tribunal tried three Germans and one Ukrainian collaborator unlucky enough to be captured, as well as six individuals in absentia. The proceedings were filmed and made into a powerful Spanish-language documentary (Paso a la Justicia!) which shows the trial to have been a serious and dignified affair. The verdict of the court was reprinted in Nazi Crimes in Ukraine (Academy of Sciences, 1987) and is reproduced below.

Verdict of the Military Tribunal in the Case of Atrocities Committed by German-fascist Invaders in the City of Kharkov and Kharkov region during their Temporary Occupation (December 15-18, 1943)

In the Name of the Union of Soviet Socialist Republics

On 15 -18 December 1943, the Military Tribunal of the 4th Ukrainian Front, composed of the Presiding Judge, Major-General A.N. Myasnikov, chairman of the Military Tribunal of the Front; judges - Colonel M.A. Kharchev and Major S.S. Zapolsky; secretary - Captain N.M. Kandybin, with the participation of the

State Prosecutor Colonel N.K. Dunayev, military procurator, and defense counsels assigned by the court lawyers N.V. Kommodov, S.K. Kaznacheyev and N.P. Belov in an open trial in the city of Kharkov examined the case of atrocities committed by German-fascist invaders in the city of Kharkov and Kharkov Region at which the following were tried:

1. Wilhelm Langheld, born 1891 in the city of Frankfurt on the Main (Germany), German, member of the Nazi party since 1933, officer in the German Army's military counterespionage, captain.

2. Hans Ritz, born 1919 in the city of Marienwerder (Germany), German, higher education, member of the Nazi Party since 1937, deputy commander of an SS company, SS-Untersturmfuhrer.

3. Reinhard Retzlaw, born 1907 in the city of Berlin, German, secondary education, official of the German secret field police in the city of Kharkov, Senior Lance-Corporal.**4.** Mikhail Petrovich Bulanov, born 1917 in the station of Dzhanibek, Kazakh SSR, Russian, non-Party man.

All four had committed crimes specified in Part 1 of the Decree of the Presidium of the Supreme Soviet of the Union of Soviet Socialist Republics dated 19 April 1943.

The material of the preliminary and court investigation of the Front's Military Tribunal established: Having perfidiously attacked the Soviet Union and temporarily occupied part of her territory, German-fascist troops, on direct orders from Hitler's government, despite the fact that Germany had signed and ratified international conventions on the rules of war conduct, brutally exterminated peaceful population, deported to German slavery hundreds of thousands of citizens, robbed, burned, and destroyed material and cultural valuables of the Soviet people.

On the territory of the city of Kharkov and Kharkov Region acts of atrocity and violence were committed against Soviet peaceful inhabitants by officers and men of: the SS "Adolph Hitler" Division commanded by SS Obergruppenfuhrer Sepp Dietrich; the SS Dead Head Division commanded by SS Gruppenfuhrer Simon; German punitive bodies; the Kharkov "SD Sonderkommando" led by Sturmbannfuhrer Hanebitter; the German secret field police group in the city of Kharkov headed by Police Commissioner Karkhan; and the defendants in this case Wilhelm Langheld, Hans Ritz, Reinhard Retzlaw, as well as their accomplice Mikhail Bulanov, traitor to the homeland.

During the temporary occupation of the city of Kharkov and Kharkov Region, the German-fascist invaders had shot, hung, burned alive and poisoned by carbon monoxide gas more than 30,000 peaceful completely innocent citizens, including women, old people and children.

Thus, in November 1941 in the city of Kharkov, some 20,000 peaceful Soviet citizens on orders of the Gestapo, were moved from their city apartments to barracks located on the territory of the Kharkov Tractor Plant. Subsequently, in groups of 200-300 persons, they were sent to the nearest ravine and shot.

The German Command, carrying out the direct orders of the piratical Hitlerite government on the extermination of the Soviet people, did not hesitate also in killing patients and wounded Soviet citizens, including children, who had been hospitalized.

Thus, in December 1941, the Gestapo shot 435 patients being treated at the Kharkov Regional Hospital, and among them were many elderly people and children.

In March 1943, 800 wounded officers and men of the Red Army, who were being treated at the 1st Army Marshalling Hospital of the 69th Army located in Kharkov on Trinkler Street, were shot and burned alive.

Numerous arrested innocent Soviet citizens were subjugated to brutal torture and all types of humiliation, in the Fascist torture-chambers of the Gestapo and other punitive organs. It was often the case that such interrogations were fatal. Regardless of generally accepted laws and customs of war conduct, the German Command forcibly put peaceful Soviet citizens, who had been seized on the temporary occupied territory of the Soviet Union, into prisoner of war camps and considered them as being war prisoners.At these camps there took place, through torture, shootings, starvation and inhuman conditions, the mass annihilation of prisoners of war and the civil population kept in these camps.

The German-fasicist invaders used the so-called "gazenwagens" -- large, enclosed trucks -- for the mass killings of Soviet citizens. [The Russians called them "dushegubki", i.e. murdergas vans.] The German-fascist invaders forced Soviet citizens into these gas vans and suffocated them by filling the vehicles with a special deadly gas -- carbon monoxide.

With the purport of covering up the traces of their monstrous crimes and mass extermination of Soviet people by way of poisoning them with carbon monoxide in the "gazenwagens", the German-fascist criminals burned the bodies of their victims.

During the successful Red Army offensive in the summer of 1943 and the liberation of the city of Kharkov and Kharkov Region from the German occupants, the monstrous crimes committed by the German-fascist criminals were discovered by Soviet bodies and corroborated at preliminary and court investigations.

Having listened to the explanations of the defendants, testimonies of witnesses, conclusions of forensic medical experts, as well as the speeches of the State Prosecutor and the defence, the Military Tribunal established the guilt of each of the defendants in the following:

1. Wilheln Langheld, as an officer of the German military counterintelligence, participated actively in the shootings and atrocities committed against prisoners of war and the civil population, in the interrogations of war prisoners and by means of torture and provocations tried to obtain false evidence. He was personally involved in the fabrication of a number of cases on the basis of which one hundred completely innocent prisoners of war and civilians were shot.

2. Hans Ritz, as Deputy Commander of an SS company attached to the Kharkov SD Sonderkommando, personally took part in the torture and shootings of peaceful Soviet citizens in the vicinity of the village of Podvorki near Kharkov, organized the shootings carried out by the SD Sonderkommando in the city of Taganrog, and interrogated prisoners beating them with rods and rubber hoses, trying to obtain fictitious evidence.

3. Reinhard Retzlaw, as an official of the German secret field police in the city of Kharkov, conducted investigations of cases pertaining to arrested Soviet citizens, tried to wring out of them through torture -- pulling out the hair of prisoners and sticking pins into them -- false evidence, compiled fictitious conclusions in relation to 28 Soviet citizens allegedly guilty of anti-German activities, as a result of which some of them were shot and the rest killed in gas vans. He personally forced Soviet citizens into a bus assigned for extermination of people, accompanied the gas vans to the place of unloading, and took part in the cremation of the bodies of his victims.

4. Mikhail Petrovich Bulanov, traitor of the Socialist homeland, voluntarily went over to the enemy's side, worked for the Germans as a chauffer of the Kharkov branch of the Gestapo, participated personally in the extermination of Soviet citizens by means of the gas vans, took Soviet citizens out to be shot and participated in the shooting of 60 children.

In this way, the guilt of all the above-listed defendants in the crimes specified in Part 1 of the Decree of the Presidium of the Supreme Soviet of the USSR dated April 19, 1943 was proven both in the preliminary investigation and in court proceedings.

Governed by Article 296 of the Criminal Code of the Ukrainian SSR and Decree of the Presidium of the Supreme Soviet of the USSR dated April 19, 1943, the Military Tribunal of the Front sentences Wilhelm Langheld, Hans Ritz, Reinhard Retzlaw and Mikhail Petrovich Bulanov to death by hanging. The verdict is definite and cannot be appealed.

On 19 December 1943, the death sentences decreed by the Military Tribunal of the 4th Ukrainian Front for the defendents Langheld, Ritz, Retzlaw, and Bulanov were carried out in Kharkov's main square. Soviet press accounts stated that 40,000 citizens gathered in the square and greeted the hangings with stormy applause.

It is unclear why the Soviets included such sweeping charges against two Waffen-SS divisions (1. SS-Panzer-Division *Leibstandarte Adolf Hitler* and 3. SS-Panzer-Division *Totenkopf*) and their commanders in this verdict. While two limited allegations against these units were made (see *Kharkov 2* and *Kharkov 4*), no evidence of large-scale killings by these Waffen-SS divisions was ever produced by the Soviets. There is not even circumstantial evidence that these divisions murdered any of the twenty thousand Kharkov civilians usually been attributed to them (see *Kharkov 3* for a full discussion of this case). The mass graves found at Kharkov and the overwhelming majority of civilians killed there were the result of Sonderkommando 4a operations in the region. As previously noted, however, this unit was partially composed of Waffen-SS personnel and for these operations also had the assistance of another unidentified Waffen-SS unit.

Sources
(Gutman, 1990, pp. 796-797)
(IMT, 1948/1971, vol. 22, p. 352)
(Academy of Sciences..., 1987, pp. 279-283)
(Kladov, 1944)
(Ecer, 1944)
(Lauterbach, 1945)
(Anonymous, 1944)
(Paso a la Justicia! -- A Step Toward Justice! - The Trial in the Case of the Atrocities Committed
by the Germans in the city of Kharkov and the Surrounding Region, U.S. National Archives,
NWDNM(m)-242-MID-3053-R)

Kharkov 2 (USSR)

It was claimed by witnesses at the Kharkov War Crimes Trial on 15 - 18 December 1943 (see Kharkov 1 for further details on the trial) that elements of the 1. SS-Panzer-Division Leibstandarte Adolf Hitler (CO: SS-Oberstgruppenführer Josef "Sepp" Dietrich) butchered hundreds of wounded Soviet soldiers after fighting their way into the city. On 13 March 1943 the Waffen-SS troopers arrived at the 1st Army Marshalling Hospital of the 69th Soviet Army in Trinkler Street. They sealed the doors of building #8 and then threw an incendiary device into the building. It quickly caught fire; any wounded who fled the building to save themselves were immediately gunned down by the waiting SS troopers. The next day several SS men returned, drove the medical personnel from the remaining hospital wards, and shot all of the hospital's wounded. Approximately 800 wounded POWs were murdered in this two day action.

Unfortunately, as is the case with a number of Soviet claims, the alleged atrocities at the hospital are difficult to prove either way. The Soviet authorities

waited until 1967 to see that the alleged perpetrators were brought to justice. At this time they submitted evidence to the West German Government that consisted of the findings of a Soviet War Crimes Commission held in September 1943. In response German judicial authorities performed a lengthy series of inquiries, interviewing 688 witnesses, the vast majority of whom were former members of the Leibstandarte Adolf Hitler. It was established that the Soviet hospital was located within the offensive zone of the 1. SS-Panzergrenadier-Regiment and that the main Soviet defensive belt lay nearby. The hospital may have been accidentally caught up in the vicious street fighting. In the end, the court ruled that there was insufficient evidence for individual culprits to be identified and no further action was taken.

Wykes has claimed that the divisional commander, SS-Oberstgruppenführer Josef "Sepp" Dietrich, showed little compunction "in ordering a Leibstandarte Schrecklichkeit (terror) band to beat to death 200 wounded in a Kharkov hospital before setting the building alight. The attackers in this gruesome episode used their Leibstandarte belts, the buckles of which displayed the motto "My Honour is My Loyalty" (Meine Ehre heisst Treue). 'It did not seem disgraceful,' one of them said at Nuremberg. 'It was an order and it was for the Führer and the Reich. We would not have been ordered to do it if it had not been necessary." As has been noted elsewhere, Wykes' book is error-ridden and unreliable. Since he gives no citation for this version of events, it should be treated as an unsubstantiated rumor.

Sources
(Academy of Sciences..., 1987, pp. 279-283)
(Wykes, 1974)
(Messenger, 1988, pp. 115-166 & 210-211)
(Stein, 1966, p. 136)

Kharkov 3 (USSR)

Following the debacle at Stalingrad, the Soviets continued their advances in the Ukraine against the shattered German forces. On 15 February 1943 the Soviets liberated the city of Kharkov and continued to drive westward. When the Soviet offensive finally ran out of steam in late February, German Field Marshal von Manstein launched a devastating counterattack spearheaded by the SS-Panzer-Korps commanded by SS-Obergruppenführer Paul Hausser. This corps was composed of three elite Waffen-SS divisions : 1.SS-Panzer-Division Leibstandarte Adolf Hitler (CO: SS-Obergruppenführer Josef "Sepp" Dietrich), 2. SS-Panzer-Division Das Reich (CO: SS-Oberführer Herbert Ernst Vahl; after 4/3/43 SS-Gruppenführer Walter Krüger), and 3. SS-Panzer-Division Totenkopf (CO: SS-Gruppenführer Max Simon). By 16 March 1943, the SS-Panzer-Korps had crushed the Soviet offensive and retaken Kharkov. The German counteroffensive drove the Soviets back to Belgorod and the front stabilized on 1 April.

All three Waffen-SS divisions took very heavy losses during this offensive. Accordingly, once the front had stabilized LAH and Das Reich were pulled back to rear areas west of Kharkov for rest and refitting. Totenkopf remained in position and refitted in the Belgorod area. In July the SS-Panzer-Korps took part in Operation Citadel, the German offensive to eliminate the Kursk salient. When this offensive was halted on 13 July, the Korps was sent to Kharkov for a week of further refitting. On 3 August 1943 LAH was dispatched to stabilize the tottering Axis situation in Italy. Das Reich remained in defensive positions to the west of Kharkov, while Totenkopf was dispatched south to heavy defensive fighting along the Mius River. The Soviets made renewed attacks against Kharkov causing Totenkopf to be recalled to the area by mid-August where it joined Das Reich in its defensive positions west of the city. The Soviets liberated Kharkov again on 23 August 1943 despite the best efforts of the two Waffen-SS divisions. Following liberation, the Soviets discovered several mass graves in the Kharkov area. In September 1943 they set up a commission to perform investigations which ultimately led to a war-crimes trial held 15 - 18 December 1943 (see Kharkov 1). At this trial, SS-Obergruppenführer Dietrich (commander of LAH), SS-Gruppenführer Simon (commander of Totenkopf), and several other officers were condemned to death in absentia for various alleged crimes. In his closing speech at the post-war Nuremberg Trials, General R.A. Rudenko (Chief Prosecutor for the USSR) restated the Kharkov Trial findings and charged that "the units of the SS -- particularly the SS Division of Adolf Hitler under the leadership of Ober-gruppenführer Dietrich, and the SS Division "Totenkopf" under the leadership of Obergruppenführer Simon, are responsible for the extermination of more than 20,000 peaceful citizens of Kharkov, for the shooting and burning alive of prisoners of war." Rudenko claimed that these murders took place between March 1943 and August 1943. The Russian representatives never substantiated these charges, nor did they press for the extradition of those convicted in absentia. The Nuremberg Tribunal dismissed these charges against the Waffen-SS due to a lack of any supporting documentation.

Despite a lack of evidence, this Soviet claim against the Waffen-SS has garnered plenty of supporters. The charge has become an accepted part of the popular lore surrounding the Waffen-SS: Hitler's elite sullied one of their greatest battlefield victories with a large-scale post-battle massacre of civilians. Even some academics (Stein, for example) have looked at the non-evidence and concluded that based on Waffen-SS behavior elsewhere, the Russian charges are probably true. The most that can be reliably said against the SS-Panzer-Korps is that it impressed 25,000 Russians as forced laborers for the construction of defensive positions in and around Kharkov. Undoubtedly, some may have died as a result of their forced employment. In defense of the SS-Panzer-Korps several points should be made. First of all, there is no evidence that these mass killings ever occurred. With the exception of two instances (see Kharkov 2 and Kharkov 4), all Soviet and German evidence indicates that the bodies found at Kharkov were the result of Einsatzgruppppen operations (see Kharkov 1). Secondly, the historical record clearly shows that the three Waffen-SS divisions were almost continuously engaged in heavy combat throughout the period of March -August 1943. It seems unlikely that they would have taken the time to execute such a large mass of forced laborers. Finally, for reasons unknown, the Soviets have not included the Das Reich division in their accusations. This is certainly strange considering the close battlefield relationships between the three Waffen-SS divisions at this time.

Sources
(Stein, 1966, pp. 136 & 273)
(Sydnor, 1977, pp. 295-296)

(Creel, 1944)

(Weingartner, 1974, p. 152)

(Madeja, 1992)

(Lehmann, 1977-1987)

(IMT, 1948/1971, vol. 22, p. 352)

(Messenger, 1988, pp. 115-1166)

Kharkov 4 (USSR)

As part of the Soviet charges regarding German atrocities in the Kharkov region, the accusation was made that members of the 7. Kompanie / SS-Panzergrenadier-Regiment 5 Thule / 3. SS-Panzer-Division Totenkopf (divisional CO: SS-Gruppenführer Max Simon) executed 40 Soviet POWs in August 1943 during fighting in the city of Kharkov. When queried concerning this atrocity at the Nuremberg Trials, former SS-Obergruppenführer Paul Hausser objected that Totenkopf could not be responsible since it was heavily engaged in defensive fighting far to the south along the Mius River. In this instance, Hausser was mistaken. Totenkopf was engaged defensively along the Mius in late-July, but was back in the Kharkov area by mid-August. It is unclear whether any elements of the division actually entered the city during this round of fighting; the bulk of the division occupied positions west of Kharkov. Nevertheless, a final judgment on this atrocity cannot be made given the poor level of documentation of the Soviet allegations.

Sources

(IMT, 1948/1971, vol .20, p. 397)

(Sydnor, 1977)

Kiev Region (USSR)

In February 1942 a special cultural artifact looting group under SS-Sturmbannführer Prof. Herbert Jankuhn was proposed by the Ahnenerbe (SS archaeological wing). Reichsführer-SS Heinrich Himmler personally approved of the plan and ordered Jankuhn's unit attached to the 5. SS-Panzer-Division Wiking (CO: SS-Gruppenführer Felix Steiner) which was directed to give it "every support possible." The unit operated in the Kiev region of southern Russia looting museum holdings and transferring them to SS collection points for eventual shipment to Germany. Jankuhn's many

"preservation efforts" included looting the Museum of Prehistoric Art in the Lavra Monastery and the Museum of Berdichev. By September 1943, Russian offensives forced the unit to cease its operations and evacuate the area.

Sources

(Nicholas, 1994, p. 197)

(U.S. National Archives Record Group 260, Records of the U.S. Occupation Headquarters, World War II, Ardelia Hall Collection: Records of the Collecting Points, Ahnenerbe Documents 225-227)

Klisoura (Greece)

Following a disastrous year on the Eastern Front, the 4. SS-Polizei-Panzergrenadier-Division (CO: SS-Brigadeführer Fritz Schmedes) was sent to northern and central Greece for resting, training, and refitting. There they were involved in numerous anti-partisan actions. At the beginning of May 1944, Greek partisans attacked one of the unit's convoys approximately 2.5 kilometers from the town of Klisoura (southwest of Mount Olympus, near Elasson) resulting in a handful of Waffen-SS casualties. After the partisans had withdrawn, the Germans sent in an anti-partisan unit to search Klisoura, but they found nothing. On 5 May 1944, the 7. SS-Panzergrenadier-Regiment / 4. SS Polizei-Panzergrenadier-Division entered Klisoura to retaliate for the deaths of two of their comrades in the earlier ambush. They rounded up and shot 215 civilians including 50 children under the age of ten and 128 women. Some revisionists (e.g., Theile) have sought to explain away this atrocity with unsupported and erroneous claims of heavy SS casualties in the original ambush.

Sources

(Zöller & Leszczynski, 1965, pp. 62 & 164)

(Bender & Taylor, 1969-1982, vol.2, p. 121)

(Stein, 1966, p. 277)

(Höhne, 1971, p. 531)

(Mazower, 1993, p. 180)

(Theile, 1997, p. 394)

(Germany, 1949-1953, pp. 831-832)

Kopaonik Mountains (Yugoslavia)

During Fall / Winter 1942, the 7. SS-Freiwilligen-Gebirgs-Division Prinz Eugen (CO: SS-Obergruppenführer Artur Phleps) conducted a series of operations against Chetnik partisans under Major Keserovic in the Kopaonik Mountains around Kriva Reka (Serbia) that included mass killings of innocent civilians. In his orders to the division dated 5 October, SS-Obergruppenführer Phleps stressed that ".... the entire population of this area must be considered rebel sympathizers." In mid-October, Prinz Eugen's Kampfgruppe Süd (composed primarily of the I. and III. Bataillon / SS-Gebirgsjäger-Regiment 2) commanded by SS-Obersturmbannführer August Schmidhuber murdered approximately 300 civilians in towns along the Kapaonik Mountains, northeast of Novi Pazar. Photographs of some of the victims were taken by a Waffen-SS trooper and later published in the Berliner Illustrierte Zeitung (1942, no. 45). The captions for the four photos claimed that the local populace invited the Waffen-SS to protect them from terror bands and that the bodies shown were those of partisans killed in action.

Sources

(Glisich, 1970, pp. 128-131)
(Kumm, 1978)

Kosutica (Yugoslavia)

On 12 July 1943, elements of the 7. SS-Freiwilligen-Gebirgs-Division Prinz Eugen (CO: SS-Brigadeführer Carl Ritter von Oberkamp) operating out of the Zenica-Sarajevo area executed 40 unarmed Bosnian Muslim civilians at Kosutica, 57 kilometers southwest of Banja Luka. Einsatzkommando 2 reported that the SS troopers took this action because they had supposedly been fired upon from the town's church. The atrocity occurred at a delicate moment in SS-Muslim relations: the primarily Bosnian Muslim 13. Waffen-Gebirgs-Division der SS Handschar (kroatisches Nr. 1) had just begun its training and Reichsführer-SS Heinrich Himmler did not want anything to spoil his cordial relations with the Bosnian Muslims. In order to quell the fears of its new ally, the SS offered its profoundest apologies for the massacre and directed relief supplies to Bosnia-Herzegovina. The officer responsible

for the killings, Carl Juels, was tried before an SS military court. He was convicted, sentenced to eight year's imprisonment, and dismissed from the SS. The actual time he served in prison is unknown.

Sources
(Höhne, 1971, pp. 530-531)
(Kumm, 1978)
(Lepre, 1997, pp. 50 & 112)
(letter from von Reinholz to Einsatzgruppe E, 15 July 1943, U.S. National Archives, Records of the RFSS [T-175], roll 140)
(Gen. Kdo. V. SS-Geb. Korps, Abt. Ia Tgb. Nr. 77/43 geh., v. 7.9. 1943, U.S. National Archives, Records of the RFSS [T-175], roll 31, ff 2601899)
(Personnel file of Carl Juels, U.S. National Archives, Berlin Document Center records)

Kriva Reka (Yugoslavia)

As part of the German effort to disarm Chetnik partisan bands in Yugoslavia during the Fall / Winter 1942, SS-Obergruppenführer Artur Phleps issued orders on 5 October for operations against the partisans under Major Keserovic in the Kopaonik Mountains around Kriva Reka (40 kilometers southwest of Krusevac, Serbia). In these orders SS-Obergruppenführer Artur Phleps stressed that ".... the entire population of the area must be considered rebel sympathizers." The operation was scheduled to begin 6 October and included elements of the 7. SS-Freiwilligen-Gebirgs-Division Prinz Eugen (which he commanded) and the 9th Bulgarian Infantry Division. The operation showed immediate successes as the combined German-Bulgarian forces gained ground and also disarmed various partisan detachments. On 11 October SS-Gebirgsjäger-Regiment 2 (CO: SS-Obersturmbannführer August Schmidhuber) and elements of the 9th Bulgarian division surrounded the village of Kriva Reka. The next day, although the locals offered no resistance, the Germans and Bulgarians began destroying houses and indiscriminately killing men, women, and children. Approximately 70 townspeople were collected and detained in the local church overnight. The next morning (13 October) elements of I. Bataillon / SS-Gebirgsjäger-Regiment 2 (CO: SS-Hauptsturmführer Kaaserer) sealed the church and then detonated explosives which they had previously emplaced. The ruins of the church were then set on fire by the Waffen-SS troopers. The action in the town continued that day with further massacres, looting, and destruction. A total of 320 men, women, and children were killed; only 20 houses remained standing in the town when it was all over.

News of the massacre spread throughout Serbia and talk of the terrible Waffen-SS division Prinz Eugen was on everyone's lips. In an effort to quell this concern on the part of the Serbian populace, the military commander for Serbia, General Paul Bader, declared official condolences for the dead and ordered that in the future detainment and execution without cause would be forbidden. General Bader also went as far as warning SS-Obergruppenführer Phleps that such actions should not be taken in the future because of the negative impact that they have on the German image in Serbia. These efforts were to no avail however, since Himmler approved of and took great delight in the division's "balkan methods." The depradations of Prinz Eugen continued unabated.

At the Nuremberg Trials, the prosecution cited an unnumbered document, apparently the text of a Soviet interrogation of former SS-Brigadeführer August Schmidhuber: "A war correspondent told me that the commander of my first battalion, Kassere, had a large number of citizens locked up in a church in Kriva Reka and then ordered the church to be blown up. I do not know how many persons perished." Former SS-Obergruppenführer Paul Hausser objected that this was hearsay evidence, but the prosecution countered that SS-Brigadeführer Schmidhuber did not doubt that the atrocity had occurred. This trial interchange has led some, Sauer for instance, to mistakenly conclude that the atrocity occurred at some point during SS-Brigadeführer Schmidhuber's command of the division in 1945.

Sources
(Glisich, 1970, pp. 128-131)
(Sauer, 1977, p. 35)
(IMT, 1948/1971, vol. 20, pp. 401-402)
(Kumm, 1978)

Krivodol (Yugoslavia)

On 28 March 1944 elements of the 7. SS-Freiwilligen-Gebirgs-Division Prinz Eugen (CO: SS-Brigadeführer Otto Kumm) with the help of the 369. Infanterie Division (CO: Generalleutnant Fritz Neidholdt) fired the town of Krivodol, 53 kilometers west of Mostar in Bosnia-Herzegovina, and shot 300 innocent civilians as part of a larger säuberungsaktion ("cleansing action") in the region.

Sources
(Zöller & Leszczynski, 1965, p. 62)
(Kumm, 1978)

Ksiazki (Poland)

On 8 September 1939 at the town of Ksiazki (northeast of Torun, Pomerania) members of SS-Totenkopfsturmbann Heimwehr Danzig (CO: SS-Obersturmbannführer Hans Friedemann Götze) executed 3 Polish POWs and 30 Polish civilians in retaliation for the detainment of seven local ethnic Germans. In November 1939, this unit was incorporated into the fledgling 3. SS-Panzer-Division Totenkopf.

Sources
(Sydnor, 1977, p. 41)
(Datner, 1964, p. 305)
(Questionnaire of C.C.I.N.C. in Poland, Pomerania, vol. III, p. 437)

Kukes (Albania)

On 11 August 1944 elements of the 21. SS-Freiwilligen-Gebirgs-Division Skanderbeg (CO: SS-Oberführer August Schmidhuber) hung an unspecified number of civilians in retaliation for partisan attacks just east of the town of Kukes (Kosoves Province, 96 kilometers northeast of Tirana).

Source
(Zöller & Leszczynski, 1965, p. 62)

Lago Maggiore (Italy)

The murder of sixty Jews on 22/24 September 1943 at Lago Maggiore (30 kilometers north of Novara in northwestern Italy) by elements of the 1. SS-Panzer-Division *Leibstandarte Adolf Hitler* is one of the few atrocities committed by Waffen-SS personnel that is acknowledged by some apologists such as Lehmann. The physical evidence and eyewitness testimony concerning the Waffen-SS troopers' actions is such that the accusations have never been denied: most apologists prefer to just ignore that the incident ever happened. This does not imply, however, that justice was served in this case. Mid-July 1943 found the 1. SS-Panzer-Division *Leibstandarte Adolf Hitler* (CO: SS-Brigadeführer Theodor Wisch) in the Ukrainian city of Kharkov resting and refitting from its heavy losses suffered during the Operation Citadel offensive against the Kursk salient. When the Italian Fascist government began to totter in early August, Hitler transferred *LAH* to Italy to restore the situation. The final collapse of Mussolini's government in September prompted the division to perform general security operations including the disarming of Italian troops in northern Italy.

 On 14 September SS-Hauptsturmführer Hans Becker, commander of 1. Bataillon / SS-Panzergrenadier-Regiment 2, received orders to secure the area between Lago Maggiore and the Swiss border. For several days the battalion disarmed Italian units in the Boves-Chiusa-Lago Maggiore area. Numerous military bases were taken over and their personnel transported to detention camps. On 15 September elements of 1. Bataillon under the command of SS-Hauptsturmführer Hans Walter Krüger entered the town of Meina on Lago Maggiore. Massara's account of the events that transpired in Meina is given below. Meina, a central tourist town of note on the Lago Maggiore [a little more than 40 kilometers from Capoluogo and about 3.5 kilometers from Arona] has numerous houses, summer residences, pensione and hotels. In the early days of September 1943, some of the untenanted houses were occupied by "men of importance" of the Regime and their families. Some Jewish families resided as guests at the Hotel Meina. The SS, as soon as they entered Meina on 15 September and in their first sweeps through the Municipio, gathered lists of the Jews residing or temporarily sheltered in private homes or in hotels. They also surrounded the Hotel Meina, thus proving their previous knowledge of the presence of the Jews there. The families housed at the Hotel Meina came from Greece (for the most part) and Capoluogo (Lombardy).

 The owner of the Hotel Meina and the commandant Behar, a Turkish Jew, sought to protect them through an intervention agreement between Hitler's Germany and the Turkish Government. Those housed at the Hotel Meina were : the family Fernandez Diaz (composed of the couple Pietro and Liliana Skialon, their children Giovanni aged 15, Roberto aged 12, and Bianca aged 8, and the grandfather Moishe Dino aged 76), the family Mosseri (composed of the couple Marco and Betton Ester, their son Renato aged 22 and his fiancee Odette Uziel aged 19 years), Raoul and Valeria Torres, Mario and Lotte Frölich Mazzucchelli (dinner guests from Milan), the farmer Daniele Modiano, and businessman Vittorio Pombas. Also present were the barman of the hotel, Cori Vitale, and the Jewish guests.

 The alarm was given by one of the proprietor's sons as he ran through the hotel halls yelling "the Germans, the Germans!" The couple Mazzucchelli, who were found in the reading room, were the first overtaken and shut up inside their room. In that moment the only people outside of the hotel were Pietro Fernandez Diaz and his 3 children. They noticed the presence of the SS and immediately returned inside the hotel in order to unite their family.

 Commanding the SS was Captain Hans Walter Krüger. He entered the hall of the hotel, followed by his SS troopers, and ordered all of the guests to stay in their rooms. The SS inspected the hotel register and the documents in the porter's lodge and then passed from room to room conducting a muster. All of the Jews were escorted to the last floor, the area of the servant's quarters.

 The lawyer from Lombard Mario Mazzucchelli, Aryan and of the Catholic faith, was allowed to leave the hotel. At that time Mazzucchelli, in an effort to aid his fellow man, went around town and knocked on numerous doors of the important fascists and the Nazi commander -- many were "surprised" at what was occurring and promised to look into it. When, on 21 September, Mazzucchelli returned to Meina, the situation appeared to have improved. The Jews were still in the lodgings of the servants, but they were allowed to descend, at dinner time, to the hotel restaurant.

At sunset on 22 September, SS-Captain Krüger ordered the Jews to eat in their rooms. Afterwards he passed through each of the rooms instructing the prisoners that they were going to be taken to the Mayor where they would be interrogated by officials. The trips to the interrogation, explained Krüger, would be done in small groups since they only had one vehicle at their disposal.

At about 9:30, the prisoners were taken out of their rooms and lined up along the back wall of the upstairs corridor. The first group consisted of Lotte Mazzucchelli, the couple Marco and Betton Ester Mosseri, and the barman Cori Vitale. They were part of the first convoy; the others remained in the lobby expectantly. By now, at least for the adults, the illusion of safety had vanished; they all had the perception that they were in the antechamber of death. At about one in the morning on 23 September the SS repeated their "summons" --- it was the turn of Liliana Skialon, her husband Pietro, and the two young Mosseri, Renato and Odette. From their waiting place in the hotel lobby the Jews could plainly hear the shouts and the derisive laughter of the SS, drunk on alcohol and on blood. At three, the final group of the night was formed of the couple Raoul and Valerie Torres, the country farmer Daniel Modiano and the business man Vittorio Pombas. The three children of the couple Fernandez Diaz and the grandfather Dino were driven back to their room on the last floor. The bodies of those murdered were then taken by the SS to a remote locale in the territory of Meina (near Casa Cantoniera, Sempione il lago) and dropped just offshore into the lake. The corpses were tied up with barbed wire to a large stone, brought out to an open space, and cast into the lake. On the following day, in an effort to purify the water, the SS troopers used grapples and bayonets to submerge any floating bodies. On the morning of 23 September there was a collection of the "booty" and a distribution of articles seized during the raid by the SS troopers; some articles were sold openly in the marketplace. Then began the final act of the tragedy of Meina.

The "aryan" clients of the Hotel Meina were ordered to eat supper in their rooms and then remain there the entire night. The youths Gianni, Roberto, Bianca Fernandez Diaz and their grandfather Dino Moise were slaughtered in the room on the last floor; terrible shouts of the youthful victims begging for pity on

the old grandfather..... afterwards the silence, a heavy silence..... the tragedy was complete. Afterwards the transport to the lakeshore. The SS bound the young together with iron wire, hand to hand, foot to foot, threw them into the lake and held them under with the force of oars.

When word of the massacre leaked out in early October, the divisional commander SS-Brigadeführer Wisch ordered an investigation. However, before much could occur the division was redeployed to heavy defensive fighting on the Eastern Front and the matter was dropped by the divisional court. Five former *LAH* officers -- SS-Hauptsturmführer Hans Walter Krüger, SS-Untersturmführer Karl Herbert Schnelle, SS-Untersturmführer Friedrich Röhwer, SS-? Oskar Schultz, and SS-? Otto Ludwig Leithe -- were tried by West German authorities after the war. Hans Becker was not tried as he was killed in action in Normandy on 20 August 1944. The Schwurgericht Osnabrück found that on 22/24 September 1943 the five defendants and other members of 1. Bataillon / SS-Panzergrenadier-Regiment 2 in some villages along Lago Maggiore seized Jews and later killed them.

The court decision stated that :

1) the troops had strict orders to abstain from violent actions against the civil populace
2) Italian Jews at that time were not being hunted by German organizations
3) the troops knew that criminal orders should not be carried out
4) a company commander, who had ordered the Jewish executions, made up a plausible account to serve as a cover for it
5) for that reason the crimes were hidden from their superior officers

On 5 July 1968 the Schwurgericht Osnabrück sentenced the five defendants to death because of their responsibility for the murders at Meina. The defendants immediately submitted an appeal to the Bundesgerichtshof in Berlin. In April 1970 this federal court caused great consternation when it overturned the lower court ruling and acquitted the defendants on the grounds that they were only following orders and that the statute of limitations had expired anyway.

Sources
(Artzt, 1974, p. 111)
(Lehmann, 1977-1987, vol. 3, pp. 287-336)
(Massara, 1984, pp. 169-175)
(Mayda, 1978)

Lahoysk (USSR)

During the southerly march of the 2. SS-Panzer-Division *Das Reich* (CO: SS-Obergruppenführer Paul Hausser) to participate in the encirclement battles around Kiev in September 1941, an unidentified rear-area company of the division assisted elements of Einsatzgruppe B (CO: SS-Brigadeführer Arthur Nebe) in executing 920 Jews at the town of Lahoysk, near Minsk. The operation was officially noted in the Einsatzgruppen reports to Berlin (Ereignismeldung UdSSR.....) :

> "A large-scale anti-Jewish action was carried out in the village of Lahoysk. In the course of this action, 920 Jews were executed with the support of a unit of the SS Division Reich. The village may now be described as 'free of Jews' (Judenfrei)."

Although Hausser was questioned about Waffen-SS atrocities during the Nuremberg Trials, this particular incident went unmentioned and remains uninvestigated to this day. Theile has labelled this atrocity a post-war fabrication for which no supporting evidence exists, despite its prominent mention in an official German war-time communique.

Sources
(Stein, 1966, p. 274)
(Reitlinger, 1957, p. 169)
(Theile, 1997, p. 391)
(Ereignismeldung UdSSR nr. 92 / Berlin, 23 September 1941 in Arad et.al., 1989, p. 151)
(IMT, 1948/1971, Document NO 3143, Case IX)

Le Paradis (France)

During the French Campaign of 1940, the 3. SS-Panzer-Division *Totenkopf* (CO: SS-Gruppenführer Theodor Eicke) battled elements of the British Expeditionary Force for control of La Basse Canal in northern France. The *Totenkopf* division crossed the canal near Bethune only after taking serious casualties. Once across the canal, the situation did not get any better for the Waffen-SS. Their opponent, the British 2nd Division, was sacrificing itself in order to allow other British units to escape towards Lys. The 4th Brigade of the 2nd Division held the canal line between Robecq - Bethune. Repeated attacks by *Totenkopf* accompanied by heavy SS casualties slowly forced the British defenders back towards the villages of Le Paradis and Locon. There, the 1st Royal Scots, 2nd Royal Norfolk, and the I/8th Lancashire Fusiliers decided to make a final stand. On 27 May 1940 *Totenkopf* began its advance north towards Merville. The 4. Kompanie / 1. Bataillon / SS-Panzergrenadier-Regiment 6 (kompanie CO: SS-Obersturmbannführer Fritz Knöchlein) was held up by the determined resistance of approximately 100 men from the 2nd Royal Norfolk Regiment at a small farm in Le Paradis. When it became obvious to the British that further resistance was useless, they surrendered. After being searched and stripped of their equipment, the Norfolk POWs --- most of them wounded --- were marched across the road to a barn, lined up, and massacred with the fire from two previously set up machine-guns. After the execution, SS-Obersturmbannführer Knöchlein and his men searched the pile of bodies for survivors. Any who still showed signs of life were then shot or bayoneted to death. Several French civilians who witnessed the slaughter were threatened by the SS troopers and chased off. After an hour or so, the SS troopers rejoined their regiment on its drive towards Merville. Two badly wounded Norfolks survived, however. Privates Albert Pooley and William O'Callaghan hid in a pigsty on a nearby farm for several days. They were cared for by villagers, but finally surrendered to a medical company of the 251. Infanterie-Division because of the severity of their wounds. Pooley was repatriated to England in 1943 due to ongoing health problems; O'Callaghan returned to Britain at war's end. The bodies of the executed British POWs were later buried in a mass grave by the Germans. In 1942 French authorities exhumed the bodies and reburied them in the Le Paradis churchyard.

 Complaints against SS-Obersturmbannführer Knöchlein were soon made by some of his fellow *Totenkopf* officers. One even challenged him to a duel for "the honor of the regiment." General Hoeppner, commander of the XVI Panzer Korps, demanded action against the guilty parties. However, no serious investigation of the crime was ever pursued : a Wehrmacht legal inquiry into the shootings was quashed on the direct orders of Reichsführer-SS Heinrich Himmler. Knöchlein went on to further command positions culminating in his appointment as commander of SS-Freiwilligen-Panzergrenadier-Regiment 23 *Norge* (11. SS-Freiwilligen-Panzergrenadier-Division *Nordland*) in April 1944. He was also awarded the Ritterkreuz (Knight's Cross) for valor on the Eastern Front.

In September 1946 Pooley paid a return visit to Le Paradis. At this time British authorities began inquiries into the claims of Pooley and O'Callaghan that atrocities had been committed against the Norfolks. During a search of POW camps for war criminals in late 1946, Knöchlein was recognized and arrested by Allied authorities. On 11 October 1948, he was tried by a British military tribunal at Altona near Hamburg for the deliberate murder of the Norfolk POWs. Both Pooley and O'Callaghan, along with a number of villagers from Le Paradis, gave testimony against him during this trial. Knöchlein attempted to justify his crime by claiming that British soldiers had committed war crimes and thus his actions were completely legal under an old German law which provided for the establishment of emergency battlefield courts known as *Standgerichte*. It was a clever ruse, but failed to convince the judges on three counts: *first*, no evidence of British crimes was ever produced, *second*, there was no evidence that any "emergency" court had been established at Le Paradis and *third*, the POWs had been shot out of hand without any legal considerations taking place. Fritz Knöchlein was convicted of all charges on 25 October 1948 and hung on 28 January 1949 at Hameln.

Waffen-SS apologists, such as Krätschmer, continue to claim that the fighting around La Basse Canal was characterized by atrocities on both sides. Some have even restated Knöchlein's specific charges that the killings were in retaliation for the British troops using dum-dum ammunition against his men. Such claims have been shown to be without any basis in fact.

Sources
(*Krätschmer, 1982, pp. 803-805*)
(*Reitlinger, 1957, p. 148*)
(*Stein, 1966, pp. 76-78*)
(*Windrow, 1988, p. 12*)
(*Bender & Taylor, 1969-1982, vol. 2, p. 102*)

(*Quarrie, 1987, pp. 78-79*)
(*Sydnor, 1977, pp. 106-109*)
(*Jolly, 1956*)

L'Arbresle (France)

On 19 June 1940, elements of 5. Kompanie / 2. Bataillon / SS-Panzergrenadier-Regiment 6 / 3. SS-Panzer-Division *Totenkopf* (divisional CO: SS-Gruppenführer Theodor Eicke) fought a vicious battle against French Moroccan troops left as rearguards near L'Arbresle, 19 kilometers northwest of Lyon. The SS troopers denied quarter to the 30 Moroccans -- they were not allowed to surrender -- and killed every one of them. With the exception of the *Le Paradis* massacre, such denial of quarter appears to have been reserved for "inferior" black troops by *Totenkopf* personnel during the invasion of France.

Source
(*Sydnor, 1977, pp. 116-117*)

Larisa (Greece)

It has been claimed that the 4. SS-Polizei-Panzergrenadier-Division committed unspecified atrocities during its 1944 operations in the area of Larisa (eastern-central Greece). No further information has been found regarding this accusation.

Source
(*Windrow, 1988, p. 13*)

Legatori (Yugoslavia)

On 28 March 1944 elements of the 7. SS-Freiwilligen-Gebirgs-Division *Prinz Eugen* (CO: SS-Brigadeführer Otto Kumm) with the help of the 369. Infanterie Division (CO: Generalleutnant Fritz Neidholdt) fired the town of Legatori in Bosnia/Herzegovina and shot 40 civilians as part of a larger *säuberungsaktion* ("cleansing action") in the region.

Sources
(*Zöller & Leszczynski, 1965, p. 62*)
(*Kumm, 1978*)

Lentilly (France)

On 19 June 1940 elements of 3. Bataillon / SS-Panzer-grenadier-Regiment 5 / 3. SS-Panzer-Division *Totenkopf* (divisional CO: SS-Gruppenführer Theodor Eicke) engaged French forces that included Colonial Moroccan troops near the town of Lentilly (15 kilometers northwest of Lyon). The battalion's daily report (Tagesmeldung) noted that they captured 24 white French prisoners while "24 Negroes fell in combat." The daily report also describes another encounter in which Negroes were "put out of action" and concludes with the comment that the day's fighting yielded "25 French prisoners and 44 dead Negroes." As noted in connection with the *L'Arbresle* atrocity, *Totenkopf* personnel treated "inferior" black Moroccan troops in a manner consistent with their SS ideological indoctrination.

Source
(Sydnor, 1977, p. 117)

Lidice (Czechoslovakia)

During his reign as Protector of Bohemia and Moravia, SS-Obergruppenführer Reinhard Heydrich earned the nicknames "Butcher of Prague" and "Heydrich the Hangman" due his brutal methods of suppressing opposition to the Nazi occupation. On 27 May 1942, he was assassinated by Czech agents parachuted in at the behest of British Intelligence. He finally died of his wounds on 4 June 1942. Hitler was enraged that this exemplar of "aryan manhood" had been cut done so treacherously and ordered his security services to leave no stone unturned in their search for the assassins and their accomplices.

 Through the use of paid informants, the Germans discovered the hiding place of the assassins in Prague. On 5 June, elements of the SS-Infanterie-Ersatz-Bataillon *Deutschland* (CO: ?) [a training unit of the 2. SS-Panzer-Division *Das Reich*] surrounded the Greek Orthodox Karel Boromejsky Church. After destroying the altar and sledgehammering the walls of the church, the SS troopers discovered a false crypt concealing the assassins. After a short firefight, the two Czech patriots were dead. The SS investigators believed that several small Czech towns, such as Lidice near Kladno, were also involved in Heydrich's death. Hitler, whose desire for revenge was not satisfied by the deaths of the two assassins, ordered Heydrich's replacement SS-Gruppenführer Karl Hermann Frank to wipe Lidice from the face of the earth.

On the evening of 9 June 1942 the town was surrounded by a Schutzpolizei regiment under the command of Oberst der Schutzpolizei Max Rostock. Later in the evening this regiment was relieved by Heeres-Ersatz-Bataillon 480 based in Slany. The Schutzpolizei then arrested all of the town's inhabitants : 173 men were locked into the mayor's barn; 198 women and 98 children were trucked to a gymnasium in nearby Kladno where they were guarded by a platoon of Czech Protectorate gendarmes. After the arrival of two further platoons of gendarmes from Prague, Lidice was thoroughly looted and the goods transported to the Gestapo headquarters in Kladno.

At daybreak on 10 June, all of the men were taken out and shot by a Schutzpolizei platoon in a nearby orchard. At 7:00 am, Lidice was fired with 500 liters of gasoline supplied by the Gestapo and the Wehrmacht. By 10:00 am, all of the houses in the town were on fire. On 11 June 1942, a group of Jews was transported from the Theresienstadt Ghetto and forced to bury the bodies of Lidice's men in a mass grave. Later that day an unidentified Waffen-SS pioniere platoon (most likely, either elements of the *Deutschland* training battalion or SS-Totenkopf-Infanterie-Ersatz-Bataillon II *Prag*) numbering some 37 personnel began blowing up those walls of the town that had survived the fire. Lidice's crumbled remains were then dug up and the area completely landscaped into meadows by the Reichsarbeitdienst in a massive effort lasting several months.

On 13 June the women and children of Lidice were separated by their German captors. The women were sent to various German concentration camps : of 198 women deported, only 143 survived at war's end. The children of Lidice were sent to Gniesenau in occupied Poland where they were sorted according to physical appearance. Those possessing "aryan" characteristics as defined by SS racial experts were adopted into German families through the Lebensborn (SS maternity home and orphanage organization). The rest of the children were killed in carbon monoxide gas vans at the Chelmno extermination camp in Poland. Only 16 of the 104 children taken from the village were traced and returned to their surviving relatives after the war.

Other nearby Czech towns also received the "Lidice treatment" following Heydrich's assassination. The Germans claimed that the towns had sheltered the assassins and also served as partisan weapon depots and radio stations. No substantive evidence to support these claims has ever surfaced; although this has not prevented Nazi apologists from using them as the basis for legitimizing these murderous actions. While the Waffen-SS role in the Lidice affair was certainly limited, it serves to further illustrate their participation in "security operations" that were little more than glorified murder campaigns.

Sources
(Bradley, 1972)
(Wykes, 1973)
(Reitlinger, 1957, p. 216)
(Rückerl, 1980, p. 145)
(Krausnick, 1981, p. 27)
(Czechoslovak Republic, 1942)
(Weiner, 1969, pp. 116-120)

Liga (Yugoslavia)

During Fall 1942, the 7. SS-Freiwilligen-Gebirgs-Division *Prinz Eugen* (CO: SS-Obergruppenführer Artur Phleps) conducted a series of operations against Chetnik partisans under Major Keserovic in the Kapaonik Mountains around Kriva Reka (Serbia) that included the mass killings of innocent civilians. In his orders to the division dated 5 October, SS-Obergruppenführer Phleps stressed that ".... the entire population of this area must be considered rebel sympathizers." In mid-October, elements of the *Prinz Eugen* division executed 104 civilians in the neighborhood of Liga and Krusevac.

Sources
(Glisich, 1970, pp. 128-131)
(Kumm, 1978)

Lithuania

It has been alleged that an unidentified East Prussian Allgemeine SS-Reiterstandarte was involved in a *Judenbeschaffungsaktion* ("Jewish supply operation") and shot many hundreds of Jews in the Lithuanian border area at an unspecified date. Three such units were stationed in East Prussia : SS-Reiterstandarte 1 (Insterburg), SS-Reiterstandarte 3 (Lyck), and SS-Reiterstandarte 20 (Tilsit). With the commencement of the war, these units regularly supplied personnel to the Waffen-SS and, specifically, to the 8. SS-Kavallerie-Division *Florian Geyer*. Without additional information, little can be said about this claim. For a listing of Allgemeine SS-Reiterstandarte commanders throughout the war, see Yerger.

Sources
(Krausnick & Wilhelm, 1981, p. 601)
(Rüter-Ehlermann et al., 1978, Band XIX, p. 374)
(Yerger, 1997, pp. 214-221)

Livarot (France)

On 21 August 1944 while defending the town of Livarot against German counterattacks, D Company, 1/6th Queens Regiment of the British 7th Armoured Division was purportedly overrun by elements of the 27. SS-Freiwilligen-Grenadier-Division *Langemarck* (flämische Nr. 1) [SS-Obersturmbannführer Konrad Schellong]. All of the British wounded and prisoners were then hacked to death with pick-axes. The perperators were identified by their uniform cuff-bands bearing the legend "Langemarck."This claim is problematical as all documentary evidence indicates that the *Langemarck* division served exclusively on the Eastern Front. In fact, at the time of this claimed atrocity the division was undergoing reorganization at Breslau in eastern Germany. It is possible that the unit responsible was either a reserve or some other minor support component of the division that was deployed separately. Alternately, the perpetrators could have been former *Langemarck* personnel attached to the 12. SS-Panzer-Division *Hitler Jugend* (CO: SS-Brigadeführer Kurt Meyer) remnants of which were opposing the British 7th Armoured Division's advance in this area. Waffen-SS personnel often retained the uniform cuff-bands from their original units.

Source
(Delaforce, 1994, pp. 73-78)

Lodz (Poland)

During it advance through Poland in September 1939 (most likely on 8 September), elements of II. Bataillon / *Leibstandarte Adolf Hitler* Regiment under the command of SS-Obersturmbannführer Carl Ritter von Oberkamp tortured an unknown number of civilians in the city of Lodz. The structure of the battalion at this time was as follows:

5. Kompanie	SS-Hauptsturmführer Wilhelm Mohnke
6. Kompanie	SS-Hauptsturmführer Otto Baum
7. Kompanie	SS-Hauptsturmführer Seppel Lange
8. Kompanie	SS-Hauptsturmführer August Dieterichs

SS-Hauptsturmführer Lange was killed in action on 12 September 1939 and replaced by SS-Hauptsturmführer Artur Klingemeier. There is no evidence that legal proceedings were ever instigated with respect to these crimes. Carl Ritter von Oberkamp was executed in 1947 by the Yugoslavian authorities for numerous atrocities committed against Balkan civilians.

Sources
(Sayer & Botting, 1989, p. 20)
(United Nations War Crimes Commission file number 284/P/G/29)

Lotoschinsk Psychiatric Clinic (USSR)

The four Einsatzgruppen operating behind the frontlines in the USSR reported exterminating tens of thousands of "asocials"(Gypsies and the mentally ill) during the course of their killing operations that were poorly disguised as anti-partisan campaigns. For example, late in 1941 unidentified elements of Einsatzgruppe B were responsible for the murder of 700 patients at the Lotoschinsk Psychiatric Clinic (south of Smolensk). The majority of the patients were either gassed or shot immediately. However, some were starved to death, left outside to die of exposure, or even hunted down on horseback for sport.

Source
(Burleigh, 1994, pp. 230-231)

Lublin (Poland)

Following numerous complaints concerning the excesses of its personnel, SS-Sonderkommando Dirlewanger (CO: SS-Oberführer Dr. Oskar Dirlewanger) was transferred in 1941 from the Krakow area and placed under the command of SSPf Lublin SS-Gruppenführer Ulrich "Odilo" Globocnik. The unit immediately began to terrorize the city's Jewish ghetto. Later investigations by SS-Hauptsturmführer Dr. Konrad Morgen and the Sicherheitspolizei Lublin demonstrated that the sonderkommando arrested Polish civilians illegally and arbitrarily, plundered their belongings, and extorted money from interned Jews. Even worse, however, Dirlewanger and a circle of his cronies were known to torture female prisoners -- with an especial fondness for young Jewesses. The unfortunate women were stripped naked and injected with strychnine. Dirlewanger would casually smoke cigarettes while watching the women slowly die. Their bodies were then supposedly dismembered, cut into small pieces, mixed with horsemeat, and boiled into soap. Such claims are reminiscent of the completely discredited allegations at the Nuremberg Trials that soap was produced from Jewish corpses at the German death camps in Poland. Despite interference run by SS ministry officials on behalf of the sonderkommando, the unending complaints of SS officials on the ground in Poland eventually sealed the unit's fate. In February 1942, SS-Sonderkommando Dirlewanger was upgraded and transferred to the control of HSSPf Russland Mitte und Weissruthenien SS-Obergruppenführer Erich von dem Bach-Zelewski to undertake anti-partisan and extermination operations in the USSR.

The unit eventually went on to become the 36. Waffen-Grenadier-Division der SS.

Sources
(Germany [U.S. Zone], 1949-1953, vol. 4, pp. 36-40)
(MacLean, 1998, pp. 58-66)

Lublin -- Aktion Erntefest (Poland)

As the Operation Reinhardt extermination program picked up its pace in 1943, a number of spirited armed revolts were undertaken by Jews imprisoned in ghettos and concentration camps throughout Poland (uprisings at Warsaw Ghetto, Bialystok Ghetto, and Treblinka death camp; breakout from Sobibor death camp). In order to forestall further security problems, in late October 1943 Reichsführer-SS Heinrich Himmler directed SS-Obergruppenführer Friedrich Wilhelm Krüger (HSSPf Generalgouvernement) who in turn ordered SS-Gruppenführer Jakob Sporrenberg (SSPf Lublin) to liquidate the entire populations of the Majdanek, Trawniki, and Poniatowa concentration camps.

On the evening of 2 November 1943 SS-Gruppenführer Sporrenberg met with his commanders for the operation to be codenamed *Aktion Erntefest* (Operation Harvest Festival) : SS-Obersturmbannführer Dr. Karl Pütz (KdS Lublin) and the Ordnungspolizei representative for Lublin. An assortment of rear-area occupation and training forces were gathered which included Waffen-SS, Polizei, Polizei-Kavallerie, and Ordnungspolizei units from the Lublin, Radom, Krakow, and Warsaw districts. Several of the units were deployed that evening to surround the camps and to provide logistical support for the coming operation.

On the following morning all Jewish prisoners from satellite camps in the Majdanek area were rounded up and marched to the camp by elements of the SS-Panzergrenadier-Ausbildungs-und Ersatz-Bataillon 3 *Warschau* (CO: SS-Obersturmbannführer Walther Bellwidt). Some tried to flee along the march route, but they were immediately gunned down by their Waffen-SS escorts. Once at the camp, the prisoners were separated into groups of approximately fifty, relieved of their valuables, and then ordered to undress completely. The prisoners were then run outside to stand before a series of hastily dug graves where they were mown down by machine-gun fire. Any survivors were finished off with individual pistol shots. Approximately 17 - 18,000 people were executed at Majdanek concentration camp that day. At the same time, similar events were occurring at Trawniki concentration camp where an unidentified Waffen-SS battalion also assisted with the killings. The Jews brought to Poniatowa camp were not massacred until the following day. At both Majdanek and Poniatowa the executioners set up loud speakers and played dance music in an attempt to cover up the noise of the firing squads and the terrible screams of their victims. SS-Gruppenführer Sporrenberg observed the operations from overhead in his Fieseler Storch reconnaissance aircraft. In all, a total of 42,000 Jews from camps in the greater Lublin area were murdered in the two-day operation. Following the mass killings, Jewish "cremation commandos" were forced to destroy all evidence of atrocities at the three camps. Afterwards, they were also executed.

Jakob Sporrenberg was arrested by the British on 11 May 1945. He was later remanded to Polish custody and tried for his role in the *Aktion Erntefest* massacres. He was sentenced to death and hung on 22 September 1950. Dr. Karl Pütz was also tried and executed after the war by the Polish authorities. Friedrich Wilhelm Krüger committed suicide on 10 May 1945 at Gundershausen, near Branau am Inn. The fate of Walther Bellwidt is unknown.

Sources
(Arad, 1987, pp. 365-369)
(Browning, 1992)
(Grabitz and Scheffler, 1988, pp. 328-335)

Lublin District (Poland)

In early June 1941, elements of SS-Totenkopfstandarte 14 (CO: SS-Obersturmbannführer Georg Martin) murdered an undetermined number of civilian Poles and Jews while expropriating farm animals and produce in the Lublin District. One month later, this unit was incorporated into the newly-forming 2. SS-Infanterie (mot.)-Brigade.

Source
(Sydnor, 1977, p. 324)

Lublin District/Majdanek

(Poland)

During the Nuremberg Trials, the prosecution introduced the following affidavit by Izrael Eizenberg attesting to Waffen-SS involvement in numerous war crimes :

I lived in Lublin and from there I was sent to Maidanek in the beginning of 1942. However, as a prisoner I continued to work for the Germans, who employed me as an expert for electro-mechanical jobs in the various SS buildings and SS offices in Lublin. I worked as an electro-mechanic in the palace building of the SS and Police Leader Globocznik and in the headquarters of the SS in Lublin, Warsaw Street 21. The Waffen-SS were also there. On the outer wall the notice *Waffen-SS* could be seen and on the pass which I received at the entrance, the words *Waffen-SS* were also marked. I knew all the officers, for instance, Oberscharführer Riedel, Rottenführer Mohrwinkel, Unterscharführer Schramm and so on. I know that the leaders of the Waffen-SS, as well as the regiment of the Waffen-SS -- whose seat was in the same building where I worked -- participated directly in all the expulsions of the Jews from the district of Lublin. During these expulsions thousands of persons were killed on the spot and the rest sent away for extermination. I myself have seen how, in the winter of 1941, the Waffen-SS of 21 Warsaw Street participated in the deportation of several hundred Jews to Maidanek, whereby several persons were killed on the spot. At that time my father was also deported because of his long beard, as this action was mainly concerned Jews with beards. I know that Rottenführer Mohrwinkel directed this action and was promoted to the rank of Untersturmführer in appreciation of his work. I worked for the Waffen-SS until November 1942, that is, until I was transported to Radom. They participated the whole time in all the crimes of the SS in Lublin and in the district. I wish to point out that these SS men kept their horses in the stables on the airdrome where there was a notice *Mounted Regiment Waffen-SS.*

IMT Document D-939 (exhibit GB-563)

The individual referred to as "Globocznik" was SS-Gruppenführer Ulrich "Odilo" Globocnik who held the post of SSPf Lublin from November 1939 until September 1943. The two Waffen-SS units referred to above were part of the Truppenwirtschaftslager der Waffen-SS Lublin. As noted in the section on the HSSPf/SSPf and their various functions, it was not at all uncommon for rear-area Waffen-SS units to be temporarily assigned to "security" duties that included the commission of war crimes (deportations, mass shootings, *etc.*).

Source
(IMT, 1948/1971, vol. 36, pp. 64-65)

Lvov (Poland)

In April 1967 the infamous "Stanislawow" trial took place in Münster, West Germany in which Hans Krüger, the former Gestapo chief of the Polish town of Stanislawow during the German occupation, was charged with murdering thousands of Jews. After a year-long trial, Krüger was sentenced to life imprisonment for his involvement in the extermination of approximately 120,000 Jews. Trial documents also shed light on Waffen-SS involvement in the murder of Lvov's intellectual class.

On 2 July 1941, SS-Oberführer Dr. Eberhardt Schöngarth arrived at Lvov with SS-Einsatzgruppe zur besondere Verwendung (CO: SS-Sturmbannführer Friedrich Dern). This unit was composed of a mixture of Waffen-SS, Sicherheitspolizei, and Schutzpolizei personnel. SS-Brigadeführer Schöngarth had been ordered to arrest and execute all members of the Polish intelligentsia in Lvov. On the basis of lists previously prepared for the SS by Ukrainian deserters, Schöngarth's men rounded up a group of university professors, their wives, and their children detaining them in the Abrahamowicz school.

The following night an execution squad commanded by SS-Untersturmführer Dr. Walter Kutschmann and composed of five ethnic German Waffen-SS men and two Ukrainian police auxiliaries was formed to carry out the operations. Early in the morning on 4 July the professors and their families were taken to a secluded site in the Wulecka Hills. The Ukrainian police auxiliaries dug a pit and the unfortunate Poles were executed and dumped in it. Since this was supposed to be a "top secret" operation, the two Ukrainian police auxiliaries were then shot by their Waffen-SS comrades. A post-war Polish government exhumation crew found the bodies of the auxiliaries lying on top of the Polish victims.

Source
(Wiesenthal, 1989, p. 167)

Maille (France)

The village of Maille sits 40 kilometers south of the city of Tours astride the Paris-Bordeaux railway line in the Indre et Loire province. The Germans arrived in June 1940 and set up a base in the nearby village of Nouatre. By 1944, Maille's usual village population of 241 had been augmented by an additional 85 refugees. The war had, for the most part, entirely bypassed Maille until the summer of 1944.

The Anglo-American D-Day landings on 6 June 1944 served as a signal for heightened activities by French resistance forces. The railway line in the area was sabotaged three separate times, twice at Maille Station itself. On 11 August a downed English pilot could not be found by German search parties, undoubtedly because he had been hidden away by local residents. As advancing Allied forces neared the region, the situation reached a crisis point. Early in the evening of 24 August a truck-load of resistance fighters armed with a light machinegun raided a farm north of Maille to seize supplies. Just then, a two-vehicle German patrol appeared which the resistance fighters immediately ambushed and drove off with significant casualties.

One of the officers in the German patrol, Leutnant Gustav Schlüter, telephoned Oberst Stenger, the military commander at Tours, informing him that there had been an attack by French terrorists and asking what action should be taken in response. Leutnant Schlüter was authorized, in unclear language, to undertake a reprisal operation at Maille. He apparently spent that night organizing the attack. The next morning, 25 August, German soldiers cordoned off the village and then entered it shooting everyone on sight that they encountered. Villagers who ran away were followed to their houses, shot there, and then had their houses set on fire. Residents of the parish who approached the village on business were shot down in the surrounding fields and woods. The massacre lasted all morning after which the German soldiers withdrew. In the afternoon an 88 mm anti-aircraft gun opened fire on Maille from a nearby hill. The town was shelled until early evening. Throughout the day several German military trains traversed Maille on the way to Tours and the soldiers on-board were encouraged to fire upon the village as they passed through it. At one point in the afternoon the Germans ceased their attacks and allowed the parish priest, Father An-

dre Payon, to lead survivors from the ruined village to safety elsewhere. In all 124 residents of Maille were killed that day (35 men, 41 women, and 48 children).

In 1952 Gustav Schlüter was tried *in absentia* before the military tribunal in Bordeaux and sentenced to death. He has never been located. Conflicting testimony was given by survivors: some testified that Waffen-SS troopers carried out the massacre, while others claimed that the culprits were Wehrmacht troops from the nearby base at Nouatre. The debate continues to this day. Research has demonstrated, however, that there was only one Waffen-SS unit in the area at the time of the massacre.

In November 1943 a new division designated 17. SS-Panzergrenadier-Division *Götz von Berlichingen* began formation and training in the countryside west-southwest of Tours. The D-Day landings found the division still at only 70% of its official strength, lacking required armored vehicles and motor transport, and with only limited supplies of heavy ammunition. Nevertheless, most of the division had moved north by mid-June to counterattack the enemy landing sites. The morning of 24 August, however, found 1. Batterie / SS-Flak-Abteilung 17 (CO: SS-Obersturmführer Baier) and the light bridging column of SS-Pioniere-Bataillon 17 still stationed at the town of Saumur on the Loire River west of Tours due to a lack of motor transport. The recent news from Normandy was alarming. The German defensive positions had crumbled, Allied armored forces were roaming free, and the German armies were reeling back in defeat toward Paris and the Seine River. SS-Obersturmführer Baier immediately commandeered all available vehicles in the town -- enough to enable his unit and the pioneers to move east to the city of Tours that day with all of their equipment. Along the way he acquired two 88mm anti-aircraft guns abandoned by a retreating Luftwaffe unit to add to his battery's normal complement of four 88mm and three 20 mm anti-aircraft guns. At Tours he was contacted by his divisional HQ and ordered to defend the Loire River bridge there in order to keep open a retreat route for German units south and west of the city. Whether SS-Obersturmführer Baier would have diverted personnel from this primary mission in order to raze Maille (40 kilometers to the south) the next day is debatable.

Sources
(Bender & Taylor,1969-1982, vol. 4, p. 128-138)
(Munoz, 1999, p. 9)
(Perrigault & Meister, 2004, vol. 1, p. 341)
(Musso, 1980)
(Payon, 1945)
(Le magazine de la Touraine, juillet 1984)

Malmedy (Belgium)

Introduction

The Allied D-Day landings in France on 6 June 1944 began a summer of disaster for German forces on the Western Front. Once the Allies had broken through Germany's best armored forces and pushed out of the Normandy beachhead, the race across France began. By early Winter 1944, the Germans had for the most part been pushed all the way back to Germany itself. However, worsening weather and lengthening supply lines combined to slow the Allied offensive and gave the Germans a chance to catch their breath. Hopelessly outnumbered by the Allies in men and materiel, Hitler nonetheless decided to use his last major strategic reserves to refit a handful of divisions as quickly as possible for a surprise offensive. The goal of the German's operation was to punch a hole in the American positions along the rugged Ardennes region of southeastern Belgium. Following this breakthrough, their armored forces would attack northwest to the Meuse River, cross it, and then advance on the port of Antwerp. The Allied forces, split in half and deprived of a major port of supply, would have to come to terms with Germany. Or so Hitler believed.

   The spearhead of the German offensive was the 6. SS-Panzerarmee under the command of SS-Obergruppenführer Josef "Sepp" Dietrich. The army was composed of two armored corps that appeared strong on paper, but included numerous untested reserve units of low quality.

I. SS-Panzerkorps (CO: SS-Obergruppenführer Hermann Priess)

1. SS-Panzer-Division *Leibstandarte Adolf Hitler* (SS-Oberführer Wilhelm Mohnke)
12. SS-Panzer-Division *Hitler Jugend*; 12. Volksgrenadier-Division; 277. Volksgrenadier-Division; 3. Fallschirmjäger-Division, Panzer-Brigade 150; Volkswerfer-Brigaden 4 & 9; 388. & 402. Volksartillerie-Korps; and miscellaneous attached units

II. SS-Panzerkorps (CO: SS-Obergruppenführer Wilhelm Bittrich)

2. SS-Panzer-Division *Das Reich*; 9. SS-Panzer-Division *Hohenstaufen*; 410. Volksartillerie-Korps; and miscellaneous attached units

For our purposes, the 1. SS-Panzer-Division *Leibstandarte Adolf Hitler* is the only unit of interest. The division was deployed during the offensive as the following battlegroups (not including several divisional units held in reserve):

Kampfgruppe Peiper
(CO: SS-Obersturmbannführer Joachim "Jochen" Peiper)
SS-Panzer-Regiment 1

   SS-Panzer-Bataillon 1
   (CO: SS-Sturmbannführer Werner Pötschke)
   SS-Panzergrenadier-Bataillon 3
   (CO: SS-Sturmbannführer Josef Diefenthal)
   SS-Schwere-Panzer-Bataillon 501
   (CO: SS-Sturmbannführer Hein von Westernhagen)
   SS-Panzerartillerie-Bataillon 1
   (CO: SS-Hauptsturmführer Ludwig Kalischko)
   SS-Panzerpionier-Kompanie 9
   (CO: SS-Obersturmführer Erich Rumpf)
   SS-Panzerpionier-Kompanie 3
   (CO: SS-Obersturmführer Franz Sievers)
   SS-Panzer-AA-Kompanie 10
   (CO: SS-? Karl-Heinz Vögler)

Kampfgruppe Hansen
(CO: SS-Obersturmbannführer Max Hansen)
SS-Panzergrenadier-Regiment 1

   SS-Panzergrenadier-Bataillon 1
   (CO: SS-Sturmbannführer Emil Karst)
   SS-Panzergrenadier-Bataillon 2
   (CO: SS-Hauptsturmführer Unterkofler)
   SS-Panzergrenadier-Bataillon 3
   (CO: SS-Hauptsturmführer Karl Böttcher)
   SS-Schweres-Infanterie-Geschütz-Kompanie 13
   (CO: SS-? Voss)
   SS-Panzer-AA-Kompanie 14 (CO: SS-? Stuna)
   SS-Panzerpionier-Kompanie 15 (CO: SS-? Lenski)

SS-Panzerjäger-Bataillon 1
(CO: SS-Hauptsturmführer Karl Rettlinger)
SS-Panzer-Werfer-Bataillon 1
(CO: SS-Sturmbannführer Klaus Besch)
SS-Panzerartillerie-Abteilung 4
(CO: SS-Obersturmführer Karl-Heinz Pulvermüller)

Kampfgruppe Sandig
(CO: SS-Obersturmbannführer Rudolf Sandig)
SS-Panzergrenadier-Regiment 2

SS-Panzergrenadier-Bataillon 1
(CO: SS-Sturmbannführer Karl Richter)
SS-Panzergrenadier-Bataillon 2
(CO: SS-Hauptsturmführer Herbert Schnelle)
SS-Panzer-AA-Kompanie 14 (CO: SS-? Duppel)
SS-Panzerpionier-Kompanie 15 (CO: SS-? Staude)

Schnelle Gruppe Knittel
(CO: SS-Sturmbannführer Gustav Knittel)
SS-Panzeraufklärungs-Bataillon 1

HQ-Kompanie (CO: SS-Obersturmführer Heinz Goltz)
2. Kompanie (CO: SS-Obersturmführer Manfred Coblenz)
3. Kompanie (CO: SS-Obersturmführer Hans-Martin Leidreiter)
4. Kompanie (CO: SS-Obersturmführer Erich Wägner)

SS-Panzerartillerie-Abteilung 5
(CO: SS-Obersturmführer Butschek)
SS-Panzerpionier-Kompanie 2 (CO: SS-? Unglaube)

As part of SS-Obergruppenführer Dietrich's Army Order of the Day for 14 December 1944 he stressed that "our troops have to be preceeded by a wave of terror and fright and that no humane inhibitions should be shown." This Order of the Day was incorporated into SS-Obersturmbannführer Peiper's regimental orders for the day. These regimental orders were passed on to all company commanders during a 15 December meeting presided over by SS-Sturmbannführer Werner Pötschke. Dietrich, his chief of staff SS-Gruppenführer Fritz Krämer, and the staffs of 6. SS-Panzerarmee, I. SS-Panzer-Korps, and 1. SS-Panzer-Division LAH would rue the day that such phrasing was chosen to inspire

their troops. Under the cover of poor weather (which favored the Germans, since the Allies had uncontested air superiority), the German attack opened on 16 December 1944. While threatening advances were made by the Germans initially, Allied forces soon regrouped themselves and began to bitterly contest the advance. The Germans were stopped in their tracks without ever accomplishing one of their major objectives. By 25 December the weather had cleared and the Allied airforces began to wreak devastation upon the unprotected German forces. By mid-January 1945, the Germans had been pushed back to their original starting positions having expended their last sizable strategic reserves of men and armor. During the offensive, Kampfgruppe Peiper as the lead element of LAH advanced successively through Lanzerath, Honsfeld, Hepscheid, Büllingen, Baugnez Crossroads, Ligneauville, Stavelot, Trois Ponts, La Gleize, Cheneux, and into Stoumont. They captured Stoumont from the Americans in hand-to-hand fighting, but only at a high cost. Weakened, stalled, and surrounded at Stoumont, Kampfgruppe Peiper was forced to fight its way back to their own lines as part of the general German withdrawal.

Although his Kampfgruppe had comprised only one part of the German force arrayed for the Ardennes Offensive, Peiper's group soon became the focus of Allied attention because of claims that the unit had indiscriminately murdered hundreds of American POWs and Belgian civilians during its advance in Belgium. SS-Obersturmbannführer Peiper and many other members of 6. SS-Panzerarmee were tried by a post-war American military tribunal for a long list of atrocities. The crimes came to be collectively known as "The Malmedy Massacre" after a particularly infamous mass killing that occurred at the Baugnez Crossroads near the town of Malmedy. For the sake of clarity, all of the atrocity allegations --- with a judgement on each case's merits --- will be presented first. An account of the tortured legal proceedings and evidentiary problems that surrounded the Malmedy Trial will then follow.

The Atrocities

Baugnez Crossroads

On 17 December 1944 Kampfgruppe Peiper drove southwest from Büllingen and then advanced westward, capturing the towns of Moderscheid and Schoppen by noon. It is important to note that Kampfgruppe Peiper was arrayed and moved in three groups : the Point, the Command Group (under SS-Obersturmbannführer Peiper), and the Main Body. A little after 1:00 pm, the Point elements of Kampfgruppe Peiper sighted an American convoy near the Baugnez Crossroads intersection, several miles southeast of Malmedy.

The convoy consisted of approximately 140 men in thirty unarmored vehicles from Battery B of the U.S. 285th Artillery Observation Battalion (CO: Captain Roger L. Mills), as well as several ambulances from the 546th and 575th Medical Companies. The battery was part of the 7th Armored Division enroute to the Bastogne area from Heerlen, Holland. The German lead tanks immediately opened fire, striking a number of American vehicles. As the untested American troops abandoned their vehicles in the road and scattered looking for cover, SS grenadiers riding on the tanks dismounted to flush them out of hiding. It was soon apparent to the lone surviving American officer, Lieutenant Virgil T. Lary, that his men had little chance against the SS armored force. At 1:30 pm he gave the order to surrender; the Point Group disarmed and searched the Americans, directing them to march back towards the Baugnez Crossroads.

As Peiper and his Command Group moved through the crossroads, SS-Sturmbannführer Werner Pötschke was left behind to manage the POW situation. Peiper's group then continued its advance towards Ligneuville. SS-Sturmbannführer Pötschke flagged down several half-track mounted elements of passing units to help him : 2. platoon / SS-Panzerpionier-Kompanie 3 (CO: SS-Unterscharführer Max Beutner), SS-Panzerpionier-Kompanie 9 (CO: SS-Obersturmführer Erich Rumpf), and an attached Penal Platoon (CO: SS-Oberscharführer Wendeleit). The survivors of Battery B were rounded up, searched again, and then moved into an open field near the Cafe Bodarwe on the southwest side of the

crossroads. Additional prisoners from various units arrived at Baugnez Crossroads as the Point elements of Kampfgruppe Peiper continued to direct surrendering Americans to the rear. The prisoners were covered by machine-guns mounted as standard equipment on the two half-tracks.

At approximately 2:15 pm, as Panzer 711 (CO: SS-Untersturmführer Heinz Rehagel) of the 7. SS-Panzer-Kompanie / SS-Panzer-Regiment 1 passed by, SS-Sturmbannführer Pötschke ordered SS-Unterscharführer Beutner, SS-Obersturmführer Rumpf, and SS-Oberscharführer Wendeleit to have their men open fire on the American prisoners. First Lieutenant Lary testified that an SS man (later identified as SS-Rottenführer Georg Fleps) fired his pistol twice into the crowd of American prisoners. As these initial shots rang out, the prisoners began to scatter. First Lieutenant John Munzinger of Battery B was heard to cry out "Stand Fast." At that point, the half-track mounted machine guns and remaining SS troopers opened fire on the panicked Americans. Panzer 711 continued to drive south along the N23 road, raking the mass of prisoners with machine-gun fire. The Waffen-SS continued their murderous fusillade for several minutes.

Following this initial shooting, SS grenadiers went through the field for approximately fifteen minutes delivering kill shots to any obvious survivors. Some of the SS were laughing and joking as they went about their grisly work. They then remounted their halftracks and headed south along N23 towards Ligneuville in order to catch up with the Point and Command Group elements. The Main Body of Kampfgruppe Peiper passed through the Baugnez Crossroads until about 4:00 pm, some elements firing sporadically at the prostrate bodies of the Americans. Additional killings of POWs occurred throughout the day. For instance, some time between 3:00 and 3:30 pm Panzer 624 (CO: SS-Oberscharführer Hubert Huber) stopped at the crossroads. SS-Oberscharführer Huber found a prisoner still alive, robbed him, and then killed him. Around 3:30 pm, Panzer 114 (CO: SS-Unterscharführer Kurt Briesemeister) stopped at the crossroads when several Americans were spotted running from the massacre site. His men dismounted, chased after the escaping prisoners, and shot several dead.

Despite the efforts of Kampfgruppe Peiper, many of the Americans were still alive, though wounded in varying degrees. At 4:00 pm most of the remaining survivors stood up and escaped to the shelter of nearby woods. A few remained in the field until after dark and then escaped. Survivors were taken to Malmedy by a reconnaissance unit of the U.S. 291st Combat Engineer Battalion. Of the 111 American prisoners that the Waffen-SS had herded into the field by the Baugnez Crossroads, 82 had been murdered.

The victims came from a variety of units :

Battery B / 285th Field Artillery Observation Battalion -- 66

HQ Battery / 285th Field Artillery Observation Battalion -- 3

200th Field Artillery Battalion -- 2

Reconnaissance Company / 32nd Armored Regiment / 3rd Armored Division -- 8

546th Ambulance Company -- 2

86th Engineer Battalion (Heavy Pontoon) -- 1

A total of fifty-four Americans (29 from execution site itself and the remainder from surrounding areas) survived to testify concerning the behaviour of Kampfgruppe Peiper at the Baugnez Crossroads that day. SS-Obersturmbannführer Peiper's first inkling of the massacre came in a verbal report by a subordinate to him on the morning of 18 December outside of La Gleize. During the Malmedy Trial, SS-Obergruppenführer Dietrich (commander of the 6. SS-Panzerarmee) claimed to have undertaken an internal investigation of the incident, but no evidence was produced to support his assertion. On the contrary, it appears that SS-Obersturmbannführer Peiper never disclosed to his superior officers that anything amiss had occurred at the crossroads. This is supported by the trial testimony of SS-Obergruppenführer Dietrich and SS-Gruppenführer Krämer that the first they heard of the massacre was from Allied radio broadcasts. Interestingly, an official document nominating Peiper for the

Swords to his Knight's Cross containing a summary of his exploits during this offensive mentions the "annihilation" of an enemy motorized column at Baugnez (*Vorschlag Nr. 1 für....*). Two of the Waffen-SS officers in charge at the massacre site did not survive the war to answer for their actions : SS-Unterscharführer Beutner was killed during heavy fighting in Stoumont a few days later; SS-Sturmbannführer Pötschke was killed in action on 15 March 1945 at Veszprem, Hungary. The fate of the other two officers is unknown. Most Waffen-SS apologists subscribe to one of two explanations for this unprovoked massacre: a) the Americans tried to make an escape attempt and were gunned down doing so or b) the Americans were captured by Point elements of the kampfgruppe who disarmed and directed them to the rear; the following Command Group mistook them for combatants and opened fire. The mass of documentary and forensic evidence contradicts such interpretations in no uncertain terms.

Büllingen

During the Malmedy Trial, elements of Kampfgruppe Peiper were charged with murdering 62 - 90 American POWs and nine Belgian civilians in thirteen separate instances on 17 December 1944 in the town of Büllingen. Fifty POWs were massacred at a gasoline depot after being forced to fuel up SS vehicles. The remainder were killed in a number of smaller actions (*United States vs. Valentine Bersin et. al.*, 153/2/000696-711) : on a road near Büllingen a half-track from 3. SS-Panzer-Kompanie under the command of SS-Scharführer Sepp Witkowski gunned down 6 - 8 POWs marching towards the rear; near Büllingen airfield another halftrack of the same company mowed down two separate groups of 5 - 8 POWs each; elements of the same company lined up 8 POWs against a house in the town and shot them; a short time later an additional 15 - 20 POWs were gunned down at the same spot. The prosecution, however, was unable to produce any evidence in support of the alleged civilian deaths beyond the problematic pre-trial confessions of the Waffen-SS defendants themselves. Belgian authorities testified that the SS had not killed any civilians in the town. On the contrary, SS-Obersturmbannführer Peiper claimed to have seen Belgian civilians firing on his grenadiers from the windows of houses in Büllingen (*United States vs Valentine Bersin. et. al.*, 153/3/000145 (1924)).

Butai

On 18 December 1944, SS-Panzer-Kompanie 6 (CO: SS-Obersturmführer Benno Junker) and SS-Panzer-Kompanie 7 (CO: SS-Hauptsturmführer Oskar Klingelhöfer) impressed a Belgian civilian named Fernand Hopa as a guide during Kampfgruppe Peiper's advance towards Trois Ponts. Hopa was later executed and his body dumped near the village of Butai.

Cheneux

During the Malmedy Trial, point elements of Kampfgruppe Peiper were charged with murdering 41 - 51 American POWs in two separate incidents on 18 December 1944 in the town of Cheneux. The first incident followed a devastating American fighter-bomber strike on the Kampfgruppe near Cheneux. Approximately 30 - 40 POWs were collected on the outskirts of town and cut down by machine gun fire from 4 -5 tanks and one halftrack. The prosecution, however, was unable to produce any evidence in support of the second of these allegations beyond the problematic pre-trial confessions of the Waffen-SS defendants themselves.

Honsfeld

During the Malmedy Trial, elements of Kampfgruppe Peiper were charged with murdering 59 - 64 American POWs and 3 Belgian civilians in seven separate instances on 17 December 1944 in the town of Honsfeld. Following serious house-to-house fighting, 12 members of the 394th Infantry Regiment / U.S. 99th Infantry Division surrendered under a white flag and were immediately gunned down. Another 25 members of the U.S. 612th Tank Destroyer Battalion were also executed in the central part of town by members of the Kampfgruppe. Later that morning on the outskirts of town, two separate groups of POWs (one composed of 15 - 20 individuals, the other 7) were slain. The prosecution team was unable to provide definitive evidence with regard to the claimed civilian deaths.

La Gleize

During the Malmedy Trial, elements of Kampfgruppe Peiper were charged with murdering 175 - 311 American POWs and five Belgian civilians in a number of separate instances occurring from 18 - 23 December 1944 in the town of La Gleize. Up to sixty POWs were supposedly shot on 18 December in various incidents. Approximately 80 - 100 POWs were allegedly executed by small-arms fire on the grounds of the La Gleize school (*United States vs. Valentine Bersin et. al.*, 153/2/000664-76). SS-Obersturmbannführer Peiper was also alleged to have had POWs who refused to work executed on 22 December (*United States vs. Valentine Bersin, et. al.*, 153/2/000457-59). Three of the Belgian civilians were killed on 18 December as tanks of SS-Panzer-Kompanie 1 (CO: SS-Untersturmführer Hans Hennecke) randomly sprayed houses with machine-gun fire in a search for possible American positions. The remaining Belgians were killed several minutes later at the Cheneux Bridge when SS-Untersturmführer Hennecke's Panther tank swept the bridge with machine-gun fire even though only civilians were present.

Of all the charges leveled against Kampfgruppe Peiper, those involving the killing of U.S. POWs at La Gleize were the weakest and, as investigation showed, most likely spurious. The prosecution was unable to produce any evidence in support of their allegations beyond the problematic pre-trial confessions of the Waffen-SS defendants themselves. The defense case presented before the American military tribunal was air-tight. First of all, there was incontrovertible evidence that Kampfgruppe Peiper had held 150 American POWs in La Gleize and freed all of them unharmed before they retreated back to the German lines. To make matters worse, the defence produced an American officer (Major Hal D. McCown, CO 2nd Batallion / U.S. 119th Infantry Regiment captured by Peiper at Stoumont), a Belgian cure, and numerous Belgian civilians all of whom were positive that no killings of U.S. POWs had taken place in La Gleize. Even the revelation by SS-Obersturmbannführer Peiper that at least nine American POWs were shot trying to escape from work details (*United States vs. Valentine Bersin et. al.*, 153/1/000050-51) could not save the prosecution's bungled approach to this case. The charge of mass killings at La Gleize was disproven and the prosecution greatly embarrassed by this fiasco. The defendant's pre-trial confessions that originated these allegations were later shown to be the product of machinations by over-zealous prosecutors (see *The Legal Proceedings*, below).

Ligneuville

During the Malmedy Trial, elements of Kampfgruppe Peiper were charged with murdering 48 - 58 American POWs in various incidents on 17 December 1944 in the town of Ligneuville. SS-Oberführer Wilhelm Mohnke, commander of the 1. SS-Panzer-Division *Leibstandarte Adolf Hitler,* established his headquarters in the Hotel du Moulin. The bodies of eight members of the U.S. 27th Armored Infantry Battalion were found behind the Hotel du Moulin in Ligneuville and from their disposition it was clear that they had been executed (all were shot in the head). At the January-February 1945 SHAEF Standing Court of Inquiry hearings on Waffen-SS atrocities during the Ardennes Offensive, U.S. Army Staff-Sergeant George Clevinger testified that he and five other enlisted men had surrendered to Waffen-SS troops at Ligneuville on 17 December. They were searched, taken behind the Hotel du Moulin, lined up, and then shot. Clevinger was only grazed by a bullet and successfully played dead until the Germans departed. It was later determined that the killings outside of Mohnke's headquarters had been perpetrated by members of SS-Panzerpionier-Kompanie 9 (CO: SS-Obersturmführer Erich Rumpf). The prosecution was unable to provide definitive evidence for the remainder of the claimed killings.

Ligneuville-Stoumont Road

During the Malmedy Trial it was proven that the crew of a halftrack from Kampfgruppe Peiper gunned down fifteen American POWs on 17 December 1944 near a farmhouse on the Ligneuville-Stoumont Road.

Lutre Bois

During the Malmedy Trial, it was proven that a member of Kampfgruppe Peiper killed a Belgian civilian in an unprovoked assault on 31 December 1944 in the town of Lutre Bois.

Parfondruy

Between 19 - 21 December 1944 members of the HQ-Kompanie (CO: SS-Obersturmführer Heinz Goltz) and 2. SS-Panzeraufklärungs-Kompanie (CO: SS-Obersturmführer Manfred Coblenz) of SS-Panzeraufklärungs-Abteilung 1 / Schnelle Gruppe Knittel murdered at least eleven Belgian civilians in their homes in the village of Parfondruy, near Stavelot. Many of the victims were shot as they lay in their beds. The bodies were discovered on 22 December after D Company / U.S. 117th Infantry Regiment recaptured the village. In July 1948, Heinz Goltz was sentenced by Belgian authorities to fifteen years' imprisonment for these and other atrocities committed in the Stavelot area. Manfred Coblenz was found guilty at the Malmedy Trials and sentenced to life imprisonment; he was released in 1951.

Petit Thier

During the Malmedy Trial Otto Wichmann, formerly an SS-Scharführer of the headquarters company of SS-Panzer-Regiment 1, testified that on either 10 or 13 January 1945 he took a starving, frost-bitten American POW who had emerged out of some nearby woods into a field up the road from the Chateau Blanche Fontaine (then serving as regimental HQ) and executed him by small-arms fire. This execution was performed on the direct order of SS-Sturmbannführer Dr. Kurt Sickel (senior regimental medical officer) and in the presence of SS-Obersturmbannführer Peiper, SS-Sturmbannführer Dr. Sickel, and SS- Sturmbannführer Hein von Westernhagen (CO: SS-Schwere-Panzer-Abteilung 501). Both Peiper and Sickel confirmed this account in their trial testimony (*United States vs. Valentin Bersin, et. al.,* 153/2/000423-29).

Reynolds (1995), however, has pointed out that the *LAH* division had moved south on 27 December 1944 to attack the American salient at Bastogne. It seems highly unlikely that Peiper, the chief regimental medical officer, and the commander of the division's heavy tank unit would have remained behind as their comrades went back into action. Following a series of unsuccessful attacks, the remnants of *LAH* were pulled back on 12 January 1945 to an area west of Köln for rest and refitting. Reynolds (1995) speculates that Peiper and Sickel may have confirmed the murder accusation against them in order to conceal the fact that Peiper suffered a nervous breakdown in January 1945 as a result of the failed Ardennes offensive. In any case, this accusation --- like all of the others resting solely on Waffen-SS testimony --- remains unresolved.

Rahier

At approximately 1615 hours on 18 December 1944 a jeep with two passengers from the U.S. 1111th Engineer Combat Group headquarters collided with the lead Panther tank of SS-Panzer-Kompanie 1 (CO: SS-Untersturmführer Hans Hennecke). One of the Americans was killed instantly. At the Malmedy Trials, SS-Scharführer Paul Zwigart was sentenced to death for allegedly executing the surviving American. Zwigart vehemently denied any involvement in or knowledge of this killing.

Stavelot

During the Malmedy Trial, elements of Kampfgruppe Peiper (SS-Panzer-Kompanie 6 [CO: SS-Obersturmführer Benno Junker], SS-Panzer-Kompanie 7 [CO: SS-Hauptsturmführer Oskar Klingelhöfer], and SS-Panzer-Pionier-Kompanie 3 [CO: SS-Obersturmführer Franz Sievers]), Kampfgruppe Hansen (SS-Panzergrenadier-Bataillon 2 [CO: SS-Untersturmführer Friedrich Pfeifer]), and all of Schnelle Gruppe Knittel (CO: SS-Sturmbannführer Gustav Knittel) were implicated in the murders of eight American POWs and 93 Belgian civilians in various incidents from 18 - 21 December 1944 in the town of Stavelot. The physical evidence and eyewitness testimony in this case were overwhelmingly against the defendants. On 18 December, two civilians along the Stavelot-La Gleize Road (*United States vs. Valentine Bersin et. al.*, 153/2/000120-24) and several women in the town itself (*United States vs. Valentine Bersin, et. al.*, 153/1/001035-41) were indiscriminately killed in full view of witnesses. On the night of 18 December two residents were shot in their beds while they lay alseep. Andre Achille and Henri Delacourt testified that they and nineteen other Stavelot men were rounded up by Waffen-SS troopers and packed into an 8' x 12' shed. A machine gun was set up and two belts of ammunition were fired into the shed. Several SS grenadiers entered the shed and fired kill shots to finish off anyone who showed signs of life. The troopers then piled straw on the bodies and set it on fire. Amazingly, eight persons --- the two witnesses among them --- survived and managed to escape (*United States vs. Valentine Bersin et. al.*, 153/1/001046-52). On the night of 19 December, 23 civilians (2 men, 8 women, and 13 children) sheltering in the cellar of the La Gaye house on the road to Trois Ponts were ordered outside by Waffen-SS troopers and then mowed them down with small-arms fire. Madame Regina Gregoire testified that two Waffen-SS troopers opened fire on a group of Stavelot civilians, some of whom were killed (*United States vs. Valentine Bersin et. al.*, 153/1/001107-17). Antoine Colinet saw a machine-pistol wielding SS tank crewman open fire and kill civilians at random (*United States vs. Valentine Bersin et. al.*, 153/1/001022-27). At least one tank on the road to La Gleize opened fire on a group of 15 - 20 women, killing and wounding eight of them. Two civilians were also shot execution style under a railway bridge near town. Numerous other instances were also cited before the tribunal (*United States vs. Valentine Bersin et. al.*, 153/2/000034-35; 153/2/000074-80; 153/2/000457-59).

SS-Obersturmbannführer Peiper tried to deflect this preponderance of evidence by claiming that the civilians killed by his men were partisans who opened fire on his column as it passed through Stavelot. He also claimed that German wounded, left unguarded at a regimental first aid station, were tortured by armed civilians (*United States vs. Valentine Bersin, et. al.*, 153/3/000159 (1938)). While Communist resistance fighters of the *Armee Belge des Partisans du Front de l'Independance et de la Liberation* were active against German troops in the Ardennes, no evidence was ever found to support any of SS-Obersturmbannführer Peiper's allegations.

It was also alleged, second-hand, that unspecified personnel from 9. SS-Panzer-Division *Hohenstaufen* murdered approximately 50 civilians in Stavelot supposedly in revenge for partisan activities in the area the previous September (see IMT, 1948/1971, vol. 6, pp. 541-542). This is certainly possible since elements of the division were transferred from fighting to the north at St. Vith in order to shore up Kampfgruppe Peiper sometime after 21 December. The evidence is far from clear, however, and other explanations may be equally likely. The allegation could be mistaken or, perhaps, there were individuals under Peiper's command who had transferred from *Hohenstaufen* and retained their cuff-bands, a not uncommon practice among Waffen-SS personnel.

Stoumont

During the Malmedy Trial, elements of Kampfgruppe Peiper and Schnelle Gruppe Knittel were charged with murdering 104 - 109 American POWs and one Belgian civilian in 24 separate incidents on 19 December 1944 in the town of Stoumont. During the morning 7 POWs were shot by members of SS-Panzergrenadier-Kompanie 11 (CO: SS-? Heinz Tomhardt) at the edge of a pasture. A total of 9 POWs and 1 civilian were shot in a chicken house and its adjacent fields by elements of SS-Panzerpionier-Kompanie 3 (CO: SS-Obersturmführer Franz Sievers). Tank crews were also hard at work : 30 - 45 POWs were machine-gunned to death by an unidentified Panzer Mk IV and by tanks of SS-Panzer-Kompanie 2 (CO: SS-Obersturmführer Friedrich Christ) in two separate instances. At 2:00 pm another 25 POWs were gunned down by machine-gun fire from elements of SS-Panzeraufklärungs-Kompanie 2 at a spot approximately two miles west of Stoumont. It has also been alleged that on the afternoon of 19 December, SS-Obersturmbannführer Peiper had at least one POW interrogated and shot (*United States vs. Valentine Bersin et. al.*, 153/2/000457-459). In a post-war interview the former commander of SS-Panzeraufklärungs-Kompanie 2 / Schnelle Gruppe Knittel, Manfred Coblenz, confirmed that an unknown number of U.S. POWs had been executed on the orders of the third platoon commander, SS-Untersturmführer Siebert. The ostensible reason for the killings was that the platoon could not spare anyone to guard the prisoners.

Trois Ponts

During the Malmedy Trial it was proven that elements of Kampfgruppe Peiper murdered eleven American POWs and four Belgian civilians in various incidents in the town of Trois Ponts (dates unspecified).

Wanne

During the Malmedy Trial it was proven that elements of SS-Panzer-Kompanie 1 (CO: SS-Obersturmführer Kremser) and SS-Panzer-Kompanie 7 (CO: SS-Hauptsturmführer Oskar Klingelhöfer) murdered six Belgian civilians in three separate incidents on 20 - 21 December 1944 in the town of Wanne. The shootings were ordered by divisional commander SS-Oberführer Wilhelm Mohnke as a reprisal for the alleged discovery of a radio transmitter in the town. Originally, the execution order covered all male inhabitants of Wanne over the age of 16 but for reasons never made clear the reprisal action was suspended after a half-dozen killings.

Wereth

On 17 December elements of SS-Panzergrenadier-Bataillon 1 (CO: SS-Sturmbannführer Emil Karst) and/or SS-Panzerjäger-Bataillon 1 (CO: SS-Hauptsturmführer Karl Rettlinger) executed 11 African-Americans of the U.S. 333rd Field Artillery Battalion. During the opening of the German offensive on the previous day, the Americans became separated from their unit and took refuge with civilians in Wereth. They were captured by Waffen-SS troopers who occupied the town the following day. The prisoners were held under guard until dark and then run out of town by a group of their captors. The Americans were never seen alive again. In Spring 1945 thawing snow revealed their bodies dumped in a roadside ditch just outside of town. Autopsies revealed that the prisoners had been beaten, shot and bayonetted to death. Some of their bodies also bore the marks of tracked-vehicles indicating that an attempt had been made to conceal the nature of the fatal injuries. The massacre was initially treated as a war crime, but the investigation was dropped when the U.S. Army was unable to identify the culprits. Oddly enough, the fate of the murdered soldiers remained classified for more than 50 years. Immediate family members only learned of the circumstances of their loved one's deaths as a result of a 1997 investigation by American television journalists. While none of the victims are buried there, a small monument has been erected by Belgian civilians at the massacre site.

The Legal Proceedings

The Inspector General's Office, under Colonel Rosser M. Hunter, at the First U.S. Army Headquarters in Spa, Belgium learned of the massacre at Baugnez Crossroads, within four hours of its occurrence. The crossroads was not recaptured by American forces until 13 January 1945. The bodies were searched for (there had been a heavy snowfall in the intervening time), uncovered, numbered, and photographed in place. They were well preserved due to the cold weather. A considerable number of the dead had been frozen with their hands still above their heads. The bodies were then removed to Malmedy for thawing, re-photographing, and examination. Autopsies were performed on 14 - 16 January. The causes of death varied, but were consistent with the accounts given by survivors : shot in head (40), shrapnel wounds (3), bleeding (4), blow to head (3), HE shells (3), concussion (1), crushed (3), MG or small arms fire (19), and unknown (6). There was also evidence that some of the bodies had been robbed and/or mutilated. The bodies were interred on 17 January in the Henri Chapelle American Military Cemetary in Belgium. Between February and April 1945, an additional fifteen bodies of murdered American POWs would be found in areas around the Buagnez Crossroads.

On 27 January 1945 the 1st Army Inspector General's Office completed its preliminary report. Three days later, a SHAEF Standing Court of Inquiry opened hearings on what was now called the Malmedy case taking evidence from twenty-nine survivors and four Belgian civilians. Aside from the copious documentation gathered concerning the events at Baugnez Crossroads, these hearings also generated evidence of other atrocities committed by the Waffen-SS. The SHAEF Standing Court of Inquiry issued its final report in March 1945, finding that at least 72 Americans had been killed in violation of international law and that other atrocities were probable. In June 1945, the rounding up of Waffen-SS suspects from Allied POW camps and the construction of a legal case against them began in earnest.

The Malmedy case was initially assigned to Captain Dwight Fanton (U.S. Forces European Theater, War Crimes Branch, Investigation Section). Slowly all of the surviving members of Kampfgruppe Peiper and the staffs of 6. SS-Panzerarmee, I. SS-Panzerkorps, and 1. SS-Panzer-Division *LAH* (approximately 1000 individuals) were gathered together and held at Zuffenhausen near Ludwigsburg. The former commander of 1. SS-Panzer-Division *LAH*, Wilhelm Mohnke, was in Soviet custody and unavailable for the trial. Six months of questioning yielded few tangible results; the prisoners stuck together and refused to talk about the alleged atrocities. Hard core suspects in the case were then transferred solitary confinement at Schwäbisch Hall prison, near Heil-

bronn. In mid-November 1945, the investigation team was expanded to include Captain Raphael Shumacker, First Lieutenant William R. Perl, civilians Morris Elowitz and Harry Thon, Lieutenant Colonel Burton F. Ellis, and Lieutenant Colonel Homer B. Crawford. Under this new team intensive interrogations were instigated and results began to come in.

By April 1946 the investigating team, now headed by Lieutenant Colonel Ellis, had accumulated a substantial body of evidence suggesting that large numbers of prisoners and Belgian civilians had been murdered by the various kampfgruppes at numerous locales. The overwhelming weight of evidence assembled by the investigators consisted of sworn statements by defendants who were implicated in some of the criminal acts. Without these confessions, the legal case against them with regard to many of the allegations would have been very weak indeed. Instead, to outside observers, the case appeared to be running overwhelmingly against the defendants.

At 10:00 am on 16 May 1946 the Malmedy Trial (officially known as Case # 6-24, *United States vs. Valentine Bersin, et. al.*) began at Dachau before an American General Military Government Court. Brigadier General Josiah T. Dalbey sat as President of the Court; he was assisted by six U.S. Army colonels and legal advisor Colonel Abraham H. Rosenfeld. The prosecution team consisted of Lieutenant Colonel Ellis (as chief prosecutor), Lieutenant Colonel Homer B. Crawford, Captain Raphael Shumacker, First Lieutenant Robert E. Byrne, Mr. Morris Elowitz, and Lieutenant William R. Perl. The defendants numbered 74 including : 15 junior officers, 51 enlisted men or NCOs, and 8 higher-ranking officers. Only 30 had been directly involved with events at the Baugnez Crossroads. The defense team consisted of Colonel Willis M. Everett Jr. (as chief counsel), Lieutenant Colonel Granger G. Sutton, Herbert J. Strong, Captain Benjamin Narvid, Lieutenant Wilbert Wahler, Lieutenant Colonel John Dwinnell, as well as two U.S. Army attorneys and six somewhat unwilling German attorneys. The defense team had been afforded only one month to prepare its case.

One of the stumbling blocks in the trial was the fact that the purpose of military government courts was not to fulfill some abstract concept of justice, but rather to preserve the security of Allied Forces and their rear areas. Procedural technicalities that were considered valid in civil courts had no standing in military courts. Sweeping and potentially arbitrary authority was vested in the tribunal judges who determined what evidence could be introduced into the proceedings. Many of the legal appeals filed by the defense subsequent to the Malmedy Trial grew out of these crucial procedural differences.

On the opening day, the prosecution declared itself ready to prove the murder of 538 - 749 American POWs and over 90 Belgian civilians. Their case was straightforward and simple. The prosecution asserted that SS-Obergruppenführer Dietrich had ordered his subordinates to execute POWs, citing his 14 December 1944 Order of the Day for the 6. SS-Panzerarmee. While there was a substantial amount of physical evidence for atrocities having occurred at the Baugnez Crossroads and a number of other localities (see entries above), for many of the charges there was no evidence beyond the pre-trial confessions of the defendants themselves. Most of the junior ranks of Kampfgruppe Peiper who stood accused of these atrocities stated in their pretrial statements that they had shot prisoners on the orders of their superior officers. The large discrepancy in the claimed body count seemed to indicate that the prosecution wasn't sure exactly what it could prove.

The defense argued that the POWs at the Baugnez Crossroads tried to escape and that the shooting, while regrettable, was entirely justified. The proof offered to support this contention was non-existant, in fact all of the physical evidence and survivor testimony contradicted this defense thesis. At the start of the trial, all of the defendants recanted their pre-trial confessions. They alleged that the U.S. interrogation team used mental and physical abuse to secure the confessions. Torture, mock trials and hangings, beatings, starvation, and threats against family members were supposedly used to stimulate the defendant's memories. The interrogator's were also accused of fabricating confessions and forcing defendants to sign off on them. Lieutenant Colonel Everett claimed that all of the confessions were inadmissable due to the manner in which they were obtained. He also objected to the mass trial, since it often caused the defendants to testify in a manner which cleared themselves while implicating others. The prosecution team and interrogators denied ever physically abusing any of the accused or of fabricating their confessions.

In his defense concerning the infamous 6. SS-Panzerarmee Order of the Day, Sepp Dietrich claimed that it was meant as rhetoric to inspire his troops on the eve of a crucial engagement. No specific order authorizing the killing of POWs could be found in German files, although the defense was quick to point out that such orders were issued by some American units after news of the atrocities leaked out. Former staff officers from 6. SS-Panzerarmee testified that prisoners were scrupulously handled in accordance with the laws of war. Jochen Peiper made the most telling point, however, when he denied issuing orders permitting the execution of POWs : such orders were unnecessary since it was obvious to experienced officers that POWs had to be shot "when local conditions required it." (*United States vs. Valentine Bersin et. al.*, 153/2/000115-16).

On 11 July 1946, after 2 hours and 20 minutes of deliberation, the tribunal judges returned 73 guilty verdicts against the defendants (one individual was cleared of all charges and dismissed). The tribunal reconvened five days later and issued 43 death sentences, 22 life sentences, and 8 sentences of 10, 15, or 20 years imprisonment. Jochen Peiper received a death sentence, Sepp Dietrich received life imprisonment, and Hermann Priess was sentenced to 20 years imprisonment. On 17 July, the prisoners were sent to Landsberg Prison to await execution or begin serving their sentences. Friends and relatives immediately requested clemency for the defendants.

On 28 December 1946 Lieutenant Colonel Everett formally filed a petition for review of the cases on the basis that the rules of evidence had been adapted as the court saw fit and that the court had been pressured by public opinion into finding the defendants guilty. He felt that while his clients may have committed atrocities, justice had not been served properly. Lieutenant Colonel Everett believed that the pre-trial confessions had been extorted and then legitimated by a court biased against the defendants from the very beginning. He was also convinced that the crimes for which his clients had been tried and convicted were also committed by U.S. Army personnel. A review was already underway, however, and had been entrusted to Maximilian Kössler of the U.S. Judge Advocate General's Office. Not all was well since by January 1947 the U.S. press was beginning to report that there had been irregularities in the trial. The Deputy Judge Advocate for War Crimes, Lieutenant Colonel Clio E. Straight, replaced Kössler in February 1947 restarting the review that his predecessor had begun. On 20 October 1947, Lieutenant Colonel Straight completed his review and began to write a case opinion for the theater commander. Lieutenant Colonel Straight's final recommendations were sent directly to the Theater Judge Advocate, Colonel James L. Harbaugh, Jr. (*Report of Proceedings of Administration of Justice Review Board*, Headquarters, European Command, 7 July 1948). On the grounds that many of the defendants were young, intellectually limited, and acting under orders, Lieutenant Colonel Straight advised that all death sentences be commuted to terms of 25 years imprisonment, that the case against one defendant be dropped due to a lack of evidence, that 17 of the 22 life sentences be dismissed entirely, and that the remaining life sentences be reduced to terms of 10 - 15 years imprisonment.

Disturbed by these findings, Colonel Harbaugh assigned a new board, chaired by Colonel Howard F. Bresee, to review the Malmedy Trial proceedings. In its report released on 8 February 1948, the board concluded that there was evidence of improper pre-trial investigations, as well as improper procedural rulings by the Dachau tribunal (*War Crimes Board of Review and Recommendations in the Case of United States vs Valentine Bersin, et. al.*). They openly accused the army investigators of conduct at best inept, at worst unprincipled, and the army judges of consistent bias to the advantage of the prosecution. The Bresee report recommended that 29 cases be dismissed, 32 sentences be reduced, and only 12 death sentences be upheld. In preparing his final recommendations to General Lucius D. Clay (Chief of Military Government, American Zone of Occupation) Colonel Harbaugh took a position midway between the Straight and Bresee reports by calling for 13 case dismissals, 13 death sentences, and 47 prison terms of varying lengths. On 20 March 1948 Colonel Harbaugh's recommendations were adopted by General Clay.

Despite these reviews, there was rising agitation on both sides of the Atlantic with regard to war crimes in general, and over the Malmedy Trial in particular. Unlikely bedfellows were made as pacifists and civil libertarians joined with unrepentant Nazis and anti-Semites in condemnation of the legal proceedings. Dr. Rudolf Aschenauer, a former Nazi Party member and defending council for the murderous Einsatzgruppe commander Otto Ohlendorf, became the primary spokesman for the Malmedy defendants. On 14 May 1948 Willis Everett, by now a civilian, filed an unsuccessful plea of *habeas corpus* before the United States Supreme Court.

In an attempt to head off further criticism, on 23 July 1948 Secretary of the Army Kenneth C. Royall established the three-man Simpson Commission to review all of the Malmedy Trial death sentences. The commission's final report advised that all death penalties be commuted to terms of life imprisonment. Judge Le Roy van Roden, a member of the Simpson Commission, returned to the U.S. in early Fall 1948 and publicly supported the most extreme allegations of investigational misconduct made by Willis Everett and the German defendants. His influence was quickly felt; by mid-October the U.S. press had begun to change its tune. The arrival of the Cold War in Autumn 1948 combined with Judge Van Roden's continuing harangues about the "injustice" of the Malmedy Trials led to press opinion radically in favor of the defendants by Spring 1949.

Meanwhile, a simultaneous review was begun by General Clay's Administration of Justice Review Board. Its final report gave no specific recommendations (*Headquarters European Command. Final Report of Administration of Justice Review Board*, 14 February 1949). General Clay was aware of the public uproar in the U.S. and was also a target of the defendants' numerous lobbyists. Later that month, Senator William Langer (R, ND) introduced Senate Resolution 39 calling for hearings on American military justice in Europe. On 3 March, Secretary of the Army Royall ordered General Clay to delay all executions until further notice. General Clay personally reviewed the Malmedy cases and advised that six of remaining twelve death sentences should be carried out.

In spite of the endless reviews that had already taken place, the Senate Armed Services Committee (pursuant to Senate Resolution 42 introduced by Senator Langer) appointed a subcommittee on 29 March to pursue Malmedy Trial hearings. The subcommittee consisted of Senators Millard Tydings (as chairman), Raymond E. Baldwin (CT), Estes Kefauver (TN), Lester C. Hunt (WY), and Joseph McCarthy (WI). Conflict of interest accusations immediately surfaced since Senators Baldwin and Kefauver were friends with members of the Malmedy prosecution team. The hearings opened on

18 April and Senator McCarthy quickly took center stage and began attacking the Malmedy prosecutors and their interrogation methods. It was soon apparent that McCarthy was at loggerheads with the rest of the subcommittee.

Events were not progressing to Senator McCarthy's liking, however. Summoned before the Senate subcommittee, an embarrassed Judge Van Roden denied his earlier vocal criticisms of the Malmedy Trial and admitted that he had no hard evidence of prosecutorial abuses. For their part, the prosecution team denied that they had tortured any of the defendants in order to secure damning confessions. It was over the credibility of Lieutenant Perl's testimony that Senator McCarthy precipitated a crisis that led to his withdrawal from the hearings. McCarthy began by demanding that witnesses take a lie-detector test. When the subcommittee rejected this proposal, he denounced the hearings as a whitewash and quit. Senator Baldwin angrily accused him of being more willing to believe the word of an SS officer than of an American officer under oath. The hearings continued more placidly without the junior senator from Wisconsin and the subcommittee even traveled to Germany to gather evidence. The Senate subcommittee issued its report on 13 October 1949 (*Malmedy Massacre Investigation. Report of Subcommittee on Armed Services, United States Senate*, Washington) and specifically found no evidence that defendants were physically mistreated and generally found little reason to criticize the investigations and trial.

As it turned out, all of the work and the numerous reviews were for naught. Political changes --- the ongoing Cold War, the end of U.S. Military Government in Germany, unceasing public pressure in Germany, *etc.* --- were combining to unravel the Malmedy Trial convictions. During the latter half of 1949 and throughout the next two years there was a continuous flood of protest over the trial, much of it generated by Waffen-SS apologists such as Aschenauer, Greil, and Ziemssen. Yet another judicial review was launched in Autumn 1950 which embraced both death sentences as well as prison sentences. At the same time, the outbreak of the Korean War resulted in further increased European tensions and once again the Western Allies looked to West Germany to strengthen defences against the Communists. On 31 January 1951, General Thomas T. Handy (Commander in Chief, U.S. European Command) announced

clemency for the six remaining Malmedy death-row defendants (including Peiper). Vocal criticism from veterans' groups in the United States fell on deaf ears.

With the end of U.S. Military Government rule in Germany, war crimes' prisoners were transferred to German jurisdiction. A review board was formed of three German representatives and 1 each from the U.S., Britain, and France for the remaining cases. In 1954 Jochen Peiper's life sentence was reduced to 35 years, while Hermann Priess was paroled. On 22 October 1955, Sepp Dietrich was released from prison. By the summer of 1956 only three Malmedy defendants still remained in custody. Jochen Peiper, the last defendant to be released, was paroled on 22 December 1956.

Aftermath

In 1946 a group of sentimental Belgians erected a monument at the Baugnez Crossroads in honor of the murdered Americans. They built a curved stone wall mounted with slate plaques, each bearing the name of one who fell in the nearby field.

The post-trial fates of Hermann Priess and Fritz Krämer remain unknown. Following his parole, Jupp Diefenthal retired in seclusion to the Ardennes.

On 14 May 1957 Sepp Dietrich was imprisoned and brought to trial before the Landgericht München for his key role in the killing of SA leaders during the "Night of Long Knives" putsch in 1934. He was eventually released from custody on 2 February 1959 and died of natural causes at Ludwigsburg on 21 April 1966.

In June 1964 West German officials announced that Jochen Peiper was once more under investigation, this time for atrocities committed in northern Italy in 1943. On 11 December 1968, Italian authorities accused Peiper and two of his former subordinates with murder before the Landgericht Stuttgart. Despite extensive evidence to the contrary, the court ruled in February 1969 that there was insufficient evidence for formal charges to be made against the accused. In 1972 Peiper settled into anonymous retirement in the town of Traves in southeastern France. In 1975, he was recognized by a shopkeeper in the nearby town of Vesoul who tipped off French journalist Pierre Durand. After a lengthy investigation, Durand published an article exposing Peiper in the 22 June 1976 edition of the newspaper L-Humanite and calling for his deportation. Peiper began to receive threats, was harrassed by his neighbors, and was warned to leave France by Bastille Day (July 14). Instead, he sent his wife away and remained at home armed with a pistol and rifle. On the evening of 14 July 1976 he stood guard over his property. During the night neighbors heard a gun battle break out. By the time police arrived, Peiper lay dead inside his burning house. His unknown assailants have never been found.

Conclusions

The Malmedy Trial controversy has lasted for some six decades and will never be resolved until the extreme positions of the opposing sides are rejected. Clearly there exists a copious amount of evidence that Kampfgruppe Peiper committed atrocities against both American POWs and Belgian civilians at several points along its attack corridor. The only remaining doubt concerns the exact number of "incidents" and victims. The scale and fluidity of modern warfare rendered it improbable that the investigators could ever produce a full accounting of the kampfgruppe's crimes. On the other hand, it is also clear that the American interrogation team subjected the defendants to improper physical and psychological duress in an attempt to obtain information. In the end, they were rewarded with a number of spurious confessions which they accepted at face value, much to the detriment of their legal case against the accused. However much we may wish to condemn the unprofessional, dishonest, and mean-spirrited behavior of the investigators, their actions in no way serve to wash away the innocent blood of those deliberately murdered by the men of Kampfgruppe Peiper.

Sources

(Stein, 1966, pp. 253 & 278-281)

(Reynolds, 1995)

(Quarrie, 1986, pp. 41-44)

(Krätschmer, 1982, pp. 388-398)

(Greil, 1977)

(Greil, 1958)

(Cuppens, 1989)

(Kavanaugh, 1996)

(Pallud, 1987, pp. 26-28 & 54)

(Weingartner, 1974, pp. 149-151)

(Jurado & Hannon, 1985)

(Infield, 1990, pp. 7-12)

(Messenger, 1988, pp. 155-214)

(Weingartner, 1979)

(Greil, 1958)

(Ziemssen, 1981)

(U.S. National Archives War Crimes Files, Malmedy, United States vs. Valentine Bersin et. al., Dachau, RG 153 [Boxes 69 - 73] and RG 338 [Boxes 1 - 70], Case 6-24, NARA Suitland Reference Branch, Suitland, MD)

(Technical Manual for Legal and Prison Officers, 2nd Edition, Washington DC, 1945)

(Vorschlag Nr. 1 für die Verleihung der Schwerter zum Eichenlaub des Ritterkreuzes des EK,

U.S. National Archives, Berlin Document Center records, Malmedy Defendants' Files)

("Army to Present......, 1998) (Whistine, 1998)

Miscellaneous Atrocities

The following listing consists of atrocity claims for which additional information is extant, but not presented at this time. These claims are sourced from United Nations War Crimes Commission (UNWCC) summary reports that were submitted to the International Military Tribunal in Nuremberg (see *Sources* below). The original UNWCC documentation supporting these claims has only recently been made accessible to bona fide researchers. Nonetheless, the application and review process required in order to view UNWCC files is still sufficiently daunting as to preclude my following these leads at the present time. Unless noted otherwise, the listed claims are from IMT document D-961.

1. SS-Panzer-Division Leibstandarte Adolf Hitler

Sub-Unit	Date	Location	Charge
?	12/41 - 1/42	Taganrog, USSR	genocide (USSR-396)
?	3/43	Smyev, USSR	village razed
2. Regiment	8/20/44	St. Denis, France	village razed
?	8/24/44	Leshoguen, France	5 Allied POWs shot
?	9/6/44	Navaugle, France	civilians shot
?	9/7/44	Nerstal, France	civilians/forced labor

2. SS-Panzer-Division Das Reich

Sub-Unit	Date	Location	Charge
3. Regiment	5/44	Aussone, France	civilians shot
4. Regiment	5/44	Montauban, France	civilians shot
3. Regiment	5/44	Tarbes, France	civilians shot
?	5/12/44	Toulouse, France	6 villages razed
3. Regiment	6/44	Miremont, France	Jewish civilians shot
4. Regiment	6/44	Limoges, France	civilians shot
4. Regiment	6/44	Vergt de Biron, France	24 civilians shot
4. Regiment	6/44	Yuret, France	rape and murder
3. Regiment	6/10/44	Marsoulas, France	civilians shot
3. Regiment	6/14/44	Flavigny, France	murder
3. Regiment	6/17/44	Bazens, France	murder
2. Regiment	6/18/44	Angouleme, France	civilians shot
3. Regiment	6/26/44	Justiniac, France	murder
3. Regiment	9/3/44	Permez, France	murder

3. SS-Panzer-Division Totenkopf

Sub-Unit	Date	Location	Charge
3. Bataillon	7/42	Brno, USSR	40 civilians shot
1. Regiment	8/43	Kharov, USSR	40 POWs shot

4. SS-Polizei-Panzergrenadier-Division

Sub-Unit	Date	Location	Charge
?	1941	Pskov, USSR	genocide (USSR-396)

5. SS-Panzer-Division Wiking

Sub-Unit	Date	Location	Charge
Germania Rgt.	1940	St. Venant, France	British POWs shot
7 Co./Germania	4/27/41	Jussey, France	civilians shot
?	12/41 - 1/42	Taganrog, USSR	genocide (USSR-396)

9. SS-Panzer-Division Hohenstaufen

Sub-Unit	Date	Location	Charge
?	2/44	Gard, France	civilians shot ?
	3/2/44	Nimes, France	civilians shot ?
	9/44	Arnhem, Netherlands	British POWs shot

11. SS-Freiwilligen-Panzergrenadier-Division Nordland

Sub-Unit	Date	Location	Charge
?	7/15/44	France	24 U.S. POWs shot

Note: All evidence indicates that this division served exclusively on the Eastern Front. If this claim is true, then the murders may have been committed by detached divisional elements or former Nordland personnel attached to a new unit but still retaining their old cuff-bands (a common Waffen-SS practice).

12. SS-Panzer-Division Hitlerjugend

Sub-Unit	Date	Location	Charge
Flak Abt.	3/44	Franco-Belgian border	civilians shot
25. Regiment	8/31/44	Plomion, France	murder, torture
26. Regiment	8/44	St. Martin, France	civilians shot

16. SS-Panzergrenadier-Division Reichsführer-SS

Sub-Unit	Date	Location	Charge
?	6/29/44	Guardistallo, Italy	46 civilians shot
?	7/44	Hungary	civilians killed

17. SS-Panzergrenadier-Division Götz von Berlichingen

Sub-Unit	Date	Location	Charge
?	7/3/44	des Verrieres, France	U.S. POWs shot
?	7/19/44	Poitiers, France	30 U.S. POWs shot
?	8/5/44	Lussac, France	civilians shot

Sources

(Nuremberg Document D-961, UNWCC,
"Crimes committed by Waffen-SS Units",
Record Group FO 645/106, Imperial War Museum, London)
(Nuremberg Document USSR-396, UNWCC,
"Excerpts from the Report of the Extraordinary
Commission",
Zentrale Stelle der Landesjustizverwaltungen, file 114 AR, Nr. 1055/1971)

Monte Sol (Italy)

At the end of May 1944 the 16. SS-Panzergrenadier-Division *Reichsführer-SS* (CO: SS-Gruppenführer Max Simon) was transferred from Hungary to the Ligurian Coast of Italy and deployed from Massa (30 km north of Livorno) to Cecina (40 km south of Livorno). Throughout the month of June 1944 the division engaged British forces along the Cecina and Arno Fronts. It also conducted sporadic fighting against partisans in compliance with the 17 June orders of Field Marshal Albert Kesselring, overall commander of German forces in Italy, that all partisan bands were to be ruthlessly exterminated. On 1 July, Field Marshal Kesselring issued a new order with regard to partisan warfare : when partisans are present in a town in large numbers, they undoubtedly live there --- accordingly, some percentage of the male inhabitants should be shot and the town fired.

Fifteen miles south of the city of Bologna, almost at the northern tip of the Appenine Mountains, lay a prominent height named Monte Sol. The mountain's 2,000-foot summit dominated the entire countryside and played host to a partisan brigade named the *Stella Rossa* (Red Star) led by Il Lupo ("The Wolf", aka Mario Musolesi). The *Stella Rossa* preferred to attack German convoys in the Setta valley, along Autostrada 325, along the Reno Highway, and the railroad line to Pistoia. They then invariably retreated to their mountain hideouts and let the local peasants suffer the inevitable German reprisals. The month of July 1944 was marked by an escalating cycle of partisan attacks and German

reprisals. By mid-August, the brigade had grown to approximately 1,000 effectives and the Monte Sol area was entirely off limits to the German military due to partisan activities. Hardly any traffic moved on the roads and the railroad line was damaged beyond use. During September, the *Stella Rossa* continued their campaign against the German occupiers with numerous instances of sabotage and ambush attacks in the Reno and Setta valleys. At the end of the month, the *Reichsführer-SS* division was ordered to encircle and destroy this troublesome partisan band with the assistance of several Wehrmacht units.

SS-Sturmbannführer Walter Reder, in command of SS-Panzeraufklärungs-Abteilung 16, led the assault on the *Stella Rossa* partisan brigade. At three in the morning on 29 September 1944 the Waffen-SS troopers broke camp, forded the Setta River, and marched on Monte Sol in an ice-cold rain. Heavy fighting followed and Waffen-SS operations lasted in the area until the fifth of October. Reder's offensive drove the *Stella Rossa* back up the slopes of Monte Sol where the partisans finally were forced to make a last stand. They were virtually all killed, including Musolesi and his entire staff. Additionally, large numbers of dead women and children were found in "partisan defensive positions" and scattered about the mountain by civilians returning to the area after the battle. German authorities dismissed these bodies as either partisans or unfortunates who were accidentally killed as bystanders during combat. Reder's losses were, by comparison, relatively minor : 24 dead, 40 wounded, and 6 missing.

The first hint of a possible atrocity came out when a member of SS-Panzeraufklärungs-Abteilung 16, Julien Legoli, was captured by the Americans several days after the offensive against the *Stella Rossa*. Since he was an Alsatian, Legoli was remanded to French authorities. He testified to French military officials that SS-Sturmbannführer Reder had ordered all civilians in the operation's zone, including the old and infirm, to be shot. On the basis of this testimony, Reder's name was put on a list of war criminals being compiled for post-war use.

For some time, unverified rumors flew among the Italian populace around Bologna that the *Reichsführer-SS* division had massacred hundreds, if not thousands, of innocent civilians on Monte Sol. After the war, Italian Communists tried to exploit the incident by coopting the *Stella Rossa* brigade as a Communist organization, which it was not. The rout and annihilation of the partisan band was recast as a major fight to the death by a brave band of Communists against four German divisions, during which the bestial Waffen-SS massacred countless innocent civilians. Italian centrist and right-wing politicians, battling the Communists for the control of the country, had no choice but to dismiss the entire story as a fabrication. Such a conclusion naturally received considerable support from many Waffen-SS apologists.

In 1949 when the political situation was sufficiently stabilized, the martyrdom of the inhabitants of Monte Sol was finally officially recognized. The Gold Medal, Italy's highest decoration, was presented to the entire commune of Marzabotto (the town of Marzabotto was a part of the commune of Marzabotto which embraced the Monte Sol area). An ornate marble bone crypt was built in Marzabotto, and the names of the known dead chiselled into plaques.

Meanwhile, SS-Sturmbannführer Reder was arrested on 8 May 1945 by Americans at a Salzburg hospital. He was soon released to house arrest in Salzburg pending further action in his case. At the request of Italian authorities, however, Reder was re-interned in September 1945 at the Glasenbach POW camp (near Hallein). In September 1947, Reder was remanded to British custody so that he could testify in the trials of Field Marshal Kesselring and his former divisional commander SS-Gruppenführer Max Simon. Kesselring was sentenced to death by a British court for assorted war crimes in Italy (including Monte Sol), but this was later reduced to life imprisonment and then commuted altogether. Simon, who had been earlier implicated in atrocities in Poland and the USSR (see *Einsatzgruppe in Poland* and *Kharkov 3*, respectively), was condemned to death by a British court in Padua for crimes occurring during his command of 16. SS-Panzergrenadier-Division *Reichsführer-SS* in Italy. Simon's sentence was also commuted and he was freed in 1954. Walter Reder was finally remanded to Italian custody on 13 May 1948 in order to stand trial for his role in the atrocities at Monte Sol.

Three and one-half years were spent putting together the following accusations against Reder, a number of which covered atrocities unrelated to the events at Monte Sol :

1) 12 August 1944 - Santa Anna di Stazzema
   -- see this entry elsewhere
2) 19 August 1944 - Bardine de San Terenzo
   -- see this entry elsewhere
3) 24-26 August 1944 - Vinca di Fivizzano, Gragnola, Monzone, Ponte S. Lucia
   -- see these entries elsewhere
4) 29/30 September and 1 & 5 October 1944
   -- Marzabotto, Casaglia, Cerpiano, Caprara, S. Giovanni di Sopra and di Sotto, Casoni di Bavellino, Casoni di Riomoneta
5) 19 August 1944 - Valla
   -- see entry elsewhere
6) numerous other minor charges

Reders' trial for these war crimes lasted from 19 - 30 October 1951 before an Italian Military Tribunal in Bologna. It was demonstrated that before the events at Monte Sol, he had plenty of experience exterminating innocent civilians in Poland, the Ukraine, and in the mountains of northern Italy. In one incident, Reder's Waffen-SS troopers posed 107 men, women, and children before "hooded cameras," then removed the hoods, and machine-gunned the group to death. A young girl shielded from the bullets by falling bodies lived to tell the story. In another of Reder's reprisal actions, he had 53 Italian laborers strangled and hung on a barbed-wire fence as an example for any partisans in the area. Many of the survivors of Monte Sol testified against Reder, accusing him of personally performing many atrocities. The survivors remembered Reder well because of his missing left hand. Former Waffen-SS men were interviewed in Germany and their depositions made part of the trial record. Evidence for the following crimes on Monte Sol was produced during the trial:

Caprara -- three young women were found tied to a chestnut tree, skirts raised, with branches protruding from their vaginas

Casaglia -- an indeterminate number of civilians were herded into a cemetary and machine-gunned

Casoni di Bavellino -- see Marzabotto below

Casoni di Riomoneta -- see Marzabotto below

Cerpiano -- 49 civilians were herded into a church oratory and then grenades were thrown in, a few survived

Creda

-- 90 civilians were rounded up into a farmshed;they were then shot and grenaded; a few survived

Marzabotto

-- approximately 1800 civilians murdered by various means

Pioppe di Salvaro

-- 45 civilians executed

San Giovanni di Sopra & di Sotto

-- see Marzabotto above

Sperticano

-- 116 civilians executed

The exact number of civilians murdered on Monte Sol will never be known. During Reder's trial, Italian military authorities cited 1830 victims as an educated guess. One of the marble bone crypts in Marzabotto contains 1200 sets of identified remains while another crypt contains 300 sets of unidentified remains. A post-war census by the Italian Government indicated that the region's population had dropped by approximately 2000 individuals; most of those missing were women and children.

The prosecution introduced extensive testimony only in those cases where it was clear that Reder was personally responsible in some fashion. As a result, he was found guilty of only half the atrocities that were actually committed by his men on Monte Sol. The Italian Military Tribunal in Bologna found Reder guilty of murder for charges 2, 3, 4, and 5; guilty of destruction for charges 2, 3, and 4; and innocent of charges 1 and 6. Since Italy had no death sentence, Walter Reder was sentenced on 31 October 1951 to life imprisonment for his role in the crimes at Monte Sol and numerous other localities.

His lawyers filed an immediate appeal based on irregularities in the trial proceedings. First of all, the Italian Military Tribunal did not follow all of the rules set out under Article 19 of the International Military Tribunal statutes. Although pre-trial preparations took three and a half years, Reder was not informed of the charges against him until two months prior to trial. Additionally, he was not allowed to retain German legal counsel. The defense also claimed that it was hindered in making its case and presenting its arguments. Finally, the defense objected to the fact that the Tribunal had accepted the statement of Julien Legoli

at face value. Legoli was never called to testify before the court (in fact, no effort was even made to find him after the war). Thus, the defense had no opportunity to question Legoli's highly-damaging statement that Reder had authorized the mass killings. In his appeal, Reder restated his claim that Marzabotto was not in his operational area and that neither he nor anyone from his unit ever entered the town. The Supreme Italian Military Court in Rome dismissed the appeal --- while irregularities had occurred during the trial, they did not change the basic facts of what had happened at Monte Sol.

On 16 May 1954, Reder began his life sentence at the Gaeta Military Prison (Reclusorio Militare Gaeta/Latina), located south of Naples. By this time, newspapers in West Germany and Austria were decrying Reder's trial as rigged. Official protests against his imprisonment were issued by politicians on the floor of the Austrian parliament. Money and gifts were sent by strangers to Reder in his oversized and comfortable cell (including a kitchen, a balcony with view, and occasional female visitors). Petitions began to circulate for his release.

In 1955 right-wing politicians talked the Austrian government into granting Reder citizenship in violation of the usual practices (he had naturalized from Austrian to German in 1934 and was not eligible to reclaim his former citizenship). The Austrian government also decided to assume his case, including legal costs and other expenses. It even went so far as to assign a Foreign Ministry civil servant to handle his affairs. Bouyed by these successes, the European right-wing began to heavily sell the image of Reder as that of an innocent martyr and Austria's last prisoner of war. Interestingly enough, the various factions supporting Reder never could agree as to why his sentence was unjust -- some argued that the massacres were simply the unavoidable result of guerilla warfare (anti-partisan warfare can't follow the rules of war and still be effective), others that the partisans themselves were guilty of massacres and thus deserved what they got, others that the dead civilians were the result of Allied attacks, and still others that the atrocities were a hoax. Despite the overwhelming evidence against Reder, he has found numerous champions among right-wing and Neo-Nazi writers such as Lothar Greil, Rudolf Aschenauer, and F.J.P. Veale.

In 1957, Reder along with five other prisoners at Gaeta, under the name of "Gaeta-Hilfe," began a petition for their release. In the Spring of 1958, this petition (signed by approximately 280,000 soldiers from 35 different countries and comprising 26 bound volumes) was presented by a delegation to a judicial tribunal in Rome. It was accompanied by diplomatic actions, both inside and outside of Italy, to release the prisoners. While other individuals were paroled, Reder was passed over time and again by all amnesties. Austrian politicians and representatives of the Catholic Church continued to seek clemency for Reder on humanitarian grounds; he filed countless legal appeals in the intervening years, all to no avail.

On 26 July 1980, the Military Tribunal of Bari announced that Walter Reder would receive premature release due to his repentance and new-found Christian belief. He was finally released on 25 January 1985 after being in one form of custody or another for nearly 40 years. Austrian Defense Minister Frischenschlager met Reder at the Vienna airport like the prodigal son, causing a short-lived political scandal until the Minister apologized for his "mistake." Once free, Walter Reder's unrepentant statements and behavior soon demonstrated that his "turning over a new leaf" was a scam, pure and simple. Reder later died in Vienna on 26 April 1991.

Sources

(Kunz, 1967)
(Stein, 1966, p. 276)
(Olsen, 1968)
(Bender & Taylor, 1969-1982, vol. 4, pp. 113-115)
(Veale, 1968)
(Greil, 1977)
(Ortner, 1986)
(Bundesverband, 1985, pp. 29-32)
(Krätschmer, 1982, pp. 468-472)
(Greil, 1959)
(Aschenauer, 1978)

Mussidan (France)

"Early in the morning of June 11th, 1944 a force of F.F.I. [Forces Francaises de l'Interieur, i.e. French partisans] arrived in trucks in the town of Mussidan [Department of Dordogne, 30 km southwest of Perigueux].

There they went to the R.R. station to attack the German train which patrolled the tracks between that town and St. Astier. On the train's arrival a fight began and the population of the town went into hiding. During the fight eleven Germans were killed and eight taken prisoner, but the F.F.I. had to withdraw from the town about 12:30 pm when a detachment of the SS Division Das Reich [2. SS-Panzer-Division Das Reich (CO: SS-Brigadeführer Heinz Lammerding)], enroute from Perigeux to Bordeaux, arrived on the scene.

Once in command of the situation the commanding officer of the SS started a roundup of all males in the town between 16 and 60 years old. By 3:00 pm, 350 were taken to the Mairie and their papers examined. Some 48 were then selected from the 350 and 10 of these 48 were closely questioned and beaten in order to get some information from them. Why the remaining 38 were selected is not clear but their selection seems to have been influenced by their appearance because the worst dressed were usually included. At 10:30 pm that night word came from the Perigeux headquarters to shoot all 48 and this order was carried out under the personal supervision of the chief Gestapo agent, Hombrech.

The Mayor of Mussidan, that same evening was arrested at 8:30 pm and taken to the Mairie. There he was beaten with a wooden club and asked to give information which he either would not or could not give. About 10:00 pm he managed somehow to escape from the Mairie but was soon recaptured and killed. His secretary was also killed. The German authorities refused to permit any flowers or funeral processions in burying the victims and only permitted three members of each victim's family to be present."

Source

(U.S. National Archives, Records of the Office of the Judge Advocate General [Army], French War Crime Cases, RG-153, 151 / File Number 000-11-175, Case Summary)

The Netherlands

In April 1941, SS-Standarte Nordwest was formed from Dutch volunteers with a cadre of German Waffen-SS officers. Following the German invasion of the USSR, the unit was disbanded and the bulk of its strength reallocated to other Dutch/Flemish Waffen-SS units as replacements. One battalion, redesignated SS-Wacht-Bataillon *Nordwest*, was returned to the Netherlands for guard duties at KL Westerbork (Drente), KL Vught (southern Netherlands), and KL Amersfoort (Utrecht). These concentration camps served as holding points for Dutch and French Jews awaiting transport to the extermination centers in Poland. In September 1944, this battalion was redesignated SS-Panzerjäger-Abteilung *Nordwest* and incorporated into 34. SS-Grenadier-Division *Landstorm Nederland*.

Source
(Littlejohn, 1972)

Niksic (Yugoslavia)

During the course of the Nuremberg Trials, the prosecution cited Document D-940, an extract from the Yugoslav State Commission Report :

> "At the end of May 1943 the Prinz Eugen Division [7. SS-Freiwilligen-Gebirgs-Division Prinz Eugen] came to Montenegro [Crna Gora] to the area of Niksic in order to take part in the fifth enemy offensive with the Italian troops. This offensive was called 'Action Black' by the German occupying forces. Proceeding from Herzegovina, parts of the division fell upon the peaceful villages of the Niksic District [and] commenced to commit outrageous crimes on the peaceful villages.... Everything they came across they burned down, murdered and pillaged. The officers and men of the SS Division Prinz Eugen committed crimes of an outrageous cruelty on this occasion. The victims were shot, slaughtered, and tortured, or burned to death in burning houses.... Infants with their mothers, pregnant women, and frail old people were also murdered. In short, every civilian met with by these troops in these villages was murdered. In many cases whole families who, not expecting such treatment or lacking the time for escape, had remained quietly in their homes, were annihilated and murdered. Whole families were thrown into burning houses in many cases and thus burned. It has been established from the investigations entered upon that 121 persons, mostly women, including 30 persons aged 60-92 years and 29 children of ages ranging from 6 months to 14 years, were executed on this occasion in the horrible manner narrated above."

The report goes on to detail the seizing of livestock, and the looting of valuables from these villages by the troops. The report also names the individuals responsible for issuing the orders to carry out this action : SS-Gruppenführer Artur Phleps (the divisional commanding officer), SS-Brigadeführer Carl Ritter von Oberkamp, SS-Brigadeführer August Schmidhuber, SS-Sturmbannführer Rudolf Bachmann, SS-Sturmbannführer Bernhard Dietsche, and another ten Waffen-SS junior officers.

Sources

(Sauer, 1977, p. 46)
(IMT, 1948/1971, vol. 20, pp. 374-376)

Niksic-Avtovac Railroad Line
(Yugoslavia)

During the Nuremberg Trials, the prosecution cited document D-944 (exhibit GB-566), a statement from the Yugoslav War Crimes Commission taken from a member of the SS, Leander Holtzer:

> "In August 1943, on the orders of the same person (i.e., SS-Obersturmbannführer Wagner), the 23rd Company [7. SS-Freiwilligen-Gebirgs-Division], under the command of SS-Untersturmbannführer Schuh, set fire to a village on the railway line Niksic-Avtovac [railroad line northwest from Niksic (Crna Gora) approximately fifty kilometers to Avtovac (Bosnia-Herzegovina)]; and the inhabitants of the village were shot. The order for the shooting came from Jablanica..."

When asked to respond to this allegation, former SS-Obergruppenführer Paul Hausser objected that the Waffen-SS did not use a numbering scheme that would have included a "23rd Company." However, he then went on to say that he was not familiar with the *Prinz Eugen* division. If the atrocities did occur, however, then in his opinion they were the result of the unit having too many Volksdeutsche personnel. Hausser was incorrect; *Prinz Eugen* did possess a 23rd Company as part of its IV Bataillon / SS-Gebirgsjäger-Regiment 1. However, the battalion commander at this time was SS-Sturmbannführer Horst Strathmann.

The former battalion commander, SS-Obersturmbannführer Jürgen Wagner, had already been assigned to command the 23. SS-Freiwilligen-Panzergrenadier-Division *Nederland* which had recently been deployed to Yugoslavia for working up and training.

Sources

(IMT, 1948/1971, vol. 20, p. 398)
(Kumm, 1978)

Nisko (Poland)

During the month of September 1939, an unspecified number of Jews, Polish POWs, and Polish political and religious leaders were tortured and then executed by Waffen-SS elements of Einsatzgruppe II (CO: SS-Obersturmbannführer Dr. Emanuel Schäfer) at the town of Nisko (north of Rzeszow, south-central Poland) in the course of "cleansing and security" measures in the operational zone of the 10th Army. These atrocities were carried out by either SS-Totenkopfstandarte I *Oberbayern* (CO: SS-Sturmbannführer Max Simon) or SS-Totenkopfstandarte III *Thüringen* (CO: ?). They were the only Waffen-SS formations operating behind the 10th Army at this time that had the firepower and mobility to conduct such large-scale killing operations. On 1 November 1940, both units were designated as cadre for the newly activated SS-Totenkopfdivision (later 3. SS-Panzer-Division *Totenkopf*).

Source
(Sydnor, 1977, p. 41)

Normandy (France)

Introduction

On 6 June 1944 the long awaited Anglo-American invasion of Nazi-occupied Europe began with landings on the beaches of Normandy. The 3rd Canadian Infantry Division (CO: Major-General R.F.L. Keller) was part of the 1st British Corps and was assigned to attack through the gap between Bayeux and Caen, while British divisions on their flanks captured the two towns. The Canadian attack was led by the 7th

Canadian Infantry Brigade (CO: Brigadier H.W. Foster), on the right flank, and the 8th Canadian Infantry Brigade (CO: Brigadier K.G. Blackader), on the left flank. Each unit was supported by a regiment of the 2nd Canadian Armoured Brigade. Brigadier D.G. Cunningham's 9th Canadian Infantry Brigade was held in reserve. By the end of the first day, none of the attack objectives had been met : the 7th Brigade was bogged down near Creully, while the 8th Brigade was short of its objectives northwest of Caen. The 6th Canadian Armoured Regiment *1st Hussars* advanced as far as Bretteville l'Orgueilleuse, but was forced to withdraw as a result of Waffen-SS counterattacks. The 9th Brigade, along with the North Nova Scotia Highlanders (CO: Lieutenant-Colonel C. Petch) and the 27th Canadian Armoured Regiment *Sherbrooke Fusiliers* (CO: Lieutenant-Colonel M.B.K. Gordon) were pulled out of reserve and brought up to assault enemy positions in the area, but they too were halted four miles north of Caen by fierce counterattacks. Faced with the determined and fanatical opposition of Waffen-SS units, the Canadians would not capture Caen until over a month later.

Standing between the Canadian forces and their first day's objectives was the elite 12. SS-Panzer-Division *Hitlerjugend* (CO: SS-Brigadeführer Fritz Witt). *Hitlerjugend* was a newly-formed division composed of 17 - 21 year old Hitler Youths and a cadre of experienced personnel from the 1. SS-Panzer-Division *Leibstandarte Adolf Hitler*. As this division would later be accused of committing numerous war crimes in the area of Caen, it will be helpful to examine the command structure of its five main combat components.

SS-Panzergrenadier-Regiment 25
CO: SS-Brigadeführer Kurt Meyer

I.	Bataillon	CO: SS-Sturmbannführer Hans Waldmüller
II.	Bataillon	CO: SS-? Hans Scappini
III.	Bataillon	CO: SS-Obersturmbannführer Karl-Heinz Milius

SS-Panzergrenadier-Regiment 26
CO: SS-Standartenführer Wilhelm Mohnke

I.	Bataillon	CO: SS-Sturmbannführer Bernhard Krause
II.	Bataillon	CO: SS-Sturmbannführer Bernhard Siebken
III.	Bataillon	CO: SS-Sturmbannführer Erich Olboeter

SS-Panzer-Regiment 12
CO: SS-Sturmbannführer Max Wünsche

I. Abteilung   CO: SS-Sturmbannführer Arnold Jürgensen
II. Abteilung   CO: SS-Sturmbannführer Karl-Heinz Prinz

SS-Panzerpionier-Abteilung 12
CO: SS-Sturmbannführer Siegfried Müller

SS-Panzeraufklärungs-Abteilung 12
CO: SS-Sturmbannführer Gerhard Bremer

On the right flank of their advance, things had gone fairly well for the Canadians. SS-Panzergrenadier-Regiment 26 was not yet fully in position and against light resistance the 7th Canadian Infantry Brigade reached most of its objectives (the Royal Winnipeg Rifles had taken Putot-en-Bessin and the Regina Rifles were in Norrey-en-Bessin). Along with the North Nova Scotia Highlanders, these two units commanded the vital Caen-Bayeux road and railway corridor. On 8 June they were fiercely attacked by assorted elements of the Hitlerjugend division. The Royal Winnipeg Rifles were overrun and suffered heavy losses at the hands of SS-Panzergrenadier-Regiment 26. The North Nova Scotia Highlanders were forced to retreat, recovered their positions, and then held on to them through a week of constant shellfire. The Regina Rifles position was penetrated on the night of 8/9 June by elements of SS-Panzergrenadier-Regiment 25 and SS-Panzer-Regiment 12 in an attack led personally by SS-Brigadeführer Meyer. After a night of valiant and determined defense, the Canadians were finally able to drive off their attackers with the loss of many tanks. The 7th Brigade survived intact and held onto its assigned positions until they later took part in the attack on Caen.

Meanwhile, the 8th Brigade moved forward to attack key German positions. On 11 June the Queen's Own Rifles, supported by two armoured regiments, unsuccessfully attempted to seize the heights south of Putot-en-Bessin and reached the town of le Mesnil-Patry but were forced to withdraw. On 16/17 June they attacked again and reoccupied these positions without serious opposition. On 17 June the commander of Hitlerjugend, SS-Brigadeführer Fritz Witt, was killed as a result of naval bombardment. His replacement, SS-Brigadeführer Meyer, immediately reorganized the slowly crumbling German line. The 3rd Canadian Division continued to hold its positions along the line from Villons-les-Buissons on the east to Putot-en-Bessin on the west throughout heavy combat for the balance of the month of June, until it advanced towards Carpiquet and Caen in early July.

The first indications that a ruthless policy was being implemented by the Germans regarding the treatment of prisoners were seen early on in the fighting. Reports came in to British and Canadian headquarters claiming that unarmed Allied prisoners of war were being summarily executed. Most of these reports originated from the sector of the front held by Hitlerjugend. For the sake of clarity, all of the atrocities attributable to Hitlerjugend personnel will be reviewed first. This will then be followed with an account of the post-war legal proceedings related to these atrocities.

The Atrocities

Ancienne Abbaye Ardenne

SS-Brigadeführer Kurt Meyer, commander of SS-Panzergrenadier-Regiment 25, established his regimental headquarters at the Ancienne Abbaye Ardenne (2.5 kilometers northwest of Caen) at the start of the fighting in Normandy. On 7/8 June 1944 approximately eighteen Canadian POWs were interrogated and executed at the abbey. On 17 June two additional Canadian prisoners were interrogated and then murdered there. After the war, charges related to these incidents were brought against Kurt Meyer based on the testimony of French civilians and former Waffen-SS personnel. The key eyewitness was former SS-Sturmmann Jan Jesionek, a conscript in the 15. SS-Panzeraufklärungs-Kompanie who had served with the unit since its formation. He testified that on the morning of 8 June he was dispatched to the abbey to pick up a motorcycle. While there, he saw seven Canadian POWs brought in. SS-Brigadeführer Meyer appeared visibly upset that the prisoners had been taken, opining that "They only eat up our rations. In the future no more prisoners are to be taken." The POWs were questioned and then taken individually into the abbey gardens and shot by an unidentified SS-Unterscharführer. Jesionek led investigators to the abbey where he claimed that the murders had taken place. A search was made and the bodies of eighteen Canadian soldiers (members of the Stormont, Dundas and Glengarry Highlanders; Royal Canadian Armoured Corps; and North Nova Scotia Highlanders) were discovered in five different well-concealed graves. Forensic examination revealed that all of the victims died as a result of close range pistol shots fired into the base of the skull, multiple bullet wounds, or the application of a blunt instrument to the head.

Argentan

On 7 June 1944 three downed American flyers were shot by elements of the 12. SS-Panzer-Division *Hitlerjugend* near the Caen-Falaise road, north of the town of Argentan.

Authie / Buron

Following the bitter fighting of 7 June 1944 in and around the villages of Authie and Buron (four kilometers northwest of Caen), thirty-one Canadian POWs (26 North Nova Scotia Highlanders, 2 Cameron Highlanders of Ottawa and 3 Sherbrooke Fusiliers), many of whom were wounded and disabled, were murdered in a number of incidents by members of 3. Bataillon / SS-Panzergrenadier-Regiment 25 (CO: SS-Obersturmbannführer Karl-Heinz Milius) and II. Abteilung / SS-Panzer-Regiment 12 (CO: SS-Sturmbannführer Karl-Heinz Prinz). The bodies were left unburied for the most part. In some cases, Waffen-SS grenadiers deliberately moved the victims out into roadways so that passing tanks and other vehicles would crush them and the manner of their death beyond recognition.

Bretteville l'Orgueilleuse

On 9 June 1944 Riflemen L.W. Lee and E.N. Gilbank of the Regina Rifles were captured by the crew of a disabled Waffen-SS tank near the town of Bretteville l'Orgueilleuse. The two Canadian POWs were forced to run five hundred yards to the south where they were interrogated by a Waffen-SS tank commander. This officer, apparently dissatisfied with the information he received, turned a machine-pistol on the prisoners and gunned them down. Rifleman Gilbank was killed immediately; Rifleman Lee was only wounded

and played dead. He eventually escaped back across the lines to his battalion. It was later determined that 1. and 3. Kompanie of SS-Panzer-Regiment 12, commanded by SS-Hauptsturmführers Anton Berlin and Rudolf Ribbentrop respectively, were operating in the area at the time of this atrocity. Neither of the company commanders were ever apprehended for interrogation.

Chateau d'Audrieu

One of the first major atrocities took place on 8 June 1944 at the headquarters SS-Panzeraufklärungs-Abteilung 12 located at Chateau d'Audrieu near Pavie, thirteen kilometers west of Caen. Three Canadian POWs were escorted into a patch of woods behind the chateau and, at the direction of an officer, were shot by their Waffen-SS guards. Soon thereafter another three Canadians (Riflemen D.S. Gold, J.D. McIntosh, and W. Thomas of the Royal Winnipeg Rifles) were taken into the same woods and executed. At 4:30 pm, thirteen more prisoners (all from the 9th Platoon / A Company / Royal Winnipeg Rifles) were shot by several Waffen-SS grenadiers within plain view of numerous officers and NCOs from the SS headquarters. An additional seven Canadian POWs were also executed later that same day.

This was among the first cases to be investigated by Canadian authorities after the war. Mass graves were located and the bodies of 26 Allied soldiers were exhumed. Autopsies were then performed by Canadian Army pathologist, Lieutenant-Colonel R.A.H. Mac-Keen. Twenty-four witnesses, both French civilians and Canadian Army personnel, were subsequently questioned concerning the events at Chateau d'Audrieu. According to his own testimony, SS-Hauptsturmführer Gerd von Reitzenstein was the acting commander at the time of these atrocities because the regular commander, SS-Brigadeführer Gerhard Bremer, had been wounded by an artillery barrage early that morning. He claimed to have ordered the shootings in retaliation for his commander's wounding. However, SHAEF investigators (see *The Legal Proceedings*, below) had already proven that SS-Sturmbannführer Bremer was not injured until after the killings had taken place and French civilian eyewitnesses placed him at the scene of the murders. Also implicated by evidence uncovered during the investigations were SS-Obersturmbannführer Hansman and SS-Oberscharführer Leopold Stun, as the officers in charge of the executions. The firing squads were composed of motorcycle dispatch riders attached to the SS-Panzeraufklärungs-Abteilung 12 headquarters.

Fontenay-le-Pesnel

On the morning of 8 June 1944 the Royal Winnipeg Rifles and Cameron Highlanders of Ottawa, supported by guns of the 3rd Canadian Anti-Tank Regiment RCA, were holding positions near the village of Putot-en-Bessin. They were attacked by 2. Bataillon / SS-Panzergrenadier-Regiment 26 and pushed out of the village for a few hours. The 5. and 7. Kompanie of the 2. Bataillon captured 25 - 30 Canadians during the fighting. The prisoners were evacuated by their captors through the battalion headquarters (CO: SS-Sturmbannführer Bernhard Siebken) at le Mesnil-Patry where another group of Canadian prisoners was added making a total of forty POWs in the group. Later that evening the prisoners were marched south towards the Caen - Fontenay-le-Pesnel road. The group encountered an SS officer who relayed orders to the guards. The prisoners were marched until they were within one hundred yards of the Caen road at which point they were turned off into a neighboring field. They were instructed to sit down and rest, close together. Soon thereafter, a half-track turned into the field and a number of Waffen-SS grenadiers dismounted. The Germans talked amongst themselves briefly, formed a line, advanced on the prisoners, and began firing into the surprised crowd. Thirty-five of the Canadians were killed in the ensuing massacre; five escaped into a nearby wheatfield (Corporal H.C. McLean, Riflemen G.J. Ferris, A. Desjarlais, and J. MacDougall of the Royal Winnipeg Rifles and Gunner W.F. Clark of the 3rd Anti-Tank). The survivors were later recaptured by other German units and sent to POW camps for the duration of the war. Post-war investigations yielded a shallow mass grave containing thirty-one bodies and two smaller graves nearby with the bodies of the remaining victims. The testimony of the survivors corroborated statements previously taken from Lieutenant D.A. James and Rifleman W.R. LeBarr who had themselves escaped from other Waffen-SS guards after witnessing the mass execution from a distance. The exact identity of the guilty parties was never determined despite painstaking investigation.

Galmanche

On the night of 7 June 1994 Captain W.L. Brown (a chaplain), Lieutenant W.F. Granger, and Lance-Corporal J.H. Greenwood of the Sherbrooke Fusiliers encountered a patrol from 1. Bataillon / SS-Panzergrenadier-Regiment 25 (CO: SS-Sturmbannführer Hans Waldmüller) who opened fire on them. Lieutenant Granger was wounded and left for dead; Lance-Corporal Greenwood was killed outright and Captain Brown taken prisoner. At the time of his capture the chaplain was unarmed and wearing a clerical collar and a Red Cross armband. Lieutenant Granger eventually made it back to friendly lines. Approximately one month later Captain Brown's surprisingly well-preserved body was recovered. Forensic examination revealed that he had died as a result of a bayonet or knife wound to the thorax. For reasons unknown, Captain Brown was denied quarter and killed despite his special status as a POW and cleric.

le Haut du Bosq

At 4:00 pm on 11 June 1944 three Canadian soldiers (Rifleman A.R. Owens of the Royal Winnipeg Rifles; Sappers J. Ionel and G.A. Benner of the Royal Canadian Engineers) were brought as prisoners to the headquarters of SS-Panzergrenadier-Regiment 26 located in an orchard at Forme du Bosq, near the village of le Haut du Bosq. They were interrogated for approximately twenty minutes by regimental commander SS-Obersturmbannführer Wilhelm Mohnke in the presence of his adjutant (SS-Hauptsturmführer Kaiser) and numerous other members of the regiment. SS-Obersturmbannführer Mohnke was clearly upset, shouting and gesticulating in an angry manner throughout the interrogation. The prisoners were then searched, had their identity papers thrown away, and were marched to the edge of a deep bomb crater. An SS-Scharführer mowed them down with his machine-pistol and then two Waffen-SS Feldgendarmerie stepped forward and delivered single pistol-shots to the head. SS-Obersturmbannführer Mohnke and his staff watched the entire proceedings. After the war, at the direction of several eyewitnesses (former Waffen-SS conscripts Withold Stangenberg and Heinz Schmidt), the POW's identity papers were found as well as the crater containing their remains. Forensic examinations demonstrated that the prisoners had died from multiple bullet wounds. Additional confirmation of SS-Obersturmbannführer Mohnke's responsibility for these and other crimes committed by his regiment was obtained on 16 March 1946 when Bernard Siebken (former commander of the 2. Bataillon / SS-Panzergrenadier-Regiment 26) testified that during the early days of fighting Mohnke ordered that prisoners should be shot after interrogation.

le Mesnil-Patry 1

At 9:00 am on 9 June 1944 three wounded Canadians (Riflemen F.W. Holness and E.C. Baskerville of the Royal Winnipeg Rifles; Private H.S. Angel of the Cameron Highlanders of Ottawa) were brought to an aid station of 2. Bataillon / SS-Panzergrenadier-Regiment 26 located in a farmhouse on the outskirts of le Mesnil-Patry, eleven kilometers west of Caen. Madame St. Martin, a resident of the farmhouse, witnessed the following events. The prisoners had their wounds dressed and were then interrogated by a Waffen-SS medical officer. Another Waffen-SS officer arrived and ordered the prisoners out of the house and into the garden. At this second officer's command, the Canadians were executed by four Waffen-SS grenadiers armed with machine pistols. The officer then shot each of the prisoners once in the head with his sidearm. The bodies were left where they lay for several days and then only partially buried. They were found on 1 July when British troops liberated the area.

From captured Waffen-SS personnel it was learned that the Canadians had been captured by 7. Kompanie / 2. Bataillon / SS-Panzergrenadier-Regiment 26 (CO: SS-Obersturmführer August Henne). They were taken to the battalion headquarters of SS-Sturmbannführer Bernard Siebken. The prisoners were then moved on to the aid station cited above. SS-Obersturmbannführer Andersen (Siebken's adjutant) would normally have

had the responsibility for the evacuation of prisoners. Some evidence indicated that the officer in charge of the executions may have been a company commander named Polansky. During his post-war trial Bernhard Siebken confirmed much of the evidence in this case, but maintained that he knew nothing of the killings.

le Mesnil-Patry 2

A post-war search turned up the bodies of three Canadian POWs (Trooper A. Bowes and Trooper G.H. Scriven of the 6th Canadian Armoured Regiment *1st Hussars*; CSM J. Forbes of the Queen's Own Rifles) buried near the site of another massacre (see *le Mesnil-Patry 1*, above). Forensic examination established that the prisoners had died as a result of pistol shots to the head. Once again it appears that wounded prisoners were brought to an aid station in the area of 2. Bataillon / SS-Panzergrenadier-Regiment 26 (CO: SS-Sturmbannführer Bernhard Siebken) and then were executed. At 9:30 am on 9 June 1944, two French civilians, Madame St. Martin and M. Poisson, witnessed this execution of Canadian POWs by a Waffen-SS firing squad composed of five soldiers and an officer. Numerous Waffen-SS grenadiers and officers milled about taking in the spectacle. After one volley of fire, the officer in charge drew his revolver and delivered a *coup de grace* to each victim.

les Fains

On 12 June 1944 Sapper R.R. Forbes (a British member of the Royal Canadian Engineers) was gunned down from behind near the village of les Fains as he was being marched along a road by an escort from the 3. Bataillon / SS-Panzergrenadier-Regiment 26 (CO: SS-Sturmbannführer Erich Olboeter). Four other British POWs met their deaths under similar circumstances two days later in this same area. The killings were witnessed by several French civilians.

les Saullets 1

On 11 June 1944 three members of the 6th Canadian Armoured Regiment *1st Hussars* (Sergeant E.S. Payne, Trooper H.L. Preston and Trooper R.C. McClean) were captured by unidentified elements of *Hitler Jugend* near the village of les Saullets. The POWs were interrogated by an officer and then marched toward the rear under guard. Without any warning, the Waffen-SS grenadiers opened fire on their prisoners. Trooper Preston was killed outright; the other two Canadians were only wounded. They feigned death and later escaped back to friendly lines. Post-war investigations determined that their captors were either from the 2. Bataillon / SS-Panzergrenadier-Regiment 26 or 3. Kompanie / SS-Panzerpionier-Abteilung 12.

les Saullets 2

On 11 June 1944, a tank crew from the 6th Canadian Armoured Regiment *1st Hussars* (Captain H.L. Smuck, Private A.H. Charron, Troopers A.M. LeClair and A.B. Hancock) was reported as missing in action following an unsuccessful attack on the village of les Saullets. During post-war investigations, former Waffen-SS personnel testified that the tank crew was taken prisoner by members of 7. Kompanie / 2. Bataillon / SS-Panzergrenadier-Regiment 26 (CO: SS-Obersturmführer August Henne). SS-Obersturmführer Henne claimed to have dispatched the POWs to battalion headquarters under guard of SS-Sturmmann Mischke. The Canadian's bodies were found by investigators in a common grave lying close to the path between the unit's company and battalion HQ positions. Forensic examinations demonstrated that the prisoners had not been killed in combat or while resisting their captors.

Mouen

At 6:00 pm on 17 June 1944 seven exhausted Canadian POWs (six from the Queen's Own Rifles and one from the 6th Canadian Armoured Regiment *1st Hussars*) were brought to the rear area headquarters of SS-Panzerpionier-Abteilung 12 (CO: SS-Sturmbannführer Siegfried Müller) in the village of Mouen, eight kilometers southwest of Caen. Here they were interrogated by an officer. Four hours later, this officer had the prisoners marched to the outskirts of the village where they were executed by a group of fourteen Waffen-SS grenadiers led by an NCO. The following day local civilians were impressed to dig a grave and bury the bodies. It was later determined that SS-Sturmbannführer Müller had ordered his company commanders to take no prisoners. The names of the interrogating officer, the NCO in charge of the execution, and the firing squad members were never determined.

St. Sulpice

On 8 June 1944 a downed U.S. Army Air Force pilot who had crash-landed near Rugles was handed over to a detachment of SS-Panzeraufklärungs-Abteilung 12 commanded by SS-Untersturmführer Kirchner. SS-Untersturmführer Kirchner handed the prisoner over to SS-Unterscharführer Hugo Wolf who took him to a chateau near St. Sulpice where two officers of the Abteilung killed in an Allied air attack earlier that day lay in state. SS-Unterscharführer Wolf explained how his comrades had been killed and then drew his pistol and shot the pilot to death.

The Legal Proceedings

Following the liberation of Caen in July 1944, the earlier reports of Waffen-SS atrocities seemed to be borne out by the discovery of the buried and unburied bodies of Allied soldiers bearing physical indications that they had been executed by their captors. Accordingly, General Bernard L. Montgomery (commander of the 21st Army Group) and General Dwight D. Eisenhower (Supreme Commander, Allied Expeditionary Force) created courts of inquiry to investigate the facts surrounding the various alleged atrocities. The first investigations made were of the shootings near Mouen. Once the scope and nature of the atrocities had been ascertained, the two courts of inquiry were merged into a SHAEF Standing Court of Inquiry under the direction of Major-General R.W. Barker. The SHAEF Court continued to function after the German capitulation on 8 May 1945. Meanwhile, a Canadian legal team (No. 1 Canadian War Crimes Investigation Unit) was established to support the work of the SHAEF Court with investigations of concern to the Canadian armed forces.

The investigations by the various courts established that 156 Canadian, 4 British, and 3 American POWs had been murdered by members of the 12. SS-Panzer-Division Hitlerjugend. The testimony of eyewitnesses, both French civilians and a handful of POWs who survived execution attempts, was invariably supported by the results of forensic examinations. The standard method of execution had been by a single aimed pistol shot fired from the rear into the base of the victim's skull. In cases where firing squads were involved, Schmeisser machine pistols seem to have been the weapon of choice. In several cases the victim's skull had suffered so much damage that it was concluded they had been bludgeoned to death. In most cases, it was not a question of whether a war crime had been committed, but by whom and under what authority (if any). In a number of instances, witnesses testified that the officers directing atrocities bore a cuff-band on their left sleeves that read Adolf Hitler in German script. This cuff-band was only worn by former personnel of the 1. SS-Panzer-Division Leibstandarte Adolf Hitler which had provided a sizable cadre for the formation of the Hitlerjugend division. Indications were that many more prisoners were also murdered after capture, but definite proof was lacking in these cases.

The SHAEF Standing Court of Inquiry concluded that the policy of denying quarter and executing prisoners after interrogation, if not ordered, was at least tolerated by regimental and divisional commanders. On the basis of their investigations, the court recommended that Kurt Meyer, Wilhelm Mohnke, Gerhard Bremer, Karl-Heinz Milius, and Siegfried Müller be tried for denying quarter to POWs and failing to prevent violations of the laws of war. The court also recommended that Gerhard Bremer, Siegfried Müller, Gerd von Reitzenstein, SS-Untersturmführers Kirchner and Schenk, SS-Stabscharführer Hagetorn, Hugo Wolf, and Leopold Stun be charged with murder as direct perpetrators or as accessories before and/or after the fact. Unfortunately, most of the suspects had not survived the war. Hans Waldmüller was killed on 8 September 1944 by Belgian partisans near Basse-Bodeux. Arnold Jürgensen was killed in action during the Ardennes Offensive in December 1944. Bernhard Krause was killed in action on 19 February 1945 near Muzsla, Hungary. Erich Olboeter was mortally wounded by Belgian partisans and died on 2 September 1944 at the Lazarett Charleville, Belgium. Karl-Heinz Prinz was killed in action on 14 August 1944 during the battle for Hill 159. SS-Stabscharführer Hagetorn was killed in action. Siegfried Müller and Max Wünsche survived the war and were investigated, though never brought

to trial. Gerhard Bremer was in French custody until 1948, but was never investigated with regard to these crimes. Wilhelm Mohnke was in Soviet custody until 1955. On 8 November 1945 he was placed on a list of wanted war criminals (CROWCASS --- Central Registry of War Criminals and Security Suspects) but was never investigated with regard to these crimes following his return to the West. The fates of Hans Scappini and Karl-Heinz Milius are unknown.

As it turned out, only Bernhard Siebken and Kurt Meyer ever stood trial for their involvement in atrocities during the Normandy fighting. Bernhard Siebken was apprehended in May 1945 and held in Fischbeck POW camp near Hameln, Germany. Due to the sudden and untimely disbandment of the No. 1 Canadian War Crimes Investigative Unit, his case was transferred to the British military authorities. Following a lengthy investigation, a preliminary hearing was held on 28 August 1948 before a British Military Court in Hamburg. The defendants were Bernhard Siebken, Dietrich Schnabel (his orderly officer), Heinrich Albers, and Fritz Bundschuh (both medical orderlies from the II. Bataillon / SS-Panzergrenadier-Regiment 26 first aid post). They were to be tried for the atrocity known as le Mesnil-Patry 1, with Albers and Bundschuh as the identified gunmen.

The trial began on 21 October 1948 and was presided over by Lieutenant-Colonel H.R. Bentley. The defense did not deny that the three Canadian soldiers had been executed but insisted that the killings were legal reprisals. The prosecution case was built around the eyewitness testimony of French civilian witnesses and the demonstration that international law does not allow reprisals against prisoners of war. After three weeks of testimony and cross-examination, a verdict was reached. Albers and Bundschuh were found to have participated in the killings, but were judged not guilty on the grounds that they were simple men who could not appreciate the illegality of their actions. Bernhard Siebken was found guilty of ordering the executions and condemned to death. Dietrich Schnabel was found guilty of carrying out the executions and condemned to death.

There now began a period of legal maneuvering on behalf of the condemned. The defence team submitted a petition to have the verdict overturned. The case was reviewed by Deputy Judge Advocate General Brigadier Lord Russell who moved to deny the defense petition in his report of 27 November 1948 to the Commander-in-Chief British Army of the Rhine. On 30 December 1948 the defense submitted a plea for clemency to General Sir Brian Robertson (C-in-C, British Zone of Occupation in Germany). This plea was rejected as was a personal plea for clemency, dated 3 January 1949, from Bernhard Siebken himself. On 20 January 1949 Bernhard Siebken and Dietrich Schnabel were hung in a British Military Gaol at Hameln, Germany.

Kurt Meyer was captured by Belgian partisans on 6 September 1944 and handed over to the Americans the next day. He was eventually remanded to British custody. In his initial interrogations, Meyer disavowed any knowledge of the killings at Ancienne Abbaye Ardenne and even claimed that the victims could not have been murdered but had probably died in combat. In an interrogation session on 15 October 1945, however, Meyer asked to amend his previous testimony. He then claimed that on 10/11 June 1944 two of his subordinates reported the presence of unburied bodies of executed Canadian POWs on the abbey grounds. Meyer claimed to be greatly upset by this news and ordered an investigation to determine who was responsible for these killings. He also ordered the bodies to be buried (they were, in carefully-concealed unmarked graves). Nothing came of Meyer's alleged investigation.

He was brought to trial by a Canadian Military Court on 10 December 1945 at Aurich, Germany. The court was presided over by Major-General H.W. Foster, with Lieutenant-Colonel B.J.S. McDonald as prosecutor and Lieutenant-Colonel Maurice W. Andrew as defense counsel. Meyer was charged with counselling his troops to deny quarter, killing POWs at the towns of Buron and Authie, and killing POWs at the Ancienne Abbaye Ardenne. He pleaded not guilty to all charges. Meyer's defense was largely ineffective due to the fact that he changed alibis and that the eyewitness testimony of French civilians showed his version of the events at the abbey to be a complete fabrication. On 27 December 1945 Meyer was found guilty of ordering his troops to deny quarter and held responsible for the deaths of the eighteen Canadian POWs at the abbey. The next day he was sentenced to death by firing squad.

Meyer's trial and verdict were widely criticized, and not only by the usual group of germanophiles and Waffen-SS apologists. At least one high-ranking Canadian Army officer complained that it was unfair to hold Meyer responsible for his men's actions since some Canadians had killed German POWs in Normandy. The lobbying efforts on his behalf were ceaseless. On 13 January 1946 Major-General Chris Vokes, commander of the Canadian Army Occupation force in Germany, commuted Meyer's sentence to life imprisonment on the grounds that the evidence against him was purely circumstantial. He was sent to Dorchester Penitentiary (New Brunswick, Canada) and employed preparing lengthy tactical studies on Soviet forces for the National Defense Headquarters (Ottawa). In October 1951, the Canadian Government transferred Meyer to a British prison at Werl, Germany. By the summer of 1952, his health was failing and he had to be hospitalized. On 7 September 1954 Meyer was paroled from prison due to his chronic health problems. An unrepentant National Socialist to the end, by 1956 he had become a principal spokesmen for HIAG. On 23 December 1961 Kurt Meyer died of a heart attack.

Aftermath

The only question left unresolved by the numerous legal investigations was whether or not POWs had been killed on the spur of the moment or as a result of direct orders from regimental commanders. In the case of Bernhard Siebken, it was undeniable that his superior --- Wilhelm Mohnke --- had ordered the executions to take place. There was evidence, however, that Siebken attempted to prevent the murder of POWs. However, with Mohnke unavailable for trial, Siebken was the only available scapegoat. Other cases, such as that of Kurt Meyer, were more certain. It is implausible in the extreme that executions could occur right outside of a regimental commander's HQ without him having any knowledge of the crimes. At his trial, Meyer stated that the killings were probably committed, as a result of their long experience on the Eastern Front, by former LAH personnel serving in the Hitlerjugend division. Despite his use of self-serving and contradictory alibis, Meyer's appraisal in this instance was unusually honest and perceptive. Nonetheless, practices that passed as "standard operating procedure" on the

Eastern Front were still war crimes.

This series of war crimes in Normandy has recently received considerable press attention in Canada. Investigators have concluded that the post-war Canadian political and military bureaucracies ceased prosecuting war criminals as part of a larger Allied quid pro quo to get West Germany on board in the Cold War against the Soviet Union. Unsurprisingly, many Canadians feel that these men were twice victimized: first by the Waffen-SS who murdered them and then by uncaring Canadian bureaucrats who declined bringing their killers to justice out of political expediency.

Sources

(Supplementary Report of SHAEF Court of Inquiry re Shooting of Allied Prisoners of War
by 12 SS Panzer Division [Hitler-Jugend] Normandy, France, 7 - 26 June 1944; U.S. National Archives RG 218)
(Reitlinger, 1957, p. 197)
(Stein, 1966, pp. 277-278)
(Luther, 1987, pp. 181-94 & 238-245)
(Krätschmer, 1982)
(Margolian, 1998)
(Datner, 1964, pp. 451-461)
(Bender & Taylor, 1969-1982, vol. 3, p. 114)
(MacDonald, 1954, pp. 3-70)
(Proceedings of the SHAEF Court of Inquiry, France, 20 August 1944; U.S. National Archives RG 218)
(Records of Proceedings [revised] of the Trial by Canadian Military Court of SS-Brigadeführer Kurt Meyer; U.S. National Archives RG 238)
(Record of Trial of Bernhard Siebken, et. al. before a British Military Court in Hamburg on 28 August and 21 October - 9 November 1948; Public Records Office; Kew; WO235/796)

Norway

On 7 October 1942, KdS Trondheim SS-Obersturmbannführer Gerhard Flesch ordered the arrest of all Jewish males over fourteen years of age. On 26 October 1942, Norwegian Secret Police, Oslo Police, and elements of the Germanske SS-Norge division (Norwegian SS volunteers) began the roundup of all Jewish men in Norway between the ages of 15 and 65. They were armed with prepared mimeographed sheets and conducted door-to door searches. The arrested Jews were held at a temporary camp in Berg. On 25 No-

vember 1942, the same units with the help of the Hird (a Norwegian Quisling party formation) took all remaining Norwegian Jews --- women, children, and the elderly --- into custody. The following day, all of the detained Jews (532) were loaded aboard the German Kriegsmarine transport ship Donau and shipped to Stettin, Germany. They were then transported by train to the Auschwitz death camp. Roundups by these same units continued throughout Winter 1942/43. In February 1943, an additional 158 detained Jews from Trondheim and northern Norway were shipped to Stettin on the Kriegsmarine ship Gotenland and then forwarded to the Auschwitz death camp by train. A total of 800 - 1,000 Norwegian Jews were sent to their deaths as a result of these operations. In March 1943, personnel from the Germanske SS-Norge was incorporated into the newly forming 11. SS-Freiwilligen-Panzergrenadier-Division Nordland.

Sources

(Braham, 1983, pp. 124-131)
(Hilberg, 1985, vol. 2, pp. 555-557)

Noville-lez-Bastogne (Belgium)

On 21 December 1944 an unidentified unit composed of French-speaking personnel wearing Waffen-SS uniforms with a helmet device bearing the French tricolor entered the village of Noville-lez-Bastogne. The village was largely deserted as many of its inhabitants had earlier hidden in nearby caves and the local forest in order to escape the fighting resulting from the German Ardennes Offensive. The commanding officer interrogated the few villagers who had remained behind and demanded information about resistance fighters in the area. When information was not forthcoming he selected seven civilians (MM. l'abbe Louis Delvaux, Emile Rosiere, Auguste Lutgen, Rene Deprez, Germain Deprez, Romain Henkinet and Roger Beaujean) to be executed as a warning. The victims were marched to the ruins of the Gregoire estate along the road from Bastogne to Houffalize and then gunned down with small-arms fire.

The identity of the responsible unit remains uncertain. Some elements of the 33. Waffen-Grenadier-Division der SS Charlemagne (französische Nr. 1) may have worn a combination of Waffen-SS uniforms with helmets bearing the French tricolor. Surviving villagers testified that one of the soldier's claimed that his unit was part of a Gestapo special detachment hunting resistance members.

Source
(Royaume de Belgique...., 1948, pp. 26-30)

Novi Sad (Yugoslavia)

In January 1942 Hungarian army and police units, with the aid of local ethnic Hungarians and Germans, carried out a series of killing operations against Serbians and Jews in the Backa region. The putative excuse for these massacres was an earlier armed skirmish with a detachment of partisans, in which four Hungarian policemen lost their lives. Although the partisan detachment was destroyed, the Hungarian Government instituted martial law in the districts of Titel, Zabalj, Novi Sad, and Stari Becej. The main goal of these operations was to make ethnic Hungarians and Germans the dominant population in the region.

The bloodiest massacre occurred in the prefect of Novi Sad (Autonomous Serbia) and included the towns of Novi Sad, Srbobran, and Stari Becej (see separate entry). In the course of three days, 21 - 23 January 1942, the Hungarians and their allies murdered 430 Serbs and 870 Jews. The operation was entrusted to the commander of the 5th Szegedin Army, General Ferenc Feketehalmy-Czeydner. The first day of the raid passed with only a few killings. On the second day the "examination committee" that had been detailed to select candidates for execution sent only a handful of individuals to their deaths. The leaders of the raid, General Feketehalmy-Czeydner and his adjutant Colonel Josef Grassy (CO: 13th Honved Infantry Division), were not satisfied with either the speed or the results of the operation. In order to provide an excuse for more drastic action, they arranged a simulated "fight" between the police forces and the "partisans" on the night of 22 January.

The following morning, with the temperature at 30 degrees below zero, Hungarian troops and police forces began hunting down the Serbian and Jewish residents of Novi Sad. The first mass execution occurred in Miletic Street : a group of 30 - 40 men, women, and children were ordered to lie down in the road and were then executed by rifle-fire. Simultaneously, another massacre was carried out at the intersection of Miletic and Grckoskolska streets. The executions at this intersection lasted from 9:30 am until 12:00 noon. Afterwards, a group of sixty individuals was murdered at the Beograd pier. The bodies were stripped naked, their gold teeth pulled out and valuables looted, and then they were pushed into the frozen Danube through a hole in the ice. Numerous killings also took place in the Uspenski Greek Orthodox cemetary, where 250 corpses were later found piled together. At the NAK football field, Hungarian soldiers stripped their victims and ordered them to run, falsely promising to save the lives of the fastest ones. All were mowed down by machine-gun fire. Most of Novi Sad's Jews were killed outside of the town at a popular bathing place known as The Strand. They were brought from the town by truck or driven there on foot from the various collection points in Novi Sad. At 4:00 pm, a Hungarian officer arrived at the Strand and ordered soldiers to halt the executions. This day-long killing frenzy was followed by uncontrolled ransacking and looting of the victim's houses. The numerous corpses lying about Novi Sad were searched both before and after execution: fingers were cut off to secure rings, ear-rings were torn from women's heads, and jaws broken up for the gold teeth they contained.

Following the operations at Novi Sad, a grateful Hungarian government conferred orders and medals on all those responsible for these massacres. Colonel Grassy, who had overseen the killings in Novi Sad for his superior General Feketehalmy-Czeydner, was personally promoted to the rank of Major-General by Admiral Miklos Horthy, the Hungarian Regent. The links to the Waffen-SS came several years later. General Feketehalmy-Czeydner saw active duty with the Waffen-SS from 1 July 1944 until the war's end under the name of SS-Obergruppenführer Franz Zeidner. Major-General Grassy saw active duty with the Waffen-SS and held the rank of Waffen-Generalleutnant der SS. At various times he served as the commanding officer of the 25. Waffen-Grenadier-Division der SS *Hunyadi* (ungarische Nr. 1) and 26. Waffen-Grenadier-Division der SS (ungarische Nr. 2). Both of these divisions contained personnel who participated in the Hungarian massacres at Novi Sad, Stari Becej, and Srbobran.

Source
(Löwenthal, 1957, pp. 27-30)

Oradour-sur-Glane (France)

Introduction

In April 1944 the remnants of 2. SS-Panzer-Division Das Reich (CO: SS-Brigadeführer Heinz Lammerding) was sent to the Montauban area in southwest France for refitting following heavy defensive engagements on the Eastern Front. The 2,500 survivors of Kampfgruppe Lammerding were bolstered by 9,000 recruits composed mostly of Hungarian, Rumanian, and Alsatian Volksdeutsche, as well as some redundant ground personnel from the Luftwaffe that were drafted piecemeal into the Waffen-SS. In the last weeks before the Anglo-American invasion of Europe on D-Day (6 June 1944), Das Reich was involved in a series of anti-partisan operations and made the price of resistance very clear to the surrounding countryside. Numerous small partisan actions resulted in reprisals against the innocent civilians of nearby communities.

At dawn on 8 June *Das Reich* moved out of the Montauban area and began its advance towards the Normandy beaches far to the north in order to counterattack the Anglo-American invasion force. The division's general line of advance to the beaches was: Montauban, Caussade, Cahors, Souillac/Argentat, Brive, Salon-la-Tour, Limoges, Poitiers, Saumur/Tours, Sable/Le Mans, Mayenne, Domfront, Mortain/Tinchebray, Villers Bocage/St. Lo/Coutances. Prior to the invasion, SHAEF called upon French resistance forces (Maquis) to fight the Germans and delay reinforcement of the Normandy theater as much as possible. As a result of Maquis ambushes in the Montauban area, *Das Reich* lost fifteen men killed and thirty wounded over the course of several days. The inevitable German reprisals followed each resistance attack; some reprisals were performed for no specific reason beyond terrorizing the civil population. One reprisal in particular would come to symbolize Waffen-SS barbarity : the massacre at Oradour-sur-Glane.

The Events

On 8 June, SS-Panzergrenadier-Regiment 4 *Der Führer* (CO: SS-Standartenführer Sylvester Stadler) arrived in the Limoges area after the long drive north from Montauban. At dusk on 9 June SS-Sturmbannführer Helmut Kämpfe, commander of the regiment's third battalion, drove off alone in his command car to scout the road ahead. He was captured at the tiny hamlet of La Bussiere in the commune of St. Leonard-de-Noblat by the Maquis. Elements of his battalion came by ten minutes later and found his car abandoned with the motor still running. The enraged Waffen-SS troopers began searching the village for him with the assistance of a number of local militiamen. Two innocent farmers, Pierre Mon Just and Pierre Malaguise, from La Bussiere were executed after an impromptu interrogation. The resistance forces, however, had already spirited off SS-Sturmbannführer Kämpfe to the neighboring commune of Chessioux. The men of the *Der Führer* regiment continued to search the Limousin area for their missing officer into the next day.

At 2:15 pm on 10 June, battalion commander SS-Sturmbannführer Adolf Diekmann and 3. Kompanie / 1. Bataillon / SS-Panzergrenadier-Regiment 4 *Der Führer* (CO: SS-Hauptsturmführer Otto Kahn) arrived at the village of Oradour-sur-Glane, near Limoges. The men of 3. Kompanie dismounted from their vehicles, fanned out, and began rounding up everyone they could find. The Waffen-SS troopers assured the villagers that they only wanted to perform a check of identity papers. By 2:45 pm all of the civilians were gathered in the Champ de Foire, with the men on one side, and the women and children on the other. At this point, small groups of Waffen-SS went around the town and shot the infirm in their beds where they lay. The mass of women and children were then moved into the village church. The men were herded by Waffen-SS troopers under the command of SS-Untersturmführer Heinz Barth into six sheds and informed that the town was to be searched for hidden weapons. A single gunshot was heard from the square: this was the signal for the massacre to begin. The Waffen-SS guards at the sheds gunned down the six groups of men; the sheds were then set on fire. Amazingly, a few lucky individuals were only wounded, played dead, and then escaped from the sheds under cover of all the smoke. Meanwhile in the church packed with over four hundred women and children, the Waffen-SS troopers brought in an incendiary charge, lit it, and then hastily retired. At the first sound of shooting from the other execution sites, they raked the church interior with grenades and small-arms fire. The incendiary charge went off and soon the church caught on fire. The Waffen-SS troopers added straw to the blaze and then retreated to a safe distance. Amidst all of the panic and confusion, a few of the women and children were only wounded and escaped unseen from the church. Eventually, the blazing church roof collapsed in on itself.

The Waffen-SS then looted and fired the entire village. More civilians, those who successfully hid and were missed in the initial roundup, were driven out of their refuges by the flames and shot dead by patrolling troopers. At 11:00 am the next day, SS-Sturmbannführer Diekmann's battalion departed from the smoking remains of Oradour-sur-Glane well-stocked with looted provisions and valuables. Left behind in the rubble were the bodies of 642 civlians (including 207 children). SS-Sturmbannführer Diekmann's regimental after-action report was brief and to the point:

I. Bataillon/SS 'DF' occupied Oradour on 10 June 1944 at 13:30 hours. After a search the town was fired. Munitions had been found in nearly every house. 548 enemy dead. Germans - 1 killed, 1 wounded.

[excerpts from "Tagesbericht des SS-Panzer-Grenadier-Regiment 4 'Der Führer' über die Zerstörung von Oradour, 1944" (dated 11 June 1944) reproduced in Schröder (1979)]

SS-Sturmbannführer Kämpfe was subsequently executed by his Maquis captors when they learned of the massacre at Oradour-sur-Glane. (Although some sources claim that he was shot while trying to escape, or that he was shot at a much later date. The German war graves maintenance association has registered Helmut Kämpfe's death as 10 June 1944).

Revisionist Variations

Despite the fact that the massacre at Oradour is one of the best documented atrocities committed by the Waffen-SS, apologists have offered up half-baked explanations in an attempt to restore Waffen-SS honor. As usual, their *modus operandi* is to simply ignore mountains of physical evidence and eyewitness testimony and to concoct a story that completely exculpates the Waffen-SS perpetrators of any guilt. Otto Weidinger, a former high-ranking officer of the *Das Reich* division

and a defendant at the post-war Oradour trial, has written the most widely circulated revisionist account of the massacre (Weidinger, 1984). It will be instructive to quote him at some length:

"Kämpfe had driven ahead of the route column because he wanted to thank the mayor of a town along the battalion's route for having restored a destroyed bridge on Kämpfe's instructions during the course of that day.... [Kämpfe disappears/the search begins] ....In the meantime the office of the Sicherheitsdienst in Limoges informed the regiment that, according to reports from its French agents, there was a command post of the Maquis in Oradour-sur-Glane.... In the early morning hours Kämpfe's identity papers had been found in the main thoroughfare in the centre of Limoges by a motor-cycle dispatch rider and handed in to the regiment. From this it could be deduced that Kämpfe had been driven through the town to another location during the night by the Maquisards.

During the morning the commander of I/DF, Sturmbannführer Diekmann, came to regimental headquarters and reported as follows: In St. Junien, his billeting area, two French civilians had come to him and reported that a high-ranking German officer was being held captive by the Maquisards in Oradour-sur-Glane. The officer was to be ceremoniously executed and burnt during the evening of that same day. The entire population of Oradour-sur-Glane was collaborating with the Maquisards. And in the village there were high-level Maquis staff.... Sturmbannführer Diekmann consequently asked permission of Standartenführer Stadler to be able to drive there straight away with a company and free Kämpfe, who was a personal friend of his.... Stadler thereupon gave Diekmann approval for his intended mission, although he stipulated that Diekmann should try, under all circumstances, to negotiate the release of Kämpfe and only occupy the village and free Kämpfe by force if negotiation failed. Should Kämpfe not be found, a large number of prisoners were to be taken -- leaders of the Maquis if possible -- so that another attempt at negotiating an exchange could be made afterwards....

In the late afternoon of 10 June, Sturmbann-nführer Diekmann returned to the regiment and reported as follows to the regimental commander: He had driven with the 3rd company to Oradour-sur-Glane. There the company had met with resistance. When the village was taken, Kämpfe was not to be found but he did find a number of murdered German soldiers. The population had taken part in the resistance. In the ensuing search of the houses a large number of weapons and quantities of ammunition were found. He had then had all male inhabitants of the village -- about 180 -- rounded up and shot. The houses in which the weapons and ammunition had been found were burned down. The flames had sprung over to the church, which was burnt out to the accompaniment of violent explosions. As later investigations showed, Diekmann said nothing of the deaths of women and children in his first report. He answered no when asked if he had brought back any captured Maquisards. Standartenführer Stadler was extremely shocked when he had heard the report... He was particularly angry at the fact that Diekmann, contrary to his orders, had not brought back any captured Maquisards or their leaders. Very much disgruntled he dismissed Diekmann, telling him to write a full and accurate report about the events in Oradour-sur-Glane.... As soon as the division's commander, Brigadeführer Lammerding, arrived, Stadler reported the incident in Oradour-sur-Glane and asked for a court-martial investigation of Diekmann's conduct. This was promised him as soon as the situation permitted.... An announcement by an enemy broadcaster was also picked up saying that Sturmbannführer Kämpfe had been shot as retribution for the destruction of Oradour. Much later, when the heavy defensive battles in Normandy were well under way, the division received an official complaint from the Prefect of Limoges via the commander-in-chief for France concerning the incident in Oradour-sur-Glane. The division and the regiment had to produce a statement. At this point, for the first time, French reports about Oradour became known, according to which the entire population of the village had been killed.

Immediately after the arrival of the division in Normandy an inquest was begun into the events of Oradour-sur-Glane. Diekmann, the company commander Kahn, the regimental adjutant, Hauptsturmführer Werner, and several Unterführer were heard by the division's disciplinary court.... Lammerding left details of the war-time inquest into Diekmann's actions, details known to the legal-aid office and thus to the Federal German government at the time of the Bordeaux trial : On the way into the village of Oradour-sur-Glane Diekmann had discovered, among other things, the remains of a German medical squad, who together with their wounded -- the driver and the person beside him were tied to the steering wheel -- had apparently been burnt alive. Proof of this was handed over to Lammerding after the war and also passed on to the legal-aid office. Quite apart from the women and children who died in the church, these new facts cast a different light on Diekmann's decision to burn the village to the ground and shoot the male inhabitants. The military inquest in Normandy could not be concluded because Diekmann fell during the first days of action and his battalion suffered losses of 70 to 80% in dead, missing, and wounded. The commander of the 3rd company, Hauptsturmführer Kahn, was further-more wounded (loss an arm) and was also no longer available for further investigations into the matter. The inquest was terminated and submitted to the commanding authorities as a closed file. The findings of the division's disciplinary court.... were lost in action....."

But Weidinger did not stop there. He also offered "proof" that not even the French inhabitants of the Oradour-sur-Glane area believed the Allied propaganda story of Waffen-SS atrocities:

"An affidavit by the retired lieutenant colonel in the Bundeswehr, Eberhard Matthes, who visited Oradour-sur-Glane twice after the war and reported as follows about what he experienced there.... the church had not been set fire to by the Germans in the first place. On the contrary,

SS soldiers had risked their own lives to save several women and children from the burning church. Two women in the group around me [French civilians] even said that they themselves had been rescued by German soldiers, otherwise they would not be standing there that day.... On 13 April 1981 retired lieutenant colonel Eberhard Matthes added to his sworn affidavit of 16 November 1980 by stating that in November 1963 the women who had claimed to have been rescued from the burning church by soldiers in German uniform had also told him, among other things, that the firing outside the church had not begun until the church interior had started to burn following an explosion.From this one can conclude that the explosion in the church may have been the real reason for the shooting of the male population. When elderly women in Oradour say such things to an officer of the German Bundeswehr, the whole Oradour complex appears in a new light. The responsibility for burning down the church with the women and children trapped inside it is thus removed from Diekmann's shoulders."

Weidinger then forged ahead to his conclusion, which was an indictment of war crimes trials in general and the Oradour case in particular:

"Shortly after the division continued its march towards the invasion front, Oradour took over the first place in the Allied war propaganda against Germany.... The defamation of the Waffen SS was pursued very zealously after the war, particularly in the case of Oradour, by much of the new German press, taken over by the mass media radio and television and continues to this day, despite all counter-presentations.... From its very beginnings the division placed considerable emphasis on the strictest discipline, and this could be ensured, if need be, by severe judgements on the part of the division's disciplinary court.

A third of 3rd company consisted of Alsatians who had been called up to the Waffen SS. And it was precisely the platoon with the Alsatians that was present at the church in Oradour.... Whilst on remand with the men of the 3rd company in Bordeaux, the author inquired of them to discover in what frame of mind Sturmbannführer Diekmann had been in when in Oradour-sur-Glane. They all said that he had walked up and down the street with an expression of cold and grim determination on his face -- apparently after talking to the mayor -- and that nobody could have dared to disobey him. The men were thus acting under absolutely binding orders, and this was not taken into consideration by the court either. War really can be cruel when it forces young and blameless men into such a corner, torn between the pressure of their conscience and the call for absolute obedience. None of them could ever have possibly met with such a situation in times of peace and in civilian life.... The "right of the victor" has meant that up to the present day no crime committed by the Maquisards, no matter how grave, has ever been judged before a court, whilst the whole guilt was placed upon the shoulders of the loser of the war, the German people, even though there can be no doubt that this fight was initiated by the Maquisards.... Why did the Maquisards blow up the explosives that they had stored in the church? One can only guess. Perhaps to prevent them falling into the hands of the Germans? Or to make the burning church a flaming beacon to signal a general revolt by the French against their German occupiers and to stir up hatred against the Germans?.... If France however, with the communist FTPF at the forefront, wanted to conduct its struggle for liberation in violation of bilateral and international agreements [i.e., the Franco-German armistice agreements of 1940], it had to expect and accept rigorous German reprisals.... Das Reich Division never dealt the first blow, its actions against the Maquisards were always mere reactions to the crimes committed against German soldiers and civilians by the Maquisards."

Weidinger's defense of the atrocities at Oradour-sur-Glane contains the hallmarks of revisionism favored by Waffen-SS apologists. The actual sequence of events related to the atrocity is discarded almost entirely and replaced by a completely fictitious scenario. Every critical aspect of Weidinger's account

--- that Oradour-sur-Glane was a center of Maquis activity, the entire account of his regiment's operations in the village, the alleged after-action investigations into Diekmann's operations, that a murdered German medical squad was found outside of the village, that the Maquis blew up the village church -- is a post-war invention. Weidinger would have us believe that the victims were not innocent civilians, but partisans. The women and children were not killed by the men of 3. Kompanie, but by their own countrymen in a cynical attempt to foment hatred against the Germans occupiers. The only individuals the Waffen-SS did kill were partisans anyway (the men) and they merited such a fate. Even if they didn't deserve such treatment, war is a nasty business full of crimes which are never legally investigated. Besides, don't we also have the sworn affidavit of a German officer stating that two French civilians told him that the historical version of the massacre was merely Allied war propaganda? Weidinger's revisionism would be laughable if not for the hundreds of innocents massacred at Oradour-sur-Glane.

Numerous Waffen-SS apologists have adopted Weidinger's account and repeated it for the benefit of their readers [for instance, Krätschmer (1982) and Woltersdorf (1989)]. Greil (1992) altered the account slightly by claiming that SS-Sturmbannführer Kämpfe was actually burned to death by the Maquis on 10 June 1944. Theile (1997) reached new depths of unsupported speculation when he implied that the reprisal occurred because the charred remains of SS-Sturmbannführer Kämpfe were found in an Oradour bakery oven when the village was searched by 3. Kompanie. The editors of a Waffen-SS tribute volume entitled Wenn alle Brüder schweigen noted that the atrocity was "a reaction to an attack carried out by the French resistance movement. In this case, however, a company leader of the Das Reich division committed an excess which obliges one to share in the grief and sympathy for the victims. Nonetheless, it should be remembered that Oradour involved one company, whereas the Das Reich division contained about seventy companies altogether." This particular rationalization would have us believe that: Yes, the atrocity was bad.... but the French civilians deserved it.... and besides, only a few Waffen-SS men were involved anyway. In trying to cover all objections at once, the apologist's argument collapses under the sheer weight of its own inherent self-contradictions.

Variant accounts of the massacre at Oradour-sur-Glane, not authored by germanophiles or Waffen-SS apologists, have also appeared in print. For reasons unknown, Stein (1966) has mistakenly attributed the massacre as a reprisal resulting from the killing of an SS officer by a French resistance sniper. Considering the extensive evidence that exists and notoriety of the Oradour case, it is distressing that an academic would make such an obvious mistake. More interesting is Robin Mackness' (1988) account that plays on the modern penchant for conspiracy theories. He claims that the Maquis ambushed a small German convoy near St. Junien on 9 June 1944. They killed the guards and made off with thirty boxes of gold bullion. The Waffen-SS raid on Oradour-sur-Glane the next day was an attempt to recover the bullion. Mackness claims that the gold was hidden in France until 1982, when a mystery man named "Raoul" tried to get him to transport it to Switzerland. Mackness' account ignores reams of evidence and is as devoid of proof as Weidinger's version, but serves the same purpose of blurring Waffen-SS responsibility for the unprovoked mass murder of civilians.

The Legal Proceedings

After the war, the operations of the 2. SS-Panzer-Division Das Reich during its march to the Normandy theater were thoroughly investigated by a French Military Tribunal sitting at Bordeaux. The Oradour-sur-Glane massacre trial began on 13 January 1953 with 64 members of 3. Kompanie / 1. Bataillon / SS-Panzergrenadier-Regiment 4 Der Fuhrer and the Das Reich command staff charged with complicity in the massacre. The majority of the responsible personnel were unavailable for trial since they had subsequently been killed in action during fighting in Normandy, the Ardennes, Hungary, and Austria. This included the former battalion commander in charge of the operations in Oradour, Adolf Diekmann, who died on 29 June 1944 near Noyers in Normandy. Otto Kahn was badly wounded in Normandy (losing an arm), bounced through a series of reservist positions, and then disappeared at war's end. It is believed that he lived and died in Sweden under an assumed identity with his family. Both Heinz Lammerding and Sylvester Stadler denied responsibility in the affair and successfully fought extradition to France. Lammerding died of cancer on 13 January 1971 at Bad Tölz, West Germany. Stadler, who enjoyed a good post-war reputation due to his kindly treatment of Allied POWs in Normandy, went on to a career in business management and died in Germany on 23 August 1995. In all, a total of 21 defendants were physically brought before the tribunal for trial. Since fourteen of the defendants were Alsatians, a formidable protest movement on their behalf quickly materialized in the French province of Alsace-Lorraine.

After reviewing the voluminous physical, documentary, and testimonial evidence offered by the prosecution, the French Military Tribunal found the defendants guilty as charged in the mass murder of 642 innocent civilians at the town of Oradour-sur-Glane. On 12 March 1953, the following sentences were handed down:

forty-four German defendants
were sentenced to death in absentia

one Alsatian defendant was sentenced to death

five German defendants were
sentenced to 8 - 12 years hard labor each

thirteen Alsatian defendants were
sentenced to 4 - 8 years hard labor each

one German defendant was acquitted of all charges

The response in Alsace-Lorraine was immediate: an unprecedented public furor erupted. One week after the verdicts were delivered, the French Assembly, fearful of serious political repurcussions if nothing was done to restore calm, pardoned all of the Alsatian defendents sentenced to hard labor. They were immediately released from custody. The two defendents awaiting execution had their sentences commuted to life imprisonment. The five Germans still in custody, however, were led away to begin their prison terms. Their sentences were reduced several times and all were paroled after serving only a few months in jail. The two defendants serving life sentences were even-

tually released in 1959. As is not unusual in French war crimes trials involving French perpetrators, the complete release of all court records concerning the massacre at Oradour-sur-Glane will not occur until the year 2039. Whether this is to protect the individuals involved or France's wounded pride at the prevalence of collaboration with her enemies is open for debate.

In a separate set of legal proceedings conducted by East German authorities in 1983, Heinz Barth was belatedly tried and sentenced to life imprisonment for his role in the massacre. In court he claimed that there were no Maquis weapons-caches in Oradour and that he did not know why the order had been given to kill everyone in the town. Barth was released from prison in 1997 due to ill-health and on the grounds that he was repentent. At the time of this writing, he still lives in Germany.

Aftermath

The atrocity at Oradour-sur-Glane and its subsequent trial is perhaps the best example of the inherent difficulty society's face in coming to terms with war crimes. The evidence against the defendants was both extensive and incontrovertible. Nonetheless the French Military Tribunal was quite lenient towards the defendants.... and even these verdicts were quickly undermined by public and political pressure. Most of the defendants were fellow Frenchmen (Alsatians) and there was an inherent discomfort in acknowledging their responsibility for such terrible crimes. The occupation by Germany had left skeletons in many French closets and most people felt that they were best left undisturbed.

One key question unanswered throughout the investigation and legal proceedings was: Why Oradour-sur-Glane? The official SS explanation, long since disproven, was that the village was a focus of resistance activities and that Helmut Kämpfe was being detained there. Unfortunately, there is no longer any prospect of discovering the definitive truth about Adolf Diekmann's motive in moving against Oradour-sur-Glane. All of the Waffen-SS personnel who could clarify the situation are either dead, have motives to lie, or are incommunicative. It seems quite likely that Diekmann singled out Oradour-sur-Glane on the basis of deceptive information from a malignant French source with

motives of its own. Perhaps when the full records of the Bordeaux Tribunal are opened in the year 2039 light will be shed on this missing piece of the puzzle.
 The French, for their part, lost little time in memorializing the massacre in a fashion most amenable to fostering a particular historical vision. As Farmer (1999) noted, "the complexity of the historical context... [has been]... pared away to produce a simple tale of French innocence violated by Nazi barbarism." On 10 May 1946 the National Assembly passed legislation designating Oradour a historical monument. It was quickly signed into law by the French President. With the ruins of Oradour expropriated by the state and slated for eternal preservation, construction work began in 1947 on a new adjoining replacement town. In the intervening years, the martyred village of Oradour has become *the* symbol of French suffering under the Nazi occupation. French preservation efforts have slowed, but not halted, the village's return to the elements. This slow decay and the eventual loss of the "war generation" spurred the 1997 construction of a permanent museum adjoining the ruins to forever preserve the memory of the massacre.

Sources

(Stein, 1966, pp. 276-277)
(Quarrie, 1986, p. 73)
(Reitlinger, 1957, pp. 170 & 400-401)
(Farmer, 1999, p. 29)
(Woltersdorf, 1989, p. 205)
(Greil, 1992, pp. 64-66)
(Mackness, 1988)
(Weidinger, 1984)
(Krätschmer, 1982, pp. 604-606 & 672)
(Hastings, 1981)
(Schröder, 1979, pp. 80-81)
(Pauchou, 1945)
(Bundesverband der ....., 1985, p. 33)
(Theile, 1997, pp. 419-429)
(Taege, 1981)
(Taege, 1985)

Osekovo (Yugoslavia)

During the Nuremberg Trials, the prosecution cited document D-578 (exhibit GB-553) --- a report by Colonel Pericic, commanding officer of the 1. Gebirgsjäger-Brigade, dated 26 September 1943, on the activities of the 7. SS-Freiwilligen-Gebirgs-Division Prinz Eugen (CO: SS-Brigadeführer Carl Ritter von Oberkamp) in the area of Popovaca, Bosnia : "On 16 September 1943 an SS unit of 80 men marched from Popovaca to Osekovo [seventeen kilometers east-northeast of Sisak, Croatia] for the compulsory purchase of cattle. I was not notified by anybody about the arrival of this unit in the technical operations area of the [1. Gebirgsjäger-Brigade] and about the activity of this unit in the area for which I alone am responsible. A short time after their arrival in Osekovo this unit was attacked by partisans. Under the pressure of the numerically superior partisans, this unit had to retreat in the direction of the railway station, which they succeeded in doing, but they had four men seriously and several lightly wounded, among them the unit commander. One man was missing, and they also lost an armored car. The unit commander then reported from Popovaca by telephone that when he had to retreat, he had killed all persons who were in the open because he had no chance to distinguish between the loyal population and the partisans. He himself said that he killed about 100 persons in this incident." Clearly, the unprovoked killing of civilians because they might be partisans is a war crime. Given the Waffen-SS tendency to explain away unprovoked massacres as legitimate anti-partisan actions, the killings at Osekovo may well have been the result of post-ambush retributions against an innocent civil populace once the partisans had disengaged (such as occurred at Dhistomon).

Source
(IMT, 1948/1971, vol. 20, p. 373)

Otok Cornji (Yugoslavia)

On the direct orders of Generalmajor Hubertus Lamey (CO: 118. Jäger-Division), a combat group under the command of SS-Sturmbannführer Bernhard Dietsche consisting of a battalion of the 7. SS-Freiwilligen-Gebirgs-Division Prinz Eugen (CO: SS-Brigadeführer Otto Kumm) and a battalion of the 369. Infanterie-

Division (CO: Generalleutnant Fritz Neidholdt) carried out a säuberungsaktion ("cleansing action") beginning on 27 March 1944 in the Sinj region (Croatia) in retaliation for the destruction of a German supply column. The following day this combat group overran the villages of Otok Cornji (24 km northeast of Split), Ruda (28 km east-northeast of Split), and Dolac Donji (17 km east of Split). In a single day they murdered 834 men, women and children. The mass executions were carried out in each village in the same manner: the inhabitants were gathered together and then killed with machine-gun fire and grenades. No one was spared, not even those who offered the troopers hospitality out of fear. They also robbed the bodies of their victims removing rings, watches, etc. The Germans then looted houses and businesses for anything of value before firing each town.

Sources
(Zöller & Leszczynski, 1965, p. 62)
(Kumm, 1978)
(IMT, 1948/1971, vol. 20, pp. 374-376)
(IMT, 1948/1971, vol. 36, pp. 70-72,
document D-945 [exhibit GB-554])

Ovrlje (Yugoslavia)

On 28 March 1944 elements of the 7. SS-Freiwilligen-Gebirgs-Division *Prinz Eugen* (CO: SS-Brigadeführer Otto Kumm) with the help of the 369. Infanterie Division (CO: Generalleutnant Fritz Neidholdt) fired the town of Ovrlje (eighty kilometers southwest of Travnik, Bosnia-Herzegovina) and shot 150 civilians as part of a larger *säuberungsaktion* ("cleansing action") in the region.

Sources
(Zöller & Leszczynski, 1965, p. 62)
(Kumm, 1978)

Owinsk (Poland)

In late October 1939, a unit of thirty men from SS-Totenkopfstandarte 12 (CO: SS-Obersturmbannführer Sacks) occupied the asylum at Owinsk (north of Poznan) and began the systematic liquidation of the psychiatric patients housed there. These murders were part of a larger operation aimed at freeing up German and Polish psychiatric institutions so that they could be coverted to military barracks and hospitals. The Waffen-SS troopers were soon aided in their killing operations by local ethnic German civilians. The first patients murdered were those diagnosed as criminally insane. They were bound, loaded into trucks, and driven off by rifle- and spade-bearing Waffen-SS guards. The trucks returned empty later that day; the guards' shovels were spotted with dirt and blood. It did not take long for the remaining inmates to realize what was happening to their fellow patients. Any resistance was forestalled through the use of sedatives. In less than one month the unit murdered all of the asylum's nine hundred patients. In August 1940, SS-Totenkopfstandarte 12 was incorporated into the 3. SS-Panzer-Division Totenkopf as replacements.

Sources
(Sydnor, 1977, p. 42)
(Burleigh, 1994, pp. 132-133)

Padule di Fucecchio (Italy)

Sometime after 12 August 1944 elements of SS-Panzeraufklärungs-Abteilung 16 / 16. SS-Panzergrenadier-Division Reichsführer-SS (abteilung CO: SS-Sturmbannführer Walter Reder) executed 120 residents of this northern Italian town in the vicinity of Bologna. This atrocity occurred during a large anti-partisan sweep that resulted in the deaths of many civilians. After the war, SS-Sturmbannführer Reder was tried before an Italian Military Tribunal for this and numerous other atrocities committed in the Bologna region. The court found him innocent of direct involvement in the massacre at Padule di Fucecchio. For a full accounting of SS-Sturmbannführer Reder's operations in northern Italy and his subsequent post-war trial, see the entry for Monte Sol.

Source
(Bender & Taylor, 1969-1982, vol. 4, p. 114)

Palmiry Forest (Poland)

Beginning in November 1939, 1700 Polish civilians were executed in the Palmiry Forest (30 km northwest of Warsaw) by elements of Einsatzgruppe IV (CO: SS-Brigadeführer Lothar Beutel). Most of the executions took place in the Kampinowskie woods outside the village of Palmiry at the site of a Polish artillery dump that had been dismantled by the Germans. Execution pits were dug on site prior to the killings. The victims, primarily Polish intellectuals and civic leaders, were brought by truck from Pawiak prison in Warsaw. Upon arrival, they were blindfolded and then machine-gunned to death. During post-war excavations conducted by the Polish Red Cross and the Main Commission for the Investigation of Nazi Crimes in Poland, 800 bodies were recovered. One of the largest killing operations took place on 20-21 June 1940 as a part of Aktion AB: 358 civilians were executed.

Sources
(Krausnick, 1981, p. 95)
(Gumkowski & Leszczynski, 1961, p. 112)

Pancevo (Yugoslavia)

At the Nuremberg Trials of Major German War Criminals the prosecution cited document D-944 (exhibit GB-566), a statement from the Yugoslav War Crimes Commission taken from a member of the Waffen-SS named Leander Holtzer: "The shootings in Pancevo [Serbia (APV)] were carried out by the police agent Gross, former master dyer, and Brunn, a former master miller from the SS Division Prinz Eugen [7. SS-Freiwilligen-Gebirgs-Division Prinz Eugen], from Pancevo. The latter received a reward of 20,000 dinars for the hangings at the cemetary." The victims of this action were civilian hostages. Photographs of the executions are on file at the Bildarchiv Pruessischer Kulturbesitz (Berlin). No further information regarding these atrocities has been forthcoming.

Sources
(IMT, 1948/1971, vol 20, p. 398)
(USHMM, Genocide in Yugoslavia....)

Pinsk (USSR)

When the German Wehrmacht captured the Soviet city of Pinsk on 4 July 1941, the Jewish population is estimated to have exceeded 30,000 individuals. On 9 July elements of Waffen-SS Bataillon zbV (CO: SS-Sturmbannführer Friedrich Dern) arrived in Pinsk and began anti-Jewish operations at the direction of SS-Oberführer Dr. Eberhardt Schöngarth. An unknown number of civilians were killed.

From 4 - 15 August 1941, elements of the Reitenden Abteilung / SS-Kavallerie-Regiment 2 (CO: SS-Sturmbannführer Franz Magill conducted numerous operations in and around Pinsk whose sole aim was the extermination of the Jewish population.

On 4 August the commander of 1. Schwadron / Reitenden Abteilung, SS-Hauptsturmführer Stephan Charwat, issued an order for all Jewish men between the ages of 16 - 50 years to report to the Güterbahnhof the next morning for three days of work detail. Many Jews showed up "willingly;" others were rounded up at gunpoint by members of 1. Schwadron with the assistance of local Ukrainian militia. The approximately 2,000 Jews were then marched one hour outside of Pinsk to woods near the village of Possienicze. Once in the woods they were relieved of their overcoats and shoes. The Jews were then taken in small groups to previously dug mass graves where they were systematically gunned down. The following day (6 August) another 100 Jews were marched out of Pinsk to cover the mass graves with soil. Once their job was done, they too were murdered by soldiers from 1. Schwadron.

On 5 August elements of 2. Schwadron (CO: SS-Hauptsturmführer Walter Dunsch) entered Janow and rounded up 120 Jews into the town marketplace. They were then marched about 1,000 meters outside of town where they were shot and quickly covered with dirt. The unit then continued its advance along the line Luniniec - Baranowicze and executed another 100 Jews from 6 - 16 August.

On 7 August elements of 1. Schwadron and 4. Schwadron / Reitenden Abteilung (CO: SS-Obersturmführer Kurt Wegener) along with local Ukrainian militia rounded up another 1,000 Jews in Pinsk for a "work detail" and took them on a one-way trip to the surrounding forests. On 9 August, the two squadrons were ordered to suspend their killing operations in Pinsk and to resume combing the region surrounding the city for more Jews. From 9 - 14 August, advancing along the line Luniniec - Bostyn, 1. Schwadron executed another 100 Jewish civilians. At the same time, 4. Schwadron advanced along the line Luniniec - Mokroc killing some 200 Jews in the process.

On 10 August elements of 3. Schwadron (CO: SS-Hauptsturmführer Hans-Viktor von Zastrow) entered Davidgrodek and, with the help of local Ukrainian militia, rounded up 300 Jewish men. The victims were marched off to firing squads and hastily dug graves nearby. The next day the town's Jewish women and children met a similar fate at the hands of the Ukrainian militia. On 15 August elements of 3. Schwadron executed approximately 30 Jews in two separate unnamed villages.

As of 20 August the various elements of the Reitenden Abteilung under SS-Sturmbannführer Magill had murdered 4,500 Jews in the Pinsk area (Ereignismeldung UdSSR Nr. 58 in *Arad et.al., 1989*). On 3 September elements of 3. Schwadron shot an unspecified number of Jews at Mosyr. The remainder of Pinsk's Jews, primarily women and children, would survive for more than a year. On 29 October 1942, the 20,000 surviving Jews of Pinsk were murdered by 2 companies of Ordnungspolizei, aided by an unidentified SS-Kavallerie detachment which guarded the execution site and shot escapees.

Little justice would be dealt out to the murderers of the Pinsk Jewish community. Stephan Charwat and Hans-Viktor von Zastrow did not survive the war. Friedrich Dern's fate is unknown. Eberhardt Schöngarth was executed by British authorities on 15 May 1946 for crimes he committed as BdS Haag [Holland]. In 1963 Franz Magill, Kurt Wegener, Walter Dunsch, and Hans-Walter Nenntwich (a former member of 2. Schwadron) were taken into custody by West German authorities. They were tried together before the Landgericht Braunschweig; Franz Magill was charged with the deaths of over 5,300 civilians. Most of the defendants adopted the usual defense of "following orders" and claimed that they were fighting partisans, not killing civilians. Hans-Walter Nenntwich had the most interesting defense in that he claimed to have killed only a few Jews and to have actively saved at least one (an attractive, elegantly dressed blonde-haired Jewish woman). On 20 April 1964 the court sentenced Magill and Wegener to 5 years' imprisonment each, Dunsch to 4 years 6 months imprisonment, and Nenntwich to four years' imprisonment. The sentences of Dunsch, Wegener, and Nenntwich were later (17 November 1964) overturned on technicalities by the 5. Strafsenat des Bundesgerichtshofs.

Sources
(Büchler, 1986, pp. 16-17)
(Reitlinger, 1961, p. 226)
(Yerger, 1996, pp. 90-91)
(Arad et al., 1989)
(NMT, 1949-1953, case IX, transcript 724
[Evidence, Ohlendorf])
(Rüter-Ehlermann et al., 1968-1981,
Band 20, Lfd. Nr. 570, pp. 23-105)

Podvolochisk (USSR)

At the Nuremberg Trials of Major German War Criminals the prosecution cited document D-955 (exhibit GB-565), the affidavit of the merchant Mojzesz Goldberg: "On 23 June 1941, I was called up into the Soviet Army in Lemberg [Lvov]. In the middle of July, I was taken prisoner by the Germans. At a locality 5 kilometers from Podwoloczysk the SS companies sought the Jews out of the whole mass of prisoners and shot them on the spot. I remained alive as they did not recognize me as a Jew. I stress the fact that it was the Waffen-SS who did this." The identity of the Waffen-SS unit responsible for this atrocity is unknown.

Source
(IMT, 1948/1971, vol 20, p. 388)

Poland

Generalmajor Herbert Loch, commander of 17. Infanterie-Division during the 1939 invasion of Poland, was disparaging of Waffen-SS battlefield performance and complained about the Leibstandarte's (1. SS-Panzer-Division Leibstandarte Adolf Hitler) wild firing and tendency to automatically fire villages as they passed through them. From all accounts, "trigger happiness" was a marked characteristic of many Waffen-SS formations during the first two years of the war. The decidedly unprofessional and murderous behavior of the SS-Totenkopf units, particularly during and after the Polish campaign, provoked an attitude of disgust among numerous senior officers in the Wehrmacht.

Sources
(Messenger, 1988, p. 74)
(Sydnor, 1977, p. 42) (Madeja, 1985)

Poland -- Miscellaneous Atrocities

The following crimes are taken from extensive tables given in Datner et al. (1962). The abbreviations used to identify the perpetrators are as follows: SS (Schutzstaffel), G (Geheime Staatspolizei), W (Wehrmacht), P (Polizei), Selbst (Volksdeutsche Selbstschutz) and RAD (Reichsarbeitdienst). In all likelihood, the crimes occurring in 1939-1940 were committed primarily by Einsatzgruppen and/or Totenkopfstandarten personnel. Both of these groups later became part of the Waffen-SS.

Date	Locality	# of Victims	Perpetrators
	(Danzig-Westpreussen Province / Starogard District)		
9/2 - 12/1/40	Starogard	190	SS, Gest, Selbst
9/39 - 5/40	Szpegawsk	7000 from Tczew & Starogard	SS, Selbst
10/39?	Skorcz, Zajaczek Forest	100 from Skorcz area	SS, Selbst
1/20-25/45	Starogard military grounds	150	SS, Gest
1/45	Lubichowo	19 (17 women)	SS
2/45	Skorcz	70 Jewish women ditchdiggers	SS
	(Danzig-Westpreussen Province / Koscierzyna District)		
10/39	Skarszewy	357	SS, Gest, Selbst
10/39	Jaroszewy	53	SS, Selbst
10/39	Nowy Wiec	43	SS, Selbst
	(Danzig-Westpreussen Province / Tczew District)		
9/39 - 1/23/40	Tczew	40	SS
	(Danzig-Westpreussen Province / Chojnice District)		
9-10/39	Chojnice	208 mental patients	SS, G, W,Selbst
9/39 - 1/40	Chojnice	1030 (includes 200 prisoners from Kamien Pomorski prison)	SS, G, W,Selbst
1/45	Chojnice	1600 (Bydgoszcz, Grudziadz, Warsaw)	SS, G, W
2/5/45	Lesno	200 Jews	SS, G
	(Danzig-Westpreussen Province / Tuchola District)		
11/2-10/39	Tuchola	140	SS, Selbst
11/1/40	Bralewnica	11	SS, G
2/45	Sliwice	100 Jews from Grudziadz	SS
	(Danzig-Westpreussen Province / Swiecie District)		
1/39 - 1/40	Luszkowko	3000 (includes mental patients Selbst,	SSfrom Swiecie)
10/15 - 12/40	Grupa drilling ground	6500 (from Grudziadz area)	SS, RAD,Selbst
	Danzig-Westpreussen Province / Grudziadz District)		
10/39	Bialochowo	135	Selbst, SS
	(Danzig-Westpreussen Province / Sepolno District)		
9/20 - 11/15/39	Karolewo	8000 (Bydgoszcz, Sepolno, etc.)	W, Selbst, SS
1/26/45	Wiecbork	19 children	SS
	(Danzig-Westpreussen Province / Wyrzysk District)		
10-11/39	Sadki & Lelazne	86 (Anielin, Debianka, etc.)	Selbst, SS
	(Danzig-Westpreussen Province / Bydgoszcz District)		
9/39	Bydgoszcz	28	G, SS, Pol
11/13/39	Bydgoszcz	100	G, SS
	(Danzig-Westpreussen Province / Wabrzezno District)		
11-12/39	Lopatki sand pit	2000 (district residents)	SS, G

Date	Locality	# of Victims	Perpetrators
	(Danzig-Westpreussen / Brodnica District)		
9/21/39	Buk-Goralski	12	SS, Selbst
1/28/45	Malki	75 Jewish women	SS
	(- / Szubin District)		
9/5 - 10/30/39	Kcynia	35	SS, locals
	(- / Torun District)		
10/11/41	Olek	18	SS
	(- / Rypin District)		
10/11-13/39	Rusinowo	150	SS, G, Pol,Selbst
10/39	Rypin	1084	SS, Pol, Selbst
	(- / Inowroclaw District)		
10/39	Zajeziorze	63	SS, G, Pol
11/39	Zajezierze-Swietokrzyz	450 (from Inowroclaw Prison)	SS, G, Pol
	(- / Wejherowo District)		
11-12/39	Piasnica	at least several thousand	SS, G, Selbst
	(Wartheland Province / Lodz Voivodship / Leczyca District)		
9/9/39	Kowalewice	21 (Kowalewice, Ozorkow)	SS
	(- / - / Lodz District)		
9/14/39	Aleksandrow	20	SS
3/20/42	Zgierz	100	W, SS
	(- / - / Brzeziny District)		
9/8-14/39	Biesiekierz area	50	SS
	(- / - / Sieradz District)		
6-9/44	Zdunska Wola	200	SS, Pol
	(Wartheland Province / Poznan Voivodship / Oborniki District)		
Autumn 1939	Roznowo Mlyn	3000	SS, G
	(- / - / Nowy Tomysl District)		
10/40	Bolewice	100 (Buk, Grodzisk, Lwowek, etc.)	G, SS
	(- / - / Poznan District)		
12/39	Dabrowka	70	G, SS
1939-40	Debienko forest	334 (Poznan; 114 women)	G, SS
1/6/40	Dabrowka	1200 (Poznan)	G, SS
1-3/40	Wypalanki	350 (Poznan, Koscian)	G, SS
4/24 - 5/25/40	Wypalanki	100	G, SS
7/16-27/40	Wypalanki	150 (Poznan, Koscian)	G, SS
8/40	Wypalanki	20 (Poznan, Koscian)	G, SS
?	Dabrowka	1225	G, SS
1945	Debienko forest	1260 (Poznan)	G, SS
	(- / - / Gniezno District)		
9/9-10/39	Klecko	300 (Klecko, Gniezno, Chodziez)	W, SS
	(- / - / Srem District)		
10/20/39	Ksiaza	17 (Dolsko, Ksiaza)	SS
10/20/39	Srem	19	SS

Date	Locality	# of Victims	Perpetrators
	(- / - / Konin District)		
11/10-11/39	Konin Jewish Cemetary	200	SS, Pol
Autumn 1939	Konin	100	SS, Pol
	(- / - / Kolo District)		
3/40	Koscielec	30	G, SS
	(- / - / Turek District)		
10-11/40	Turek sandpit	20	SS, G
	(- / - / Leszno District)		
10/21/39	Leszno	20	SS, G, Pol
	(- / - / Krotoszyn District)		
9/15/39	Rozopole	18	SS
	(- / - / Pleszew District)		
11/41	Jedlec	100	SS
	(- / - / Kalisz District)		
1/19/45	Skarszew	55 (from area prisons)	G, SS, Pol
	(- / - / Kepno District)		
9/1-2/39	Wyszanow	59 (Wyszanow, Torzeniec)	W, SS
	(Regierungsbezirk Kattowitz / Katowice Voivodship / Zawiercie District)		
9/4/39	Siewierz	10	SS
	(- / - / Katowice District)		
9/39	Panewnik	20 (Katowice)	SS
	(Regierungsbezirk Ziehenau / Warsaw Voivodship / Dzialdowo District)		
10/39 - 44	Dzialdowo	1000	SS, G
2/40 - 9/44	Komorniki	12,000	SS, G, Pol,Selbst
4/40 - ?	Bialuty	15,000	SS, G
5/40	Bursz	48 (Dzialdowo)	W, SS
12/18/44	Rumoka	21 SS	
	(- / - / Ciechanow District)		
2/5/40 - ?	Oscislowo	1700 (disabled from district)	SS, G
2/5/40 - 45	Oscislowo	300	SS, G
	(- / - / Makow Mazowiecki District)		
2/12/40	Sewerynowo	500	G, SS
	(- / - / Pultusk District)		
?	Pultusk Poplawy forest	120 (Jablonna, Legionowo)	SS

Polish Corridor (Poland)

On 3 July 1939 SS-Wachsturmbann Eimann (CO: SS-Sturmbannführer Kurt Eimann), consisting of 400 effectives and motor transport, was organized at Danzig for special duties including the protection of Danzig during the German campaign against Poland.

Among its first operations was the mass execution of the Polish postmen who had defended the Danzig main post office during the German invasion. After 13 September 1939 the unit operated as a part of Einsatzgruppe IV (CO: SS-Brigadeführer Lothar Beutel) in the area between Karthaus and Neustadt in the Polish Corridor and carried out an undetermined number of massacres of Polish Jews. In October 1939, SS-Wachsturmbann Eimann was split up. Approximately half of its personnel were detailed to concentration camp guard duties at Neufahrwasser, Stutthof, and Grenzdorf while the remainder carried out numerous extermination actions against Polish psychiatric patients (see Szpegawsk). In January 1940, the unit was disbanded and its personnel distributed to various SS-Totenkopfverbände serving as replacement/training elements for the Totenkopf Division (3. SS-Panzer-Division Totenkopf).

Sources
(Sydnor, 1977, p. 41)
(Burleigh, 1994, pp. 130-132)

Prague (Czechoslovakia)

On 5 May 1945 Czech partisans in Prague began an armed uprising to coincide with the arrival of Soviet forces near the city's outskirts. Waffen-SS units throughout the city went on a rampage. They rooted out thousands of civilians from their homes and shot them in the street. Some bodies even bore evidence of torture and mutilation. The Waffen-SS also used civilians as hostage-shields when moving through the city to engage partisan and Soviet forces. Although a definitive identification is lacking, the perpetrators of these atrocities were most likely from SS-Wach-Bataillon 2 Prag, SS-Wach-Bataillon Böhmen-Mähren, and/or the Waffen-SS Troop Supply Depot in the city. The presence of any other Waffen-SS units in Prague at this time has yet to be confirmed.

Source
(IMT, 1948/1971, vol. 36, pp. 86-93, document D-959 [exhibit GB-571])

Pripet Marshes (USSR)

Following their invasion of the Soviet Union on 22 June 1941, it became clear to the Germans that significant problems were developing in their rear-areas. Numerous Soviet units were bypassed by the swiftly advancing German lead elements and needed to be neutralized. Additionally, the first stirrings of an underground partisan movement against the invaders were being felt. Always lurking amidst these valid security concerns was the specter of Nazi racial ideology and its concomitant extermination programs. Among the second-line German units assigned to such "pacification" operations were SS-Kavallerie-Regiment 1 (CO: SS-Standartenführer Hermann Fegelein) and SS-Kavallerie-Regiment 2 (CO: SS-Standartenführer Heino Hierthes), as well as two semi-autonomous advance units: Vorausabteilung SS-Kavallerie-Regiment 1 (CO: SS-Hauptsturmführer Christian Reinhardt) and Vorausabteilung SS-Kavallerie-Regiment 2 (CO: SS-Sturmbannführer Albert Fassbender).

One of this cavalry group's earliest operations was Einsatz Pripjet Sümpfe carried out in the Pripet Marshes of western Russia from 28 July - 31 August 1941 at the direction of Reichsführer-SS Heinrich Himmler. The goal of the operation was ostensibly to clear out elements of the Soviet 36th and 37th Cavalry Divisions and 121st Rifle Division that had broken through German lines on 25 - 27 July 1941 and taken refuge in the swamps. In his official directive for the operation RFSS Himmler was quite clear on how the civil populace of the region was to be treated:

> 2. If the population serves as the enemy of Germany, is racially or humanly inferior, or indeed, as it often is in the marsh areas, made up of fleeing criminals, then all people that are suspected of helping the partisans are to be shot, while females and children are to be evacuated and cattle and food are to be apprehended and secured. These villages are then to be burned to the ground.

3. Either the villages and settlments are a network of strongpoints, whose residents kill partisans and pillagers and inform us of them, or they cease to exist. No enemy will be allowed to find support, food, or shelter in these areas.

[Kommandosonderbefehl - Richtlinien für die Durchkämmung und Durchstreifen von Sumpfgebieten durch Reitereinheiten, dated 28 July 1941; cited in Rüter-Ehlermann et. al., p. 43]

The operation took place in two distinct phases (29 July - 13 August; 15 August - 30 August). That this "cleansing action" was little more than a glorified murder campaign can be seen from the SS-Kavallerie after-action reports of 13 August and 16 September 1941. For further operational details on Einsatz Pripjet Sümpfe see the entries for *Pinsk* and *SS-Kavallerie-Brigade Operations and Atrocities in the USSR*. At the cost of 17 dead and 76 wounded, the units posted the following impressive figures:

Partisans killed	1,001
Red Army soldiers killed	699
Prisoners taken	830
Plunderers killed	14, 178

(SS-Kav-Brigade 1 an den HSSPf beim Befehlshaber des rückwartigen Heeresgebietes Mitte, 16.9.1941, Central State Archives CSSR 147)

"Plunderers," of course, was yet another euphemism for Jewish civilians. In an effort to conserve ammunition, on 1 August Himmler had ordered the brigade to drown women and children in the swamp. However, in his report dated 12 August 1941 SS-Sturmbannführer Magill stated that: "Driving women and children into the swamp was not successful, because the swamp was not so deep that sinking under could occur. After a depth of one meter, for the most part one hit firm ground, so that sinking under was not possible (Bericht über den Verlauf der Pripjet-Aktion vom 27.7 - 11.8.1941 in Baade)." They had to be shot after all.

These wildly disparate casualty figures, as well as the recovery of proportionately little military material, belie the after-action reports of SS-Kavallerie command-ers claiming that their opponents were well-equipped and fought fiercely in well-prepared defensive positions. When these SS-Kavallerie units did finally face such opponents during front-line deployments (December 1941 - Summer 1942), they were bled-white by staggering losses. Franz Magill and other personnel were tried for some of these killings after the war (see *Pinsk*).

The unit, now bearing its final divisional designation (8. SS-Kavallerie-Division *Florian Geyer*), also participated in the Operation Hornung anti-partisan sweep of the Pripet Marsh region from 8 - 26 February 1943. The after-action report of the KdS Belorussiya reveals Hornung to have been another extermination campaign disguised as a military operation.

The final results of the operation were:
Losses of the enemy:
    2,219 dead
    7,378 received special treatment
    65 prisoners
    3,300 Jews

Our own losses:
2/27 German dead/non-German dead
12/26 German wounded/non-German wounded

Booty in weapons:	172 rifles
	14 pistols
	2 heavy machineguns
	6 light machineguns
	5 machine pistols
	1 gun

The exact nature and extent of *Florian Geyer*'s contribution to this operation have yet to be clarified. The division also took part in extensive "cleansing actions" in the Pripet Marshes in the spring, summer, autumn of 1943 that claimed the lives of over 15,000 Soviet partisans and resulted, as usual, in the indiscriminate murder of an undetermined number of Soviet civilians. Interestingly, at this time SS-Oberführer Heinz Lammerding was chief of staff to SS-Obergruppenführer Erich von dem Bach-Zelewski (Chief of Anti-partisan Forces). In this capacity, SS-Oberführer Lammerding planned and helped conduct many of the "cleansing actions" of 1943.

He later commanded the 2. SS-Panzer-Division *Das Reich* at the time of its Tulle and Oradour sur Glane atrocities.

Sources

(Stein, 1966, p. 275)
(Krausnick, 1981, p. 222)
(Browning, 1992a, p. 107)
(Birn, 1986, p. 171)
(Cooper, 1979, p. 87)
(Sydnor, 1977, p. 316)
(Baade et al., 1965, pp. 208-228)
(Yerger, 1996, pp. 97-110)
(Schröder, 1979, p. 82)
(Rüter-Ehlermann et al., 1968-1981, Band 20, Lfd. Nr. 570, pp. 23-105)

Pristina (Yugoslavia)

In April 1944, the 21. Waffen-Grenadier-Division der SS Skanderbeg [albanische nr. 1] (CO: SS-Brigadeführer Josef Fitzhum) arrested 300 Jews in Pristina (Kosovo Province), Yugoslavia. They were later deported to concentration camps.

Source

(Militärbefehlshaber Südost - Chief of Staff von Geitner to Army Group F; 16.4.44; Nuremberg Documents Collection NOKW-668, International Law Library, Columbia University, New York City)

Putten (Netherlands)

On the night of 30 September 1944, two weeks after the Allied Market Garden airborne offensive, Dutch partisans ambushed a vehicle carrying four officers of the Fallschirm-Panzer-Ersatz und-Ausbildungs-Brigade 4. This training and replacement element of the Luftwaffe's 1. Fallschirm-Panzer Division Hermann Göring was stationed at Harderwijk, near Putten. The attack did not go off as planned. One of the officers was wounded and taken prisoner. Another badly wounded officer escaped to a nearby farm; he died in a hospital the next day. In all the confusion, the remaining two officers escaped and returned to their unit. Upon hearing of the ambush, their commander, Oberst Fritz W.H. Fullriede, ordered his brigade to cordon off Putten and find their captured comrade. Early the next morning the Luftwaffe troops began searching Putten and detaining its citizens. Eight inhabitants who tried to flee were shot out of hand. The Wehrmacht Chief of Staff for the Netherlands, Generalleutnant Heinz Helmuth von Wühlisch, ordered additional elements of the brigade stationed in Utrecht and Amersfoort to proceed to Putten and support operations there. Generalleutnant von Wühlisch also instructed Oberst Fullriede to arrest the entire town's population. With the assistance of Dutch Police officers, the Germans meticulously searched the town and its outskirts building by building. Women and children were locked in the Dutch Reformed Old Church. The men were gathered together in the school on the market square. Oberst Fullriede declared that if the captive officer was released within 24 hours, no further actions would be taken. Even though he was quickly released by the partisans, repressive actions were instituted anyway.

Following deliberations among General der Flieger Friedrich Christian Christiansen (Befehlshaber der Wehrmacht, Nederland), SS-Obergruppenführer Hans Albin Rauter (HSSPf Nederland) and other high-ranking German representatives, Oberst Fullriede was ordered to deport the male population of the town between the ages of 18 and 50. The women and children were to be evacuated and the entire town fired, excluding the homes of German sympathizers. The next day, October 1st, the women and children were released on the condition that they return the following morning with food and clothing for the captive men. The men were then marched to the church and held there at gunpoint overnight. The next morning, the women returned with the supplies as promised. The 660 men were handed over to elements of SS-Wach-Bataillon *Nordwest* (CO: ?) and taken by train to a detention camp near Amersfoort. Along the way 12 escaped their SS guards. Over the course of the next week an additional 49 men were released from detention for various reasons. The remaining inhabitants of Putten -- women, children, and men over the age of 50 -- were declared "refugees" and driven from the town by Oberst Fullriede's troops. The town was fired that night and when the "refugees" returned a few days later over one hundred houses had been destroyed. Nine days later the remaining 589 Putten men taken captive were sent by train from Amersfoort to KL Neuengamme near Hamburg. Only 49 survived the camp's appalling conditions and returned to the Netherlands after the war. Five died soon thereafter as a result of their ordeal in the concentration camp. In total, 548 innocent civilians had been killed, 300 women widowed, and 750 children orphaned.

Later in October 1944, the personnel of SS-Wach-Bataillon *Nordwest* were incorporated into the 34. SS-Panzergrenadier-Division *Landstorm Nederland*, as SS-Panzerjäger-Abteilung 60. They spent the remainder of 1944 into early 1945 engaged in anti-partisan and security operations in the Netherlands. In 1946 Heinz von Wühlisch committed suicide in a Dutch prison while awaiting trial. Friedrich Christiansen and Fritz W.H. Fullriede were tried by the Dutch in 1948. Christiansen was sentenced to 12 years' imprisonment with credit for time served. He was granted clemency and released three years later due to his advanced age (72) and failing health. Fullriede was sentenced to 2 1/2 years' imprisonment on account of his purported reluctance in carrying out his superior's orders. He had not burned down the entire town as ordered and had dealt more leniently with the women and children than instructed. After release from prison, Fullriede emigrated to South Africa.

Several accounts have mistakenly identified the 1. Fallschirm-Panzer Division *Hermann Göring* as a Waffen-SS unit. This is probably attributable to the similarity in uniforms worn (identical army pattern field uniforms, camouflage jackets, tunic cuffbands with divisional names) and the fact that a Waffen-SS unit did take part in the operations at Putten.

Sources
(Sauer, 1977, p. 26)
(Komitee der....., 1960, p. 555)
(de Keizer, 1996)
(IMT, 1948/1971, Documents F-719 and RF-409)
(Groen & van Maanen, 1977)
(Angolia & Schlicht, 1997, vol. 2, pp. 248-285)
(Madeja, 1992, pp. 180-183)

Radom (Poland)

For the time period of Autumn 1939 through Summer 1940 security in the region between Warsaw and Radom was the responsibility of SS-Totenkopfstandarte 11 (CO: SS-Obersturmbannführer Prof. Karl Diebitsch). The unit's performance was characterized by numerous unwarranted executions of civilians, public drunkeness, and the looting of private residences. On 23 November 1940 the unit was incorporated as replacements into the 2. SS-Panzer-Division Das Reich.

Source
(Sydnor, 1977, p. 43)

Radom 2 (Poland)

At the Nuremberg Trials of Major German Criminals the prosecution cited document D-955 (exhibit GB-565), the affidavit of the merchant Mojzesz Goldberg:

After my captivity [as a Soviet POW in German hands, he was not recognized as a Jew] was ended, I lived in Radom and worked from June 1942 to July 1944 for the Waffen-SS at 3 places: the SS Veterinary Reinforcement Detachment, Koscinski Street; the Garrison Administration of the Waffen-SS, Planty 11; and the Building Directorate of the Waffen-SS, Slowacki Street 27. As I worked so long for the SS, I know the names and faces of all of the officers and NCOs of the above-named detachments of the Waffen-SS very well. At the head of the SS Veterinary Reinforcement Detachment [SS-Veterinär-Ersatz-Abteilung] were SS-Sturmbannführer Dr. [Heinrich] Held and SS-Hauptsturmführer [Dr. Richard] Schreiner; at the head of the Garrison Administration there was SS-Obersturmführer Grabau and at the head of the Building Directorate, SS-Oberscharführer Seiler. All the persons mentioned took a direct part, together with their companies, in carrying out the expulsions in Radom on 5, 16, and 17 August 1942, during which some thousands of people were shot on the spot. I know that the SS Veterinary Reinforcement companies went to the provincial towns to carry out the 'expulsions' of Jews. I heard individual soldiers boasting about the number of Jews they had killed. I know from their own stories that these same companies participated in the actions against Polish partisans and also set the surrounding Polish villages on fire.

It was not unusual for rear-area Waffen-SS and Polizei support units to be called upon for what were euphemistically described as "security operations" such as these events at Radom.

Source
(IMT, 1948/1971, vol. 36, pp. 84-85)

Radomyshl' (USSR)

"Following an urgent call for help from the local commander of Radomyshl, a sub-unit [of Einsatzgruppe C] and part of a Waffen-SS platoon moved in and immediately found unbearable conditions. The newly established mayor was unmasked as an informer for the NKVD and CP member since 1925. It was proven that until recently he had contact with Communist bands. His deputy was a Bolshevik as well. Furthermore, a citizen was discovered who caused the deportation of Ethnic Germans and Ukrainian families. Finally, also Jews were arrested who openly opposed the German Military, refusing to work for the OT, *etc.* In the course of these actions, nine out of 113 persons arrested were shot."

The Waffen-SS platoon involved was in all likelihood from the 1. SS-Infanterie-Brigade (CO: SS-Brigadeführer Richard Hermann) which was conducting security operations in the area at the time. It is possible that the platoon came from either the 1. SS-Panzer-Division *Leibstandarte Adolf Hitler* (CO: SS-Obergruppenführer Josef Dietrich) or the 5. SS-Panzer-Division *Wiking* (CO: SS-Gruppenführer Felix Steiner) which were also in the general vicinity. In any event, this incident again demonstrates the linkage between the Waffen-SS and the murderous Einsatzgruppe which has been consistently denied by apologists.

Source
(Ereignismeldung UdSSR Nr. 58 / dated: Berlin, 20 August 1941 in Arad et al., 1989, p. 96)

Rawa Mazowiecka (Poland)

The torture and mass execution of an undetermined number of Jews, political and religious leaders, and Polish POWs occurred on 15 September 1939 (and possibly other dates) at the Polish town of Rawa Mazowiecka, east of Lodz in central Poland. Photos of the victims can be found in Poznanski. These atrocities were committed by either SS-Totenkopfstandarte I *Oberbayern* (CO: SS-Sturmbannführer Max Simon) or SS-Totenkopfstandarte III *Thüringen* (CO: ?), both of which were detailed to "cleansing and security" measures in the operational zone of the 10th Army as part of Einsatzgruppe II (CO: SS-Obersturmbannführer Dr. Emanuel Schäfer). They were the only Waffen-SS formations operating in the area during the month of September that had the size, firepower, and mobility to conduct such large-scale massacres. On 1 November 1940, both units were designated as cadre for the newly activated SS-Totenkopfdivision (forerunner of the 3. SS-Panzer-Division *Totenkopf*).

Sources
(Sydnor, 1977, p. 41)
(Poznanski, 1963)

Razori (Yugoslavia)

At the Nuremberg Trials of Major German War Criminals the prosecution cited photograph #47 and document D-944 (exhibit GB-566: The Report of the Yugoslav War Crimes Commission)..... "On 9 June 1944 and on the following days the SS troops from Trieste committed atrocities and crimes against the Slovene population in the Slovene coastal area, as we have already stated above.... On that day Hitler's criminals captured two soldiers of the Yugoslav Liberation Army and the Slovene partisan battalions. They brought them to Razori [near Dobrana, 35 km southeast of Ljubljana (Slovenia)], where they mutilated their faces with bayonets, put out their eyes, and then asked them if they could see comrade Tito now. Thereupon they called the peasants together and beheaded the two victims before Sedej's house. They then placed the heads on a table. Later, after a battle, the photographs were found on a fallen German. From this it can be seen that they confirm the above-described incident, namely the crime of bloodthirsty German executioners at

Razori." The unit blamed for this atrocity was the 7. SS-Freiwilligen-Gebirgs-Division *Prinz Eugen* (CO: SS-Brigadeführer Otto Kumm).

Source
(IMT, 1948/1971, vol. 20, p. 403)

Ripac (Yugoslavia)

At the Nuremberg Trials of Major German War Criminals the prosecution cited document USSR-133, a letter of information from the German High Command to the Italian High Command describing activities of the 7. SS-Freiwilligen-Gebirgs-Division Prinz Eugen (CO: SS-Obergruppenführer Artur Phleps) during the 20 January - 15 March 1943 Unternehmen Weiss I/II operations against Tito's partisans in western Bosnia: "The western group of the SS division is near Ripac [7 kilometers southeast of Bihac, Bosnia-Herzegovina] in front of barricades, which are being removed.... As a result of the successful engagement, 23 dead and 34 wounded and more than 100 enemy dead have been counted, 47 prisoners shot, and 363 provisionally apprehended."

Prinz Eugen's Kampfgruppe West (CO: SS-Obersturmbannführer August Schmidhuber) was composed primarily of the II. and III. Bataillon of SS-Gebirgsjäger-Regiment 2 and bolstered by miscellaneous regimental support elements. The Kampfgruppe moved through the Ripac area on 30/31 January 1943. Exactly what was meant by *provisionally apprehended* is unclear. Given the track record of German euphemisms for killing, these individuals may have met the same fate as the 47 unarmed prisoners that the Waffen-SS troopers murdered on the spot.

Sources
(IMT, 1948/1971, vol. 20, pp. 403-404)
(Kumm, 1978)

Rostov-na-Donu (USSR)

It has been claimed that after the first battle for Rostov on the Don River in November 1941, elements of the 1. SS-Panzer-Division Leibstandarte Adolf Hitler (CO: SS-Obergruppenführer Josef Dietrich) executed surrendering Soviet garrison forces since in SS-Obergruppenführer Dietrich's view "it was a waste of time observing the usual formalities when to do so would have held up the action; dealing with prisoners is always a waste of time unless you can squeeze some useful information out of them." Since the source making this accusation is littered with numerous egregious errors of fact, this particular atrocity claim should be treated as an unsubstantiated rumor.

Source
(Wykes, 1974)

Rozan (Poland)

On 9 September 1939 an SS-Sturmmann of the SS-Artillerie-Regiment (attached to Panzer-Division Kempf operating as part of the German Third Army) and a Wehrmacht Geheime Feldpolizei Stabsfeldwebel herded 50 Jews of a forced labor detail performing bridge repair on the river Narew into a synagogue in Rozan (north-northeast of Warsaw) and shot them. The men were arrested, court-martialed, and on 13 September 1939 found guilty of manslaughter by a three-man court comprised of a Wehrmacht judge and two SS jurors. The SS-Sturmmann was sentenced to 3 years imprisonment and the GFP-Stabsfeldwebel received a sentence of nine years hard labor. The prosecutor, however, wanted the death penalty for both men and appealed the sentences to Berlin. Upon review, a senior Wehrmacht judge upheld the sentence for the SS-Sturmmann on the grounds that "he was in a state of irritation as a result of the many atrocities committed by the Poles against ethnic Germans. As an SS man he was also particularly sensitive to the sight of Jews and the hostile attitude of Jewry to Germans; and thus acted quite unpremeditatively in a spirit of youthful enthusiasm." In the case of the GFP-Stabsfeldwebel, the sentence was reduced to 3 years hard labor. Before either man spent a day in prison however, their sentences were set aside by Field Marshal von Brauchitsch and then dropped altogether under the provisions of a general amnesty.

Sources

(Krausnick and Wilhelm, 1981, p. 81)

(Stein, 1966, p. 271)

(Reitlinger, 1957, p. 125)

(de Zayas, 1990, p. 141)

(Diary of Chief of the General Staff Halder, 10.9.39, Nuremberg Documents Collection NOKW-3140, International Law Library, Columbia University, New York City)

(Oberkriegsgerichtsrat 3. Armee to Oberstkriegsgerichtsrat Generalquartiermeister, 14.9.39,

in: IMT, 1948/1971, vol. 20, Nuremberg Document D-421)

Ruzyn (Czechoslovakia)

On 28 October 1939, the people of Prague demonstrated their loyalty to the Republic by observing the day as national holiday just as had been done for the previous 20 years. The German authorities used force to suppress the demonstrations. Among those arrested was a young medical student attending Charles University who later died of wounds received at the hands of the Gestapo. The University students were prohibited by the German authorities from attending the youth's funeral on 15 November, but they gathered in front of the church anyway. Afterwards the crowd of students marched on the Old Town Square where they had a bloody confrontation with German police. On the following day, Reich Protector Constantin von Neurath and State Secretary Karl-Hermann Frank travelled to Berlin and were met by an infuriated Führer. On Hitler's command, strong SA and SS motorised regiments were immediately dispatched to Prague to quell the rebellious Czechs. On the night of 16 November German military forces assaulted the student's dormitory at Charles University seizing students in their nightclothes. Numerous students were killed outright; a dozen others were brutally beaten and then transported to the Air Force barracks at Ruzyn, east of Prague. There, they were subjected to torture and the next morning (17 November) executed by firing squads from the 6. SS-Totenkopfstandarte (CO: SS-Oberführer Bernhard Voss). In the summer of 1940, this unit was incorporated into SS-Kampfgruppe Nord (later the 6. SS-Gebirgs-Division Nord).

Bernhard Voss, held in American custody after the war, was interrogated by Colonel Dr. B. Ecer on 21 June 1945 at Wiesbaden regarding the murder of the Czech students. Voss was remanded to Czech custody and returned to Prague. There he was tried and executed.

Sources

(Czechoslovak Republic, 1945, pp. 468-469)

(Theile, 1997, p. 152)

(IMT, 1948/1971, vol. 36, pp. 86-93, document D-959 [exhibit GB-571])

St. Germain-du-Belair (France)

During the Nuremberg Trial of Major German War Criminals, the accusation was made that SS-Panzergrenadier-Regiment 3 Deutschland / 2. SS-Panzer-Division Das Reich burned the town of St. Germain-du-Belair (Department of Lot, 30 kilometers southeast of Sarlat) in June 1944. No evidence was offered to support this charge. Das Reich was deployed to the fighting in Normandy at this time. The divisional commander was SS-Brigadeführer Heinz Lammerding; the CO of SS-Panzergrenadier-Regiment Deutschland was SS-Sturmbannführer Gunther-Eberhardt Wisliceny. If this atrocity did occur, it would most likely have been committed by stragglers during the unit's march up from Montauban in southwestern France, shortly after 6 June 1944.

Source
(IMT, 1948/1971, vol. 20, p. 396)

Sajmiste Camp, Belgrade

(Yugoslavia)

At the end of February 1942, the Germans informed the women internees of Sajmiste Camp that the camp was to be gradually evacuated and invited them to apply voluntarily. Volunteers were transported in a large enclosed car (with a capacity of about 100 people), in which they were suffocated with carbon monoxide gas. The last such transport left Sajmiste Camp on 10 May 1942. Of approximately 8,000 prisoners only six women remained alive. In December 1946 the Military Tribunal of the Belgrade Garrison investigated the whereabouts of these thousands of women and children. Former SS-Obersturmbannführer Ludwig Teichmann (SD Serbien and a staff member of Einsatzgruppe Serbien) stated "that a special command from Berlin had liquidated the remaining Jews in the Sajmiste camp by means of poison cars" and estimated their number at about 7,000. This is supported by telegram No. 3113 (dated 9 June 1942) from SS-Oberführer Emanuel Schäfer (KdS Belgrade) to the RSHA Hauptamt (Berlin) stating that the "SS drivers Götz and Mayer had accomplished their special mission, so that the said persons and the cars mentioned above may be returned." Additional details are being sought to determine what if any Waffen-SS personnel took part in these actions.

Source
(Löwenthal, 1957, p. 5)

Sancaku (Yugoslavia)

In Fall 1942 the 7. SS-Freiwilligen-Gebirgs-Division Prinz Eugen (CO: SS-Obergruppenführer Artur Phleps) began a series of anti-partisan actions against Chetnik forces in Serbia that included the mass killings of innocent civilians. In his divisional orders dated 5 October, SS-Obergruppenführer Phleps stressed to his officers that "…. the entire population of this area must be considered rebel sympathizers." A number of these "cleansing actions" took place in the Zapadne Morave river valley (running from Cacak - Kraljevo - Krusevac), especially in around the town of Sancaku from middle to late October.

Sources
(Glisich, 1970, pp. 128-131)
(Kumm, 1978)

Sant'Anna di Stazzema (Italy)

On 12 August 1944 this town (Lucca province, Tuscany) was burned to the ground and 540 residents were killed by elements of SS-Panzeraufklärungs-Abtei-lung 16 / 16. SS-Panzergrenadier-Division Reichsführer-SS (abteilung CO: SS-Sturmbannführer Walter Reder). Approximately 80% of those killed were women, children and the elderly. An estimated 400 Waffen-SS troopers entered Sant'Anna di Stazzema shooting villagers down in groups and killing many others by tossing handgrenades in their homes. More than 130 villagers were shot to death en masse while kneeling in prayer with their priest before the doors to the town church. Waffen-SS troopers then burned the bodies using petrol and wooden pews looted from the church. An additional 150 residents of the neighboring villages of Vaccareccia, Mulino Rosso, Valdicastello and Capezzano di Pietrasanta were also murdered at various times throughout the day.

After the war, SS-Sturmbannführer Reder was tried before an Italian Military Tribunal for this and numerous other atrocities committed in the Bologna area. He was acquitted of direct involvement in the crimes at Sant'Anna di Stazzema. For a full accounting of SS-Sturmbannführer Reder's operations in northern Italy and his subsequent post-war trial see the entry for
Monte Sol.

In 2002 German officials pursued inquiries into the massacre, but no charges were filed despite several years of work. After a year of its own proceedings, an Italian military court sitting at La Spezia in June 2005 found ten former Reichsführer-SS unit members guilty of war crimes and sentenced them in absentia to life imprisonment. Immediately following the Italian verdicts, German officials announced that they were reopening investigations involving 14 former unit members.

Sources
(Bender & Taylor, 1969-1982, vol. 4, p. 114)
(Schreiber, 1996)
("10 former SS soldiers get life sentences in Italy", Deutsche Presse-Agentur, 23 June 2005)
("German authorities reopen Nazi war crimes case", Deutsche Presse-Agentur, 24 June 2005)
("Späte Sühne für SS-Massaker", Neue Zürcher Zeitung, 23 June 2005)
("Gedenken an SS-Massaker in der Toskana", Die Presse, 12 August 2004)

Sava River / Brcko (Yugoslavia)

It has been alleged that during the course of Unternehmen Vollmond, an anti-partisan operation lasting from 7 April - 15 June 1944 in northeastern Bosnia, elements of 13. Waffen-Gebirgs-Division der SS Handschar [kroatisches Nr. 1] (CO: SS-Brigadeführer Karl-Gustav Sauberzweig) murdered approximately 500 partisan POWs in a forest north of the Sava River, as well as another 40 partisan POWs in the town of Brcko. One author has even identified specific victims (see Peric, below).

Sources
(Lepre, 1997, pp. 213-223)
(J.J. Peric, "13. SS 'Handzar' divizija i njen slom u istocna Bosni", Istocna Bosna u NOB-u 1941-45, vol. 2, p. 587)

2. SS-Infanterie (mot.)-Brigade Operations and Atrocities in the USSR

All entries are from the *Kriegstagebuch Kommandostab RF-SS* reproduced in Baade (1965), unless otherwise noted. Operations are sometimes cited for specific brigade sub-units: SS-Infanterie-Regiments 4, 5, and 14 (SS-I.R. 4,5, 14). It should be pointed out that the designations "security operation" and "cleansing operation" were often euphemisms for a killing action; any such designation should be considered suspect. The commanding officers of the brigade at this time were: SS-Brigadeführer Kurt Knoblauch (12/40 - 4/41), SS-Brigadeführer Karl von Treuenfeld (4/41 - 7/5/41), and SS-Brigadeführer Göttfried Klingemann (7/5/41 - 1/26/43).

6/20/41   As of 6/21/41, 2. SS-Infanterie-Brigade (mot.) is under Kdo.Stb. RF-SS control.
6/24/41   SS-I.R. 4 conducted a cleansing operation along the Lazdijai-Seirijai road.
7/4/41   One battalion of SS-I.R. 4 deployed to Minsk, Baranowice and Vilna to assist elements of Einsatzgruppe A in anti-Jewish operations [Zentrale Stelle CSSR II, Band 3, Bild 95].

8/30/41   2. SS-Infanterie-Brigade subordinated to HSSPf Nord [Prützmann] and marched to Mitau.
9/9/41   Elements SS-I.R. 4 conducted road security operations in the Rozhdestvenskiy region.

9/16/41   2. SS-Infanterie-Brigade conducted road secrity in the Wyriza region.
9/24/41   2. SS-Inf-Brigade conducted a cleansing operation along the Novgorod-Imla-Medes road.
9/25/41   2. SS-Inf-Brigade conducted security operations along the Novgorod-Petersburg road.
9/26/41   2. SS-Infanterie-Brigade conducted security operations along the Livenskaya-Tosno road.
9/27/41   SS-I.R. 4 conducted security operations south of the Kalja-Tosno road.
9/29/41   2. SS-Infanterie-Brigade conducted security operations south of Tosno. 74 partisans were executed.
10/1-6/41 2. SS-Infanterie-Brigade conducted anti-partisan operations in the Lyuban' area.

Siatista (Greece)

At an unspecified date in 1944, an unknown number of female hostages were shot at the town of Siatista (north-central Greece) during a reprisal operation by members of 7. Regiment / 4. SS-Polizei-Panzergrenadier-Division on the orders of the regimental commander, SS-Standartenführer Karl Schümers. SS-Standartenführer Schümers was later killed in action in northern Greece on 16 August 1944.

Source
(Mazower, 1993, p. 211)

Sinj (Yugoslavia)

At the Nuremberg Trials of Major German War Criminals, the prosecution cited document USSR-513, a Waffen-SS proclamation : "On 3 November 1943, around 2000 hours, a German soldier on the Velika Street in Sinj [Croatia] was ambushed and killed. Since, despite all efforts, the culprit has not been found and the populace has not supported us in this matter, 24 civilians will be shot and one hanged. The sentence will be carried out on 5 November 1943 at 0530 hours." -- Signed -- "Breimaier, SS-Sturmbannführer and Battalion Commander." The officer issuing this reprisal measure was SS-Sturmbannführer Wilhelm Breimaier (CO; II. Bataillon / 13. Regiment / 7. SS-Freiwilligen-Gebirgs-Division Prinz Eugen). Under questioning during the Nuremberg Trials, former SS-Obergruppenführer Paul Hausser stated that these killings were illegal, unless a court-martial was held beforehand. The history of German occupation policy leaves little doubt that these reprisals were carried out without benefit of any legal inquiries.

Source
(IMT, 1948/1971, vol. 20, pp. 402-403)

Sladovil (Yugoslavia)

On 28 March 1944 elements of the 7. SS-Freiwilligen-Gebirgs-Division Prinz Eugen (CO: SS-Brigadeführer Otto Kumm) with the help of 369. Infanterie-Division (CO: Generalleutnant Fritz Neidholdt) fired the town of Sladovil and shot 7 civilians as part of a larger "cleansing action" in the region.

Sources
(Zöller & Leszczynski, 1965, p. 62)
(Kumm, 1978)

Slovak National Uprising (Czechoslovakia)

As the military situation continued to deteriorate for the Germans on the Eastern Front, their formerly enthusiastic eastern European allies could clearly see the writing on the wall. Faced with an impending Soviet invasion, Slovak politicians and elements of the Slovak Army planned a revolt against the pro-German government of President Joseph Tiso at Neusohl in the Carpathians. On 23 August 1944, members of the Cabinet under Defense Minister General Catlos and backed by a group of the Army under General Golian seized power and declared an armistice with the Soviets.

Two Soviet airborne brigades were flown in and dropped behind the German lines to reinforce the rebel government. The situation was critical for the Germans: the retreat route of the hardpressed German 8th Army in Galicia was now blocked off and another disastrous encirclement appeared in the making. SS-Obergruppenführer Gottlob Berger, from the SS-Hauptamt, was made C-in-C Slovakia in late August. However, it was soon apparent that he was not cut out for the job. Two weeks later he was replaced by SS-Obergruppenführer Hermann Höfle who was given the title HSSPf Slovakia. Under SS-Obergruppenführer Höfle, the Germans regained the initiative from the faltering rebel government. The immediate need for a strong offensive force was met by forming an ad hoc armored regiment designated SS-Panzergrenadier-Regiment Schill (CO: SS-Obersturmbannführer Klotz) from a Waffen SS school and a training/replacement battalion in neighboring Böhmen-Mähren (staff and cadets from the SS-Panzergrenadier-Schule Kienschlag and SS-Panzergrenadier-Ausbildungs-und Ersatz-Bataillon 10 in Brünn). Other Waffen-SS units that could be spared were rushed to Slovakia including: elements of 14. Waffen-Grenadier-Division der SS (ukrainische Nr. 1) were deployed (III. Bataillon/Waffen-Grenadier-Regiment der SS 29; a light infantry gun platoon; and an anti-tank gun section) as SS-Kampfgruppe Beyersdorff under the command of SS-Obersturmbannführer Friedrich Beyersdorff; elements of 18 SS-Freiwilligen-Panzergrenadier-Division Horst Wessel (CO: SS-Brigadeführer August-Wilhelm Trabandt); and SS-Sturmbrigade Dirlewanger (CO: SS-Oberführer Dr. Oskar Dirlewanger).

As SS-Panzergrenadier-Regiment Schill advanced on the rebel government stronghold at Neusohl, the remaining units moved into Slovakia from the east. The Slovak rebels, poorly equipped and organized, were no match for the German units arrayed against them. In the course of its operations, SS-Kampfgruppe Beyersdorff murdered several thousand innocent civilians in the Puchorem/Strba region. By the end of October Slovakia was pacified and its leaders had been spirited off by Reichsführer-SS Himmler's Sicherheitsdienst to an unsavory fate in the concentration camp system. An integral part of the German's pacification activities were the anti-Jewish operations of Einsatzgruppe H (EGr 8) under the command of SS-Obersturmbannführer Dr. Josef Witiska. From September - October, Einsatzgruppe H rounded up 13-14,000 Jews with the assistance of the Waffen-SS units in Slovakia. Their fates were as follows:

7,936 deported to KL Auschwitz (few survivors)
4,370 deported to KL Sachsenhausen & KL Theresienstadt (few surviviors) remainder shot during operations in Slovakia

Sources
(Höhne, 1971, p. 616)
(Bender & Taylor, 1969-1982, vol. 4, pp. 38-40)
(Korman, 1990, pp. 67-71)
(Yad Vashem, Testimony of Dr. Bedrich Steiner, Eichmann Trial Transcript, May 24, 1961, session 50, pp. W1, X1)

Smilici (Yugoslavia)

On 28 March 1944 elements of the 7. SS-Freiwilligen-Gebirgs-Division Prinz Eugen (CO: SS-Brigadeführer Otto Kumm) with the help of 369. Infanterie-Division (CO: Generalleutnant Fritz Neidholdt) fired the town of Smilici and shot 5 civilians as part of a larger "cleansing action" in the region.

Sources
(Zöller & Leszczynski, 1965, p. 62)
(Kumm, 1978)

Soltysy-Zabuce (Poland)

On 13 May 1944, elements of the galizisches SS-Freiwilligen-Regiment 5 (CO: ?) carried out operations in Soltysy and Zabuce on the eastern side of the Bug River (23 kilometers south of Wlodawa). They captured six bandits and killed 35 bandits and "bandit helpers" who fled or tried to resist. They then fired the towns and destroyed 80% of the houses. Sixteen houses supposedly exploded due to stored munitions. This regiment

was formed in May 1943 with excess volunteers from the 14. Waffen-Grenadier-Division der SS (ukrainische Nr. 1) and performed extensive security duties in Poland.

Source
(U.S. Holocaust Memorial Museum, Der SS und Polizeiführer im Distrikt Lublin, HSSPf Ost Führungsstab Ia - Tgb. Nr. 572/44g, dated 16 May 1944, Lublin)

Sosnowiec (Poland)

From 1-8 August 1943, personnel (at times totalling as many as 690 effectives) from the Polizei-Reitschule Bendsburg, 1. Polizei-Kompanie Sosnowitz, Ausbildungs-Kompanie Maczki, and supporting units from Gleiwitz and Kattowitz performed a "Jewish action" in the Sosnowiec area of Upper Silesia (east of Kattowitz). Hilberg has identified the Polizei-Reitschule Bendsburg as a Waffen-SS cavalry school, but this is an inaccurate statement. While the German Schutzpolizei was considered part of the overall SS organization, Schupo units were not a part of the Waffen-SS. In some instances Schupo personnel were transferred wholesale into the Waffen-SS as replacements or as the cadre of newly-forming units, but this only serves to reinforce the technical distinction between the two organizations.

Sources
(Hilberg, 1985, vol. 2, pp. 485-486)
(Polizeipräsident Sosnowitz to Regierungspräsident Kattowitz; 1.8.43 in: Centralna Zydowska..., 1946, vol. 2, p. 60)
(Polizeipräsident Sosnowitz to Regierungspräsident Kattowitz; 4.8.43 in: ibid, vol. 2, p. 63)
(Polizeipräsident Sosnowitz to Regierungspräsident Kattowitz; 7.8.43 in: ibid, vol. 2, p. 67)
(IdO Schlesien in Breslau to Polizeipräsident Sosnowitz; 25.8.43 in: ibid, vol. 2, p. 70)
(Polizeipräsident Sosnowitz to IdO Breslau; 14.8.43 in: ibid, vol. 2, p. 71)

Split - Sinj region (Yugoslavia)

It has been alleged that in March 1944 elements of the 7. SS-Freiwilligen-Gebirgs-Division Prinz Eugen (commander SS-Brigadeführer Otto Kumm) massacred approximately 400 Croatian women and children in the Split-Sinj region. According to a statement of the Yugoslav State Commission on War Crimes (document USSR-520), the SS unit followed up this massacre with similar operations against the villages of Srijane (12 km east-southeast of Split), Bisko (30 km northeast of Split), Gornji Dolac (30 km northeast of Split), and Putisic (18 km east of Split). German sources have denied that any of these events ever occurred. There is also no evidence to date that any elements of Prinz Eugen were deployed in the areas stated at the times specified.

Sources
(Vukcevich, 1990, p. 354)
(IMT, 1948/1971, vol. 20, pp. 400-401)
(Kumm, 1978)

SS-Kavallerie Operations and Atrocities in Poland

In the second week of September 1939 the SS-Totenkopf-Reiterstandarte was authorized and began formation in Berlin. The unit consisted primarily of Waffen-SS recruits, along with some cadres of Schutzpolizei and Allgemeine-SS cavalry personnel. The unit consisted of 4 squadrons and had the following command structure:

CO SS-Totenkopf-Reiterstandarte :
SS-Standartenführer Hermann Fegelein
CO 1. Schwadron : SS-Sturmbannführer Franz Magill
CO 2. Schwadron : SS-Obersturmführer
                   Herbert Schönfeldt
CO 3. Schwadron : SS-Sturmbannführer Rudolf Ruge
CO 4. Schwadron : SS-Hauptsturmführer Rolf Becher
  On the orders of Reichsführer-SS Heinrich Himmler, the unit was subordinated to HSSPf Ost and deployed at the end of September to perform security and pacification operations in Occupied Poland. In large measure, many of these operations were thinly disguised extermination, looting, and forced resettlement operations directed at Poland's civil populace --- especially its Jewish communities.

9/27 - 11/39---
   This initial period of deployment was characterized by the 1. Schwadron and 4.Schwadron conducting search and seizure operations in Lodz, Zgierz, Kaly, Andere jow, Orla, Grodnici, Krasnodeby, Bzura, Ruta Alexandrow, Jastrzebia, Bruzyczka, Piaskowice,Sobien, Zgierz, Mileszki, Brzeziny, Lucmierz, Wiskitno, Ruda, Dabrowa, Krosniewice,Strykow,and Rydzyny. The remaining two squadrons were employed constructing barracks for the unit.

10/6/39---
   4. Schwadron carries out a "special assignment" in Kutno.

10/12/39---
   4. Schwadron "pacifies" the prisoners at Zgierz Prison.

11/39 - 4/40---
   The unit was expanded and reorganized into twelve dispersed squadrons concen trated in central and eastern Poland as follows:

Warsaw :
Stab (CO: SS-Standartenführer Hermann Fegelein)
Medical (CO: SS-Untersturmführer Dr. Karl Reinsch)
1. Schwadron
 (CO: SS-Hauptsturmführer Waldemar Fegelein)
9. Schwadron
(CO: SS-Hauptsturmführer Rolf Becher)
[note: this squadron was later moved to Lodz]
Garwolin :
2. Schwadron
(CO: SS-Sturmbannführer Rudolf Ruge)
Seroczyn :
3. Schwadron
(CO: SS-Hauptsturmführer Gustav Lombard)
Zamosc :
4. Schwadron (CO: SS-Sturmbannführer Josef Fritz)
Chelm :
5. Schwadron
(CO: SS-Hauptsturmführer Wilhelm Reichenwallner)

Tarnov :

6. Schwadron

(CO: SS-HauptsturmführerHans-Viktor von Zastrow)

Krakau :

7. Schwadron

(CO: SS-Hauptsturmführer Herbert Schönfeldt)

12. Schwadron

(CO: SS-Hauptsturmführer Arno Paul)

Kielce :

8. Schwadron

(CO: SS-Hauptsturmführer Walter Dunsch)

Kamiena :

10. Schwadron

(CO: SS-Obersturmführer Franz Rinner)

Lublin :

11. Schwadron

(CO: SS-Sturmbannführer Franz Magill)

11/39--- 1. Schwadron carries out an unspecified number of executions.

12/39--- 5. Schwadron ordered to transport 1,000 prisoners from Chelm to Sokal. During the march, 440 prisoners were "shot to death while trying to escape."

1/13/40--- 5.Schwadron with the assistance of Feld polizei executes 560 prisoners in the forest near Ruda.

3/30/40--- During an anti-partisan operation in the forests near Kamiena, the 1, 2, 3, 7, 8, 9, 10, and 12 Schwadronen with the aid of Polizei-Bataillon 51 round up and execute the entire male population of the area. Women and children are sent to work camps.

4/40--- The unit is expanded and reorganized:

1. SS-Totenkopf-Reiterstandarte

(CO: SS-Standartenführer Hermann Fegelein)

Seroczyn: 1. Schwadron (former 3rd)

Kielce: 2. Schwadron (former 8th)

Krakau: 3. Schwadron (former 7th) and 6. Schwadron (former 12th)

Tarnov: 4. Schwadron (former 6th)

Warsaw: 5. Schwadron (former 1st)

2. SS-Totenkopf-Reiterstandarte

(CO: SS-Sturmbannführer Franz Magill)

Garwolin: 1. Schwadron (former 2nd)

Chelm: 2. Schwadron (former 5th)

Zamosc: 3. Schwadron (former 4th)

Kamienna: 5. Schwadron (former 10th)

Lublin: 6. Schwadron (former 11th)

5/40--- Units are deployed to threaten and motivate local farming communities into cooperating with the Occupying Government's resettlement and agricultural plans.

8/40--- In retaliation for alleged malingering of the general populace, elements of 1. and 2. SS-Totenkopf-Reiterstandarte round up all Jewish males and 1,500 Poles in Krakau and deport them to labor camps.

8/30/40--- 1. Schwadron / 1. SS-Totenkopf-Reiterstandarte executes 87 Polish civilians in Warsaw.

9/19-20/40--- Elements of 1. SS-Totenkopf-Reiterstandarte execute 200 civilians at Warsaw and deport 1,600 to labor camps. Additionally, 700 Jews are rounded up at Otwock and deported to labor camps.

11/40 - 3/41--- This period saw little field activity by the SS cavalry. For further information see *SS-Kavallerie-Brigade Operations and Atrocities in the USSR* and *8. SS-Kavallerie-Division Florian Geyer*.

Source
(Yerger, 1996)

SS-Kavallerie-Regiment/Brigade Operations and Atrocities in the USSR

All of the following material related to specific operations is from the *Kriegstagebuch Kommandostab RF-SS* (reproduced in Baade, 1965) unless otherwise noted. Operations are sometimes cited for specific brigade sub-units: SS-Kavallerie-Regiments 1 and 2 (SS-Kav.-Regt. 1 or 2). It should be pointed out that the designation "security operation" was often used as a euphemism for exterminations; any such designation should be considered suspect. At the start of the German invasion of the USSR, the

Waffen-SS cavalry units had not been officially brigaded together despite operating in unison. Their command structure at the start of the invasion was as follows:
CO SS-Kavallerie-Regiment 1:
SS-Standartenführer Hermann Fegelein
CO Reitende Abteilung:
SS-Hauptsturmführer Gustav Lombard
CO SS-Kavallerie-Regiment 2:
SS-Standartenführer Heino Hierthes
CO Reitende Abteilung:
SS-Hauptsturmführer Herbert Schönfeldt
SS-Sturmbannführer Franz Magill (as of 7/30/41)

The regiments were primarily detailed to anti-partisan and extermination operations behind the front-lines. For details on the formation and history of these units see *SS-Totenkopf-Kavallerie Operations and Atrocities in Poland*.

6/21/41--- SS-Kav.-Regt. 1 and SS-Kav.-Regt. 2 subordinated to Kommandostab RF-SS.

7/19/41--- SS-Kav.-Regts. 1 and 2 detailed to Baranovichi. Conducted cleansing operation in Grodno-Nyshin-Sluch'-Bobruysk-Lyakhovichi area of the Pripet-Sümpfe under the direction of HSSPf von dem Bach-Zelewski.

7/19 - 8/31/41--- Einsatz Pripjetsümpfe (for details see entries for *Pinsk* and *Pripet Marshes*).

Abschrift Reinhardt (SS-Hauptsturmführer) an SS-Kav-Regt 1, "Bericht über die Tätigkeit der Voraus Abteilung vom 27.7 - 3.8.41"/ [areas of operation]:

7/27---	Lyakhovichi-Dorohi Stare road
7/28---	Dorohi Stare-Budenichi-Osewiec
7/29---	Pasieka-Budenichi-Dubrovo-Schtschity-Mokawicze
7/30---	Lyuban'-Troitschany-Glussk-Dubrovo-Pasieka-Ruchowo
7/31---	same as previous day and Novo Andrevskaya
8/1---	Troitschany-Dorohi Stare
8/2---	sweep of whole region
8/3---	sweep of whole region; Shiwun

Abschrift Fassbender (SS-Sturmbannführer) an SS-Kav-Regt 1, "Bericht über die Tätigkeit der Voraus Abteilung vom 3.8 - 12.8.41"/ [areas of operation]:

8/4---	Lyaskovichi-Shiwun-Reppin
8/5---	Zabolot'ye-Poretje-Reppin
8/6---	Buda-Repplof-Poretje
8/8---	Buda
8/9---	Glussk
8/10---	Dorohi Stare

8/2/41--- Formation of 3. SS-Ersatz-Schwadron (Rennstall, Gestüte, Reitschule München) at Baranovichi. Official formation of SS-Kavallerie-Brigade from SS-Kavallerie-Regiments 1 and 2 with the following command structure:

Brigade CO: SS-Standartenführer Hermann Fegelein
SS-Kav.-Regt. 1
CO:SS-Sturmbannführer Gustav Lombard
SS-Kav.-Regt. 2
CO:SS-Standartenführer Hermann Schliefenbaum
Vorausabteilung
CO:SS-Sturmbannführer Albert Fassbender

8/17/41--- Second action of the SS-Kavallerie-Brigade against the Pripjet-Sümpfe from the start line Makarichi-Bobrik-Bol'Shiye Gorodyatichi-Ubybaczki-Yuntseviche-Lyuban'-Urech'ye-Sorchi.
8/23/41--- SS-Hauptsturmführer Waldemar Fegelein, in temporary command of SS-Kavallerie-Regiment 1, orders the execution of the entire male Jewish population of the town of Starobin (exact number unspecified) in reprisal for the murder of the town's mayor. An additional 21 "suspicious" civilians are also executed. [Yerger, 1996, pp. 107-108] [U.S. Holocaust Memorial Museum *Selected Documents from the Military Historical Institute (Prague)*, Reel 2, Kommandostab RF-SS Karton 24, 1941-43, unit report dated 4 September 1941]

9/7/41--- SS-Kavallerie-Brigade conducts security operations in the area between the Dnepr and Pripjet and the line Retschiza-Pticha.

9/10/41--- SS-Kavallerie-Regiment 1 "kills 384 partisans in combat" during operations at Krassnyi Ostroff at the cost of 2 SS horses. [Yerger, 1996, pp. 107-108]

9/22/41--- Unit ends up old operations and begins operations in the Dnepr-Szos region.
late 9/41--- Unit operating in the Gomel area [Büchler, 1986].

9/26/41--- SS-Kavallerie-Brigade reports killing "284 partisans and 87 criminals" during operations in the Gomel region. [Yerger, 1996, p. 129]

9/28/41--- In addition to the 15,878 civilians that the brigade exterminated during Einsatz Pripjetsümpfe, SS-Standartenführer Fegelein reports that a total of 31,403 prisoners had been taken. These individuals have never been accounted for and considering the murderous activities of the SS-Kavallerie-Brigade during 1941 it is probable that they were also executed.

early 10/41--- cleansing operations in the Vitebsk and Toropetz areas [Büchler, 1986].

mid 10/41--- cleansing operations in the Velikye Luki and Rzhew area [Büchler, 1986].

11/9/41--- Unit executes 44 "partisans."

11/10/41--- SS-Kavallerie-Brigade reduces claimed enemy strong point at Berjosawthal and subjects 519 suspected partisans to "strong handling"

11/12/41--- Another 20 suspected partisans "strongly handled".
(SS-Kavallerie-Brigade reports that from 10/18/41 - 11/18/41 the unit killed or executed approximately 3,300 suspected partisans at the cost of 7 dead and 9 wounded! [Yerger, 1996, pp. 134-141])

With the reversal of German military fortunes in the Winter of 1941/42, the brigade was removed from its rear-area "security" duties and assigned a front-line defensive role. It began to suffer correspondingly heavy losses. In mid-April 1942, the battleworthy remnants of the brigade were formed into Kampfgruppe Zehender while the remainder of the unit was sent to Truppenübungsplatz Debica (Poland) for refitting. Aside from its front-line commitments, the kampfgruppe also took part in the following anti-partisan operations in the USSR: Nordpol, Karlsbad, Karlsbad II, Sumpffieber, Frieda. In August 1942 the kampfgruppe was withdrawn to Debica to participate in the formation of the SS-Kavallerie-Division (see 8. SS-Kavallerie-Division *Florian Geyer*).

Stara Cernova (Czechoslovakia)

On 28 September 1944 at point 852 (near Hill 1211, 8 kilometers south of Stara Cernova [southwest of Ruzomberok, northwestern Slovakia]), elements of 1. Bataillon / SS-Panzergrenadier-Regiment 39 (CO: SS-Hauptsturmführer Arno Liebenau) of 18. SS-Panzergrenadier-Division Horst Wessel seized eight fleeing Jews and turned them over to the divisional Feldgendarmerie for "special handling." It is interesting that despite constant defensive actions against overwhelming Soviet forces, the Waffen-SS troopers still had some spare time for persecuting Jews.

Source
(1. Bataillon/SS-Panzergrenadier-Regiment 39
Kriegstagebuch, 1.5.44 - 31.12.44,
U.S. Holocaust Memorial Museum, RG-48.004M, reel 3,
FN 300196 - FN 300230
[Kriegsarchiv SS, Military Historical Institute Prague])

Stari Becej (Yugoslavia)

As part of the effort by Hungarian occupation authorities to make ethnic Hungarians and Germans the dominant population in the Backa region (see *Novi Sad*), a series of large-scale killings of Serbs and Jews was carried out during the month of January 1942 in the town of Stari Becej (37 kilometers east of Becej, Autonomous Serbia). These operations were conducted under the guise of anti-partisan operations. Individual executions began on 10 January and several massacres were carried out from 26 - 28 January by Hungarian army and police personnel. These killing operations were planned and executed by Colonel Ladislaus Deak. Approximately two hundred civilians, half of whom were Jews, were murdered during the operations. The victims were robbed both before and after execution: fingers were cut off to secure rings, ear-rings were torn off women's heads, and jaws were broken up for the gold teeth they contained. This killing frenzy was followed by uncontrolled ransacking and looting of the victim's homes.

After the operations at Stari Becej, a grateful Hungarian government conferred orders and medals on all those responsible for these massacres. The links to the Waffen-SS came several years later. Colonel Deak later served in the Waffen-SS as a Waffen-Oberführer der SS and commanded Waffen-Grenadier-Regiment der SS 61 / 25. Waffen-Grenadier-Division der SS *Hunyadi* (ungarische Nr. 1). Numerous personnel who participated in these massacres also served in this division and its sister unit, the 26. Waffen-Grenadier-Division der SS (ungarische Nr. 2).

Source
(*Löwenthal, 1957, p. 30*)

Staro-Konstantinov (USSR)

"After the German troops entered Staro-Konstantinov (the present seat of the Higher-SS, the Police Chief, and of the Military Commander of the Rear Area), Jews were employed for cleaning the barracks. Since the Jews did not report for work lately, the military authorities had to round up the Jewish labor force early in the day. The Jews were impertinent and even refused to work. Out of about 1,000 Jews that were recruited for field work, only 70 appeared on the following day. Moreover, it was established that harvesters were sabotaged. Finally, the Jewish Council of Elders spread the rumor that the Russians were advancing again; whereupon the Jews publicly threatened and abused the Ukrainians. Finally it was established that Jews were conducting a flourishing trade with stolen cattle and goods. In reprisal, the 1 SS-Brigade carried out an action against the Jews in the course of which 300 male and 139 female Jews were shot."

(*Ereignismeldung UdSSr Nr. 59, Berlin, 21 August 1941 from Arad et al.*)

The 1. SS-Infanterie (mot.) Brigade, under the command of SS-Brigadeführer Richard Hermann, was a rear-area Waffen-SS unit responsible for numerous anti-partisan and killing operations. It also supplied replacements to the main-series Waffen-SS divisions in 1941/1942 and later provided cadre to both the 20. Waffen-Grenadier-Division der SS (estnische Nr. 1) and the 18. SS-Freiwilligen-Panzergrenadier-Division

Horst Wessel.

Woltersdorf relates the entry of the 2. SS-Panzer-Division Das Reich into Staro-Konstantinov. All able-bodied men were required to leave their captured villages and head west, under threat of being shot. This was posted on placards; the locals were cooperative and no one was shot. The placards were later captured by the Soviets and formed the basis (according to the author) for the later atrocity claims. Although Das Reich was not involved in the reprisal action, Woltersdorf is convinced that absolutely nothing happened at Staro-Konstantinov. Woltersdorf's apologist position renders his objectivity and veracity problematic.

Sources
(*Arad et al., 1989, p. 100*)
(*Woltersdorf, 1989, pp. 200-201 & 209-210*)

Staroverovka (USSR)

At the Nuremberg Trials of Major German War Criminals, the Soviet prosecutor claimed that the 2. Regiment / 1. SS-Panzer-Division Leibstandarte Adolf Hitler (regimental CO: ?) burned the town of Staroverovka in Spring 1943 during the fighting around Kharkov. No evidence was ever produced to support this charge.

Source
(*IMT, 1948/1971, vol. 20, p. 394*)

Szpegawsk (Poland)

Following the campaign in Poland, SS-Wachsturmbann Eimann (CO: SS-Sturmbannführer Kurt Eimann) spent the month of October 1939 executing patients from Pomeranian psychiatric hospitals which were being cleared for use as Waffen-SS barracks and military hospitals. They performed the following "cleansing actions" at the Klinik Kocborow near Szpegawsk:

3 October	115 patients executed
17 October	151 " "
20 October	149 " "
21 October	89 " "

Patients from other clinics were taken by train from Stralsund, Lauenburg, Überkmunde, and Treptow to Danzig-Neustadt. They were then transferred to trucks and driven to the forest near Piasznicz. Upon arrival, patients were led off individually into the woods, shot in the back of the neck, and then dumped into graves dug by prisoners from KL Stutthof. At day's end the trucks returned to Danzig empty, except for the Waffen-SS troopers and their victim's clothing. After several weeks, the operation wound down with the execution of the gravediggers to eliminate any potential witnesses. The mass graves were then obscured with soil and vegetation. The final count of patients murdered by the unit is uncertain, although in a report dated 9 January 1940 SS-Sturmbannführer Eimann estimated the figure to be in excess of three thousand (*Bericht.....*).

In January 1940 the unit was disbanded and its personnel distrbuted to various SS-Totenkopfverbände serving as replacement/training elements for the Totenkopf Division (3. SS-Panzer-Division *Totenkopf*). SS-Sturmbannführer Eimann later served with distinction in the II-SS-Panzerkorps in Normandy and the Ardennes. After the war, he was briefly detained but then released. He was finally brought to trial in 1962 and sentenced to four years imprisonment in 1968 for his role in the murders of an estimated 1,200 psychiatric patients.

Sources
(Röhr et al., 1989)
(Burleigh, 1994, pp. 130-132)
(Bericht über Aufstellung, Einsatz, und Tätigkeit des SS-Wachsturmbann E / U.S. National Archives, Berlin Document Center personal file on Kurt Eimann HSSPf Danzig-Westpreussen)
(Fall Eimann, Zentrale Stelle der Landesjustizverwaltungen, V 203, AR-Nr 1101 [1962])

Tarnow (Poland)

The beginning of June 1942 saw the commencement of the first large-scale extermination operations (disguised as resettlement programs) targeting the Jewish populace in Nazi-occupied Poland. The city of Tarnow, 85 kilometers east of Krakau, had a Jewish population of approximately 26,000 crowded into its small ghetto. Under the direction of SSPf Krakau SS-Oberführer Julian Scherner, the extermination of the Tarnow Jews began on 11 June 1942. All those who were unable to work (the elderly, children, and the physically and mentally ill) were rounded up by the Tarnow Stadtpolizeiabteilung, Tarnow Sicherheitspolizei, and a Waffen-SS company from

nearby Truppenübungsplatz Debica [unit and commander unidentified]. They were registered and had the letter "K" stamped on their identity cards. In small groups they were then marched out of the city to a nearby forest where they were shot and buried in mass graves. Approximately 4,000 individuals were murdered in this manner. In the following weeks an additional 8,000 Jews were registered and sent by train to Vernichtungslager Belzec where they were gassed to death. The second "resettlement" occurred in September 1942 when 8,000 Jews were sent to their deaths at VL Belzec. Two months later (November 1942) the third "resettlement" resulted in another 4,000 Jews being sent to VL Belzec where they were gassed upon arrival. In late August - early September 1943, the Tarnow Ghetto was largely cleared during a final operation that resulted in the transfer of approximately 2,000 Jews to Arbeitslager Krakau-Plaszow.

Source
(Rüter-Ehlermann et al., 1968-1981, Band 20, Lfd. Nr. 571, pp. 114-122)

Tavaux-et-Pontsericourt (France)

"On the 30th August 1944, about 50 soldiers of the Adolf Hitler SS Division arrived at Tavaux-et-Pontsericourt (10 kilometers south of Vervins in the Department of Aisne), where they shot in the streets and the houses of the village a total of 22 persons only two of whom survived. Many of the bodies were burnt as the Germans fired the town. The youngest victim was a two year old boy, seven victims were over seventy. The wife of a FFI leader, Mme. Maujeon, after having been tortured and wounded, was drenched with petrol and burnt alive in the presence of her children. When the children the oldest of whom is 9 years old, refused to divulge the whereabouts of their father, they were locked in the cellar and the house set alight. Fortunately the neighbors rescued the children as the SS troops were leaving. 83 houses were burnt in this village."

The unit in question was the 1. SS-Panzer-Division *Leibstandarte Adolf Hitler* (CO: SS-Oberführer Wilhelm Mohnke).

Source
(U.S. National Archives RG-153, 151 -- Records of the Office of the Judge Advocate General (Army), French War Crime Cases, File Number 000-11127)

Ternopol' (USSR)

The Einsatzgruppen report for 16 July 1941 (Ereignismeldung UdSSR Nr. 24; Berlin, July 16, 1941; Einsatzgruppe C cited in Arad et al.) states that, "at Tarnopol 10 (German) soldiers were also found among the murdered in the prison, 1 of them a lieutenant of the air force, 6 pilots, and 3 soldiers of the mountain troops. Of the Jews assigned to disinter the corpses, about 180 were slain, some in the prison courtyard, some in the streets. Moreover, Jewish residences were destroyed by members of the Waffen-SS with hand grenades, and then set on fire."

Three separate Waffen-SS units were passing through the Ternopol' area during this time period: 5. SS-Panzer-Division *Wiking* under the command of SS-Obergruppenführer Felix Steiner, 1. SS-Infanterie (mot.)-Brigade under the command of SS-Brigadeführer Richard Hermann, and Sonderkommando 4b of Einsatzgruppe C under the command of SS-Obersturmbannführer Günther Herrmann. The exact identity of the Waffen-SS troopers engaged in these killings remains unresolved. Despite the fact that it was an extermination unit, Sonderkommando 4b is an unlikely candidate for the crime since it did not receive its Waffen-SS component until late-July 1941.

Source
(Arad et al., 1989, pp. 32-33)

Topoli (Yugoslavia)

The 7. SS-Freiwilligen-Gebirgs-Division Prinz Eugen (CO: SS-Obergruppenführer Artur Phleps) had a garrison in Topoli which perpetrated a series of crimes in the district during November - December 1942. Approximately thirty civilians were detained, tortured, and then executed on the basis of their "confessions" by members of the II. Bataillon/SS-Gebirgsjäger-Regiment 2 (CO: SS-Hauptsturmführer Dietsche.

Sources
(Glisich, 1970, pp. 128-131)
(Kumm, 1978)

Torzeniec (Poland)

On 1 September 1939, thirty four civilians were executed at Torzeniec (south of Kalisz in central Poland) by members of the Leibstandarte Adolf Hitler Regiment's Pionierzug (CO: SS-Obersturmführer Christian "Cissy" Hansen). This regiment later served as cadre for the 1. SS-Panzer-Division Leibstandarte Adolf Hitler. The fate of SS-Obersturmführer Hansen remains undetermined.

Sources
(Röhr et al., 1989)
(Lehmann, 1977-1987)

Tosno (USSR)

"On October 20, 1941, at 8 o'clock, in Tosno, in co-operation with the Second SS Brigade as well as the Field Police, a screening of all persons in this locality took place. All of Tosno was surrounded by units of the SS Brigade and all houses searched according to a pre-arranged plan. The men were led to a large square and screened by a Kommando of the Security Police. Altogether, 156 persons had to be executed in the period from October 15 to October 23."

The unit referred to above is the 2. SS-Infanterie (mot.) Brigade, under the command of SS-Brigadeführer Göttfried Klingemann, which performed rear-area security duties and "cleansing actions" in the USSR. The unit also supplied replacements for the main-series Waffen-SS divisions decimated in the 1941-1942 campaign and was dissolved on 23 January 1943 to serve as cadre for the newly-forming Lettische Legion (future 19. Waffen-Grenadier-Division der SS [lettische Nr. 2]).

Source
(Ereignismeldung UdSSR Nr. 130, Berlin, 6 November 1941 in Arad et al., 1989, p. 222)

Troyes (France)

From 22 - 26 August 1944 assorted elements of the 51. SS-Panzergrenadier-Brigade (CO: SS-Sturmbannführer Walter Jöckel) killed several hundred civilians in the Troyes region during the post-Normandy Breakout retreat of German forces across France. Since the brigade was engaged with both elements of the U.S.

4th Armored Division and French partisans throughout this time period, it is uncertain how many of the dead were legitimately killed in combat and how many were innocents murdered as a part of reprisals. On 8 September 1944 the unit was incorporated into the 17. SS-Panzergrenadier-Division Götz von Berlichingen. In 1952 several former brigade members were tried in absentia for these executions by a French military tribunal in Metz.

Sources
(Wiggers, 1990)
(Militärarchiv Freiburg, SS Ordner Blatt 4)
(Bender & Taylor, 1969-1982, vol. 4, pp. 136-140)
(Stöber, 1966, p. 40)

Tulle (France)

In April 1944 the remnants of the 2. SS-Panzer-Division Das Reich (CO: SS-Brigadeführer Heinz Lammerding) was sent to the Montauban area of southwestern France for refitting following its participation in heavy defensive battles on the Eastern Front. The 2,500 survivors of Kampfgruppe Lammerding were bolstered by 9,000 recruits, many of them Hungarian, Rumanian, and Alsatian Volksdeutsche. In the weeks prior to the Allied amphibious invasion in Normandy, the reforming Das Reich division made the price of resistance to the German occupation very clear to the surrounding countryside. Numerous minor incidents of resistance activities resulted in savage reprisals against innocent civilians.

The Anglo-American invasion on 6 June 1944 resulted in the mobilization of numerous German reserve units throughout France. At dawn on 8 June the scattered elements of *Das Reich* assembled and moved out of Montauban area towards the Normandy beaches. The division was arrayed in three main columns and traveled along the general route: Montauban, Caussade, Cahors, Souillac/Argentat, Brive, Salon-la-Tour, Limoges, Poitiers, Saumur/Tours, Sable/Le Mans, Mayenne, Domfront, Mortain/Tinchebray, Villers Bocage/St. Lo/Coutances. Opposing their advance to the north were semi-organized forces of the French Resistance (FTP: Franc-Tireurs et Partisans, a.k.a. the Maquis). The goal of the FTP was to delay German reinforcements from reaching Normandy as long as possible. The over-

blown assessments of French Resistance historians notwithstanding, *Das Reich* was delayed by perhaps two days and lost only 15 men killed and 30 wounded as a result of FTP operations in this region.

The provinicial town of Tulle was along the division's march route. The German garrison at Tulle consisted of 700 men of III. Bataillon / 95. Security Regiment, 500 French militiamen of questionable reliability, assorted Sicherheitsdienst (SD) personnel, and a handful of Wehrmacht Feldgendarmerie. FTP forces in the district reportedly numbered five thousand, but this is surely a gross over-estimate.

FTP forces attacked the garrison at 5:00 am on 7 June. Almost immediately, the French militiamen capitulated to their countrymen and, in some instances, added their numbers to that of the partisans. Fighting continued throughout the town all that day. Outnumbered and poorly-led, the German garrison was forced to consolidate themselves at the high points in the town (the Ecole Normale, an arms factory, and a school in front of the arms factory). House-to-house fighting continued on 8 June and by late afternoon the German forces in the Ecole Normale had been subdued.

At 9:00 pm that night SS-Panzeraufklärungs-Abteilung 2 / 2. SS-Panzer-Division Das Reich under the command of SS-Sturmbannführer Heinrich Wulf arrived to relieve the garrison. Thoroughly cowed by the arrival of an armored force, the FTP fighters fled without offering any resistance. This is contrary to erroneous apologist claims that Tulle was retaken only after heavy combat resulting in significant Waffen-SS losses. In less than twenty minutes SS-Panzeraufklärungs-Abteilung 2 had retaken and secured the town. The German garrison had lost 139 killed and 40 wounded in its two-day battle with the partisans. The bodies of at least 40 German soldiers of III. Bataillon / 95. Security Regiment were found in front of their billet, horribly mutilated. According to the eyewitness accounts of inhabitants of Tulle, the German defenders had laid down their weapons and surrendered to the FTP after the latter had set fire to the Ecole Normale building. The unarmed German prisoners were then tortured and executed on the spot. In the course of the day further bodies bearing evidences of torture were discovered. A total of 64 mutilated German dead were eventually found scattered throughout Tulle.

At dawn on 9 June, two companies of Waffen-SS

troopers swept Tulle in a house-to-house search; SS-Sturmbannführer Aurel Kowatsch (*Das Reich* divisional 1c staff officer) was in charge of the operation. By 10:00 am, approximately three thousand French civilians were gathered in the yard of the arms factory. At the insistence of SS-Obersturmführer Walter Schmald (Tulle SD), SS-Sturmbannführer Kowatsch ordered reprisals for the German garrison members who had surrendered and been tortured to death by the FTP. Notices to this effect were posted around Tulle to serve as warnings to the citizenry.

With the unwilling assistance of the mayor, administrative officials, and the manager of the ammunition factory, all non-residents and "suspicious" persons were culled out of the assembled crowd by SS-Sturmbannführer Kowatsch; the remainder were released throughout the course of the day. Of those suspected of having been involved in the crime, 120 men between the ages of 17 and 42 years old were selected and sentenced to be hanged. A number of these were spared execution due to last minute intercessions by various parties. Finally, some 98 suspected persons remained. SS-Sturmbannführer Kowatsch, assisted by a pionier platoon under SS-Hauptscharführer Otto Hoff from SS-Panzeraufklärungs-Abteilung 2, executed the "suspects." They were hung throughout Tulle between 16:00 and 19:00 hours; victims were strung up from lampposts, balconies, *etc.* The bodies were then cut down, loaded into trucks, and tossed on the town rubbish dump. The Waffen-SS also deported 311 men from Tulle. 162 were soon returned, while the other 149 were sent to Dachau. Only 49 of those sent to Dachau survived the war.

On 5 July 1951 the Tulle Trial opened in Bordeaux. Three main defendants were tried : Heinrich Wulf, Otto Hoff, and an interpreter named Paulette Geissler. Heinz Lammerding had successfully fought extradition from West Germany and was tried *in absentia*. Since former Aurel Kowatsch's whereabouts were uncertain at the time of the trial (reportedly killed in Normandy in June 1944), he was also tried *in absentia*.

In general, the defense argued that the reprisals were justified by the illegal actions of the FTP forces. From his refuge in Germany, Heinz Lammerding claimed that he was out of contact with SS-Panzer-aufklärungs-Abteilung 2 and thus not responsible for the murders at Tulle. However, both Albert Stuckler (a former SS-Sturmbannführer and senior divisional staff officer) and Heinrich Wulf testified that SS-Brigadeführer Lammerding reached Tulle by 1:00 pm on 9 June and was fully aware of the reprisal proceedings. If anyone still doubted that the reprisals in Tulle were in accord with official policies set by Lammerding, the text of a divisional memorandum (dated 9 June 1944) concerning anti-guerilla operations was entered into the court records.

All of the defendants were found guilty. Heinrich Wulf was sentenced to ten years hard labor and a ten year ban from entering France, Otto Hoff was sentenced to life imprisonment for his role as the main hangman, and Paulette Geissler was sentenced to three years imprisonment for her collaboration. Heinz Lammerding and Aurel Kowatsch were sentenced to death *in absentia*. As with many other war crimes cases, none of the defendants served out their full sentences. Paulette Geissler was set free in a matter of months. Heinrich Wulf was pardoned and released in May 1952. Otto Hoff's sentence was overturned on appeal and he was released in 1953. Heinz Lammerding lived undisturbed in West Germany until his death on 13 January 1971 in Bad Tölz.

Post-trial commentary on the murders at Tulle has run a wide gamut. Typical of the apologetic comments is that of Theile (1997): "... it is with almost 100% certainty that the 98 executed belonged to the Communist-led faction of the Maquis... the reprisals taken by *Das Reich* at Tulle were justified." Even otherwise level-headed writers have felt compelled to give the Waffen-SS the benefit of the doubt in this case, as in the example of Quarrie (1986): "It is, perhaps, possible to justify this as a genuine act of war rather than the massacre of innocents that it has been described as elsewhere." Both of these opinions conveniently ignore the fact that the Waffen-SS had no evidence linking the murdered "suspects" to the FTP forces --- those executed were innocent visitors to Tulle and marginalized residents. Weidinger (1984), a former officer of the *Das Reich* division, took a page from the defense's strategy and claimed that since acts of resistance were illegal under provisions of the Hague Convention and the terms of the Franco-German armistice, any German reprisals were automatically justified. In a surprising commentary, the editors of *Wenn alle Brüder schweigen* (a publication of the Bundesverband der Soldaten der ehemaligen Waffen-SS: the Association of Soldiers of the Former Waffen-SS) correctly characterized these murders as an extra-legal reprisal action. The commission of crimes by FTP forces in no way served to justify the barbarous acts visited by the Waffen-SS on the innocent residents of Tulle.

Sources
(Reitlinger, 1957, pp. 400-401)
(Quarrie, 1986, p. 73)
(Theile, 1997, pp. 411-419)
(Bundesverband..., 1985, pp. 32-33)
(Weidinger, 1984)
(Hastings, 1981)
(Taege, 1981)
(Taege, 1985)

Tuzla (Yugoslavia)

"(At Tuzla in Bosnia-Herzegovina)..... 18 physicians and apothecaries and 40 members of their families also joined the National Liberation Army. Two of them were made prisoners and executed by the Germans, and 21 members of their families, the old, women, and children were slain by the SS troops of the "Sword Division." The unit referred to is the 13. SS-Freiwilligen-Gebirgs-Division Handschar. Since no date for these murders is given by the source, it is impossible to assign responsibility for these acts to any specific unit commander.

Source
(Löwenthal, 1957, p. 14)

Ushomir (USSR)

"In Ushomir where the 1st SS brigade shot all male Jews, bands led by four Jews entered two hours after the brigade left and set fire to 48 houses."

*(Ereignismeldung UdSSR Nr. 86, Berlin,
17 September 1941 from Arad et al.)*

The 1. SS-Infanterie (mot.) Brigade, under the command of SS-Brigadeführer Richard Hermann, was a rear-area Waffen-SS unit responsible for numerous anti-partisan and extermination operations. It also supplied replacements to the main-series Waffen-SS divisions in 1941/1942 and later provided cadre to both the 20. Waffen-Grenadier-Division der SS (estnische Nr. 1) and the 18. Freiwilligen-Panzergrenadier-Division Horst Wessel.

Source
(Arad et al., 1989, p. 134)

Valla (Italy)

On 19 August 1944 elements of SS-Panzeraufklärungs-Abteilung 16 / 16. SS-Panzergrenadier-Division Reichsführer-SS (abteilung CO: SS-Sturmbannführer Walter Reder) entered this northern Italian town near Bologna and executed 107 residents. This atrocity occurred as part of a large anti-partisan sweep that resulted in the deaths of many civilians. After the war, SS-Sturmbannführer Reder was tried before an Italian Military Tribunal for this and numerous other atrocities committed in the Bologna area. The court found Reder guilty of the murders at Valla. For a full accounting of SS-Sturmbannführer Reder's operations in northern Italy and his subsequent post-war trial see the entry for Monte Sol.

Source
(Kunz, 1967)

Vinca di Fivizzano (Italy)

From 24-26 August 1944 elements of SS-Panzeraufklärungs-Abteilung 16 / 16. SS-Panzergrenadier-Division Reichsführer-SS (abteilung CO: SS-Sturmbannführer Walter Reder) fired the northern Italian towns of Vinca di Fivizzano, Gragnola, Monzone, and Ponte Santa Lucia (all near Bologna) and executed over 200 civilians. This atrocity occurred as part of a large anti-partisan sweep that resulted in the deaths of many civilians. After the war, SS-Sturmbannführer Reder was tried before an Italian Military Tribunal for this and numerous other atrocities committed in the Bologna area. The court found

Reder guilty of the murders and wanton destruction that took place at the aforementioned towns. For a full accounting of SS-Sturmbannführer Reder's operations in northern Italy and his subsequent post-war trial see the entry for Monte Sol.

Source
(Kunz, 1967)

Vostane (Yugoslavia)

On 28 March 1944 elements of the 7. SS-Freiwilligen-Gebirgs-Division Prinz Eugen (CO: SS-Brigadeführer Otto Kumm) with the help of 369. Infanterie Division (CO: Generalleutnant Fritz Neidholdt) fired the town of Vostane (near Sredevici in Bosnia-Herzegovina, 45 kilometers northeast of Split) and shot 645 civilians as part of a larger "cleansing action" in the region.

Sources
(Zöller & Leszczynski, 1965, p. 62)
(Kumm, 1978)

Warsaw Ghetto Uprising (Poland)

22 July 1942 --- German authorities announced that most Jews would be resettled from the Warsaw Ghetto. Shipments of about 5000 persons per day begin to the Treblinka death camp.

12 September 1942 --- The Great Liquidation of the Warsaw Ghetto officially ends. Approximately 310,000 Jews have been shipped to the Treblinka death camp; nearly six thousand have been killed in the Ghetto while resisting relocation. A total number of 60,000 Jews remain in the Ghetto.

Late 1942 ---
News of the "resettlers" fate (i.e., extermination) caused the Jews remaining in the Ghetto to arm themselves. Rumors circulated that the Ghetto would soon be liquidated completely.

11 January 1943 ---
Reichsführer-SS Heinrich Himmler ordered the final liquidation of the Warsaw Ghetto stipulating that operations be completed by 15 February 1943.

18 January 1943 ---
SS-Oberführer Dr. Ferdinand von Sammern-Frankenegg, in his role as SSPf Warschau, invaded the Ghetto with a mixed force of German, Latvian, and Lithuanian security units (1,000 effectives) supported by armored cars, field guns, and Polish police units. Fierce fighting ensued.

22 January 1943 ---
SS-Oberführer Sammern-Frankenegg withdrew his forces from the Ghetto. His losses totalled sixty killed and wounded; 1,000 Jews were killed and 5,500 deported to Treblinka.

April 1943 ---
Unimpressed with the pace of operations, Reichsführer-SS Himmler assigned SS-Brigadeführer Jürgen Stroop (who had extensive prior experience with extermination actions) to complete the Ghetto liquidation.

17 April 1943 ---
SS-Brigadeführer Stroop arrived to take command and pursue the final liquidation. By now the Ghetto could muster some 3,000 defenders armed with a motley collection of revolvers, grenades, molotov cocktails, some rifles, and a small number of captured sub-machine guns. The defenders were split between three main cooperating groups: ZOB (Zydowska Organizacja Bojowa -- Jewish Fighting Organization, 600-800 effectives), ZZW (Zydowski Zwiazek Wojskowy -- Jewish Military Union, 400 effectives), and independents (2,000 effectives).

18 April 1943 ---
Polish police units surrounded the Ghetto walls.

19 April 1943 ---
At SS-Brigadeführer Stroop's direction, SS-Oberführer Sammern-Frankenegg led an expanded force (Jewish Ghetto police, Polish police, 250 SS-Ordnungspolizei, an unknown number of Ukrainian, Lithuanian, and Latvian police, armored cars, 15 Renault tanks) into the Ghetto. Confused fighting broke out. SS-Oberführer Sammern-Frankenegg withdrew his force and was summarily replaced by SS-Brigadeführer Stroop as SSPf Warschau. (SS-Oberführer Sammern-Frankenegg was transferred to security duties in Croatia where

he was later killed by partisans.) SS-Brigadeführer Stroop reorganized his forces with the assistance of his staff, including SS-Obersturmbannführer Franz Konrad. SS-Obersturmbannführer Ludwig Hahn was formally placed in command of all SD and Wehrmacht elements. SS-Brigadeführer Stroop employed the following units for the reduction of the Ghetto:

Staff Headquarters (6 officers/5 NCOs)
SS-Panzergrenadier-Ausbildungs-und Ersatz-Bataillon 3 Warschau (4 officers / 440 effectives)
CO: SS-Obersturmbannführer Walther Bellwidt
SS-Kavallerie-Ausbildungs-und Ersatz-Bataillon 1 Warschau (5 officers / 381 effectives)
CO: SS-Hauptsturmführer Willi Plänk
I. Bataillon / 22. SS-Polizei-Regiment Warschau (3 officers / 94 effectives)
III. Bataillon / 22. SS-Polizei-Regiment Warschau (3 officers / 134 effectives)
III. Bataillon / 23. SS-Polizei-Regiment Krakow (strength unknown)
Technische Nothilfe (1 officer / 6 effectives)
Polish Police (4 officers / 363 gendarmes)
Polish Firemen (166 effectives)
Sicherheitsdienst (SD) [3 officers / 32 effectives]
Leichte Flakalarmbatterie III/8 Warschau (2 officers / 22 effectives)
Pionierkommando der Eisenbahn Panzerzug-Ersatz Abteilung Rembertow (2 officers / 42 effectives)
Reserve Pionier-Bataillon 14 Gora-Kalwaria (1 officer / 34 effectives)
Trawniki Bataillon (Ukrainian AL guards) [2 officers / 335 effectives]
Luftwaffe ground personnel (directing attacks by He-217 bombers) [strength unknown]

Support Elements:	
	1 10 cm howitzer
	1 flamethrower
	18 Wehrmacht pioniers
	2 Wehrmacht medics
	3 2.28 cm Flak
	1 Renault tank
	2 armored half-tracks

SS-Brigadeführer Stroop officially reported having 36 officers and 2,054 other ranks at his disposal. However, he did not include the Luftwaffe ground personnel

and the III. Bataillon / 23. SS-Polizei-Regiment Krakow in his total. Also, the normal complement for the two Waffen-SS training and reserve battalions would be 1000 effectives each, considerably more than the numbers reported. According to the well-informed Polish intelligence service, SS-Brigadeführer Stroop had five thousand troops at work reducing the Ghetto. Thus, it appears that SS-Brigadeführer Stroop may have purposely understated the force needed to quell the Ghetto insurrection in order to save face. This supposition is bolstered by an examination of SS-Brigadeführer Stroop's own casualty reports which cite the following battalions not included in his list of units employed in the operation (compare pages 2 through 7 of Stroop's after-action report): SS-Panzergrenadier-Ausbildungs-und Ersatz-Bataillon 1 (CO: ?), SS-Panzergrenadier-Ausbildungs-und Ersatz-Bataillon 2 (CO: ?), SS-Panzergrenadier-Ausbildungs-und Ersatz-Bataillon 4 (CO: ?), and SS-Panzergrenadier-Ausbildungs-und Ersatz-Bataillon 5 (CO: ?). On a related note, Dawidowicz (1976) makes reference to the arrival of Latvian Waffen-SS reinforcements on 20 April 1943. It appears that this is a mistaken reference to the arrival of Latvian auxiliaries drawn from SS-Arbeitslager Trawniki (near Lublin).

Following this reorganization, SS-Brigadeführer Stroop personally led his forces back into the Ghetto to continue the fight. During the course of the afternoon, Waffen-SS troopers and others broke into the hospital at 6 Gesia Street. New-born babies were killed by having their heads smashed against walls; their mothers were disembowelled in their beds in the gynecological ward. The nurses and other patients were taken to the burning Werterfassung warehouse in Nalewski Street and thrown alive into the flames. SS-Brigadeführer Stroop withdrew his forces at nightfall.

20 April 1943 ---
German forces invaded the Ghetto to reengage the fight. Heavy fighting; German forces withdrew at nightfall.

21 April 1943 ---
Fighting continued. By now, the standard German procedure is to execute captured Jews (men, women, and children) on the spot.

22 April 1943 ---
The Germans fired the Ghetto in order to burn out its inhabitants. Many escapees were liquidated on the spot. The city sewers were flooded, creosoted, and gassed to drive out any hidden Jews. In his after-action report SS-Brigadeführer Stroop recalled that day's activities: "During the night, the fires we had started earlier forced the Jews to appear in front of the housing blocks to escape from the flames in any way they could. Until then, they had remained hidden in attics, cellars, and other hideouts despite our search operations. Masses of burning Jews -- entire families -- jumped from windows or tried to lower themselves using tied-together bedsheets, etc. Measures had to be taken to liquidate these as well as the other Jews immediately."

23 - 26 April 1943 ---
Fighting/burning continued. The Jewish defenders rejected SS-Brigadeführer Stroop's ultimatum to surrender.

27 April 1943 ---
Heavy losses caused the remainder of the Jewish defenders to attempt to disperse from the Ghetto into the countryside surrounding Warsaw.

28 April - 10 May 1943 ---
Scattered fighting, at times heavy, continued throughout the Ghetto. The leadership of the ZOB and ZZW resistance groups were surrounded and killed.

11 May - 30 May 1943 ---
Scattered fighting; resistance no longer a serious threat.

16 May 1943 ---
SS-Brigadeführer Stroop reported to HSSPf Generalgouvernement SS-Obergruppenführer Friedrich-Wilhelm Krüger that the operation in the Ghetto was complete: 49,065 Jews had been deported to the Treblinka death camp for extermination (6,929 perished along the way), approximately 7,000 were killed in the fighting, and an additional 5,000 – 6,000 died as a result of explosions and fires in the Ghetto. In his after-action report, SS-Brigadeführer Stroop minimized his losses claiming only 16 dead and 85 wounded for the entire operation. Polish underground estimates placed his losses at closer to 700 killed and wounded. SS-Brigadeführer Stroop's report was also silent concerning the large number of Poles that were arrested in the "Aryan" part of Warsaw during his operation and subsequently brought into the Ghetto to be executed by his men. His report did have plenty of room, however, for invective against the Jewish civilians he murdered as they are variously referred to as bandits, criminals, sub-humans, gangs, rabble, lowest elements, and creatures.

In celebration of his "victory," SS-Brigadeführer Stroop had the main Warsaw synagogue on Tlomackie Street blown up at 2015 hours.

June - July 1943 ---
Minor partisan actions in the Ghetto.

18 June 1943 ---
SS-Brigadeführer Stroop was awarded the Iron Cross First Class for suppressing the Jewish uprising and destroying the Ghetto.

Late July 1943 ---
The remaining Ghetto buildings were systematically dynamited.

At war's end, Jürgen Stroop was captured by the Americans. He was tried before the American Dachau Tribunal and on 22 March 1947 sentenced to death for numerous crimes against Greek civilians, as well as downed Allied pilots and POWs. On 30 May 1947 Stroop was remanded to Polish custody. He was tried in Warsaw for his destruction of the Ghetto and the extermination of its inhabitants. He was found guilty and condemned to death on 23 July 1951. Jürgen Stroop was hung at Warsaw's Mokotow Prison on 6 March 1952. Franz Konrad was also tried by Polish authorities and hung on 8 September 1951.

Sources
(Reitlinger, 1961, p. 478)
(Lukas, 1990, p. 181)
(Kurzman, 1976)
(Ainsztein, 1979)
(Wulf, 1961, pp. 33-43, 68, & 73)
(Dawidowicz, 1976, pp. 455-460)
(Stroop, 1979)

(Stroop, Jürgen [16 May 1943] *Es gibt keinen judischen Wohnbezirk in Warschau mehr!*, reproduced in IMT, 1948/1971, vol. 26, pp. 628-693)

Warsaw Uprising (Poland)

In July 1944 as the Soviets advanced following the destruction of Army Group Center, the German occupation authorities panicked and begin to evacuate Warsaw. The mostly-dormant Polish resistance forces decide that the time was right for an armed uprising against the Germans. Assuming that they won, the Polish Government-in-exile would retake its capital and thus compel the Soviets to recognize them, instead of installing their own puppet government. On 22 July the Soviets announced the formation of a Polish puppet government -- the Committee of National Liberation in Lublin. On 28 July, Soviet spearhead elements shelled the Warsaw suburb of Praga and broadcast radio announcements for the Poles to rise up and attack the Germans. The supporters of the Polish Government-in-exile did so; the Soviets, however, ceased their offensive towards Warsaw and let the Germans annihilate the rebellious Poles. Once the Poles were destroyed, the Soviets would resume their offensive, push the Germans out of the city, and install their own hand-picked Polish Communist government.

The Polish AK (Warsaw Army Corps) consisted of 25 - 28,000 effectives divided into three divisions under the command of General Tadeusz Komorowski (code-named "Bor"). The men of the AK were indifferently clothed, armed, and equipped with whatever they were able to scrounge up. The goal of the Polish resistance was to take over the six municipal districts of the city (City Center, Zoliborz, Wola, Ochota, Mokotow, Praga) as well as outlying districts such as Okecie. The uprising was launched on 1 August 1944. At the start of the uprising, the German garrison in Warsaw was approximately 13,000 men strong. However, only 5,000 were experienced and well-equipped troops; the majority of the German garrison consisted of over-aged, under-equipped rear-area security units.

From 2 August on, Reichsführer-SS Heinrich Himmler was personally responsible for suppressing the rebellion. By the end of the first day, the Polish AK had seized most of Warsaw. Unfortunately, in the process they took heavy casualties and failed to capture several vital bridges, defensive positions, and municipal utility stations. The Polish resistance forces suffered from a lack of properly armed personnel and poor tactical execution. As soon as they lost the initiative, the battle for Warsaw became a downhill struggle for their survival. When Hitler heard of the rebellion, he remarked laconically "Warsaw will be wiped out." The German counter-attack began on 5 August. Reichsführer-SS Himmler travelled to Posen where he initially dispatched most of the city's police force, as well as the SS-Brigades *Dirlewanger* and *Kaminski* to deal with the rebellious Poles. The units were given carte-blanche to shoot civilians and loot households. Chaos reined in the city; there were no identifiable front-lines.

The next day SS-Obergruppenführer Erich von dem Bach-Zelewski was put in overall command of the German forces and ordered by Reichsführer-SS Himmler to retake the city. The units used to quell the uprising were:

Polizeigruppe Posen (a.k.a. Kampfgruppe Reinefarth) --- four battalions of Ordnungspolizei totalling 45 officers and 2,595 effectives under the command of SS-Gruppenführer Heinz Reinefarth. Bruce (1972) claims that Reinefarth's Posen group consisted of 8,000 effectives, 37 assault guns, and a company of heavy tanks.

SS-Brigade *Kaminski* (later the 29. Waffen-Grenadier-Division der SS [russische Nr. 1]) --- only 1,700 effectives of a total strength of 6,500 effectives were deployed under the command of Waffen-Brigadeführer Bronislav Kaminski.

SS-Brigade Dirlewanger (later the 36. Waffen-Grenadier-Division der SS) --- 16 officers and 865 effectives under the command of SS-Oberführer Dr. Oskar Dirlewanger. On 20 September, the unit received 2,500 replacements (1,900 of which were former Soviet POWs from Arbeitslager Matzlau, near Danzig).elements of the 22. SS-Freiwilligen-Kavallerie-Division Maria Theresia --- at least 500 effectives under the command of ????? [Divisional commander was SS-Brigadeführer August Zehender]

miscellaneous unspecified Wehrmacht units ---
25 officers and 1,275 effectives
SS-Jäger-Bataillon 500 (CO: SS-Sturmbannführer Armin Beilhack) --- strength?; attached to SS-Brigade Dirlewanger

SS-Jäger-Bataillon 501 (CO: SS-Hauptsturmführer Rudolf Bachmann) --- strength?; attached to SS-Brigade Dirlewanger

Ostmuselmanische SS-Regiment (CO: SS-Standartenführer Harun-el-Raschid Bey) --- strength?; attached to SS-Brigade Dirlewanger

2 Wehrmacht battalions of Azerbaijani volunteers elements of 1. Panzer-Division Hermann Göring (CO: Generalmajor Wilhelm Schmalz until 9/25/44, then Generalmajor Hans-Horst Necker)

2 companies and one platoon of Ordnungspolizei
5 gun Wehrmacht artillery battery

Kampfgruppe Schmidt --- a total of 2,000 effectives: 3 battalions of the 603. Infanterie-Regiment, a battalion of grenadiers, an Ordnungspolizei battalion, miscellaneous artillery, and armored train No. 75 under the command of Oberst Wilhelm Schmidt.

Kampfgruppe von Vormann --- 1,000 East Prussian grenadiers deployed to positions in Praga holding the Poniatowski bridge (CO: ?).

a company of tanks from the 5. SS-Panzer-Division *Wiking* (4 Tigers, 1 Panther, 4 Panzer IVs, 1 assault gun)

Polizeigruppe Posen and SS-Brigade *Dirlewanger* attacked Polish AK positions in the Wola District. SS-Brigade *Kaminski* and the 22. SS-Frewilligen-Kavallerie-Division *Maria Theresia* attacked resistance positions in the Wola and Ochota Districts. The 1. Panzer-Division *Hermann Göring* worked to clear a route through Warsaw towards the Kierbedz Bridge. The German advance was slow; many units were soon on drunken, out-of-control killing and looting sprees. The *Kaminski* and *Dirlewanger* Brigades had the dubious distinction of perpetrating the worst crimes of any German units deployed in Warsaw to combat the uprising. What transpired in Wola and Ochota, the west and southwest districts of Warsaw, during the early days of August must be considered one of the war's worst crimes. In the first week of its operations, SS-Brigade *Dirlewanger* killed approximately 50,000 civilians in

the Ochota and Wola districts. Some Polish prisoners were burned alive and children were bayonetted; a number of women were tortured to death and their bodies hung upside down from balconies. Wroniszewski (1970) detailed the fighting that took place in the Ochota District, paying particular attention to the activities of SS-Brigade *Kaminski*. He compiled a map of the district showing the locations of some of the civilian massacres carried out by *Kaminski* personnel. The map indicates twelve instances of 5 - 50 victims, six instances of 50 - 200 victims, and one instance of 200+ victims. From 5 - 6 August, the brigades acted in concert to burn down three hospitals (Wilski, St. Lazarus, Charles & Mary) killing most of the staff and patients. The *Kaminski* and *Dirlewanger* brigades behaved so atrociously that they were eventually removed from the Warsaw fighting.

Meanwhile in the Wola District, SS-Gruppenführer Reinefarth's Ordnungspolizei performed orderly looting on a massive scale. Specialists were brought in to ensure that the plunder was useful and efficiently transported. Items taken included all machines, transport, raw materials, clothing, food, oils, medicines, detergents, and anything else deemed of value. The goods were loaded onto specially marked trains and trucks ("Zur Verfügung von Gauleiter Greiser" or "Kampfgruppe Reinefarth Polizeidienststelle") that went uninspected to Gauleiter Greiser in Posen. In the first ten days of August 1944 alone, 7000 railcars full of plunder were shipped out of Warsaw. No full accounting of what was "officially" taken exists, not to mention those items appropriated unofficially by the Ordnungspolizei responsible for the looting. Much of the property was then distributed to Germans living in the Posen area.

SS-Obergruppenführer von dem Bach-Zelewski slowly regained control of the situation in Warsaw. Although the Poles fought furiously, they were more than outmatched by the Germans and the Soviets refused all aid requests. While the Germans brought in seasoned Wehrmacht reinforcements --- including armor, the Poles had to be content with a few meagre air supply drops by the Anglo-Americans. Red Cross sponsored surrender talks began on 9 September 1944. The Soviets briefly renewed their offensive on 10 September, reaching the Vistula and capturing most of the Praga District by 14 September. With the exception of several ill-advised, poorly-supported and costly river-crossing attacks by elements of the communist Polish 1st Army (General Zygmunt Berling), the Soviet forces still refused, however, to come to the aid of the beleaguered Polish resistance forces on the opposite side of the Vistula. Unable to hold out any longer, the Polish AK negotiated a cease-fire on 1 October and then surrendered on 5 October. Losses (killed, wounded, and missing) for the combatants have been estimated at :

21,600	Polish AK
11,000	German and auxiliary forces
160,000 - 200,000	Polish civilians

The Germans dynamited and bulldozed almost all of Warsaw that remained following the Polish surrender. When the remains of Warsaw were later "liberated" by the Soviets, representatives of the puppet Committee of National Liberation in Lublin established themselves as the new Polish government.

None of the main German officers were ever brought to justice for the crimes committed by the troops under their command. On 25 August 1944, Waffen-Brigadeführer Bronislav Kaminski mysteriously died in an auto accident according to wartime SS sources. It is generally believed that Kaminski and several of his immediate staff were shot by their Waffen-SS masters because they were proving to be increasingly intractable servants. The brigade was broken up and its members sent as reinforcements to the 30. Waffen-Grenadier-Division der SS (russische Nr. 2) and the Vlassov Army. Dr. Oskar Dirlewanger died in French custody after the war at the Altshausen POW camp where he was recognized by former concentration camp prisoners and beaten to death. Erich von dem Bach-Zelewski lived a relatively tortured existence in West Germany after the war. He was tried at least twice for war crimes and seems to have been truly repentent for the deeds he committed, going so far as to willingly give damning testimony against himself. Erich von dem Bach-Zelewski died in prison on 8 March 1972.

Specific atrocity allegations:

Dluga Street Field Hospital

During the Nuremberg Trials of Major German War Criminals, the prosecution cited the affidavit of Bronislav Dylak contained in an official Polish report entitled The German Crime in Warsaw in 1944 (Document 4042-PS/exhibit GB-560):

"Very badly wounded in the stomach I was hospitalized in the field hospital, Dluga Street 7. On 7 September 1944 the Germans ordered the nurses and those of the inmates who were able to walk to abandon the hospital leaving behind the heavily wounded. I was in this latter group and we stayed in the ward situated in the cellar. In the whole hospital there were still a few hundred sick and heavily wounded who could not leave the hospital. Shortly after the nurses had left the hospital in the evening the German SS arrived; shooting started. First those who, with superhuman effort, left their beds and dragged themselves to the doors and the staircases to get out and save themselves were immediately killed by the Germans. Two murderers burst into our ward. One had a candle in his hand --- it was already dark. The other, with a pistol, shot and killed the men lying in beds while shouting 'bandits'. Together with a few of the inmates of our ward, I was miraculously saved because the passage to our beds was obstructed by other beds. Our hall had been partitioned into two wards; I was in the second and smaller room, the entrance to which was obstructed. In the first room all were killed; the second ward was saved by a pure miracle, maybe because someone was calling the murderers away. We heard many shots from the other wards. The execution went on throughout the hospital. Later on, the Germans checked whether everybody was dead. My comrade lying next to me stained himself with blood on his chest and head in order to simulate death. One of the Germans, speaking Ukrainian, went about among the killed and struck them in their faces with his gun. It was a terrible night. A hand grenade, thrown through the window into our ward ripped my friend's belly. Finally, the building was set on fire. The fire spread very quickly; those who tried to escape were killed. A woman in our ward succeeded in pushing aside inflammable stuff near the entrance, thereby preventing our ward from catching fire. All other wards, as well as the staircase, were on fire; the smoke, the smell of burning corpses, indescribable thirst.... Thus, out of several hundred heavily wounded at the hospital in Dluga Street 7, only a few score were left alive."

(IMT, 1948/1971, vol. 20, pp. 379-381)

[Note: The "Germans" referred to above are unidentified. The fact that one spoke Ukrainian may identify them as members of SS-Brigade *Kaminski*.]

Evacuation

"On August 7, 1944, by order of the SS people from the entire town district were compelled to leave their houses, which were at once set on fire. We went in crowds of several thousands, driven and pushed by SS-men. When anyone fell, struck by a rifle-butt, those who wanted to help were struck likewise. We went through Bednarska Street and Krakowskie Przedmiescie, towards Trebacka Street. On Marshal Square the men were separated from the women; people wept and despaired. In the Saxon garden shots were heard from the Market Place. The insurgents were firing. The SS-men began to make living barricades of us. They ordered us to lie down, beat and pushed us. Soon a rampart of living bodies was formed. People wept and cursed, but the SS-men began to fire from behind it.

The firing stopped. We went forward again under escort of SS-men. The Ukrainians robbed us of our watches and valuables, and tore our paper money into pieces....

We continued our march. A car stopped and some SS-officers got out. They looked attentively at the passers-by, took from our ranks three pretty young girls, the two sisters R. and an unknown girl, and drove off. The girls cried and tried to escape from their caresses. An old woman fell. An SS-officer shot her through the back of the head.....

In the church at Wola they stole our remaining belongings. All young girls were detained, even those of not more than 12 or 13. We older women were taken on with the children in the direction of the Western Station and then by train to Pruszkow......"

(Central Commission...., 1946-1947, vol. 1, Record No. 247, pp. 213-214)

[Note: the Waffen-SS troopers referred to above are unidentified. The "Ukrainians" referred to above were personnel from SS-Brigade Kaminski.]

Grojecka Street

"On 4 August 1944, fifty men from the SS-Brigade Kaminski surrounded some houses on Grojecka Street. They took 160 men (including young boys) to a nearby cellar and executed them by firing squad. Gasoline was poured on the corpses and lit; hand grenades were then thrown among the corpses.

(Lukas, 1990, pp. 184-219)

Maria Kazimiera Street

"On Aug. 1, 1944, I went to Zoliborz to buy some food, but owing to the outbreak of the Rising could not return to Praga where I lived. For several weeks I stayed with casual acquaintances. On Aug. 2, I went to Marymont, where I stayed at No. 29, Maria Kazimiera Street, which at that moment was in the hands of the Insurgents. On September 14 the Germans began to put down the Rising in that section in the following way: About 20 tanks came from the direction of Bielany and opened fire on various houses. The Insurgents retreated from the territory of Zoliborz without fighting.

Thus the tanks came without difficulty to No. 29, Maria Kazimiera Street. Several SS-men rushed into the courtyard throwing hand grenades into the cellars and in this way forced the frightened civilians to come out.

Then we all were told to leave. I was in the uniform of a railway worker. One of the Germans pulled off my cap and beat me for no reason. We were ordered to cross the street to a house which had previously been burnt. There were 32 of us in all, including men, women, small children and even an infant 6 months old. Here we were taken into a burnt out flat, and ordered to kneel down with our hands up facing our persecutors. A machine gun was placed before us.

The execution began at 2 pm. Several series of shots were fired into our group. I got a superficial wound in my skull. I fell; the corpses of two young men immediately fell on me. While lying I still got shots in my left arm, hand, fingers and feet. When the execution was over SS-men came back three times, killing the wounded and throwing two grenades each time. Owing to this I got pieces of shrapnel in my fingers.

So I lay for four hours, till 6 pm. Then a WH soldier came in, probably to loot the place of execution, and seeing that I moved, helped me to free myself from the corpses, comforting me and telling me not to be frightened anymore."

(Central Commission..., 1946-1947, vol. 1, Record No. 17/II, pp. 220-221)

[Note: The Waffen-SS troopers in the above account are unidentified. In all likelihood, they were not members of SS-Brigade Kaminski because they are always identified as either "Ukrainians" or "Vlasov's detachment/R.O.A." in these accounts.]

Marie Curie-Sklodowska Radium Institute

"Between ten and eleven o'clock on the morning of August 5, 1944, numerous military formations were seen approaching from the direction of the houses of Wawelska Street. Soon afterwards about a hundred soldiers in German uniforms, belonging to Vlasov's detachment (R.O.A.), rushed into the building of the Radium Institute, shouting and shooting at random.

That gang of drunken soldiers, having first secured the exits, began searching and plundering. There were at that time about 90 patients and 80 members of the staff with their families in the building. They were robbed by the soldiers of all their jewels, watches, and money and even of such trifles as fountain-pens, automatic lighters, or pocket mirrors.

The fact that the institution was a hospital, which was explained to the soldiers and was in any case obvious owing to the presence of the patients and the staff in their white coats, left the soldiers indifferent.

After having been robbed, the whole staff were driven by threat of machine-gun fire into the hospital garden, where the stage was set for an execution.

Amid insulting and threatening shouts and shots fired in all directions, the victims were lined up in rows of three and forbidden to look round; and then an order was given to set up machine-guns in their rear.

The husband of one of the patients, who slightly transgressed against the above-mentioned order, was killed on the spot by a revolver shot.

The whole party were then led in this order from the hospital garden across the Mokotow field and along streets in which lay dead bodies with skulls split open, to a camp at "Zieleniak."

There they were kept for four days and nights in the open air, without food or water. Time and again women were assaulted, dragged out and violated by the drunken soldiers. Some of the Staff of the Institute were then transported via Pruszkow to Germany. Others succeeded in escaping from the transport and stayed in the vicinity of Warsaw......

About 90 patients confined to bed remained in the hospital, and 9 members of the staff had hidden in the chimney flues, and thus avoided expulsion.

That same day the plundering and demolishing of the buildings was begun. Doors were broken down, stores, cupboards, safes, and suitcases were broken open, and glass was smashed. All the mattresses, pillows, blankets, and linen were ripped up and thrown about in the corridors and wards of the hospital. The ether and spirits were drunk and the store-rooms emptied.

More valuable things (clothing, linen, dresses, or silver) were stolen or thrown out of the windows and destroyed. Female patients were assaulted and violated.

On the next day, August 6, 1944, the barbarity of the drunken soldiers reached its climax. Some of the seriously sick and wounded, lying on the ground floor (about 15 in number), were killed with revolver shots, after which their mattresses were set on fire under their dead bodies. As not all the shots hit their mark, and those that did were not always fatal, some women who were too weak and ill to move were burnt alive. Only one of them, although badly burned and very weak, dragged herself out of bed and crawling on all fours escaped immediate death.

While these atrocities were going on, petrol was poured on the floors and the Institute was set on fire, all the exits having first been covered by machine-guns. In spite of this three women (an X-ray assistant, a nurse and a patient) managed to slip out of the building. Two of them were caught, and after having been violated many times by the soldiers were brutally murdered. Their common grave has been found in the hospital garden, where they were buried by those who were forced to dig trenches.

The remaining patients, on the upper floors, over 70 in number, and seven members of the staff who had managed to hide themselves, remained in the burning building, making desperate efforts to find some place where they could hold out against the suffocating smoke and burning heat of the fire.

That day the unfortunate victims saved their lives for the moment, thanks to the fact that the Institute was burning comparatively slowly, owing to the absence of any great quantity of inflammable material and to the existence of fireproof parquet floors. But later all the patients and one nurse were killed.

No less terrible were the scenes which took place in the Science building of the Institute. It is true that the inmates were taken to the 'Zieleniak' camp, but the building was set on fire and the people from the adjacent building (belonging to the Navy) were brought there. The women and children were separated from the men, who were driven into the burning building under the threat of machine-gun fire. In this was eleven men perished in the presence of their families.

After committing these revolting atrocities, the soldiers left the Institute for a while. The 70 patients and the 7 members of the staff still remained in the building. The nurses stealthily cooked hot food for the patients at night and looked after them. Between August 6 and 9 Vlassov's men returned from time to time to the hospital, and took away girls of 13 or 14, whom they violated and then killed in the garden. They repeatedly carried out executions in the grounds of the Institute, after driving their victims to the spot from the city, and sometimes they sey fire to the building again.

Meanwhile the German soldiers also came with cars and carried away all the valuable objects from the hospital, such as X-ray apparatus, laboratory outfits, or furniture.

When begged by members of the staff still remaining in the building to transfer them to a safer place, they answered that they could not do so.

On August 19, Vlasov's men came back again and the final destruction of the Hospital began. The few members of the staff were ordered to leave the Institute and take out all the patients. Among the latter were three women very seriously ill, who could not even walk. One of them was carried out into the garden by a woman member of the staff, who however,

did not succeed in saving the other two, for a soldier rushed up and shot them, and then poured petrol over their bodies, which he set on fire. One of them was the woman mentioned above, who on August 8 had crawled from her burning bed and so saved her life --- but only for a fortnight.

When everybody had left, the building was set on fire: 2 members of the staff had not obeyed the order and were still hiding in a chimney.

When the soldiers noticed in the procession a very sick woman, staggering and helped along by the others (it was the one who had been carried out by a member of the staff), they ordered her to be laid down near the wall of 19, Wawelska Street, where one of them shot her, and then set fire to the body.

In the Zieleniak camp only 4 members of the Staff survived. The remainder, about 70 patients and one nurse, were drawn up three deep, and marched into the Health Centre Building, where an officer was waiting for them and shot them through the head. Their dead bodies --- indeed probably some were still alive --- were piled up in the execution room, sprinkled with petrol, and set on fire. In this way, all the patients at the Radium Institute were massacred.

Of the 9 members of the staff who remained in the building after August 5, 1944, two nurses were murdered (one of them after having been violated many times), one woman employee escaped from the burning building and was saved, four were taken to the 'Zieleniak', and two stayed hidden in the chimney flues for a couple of months. They left as late as October 1944."

(Central Commission..., 1946-1947, vol. 1, Record No. 45/II, pp. 188-193)

[Note : "Vlasov's detachment/R.O.A." refers to members of SS-Brigade Kaminski.]

The Opera House

"On Aug. 9, 1944, at ten o'clock in the morning, about twenty SS-men with revolvers rushed shouting into the courtyard of our house in Trebacka Street and ordered all the people in the flats and cellars to go out into the yard. Our street had been completely in German hands since the beginning of the Rising and there had been no military activity in it whatever. The inhabitants had stayed quietly in their flats or cellars. We came down men, women, and children. In one of the flats a paralysed old woman of about 70 named Ropelewska was left behind. Several SS-men rushed into her flat after all the inhabitants had left and set fire to her mattress; seeing this her son carried her into the yard. When we were in the yard SS-men rushed into the flats and set them on fire one after the other. Then they took us into the next yard, at No. 2, Marshall Foch Street. As Mrs. Repelewska could not walk one of the armed SS-men shot her before our eyes.

At no. 2, Foch Street, the men were separated from the women. Then we went from one house to another (Nos 2, 4, 5, 7 Foch Str.). We were brought through cellars and courtyards into the Opera House; women and children into the cellars and men to the first floor. Among the men were my father, 69, and my husband, a student, 26 years old. What happened to the men I was later told by a schoolboy, Jerzy Szajkowski, who had escaped death. The men were led upstairs to the first floor of the Opera House, their Kennkarten were taken from them, and they were divided into groups: 1) Those who had been working in German institutions, 2) foreigners, 3) the remainder. Later this third group was brought out through the doors of the boxes and killed by shots through the back of the head. The corpses fell on the stage. Thus my father and husband were murdered. The number of people killed then amounted to 500. The women, of whom there were several hundred, were divided into groups: 1) above 60, 2) women with children, 3) the rest. I succeeded, with 30 other women, in escaping from the last group. We came to the church at Wola, from where we were taken to Pruszkow. I was recently in the ruins of the Opera House. The remains of the burnt corpses are still lying there. They were murdered on August 9. I saw bones, hair, teeth, and the remains of clothing, shoes and documents. I think some women were also shot there, because there were also remains of women's dresses, and I fear that this was not the only execution there."

(Central Commission..., 1946-1947, vol. 1, Record No. 19/II, pp. 230-231)

[Note: The Waffen-SS troopers in the above account are unidentified. In all likelihood, they were not members of SS-Brigade Kaminski because they are always identified as either "Ukrainians" or "Vlasov's detachment/R.O.A." in these accounts.]

Wawelberg Apartments

"On August 7, 1944, about 9 pm, at No. 15, Gorczewska Street, the three and four-storeyed Wawelberg blocks were surrounded by Germans (SS-men). They threw hand grenades inside, surrounded the houses with machine-guns, and set them on fire from all sides. Any persons who tried to get out were killed. People in flames ran to the windows. Nobody could escape from the fire; they were all burnt alive. It was a miracle if someone escaped. I know of one woman who jumped from the second storey and thus succeeded in saving her life. The front entrance was full of the bodies of those who had tried to escape from the flames. I saw among them women with babies at the breast. The houses were completely surrounded, and I suppose there must have been about 2,000 people living in them. No one came out alive unless by miracle, as in the case of the woman I have mentioned above."

(Central Commission..., 1946-1947, vol. 1, Record No. 60, pp. 206-207)

[Note: The Waffen-SS troopers in the above account are unidentified. In all likelihood, they were not members of SS-Brigade Kaminski because they are always identified as either "Ukrainians" or "Vlasov's detachment/R.O.A." in these accounts.]

Wola District

"I lived in the suburb of Wola, at No. 45, Gorczewska Street. On August 2, 1944, SS-men ordered us to leave and go to the house opposite; our house and the neighboring ones were then burnt down. We got news on the 3rd that our position was hopeless, and that we were going to be shot. Several hundreds of people were gathered in the house. At 11 am on August 4 the Germans surrounded the house, and ordered us to get out; dreadful cries from the women and children were heard. Some shots were fired at the entrance, and many people were killed or wounded. We were driven out into the potato field and ordered to lie down in the furrows. They guarded us closely, so that there was no chance of escape. After some minutes we were ordered to get up. Then they led us under a bridge quite near. There was no doubt about our fate. A woman asked where they were taking us. The answer was : 'German women and children are dying owing to you, so you must also die.' They regrouped us, separating a group of 70 people, who were sent over the bridge towards a hill. They placed the others (among whom I was) near a wall, amid barbed wire. In different places near us shots were heard: victims of the German persecutors were being executed. We were herded together. I stood on the outskirts of our group, while at a distance of about 5 metres (16 or 17 ft.) from us one of our tormentors quietly made ready to fire a machine-gun, and another took photographs of us, as they wanted to keep a record of the execution. Several were watching us. A volley of shots rang out, followed by cries and groans. I fell wounded and lost consciousness. After a certain time I recovered my senses. I heard them finishing off the wounded I did not move, pretending to be dead. They left one German to keep watch. The murderers set the neighboring houses, large and small, on fire. The heat scorched me, the smoke choked me, and my dress began to burn, I tried cautiously to put out the flames. I was hidden by a potato basket, and when the German sentinel was looking in another direction I pushed the basket in front of me and crawled along for a few yards behind it. Suddenly the wind blew a cloud of smoke in our direction so that the sentinel could not see me. I jumped to my feet and ran into the cellar of a burning house. There I found several people slightly wounded who had succeeded in getting out from under a heap of corpses. We set to work to dig an underground passage, a difficult task amid fire and smoke. At last, after several hours of superhuman effort, the passage was finished and brought us out in the courtyard of a neighboring house, not yet on fire. This was about half past twelve at night. Someone led us out to the fields, away from the fighting and burning..... The number of persons shot in my presence may be estimated at about 500, only 3 or 4 having been saved. The murderers were SS-men."

(Central Commission..., 1946-1947, vol. 1, Record No. 53, pp. 198-205)

"I lived in the Wola district at No. 8, Elekcyjna Street. At 10 am on Aug. 5, 1944 a detachment of SS-men and Vlassov's men entered. They drove us from the cellars and brought us near the Sowinski Park at Ulrychow. They shot at us when we passed. My wife was killed on the spot: our child was wounded and cried for his mother. Soon a Ukrainian approached and killed my two-year-old child like a dog; then he approached me together with some Germans and stood on my chest to see whether I was alive or not. I shammed dead, lest I should be killed too. One of the murderers took my watch; I heard him reloading his gun. I thought he would finish me off, but he went on further, thinking I was dead. I lay thus from 10 am until 9 pm pretending to be dead, and witnessing further atrocities. During that time I saw further groups being driven out and shot near the place where I lay. The huge heap of corpses grew still bigger. Those who gave any sign of life were shot. I was buried under other corpses and nearly suffocated. The executions lasted until 5 pm. At 9 pm a group of Poles came to take the corpses away. I gave them a sign that I was alive. They helped me to get up..... I cannot state the exact number of victims, but I estimate that those among whom I lay amounted to some 3,000."

(ibid., Record No. 57)

"I lived at No. 18, Dzialdowska Street, Wola........ In stayed in the cellar of No. 18 until August 5, when, between 11 and 12 noon, the Germans ordered all of us to get out, and marched us to Wolska Street..... All the inhabitants of our house had already been escorted to the "Ursus" works in Wolska Street at the corner of Skierniewicka Str., and I too was ordered to go there..... I reached the "Ursus" works with great difficulty. Shots, cries, supplications and groans could be heard from the factory yard. We had no doubt that this was a place for mass executions. The people who stood atthe entrance were led, no, pushed in, not all at once but in groups of 20. A boy of twelve, seeing the bodies of his parents and his little brother through the half-open entrance door, fell in a fit and began to shriek. the Germans and Vlassov's men beat him and pushed him back, while he was endeavouring to get inside..... We all knew what awaited us here; there was no possibility of escape or of buying one's life; there was a crowd of Germans, Ukrainians (Vlassov's men), and cars..... In the yard I saw heaps of corpses,

3 feet high in several places..... I was in the last group of four. I begged the Vlassov's men around me to save me and the children, and they asked if I had anything with which to buy my life. I had a large amount of gold with me and gave it to them. They took it all and wanted to lead me away, but the German supervising the execution would not allow them to do so..... I fell on my right side. The shot was not fatal. The bullet [had] penetrated the back of my head from the right side and went through my cheek..... I was still conscious and saw everything that was going on around me. I witnessed other executions, lying there among the dead..... thus it went on with group after group until late in the evening. It was already quite, quite dark when the executions stopped. In the intervals between the shootings the murderers walked on the corpses, kicked them, and turned them over, finishing off those who gave any sign of life, and stealing valuables.... During these dreadful doings they sang and drank vodka..... At last I succeeded in crawling on all fours over the bodies of the dead towards the wall and looked round for a way of escape..... [found 2 other survivors].... After a long search and many attempts to get free, we at last found a hole on Skierniewicka Street and made our way out through it..... [Ukrainians] surrounded us, though we begged them to allow us to get to a hospital, as we were wounded..... We were driven in the direction of Wola in a group with other passers-by, picking up still more on the way. At a certain spot the younger and older people in the group were separated. Young men and women were put on one side and then marched towards a house of execution. This was oast Plocka Street in the direction of St. Stanislaus Church. The remaining group (including myself) were driven to St. Stanislaus Church.... The Germans were setting houses on fire; throwing people out; hunting and beating them. In the yard of the "Ursus" works people were shot by Vlassov's men under the command of a German; they say he was from the SS. As far as I can judge, there must have been 5 - 7 thousand dead in the yard of this factory. About 200 people were driven there from our block alone, which had over 40 flats (with about 4 people in each), and all were killed."

(ibid., Record No. 63)

[Note: The Waffen-SS troopers in each of the above accounts are unidentified. "Vlassov's men/Ukrainians" in Record Numbers 57 and 63 refers to members of SS-Brigade Kaminski.]

Wola Hospital

"In the summer of 1944, I was sent as a patient to Wola Hospital, where I was still, suffering from sudative pleurisy, when the Rising began. The Germans came to the Hospital on August 3 at 1 pm I was in the cellar with many other sick and wounded. On entering the cellar, the Germans fired a round from a machine-gun and several wounded men who were standing near the entrance fell dead. A few minutes later the order was given to leave the hospital. All the wounded and sick who were able to walk went with the hospital staff, while the more severely wounded were carried on stretchers. Our march was a nightmare. I felt very weak, still having drainage tubes in one side. We were driven to a shed a few metres behind a tunnel in Gorczewska Street. Many people were already there. After examining our documents, they divided us into groups, and then began to drive us out. Soon the group to which I belonged was taken out for execution. We were led towards a large house (already on fire) near the tunnel; we were ordered to form rows of twelve people, and were then driven into the yard of this house. At the entrance Ukrainians (six in number) shot from close range at every person who entered, and thus the dead fell into the flames of the burning house. I saw clearly, when waiting my turn in the first group of twelve people, doctors, assistants in white aprons and also (if I am not mistaken) some priests being shot. Among the doctors was Prof. Grzybowski; then the wounded and sick in the other rows were driven to death, and when the turn of those on stretchers came, they were shot first and the stretcher-bearers after them. It was only by a miracle that I escaped death. When I was driven to the entrance in a group of twelve, I turned to one of the officers and told him, falsely, that I myself and my two companions were Volksdeutsche (I speak German well). So the German ordered us to fall back and follow him; he led us to a German first-aid station, situated in the neighborhood. About 500 persons were shot in my presence, among them many from the Wola Hospital; others also, driven here from other streets in the Wola suburb, were with us. The volleys lasted till late into the night. At nightfall hand grenades were thrown on the heaps of corpses and in the morning a tank arrived, and demolished the burnt house, thus covering the corpses of the murdered (already partly burnt) as well as the place of execution.

The frightful smell of burning corpses was unbearable. I saw it all quite well, as I stayed in the German first-aid station (situated quite near), till the following morning."

(Central Commission..., 1946-1947, vol. 1, Record No. 80, pp. 193-195)

[Note: The "Germans" in this account are unidentified. "Ukrainians" refers to members of SS-Brigade Kaminski.]

Wolska Street

"When I was wounded and in hospital, about the middle of August (I do not remember the exact date), a group of 20 or 30 men and women were driven in. They were dreadfully burnt. They had been evacuated from the shelters under some houses in Wolska Street. When they had been in the streets, Vlassov's men threw inflammable liquid over them and drove them among the burning houses. Their clothes at once caught fire, especially the women's light dresses, and several of them could go no further. The others struggled on terribly burnt. As they could not walk any further, they were taken to the hospital. Their sufferings were awful; the eyes of some were burnt out, faces were burnt, others had open wounds on the whole body. Only one-third of these victims survived; the others died after inhuman suffering."

(Central Commission..., 1946-1947, vol. 1, Record No. 71, pp. 214-215)

[Note: "Vlassov's men" is a reference to members of SS-Brigade Kaminski.]

In an interesting case of "reverse revisionism", Madeja (1992) claimed --- contrary to overwhelmng German and Polish documentary evidence --- that SS-Brigade

Kaminski was composed of sterling individuals and committed no crimes in Warsaw. Madeja's writings clearly show him to be a Polish nationalist. Since he unaccountably identified the Ukrainians in the brigade as "Polish nationalists," he apparently fely compelled to whitewash this unit's atrocious behaviour.

Sources
(Bruce, 1972)
(Deschner, 1972)
(Luczak, 1968, pp. 163-166)
(Wroniszewski, 1970)
(Madeja, 1992)
(Stein, 1966, pp. 265-269)
(Reitlinger, 1957, p. 375)
(Lukas, 1990, pp. 184-219)
(MacLean, 1998, pp. 177-187)
(Munoz, 1991)
(IMT, 1948/1971, vol. 20, pp. 188-231)
(Central Commission....., 1946-7, vol. 1, pp. 188-223)

Warta River (Poland)

During the advance of the Leibstandarte Adolf Hitler Regiment (CO: SS-Obergruppenführer Josef "Sepp" Dietrich) towards the Warta River early in the campaign against Poland (1/6 September 1939), the unit responded to its mounting casualties by terrorizing the Polish populace. Numerous villages were fired and an unknown number of innocent civilians were randomly gunned down by the rampaging Waffen-SS troopers. There is no evidence that legal proceedings were ever instigated with respect to these crimes.

Sources
(Sayer & Botting, 1989, p. 20)
(United Nations War Crimes Commission file number 284/P/G/29)

Wloclawek (Poland)

SS-Totenkopfstandarte II Brandenburg, under the command of SS-Standartenführer Paul Nostitz, advanced into Poland on 13 September 1939 to perform "cleansing and security measures" in the operational zone of the 8th Army (large areas of Poznan and the entire west-central portion of Poland) as part of Einsatzgruppe III (CO: SS-Obersturmbannführer Dr. Herbert Fischer). On 22 September the unit arrived at the town of Wloclawek in central Poland and began a four day anti-Jewish operation that involved plundering Jewish shops, dynamiting and burning synagogues, and arresting and executing en masse large numbers of the local Jewish community. The Waffen-SS troopers also tortured several Jews into admitting responsibility for the synagogue fires. SS-Standartenführer Nostitz used this as an excuse to fine the Jewish community 100,000 zloty for arson. The precise number of Jews killed in Wloclawek is unknown, although SS-Standartenführer Nostitz had ordered 800 arrested and declared that he intended to have them all shot. By the end of the operation they were all dead. On 24 September, two of the unit's three battalions were detached and sent on an operation to Bydgoszcz. SS-Standartenführer Nostitz remained in Wloclawek with the remaining battalion.

Following the campaign in Poland, General Boehm-Tettelbach filed a report with the 8th Army commander protesting the actions taken by *Brandenburg* in Wloclawek. His impression was that *Brandenburg* had been dispatched to the town solely for the purpose of taking violent measures against the Jews. To support this assertion, the General cited SS-Standartenführer Nostitz's repeated refusal to perform normal security operations. The Waffen-SS officers and men preferred instead to remain in Wloclawek to torment Jews and other Polish civilians. General Boehm-Tettelbach also described how SS-Gruppenführer Pancke had boasted openly that the SS-Totenkopfverbande would not obey Wehrmacht orders, since they had special tasks to perform that were outside the Wehrmacht's competence. A number of the atrocity complaints specifically named *Brandenburg*'s III. Bataillon as responsible for the worst offenses. The battalion's command structure at this time was as follows:

battalion CO :
SS-Sturmbannführer Willi BettenhauiserAdjutant :
SS-Obersturmführer Lange
9. Schützenkompanie CO :
SS-Obersturmführer Otto Schöner
10. Schützenkompanie CO :
SS-Obersturmführer Otto Streich
11. Schützenkompanie CO :
SS-Hauptsturmführer Paul Kümmel
In an effort to quash these and other complaints about *Brandenburg*'s operations in Poland, Reichsführer-

SS Himmler ordered a prefunctory inquiry into the affair. In an official report (USHMM *Bericht....*) the commander of *Brandenburg*'s II. Bataillon denied the charges that III. Bataillon committed any atrocities. He stated that at 8:00 pm on 25 September 1939 the III. Bataillon had two companies surround Wloclawek while a third company searched the town and rounded up Jews for relocation. Two Jews who tried to escape were shot. The battalion commander also claimed that Wehrmacht troops looted the town, traded with the locals, and interfered with Waffen-SS operations. A second document in support of the above account was the statement of SS-Rottenführer Willi Grabosch, a member of 10. Kompanie / III. Bataillon, that he was on guard in Wloclawek on 25 September 1939 and was responsible for shooting dead the 3 escaping Jews (note numerical discrepancy with above report). Himmler publicly accepted this version of the events at Wloclawek and ignored independent reports of the mass executions that he had, in fact, authorized prior to the invasion of Poland.

On 1 November 1939, *Brandenburg* was designated as cadre for the newly activated SS-Totenkopfdivision (later the 3. SS-Panzer-Division *Totenkopf*). The fate of Paul Nostitz is uncertain, as of July 1944 he was posted to SS-Panzergrenadier-Ersatz-Bataillon 1. The fate of the officers of III. Bataillon is unknown.

Sources
(Sydnor, 1977, pp. 38-43)
(U.S. Holocaust Memorial Museum, RG-48.004M, Reel 3, FN 300041 - 300043, Kriegsarchiv SS [Military Historical Institute Prague] -- Bericht über den Einsatz des I. Bataillons der 2. SS-Totenkopfstandarte in Wloclawek and Meldung: SS-Rottenführer Willi Grabosch, both documents dated 20 October 1939, Dachau)

Wormhoudt (France)

During its advance on Dunkirk in May 1940, the Leibstandarte Adolf Hitler Regiment (CO: SS-Obergruppenführer Josef "Sepp" Dietrich) was ordered to attack from Watten towards Wormhoudt. LAH was opposed by the British 48th Infantry Division which proved a much more formidable foe than the Waffen-SS troopers had so far met during the French campaign. Defending Wormhoudt and nearby Esquelbecq were two machinegun platoons of the 4th Cheshire Regiment, the 53rd Anti-Tank Regiment RA (Worcestershire Yeomanry), and the 2nd Royal Warwicks. *LAH* launched its attack at 7:45 am on 28 May 1940. The brunt of its attack was carried by 5. Kompanie (CO: SS-Hauptsturmführer Wilhelm Mohnke) and 7. Kompanie (CO: SS-Hauptsturmführer Otto Baum) of the II. Bataillon under the command of SS-Sturmbannführer Ernst Schutzeck.

Early in the battle the regimental commander and his adjutant (SS-Obergruppenführer Dietrich and SS-Sturmbannführer Max Wünsche) were trapped by heavy British fire in a roadside ditch in no-man's land. The British resistance was the fiercest yet encountered by the men of the *LAH* and they attempted numerous tricks to subdue the stubborn defenders of Wormhoudt, including dressing as civilians and donning captured Allied uniforms. By 3:00 pm, the Waffen-SS troopers had made their way into the outskirts of Wormhoudt but only after suffering heavy losses. At this time SS-Sturmbannführer Schutzeck was severely wounded and SS-Sturmbannführer Mohnke assumed command of the battalion (SS-Obersturmführer Krämer took over as CO 5. Kompanie). Desperate house to house fighting ensued; the Waffen-SS troopers reached the village center at approximately 5:00 pm. Shortly thereafter, SS-Obergruppenführer Dietrich and his adjutant were rescued from their hiding place. The town center was firmly in German hands by 10:00 pm. Isolated pockets of British troops held out in the town until close to midnight.

A large number of British soldiers were taken prisoner by the *LAH* and were reasonably treated. After being rescued by his men, SS-Obergruppenführer Dietrich even entertained some captured British officers and presented them with armbands and SS runes as souvenirs. However, some POWs were not so lucky. According to evidence collected after the war from the villagers of Esquelbecq, some men of *LAH* were enraged by the trapping of their divisional commander, SS-Sturmbannführer Schutzeck's wounding, and the stiff British resistance. There was much talk of revenge among the Waffen-SS troopers and a number of atrocities against British POWs occurred throughout the day. Due to several complicating factors (including the loss of British unit records during the retreat to Dunkirk and the deliberate removal of ID tags by the Waffen-SS from the POWs they murdered) a final ac-

counting of the number of British POWs murdered by elements of *LAH* cannot be determined. Only those incidents for which overwhelming evidence existed will be examined. It is interesting to note that the killings of POWs ceased when SS-Obergruppenführer Dietrich was rescued and reassumed command of his troops in Wormhoudt from SS-Sturmbannführer Mohnke.

British Dressing Station

According to the Mayor of Wormhoudt and eyewitness Lance-Bombadier Tom H. Nicholls of the 53rd Anti-Tank Regiment RA (Worcestershire Yeomanry), following the capture of the town center unidentified Waffen-SS troopers killed a minimum of 20 British wounded at the British Dressing Station in Wormhoudt. Most were shot; some were bayonetted to death or drowned in a nearby horse pond. Four ambulances full of wounded were also doused with petrol, set on fire, and then riddled with small arms fire.

East of Wormhoudt

A wounded officer of the 53rd Anti-Tank Regiment RA (Worcestershire Yeomanry) saw a number of his men lined up against a wall and shot by unidentified Waffen-SS troopers along a road to the east of Wormhoudt.

La Plaine au Bois

Fifty men from D Company of the 2nd Royal Warwicks (including their company commander Captain John Frazer Lynne-Allen) were captured on the outskirts of Wormhoudt by elements of 7. Kompanie (CO: SS-Hauptsturmführer Baum). A detail of 2. Platoon (CO: SS-Untersturmführer Heinrichs) searched the prisoners, stripped them of all IDs, and marched them towards Wormhoudt. Along the way, the POWs witnessed the execution of another group of 15 - 20 British POWS against the wall of a cannery building. Their escort stopped at a cafe (the Estaminet St. Hubert) and drank their fill of wine. The POWs were then marched into the outskirts of Wormhoudt where more British soldiers were flushed out of buildings and taken prisoner. The group was then marched southwest out of town along the Ledringhem Road. Upon arriving at the II. Battalion Battle HQ, another 30 - 60 POWs (primarily from A Company / 2nd Royal Warwicks with a few members of the 4th Cheshire Regiment, the

242 Battery / 69th Medium Regiment / Royal Artillery, and D Company / 8th Battalion / 53rd Anti-Tank Regiment RA [Worcestershire Yeomanry]) were added to the group.

At this point SS-Hauptsturmführer Mohnke appeared and angrily rebuked SS-Untersturmführer Heinrichs for bringing in so many prisoners. SS-Untersturmführer Heinrichs relinquished the prisoners and his guard detail (SS-Rottenführers Oskar Senf, Werner Rüger, Max Schallwig and SS-Mann Dorth) to SS-Scharführer Walter Drescher who headed an eight man escort from Nachrichten-Kompanie 8 (SS-Scharführer Josef Sorowka and SS-Rottenführers Hans Konieczka, Dutschmann, Friedhof, Günther, Moebius, and one other). On the orders of SS-Scharführer Drescher the wounded POWs were double-marched at bayonet-point across the nearby fields. Those who could not keep up were beaten; one POW was bayonetted to death. After travelling a mile the POWs were herded into an old wooden barn at the edge of a big field in La Plaine au Bois --- five immediately escaped out a small back door (Bombadier Clarke, Driver Borland, Gunners Vickers and Salisbury, and one other).

Captain Lynne-Allen began to protest at this treatment of his men and his complaints were answered with taunts and a hand grenade. The explosion killed and wounded a number of the POWs. In the ensuing confusion Captain Lynne-Allen and Bert Evans fled from the barn. However, they were soon caught and gunned down in a nearby pond. Evans was seriously wounded but survived. The Waffen-SS guards then hurled several more grenades into the barn with devastating effect. The survivors were then ordered to come outside in groups of five. Each group was then led off a short distance and cut down with small-arms fire. After two groups had been executed, the remaining survivors refused to leave the barn. Not to be frustrated in their designs, the Waffen-SS troopers stormed into the barn and swept it with gunfire until they thought no one was left alive. In the middle of this wild firing, one of the guards (SS-Rottenführer Werner Rüger) was accidentally hit by friendly fire and severely wounded. Several guards left to get medics while the remainder hung around to insure that all of the POWs were dead. The wounded guard was evacuated to a nearby dressing station and the guards returned to their units.

Miraculously, twenty of the British POWs survived this massacre attempt. They were: 2nd Royal Warwicks -- Private Bennett, Lance-Corporal Box, Private Cooper, Charles Daley, Private Dutton, Albert Evans, Corporal Robert Gill, George Hall, George Hopper, Private Johnson, Private Kelly, John Lavelle, Alfred Tombs, Private Townsend, Reginald West, and Robert Wildsmith; 4th Cheshires -- Private Cyril Harbour, Private Robinson, Gunner Richard Parry; and Royal Artillery -- Brian Fahey. Nine of the survivors were still ambulatory and fled the barn as soon as the Waffen-SS troopers left the scene. They were all eventually captured by other German units and sent to POW camps. Soon after the massacre, several French farmers happened upon the seriously wounded soldiers in the barn but refused to help them. Four of the survivors (Bennett, Box, Kelly, and Townsend) would die as a result of their wounds in the several days that elapsed before the group was discovered by German medical personnel and evacuated to a Wehrmacht dressing station for care.

Road to Dunkirk

A gun crew from the King's Heath (Birmingham) T.A. Battery / 210. Anti-Tank Regiment was stripped and shot after surrendering to unidentified Waffen-SS troops at the cafe on the road out to Dunkirk.

Southwest of Wormhoudt

At approximately 10:00 am, unidentified members of 5. Kompanie / II. Bataillon / *LAH* (CO: SS-Hauptsturmführer Mohnke) shot seven British POWs (5 from the 2nd Royal Warwicks; 2 from the 53rd Anti-Tank Regiment RA [Worcestershire Yeomanry]) at a location southwest of Wormhoudt. These murders were witnessed by Gunner Arthur Baxter, also of the Worcestershire Yeomanry, who was wounded and playing dead nearby. Two of the victims, in a truck, were also covered with petrol and set on fire after being shot.

Town Square

At approximately 1:50 pm Lance-Corporal T.A. Oxley and three companions (a mixed party of 2nd Royal Warwicks and 4th Cheshires) were gunned down after surrendering to unidentified reconnaissance elements of II. Bataillon / *LAH* in the Wormhoudt town square. Luckily, Lance-Corporal Oxley was only wounded and able to play dead. He later also witnessed the execution of a British sergeant.

Aftermath and Early Legal Proceedings

The massacre at the barn was the news-of-the-day in the *LAH* Regimental messes until SS-Obergruppen-führer Dietrich invoked the SS oath to insure silence on the matter. However, word of the atrocity reached outsiders (such as Korvetten Kapitän Alfred Roden-bücher, an officer in the Naval Reserve of the Marine Station Commando *Baltic*) posted to the regiment to obtain combat experience. Several days after the massacre, an unidentified work party buried the bodies in an unmarked mass grave in a nearby field. In an effort to conceal the crime, German authorities relocated the mass grave in 1941 and had a French work party exhume the bodies and re-inter them in six separate graves (one in Wormhoudt, four at Esquelbecq Military Cemetary, and one unknown).

In October 1943 an exchange of wounded British and German POWs resulted in the repatriation of several Wormhoudt survivors to Britain. Upon their return, the crime became known for the first time. Preliminary statements were taken by investigators of the Royal Warwickshire Regiment. Little was done until April 1947 when all known Wormhoudt survivors received a letter from the Judge Advocate General's Office requesting them to come forward and give evidence for ongoing inquiries. Survivors were interviewed at the War Crimes Investigation Unit / London District Prisoner of War Cage by Lieutenant-Colonel Alexander P. Scotland and also brought back to Wormhoudt to familiarize investigators with the scene of the crimes. French civilian witnesses were also interviewed who confirmed specific instances of murder and also painted a picture of Waffen-SS troopers on a wild rampage for an hour or two that afternoon abandoning all pretence of observing international law and civilized values.

Meanwhile, all surviving members of II. Bataillon / *LAH* Regiment were rounded up at the London District Cage for questioning. Drescher, Heinrichs, and Dorth had all been killed in action in the USSR. Wilhelm Mohnke was rumored to be in Soviet custody, but Soviet authorities refused to provide confirmation. In any event the surviving Waffen-SS men proved less than cooperative with British investigators. They either denied that the killings at the barn occurred or

claimed that they were justified because the POWs had shot one of their guards and then tried to escape. A substantial number of the Waffen-SS men hedged their bets even further by testifying that if the killings had occurred as the British claimed, then Wilhelm Mohnke would have been responsible for issuing the orders. British investigators finally broke the case with the deathbed testimony of Oskar Senf, one of the executioners. Dying of consumption, Senf outlined in detail all of the events leading up to and including the killings at the barn. His account contradicted the testimony of his comrades, but confirmed those given by British survivors. The work of Lieutenant-Colonel Scotland and the staff at the LDC resulted in the submission of two reports to the Judge Advocate General's Office in 1947 (First Wormhoudt Inquiry Report [WCIU/LDC/1500] and Second Wormhoudt Inquiry Report [WCIU/LDC/1650]).

In September 1948 the British Government ceased to hold war crimes trials or to further investigate the accusations against war criminals. The Wormhoudt case was left unresolved; no one was ever tried for the killings. Much of the evidence developed by the LDC team clearly indicated that Wilhelm Mohnke had ordered the execution of POWs as a general practice. The fact that the murdered POWs' dog tags and other forms of ID had been removed was highly significant --- the murders were either clearly premeditated or subsequently covered up. Since the British Government had found *prima facie* evidence against Mohnke and others, the killings at Le Plaine au Bois --- under the designation "Wormhoudt Massacre" --- received a United Nations War Crimes Case Number (128/UK/G/28). The two Wormhoudt Inquiry Reports were judged by the British Government to fall under the Official Secrets Act and are unavailable to the public until 1 January 2021 (see below, however).

The Fate of Wilhelm Mohnke and Ongoing Investigations

On 22 April 1945, SS-Brigadeführer Wilhelm Mohnke was appointed commander of the central "Zitadelle" (Citadel) area of Berlin. He was captured by the Russians in Berlin on 2 May 1945 and sent to Strausberg POW camp. By 9 May 1945 Mohnke was being held in Budirka Prison (Moscow) and subject to endless interrogations about Hitler and his inner circle. He was later sent to Lubyanka Prison (Moscow) where the friendly but insistent interrogations continued. In 1949 Mohnke was tried for unspecified war crimes and sentenced to life imprisonment at Woikowo Prison camp in the Urals (300 kilometers east of Moscow). However, a growing rapprochement between the West German and Soviet Governments led to the widescale release of German POWs held in the USSR. Wilhelm Mohnke was paroled and returned to West Germany on 10 October 1955. He located his family and immediately vanished from public view.

In 1976 Mohnke was found living near Hamburg, Germany. At the prompting of Reverend Leslie Aitken the Canadian Government supplied its No. 1 Canadian War Crimes Investigation Unit case files on other atrocities committed in Normandy by elements of the 12. SS-Panzer-Division *Hitlerjugend* (then under Mohnke's command) to the West German State Prosecutor. West German authorities, however, took no action against Mohnke for his involvement in these crimes. Reverend Aitken went on to publish a semi-complete account of the Wormhoudt massacre (Aitken, 1977). This spurred on other historians who brought the matter to the attention of British Government officials. On 21 April 1988 a British Member of Parliament, Jeff Rooker, put a question on the subject of Wilhelm Mohnke and the Wormhoudt Massacre to the Home Secretary in the House of Commons. Copies of the secret LCD "Reports of Inquiry" were leaked and given to Rooker. A press field-day erupted throughout Britain about the "Nazi killer who had escaped justice." The media backlash reached all the way to West Germany, where Mohnke came out of seclusion to protest his innocence. A few months later, the Parliament Under-Secretary of State for Defense revealed the full extent of Waffen-SS crimes at Wormhoudt.

Despite the evidence made public about Mohnke's crimes against Canadian POWs (Normandy), American POWs (Malmedy), and Belgian civilians (Malmedy) and the fact that he was still on Canadian, American and United Nations "wanted" lists, none of the governments in question showed any interest in pursuing legal actions against him. Under pressure from the British Government and at the request of a survivor, West German federal prosecutors opened inquiries into the Wormhoudt Massacre. In the autumn of 1988, Mohnke suffered a mild heart attack. By early 1989 the German authorities concluded that there was insufficient evidence to bring charges against Mohnke. This judgement was hardly surprising considering the Federal Republic's poor track record of indicting and convicting war criminals. According to the most recent information available, Wilhelm Mohnke is living in retired seclusion at Barsbüttel, near Hamburg.

Sources
(Cunliffe, 1956)
(Aitken, 1977)
(Reynolds, 1995, pp. 26-7 & 262)
(Messenger, 1988, pp. 83-6 &178 & 210)
(Lehmann, 1977-1987)
(Sayer & Botting, 1989)
(Worcestershire Regiment Magazine, October 1987, p. 60)

Yefrenovka (USSR)

At the Nuremberg Trials of Major German War Criminals the accusation was made that SS-Panzergrenadier-Regiment 2 / 1. SS-Panzer-Division Leibstandarte Adolf Hitler (CO: SS-Obergruppenführer Josef "Sepp" Dietrich) burned the town of Yefrenovka and murdered its civilian population in Spring 1943. No evidence to support this accusation was ever produced by the Soviet authorities.

Source
(IMT, 1948/1971, vol. 20, p. 395)

Zakroczym (Poland)

On 28 September 1939 at Zakroczym (District Nowy Dwor Mazowiecki, northwest of Warsaw) an unidentified Waffen-SS unit shot 500 Polish POWs and 100 Polish civilians. In all likelihood, these murders were committed by one of the Einsatzgruppen operating in Poland at this time.

Sources
(Datner, 1964, p. 307)
(C.C.I.N.C. in Poland, Province of Warsaw, vol. 5, p. 915)

Zborow (Poland)

The Einsatzgruppen report for 11 July 1941 (Ereignismeldung UdSSR Nr. 19; Berlin, July 11, 1941; Einsatzgruppe C/Einsatzkommando 4b cited in *Arad et al.*) records that "600 Jews were executed at Zborow between Tarnopol and Lwow by the Waffen SS as a reprisal for Soviet cruelties." Th reprisal referred to occurred on 9 July and the report is only approximately correct in its details. Motorcycle reconnaissance patrols of the 5. SS-Panzer-Division *Wiking* (CO: SS-Gruppenführer Felix Steiner) scouting ahead of the advance from Lvov had reported that at Leichenbergen thousands of murdered civilians lay in the courtyard, halls, and cellars of the GPU prison (Soviet Secret Police, precursors to the KGB). Apparently they were innocent Ukrainian victims of the retreating Soviet security forces. These murders are undoubtedly the "Soviet cruelties" referred to in the Einsatzgruppen report. At the same time, however, the popular commander of the division's *Westland* regiment (SS-Standartenführer Hilmar Wäckerle) had just been killed in a partisan ambush and many *Wiking* troopers were thirsting for revenge.There is no doubt that elements of *Wiking* took part in the 9 July massacre. Divisional records confirm that *Wiking* supply units passed through Zborow at this time. At the post-war Einsatzgruppen Trial before the International Military Tribunal, a former member of *Wiking* gave the following testimony:

> "The members of the meat train and the bakery company systematically rounded up all Jews who could be found based on their facial characteristic and their speech, as most of them spoke Yiddish. SS-Obersturmführer Braunnagel of the bakery company and SS-Untersturmführer Kochalty were in charge of rounding them up. Then a path was formed by two rows of soldiers. Most of the soldiers were from the meat train and the bakery company, but some of them were from the 1st Mountain Hunter Division. The Jews were then forced to run down the path and while doing so the people on both sides beat them with their rifle butts and bayonets. At the end of the path stood a number of SS and Wehrmacht officers with machine pistols, with which they shot the Jews dead as soon as they had entered into the bomb crater (being used as a mass grave). (Superior officers of the regiment) were part of this group that conducted the shootings. About fifty to sixty Jews were killed in this manner."
>
> *[Statement of Günther Otto, IMT NO-4434]*

The "1st Mountain Hunter Division" mentioned is a reference to the Wehrmacht's 1. Gebirgs-Division (CO: Generalleutnant Hubert Lanz). Support for this version of events can also be found in the diaries of several members of Wiking's Finnish battalion. The above-cited Einsatzgruppen report erred in attributing 600 deaths to the Zborow massacre. All available evidence indicates that most of these deaths are attributable to operations conducted in the Lvov area at this same time by Sonderkommando 4b (SS-Obersturmbannführer Günther Herrmann). After the war, the Wiking supply column commander who had allegedly given the execution order, Heinz Karl Fanslau, was acquitted on the grounds that there was no solid evidence linking him to the order (IMT Case IV, Judgment 8104). Fanslau was later re-arrested on charges related to his activities with the SS-WVHA, tried, and sentenced to 25 years imprisonment.

Sources
(Butler, 2002, p. 45)
(Strassner, 1968, pp. 8, 15-16)
(Arad et al., 1989, p. 19)
(Reitlinger, 1957, p. 157)
(Stein, 1966, p. 272)
(Theile, 1997, p. 319)

Zdunska Wola (Poland)

During it advance through Poland in September 1939 (most likely on 7 September), elements of II. Bataillon / *Leibstandarte Adolf Hitler* Regiment under the command of SS-Obersturmbannführer Carl Ritter von Oberkamp tortured an unknown number of civilians in the town of Zdunska Wola. The structure of the battalion at this time was as follows:

5. Kompanie
SS-Hauptsturmführer Wilhelm Mohnke
6. Kompanie
SS-Hauptsturmführer Otto Baum
7. Kompanie

SS-Hauptsturmführer Seppel Lange

8. Kompanie

SS-Hauptsturmführer August Dieterichs

SS-Hauptsturmführer Lange was killed in action on 12 September 1939 and replaced by SS-Hauptsturmführer Artur Klingemeier. There is no evidence that legal proceedings were ever instigated with respect to these crimes. Carl Ritter von Oberkamp was executed in 1947 by the Yugoslavian authorities for numerous atrocities committed against Balkan civilians.

Sources

(Sayer & Botting, 1989, p. 20)

(United Nations War Crimes Commission file number 284/P/G/29)

Zwiahel region (USSR)

Between 28-30 July 1941, near the town of Zwiahel in the operational area of the 6th Army, the 1. SS-Infanterie (mot.)-Brigade under the command of SS-Brigadeführer Richard Hermann conducted an "Aktion" which resulted in the execution of 73 Russian soldiers, 165 Communist functionaries and "other persons," as well as 1,658 Jews and "bolshevist Ukrainians." This brigade was a rear-area Waffen-SS unit responsible for numerous anti-partisan and extermination operations. It also supplied replacements to the main-series Waffen-SS divisions in 1941/1942 and later provided cadre to both the 18. SS-Freiwilligen-Panzergrenadier-Division Horst Wessel and the 20. Waffen-Grenadier-Division der SS (estnische Nr. 1).

Source

(Krausnick, 1981, pp. 221-222)

Atrocities - Photos

Suspects lined up before their execution, somewhere in France.

A common and very cruel form of killing that the Waffen SS used many times during their war against the civilian population. The victims were tied up and thrown into wells to drown. Peasants worked hard to retreive the bodies from the wells so they could get a proper burial.

Waffen SS troops starting a "search" in a village. During such "searches" it was common that civilians were murdered for no reason other than that they happened to live in the house or pass by in the street at the time of the "search".

Le Paradis, Scene of the crime

Prisoners from the Royal Norfolk Regiment being marched to the rear.

The Brittish troops are being rounded up by the SS-troops after the battle. This photo is perhaps taken just before the massacre started.

One of the German victims of British sniper fire, which was used as an excuse for the SS to commit the massacre.

SS-Obersturmbannführer Fritz Knöchlein

After the massacre at Le Paradis; summer 1940. From left in the photo: SS-Stubaf. Fortenbacher (Kdr I./SS-T. IR 2), SS-Hstuf. Knöchlein (Kdr. 3.Kp./SS-T.IR 2) and on the right SS-Ostuf. Walter Reder. After the war Reder was convicted of the massacre at Marzabotto in Italy. Knöchlein was sentanced to death after the war for his involvement in the massacre at Le Paradis.

The key witnesses for the prosecutor in the trial after the war regarding the massacre at Le Paradis: O´Callaghan on the left and Pooley, on their way to appear at the court in Hamburg.

Madame Creton, standing outside the scene of the crime, helped Pooley and O´Callaghan to hide for several hours after the massacre and enabled them in that way to avoid capture by the SS and survive the war.

A temporary memorial erected by the local population at the site of the massacre.

This was once Lidice outside Prague

Photos showing the demolition of Lidice after the population has been murdered. The village was blown up, the waste removed and the whole area was turned into a newly planted forest.

Lidice after the demolition.

The man, whose death became the main excuse for comitting the massagre at Lidice, SS-Obergruppen-führer Reinhard Heydrich

Malmedy: The trial – The accused. L-R front: Dietrich, Krämer, Priess and Pieper
Second row: Coblenz, Fischer, Gruhle, Hennecke and Junker.
Third row: Knittel.

Malmedy: Victims of the Waffen SS: American soldiers who had surrendered and laid down their arms were brutally murdered by Waffen SS soldiers December 1944.

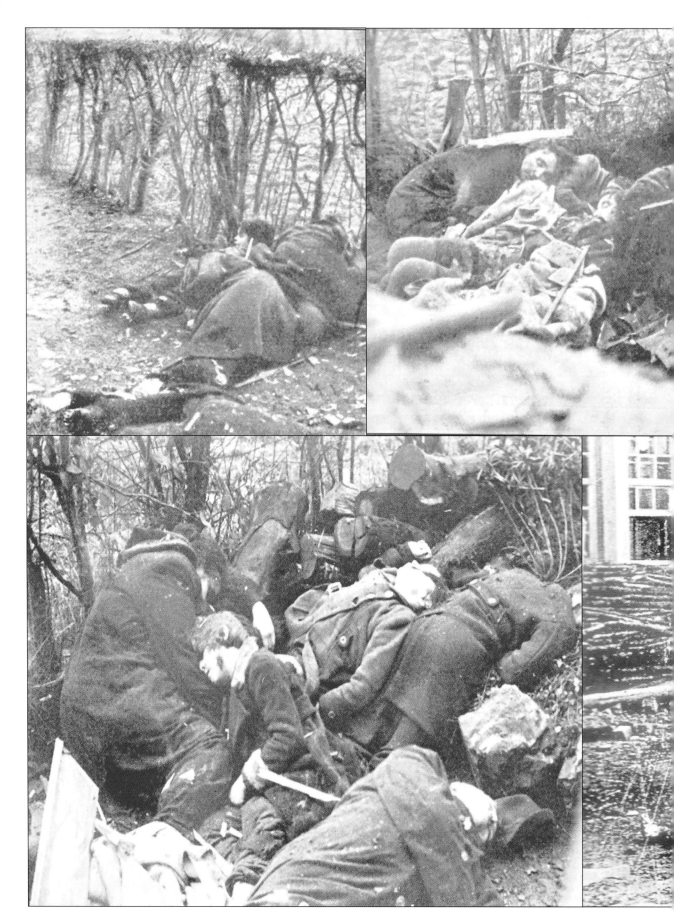

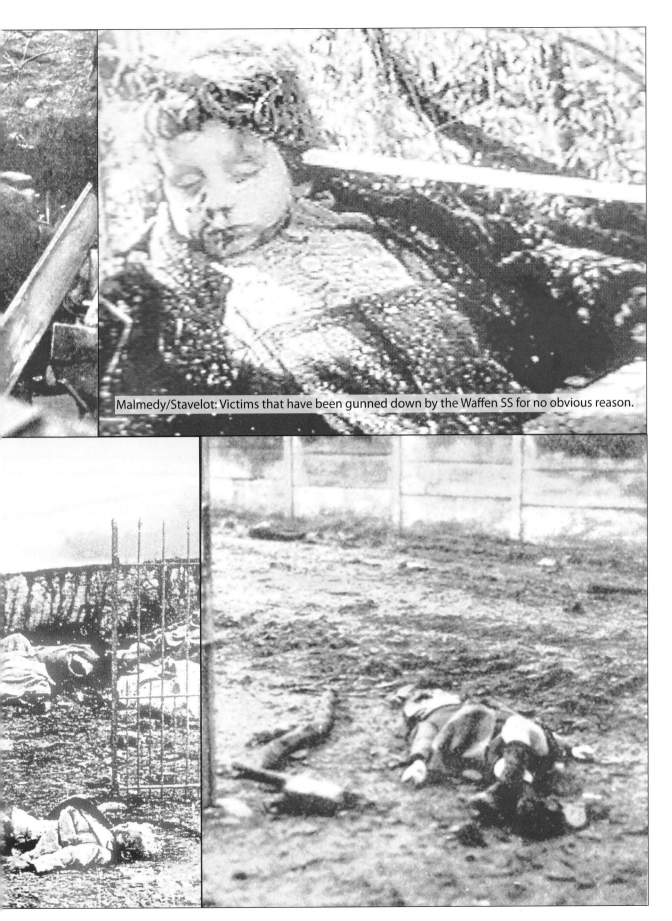

Malmedy/Stavelot: Victims that have been gunned down by the Waffen SS for no obvious reason.

183

Malmedy/Stavelot: The burial of the victims murdered by the Waffen SS troops.

Oradour: The way the church in Oradour looked before it was used as a killing ground by the Waffen SS in June 1944.

Oradour: This aerial view show how the whole village looks today.

Oradour: This is how Oradour has looked ever since that day in June 1944. The village has never been rebuilt.

The burial of some of the victims in Oradour.

Oradour: The victims are being identified before their proper burial.

Oradour Tulles: A sketch made by one of the Waffen SS soldiers taking part in the murders at Tulles in June 1944, showing the hanging of civilians from the lamp posts in Tulles.

Oradour Tulles: Murdered civilians outside Tulles, June 1944.

Warsaw Ghetto: The Waffen SS are rounding up Jews who had been hiding in cellars. They will soon be transported to the death camps.

Warsaw Ghetto: The Waffen SS are rounding up Jews who has been hiding in cellars.
They will soon be transported to the death camps.

Warsaw Ghetto: Inhabitants of the Ghetto are marched off for transportation to the extremination camps.

Warsaw uprising: Civilians being taken away for execution or transportation to a camp, where they will surely be killed.

Most of the time, civilians were shot and buried in massgraves.

A firing squad from the Waffen SS at work somewhere in the East.

Waffen SS troops burning down a village in the occupied territories. A common sight during the war in the East

A suspect is forced out of a house, he will soon be murdered. The Waffen SS soldiers are from a Einsatz group.

The most common excuse for murdering civilians – an accusation of being a Partisan.
Those suspected of being Partisans were usually hung.

Units and Organizations

Unit and Organization Master List

Waffen-SS Field Divisions:

1. SS-Panzer-Division Leibstandarte Adolf Hitler
2. SS-Panzer-Division Das Reich
3. SS-Panzer-Division Totenkopf
4. SS-Polizei-Panzergrenadier-Division
5. SS-Panzer-Division Wiking
6. SS-Gebirgs-Division Nord
7. SS-Freiwilligen-Gebirgs-Division Prinz Eugen
8. SS-Kavallerie-Division Florian Geyer
9. SS-Panzer-Division Hohenstaufen
10. SS-Panzer Division Frundsberg
11. SS-Freiwilligen-Panzergrenadier-Division Nordland
12. SS-Panzer-Division Hitlerjugend
13. Waffen-Gebirgs-Division der SS Handschar (kroatische Nr. 1)
14. Waffen-Grenadier-Division der SS (ukrainische Nr. 1)
15. Waffen-Grenadier-Division der SS (lettische Nr. 1)
16. SS-Panzergrenadier-Division Reichsführer-SS
17. SS-Panzergrenadier-Division Götz von Berlichingen
18. SS-Freiwilligen-Panzergrenadier-Division Horst Wessel
19. Waffen-Grenadier-Division der SS (lettische Nr. 2)
20. Waffen-Grenadier-Division der SS (estnische Nr. 1)
21. Waffen-Gebirgs-Division der SS Skanderbeg (albanische Nr. 1)
22. SS-Freiwilligen-Kavallerie-Division Maria Theresia
23. Waffen-Gebirgs-Division der SS Kama (kroatische Nr. 2)
23. SS-Freiwilligen-Panzergrenadier-Division Nederland
24. Waffen-Gebirgs-Division der SS Karstjäger
25. Waffen-Grenadier-Division der SS Hunyadi (ungarische Nr. 1)
26. Waffen-Grenadier-Division der SS (ungarische Nr. 2)
27. SS-Freiwilligen-Grenadier-Division Langemarck (flämische Nr. 1)
28. SS-Freiwilligen-Panzergrenadier-Division Wallonie
29. Waffen-Grenadier-Division der SS (russische Nr. 1)
29. Waffen-Grenadier-Division der SS (italienische Nr. 1)
30. Waffen-Grenadier-Division der SS (russische Nr. 2)
31. SS-Freiwilligen-Grenadier-Division
32. SS-Freiwilligen-Grenadier-Division 30 Januar
33. Waffen-Grenadier-Division der SS Charlemagne (französische Nr. 1) 34. SS-Grenadier-Division Landstorm Nederland
35. SS-Polizei-Grenadier-Division
36. Waffen-Grenadier-Division der SS
37. SS-Freiwilligen-Kavallerie-Division Lutzow
38. SS-Grenadier-Division Nibelungen

Other Waffen-SS Units and Associated Organizations:

1. SS-Infanterie (mot.) Brigade
2. SS-Infanterie (mot.) Brigade
SS-Totenkopfstandarten
Waffen-SS-Bataillon-zur besondere Verwendung
SS-Fallschirmjäger-Bataillonen 500/600
SS-Jäger-Bataillon 500
SS-Jäger-Bataillon 501
Foreign Ministry Sonderkommando Künsberg/SS-Sonderkommando Künsberg
SS-Sonderkommando 1005
Einsatzgruppen in Austria, Czechoslovakia and Poland
Einsatzgruppen in the USSR
Höheren SS-und Polizeiführer (HSSPf)

1. SS-Panzer-Division

Leibstandarte Adolf Hitler
Organizational History

17 March 1933 : SS-Stabswache Berlin formed.

May 1933 : Unit redesignated SS-Sonderkommando Zossen.

September 1933: Unit combined with SS-Sonderkommando Juterbog to form newly designated Leibstandarte SS *Adolf Hitler*.

Mid-December 1934: Unit motorized and redesignated Leibstandarte SS *Adolf Hitler* (mot.) Regiment.

12 August 1940 : Unit expanded to brigade strength, though not retitled.

June 1941 : Unit redesignated SS-Division *Leibstandarte SS Adolf Hitler*.

17 February 1942 : Cadre sent to SS-Kampfgruppe Jeckeln (later incorporated into 20. Waffen-Grenadier-Division der SS [estnische Nr. 1]).

June/September 1942 : Unit withdrawn to France for refitting.

9 September 1942 : Unit redesignated SS-Panzergrenadier-Division *Leibstandarte SS Adolf Hiler*.

5 May 1943 : Cadre sent to Estnische SS-Freiwilligen-Brigade [precursor of 20. Waffen-Grenadier-Division der SS (estnische Nr. 1)].

June 1943 : Cadre detached to form 12. SS-Panzer-Division *Hitlerjugend*.

Mid-1943 : Cadre detached to form 9. SS-Panzer-Division *Hohenstaufen*.

September/November 1943 : Unit rebuilt with young German Waffen-SS recruits in northern Italy.

22 October 1943 : Unit re-designated 1. SS-Panzer-Division *Leibstandarte SS Adolf Hitler*.

January 1944 : Unit receives final designation (see above).

February 1945 : Unit partially rebuilt after Ardennes Offensive using Luftwaffe and Kriegsmarine personnel, as well as conscripted factory workers.

Commanding Officers
- SS-Oberst-Gruppenführer Josef "Sepp" Dietrich (3/17/33-7/43)
- SS-Brigadeführer Theodor Wisch (7/43-8/20/44)
- SS-Oberführer Wilhelm Mohnke (8/20/44-2/6/45)
- SS-Brigadeführer Otto Kumm (2/6/45-5/8/45)

Main Combat Units (as of 6/44)
- SS-Panzergrenadier-Regiment LAH 1
- SS-Panzergrenadier-Regiment LAH 2
- SS-Panzer-Regiment LAH 1
- SS-Panzerartillerie-Regiment LAH 1
- SS-Panzeraufklärungs-Abteilung 1
- SS-Panzerjäger-Abteilung 1
- SS-Sturmgeschütz-Abteilung 1
- SS-Flak-Abteilung 1
- SS-Panzerpionier-Bataillon 1
- SS-Panzernachrichten-Abteilung 1

Disposition
Leibstandarte Adolf Hitler Führer-Begleit-Bataillon annihilated in Berlin on 3 May 1945 while defending the Reichskanzlerei. During the German general retreat through Austria part of the divisional rearguard was cut off and captured by the Soviets. Bulk of division surrendered on 8 May 1945 to American forces near Steyr, Austria (1,500 survivors from a June 1944 strength of 19,700).

Claimed Atrocities
- Berlin [Germany] : 27 February 1943
- Blonie [Poland] : 18 - 19 September 1939
- Boves [Italy] : 19 September 1943
- Bzura [Poland] : September 1939
- Czestochowa [Poland] : 1 - 2 October 1939

- Gejgowa/Kherson [USSR] : 16 - 18 August 1941
- Gorych [USSR] : July 1941
- Kharkov 1 [USSR] : 16+ December 1941
- Kharkov 2 [USSR] : 13 - 14 March 1943
- Kharkov 3 [USSR] : March - August 1943
- Lago Maggiore [Italy] : 22 - 24 September 1943
- Lodz [Poland] : 8 September 1939
- Malmedy [Belgium] : 17 December 1944 -13 January 1945
- Poland : September 1939
- Rostov-na-Donau [USSR] : November 1941
- Staroverovka [USSR] : Spring 1943
- Tavaux-et-Pontsericourt[France]30 August 1944
- Torzeniec [Poland] : 1 September 1939
- Warta River [Poland] : 1 - 6 September 1939
- Wormhoudt [France] : 28 May 1940
- Yefrenovka [USSR] : Spring 1943
- Zdunska Wola [Poland] : 7 September 1939
- see also *Miscellaneous Atrocities*

Security Operations

- Böhmen-Mähren [Czechoslovakia] : 28 September 1939 - 11 November 1939
- Tanny-en-Bazois, Autun [France] : 26 June 1940
- Metz, Lorraine [France] : 5 July 1940 - 28 July 1940
- Greece : 1 May 1941 - 17 May 1941
- Serbia/Croatia : 18 May 1941 - 31 May 1941
- Kiev [USSR] : 15 July 1941 - 23 July 1941
- Dnepr River Sector [USSR] : 19 August 1941 - 22 August 1941
- Kharkov [USSR] : 21 March 1943 - 31 March 1943
- Valki [USSR] : 28 March 1943
- Turin area [Italy] : 5 August 1943
- Milan, Turin, Verona [Italy] : 8 September 1943 - 12 December 1943
- Trieste [Italy] : 21 - 29 September 1943
- Pula, Rijeka [Yugoslavia] : 1 - 10 October 1943
- southeast of Laibach [Yugoslavia] : 12 - 27 October 1943

2. SS-Panzer-Division *Das Reich*

Organizational History

10 October 1939 : Formation of SS-Verfügungstruppe-Division (mot.) from SS-Standarte 1 *Deutschland*, SS-Standarte 2 *Germania* and SS-Standarte 3 *Der Führer* at Truppenübungsplatz Brdy-Wald (Pilsen).

1 April 1940 : Unit redesignated SS-Verfügungs-Division (mot.).

20 November 1940 : SS-Standarte 2 *Germania* sent as cadre to form new *Germania* division (later designated *Wiking*). Unit is redesignated SS-Division *Deutschland*.

21 December 1940 :
Unit redesignated SS-Division *Reich*.

1 September 1941 : Incorporation of 1,014 effectives (former SS-Infanterie-Regiment 5 / 2. SS-Infanterie-Brigade) as replacements.

1 November 1941 : Incorporation of SS-Totenkopf-Standarte 11 (formed from elements of SS-Totenkopf-Standarte 4 and Austrian volunteers) into SS-Infanterie-Regiment 3 *Deutschland* and SS-Infanterie-Regiment 4 *Der Führer*.

1942 : Personnel transferred to strengthen Waffen-SS guard units at the Auschwitz extermination camp.

April 1942 : Unit rebuilt at Truppenübungsplatz Bergen (Lager Fallingbostel) after heavy losses in USSR.

May 1942 : Unit redesignated SS-Division *Das Reich*.

1 June 1942 : Incorporation of SS-Infanterie-Regiment *Langemarck* at Lager Fallingbostel.

9 November 1942 : Unit upgraded and redesignated SS-Panzergrenadier-Division *Das Reich*.

January 1944 :Unit receives final designation (see above).
Commanding Officers
- SS-Obergruppenführer Paul Hausser (10/19/39 - 10/14/41) wounded

- SS-Brigadeführer Wilhelm Bittrich
  (10/14/41 - 12/31/41)
- SS-Brigadeführer Matthias Kleinheisterkamp
  (1/1/42 - 4/1/42)
- SS-Gruppenführer Georg Keppler
  (4/1/42 - 2/15/43) taken ill
- SS-Oberführer Herbert Ernst Vahl
  (2/15/43 - 4/3/43)
- SS-Gruppenführer Friedrich Wilhelm Krüger
  (4/3/43 - 11/1/43)
- SS-Brigadeführer Heinz Lammerding (12/9/43
  - 7/26/44) wounded
- SS-Obersturmbannführer Christian Tychsen
  (7/26/44 - 7/28/44) KI
- SS-Standartenführer Otto Baum
  (7/28/44 - 10/15/44)
- SS-Brigadeführer Heinz Lammerding
  (10/16/44 - 1/20/45)
- SS-Standartenführer Karl Kreutz
  (1/20/45 - 2/4/45)
- SS-Gruppenführer Werner Ostendorff
  (2/4/45 - 3/9/45) wounded
- SS-Standartenführer Rudolf Lehmann
  (3/9/45 - 4/13/45)
- SS-Standartenführer Karl Kreutz
  (4/13/45 - 5/10/45)

Main Combat Units (as of 6/44)
- SS-Panzergrenadier-Regiment 3 *Deutschland*
- SS-Panzergrenadier-Regiment 4 *Der Führer*
- SS-Panzer-Regiment 2
- SS-Panzerartillerie-Regiment 2
- SS-Panzeraufklärungs-Abteilung 2
- SS-Panzerjäger-Abteilung 2
- SS-Flak-Abteilung 2

- SS-Pionier-Bataillon 2
- SS-Nachrichten-Abteilung 2
- SS-Feldersatz-Bataillon

Disposition
In May 1945 a small portion of the division was overrun and destroyed by Soviet forces in northern Böhmen (Czechoslovakia). The remainder surrendered between 8 and 10 May 1945 to American forces near Pilsen, Böhmen.

Claimed Atrocities
- Bais [France] : 6 August 1944
- Bagneres-de-Bigorre [France] : 11 June 1944
- Carsac-de Carlux [France] : 8 June 1944
- Dunes [France] : 23 June 1944
- Fraysinnet-le-Gelat [France] : 21 May 1944
- Gabaudet [France] : 8 June 1944
- Gau Niederdonau [Austria] : April 1945
- Kharkov 3 [USSR] : March - July 1943
- Lahoysk [USSR] : September 1941
- Lidice [Czechoslovakia] : 10 June 1942
- Mussidan [France] : 11 June 1944
- Oradour-sur-Glane [France] : 10 June 1944
- Radom [Poland] : Autumn 1939 - Summer 1940
- St. Germain-du-Belair [France] : June 1944
- Staro Konstantinov [USSR] :
- Tulle [France] : 9 June 1944
- see also *Miscellaneous Atrocities*

Security Operations
- Apeldoorn, Zutphen, Helder [Holland] : 12 July 1940 - 15 December 1940
- Banat, Belgrade [Yugoslavia] : 11 April 1941 - 30 April 1941 (in Belgrade after April 12)
- Oskol, west of Weluiki [USSR] : 30 January 1943

3. SS-Panzer-Division *Totenkopf*

Organizational History

1 November 1939 : Unit activation ordered and formation begun as SS-Totenkopf-Division at SS-Truppenübungslager Dachau and later Truppenübungslager Obermünsingen. Personnel consisted of three Totenkopfstandarten (concentration camp guard regiments) - SSTK 1 *Oberbayern*, SSTK 2 *Brandenburg*, SSTK 3 *Thuringen*; the semi-autonomous security unit SS-*Heimwehr Danzig* (approximately 1500 effectives); as well as elements from the SS-Verfügungs Division, Ordnungspolizei personnel, Allgemeine SS reservists, and new Totenkopfverbande units raised during the last months of peace. Key positions on divisional staff were awarded to individuals possessing concentration camp or concentration camp inspectorate experience.

August 1940 : Incorporation of SS-Totenkopfstandarte 12 as replacements.

2 November 1940 : Incorporation of two battalions of concentration camp guards as replacements.

October 1941 : Incorporation of a company from SS-Bataillon-zur besondere Verwendung (sub-unit of Einsatzgruppe A) as replacements.

Winter 1941 - 42 : Large numbers of Waffen-SS reservists from concentration camps incorporated as replacements.

17 April 1942 : Incorporation of 500 effectives from SS-Freikorps *Dänemark* as replacements.

Spring - Summer 1942 : Incorporation of 3,000 Waffen-SS reservists, a few Danish SS volunteers, and some Volksdeutsche recruits from other Waffen-SS divisions.

Mid-October 1942 : Unit sent to France for refitting. Reinforced by 1,500 Waffen-SS reservists from Warsaw, 6,000 draftees from the RAD (Reichsarbeitdienst) released for SS service, and the 500 survivors of SS-Infanterie-Regiment 9.

9 November 1942 : Unit upgraded and redesignated SS-Panzergrenadier-Division *Totenkopf*.

Summer 1943 : Unit redesignated SS-Panzer-Division *Totenkopf.*

October 1943 : Incorporation of SS-Totenkopfstandarte *Kirkenes* from 6. SS-Gebirgs-Division *Nord* as replacements for SS-Panzergrenadier-Regiment 5 *Thule*.

February 1944 : Unit receives final designation (see above).

May - June 1944 : Unit reinforced by 4,500 personnel from the 16. SS-Panzergrenadier-Division *Reichsführer-SS*.

Commanding Officers

- SS-Gruppenführer Theodor Eicke
  (11/14/39 - 7/7/41)
- SS-Standartenführer Matthias Kleinheisterkamp
  (7/7/41 - 7/15/41)
- SS-Brigadeführer Georg Keppler
  (7/15/41 - 9/9/41)
- SS-Obergruppenführer Theodor Eicke
  (9/9/41 - 2/26/43) KIA
- SS-Gruppenfuhrer Max Simon
  (2/27/43 - 10/16/43)
- SS-Gruppenführer Hermann Priess
  (10/16/43 - 7/13/44)
- SS-Brigadeführer Helmuth Becker
  (7/13/44 - 5/9/45)

Main Combat Units (as of 6/44)

- SS-Panzergrenadier-Regiment 5 *Thule*
- SS-Panzergrenadier-Regiment 6 *Theodor Eicke*
- SS-Panzer-Regiment 3
- SS-Panzerartillerie-Regiment 3
- SS-Aufklärungs-Abteilung 3
- SS-Panzerpionier-Bataillon 3
- SS-Sturmgeschütz-Abteilung 3
- SS-Flak-Abteilung 3
- SS-Nachrichten-Abteilung 3

Disposition

The division surrendered on 9 May 1945 to American forces at Stetteldorf (northwest of Vienna) after agreeing to disarm SS-Totenkopf personnel at the nearby Mauthausen concentration camp. Less than 1,000 survivors from an original establishment strength of 19,000 men. These survivors were handed over to Soviet custody on 14 May 1945. Virtually all of them were executed or died in Siberian penal camps.

Claimed Atrocities

- Bydgoszcz 2 [Poland] :
  24 - 26 September 1939
- Ciepielow [Poland] : September 1939
- Grafeneck Castle [Germany] :
  November 1939
- Kharkov 1 [USSR] : 16+ December 1941
- Kharkov 3 [USSR] : March - August 1943
- Kharkov 4 [USSR] : August 1943
- Ksiazki [Poland] : 8 September 1939
- L'Abresle [France] : 19 June 1940
- Lentilly [France] : 19 June 1940
- Le Paradis [France] : 27 May 1940
- Lidice [Czechoslovakia] : 10 June 1942
- Nisko [Poland] : September 1939
- Owinsk [Poland] : Late-October 1939
- Polish Corridor [Poland] : September - October 1939
- Rawa Mazowiecka [Poland] :
  15 September 1939
- Szpegawsk [Poland] : October 1939
- Wloclawek [Poland] :
  22 - 25 September 1939
- see also *Miscellaneous Atrocities*

Security Operations

- Garonne; border with Spain [France] : 29 June 1940 - 8 July 1940
- Demarcation Line between Moulins & Chalons sur Saone [France] : 15 July 1940 - 27 August 1940
- Demarcation Line and the Atlantic Coast [France] : 28 August 1940 - 30 September 1940
- Angouleme, Atlantic Coast & Demarcation Line [France] : 24 October 1942 - 10 November 1942

4. SS-Polizei-Panzergrenadier-*Division*

Organizational History

18 September 1939 : Unit activation ordered and formation begun at Truppenübungsplatz Wandern.

1 October 1939 : Unit given designation SS-Polizei-Division; personnel consisted of conscripted civilian police (Ordnungspolizei Regimenten 1, 2, and 3), Allgemeine SS reservists, and Wehrmacht cadre elements (Artillerie-Regiment 228, Nachrichten-Abteilung 228).

May 1940 : Divisional personnel composition at this time -- 25% Austrian, 50% Polish Volksdeutsche, with the remainder Germans and miscellaneous Volksdeutsche from eastern Europe.

Fall 1940 : Unit deployed to occupation duties in Paris. While there it is thoroughly overhauled -- older personnel are replaced by 10,000 younger Ordnungspolizei reservists.

10 February 1942 : Unit fully integrated into the Waffen-SS and redesignated SS-Polizei-Division.

September 1943 : Unit rebuilt at various training camps in Schlesien and Böhmen-Mähren. It also receives its final designation (see above).

June 1944 : SS-Panzergrenadier-Ausbildungs und- Ersatz-Bataillon 4 mobilized and attached to division as Kampfgruppe Delfs.

mid-April 1945 : Elements of SS-Panzergrenadier-Regiment 7 detached and sent as replacements to SS-Fallschirmjäger-Bataillon 600.

18 April 1945 : Incorporation of SS-Panzergrenadier-Ausbildungs-und Ersatz-Brigade 103 as replacements.

Commanding Officers

- SS-Gruppenführer Karl Pfeffer-Wildenbruch (10/1/39 - 11/10/40)
- SS-Gruppenführer Arthur Mülverstedt (11/10/40 - 8/10/41) KIA
- SS-Brigadeführer Walter Krüger (8/18/41 - 12/15/41)

- SS-Brigadeführer Alfred Wünnenberg (12/15/41 - 6/10/43)
- SS-Brigadeführer Fritz Schmedes (6/10/43 - 7/5/44)
- SS-Brigadeführer Herbert Ernst Vahl (7/13/44 - 7/22/44) KIA
- SS-Standartenführer Karl Schümers (7/23/44 - 8/16/44) KIA
- SS-Standartenführer Helmut Dörner (8/17/44 - 8/21/44)
- SS-Brigadeführer Fritz Schmedes (8/22/44 - 11/27/44)
- SS-Standartenführer Walter Harzer (11/28/44 - 5/45)

Main Combat Units (as of 1944)
- SS-Panzergrenadier-Regiment 7
- SS-Panzergrenadier-Regiment 8
- SS-Panzer-Abteilung 4
- SS-Artillerie-Regiment 4
- SS-Panzeraufklärungs-Abteilung 4
- SS-Panzerjäger-Abteilung 4
- SS-Flak-Abteilung 4
- SS-Pionier-Bataillon 4
- SS-Nachrichten-Abteilung 4
- SS-Feldersatz-Bataillon 4

Disposition
Some elements of the division were annihilated in the defense of Berlin (April - May 1945); remnants surrendered on 2 May 1945 to American forces near Hagenau-Wittenberge.

Claimed Atrocities
- Agios Georgios [Greece] : August 1944
- Dhistomon [Greece] : 10 June 1944
- Ioannina [Greece] : 25 March 1944
- Karpenisi [Greece] : August 1944
- Klisoura [Greece] : 5 May 1944
- Larisa [Greece] : 1944
- Siatista [Greece] : 1944
- see also *Miscellaneous Atrocities*

Security Operations
- unspecified locales [Poland] : late 1939 - early 1940
- Demarcation Line [France] : 26 June 1940 - 1 July 1940
- Paris, Bures, Saint-Cloud, Osray, Cirey-sur-Blaise, Saint-Denis, Billancourt [France] : 4 August 1940
- Vyritsa, Neva River, Nikolskoye, Ivanovskoye, Tosna River, Sablino [USSR] : 26 June 1942
- Böhmen-Mähren [Czechoslovakia] and unspecified locales [Poland] : Spring 1943
- Sabac, Valjevo, Mionica, Lajkovac, Turnu, Matzdorf, Obrenovac, Koviljaca [Yugoslavia] : August 1943
- Larissa, Arta, Ptolemais, Agrinion, Pindus & Wermion Mountains [Greece] : March 1944

5. SS-Panzer-Division *Wiking*

Organizational History

1 December 1940 : Unit activation ordered and formation begun of SS-Division (mot.) *Germania*; personnel consisted of cadre from SS-Verfügungs Division (Standarte 2 *Germania*) along with Western European volunteers. Scandinavians and some SS-Totenkopf-Verbande instructors formed into *Nordland* regiment; Dutch and Fleming volunteers formed into *Westland* regiment.

1 January 1941 : Unit redesignated SS-Division *Wiking*.

February 1941 : Recruitment drive for Finnisches Freiwilligen-Bataillon der Waffen-SS begun.

February - March 1941 : Division working up at Truppenübungsplatz Heuberg.

May 1941 :Finnisches Freiwilligen-Bataillon der Waffen-SS incorporated as a closed unit into the division.

1941/1942 : Incorporation of a significant number of guard personnel from the Auschwitz extermination camp.

9 November 1942 : Unit upgraded and redesignated SS-Panzergrenadier-Division *Wiking*.

18 March 1943 : *Nordland* regiment detached and sent as cadre for the newly-forming 11. SS-Freiwilligen-Panzergrenadier-Division *Nordland*.

4 April 1943 : SS-Panzergrenadier-Bataillon *Narwa* [formerly I. Bataillon / 20. Waffen-Grenadier-Division der SS (estnische Nr. 1)] attached to division.

July 1943 : Finnisches Freiwilligen-Bataillon der Waffen-SS detached from division, returned to Finland and disbanded there.

19 October 1943 : Division upgraded and receives final designation (see above).

July 1944 : SS-Panzergrenadier-Bataillon Narwa detached and returned to the 20. Waffen-Grenadier-Division der SS (estnische Nr. 1) as replacements.

April - May 1945 : I. Bataillon / SS-Panzergrenadier-Regiment 23 *Norge* and I. Bataillon / SS-Panzergrenadier-Regiment 24 *Danmark* (both from the 11. SS-Freiwilligen-Panzergrenadier-Division *Nordland*) incorporated into division as replacements.

[Note: This division was the most European of SS divisions: Germans, Dutch, Flemish, Norwegians, Danes, Swiss, Finns, Swedes, Estonians, Walloons, and Balkan Volksdeutsche.]

Commanding Officers

- SS-Gruppenführer Felix Steiner (12/1/40 - 5/1/43)
- SS-Gruppenführer Herbert Otto Gille (5/1/43 - 8/6/44)
- SS-Standartenführer Johannes Rudolf Mühlenkamp (8/6/44 - 10/9/44)
- SS-Oberführer Karl Ullrich (10/9/44 - 5/8/45)

Main Combat Units (as of 7/44)

- SS-Panzergrenadier-Regiment 9 *Germania*
- SS-Panzergrenadier-Regiment 10 *Westland*
- SS-Panzer-Regiment 5
- SS-Artillerie-Regiment 5
- SS-Aufklärungs-Abteilung 5
- SS-Pionier-Bataillon 5
- SS-Nachrichten-Abteilung 5
- SS-Feldersatz-Bataillon 5
- SS-Panzerjäger-Abteilung 5
- SS-Sturmgeschütz-Abteilung 5
- SS-Sturmgeschütz-Batterie
- SS-Flak-Abteilung 5

Disposition

The divisional remnants surrendered on 8 May 1945 to American forces east of Graz, Austria.

Claimed Atrocities

- Zborow [Poland] : 9 July 1941
- Gau Steiermark [Austria] : March – April 1945
- see also *Miscellaneous Atrocities*

Security Operations

- Modlin, Wieliszew, Zegrze [Poland] : 23 September 1944

6. SS-Gebirgs-Division *Nord*

Organizational History

Summer 1940 : SS-Totenkopfstandarten 6 and 7 brigaded together and transferred to occupied Norway.

24 February 1941 : Addition of SS-Division-Nachrichten-Abteilung; unit renamed SS-Kampfgruppe *Nord*.

1 April 1941 : Incorporation of SS-Totenkopfstandarte 9 and SS-Totenkopfstandarte *Kirkenes* (formed from SS-Sonderbataillon *Reiz* and elements of SS-Totenkopfstandarten 9 and 12).

17 June 1941 : Unit upgraded and redesignated SS-Division *Nord*.

16 August 1941 : Incorporation of elements from SS-Infanterie-Regiment 5 (2. SS-Infanterie-Brigade).

Fall 1941 : Formation of divisional support elements at Truppenübungsplatz Wildflecken (Rhön): four Gebirgsjäger-Bataillonen, three Gebirgsartillerie-Abteilungen, and the Gebirgspionier-Bataillon.

December 1941 : SS-Totenkopfstandarte *Kirkenes* detached and sent to the Eastern Front.

1941/1942 : Interchange (transfer and receipt) of a substantial number of personnel with Waffen-SS guard units stationed at the Auschwitz extermination camp.

15 June 1942 : Unit redesignated SS-Gebirgs-Division *Nord*.

Early-Summer 1942 :
Support elements from Truppenübungsplatz Wildflecken incorporated.

October 1943 : Division receives final designation (see above). SS-Totenkopfstandarte *Kirkenes* transferred to SS-Panzergrenadier-Regiment 5 *Thule* (SS-Panzer-Division *Totenkopf*).

April 1944 : Sturmgeschütz-Batterie / SS-Panzergrenadier-Bataillon 506 detached and sent as cadre to SS-Pan

zer-Abteilung 18 (18. SS-Freiwilligen-Panzergrenadier-Division *Horst Wessel*).

Early-February 1945 : Incorporation of Volksdeutsche conscripts; officer replacements from SS-Gebirgsjäger-Schule (Austria).

Early March 1945 : Incorporation of miscellaneous Luftwaffe and Wehrmacht personnel as replacements.

Commanding Officers

- SS-Brigadeführer Richard Herrmann (6/12/40 - 5/25/41)
- SS-Brigadeführer Karl Maria Demelhuber (5/25/41 - 10/41)
- SS-Standartenführer Hans Scheider (10/41 - 3/30/42)
- SS-Brigadeführer Karl Maria Demelhuber (4/1/42 - 5/2/42)
- SS-Brigadeführer Matthias Kleinheisterkamp (5/2/42 - 12/15/43)
- SS-Gruppenführer Lothar Debes (1/15/44 - 5/22/44)
- SS-Obergruppenführer Friedrich-Wilhelm Krüger (5/44 - 8/23/44)
- SS-Standartenführer Gustav Lombard (8/23/44 - 9/1/44)
- SS-Gruppenführer Karl-Heinrich Brenner (9/1/44 - 5/45)
- SS-Standartenführer Franz Schreiber (5/45)

Main Combat Units (as of 1944)

- SS-Gebirgsjäger-Regiment 11 *Reinhard Heydrich*
- SS-Gebirgsjäger-Regiment 12 *Michael Gaissmair*
- SS-Panzergrenadier-Bataillon 506
- SS-Gebirgsartillerie-Regiment 6
- SS-Schijäger-Bataillon *Norwegen*
- SS-Gebirgspionier-Bataillon 6
- SS-Aufklärungs-Abteilung 6
- SS-Nachrichten-Abteilung 6
- SS-Flak-Abteilung 6

Disposition

Main divisional remnants surrendered on 4 May 1945 to American forces at St. Polten (Bavaria). Some minor elements surrendered to American forces in Thuringia and elsewhere in Bavaria.

Claimed Atrocities

- Ruzyn [Czechoslovakia] : 16 - 17 November 1939

7. SS-Freiwilligen-Gebirgs-Division

Prinz Eugen

Organizational History

1 March 1942 : Unit authorized as Freiwilligen-Gebirgsdivision and formation begun. Personnel primarily a mix of Volksdeutsche volunteers and conscripts from the Serbian Banat. Some previously formed units are incorporated: Serbian Selbstschutz and a Croatian-based Einsatzstaffel. Officer cadre consists of Austrian and Rumanian Volksdeutsche, as well as several officers from the 5. SS-Panzer-Division *Wiking*.

1 April 1942 : Unit redesignated as SS-Freiwilligen-Division *Prinz Eugen*.

11 April 1943 : Eighty-five man SS-Sonderkommando Lange (CO: SS-Hauptsturmführer Hans Bothmann) from Chelmno extermination camp assigned to division as SS-Feldgendarmerie.

Spring 1943 : Cadre sent to 13. Waffen-Gebirgs-Division der SS *Handschar* (kroatische Nr. 1).

1943 : Unit redesignated as SS-Freiwilligen-Gebirgs-Division *Prinz Eugen*.

22 October 1943 : Unit receives final designation (see above).

February 1944 : SS-Sonderkommando Lange returned to the re-opened Chelmno extermination camp. Divisional members in excess of 45 years old transferred to the Sonderkommando prior to its return. In August 1944, the sonderkommando was responsible for the liquidation of the Lodz Ghetto.

September 1944 : Cadre sent to 24. Waffen-Gebirgs-Division der SS *Karstjäger*.

February 1945 : Remnants of disbanded Kampfgruppe 21. Waffen-Gebirgs-Division der SS *Skanderbeg* (albanische Nr. 1) added as reinforcements to SS-Freiwilligen-Gebirgsjäger-Regiment 14. Henceforth, the regiment carries the honor title of *Skanderbeg*.

Commanding Officers

- SS-Obergruppenführer Artur Phleps (3/1/42 - 6/21/43)
- SS-Brigadeführer Carl Ritter von Oberkamp (7/3/43 - 2/1/44)
- SS-Brigadeführer Otto Kumm   (2/11/44 - 1/20/45)
- SS-Brigadeführer August Schmidhuber (1/20/45 - 5/45)

Main Combat Units (as of 12/44)

- SS-Freiwilligen-Gebirgsjäger-Regiment 13 *Artur Phleps*
- SS-Freiwilligen-Gebirgsjäger-Regiment 14
- SS-Freiwilligen-Gebirgsartillerie-Regiment 7
- SS-Radfahr-Aufklärungs-Abteilung 7
- SS-Kavallerie-Abteilung 7
- SS-Panzerjäger-Abteilung 7
- SS-Flak-Abteilung 7
- SS-Pionier-Bataillon 7
- SS-Nachrichten-Abteilung 7
- SS-Feldersatz-Bataillon 7

Disposition

Division remnants were forced to surrender on 15 May 1945 to Yugoslav partisans near the city of Krainburg (Slovenia) while attempting to cross to Allied lines. They were then subjected to a weeks-long death march ("Sühnemarsch") through Yugoslavia. Many of the prisoners were killed out of hand (members of *Prinz Eugen* were reportedly shot on 18 May 1945 by elements of the 1st Army, II Partisan Brigade). The survivors of the march (perhaps only 50%) were sent as slave laborers to the copper mines at Bor where most lost their lives. Some were also tried and executed by Yugoslav authorities for atrocities; others were subsequently murdered for various reasons. Few ever returned to the West.

Claimed Atrocities

- Blazevici [Yugoslavia] : 28 March 1944
- Blazevo, Gradac, Bozominu, Domisevina, Boronjina, Ravniste, Rodici, Ilinci [Yugoslavia] : Winter 1942
- Dola [Yugoslavia] : 7 June 1943
- Gocu, Zhescin, Biserske Livade, Raskoj, Ivanjica [Yugoslavia] : 8 - 19 October 1942
- Grubisnjici [Yugoslavia] : 28 March 1944
- Jablanica-Prozor Railline [Yugoslavia] : August 1943
- Kopaonik [Yugoslavia] : mid-October 1942
- Kosutica [Yugoslavia] : July 1943
- Kriva Reka [Yugoslavia] : 12 - 13 October 1942
- Krividol [Yugoslavia] : 28 March 1944
- Legatori [Yugoslavia] : 28 March 1944
- Liga, Krusevca [Yugoslavia] :   mid-October 1942
- Niksic [Yugoslavia] : late-May 1943
- Niksic-Avtovac Railline [Yugoslavia] :August 1943
- Osekovo [Yugoslavia] : 16 September 1943
- Otok Cornji, Ruda, Dolac Donji [Yugoslavia] : 28 March 1944
- Ovrlje [Yugoslavia] : 28 March 1944
- Pancevo [Yugoslavia] :
- Razori [Yugoslavia] : 9 June 1944
- Ripac [Yugoslavia] :   20 January - 15 March 1943
- Sancaku [Yugoslavia] : mid-late October 1942
- Sinj [Yugoslavia] : 5 November 1943
- Slavdovil [Yugoslavia] : 28 March 1944
- Smilici [Yugoslavia] : 28 March 1944
- Split - Sinj Region [Yugoslavia] : March 1944
- Topoli [Yugoslavia] : November - December 1942
- Vostane [Yugoslavia] : 28 March 1944
- numerous other locales [Yugoslavia] :   late 1942 - late 1944

Security Operations

- Kraljevo, Pec, Mitrov, Novi Pazar, Rudnica, Raska [Yugoslavia] : 9 September 1942
- Usice, Cacak, Novi Pazar, Mitrovica [Yugoslavia] : October 1942
- Vrnjacks Banja, Trstenik, Krusevac, Belgrade [Yugoslavia] : 6 November 1942
- Zagreb, Petrinja, Karlovac, Bosanski Petrovac, Bihac, Vytina, Livno [Yugoslavia] : 20 January - 15 March 1943 (Unternehmen Weiss I & II)
- Mostar, Imotski, Dresnica [Yugoslavia] : 16 March 1943

- Bijelo Polje, Dubrovnik, Mostar, Niksic, Sarajevo, Herzegovina, Montenegro [Yugoslavia] : April - May 1943 (Unternehmen Schwarz)
- Dubrovnik, Vares, Zepce, Tetovo [Yugoslavia] : 24 July 1943
- Split, Sinj, Dubrovnik, Mitkovic [Yugoslavia] : ? September - 28 September 1943 (Unternehmen Achse)
- Peljesac Island [Yugoslavia] : 23 October - 11 November 1943 (Unternehmen Herbstgewitter)
- Sarajevo, Rogatica, Goradze, Visegrad [Yugoslavia] : December 1943 (Unternehmen Kugelblitz)
-
- Vlasenica, Vares, Zavidovici, Banovici [Yugoslavia] : Christmas 1943 (Unternehmen Schneesturm)
- Zenica, Bugojno, Donji Vakuf, Kiseljak [Yugoslavia] : 4 - 18 January 1944 (Unternehmen Waldrausch)
- Mirkonjicgrad, Bugojno, Travnik, Sarajevo, Rogatica, Gorazde, Visegrad [Yugoslavia] : March 1944
- Srebrenica, Zvornik, Rogatica, Olovo, Vlasenica, Gorazde, Kladanj, Pale [Yugoslavia] : 26 April - 18 May 1944 (Unternehmen Maibaum)
- Drvar [Yugoslavia] : assault on Tito's HQ, May 1944 (Unternehmen Rösselsprung)
- Zenica, Travnik, Bugojno, Gornji Vakuf, Kiseljak, Pale, Gorazde, Foca, Konjic [Yugoslavia] : 18 June - 9 July 1944 (Unternehmen Freiejagd)
- Visegrad, Nis, Uzice, Zepce [Yugoslavia] : 4 August 1944
- Rogatica, Gorazde, Foca, Scepan Polji, Trsa, Banski Stanovi, Zabljak, Pljevlja, Boljanici [Yugoslavia] : 5 August - 22 August 1944 (Unternehmen Rübezahl)
- Nis, Leskovac, Aleksinac, Bovan, Krivi Vir, Bogovina, Krusevac, Zitorada, Merosina, Dzigolj, Ajdovac, Razbojna, Brus, Usce [Yugoslavia] : 1 October - 20 October 1944
- Rogatica, Kraljevo, Sopotnik, Otok, Brcko [Yugoslavia] : 1 November 1944 *
- Zvornik, Vukovar area [Yugoslavia] : January 1945 *
- Tovarnik, Sid, Ljuba, Novak [Yugoslavia] : 17 January - 19 January 1945 (Unternehmen Frühlingssturm)
- Virovitica, Nasice, Velika, Ceralije, Cacinci, Podrav. Slatina [Yugoslavia] : 4 - 25 February 1945 (Unternehmen Wehrwolf)
- Sarajevo, Konjic, Visoko, Kiseljak, Travnik, Zenica, Kakanj, Maglaj, Doboj [Yugoslavia] : 1 March - 17 April 1945 (Unternehmen Feuerwehr) *

Note : Operations followed by an asterisk (*) were primarily defensive operations against Soviet troops.

8. SS-Kavallerie-Division *Florian Geyer*

Organizational History

2 August 1941 : Unit formed from SS-Kavallerie-Regiment 1 and SS-Kavallerie-Regiment 2; designated as SS-Kavallerie-Brigade. For information on this unit's precursors see *SS-Kavallerie-Regiment Operations and Atrocities in Poland* and *SS-Kavallerie-Brigade Operations and Atrocities in the USSR*.

December 1941 : Unit reinforced with seven Totenkopf-Reiterschwadrone (3,600 men) from Warsaw.

March 1942 : Incorporation of Volksdeutsche reinforcements.

April 1942 : Elements temporarily detached to form SS-Kampfgruppe Zehender. This battlegroup participated in anti-partisan sweeps in Poland from 16 June to the end of August (specific locales unknown).

1 June 1942 : Unit reinforced and redesignated SS-Kavallerie-Division [unofficial title "Fegelein" or *Ost*].

August 1942 : Division working up at Truppenübungsplatz Heidelager (Debica).

15 April 1943 : SS-Kavallerie-Regiment 17 temporarily detached to form SS-Kampfgruppe Gille. SS-Pionier-Bataillon 8 permanently detached (later incorporated into 37. SS-Freiwilligen-Kavallerie-Division *Lützow*).

9 August 1943 : Incorporation of Russian Volksdeutsche as a fourth regiment (SS-Kavallerie-Regiment 18).

22 October 1943 : Unit redesignated 8. SS-Kavallerie-Division.

Late 1943 - Early 1944 : Incorporation of Volksdeutsche cavalry regiment (at least 3 squadrons).

12 March 1944 : Unit receives final designation (see above).

June 1944 : SS-Kavallerie-Regiment 17 detached and sent as cadre to the 22. SS-Freiwilligen-Kavallerie-Division *Maria Theresia*.

[Note: This unit served under control of the Reichsführer-SS as needed on security operations behind the frontlines in the USSR. It was often subordinated to local HSSPF for "cleansing operations" and also served as a replacement pool for the main-series Waffen-SS divisions decimated in 1941-1942 campaigns.]

Commanding Officers

- SS-Standartenführer Hermann Fegelein (8/2/41 - 5/1/42)
- SS-Brigadeführer Wilhelm Bittrich (5/1/42 - 11/1/42)
- SS-Standartenführer Gustav Lombard (11/1/42 - 2/1/43)
- SS-Brigadeführer Wilhelm Bittrich (2/1/43 - 2/15/43)
- SS-Brigadeführer Fritz Freitag (2/15/43 - 4/20/43)
- SS-Brigadeführer Hermann Fegelein (4/20/43 - 11/1/43)
- SS-Gruppenführer Bruno Streckenbach (11/1/43 - 4/1/44)
- SS-Brigadeführer Joachim Rumohr (4/1/44 - 2/11/45) suicide

Main Combat Units (as of 7/44)

- SS-Kavallerie-Regiment 15
- SS-Kavallerie-Regiment 16
- SS-Kavallerie-Regiment 18
- SS-Artillerie-Regiment 8
- SS-Panzer-Aufklärungs-Abteilung 8
- SS-Panzerjäger-Abteilung 8
- SS-Sturmgeschütz-Batterie
- SS-Flak-Abteilung 8
- SS-Pionier-Bataillon 8
- SS-Nachrichten-Abteilung 8
- SS-Feldersatz-Bataillon

Disposition

Division annihilated in Budapest Pocket (November 1944 - 12 February 1945) with the exception of small groups which broke out and reached German lines.

Division reformed with survivors of 22. SS-Freiwilligen-Kavallerie-Division *Maria Theresia* into SS-Kavallerie-Gruppe *Ameiser*.

Subordination

- Kommandostab RF-SS (5/41 - 8/41)
- Heeres Gruppe Mitte (8/12/41 - 4/42)
- HSSPf Center Russia (4/14/43 - 4/30/43)
- HSSPf South Russia (6/11/43 - 9/19/43)
- KGr. Schimana (5/1/43 - 6/10/43)

Claimed Atrocities

- Chelm [Poland] : 12 January 1940
- Pinsk [USSR] : 5 - 8 August 1941
- Pripet Marshes [USSR] : 19 July - 31 August 1941
- numerous rear-area locales [USSR] : late 1941 - December 1943
- see also entry *SS-Kavallerie-Brigade Operations and Atrocities in the USSR*
- see also entry *SS-Kavallerie-Regiment Operations and Atrocities in Poland*

Security Operations

- Vyazma-Bryansk area [USSR] : 2 October 1941
- Olenino-Nelidowo [USSR] : 21 February 1942 - 18 April 1942
- Occupied Territories [USSR] : 27 May 1942 - 15 June 1942
- Poland : 16 June 1942 - 31 August 1942

- Baturino, Pochinok, Simonovo, Petrovo, Soino [USSR] : 21 December 1942
- Belyj [USSR] : 25 January 1943 - 20 February 1943
- Reichskommissariat Ukraine [USSR] : 16 April 1943 - 20 August 1943
- Minsk, Bobruisk, Lapichi, Staryye Dorogi [USSR] : 19 April 1943
- Rechitsa, Khoyniki, Dnepr & Pripet Rivers [USSR] : 16 May 1943 (Unternehmen Weichsel)
- Mozyr, Ovruch, , Petrikov, Gomel [USSR] : 17 June 1943 (Unternehmen Seydlitz)
- Lutsk, Dubno, Pinsk, Vladimir-volynski [USSR] : 1 August 1943
- Belyayevks, Kharkov, Yefremovka, Berezovka [USSR] : 18 August 1943
- Dnepr River sector, Kremenchug [USSR] : 7 September 1943
- Mironovka, Lozovatka, Pasiki, Uspenskoye [USSR] : December 1943
- Croatia [Yugoslavia] : January - March 1944

9. SS-Panzer-Division *Hohenstaufen*

Organizational History
31 December 1942 :
Unit formation authorized and designated 9. SS-Panzergrenadier-Division.

January - August 1943 : Formation and training at Truppenübungsplatz Mailly le Camp (France). Personnel primarily German conscripts from the Reichsarbeitdienst (70%) and Hungarian Volksdeutsche. Cadre provided from *Leibstandarte Adolf Hitler* Ausbildungs-Bataillon (Berlin-Lichterfelde).

1 March 1943 : Unit redesignated SS-Panzergrenadier-Division *Hohenstaufen*.

22 October 1943 : Unit redesignated 9. SS-Panzergrenadier-Division *Hohenstaufen*.

26 October 1943 : Division receives final designation (see above).

12 November 1943 : Kradschützen-Kompanie 15 / SS-Panzergrenadier-Regiment 20 detached to serve as cadre for SS-Aufklärungs-Abteilung 16 / 16. SS-Panzergrenadier-Division *Reichsführer-SS*.

October 1944 : Division rebuilt with Luftwaffe personnel and miscellaneous Wehrmacht remnants.

Commanding Officers
- SS-Obergruppenführer Wilhelm Bittrich (2/15/43 - 6/28/44)
- SS-Oberführer Sylvester Stadler (6/28/44 - 7/10/44)
- SS-Standartenführer Thomas Müller (7/10/44 - 7/15/44)
- SS-Oberführer Sylvester Stadler (7/15/44 - 7/29/44) wounded
- SS-Oberführer Friedrich-Wilhelm Bock (7/29/44 - 10/10/44)
- SS-Brigadeführer Sylvester Stadler (10/10/44 - 5/8/45)

Main Combat Units
- SS-Panzergrenadier-Regiment 19
- SS-Panzergrenadier-Regiment 20
- SS-Panzer-Regiment 9
- SS-Panzerartillerie-Regiment 9
- SS-Panzerjäger-Abteilung 9
- SS-Sturmgeschütz-Abteilung 9
- SS-Nachrichten-Abteilung 9
- SS-Ausbildungs-Bataillon 9
- SS-Flak-Abteilung 9
- SS-Pionier-Bataillon 9
- SS-Feldersatz-Bataillon 9

Disposition
Division surrendered to American forces on 8 May 1945 at Steyr, Austria.

Claimed Atrocities
- Putten (Netherlands) : 31 September - 1 October 1944
- Stavelot (Belgium) : December 1944
- see also *Miscellaneous Atrocities*

Security Operations
- Forges-les-Eaux, Amiens [France] : 3 August 1943

10. SS-Panzer-Division *Frundsberg*

Organizational History
December 1942 : Unit receives authorization.

15 January 1943 : Unit designated 10. SS-Division.

1 February 1943 : Formation and training begun; personnel primarily German conscripts from Reichsarbeitdienst (RAD).

19 April 1943 : Unit redesignated 10. SS-Panzergrenadier-Division *Karl der Grösse*.

3 October 1943 :
Elements detached to serve as cadre for 17. SS-Panzergrenadier-Division *Götz von Berlichingen*.

20 November 1943 : Division receives final designation (see above).

October 1944 :

Division sustains heavy losses and is reduced to SS-Kampfgruppe *Frundsberg*.

Commanding Officers

- SS-Standartenführer Michel Lippert (2/1/43 - 2/15/43)
- SS-Brigadeführer Lothar Debes (2/15/43 - 11/15/43)
- SS-Gruppenführer Karl von Treuenfeld (11/15/43 - 5/1/44)
- SS-Brigadeführer Heinz Harmel (5/1/44 - 5/8/45)

Main Combat Units (as of 6/44)

- SS-Panzergrenadier-Regiment 21
- SS-Panzergrenadier-Regiment 22
- SS-Panzer-Regiment 10
- SS-Panzerartillerie-Regiment 10
- SS-Panzerjäger-Abteilung 10
- SS-Sturmgeschütz-Abteilung 10
- SS-Flak-Abteilung 10
- SS-Pionier-Bataillon 10
- SS-Nachrichten-Abteilung 10
- SS-Feldersatz-Bataillon 10

Disposition

Detached elements surrender on 5 May 1945 to American forces at Cottbus. Majority of unit surrenders in early May 1945 to Soviet forces at Teplitz-Schönau.

11.SS-Freiwilligen-Panzergrenadier-Division *Nordland*

Organizational History

Late 1942 : Unit receives authorization.

February - March 1943 : Formation begins at Truppenübungsplatz Grafenwöhr. Several provisional names for the unit are considered and discarded - Kampfverband *Wäräger*, Germanische-Freiwilligen-Division, 11. (germ.) SS-Panzergrenadier-Division.

17 March 1943 : Unit receives designation of 11. SS-Panzergrenadier-Freiwilligen-Division *Nordland*.

18 March 1943 : Incorporation of *Nordland* Regiment (from SS-Panzergrenadier-Division *Wiking*) as cadre.

20 March 1943 : Incorporation of SS-Freikorps *Danemark*, elements SS-Freiwilligen-Legion *Niederlande* and SS-Freiwilligen-Legion *Norwegen*. Remainder of unit personnel is primarily composed of Hungarian and Rumanian Volksdeutsche, along with a small number of Estonians, Finns, Flemings, Swiss and Swedes.

12 November 1943 : Unit receives final designation (see above).

20 March 1945 : Unit refitting in the Schwedt-Angermunde area.

March - April 1945 : Minor elements of the SS-Britische-Freikorps incorporated and then detached.

April 1945 : 1. Bataillon of SS-Panzergrenadier-Regiment 23 *Norge* and 1. Bataillon of SS-Panzergrenadier-Regiment 24 *Danmark* transferred to 5. SS-Panzer-Division *Wiking*. Unit receives Naval Replacement Battalion as reinforcements. Incorporation of Spanische-Freiwilligen-Kompanie der SS 101 (transferred from 28. SS-Freiwilligen-Panzergrenadier-Division *Wallonie*).
(Note : During 1944-1945, regular replacements for this unit were drawn primarily from Belgian, Danish, Croatian, Estonian, Latvian, Lithuanian, Dutch, and Ukrainian Volksdeutsche.)

Commanding Officers

- SS-Brigadeführer Fritz von Scholz (5/1/43 - 6/28/44) KIA
- SS-Brigadeführer Joachim Ziegler (6/28/44 - 4/26/45)
- [Arrested, then KIA on 5/1/45 during breakout attempt from Berlin]
- SS-Brigadeführer Dr. jur. Gustav Krukenberg (4/26/45 - 5/3/45)

Main Combat Units

- SS-Panzergrenadier-Regiment 23 *Norge*
- SS-Panzergrenadier-Regiment 24 *Danmark*
- SS-Panzer-Abteilung 11 *Hermann von Salza*
- SS-Artillerie-Regiment 11
- SS-Panzeraufklärungs-Abteilung 11
- SS-Panzerjäger-Abteilung 11
- SS-Feldersatz-Bataillon 11
- SS-Flak-Abteilung 11
- SS-Pionier-Bataillon 11
- SS-Nachrichten-Abteilung 11

Subordination

SS-Freiwilligen-Legion *Niederlande* was attached to the 2. SS-Infanterie (mot.) Brigade (4/22/42 - 7/23/42) and the 1. SS-Infanterie (mot.) Brigade (8/28/42 - ?).

Disposition

The division's scattered elements were annihilated in separate actions from late April - 3 May 1945 on the Oder Front and in defense of Berlin (Neukölln, Tempelhof and Charlottenburg districts).

Claimed Atrocities

- Norway : Fall/Winter 1942-43
  see also *Miscellaneous Atrocities*

Security Operations

- Girovo, Novgorod, Lake Ilmen, S-Gora, Gorenka, Pyatilipy, Glukhaya Kerest', Guzi, Maloye Zamosh'ye, Kerest River sector (Volkhov Pocket) [USSR] : 3 February 1942 (SS-Freiwilligen-Legion *Niederlande*)
- Zagreb, Sisak, Glina, Petrinja, Bosanski Novi [Northern Croatia, Yugoslavia] : September - 27 November 1943

12. SS-Panzer-Division *Hitlerjugend*

Organizational History

17 February 1943 : Activation ordered and recruitment begun. Unit formation at Truppenübungsplatz Beverloo in Belgium.

1 June 1943 : Formation continued; personnel mostly 17 year old former Hitler Jugend members (both volunteer and conscript) with cadre from 1. SS-Panzer-Division *Leibstandarte Adolf Hitler*, as well as fifty Wehrmacht officers.

24 June 1943 : Unit receives designation SS-Panzergrenadier-Division *Hitlerjugend*.

20 October 1943 : Incorporation of additional cadre from 1. SS-Panzer-Division *Leibstandarte Adolf Hitler*.

22 October 1943 : Unit receives final designation (see above).

August - September 1944 : Unit reduced to 600 effectives due to heavy defensive actions; elements temporarily detached as SS-Kampfgruppe *Waldmuller*.

Mid-September 1944 : Unit listed as SS-Kampfgruppe *Hitlerjugend*.

November 1944 : Incorporation of SS-Ausbildungs- und Ersatz-Regiment 12 a t Nienburg an der Weser.

Commanding Officers

- SS-Brigadeführer Fritz Witt (7/43 - 6/16/44) KIA
- SS-Brigadeführer Kurt Meyer (6/16/44 - 9/6/44) POW
- SS-Obersturmbannführer Hubert Meyer (9/7/44 - 11/9/44)
- SS-Brigadeführer Hugo Kraas (11/10/44 - 5/8/45)

Main Combat Units (as of 1944)

- SS-Panzergrenadier-Regiment 25
- SS-Panzergrenadier-Regiment 26

- SS-Panzer-Regiment 12
- SS-Panzerartillerie-Regiment 12
- SS-Panzeraufklärungs-Abteilung 12
- SS-Panzerjäger-Abteilung 12
- SS-Flak-Abteilung 12
- SS-Pionier-Bataillon 12
- SS-Nachrichten-Abteilung 12
- SS-Werfer-Abteilung 12
- SS-Feldersatz-Bataillon 12

Disposition
Remnants of division surrendered on 8 May 1945 to American forces at Enns, Austria (455 survivors from the December 1943 listed strength of 21,300 personnel).

Claimed Atrocities
- Ascq [France] : 1/2 April 1944
- Normandy [France] : 7 - 17 June 1944
- Gau Niederdonau : 18 April 1945
  see also *Miscellaneous Atrocities*

13. Waffen-Gebirgs-Division der SS

Handschar (kroatische Nr. 1)

Organizational History
13 February 1943 : Unit activation ordered.

1 March 1943 : Formation begun at Zagreb, Yugoslavia with the designation Kroatische SS-Freiwilligen-Division (along with the informal designations - "Kroatische Division" and "Muselmanen Division").

Spring 1943 : Formation continues; personnel primarily Bosnian Moslem and Croat volunteers (later conscripts), Croatian Volksdeutsche, and a small number of Albanians. Incorporation of cadre from 7. SS-Freiwilligen-Gebirgs-Division *Prinz Eugen*.
early July 1943 : Unit redesignated Kroatische SS-Freiwilligen-Gebirgs-Division and transferred for continued training in the Haute Loire, France.

September 1943 : Mutiny by Communist agents in the division results in the murder of several German officers and NCOs at Villefranche-de-Rouergue. Other elements of the division put down the revolt that same day. The surviving mutineers are tried by an SS court and executed. Unreliable personnel (some 825 Bosnians) are transferred to KL Dachau. Most "volunteer" for labor service with the Organisation Todt; the remainder are sent to KL Neuengamme.

October 1943 : Unit transferred for continued training at Truppenübungsplatz Neuhammer (Schlesien). Incorporation of cadres from other Waffen-SS units including two companies from the 6. SS-Gebirgs-Division *Nord*; dismissal of numerous ineffective Bosnian officers and NCOs.

9 October 1943 : Unit redesignated SS-Freiwilligen-b.h. Gebirgs-Division (kroatien).

22 October 1943 : Unit redesignated 13. SS-Freiwilligen-b.h. Gebirgs-Division (kroatien).

February 1944 : Unit deployed to security operations in Yugoslavia.

mid April 1944 : Albanian elements in division transferred to the newly forming 21. Waffen-Gebirgs-Division der SS *Skanderbeg* (albanische Nr. 1).

15 May 1944 : Unit receives final designation (see above).

mid June 1944 : SS-Aufklärungs-Abteilung 13 and miscellaneous cadre transferred to 23. Waffen-Gebirgs-Division der SS *Kama* and IX. Waffen-Gebirgs-Korps der SS (kroatisches).

August 1944 : Incorporation of 500 Croatian Volksdeutsche from the Reichsarbeitsdienst.

September 1944 : Reversal of German military fortunes on the Eastern Front leads to an epidemic of desertions among the Bosnian personnel.

24 September 1944 : Elements of division transferred to general command of IX.Waffen-Gebirgs-Korps der SS (kroatisches).

16 October 1944 : Unit transferred to northern Croatia despite warnings about troop morale. Massive desertions ensue as Bosnian personnel leave to defend their families against partisans and advancing Soviet forces.

25 October 1944 : Mass disarming of untrustworthy Moslem and Croatian personnel. Division disbanded and reformed into Regt. Gruppe 13. SS-Gebirgs *Handschar* (part of SS-Kampfgruppe Hanke) with the addition of remnants from the 23. Waffen-Gebirgs-Division der SS *Kama*. Majority of disarmed personnel formed into two labor battalions; some transferred as non-combatant auxiliaries to 1. Gebirgs-Division.

November 1944 : Continued desertions problems among remaining Bosnian personnel.

2 December 1944 : Incorporation of divisional training/replacement battalion, as well as a Hungarian infantry battalion and artillery battery.

early April 1945 : Incorporation of miscellaneous Volkssturm units, Hungarian infantry battalions, Luftwaffe ground units, and an Italian penal company.

Commanding Officers
- SS-Standartenführer Herbert von Oberwurzer (3/43 - mid 1943)
- SS-Brigadeführer Karl-Gustav Sauberzweig (mid 1943 - 6/18/44)
- SS-Brigadeführer Desiderius Hampel (6/19/44 - 5/8/45)

Main Combat Units (as of 1/44)
- SS-Freiwilligen-Gebirgsjäger-Regiment 27
- SS-Freiwilligen-Gebirgsjäger-Regiment 28
- SS-Freiwilligen-Gebirgsartillerie-Regiment 13
- SS-Pionier-Bataillon 13
- SS-Nachrichten-Abteilung 13
- SS-Flak-Kompanie 13
- SS-Aufklärungs-Abteilung 13
- SS-Panzerjäger-Abteilung 13

Disposition
On 5 May 1945 the division discharged all Bosnians who wished to return to their homeland despite warnings about the danger. Most appear to have been captured by Tito's partisans and executed in two separate large-scale massacres. The majority of the remaining divisional remnants continued marching westwards and surrendered to British forces on 5/12/45 at St. Veith an der Glan (Kärnten). Some stragglers subsequently taken prisoner by American forces. Bosnian POWs were eventually given asylum in countries throughout the Arab and Western worlds. The German divisional members were not so lucky. Thirty-eight German officers and NCOs were extradited to Yugoslavia for war crimes trials. The accused were tried by a military court from 22 - 30 August 1947. All of the defendants were found guilty. Ten were executed and the remainder drew prison sentences ranging from five years' to life imprisonment. Most of the defendants were paroled early and by 1952 all had been released.

Claimed Atrocities
- Bela Crkva [Yugoslavia] : 10 March 1944
- Sava River and Brcko [Yugoslavia] : 4/44 - 6/44
- Jablanica [Yugoslavia] : 10/44

- numerous locales [Yugoslavia] : 1944
- Tuzla [Yugoslavia] :
- Gau Steiermark [Austria] : 24-25 March 1945

Security Operations
- HQ at Brcko [Bosnia, Yugoslavia] : February 1944 - 30 September 1944
- Klostar Ivanic [Yugoslavia] : 5 November 1944

14. Waffen-Grenadier-Division

der SS(ukrainische Nr. 1)

Organizational History

28 March 1943 : Unit activation ordered.

28 April 1943 : Recruiting and formation begun. Unit designated SS-Schützen-Division *Galizien*.

May 1943 : Officer and NCO positions filled by German and Volksdeutsche cadre from various Ordnungspolizei units and the 4. SS-Polizei-Panzergrenadier-Division. Incorporation of Polizei Bataillon 201 (a fusion of the infamous Abwehr *Roland* and *Nachtigall* battalions of Ukrainian expatriate nationalists), 31st SD Punitive Detachment, and Ukrainische Schützmannschaft Bataillon 204 (auxuliary police) -- each of which participated in extermination operations in Poland and the Ukraine. Overwhelming response to recruitment drive - 80,000 Ukrainians volunteer for service. Excess volunteers are formed into galizisches SS-Freiwilligen-Regiment 4, 5, 6, 7, and 8 (all are SS-Polizei units). [Note: SS-Freiwilligen-Regiment 5 was used almost exclusively for security operations in Poland.]

30 July 1943 : Unit redesignated SS-Freiwilligen-Division *Galizien*.

October 1943 : Formation continues at Truppenübungsplatz Heidelager (Debica).

22 October 1943 : Unit redesignated 14. Galizische SS-Freiwilligen-Division.

31 January 1944 : Incorporation of galizisches SS-Freiwilligen-Regiment 6 and 7.

February 1944 : Unit working up continued at Truppenübungsplatz Neuhammer (Schlesien).

27 June 1944 : Unit redesignated 14. Waffen-Grenadier-Division der SS (galizische Nr. 1).

July 1944 : Division nearly annihilated in the Brody-

Tarnow Pocket. Some survivors reach German lines and serve as cadre for reforming division. Other survivors hide out in southern Poland and the Ukraine to pursue partisan activities against the Communists lasting into the 1950s. Those taken prisoner by the Soviets are sent to Siberian work camps; few survive their internment.

7 August 1944 : Unit begins reforming at Truppenübungsplatz Neuhammer (Schlesien) around a cadre of 3,000 survivors of the Brody-Tarnow Pocket. Incorporation of galizisches SS-Freiwilligen-Regiment 4 & 5, SS-Waffen-Grenadier-Ausbildung-und Ersatz-Regiment 14, the third battalions (never previously utilized) of the three former divisional infantry regiments, 1,000 German NCOs (Luftwaffe ground personnel), and two Jäger-Bataillonen (Hungarian and Slovakian Volksdeutsche).

12 November 1944 : Unit receives final designation (see above). Incorporation of Ukrainian Schütz-mannschaft-Bataillonen (auxiliary police) and miscellaneous refugees as reinforcements.

15 April 1945 : Incorporation of 2,500 personnel from the 10. Fallschirmjäger-Division as reinforcements.

25 April 1945 : Unit transferred to the Ukrainian National Army and redesignated 1. ukrainische Division der Ukrainischen National-Armee.

Commanding Officers
- SS-Brigadeführer Walter Schimana
  (7/15/43 - 11/19/43)
- SS-Brigadeführer Fritz Freitag
  (11/20/43 - 4/27/45)
  [committed suicide on 5/10/45 at Andra, Austria]
- Heneral-Khorunzhi M. Krat
  (4/27/45 - 5/8/45)

Main Combat Units
- Waffen-Grenadier-Regiment der SS 29
- Waffen-Grenadier-Regiment der SS 30
- Waffen-Grenadier-Regiment der SS 31
- Waffen-Artillerie-Regiment der SS 14
- Fusilier-Bataillon 14
- Flak-Abteilung 14
- Pionier-Bataillon 14
- Nachrichten-Abteilung 14
- Feldersatz-Bataillon 14

Disposition
Majority of personnel surrendered on 8-12 May 1945 to British forces near Tamsweg, Austria. Scattered elements surrendered during this same time period to American forces near Radstadt, Germany. See also July 1944 entry above.

Claimed Atrocities
- Soltysy - Zabuce [Poland] : 13 May 1944
- Slovak National Uprising [Czechoslovakia] : September - October 1944
- Gau Steiermark [Austria] : 26 April 1945
- see especially: "14. Waffen-Grenadier-Division der SS (ukrainische Nr. 1) Crimes in Poland"

Security Operations
- Chesaniv, Lubachiv, Tarnohrad, Bilohrj, Zamosc [Galicia, southeast Poland] : February - March 1944 (Kampfgruppe Beyersdorff under SS-Obersturmbannführer Friedrich Beyersdorff; not the entire division)
- Sillew area [Czechoslovakia] : late September 1944 (Kampfgruppe *Beyersdorff* re-formed)
- Slovakia : October 1944 - 26 January 1945
- Marburg and Save regions [Slovenia] : 26 January 1945 - March 1945
- Possruk (Kozjak) [Slovenia] : Mid-March 1945

15. Waffen-Grenadier-Division

der SS (lettische Nr. 1)

Organizational History

10 February 1943 : Unit activation ordered as Lettische SS-Freiwilligen-Legion.

25 February 1943 : Formation begins and unit redesignated Lettische SS-Freiwilligen-Division. Low volunteer rate leads to the introduction of conscription.

April 1943 : Incorporation of Lettische Polizei-Bataillonen 17, 27, 28 and 269.

18 May 1943 : Incorporation of cadre from 2. SS-Infanterie (mot.) Brigade.

Summer 1943 : Elements of Aufstellungsstab für die 15. (lett.) SS-Freiwilligen-Division sent as cadre to Lettische SS-Freiwilligen-Brigade [later 19. SS-Waffen-Grenadier-Division der SS (lettische Nr. 2)].

22 October 1943 : Unit redesignated 15. Lettische SS-Freiwilligen-Division.

15 June 1944 :
Unit receives final designation (see above).

August 1944 : Some elements [including Waffen-Artillerie-Regiment der SS 15] transferred to 19. Waffen-Grenadier-Division der SS (lettische Nr. 2).

Mid-August 1944 : Unit rebuilt around surviving cadre at SS-Truppenübungsplatz Westpreussen. Incorporation of SS-Ausbildungs-und Ersatz-Bataillonen 15, 19, and 20; elements of SS-Pionier-Ausbildungs-und Ersatz-Bataillon 1; and twenty thousand Latvian conscripts.

February 1945 : Waffen-Grenadier-Regiment der SS 32 sent as cadre to form 32. SS-Freiwilligen-Grenadier-Division *30 Januar*.

24 February 1945 : Unit divided into several independently operating SS-Kampfgruppen.

Commanding Officers
- SS-Brigadeführer Peter Hansen (3/26/43 - 5/43)
- SS-Brigadeführer Carl Friedrich Graf von Pückler-Burghaus (5/43 - 2/16/44)
- SS-Brigadeführer Nikolaus Heilmann (2/17/44 - 7/44) MIA
- SS-Oberführer Herbert von Oberwurzer (7/21/44 - 1/26/45) POW
- SS-Oberführer Adolf Ax (1/26/45 - 2/15/45)
- SS-Oberführer Karl Burk (2/15/45 - 5/45)

Main Combat Units
- Waffen-Grenadier-Regiment der SS 32
- Waffen-Grenadier-Regiment der SS 33
- Waffen-Grenadier-Regiment der SS 34
- Waffen-Artillerie-Regiment der SS 15
- Feldersatz-Bataillon 15
- Füsilier-Bataillon 15
- Flak-Abteilung 15
- Pionier-Bataillon 15
- Nachrichten-Abteilung 15

Disposition
On 2 May 1945 most of the division surrendered to American forces in the vicinity of Schwerin (Mecklenberg). Some elements were captured and/or annihilated by Soviet forces in defence of Berlin, Danzig and the Kurland.

16. SS-Panzergrenadier-Division

Reichsführer-SS

Organizational History

15 May 1941 : Activation and formation of Begleit-Bataillon *Reichsführer-SS.*

14 February 1943 : Expansion of Himmler's escort Begleit-Bataillon *Reichsführer-SS* to Sturmbrigade *Reichsführer-SS.*

16 June 1943 : Incorporation of a Grenadier-Bataillon from the 356. Infanterie-Division.

3 October 1943 : Unit redesignated SS-Panzergrenadier-Division *Reichsführer-SS.*

22 October 1943 : Unit receives final designation (see above).

November 1943 :
Unit brought up to divisional strength with the incorporation of elements from the 9. SS-Panzer-Division *Hohenstaufen*, an SS-Ausbildungs-Bataillon zur besondere Verwendung, and several miscellaneous Waffen-SS replacement units.

March 1944 : Incorporation of SS-Panzergrenadier-Lehr-Brigade and Begleit-Bataillon *Reichsführer-SS* (replacement for original unit). Approximately 4,500 personnel transferred to 3. SS-Panzer-Division *Totenkopf* and replaced by Hungarian Volksdeutsche.

February 1945 : SS-Panzerjäger-Abteilung 16 sent as cadre to newly forming 32. SS-Freiwilligen-Grenadier-Division *30 Januar.*

14 February - May 1945 :
Division assigned fictitious titles to confuse enemy intelligence -- "Auffrischungsgruppe 13. SS-Division"; "Erganzungsstaffel 13. SS-Panzergrenadier-Division".

3 April 1945 : Incorporation of four Luftwaffe Marsch-bataillonen as replacements.

Commanding Officers

- SS-Obersturmbannführer Karl Gesele (2/14/43 - 10/3/43) CO Sturmbrigade RF-SS
- SS-Gruppenführer Max Simon (10/16/43 - 10/24/44)
- SS-Oberführer Otto Baum (10/24/44 - 5/9/45)

Main Combat Units (as of 1944)

- SS-Panzergrenadier-Regiment 35
- SS-Panzergrenadier-Regiment 36
- SS-Panzer-Abteilung 16
- SS-Artillerie-Regiment 16
- SS-Nachrichten-Abteilung 16
- SS-Feldersatz-Bataillon 16
- SS-Panzeraufklärungs-Abteilung 16
- SS-Sturmgeschütz-Abteilung 16
- SS-Flak-Abteilung 16
- SS-Pionier-Bataillon 16

Disposition

Dispersed divisional units surrendered on 9 May 1945 to American forces at Radstadt, Austria and to British forces in the Untersteiermark area (west of Graz, Austria).

Claimed Atrocities

- various locales [Italy] :
- Padule di Fucecchio [Italy] : Mid-August 1944
- Sant'Anna di Stazzema [Italy] : 12 August 1944
- Farnocchia [Italy] : 12 August 1944
- Valla [Italy] : 19 August 1944
- Farneta Monastery [Italy] : 2 September 1944
- Monte Sol [Italy] : 29 September 1944
  see also *Miscellaneous Atrocities*

Security Operations

- Bardine de San Terenzo [Italy] : 19 August 1944
- Vinca di Fivizzano, Gragnola, Monzone, Ponte Santa Lucia [Italy] : 24 - 26 August 1944
- various locales [Italy] : September 1944

17. SS-Panzergrenadier-Division

Götz von Berlichingen

Organizational History

3 October 1943: Activation ordered and unit designated SS-Panzergrenadier-Division *Götz von Berlichingen*.

15 October 1943: Formations begun; working up in the Tours (France) area.

22 October 1943: Unit receives final designation (see above).

November 1943:
Personnel consists of cadre from 10. SS-Panzer-Division *Frundsberg*, cadre from Sturmbrigade *Reichsführer-SS*, assorted SS-Ausbildungs-und Ersatz-Bataillonen, Italian volunteers, and Rumanian Volksdeutsche.

July 1944: Incorporation of eastern volunteers as replacements (possibly Ost-Bataillonen 439 & 635).

August 1944: Heavy losses during defensive operations; unit redesignated Kampfgruppe "17. SS-Panzergrenadier-Division" and later SS-Kampfgruppe Fick.

4 September 1944: Incorporation of officers from the Metz Military Academy as replacements.

September 1944: Unit rebuilt with remnants of SS-Panzergrenadier-Brigade 49 *De Ruiter* (transferred from 23. SS-Freiwilligen-Panzergrenadier-Division *Nederland*) and remnants of SS-Panzergrenadier-Brigade 51.

Late December 1944: Incorporation of SS-Panzergrenadier-Ausbildungs-Regiment from SS-Panzergrenadier-Schule at Prosetschnitz.

2 March 1945: Incorporation of II. Abteilung, SS-Artillerie-Regiment zur besondere Verwendung (from 32. SS-Freiwilligen-Grenadier-Division).

28 March 1945: Incorporation of 4,000 replacements, including Marscheinheit "Schaffmann".

Commanding Officers

- SS-Standartenführer Otto Binge (10/43 - 1/44)
- SS-Brigadeführer Werner Ostendorff (1/44 - 6/15/44) wounded
- SS-Standartenführer Otto Binge (6/16/44 - 6/18/44)
- SS-Standartenführer Otto Baum (6/18/44 - 7/28/44)
- SS-Standartenführer Otto Binge (8/1/44 - 8/29/44)
- SS-Standartenführer Dr. Eduard Deisenhofer (8/30/44 - 9/44) MIA
- SS-Standartenführer Thomas Müller (9/44 - 9/44)
- SS-Standartenführer Gustav Mertsch (9/44 - 9/44)
- SS-Brigadeführer Werner Ostendorff (10/21/44 - 11/15/44)
- SS-Standartenführer Hans Lingner (11/15/44 - 1/9/45) POW
- SS-Obersturmbannführer (?) Lindtner (1/9/45 - 1/21/45)
- SS-Oberführer Fritz Klingenberg (1/21/45 - 3/22/45) KIA
- SS-Obersturmbannführer Vincenz Kaiser (@ 3/24/45)
- SS-Standartenführer Jakob Fick (3/24/45 - 3/26/45)
- SS-Oberführer Georg Bochmann (3/27/45 - 5/9/45)

Main Combat Units (as of 7/44)

- SS-Panzergrenadier-Regiment 37
- SS-Panzergrenadier-Regiment 38
- SS-Panzer-Abteilung 17
- SS-Artillerie-Regiment 17
- SS-Panzerjäger-Abteilung 17
- SS-Nachrichten-Abteilung 17
- SS-Feldersatz-Bataillon 17
- SS-Panzeraufklärungs-Abteilung 17
- SS-Sturmgeschütz-Abteilung 17
- SS-Flak-Abteilung 17
- SS-Pionier-Bataillon 17

Disposition

Divisional remnants surrendered to American forces on 9 May 1945 near Achensee (Bavaria) and near Maurach zum Inntal. Several hundred POWs shot and beaten to death by U.S. 42nd Infantry Division and other American units at Nürnberg, Eberstetten, Strassenkreuz Hohenkirchen-Brunntal, Oberpframmern, and at numerous small villages in the area.

Claimed Atrocities
- Graignes [France] : 12 June 1944
- Troyes [France] : 22 - 26 August 1944
- Maille [France] : 25 August 1944

see also *Miscellaneous Atrocities*

18. SS-Freiwilligen-Panzergrenadier-Division *Horst Wessel*

Organizational History
25 January 1944 : Activation ordered and formation begun at Zagreb and at Backa (Croatia), Yugoslavia. Unit designated as the 18. SS-Panzergrenadier-Division.

30 January 1944 : Unit receives final designation (see above).

April - November 1944 : Formation continues in Croatia, Rumania, and Hungary. Personnel primarily Hungarian Volksdeutsche with cadre from the 1. SS-Infanterie (mot.) Brigade. Incorporation of various SS-Ausbildungs-und Ersatz-Regimenter. Sturmgeschütz Batterie from 6. SS-Gebirgs-Division *Nord* transferred to form nucleus of SS-Panzer-Abteilung 18.

July 1944 : Elements temporarily detached as SS-Kampfgruppe Schafer (or *Horst Wessel*) and deployed to Galicia (southern Poland).

28 January 1945 : Incorporation of SS-Panzergrenadier-Ersatz-Bataillon 18.

May 1945 : Heavy losses; referred to hereafter as SS-Kampfgruppe *Horst Wessel*.

Commanding Officers
- SS-Brigadeführer August-Wilhelm Trabandt (1/25/44 - 1/3/45)
- SS-Oberführer Georg Bochmann (1/3/45 - 3/20/45) removed for insubordination
- SS-Standartenführer Heinrich Petersen (3/20/45 - 5/9/45) suicide

- Main Combat Units (as of 2/45)
- SS-Panzergrenadier-Regiment 39 (cadre: SS-Inf-Regt. 8)
- SS-Panzergrenadier-Regiment 40 (cadre: SS-Inf-Regt. 10)
- SS-Panzer Abteilung 18
- SS-Artillerie-Regiment 18
- SS-Pionier-Bataillon 18
- SS-Feldersatz-Bataillon 18
- SS-Panzerjäger-Abteilung 18

- SS-Panzeraufklärungs-Abteilung 18
- SS-Flak-Abteilung 18
- SS-Nachrichten-Abteilung 18
- SS-Panzergrenadier-Ausbildungs-Bataillon 18

Disposition

The majority of the divisional remnants surrendered in May 1945 to Soviet forces at Hirschberg (Schlesien) and at Pilsen (Böhmen, Czechoslovakia). A few survivors made it to the American lines.

Claimed Atrocities

- Stara Cernova [Czechoslovakia] : 28 September 1944
- Slovak National Uprising [Czechoslovakia] : September - October 1944
- see also entry "1. SS-Infanterie (mot.)-Brigade Operations & Atrocities in the USSR"

Security Operations

- Agram/Cilli region [Hungary] : March - April 1944
- Operation Panzerfaust [Hungary] : March - October 1944
- Zagreb/Celje [Yugoslavia] : April - June 1944 (elements)
- unspecified locales [Hungary] : July - October 1944
- Slovak National Uprising [Slovakia] : August - November 1944 (one regiment sent)
- Ostrau (Mähren) : January - 5 February 1945

19. Waffen-Grenadier-Division

der SS (lettische Nr. 2)

Organizational History

23 January 1943 : 2. SS-Infanterie-Brigade ordered to serve as cadre for "Lettische Legion".

Late-January 1943 : Unit formation begins; Schützmannschaft-Bataillonen 19 and 21 (Latvian auxiliary police) brigaded together.

8 February 1943 : Incorporation of Schützmannschaft-Bataillon 16.

29 March 1943 : Unit reinforced with 1,000 raw Latvian recruits.

April 1943 : Incorporation of Schützmannschaft-Bataillonen 24 and 26.

18 May 1943 : Unit redesignated Lettische SS-Freiwilligen-Brigade.

12 June 1943 : Incorporation of Schützmannschaft-Bataillon 18.

Summer 1943 : Incorporation of elements Aufstellungsstab für die 15.(lett.) SS-Freiwilligen-Division.

22 October 1943 : Unit redesignated 2. Lettische SS-Freiwilligen-Brigade.

7 January 1944 : Unit redesignated 19. Lettische SS-Freiwilligen-Division.

Mid-January 1944 : Incorporation of 2,000 Latvian conscripts as reinforcements.

March 1944 : Incorporation of SS-Freiwilligen-Ausbildungs-Regiment 19.

May 1944 :

Unit receives final designation (see above).

18 July 1944 :

Unit temporarily redesignated Kampfgruppe Streckenbach.

July - August 1944 :

Incorporation of Waffen-Feldersatz-Bataillon der SS 19 and miscellaneous volunteers.

Mid-August 1944 :

Incorporation of elements of the 15. Waffen-Grenadier-Division der SS (lettische Nr. 1) including the entire Waffen-Artillerie-Regiment der SS 15.

23 January 1945 :

German-speaking Latvian volunteers transferred to the Oder Front to form SS-Jagdpanzerabteilung 561 (CO: SS-Hauptsturmführer Jakob Lobmeyer).

Commanding Officers
- SS-Brigadeführer Fritz von Scholz (1/26/43 - 9/5/43)
- SS-Brigadeführer Hinrich Schüldt (9/5/43 - 3/15/44) KIA
- SS-Oberführer Friedrich-Wilhelm Bock (3/16/44 - 4/13/44)
- SS-Oberführer Bruno Streckenbach (4/15/44 - 5/12/44)
- Waffen-Oberführer Arturs Silgailis (5/12/44 - 5/19/44)
- SS-Gruppenführer Bruno Streckenbach (5/19/44 - 5/8/45)
-

Main Combat Units (as of 1945)
- Waffen-Grenadier-Regiment 42 *Voldemars Veiss*
- Waffen-Grenadier-Regiment 43 *Hinrich Schüldt*
- Waffen-Grenadier-Regiment 44
- Waffen-Artillerie-Regiment 19
- Flak-Abteilung 52
- Füsilier-Bataillon 19
- Panzerjäger-Abteilung 19
- Feldersatz-Bataillon 19
- Pionier-Bataillon 19
- Nachrichten-Abteilung 19
- Ausbildungs-Regiment 19

Disposition

The division's German cadre and others surrendered to Soviet forces on 8 May 1945 at Tukkum and Mitau (Kurland); few survived Soviet imprisonment. The majority of the Latvian personnel (5 - 8,000) retained their weapons and took to the forests as partisan bands. This irregular warfare continued in the Kurland until 1961 when the Soviets finally eliminated the last of the bands.

Claimed Atrocities
- Tosno [USSR] : 20 October 1941

20. Waffen-Grenadier-Division

der SS (estnische Nr. 1)

Organizational History

Early-August 1942 : Activation ordered.

1 October 1942 : Unit receives designation Estnische SS-Legion.

23 November 1942 :
Formation begins at SS-Truppenübungsplatz Heidelager (Debica). Cadre from SS-Totenkopf-Infanterie-Ersatz-Bataillon 3 (Brünn); also miscellaneous German and Volksdeutsche personnel. Most of the initial personnel were Estonian volunteers and conscripts.

21 January 1943 : Incorporation of 1. Kompanie / Bataillon der Waffen-SS zur besondere Verwendung. This unit had been attached to Einsatzgruppe A and participated in numerous mass murders in the USSR.

4 April 1943 : 1. Bataillon detached, renamed SS-Panzergrenadier-Bataillon *Narwa* (after several other designations) and transferred to SS-Panzergrenadier-Division *Wiking*.

5 May 1943 :
Unit redesignated Estnische SS-Freiwilligen-Brigade. Reinforced with cadre from 1. SS-Infanterie (mot.) Brigade and the incorporation of SS-Kampfgruppe Jeckeln (Polizei-Bataillon 5, cadre from 1. SS-Panzergrenadier-Division *Leibstandarte Adolf Hitler* and elements of SS-Freiwilligen-Legion *Norwegen*). [Note: both 1. SS-Infanterie (mot.) Brigade and SS-Kampfgruppe Jeckeln were extensively used in extermination actions in the USSR.]

October 1943 :
Incorporation of Estnische Schützmannschaft-Bataillon 39 and elements of Estnische Schützmannschaft-Bataillon 29.

22 October 1943 : Unit redesignated 3. Estnische SS-Freiwilligen-Brigade.

24 January 1944 : Incorporation of Estnische Freiwilligen-Bataillonen 658, 659, 660 and other Estonian security formations. Unit redesignated 20. Estnische SS-Freiwilligen-Division.

26 May 1944 : Unit receives final designation (see above).

July 1944 : Remnants of SS-Panzergrenadier-Bataillon *Narwa* reincorporated and used as cadre for SS-Fusilier-Bataillon 20.

22 August 1944 : Incorporation of 1. Bataillon / 200th Infantry Regiment (Estonian) of the Finnish Army.

October 1944 : Unit rebuilding at Truppenübungsplatz Neuhammer (Schlesien).

29 October 1944 : Incorporation of Estnische Polizei-Bataillon 287.

October 1944 - January 1945 : Incorporation of remnants Estnische Grenzschütz-Regimenter 1 through 6 (frontier guards).

April 1945 : Incorporation of an Estonian battalion and 2 Estonian Police companies as replacements.

Commanding Officers
- SS-Sturmbannführer Franz Augsberger (10/1/42 - ?)
- SS-Sturmbannführer Georg Eberhardt (? - 7/43) KIA
- SS-Brigadeführer Franz Augsberger (7/1/43 - 3/17/45) KIA
- SS-Sturmbannführer Hans-Joachim Mützelfeldt (3/17/45 - 3/20/45)
- SS-Oberführer Berthold Maack (3/20/45 - 5/8/45)

Main Combat Units (as of 11/44)
- SS-Freiwilligen-Grenadier-Regiment 45 *Estland*
- SS-Freiwilligen-Grenadier-Regiment 46
- SS-Freiwilligen-Grenadier-Regiment 47
- SS-Freiwilligen-Artillerie-Regiment 20

- Füsilier-Bataillon 20
- Panzerjäger-Abteilung 20
- Flak-Abteilung 20
- Pionier-Bataillon 20
- Nachrichten-Abteilung 20
- Ersatz-Bataillon 20

Disposition

Most of the division surrendered to Soviet forces on 8 May 1945 at Melnik (north of Prague); some made it to American lines, but were subsequently handed over to the Soviets. Few divisional personnel survived Soviet captivity. On 9 May 1945, a crowd of Prague townspeople tortured and murdered the division's wounded at the SS-Lazarett in the Sanatorium Praha-Podol.

Claimed Atrocities

- see notes above and entry "1. SS-Infanterie (mot.)-Brigade Operations & Atrocities in the USSR"

Security Operations

- Nevel area [Estonia] : November - December 1943

21. Waffen-Gebirgs-Division

der SS Skanderbeg (albanische Nr. 1)

Organizational History

April 1944 : Unit authorized and recruitment of Albanian Muslims begun. Austrians comprised the cadre of officers and NCOs.

mid April 1944 : Incorporation of Albanian reinforced battalion from 13. SS-Freiwilligen-Gebirgs-Division *Handschar*.

June 1944 : Formation at Kosovo, Yugoslavia.

September 1944 : German military reverses result in an epidemic of desertions.

Early-October 1944 : Incorporation of 3,800 Kriegsmarine personnel from Army Group E (Salonika, Greece) as replacements.

Mid-October 1944 : Unit redesignated Kampfgruppe 21. Waffen-Grenadier-Division der SS Skanderbeg. Incorporation of miscellaneous Albanian police personnel.

January 1945 : Elements of SS-Sanitäts-Abteilung 21 transferred as cadre to 32. SS-Freiwilligen-Grenadier-Division *30 Januar*.

February 1945 : Previously incorporated Kriegsmarine personnel released and sent back to Germany. The remains of the division are redesignated (on paper) as 2. Bataillon, SS-Freiwilligen-Gebirgsjäger-Regiment 14 (part of the 7. SS-Freiwilligen-Gebirgs-Division *Prinz Eugen*).

Commanding Officers

- SS-Brigadeführer Josef Fitzhum (4/44 - 6/44)

[HSSPf Albanien and CO during formation and intial training]

- SS-Oberführer August Schmidhuber (6/44 - 8/14/44)
- SS-Obersturmbannführer Alfred Graaf (8/15/44 - 5/45)

Main Combat Units
- Waffen-Gebirgsjäger-Regiment der SS 50
- Waffen-Gebirgsjäger-Regiment der SS 51
- Waffen-Gebirgsartillerie-Regiment 21
- Aufklärungs-Abteilung 21
- Panzerjäger-Abteilung 21
- Pionier-Abteilung 21
- Nachrichten-Abteilung 21
- Feldersatz-Bataillon 21

Disposition
Divisional remnants were forced to surrender as part of the 7. SS-Freiwilligen-Gebirgs-Division *Prinz Eugen* on 15 May 1945 to Yugoslav partisans near the city of Krainburg (Slovenia) while attempting to cross to Allied lines. They were then subjected to a weeks-long death march ("Sühnemarsch") through Yugoslavia. Many of the prisoners were killed out of hand (members of *Prinz Eugen* were reportedly shot on 18 May 1945 by elements of the II Partisan Brigade, 1st Army). The survivors of the march (perhaps only 50%) were sent as slave laborers to the copper mines at Bor where most lost their lives. Some were also tried and executed by Yugoslav authorities for atrocities; others were subsequently murdered for various reasons. Few ever returned to the west.

Claimed Atrocities
- Albania : May - July 1944
- Pristina [Albania] : April 1944
- Kukes [Albania] : 11 August 1944

Security Operations
- Kosovo area [Albania/Yugoslavia] : August 1944
- Gjakowica [Macedonia] : 11 - 13 September 1944 (see Munoz, p.234)
- Prizren, Novo Selo, Pec [Yugoslavia] : 23 September 1944
- Rogatica, Kraljevo, Sopotnik, Otok, Brcko [Yugoslavia] : 1 November 1944
- Zvornik, Vukovar area [Yugoslavia] : January 1945

22. SS-Freiwilligen-Kavallerie-Division *Maria Theresia*

Organizational History

1 May 1944 : Activation ordered as SS-Freiwilligen-Kavallerie-Division in the Budapest area.

June 1944 : Unit formed from two regiments of Hungarian Volksdeutsche and cadre (SS-Kavallerie-Regiment 17) from 8. SS-Kavallerie-Division *Florian Geyer*.

July 1944 : Unit redesignated SS-Division *Ungarn*.

September 1944 : Unit receives final designation (see above).

Commanding Officers
- SS-Brigadeführer August Zehender (5/44 - 2/11/45) KIA

Main Combat Units (as of 9/44)
- SS-Freiwilligen-Kavallerie-Regiment 17
- SS-Freiwilligen-Kavallerie-Regiment 52
- SS-Freiwilligen-Kavallerie-Regiment 53
- SS-Freiwilligen-Artillerie-Regiment 22
- Panzeraufklärungs-Abteilung 22
- Panzerjäger-Abteilung 22
- Flak-Abteilung 22
- Pionier-Bataillon 22
- Nachrichten-Abteilung 22
- Feldersatz-Bataillon 22

Disposition
The majority of the division was annihilated in February 1945 in defense of the Budapest Pocket. At the start of the Budapest encirclement, a small part of the division was north of the Danube between Pressburg and Wien with most of the unit's horses. Several unsuccessful attempts were made to rebuild the division at Pressburg.

Claimed Atrocities
- Warsaw Uprising [Poland] : August 1944

Security Operations
- Operation Panzerfaust [Budapest]: 16 October 1944

23. Waffen-Gebirgs-Division

der SS Kama (kroatische Nr. 2)

Organizational History

10 June 1944 : Recruitment and formation begun in Bacska region (Hungary). Personnel primarily Bosnian Muslims and Croatian Ustachi. German/Croatian cadre received from the 13. Waffen-Gebirgs-Division der SS *Handschar* (kroatische Nr. 1), including the entire SS-Aufklärungs-Abteilung 13. Division variously designated as Waffen-Gebirgs-Division SS *Kama* (kroatische Nr. 2) and 23. SS-Gebirgs-Division.

July - August 1944 : Formation continues.

September 1944 : Unit receives final designation (see above). Soviet advances halt recruiting drive (no more than 8 - 9,000 personnel).

17 October 1944 : Unit crippled by mutiny among Bosnian personnel.

Commanding Officers

- SS-Standartenführer Helmut Raithel (6/44 - 10/31/44)

Main Combat Units (as of 6/44)

- Waffen-Gebirgsjäger-Regiment der SS 55 (nominally)
- Waffen-Gebirgsjäger-Regiment der SS 56 (nominally)
- Waffen-Gebirgsartillerie-Regiment der SS 23
- Aufklärungs-Abteilung 23
- Panzerjäger-Abteilung 23
- Flak-Abteilung 23
- Pionier-Bataillon 23
- Gebirgs-Nachrichten-Abteilung 23
- Feldersatz-Bataillon 23

Disposition

The division was disbanded on 31 October 1944 as a result of the mutiny and massive desertions among the Bosnian Muslim and Croatian ranks. The majority of its remaining German personnel were sent as cadre to the newly-forming 31. SS-Freiwilligen-Grenadier-Division. Some were sent to the 13. Waffen-Gebirgs-Division der SS *Handschar*. In early 1945, SS-Pionier-Bataillon 23 was transferred to the 23. SS-Freiwilligen-Panzergrenadier-Division *Nederland*.

Claimed Atrocities

- Gau Steiermark [Austria] : November 1944 – 21 March 1945

23. SS-Freiwilligen-Panzergrenadier-Division *Nederland*

Organizational History

July - August 1943 : Elements of SS-Freiwilligen-Legion *Niederland* expanded into the 4. SS-Freiwilligen-Panzergrenadier-Brigade *Nederland*.

October 1943 : Sent to Zagreb, Croatia for continued training. Incorporation of Croatian Volksdeutsche volunteers.

September 1944 : SS-Freiwilligen-Panzergrenadier-Regiment 49 *De Ruiter* transferred to the 17. SS-Panzer-Grenadier-Division *Götz von Berlichingen*.

December 1944 : Unit accorded divisional status despite being understrength. Receives vacant divisional number and final designation (see above).

Early 1945 : Incorporation of SS-Pionier-Bataillon 23 (from the disbanded 23. Waffen-Gebirgs-Division der SS *Kama*).

February 1945 : Division shipped from the Kurland to Stettin, Germany. Heavy personnel losses when the transport ship *Moira* was sunk by the Soviets.

Commanding Officers

- SS-Brigadeführer Jürgen Wagner (7/43 - 5/45)

Main Combat Units (as of 5/44)

- SS-Freiwilligen-Panzergrenadier-Regiment 48 *General Seyffardt*
- SS-Freiwilligen-Panzergrenadier-Regiment 49 *De Ruiter*
- Artillerie-Regiment 54
- Füsilier-Bataillon 54
- Panzerjäger-Bataillon
- Pionier-Bataillon 54
- Nachrichten-Abteilung 54
- Feldersatz-Bataillon 54

Disposition

In late April 1945 the division was nearly annihilated by Soviet forces during defensive actions near Fürstenwalde. The survivors surrendered to American forces on 5 May 1945 near Magdeburg. Both the divisional commander and at least one of his adjutants (SS-Hauptsturmführer Karl-Heinz Ertel) were later tried by the Yugoslavian authorities for war crimes.

Security Operations

- Zagreb, Croatia [Yugoslavia] : October - December 1943

24. Waffen-Gebirgs-Division

der SS Karstjäger

Organizational History

10 July 1942 : Activation ordered of a counter-insurgency unit for operation in the Alpine/Cisalpine Arc (South Tyrol to Istria). Formation begun at SS-Kaserne Dachau and unit designated SS-Karstwehr-Kompanie. Personnel consists of Tyrolian, Rumanian, Hungarian, Ukrainian, Slovenian, Croatian, and Serbian Volksdeutsche. Officer/NCO cadre composed primarily of Austrians and personnel from the Posen Military Academy in Treskau.

15 November 1942 : Unit upgraded and redesignated SS-Karstwehr-Bataillon.

Summer 1943 : Unit reinforced by Istrian, Slovenian, Croatian, and Serbian Volksdeutsche volunteers.

5 December 1943:
Unit redesignated Waffen-Gebirgs(karst)jäger-Brigade der SS.

Sometime in 1944 : Incorporation of a company of Spaniards from the Brandenburg Kommandos.

18 July 1944 :
Unit accorded divisional status as Waffen-Gebirgs-(Karstjäger)-Division-SS.

9 September 1944 : Unit receives final designation (see above).

Late April 1945 : Unit reinforced with cadets from the SS Junkerschule Klagenfurt and with a cadre from 7. SS-Freiwilligen-Gebirgs-Division *Prinz Eugen*.

Commanding Officers
- SS-Standartenführer Dr. Ing. Hans Brand (7/42 - 1/44)
- SS-Sturmbannführer Josef Berschneider (? - ?)
- SS-Sturmbannführer Werner Hahn (? - ?)
- SS-Obersturmbannführer Karl Marks (late Summer 1944 - late 1944)
- SS-Obersturmbannführer Adolf Wagner (late 1944 - 5/9/45)

Main Combat Units (as of 8/44)
- SS-Gebirgs (Karstjäger) Regiment 59
- SS-Gebirgs (Karstjäger) Regiment 60 (nominal)
- SS-Gebirgs-Artillerie-Regiment 24
- SS-Gebirgs-Nachrichten-Abteilung 24

Subordination
HSSPf Adriatic Coast (7/18/44)

Disposition
The division surrendered on 9 May 1945 to British forces at Rosental near Villach (southern Austria).

Security Operations
- Isonzo Valley/Julian Alps [Italy/Yugoslavia] : Summer 1943
- Udino-Frioli region [Italy] : February 1944 - September 1944
- Trieste, Udine, Gorz sectors [Italy/Yugoslavia] : September 1944
- Julian and Karstian Alps [Italy/Yugoslavia] : April 1945

25. Waffen-Grenadier-Division

der SS Hunyadi (ungarische Nr. 1)

Organizational History

1 May 1944 : Activation ordered. Unit designated SS-Freiwilligen-Grenadier-Division *Ungarn*. Recruitment of Transylvanian and Hungarian Volksdeutsche begun.

Summer 1944 : Unit formation interrupted by advancing Soviet forces.

2 November 1944 : Unit formation resumed at Zalärgerszeg (southwest Hungary). Cadre primarily from the 13th Hungarian Honved Infantry Division (former commanding officer - Josef Grassy); remainder from Hungarian civilian volunteers. Unit redesignated 25. Waffen-Grenadier-Division der SS (ungarische Nr. 1); then receives final designation (see above).

16 November 1944 : Incorporation of SS-Kampfgruppe Deak (CO: Waffen-Oberführer der SS Ladislaus Deak) as cadre of Waffen-Grenadier-Regiment der SS 61.

Late November 1944 : Training shifted to Truppenübungsplatz Neuhammer (Schlesien) due to advancing Soviet forces.

January 1945 : Reinforced with remnants of the 30.

Waffen-Grenadier-Division der SS (russische Nr. 2).

Commanding Officers
- Waffen-Generalleutnant der SS Josef Grassy (5/44 - ?/?/45) wounded
- SS-Standartenführer Michael Broser (?/?/45 - 5/5/45)

Main Combat Units
- Waffen-Grenadier-Regiment 61
- Waffen-Grenadier-Regiment 62
- Waffen-Grenadier-Regiment 63
- Artillerie-Regiment 25
- Waffen-Schi-Bataillon
- Füsilier-Kompanie 25
- Panzerjäger-Abteilung 25
- Pionier-Bataillon 25
- Nachrichten-Abteilung 25
- Feldersatz-Bataillon 25

Disposition
Dispersed elements of the division surrendered to American forces at Salzkammergut (5/5/45) and also at Attersee (5/8/45). One half-company was annihilated in defense of Berlin (in the area of the SS-Hauptamt). Some elements adopted civilian clothing and passed themselves off as Hungarian refugees.

Claimed Atrocities
- Novi Sad [Yugoslavia] : 21 - 23 January 1942
- Stari Becej [Yugoslavia] : 26 - 28 January 1942

26. Waffen-Grenadier-Division

der SS (ungarische Nr. 2)

Organizational History

November 1944 : Unit activation ordered. Formation begun at Ragendorf-Rajka (northwestern Hungary) with a mixture of civilian recruits and Honved military personnel.

1 January 1945 : Formation continued; unit relocated to Sieradtz, Poland.

19 January 1945 :- Soviet advances threaten embryonic unit; division withdrawn to the west.

February 1945 : Unit reformed at SS-Truppenübungsplatz Neuhammer (Schlesien).
[Note - The final unit designation may have included the honor title *Gömbös* late in the war]

Commanding Officers
- Waffen-Oberführer der SS Zoltan von Pinsky (12/23/44 - 1/21/45) KIA
- SS-Brigadeführer Berthold Maack (1/22/45 - 3/20/45)
- Waffen-Generalleutnant der SS Josef Grassy (3/21/45 - ?/?/45) wounded
- SS-Sturmbannführer Ralf Tiemann (? - 5/9/45)

Main Combat Units (as of 3/45)
- Waffen-Grenadier-Regiment 64
- Waffen-Grenadier-Regiment 65
- Waffen-Grenadier-Regiment 85
- Waffen-Artillerie-Regiment 26
- Füsilier-Bataillon 26
- Panzerjäger-Abteilung 26
- Pionier-Bataillon 26
- Nachrichten-Abteilung 26

Disposition
Scattered divisional elements surrendered on 9 May 1945 to American forces at Neumarkt (Austria), Menin, and in the Regensburg area (Germany).

Claimed Atrocities
- Novi Sad [Yugoslavia] : 21 - 23 January 1942
- Stari Becej [Yugoslavia] : 26 - 28 January 1942

27. SS-Freiwilligen-Grenadier-

Division *Langemarck (flämische Nr. 1)*

Organizational History

10 April 1941 : Activation and formation at Hamburg of SS-Freiwilligen-Standarte *Nordwest* with Danish, Dutch, and Flemish volunteers.

1 October 1941 : Reorganized at Arys, East Prussia as SS-Freiwilligen-Legion *Flandern.*

31 May 1943 : Reorganized as SS-Freiwilligen-Sturmbrigade *Langemarck* and then as 6. SS-Sturmbrigade *Langemarck* at SS-Truppenübungsplätze Heidelager (Debica) and Böhmen (Milowitz). Reinforced with a Finnisches Freiwilligen-Bataillon, a Panzerjäger-Kompanie, Sturmgeschütze, Flak, and additional Flemish volunteers.

29 April 1944 : Unit refitted at SS-Truppenübungsplatz Böhmen (Milowitz).

19 July 1944 : Elements detached and sent to fight at Narwa as Kampfgruppe Rehmann.

18 September 1944 : Unit receives final designation (see above).

16 January 1945 : Reinforcements include Luftwaffe, Kriegsmarine, NSKK, Organization Todt, and Dutch Vlaamse Wacht personnel.

Commanding Officers
- SS-Sturmbannführer Michael Lippert (10/1/41 - 4/18/42)
- SS-Obersturmbannführer Josef Fitzthum (4/19/42 - 7/14/42)
- SS-Obersturmbannführer Konrad Schellong (7/15/42 - 5/45)

Main Combat Units (as of 11/44)
- SS-Freiwilligen-Panzergrenadier-Regiment 66
- SS-Freiwilligen-Panzergrenadier-Regiment 67
- SS-Freiwilligen-Panzergrenadier-Regiment 68
- SS-Füsilier-Bataillon 27

- Panzerjäger-Abteilung 27
- Artillerie-Regiment 27
- Pionier-Bataillon 27
- Nachrichten-Abteilung 27
- Feldersatz-Bataillon 27

Subordination

- 2. SS-Infanterie (mot.) Brigade (11/10/41 - 7/23/42) [as *Flandern*]
- 1. SS-Infanterie (mot.) Brigade (8/28/42) [as *Flandern*]

Disposition

Division surrendered in May 1945 to Soviet forces at Neustrehlitz and Waren.

Security Operations

- Tarasovo, Rublevo, Aviati [USSR]: 18 November 1941

Also check the entries for 1. and 2. SS-Infanterie Brigades regarding activities of *Flandern* with these units.

28. SS-Freiwilligen-Panzergrenadier-Division *Wallonie*

Organizational History

1941 : Activation and formation of Wallonische Legion (Belgian volunteers); unit designated as Wehrmacht Bataillon 373.

1 June 1943 : Wehrmacht Bataillon 373 transferred into the Waffen-SS and reformed as SS-Freiwilligen-Brigade *Wallonien*.

Summer 1943 : Unit training at Truppenübungsplatz Wildflecken.

3 July 1943 : Unit redesignated SS-Sturmbrigade *Wallonien*.

March 1944 : Unit redesignated 5. SS-Freiwilligen-Sturmbrigade *Wallonien*.

Spring 1944 : Unit rebuilt at Truppenübungsplatz Wildflecken after heavy losses at Tscherkassy.

Summer 1944 : Unit refitted near Breslau after heavy losses at Narwa.

18 September 1944 : Unit redesignated SS-Freiwilligen-Grenadier-Division *Wallonien*.

19 October 1944 :
Rebuilt under divisional designation with mixed replacements -- elements of SS-Panzergrenadier-Ausbildungs-und Ersatz-Bataillon 35 (see SS-Jäger-Bataillonen 500 & 501), Belgian Police, as well as French, Belgian and Spanish Organisation Todt members. Division redesignated 28. SS-Freiwilligen-Grenadier-Division *Wallonien*.

December 1944 : Unit receives final designation (see above).

February 1945 : Incorporation of Spanische-Freiwilligen-Kompanie der SS 101.

April 1945 : Spanische-Freiwilligen-Kompanie der SS 101 transferred to 11. SS-Freiwilligen-Panzergrenadier-Division *Nordland* for the defense of Berlin.

Commanding Officers
- (?) Lucien Lippert (? - 2/13/44) KIA
- SS-Standartenführer Leon Degrelle (2/13/44 - 5/7/45)

Main Combat Units (as of 10/44)
- SS-Freiwilligen-Panzergrenadier-Regiment 69
- SS-Freiwilligen-Panzergrenadier-Regiment 70
- SS-Freiwilligen-Panzergrenadier-Regiment 71 (nominal)
- SS-Artillerie-Regiment 28
- Panzerjäger-Abteilung 28
- Pionier-Bataillon 28
- Nachrichten-Abteilung 28

Disposition
Some divisional elements were captured by Soviet forces at Schwerin. However, most of the unit retreated to Schleswig-Holstein/Denmark and surrendered to British forces on 8 May 1945.

29. Waffen-Grenadier-Division

der SS (russische Nr. 1)

Organizational History

Late 1941 : Formation of Selbstschutz in and around Gemiende Lokot (between Orel and Kursk, USSR). Unit commanded by Bronislav Wladislawowitsch [or Mieczyslaw] Kaminski.

Late 1943 : Kaminski Brigade transferred into the Waffen-SS. Unit composed of approximately 6,500 Ukrainian mercenaries. Reinforced with criminals, concentration camp "trusties", *etc.*

April 1944 : Unit known as RONA (Russkaja Oswoboditielnaja Armija).

post-April 1944 : Unit receives final designation (see above).

Commanding Officers
- Waffen-Oberführer Bronislav Kaminski (?/42 - 8/25/44)

Disposition
Following the unit's atrocious performance during the Warsaw Uprising, Kaminski was shot under disputed circumstances on 25 August 1944 by his SS masters. The division was disbanded and supplied cadres to the 30. Waffen-Grenadier-Division der SS (russische Nr. 2) and the Vlassov Army.

Claimed Atrocities
- Lepel-Usaci region [USSR] : 11 April - 10 May 1944
- Warsaw Uprising [Poland] : August 1944
- unspecified locales [USSR] : rear areas of Army Group Center

Security Operations
- unspecified locales [USSR] - rear areas of Army Group Center

29. Waffen-Grenadier-Division

der SS (italienische Nr. 1)

Organizational History

September 1943 : Approximately 15,000 former Italian Army officers and men volunteer for service in the Waffen-SS and are sent to Truppenübungsplatz Münsingen. The group is designated as the Legione Milizia Armata.

October 1943 : Hitler and Mussolini work out an agreement regarding control of the Legione Milizia Armata. Most of the volunteers are transferred and assigned to newly-forming Italian Army units. Several thousand are retained under Waffen-SS control and formed into the SS-Legion *Italia*.

Winter 1943 : Following a brief period of training (most of the men were veterans), sub-units of SS-Legion *Italia* are sent to perform security duties in Northern Italy under control of HöSSPf Italien.

February - June 1944 : Unit reorganized, expanded and renamed several times -- 1. Italienisches-SS-Freiwilligen-Brigade, 1. Italienisches-Freiwilligen-Sturmbrigade des Milizia Armata, and 1. Sturmbrigade des Italienisches-SS-Freiwilligen-Legion.

July 1944 : Unit redesignated 9. Waffen-Grenadier-Brigade der SS (italienische Nr. 1).

7 Sept 1944 : Two infantry brigades, officer corps, and numerous support units transferred from security duties to reinforce unit; redesignated as Waffen-Grenadier-Brigade der SS (italienische Nr. 1).

9 March 1945 : Unit receives final designation (see above) and is assigned vacant divisional number, despite the fact that its sub-units operated widely dispersed throughout all of its history.

Commanding Officers
- SS-Brigadeführer Peter Hansen (9/43 - 10/43) taken ill
- SS-Standartenführer Gustav Lombard (10/43 - 12/43)
- SS-Brigadeführer Peter Hansen (12/43 - 1/45) taken ill
- SS-Standartenführer Constantin von Heldmann (1/45 - 3/9/45)

Main Combat Units (as of 9/44)
- Waffen-Grenadier-Regiment der SS 81 ("Vendetta")
- Waffen-Grenadier-Regiment der SS 82
- SS-Artillerie-Regiment 29
- SS-Panzerjäger-Abteilung 29
- SS-Nachrichten-Kompanie 29
- SS-Ersatz-Bataillon 29
- SS-Füsilier-Bataillon 29 ("Debica")
- SS-Pionier-Kompanie 29

Disposition
Fusilier battalion and minor elements of the division surrendered on 30 April 1945 to American forces near Gorgonzola. Balance of division, however, continued with anti-partisan operations in the Lake Como region until they ran out of supplies. After surrendering to local Communist partisans, most were executed *en masse*. Some personnel were reserved for later trial and summary execution for war crimes.

Security Operations
- Turin, Lake Como, Cuneous Valley : October 1943
- Lanzo Valley, Rora, Scheggia Pass : March - April 1944
- northwest Italy : June 1944
- Russoleno-Susa, Germanasca & Chisone Valleys, Lake Como, Monte Orisiera : June - August 1944
- Fenestrelle Fortress area : 4 - 10 August 1944
- Lanzo Valley : September 1944
- Viu Valley : September - October 1944
- Ossola, Valsassina Valley : October 1944
- Trebbia Valley, Castelarcuato : October 1944 - March 1945
- Bettola, Sommaglia, Po River, Nure Valley, Bobbio : April 1945

30. Waffen-Grenadier-Division

der SS (russische Nr. 2)

Organizational History

July 1944 :
Formation of Schützmannschaft-Brigade Siegling from German Ordnungspolizei cadre and the following Belorussian, Russian, Polish, Armenian, Tatar, & Ukrainian security units -- Schützmannschaft-Bataillonen (57, 60, 61, 62, 63, 64 & 101); Polizei-Gebiets-Kommandaturen (Minsk, Glebokie, Lida, Slusk, Baranowitschi, Wileika & Slonim); Polizeiführer Pripyet Sumpf; Schützmannschaft-Artillerie-Abteilung 56; Schützmannschaft-Ausbildungs-Bataillon Uretje; Fremdvölkisches-Bataillon Murawjew; russisches Bataillon 654; & Schützmannschaft-Reiter-Abteilung 68.

3 August 1944 : Unit accorded divisional status.
18 August 1944 : Unit receives final designation (see above).

Late August 1944 :
Approximately 2,300 mutinous personnel transferred to Transport Command Karlsruhe to work on the Westwall (Siegfried Line).

12 September 1944 : Return of mutinous personnel to division.

October 1944 : Unit reinforced with elements from disbanded 29. Waffen-Grenadier-Division der SS.

November 1944 : Division suffers heavy losses in defensive combat versus 1st French Armored Division.

1 January 1945 : Unit downgraded to brigade status. Approximately 5,000 unreliable individuals transferred to the Vlassov Army.

27 February 1945 : Unit redesignated Waffen-Grenadier-Brigade der SS *Weissruthenien* and then disbanded at Truppenübungsplatz Grafenwöhr.

Commanding Officers
- SS-Obersturmbannführer Hans Siegling (7/44 - 2/27/45)

Main Combat Units (as of 10/44)
- Waffen-Grenadier-Regiment der SS 75
- Waffen-Grenadier-Regiment der SS 76
- Waffen-Grenadier-Regiment der SS 77 (nominal)
- Aufklärungs-Abteilung
- Artillerie-Abteilung
- Pionier-Kompanie
- Feldersatz-Bataillon
- Nachrichten-Kompanie

Disposition

Division disbanded on 27 February 1945. Cadres supplied to the 25. Waffen-Grenadier-Division der SS *Hunyadi* (ungarische Nr. 1) and the 38. SS-Grenadier-Division *Nibelungen*.

Security Operations
- Belfort, Mulhouse, Besancon, Dijon [France] : August - October 1944
- Guemar, Ostheim, Rhine River, Neubreissach [Germany] : 25 November 1944

31. SS-Freiwilligen-Grenadier-Division

Organizational History

September - October 1944 : Formed in the Batschka region (Hungary) from Hungarian Volksdeutsche reservists, Hungarian and Yugoslavian Army remnants, and a cadre from the 23. Waffen-Gebirgs-Division der SS *Kama*. Far below normal divisional strength.

February 1945 : Füsilier-Bataillon 31 formed from 200 - 300 members of the Hungarian Arrow Cross Party *Szalasi Youth*.

Commanding Officers
- SS-Brigadeführer Gustav Lombard   (10/18/44 - 5/45)

Main Combat Units
- SS-Freiwilligen-Grenadier-Regiment 78
- SS-Freiwilligen-Grenadier-Regiment 79
- SS-Freiwilligen-Grenadier-Regiment 80
- SS-Freiwilligen-Artillerie-Regiment 31
- SS-Freiwilligen-Füsilier-Bataillon 31
- SS-Freiwilligen-Panzerjäger-Abteilung 31
- SS-Freiwilligen-Pionier-Bataillon 31
- SS-Freiwilligen-Nachrichten-Abteilung 31
- SS-Freiwilligen-Feldersatz-Bataillon 31

Disposition
The division attempted to surrender to American forces near Pilsen (Czechoslovakia) but were blocked by Soviet armored forces at Königgratz. Some elements surrendered to the Soviets. The majority of the division, however, surrendered on 8 May 1945 to Czech partisans who subsequently murdered 4,000 of them (few survivors).

Claimed Atrocities
- Crvenka [Yugoslavia] : 7 - 8 October 1944

32. SS-Freiwilligen-Grenadier-Division 30. *Januar*

Organizational History

30 January - February 1945 :
Activation at SS-Truppenübungsplatz Kurmark (Grunow-Briesen) ordered using numerous small units -- staff SS-Artillerie-Schule I (Glau); staff and recruits SS-Truppenübungsplatz Kurmark; Grenadier-Ersatztruppenteilen SS-Truppenübungsplatz Kurmark; Kampfgruppe SS-Waffen-und Unterführerschule Lauenburg (Pommern); SS-Grenadier-Ersatz-Bataillon 16 (Senftenberg) [a sub-unit of 16. SS-Panzergrenadier-Division *Reichsführer-SS*]; staff and recruits SS-Grenadier-Ersatz-Bataillon 9 (Stralsund) [a sub-unit of 9. SS-Panzer-Division *Hohenstaufen*]; Leader Reserve (Weimar); SS-Panzergrenadier-Regiment *Schill*; Kampfgruppe Becker der SS-Führerschule des WVHA (Arolsen) [CO: SS-Hauptsturmführer Karl Becker]; II. Abteilung des SS-Artillerie-Ausbildungs-und Ersatz-Regiment (Beneschau); Gruppe Mösinger (IV. Abteilung des SS-Artillerie-Ausbildungs-und Ersatz-Regiment 1, Olmütz); Gruppe Rössner (SS-Sturmgeschütz-Schule); staff Musikschule der Waffen-SS; SS-Nachrichten-Ersatz-und Ausbildungs-Abteilung (Eichstätt); SS-Gebirgsjäger-Ersatzeinheiten (Hallein, Predazzo); SS-Grenadier-Ausbildungs-und Ersatz-Bataillonen (Stralsund, Brünn, Stendahl, Nienburg, Spreenhagen); SS-Panzerjäger-Ausbildungs-und Ersatz-Abteilungen (Audorf, Beneschau); SS-Pionier-Ersatz-Bataillon (Beneschau); Latvian volunteers [from Waffen-Grenadier-Regiment 32 of 15. Waffen-Grenadier-Division der SS (lettische Nr. 1)]; SS-Sanitäts-Abteilung 21 [from 21. Waffen-Gebirgs-Division der SS *Skanderbeg* (albanische Nr. 1)]; Waffen-SS soldiers on leave in Frankfurt an der Oder, Ostpreussen, and Posen; as well as mixed stragglers. Unit designated as the 32. SS-Panzergrenadier-Division *30. Januar*.

2 March 1945 : II. Abteilung, SS-Artillerie-Regiment zur besonderen Verwendung transferred to 17. SS-Panzergrenadier-Division *Götz von Berlichingen*. Unit receives final designation (see above).

Commanding Officers

- SS-Standartenführer Johannes Rudolf Mühlen-kamp (?1/45 - 2/5/45)
- SS-Standartenführer Hellmuth Richter (2/5/45 - 2/17/45)
- SS-Oberführer Adolf Ax (2/17/45 - mid 3/45)
- SS-Standartenführer Hans Kempin (mid 3/45 - 5/6/45)
-

Main Combat Units (as of 4/45)

- SS-Freiwilligen-Grenadier-Regiment 86
- SS-Freiwilligen-Grenadier-Regiment 87
- SS-Freiwilligen-Grenadier-Regiment 88 (never completed)
- SS-Panzerjäger-Regiment 32
- SS-Artillerie-Regiment 32
- SS-Pionier-Bataillon 32
- SS-Füsilier-Bataillon 32
- SS-Nachrichten-Abteilung 32
- SS-Feldersatz-Bataillon 32
- SS-Flak-Abteilung 32
- SS-Werfer-Batterie 32

Disposition

Remnants surrendered to Americans forces on 6 May 1945 at Tangermünde.

33. Waffen-Grenadier-Division

der SS Charlemagne (französische Nr. 1)

Organizational History

1941 :
Formation of the Legion des Volontaires Francais (LVF), a Wehrmacht unit designated as the Französischen Freiwilligen Legion / Infanterie-Regiment 638 des Heeres (part of the 7. Infanterie-Division). The personnel were primarily French with a cadre of German officers and NCOs.

18 August 1943 : Formation of the Französisches SS-Freiwilligen-Grenadier-Regiment ordered at Ausbildungslager Sennheim (Elsass).

March 1944 : LVF unit passed to Waffen-SS control and incorporated into the Französisches SS-Freiwilligen-Grenadier-Regiment. Combined unit designated as the französisches SS-Freiwilligen-Brigade 7.

July 1944 : Unit redesignated as the französisches SS-Freiwilligen-Sturmbrigade 7 *Charlemagne*; composed of 1,100 effectives.

Late August 1944 : Further working up at Truppenübungsplatz Wildflecken (Fulda): incorporation of remaining LVF personnel (1,200 effectives), French Militia (2,500 effectives), French members of the NSKK, OT, and other organizations (2,300 effectives), as well as 1,200 French Navy volunteers (Schiffsstammabteilung 28 [Duisberg]).
1 September 1944 : Unit receives designation SS-Freiwilligen-Division *Charlemagne* (7,000 effectives).

January 1945 : Unit receives final designation (see above).

February 1945 : Division rebuilt at Truppenübungsplatz Hammerstein with Hungarian units originally planned for use in a never-activated fourth Hungarian SS division.

24 April 1945 : Waffen-Grenadier-Regiment 57 (composed of 300 volunteers) redesignated SS-Sturmbatail-lon *Charlemagne* (CO: SS-Hauptstürmfuhrer Henri-Jo-seph Fenet) and moved to Berlin defences.

Commanding Officers
- Waffen-Oberführer Edgar Puaud (9/1/44 - 2/45) MIA
- SS-Brigadeführer Dr. jur. Gustav Krukenberg (2/45 - 4/26/45)
- SS-Standartenführer Walter Zimmermann (4/26/45 - 5/45)

Main Combat Units (as of 2/45)
- Waffen-Grenadier-Regiment 57
- Waffen-Grenadier-Regiment 58
- Waffen-Artillerie-Abteilung der SS 57
- SS-Pionier-Kompanie
- SS-Panzerjäger-Abteilung 57
- SS-Nachrichten-Kompanie
- Ausbildungs-und Ersatz-Bataillon 33
- Marsch-Bataillon Greifenberg

Disposition
In early 1945 the division was broken into three sub-units during fighting against the Soviets in Pomerania. Two of the units were destroyed during further defensive combat in the area. The remaining unit retreated to the Baltic coast, was evacuated to Denmark, and then redeployed to Neustrelitz (near Berlin). A hastily formed group of 300 volunteers was designated SS-Sturmbataillon *Charlemagne* and sent to Berlin for the final defense of the capital. On 2 May 1945 *Charlemagne* was annihilated defending the Reichskanzlerei in Berlin against overwhelmingly superior Soviet forces. Its few survivors were mostly executed or worked to death in Soviet slave labor camps. A handful (including Fenet) were eventually returned to the West after many years of imprisonment. The personnel remaining at Neustrelitz surrendered several days later to Allied forces at Schwerin and Bad Kleinen. On 8 May 1945 elements of the 2nd Free French Armoured Division (CO: General Henri Leclerc) executed 12 "Charlemagners" at Karlstein in Bavaria. Official inquiries into the matter in December 1948 went nowhere. Those divisional elements captured by the Americans were interned as POWs for one year and then remanded to France as war criminals.

34. SS-Grenadier-Division

Landstorm Nederland

Organizational History

11 March 1943 :
Formation of Landwacht Niederlande (internal security unit of Dutch volunteers led by German Police officers).

16 October 1943 : Unit redesignated Landstorm Nederland.

16 September 1944 : Unit transferred to Waffen-SS control and redesignated SS-Freiwilligen-Grenadier-Brigade *Landstorm Nederland*. Some personnel supplied to SS-Wach-Bataillon 3.

September - October 1944 : Incorporation of SS-Wach-Bataillon *Nordwest* (concentration camp guard unit) as SS-Panzerjäger-Abteilung *Nordwest*.

November - December 1944 : Incorporation of additional Dutch and German volunteers; accorded divisional status despite being only brigade-sized.

March 1945 : Unit receives final designation (see above).

Commanding Officers
- SS-Standartenführer Viktor Knapp (3/11/43 - 5/11/44)
- SS-Standartenführer Martin Kohlroser (5/11/44 - 5/8/45)

Main Combat Units (as of 10/44)
- SS-Freiwilligen-Grenadier-Regiment 83
- SS-Freiwilligen-Grenadier-Regiment 84
- SS-Artillerie-Regiment 60
- SS-Panzerjäger-Abteilung 60 (formerly *Nordwest*)
- SS-Flak-Batterie 60
- SS-Pionier-Kompanie 60
- SS-Feldersatz-Bataillon 60
- SS-Füsilier-Kompanie

Disposition

Part of the division surrendered to British troops on 8 May 1945 at Rhein-Waal (Lower Rhine) and part to Canadian forces at Veenedal (Holland) on 12 May 1945.

Claimed Atrocities

- The Netherlands : 1941 - 1944
- Putten [Netherlands] : 30 September - 1 October 1944

Security Operations

- Apeldoorn, Hertogenbosch, The Hague, Vught [Netherlands] : 19 November 1943
- Rotterdam, Apeldoorn [Netherlands] : 11 September 1944
- Nord Brabant [Netherlands] : Late 1944 - Early 1945
- Rhenen, Arnhem, Apeldoorn, Gelderland [Netherlands] : 26 February 1945

35. SS-Polizei-Grenadier-Division

Organizational History

15 February 1945 : Unit formed from SS-Polizei-Brigade Wirth (SS-Polizei-Regimenter zur besondere Verwendung 1 and 2), SS-Polizei-Regiment 14, and Dresden Polizeischule personnel.

Early March 1945 : Incorporation of a company from SS-Junkerschule Braunschweig.

Commanding Officers

- SS-Oberführer (?) Wirth (? - 3/45)
- SS-Standartenführer Rudiger Pipkorn (3/45 - 4/24/45) MIA

Main Combat Units

- Polizei-Grenadier-Regiment 89
- Polizei-Grenadier-Regiment 90
- Polizei-Grenadier-Regiment 91
- Polizei-Füsilier-Bataillon
- SS-Panzerjäger-Abteilung
- SS-Polizei-Artillerie-Regiment
- Polizei-Pionier-Regiment
- Nachrichten-Abteilung

Disposition

Divisional remnants surrendered on 7 May 1945 to Soviet forces at Halbe.

36. Waffen-Grenadier-Division der SS

Organizational History

Early 1940 : Formation of a small "poachers" unit.

4 June 1940 : Unit transferred to Waffen-SS control.

15 June 1940 : Unit designated Wilddiebkommando Oranienburg.

1 July 1940 : Training and expansion begin under the direction of 5. SS-Totenkopfstandarte (Oranienburg) -- personnel composed exclusively of convicts.

1 September 1940 : SS-Obersturmbannführer Dr. Oskar Dirlewanger transferred from 5. SS-Totenkopfstandarte and takes over as unit CO. Unit redesignated SS-Sonderkommando Dirlewanger.

February 1942 : Unit upgraded and redesignated SS-Sonderbataillon Dirlewanger.
Summer 1942 : Unit reinforced with a company of Ukrainians and a battalion of Russians.

July 1942 : First addition of concentration camp "trusties" as replacement personnel.

Early 1943 : Unit at regimental strength.

May 1943 : Unit begins to receive regular additions of "trusties" as replacement personnel.

August 1943 : Unit reorganized as SS-Regiment Dirlewanger; replacement personnel consist of prisoners from German and SS penal institutions, as well as concentration camp "trusties".

January/February 1944 : Unit rebuilt with military personnel and concentration camp prisoners following decimation during emergency front-line combat.

Late July 1944 : Ostmuselmanische SS-Regiment with 1,000 effectives temporarily attached (until 15 September 1944).

20 September 1944 : Incorporation of 1,900 prisoners from Arbeitslager Matzlau (Danzig).

October 1944 : Incorporation of additional military convicts. Unit redesignated as SS-Sturmbrigade *Dirlewanger*.

10 November 1944 : Incorporation of 1,910 prisoners from a variety of the major concentration camps.

February 1945 : Incorporation of 1244. Grenadier-Regiment, 681. Panzerjäger-Abteilung, 687. Pioneer-Brigade, Panzer-Abteilung Stahnsdorf and personnel from SS-Junkerschule Braunschweig.

19 March 1945 : Unit upgraded to divisional status with the incorporation of Waffengruppe der SS *Krim* [Crimean] and receives final designation (see above).

Commanding Officers
- SS-Oberführer Dr. Oskar Dirlewanger (9/1/40 - 11/43) wounded
- SS-Hauptsturmführer Erwin Walser (11/43 - 1/44)
- SS-Oberführer Dr. Oskar Dirlewanger (1/44 - 2/15/45) wounded
- SS-Brigadeführer Fritz Schmedes (2/15/45 - 4/29/45)

Main Combat Units (as of 1944)
- Regiment 1
- Regiment 2
- Füsilier-Kompanie

Subordination
- HSSPf Russland Mitte and Weissruthenien (2/15/42 - 9/2/43)
- HSSPf Minsk (9/3/43 - 6/24/44)

Disposition
On 29 April 1945 most of the division was surrounded and massacred after surrendering to Soviet troops near Lausitz (southeast of Berlin). SS-Brigadeführer Schmedes and his staff escaped this fate and surrendered to American troops on 3 May 1945.

Claimed Atrocities
- Lublin [Poland] : 1941 - February 1942
- Operation Klette [USSR] : July 1942
- (see entry 1. SS-Inf.-Brigade Operations & Atrocities in the USSR)
- Warsaw Uprising [Poland] : August - September 1944
- Slovak National Uprising [Czechoslovakia] : September - December 1944

see also *Dirlewanger Brigade Operations & Atrocities in the USSR.*

Security Operations
- Wachkommando at Buggrabenbau/Otto Line (SE of Belzec, Poland) : Fall 1939
- Wachkommando at AL Dzikow [Poland]: Fall 1939 - 1940
- Krakow area [Poland] : 1941
- Lublin [Poland] : 1941 - February 1942
- [Returned to front at request of German authorities after numerous crimes in Occupied Poland]
- Lake Pelik region [USSR] : August 1943
- Minsk area (Logoysk, Glussk, Slutsk, Losha) [USSR] : 3 September 1943
- Gornovo, Lepel', Polotsk, Ulla, Berezino, Krulevshchizna, Otrubok, Peresechyno [USSR] : 5 April 1944 [Operations Regenschauer and Fruhlingsfest]
- Zen'kovichi, Prisynok, Seliba, Paraf'yanova, Minsk, Uzda [USSR] : 14 May 1944
- Rear area, Heeres Gruppe Mitte : June 1944
- Warsaw Uprising : August - September 1944
- Slowakei : September - October 1944

37. SS-Freiwilligen-Kavallerie-Division *Lutzow*

Organizational History

20 February 1945 - March 1945 :
Unit formed at Pressburg from SS-Kavallerie-Gruppe Ameiser (remnants of the 8. SS-Kavallerie-Division *Florian Geyer* and the 22. SS-Freiwilligen-Kavallerie-Division *Maria Theresia*), SS-Pionier-Bataillon 8 (previously detached from the 8. SS-Kavallerie-Division *Florian Geyer*), assorted stragglers including Hungarians of the *Honved* Division and the Arrow Cross Party *Szalasi Youth*. Although accorded divisional status, the unit only reached regimental strength.

Commanding Officers
- SS-Obersturmbannführer Waldemar Fegelein (2/20/45 - 3/45)
- SS-Standartenführer Karl Gesele (3/45 - 5/45)

Main Combat Units
- SS-Kavallerie-Regiment 92
- SS-Kavallerie-Regiment 93
- SS-Artillerie-Abteilung 37
- SS-Pionier-Bataillon 37
- SS-Feldersatz-Bataillon 37

Disposition
In early May 1945, the division surrendered to American forces at Freistadt, near Vienna.

38. SS-Grenadier-Division *Nibelungen*

Organizational History

27 March 1945 :
Activation ordered of the 38. SS-Grenadier-Division *Junkerschule* (also referred to as 38. SS-Grenadier-Division *Junkerschule Tölz* (*Nibelungen*). Formation begun at Freiburg in Breisgau.

April 1945 :
Unit formed from personnel SS-Junkerschule Tölz, Begleit-Bataillon *Reichsführer-SS*, assorted Hitler Youth, Ausbildungs-und Ersatz-Bataillon 33 (from the 33. Waffen-Grenadier-Division der SS *Charlemagne*), remnants of the 6. SS-Gebirgs-Division *Nord*, Reichsarbeitdienst personnel, older years of the Adolf-Hitler-Schule Sonthofen, and remnants of the 30. Waffen-Grenadier-Division der SS (russische Nr. 2).

12 April 1945 : Unit accorded divisional status despite being understrength (approximately 5,500 effectives). Unit receives final designation (see above).

Commanding Officers
* SS-Obersturmbannführer Richard Schulze-Kossens (3/45 - 4/45)
* SS-Gruppenführer Carl Ritter von Oberkamp (4/45 - ?)
* SS-Gruppenführer Heinz Lammerding (? - 4/24/45)
* SS-Standartenführer Martin Stange (4/25/45 - 5/8/45)

Main Combat Units (as of April 1945)
* SS-Grenadier-Regiment 95 (nominal)
* SS-Grenadier-Regiment 96 (nominal)

Disposition
On 8 May 1945 the division surrendered to American forces at Reit and Winkl am Alpenrand.

1. SS-Infanterie (mot.) Brigade

Organizational History

1 May 1941 : SS-Brigade (motorized) 1 formed at Krakau, Poland from SS-Totenkopfstandarten 8 and 10, along with miscellaneous Allgemeine SS personnel.

21 May 1941 : Unit transferred to the control of Reichsführer-SS Himmler.

24 May 1941 : Unit redesignated 1. SS-Brigade (mot.).

1 September 1941 : Unit receives final designation (see above).

Fall/Winter 1941 : Unit participated in widescale anti-partisan drives and killing operations in northern Russia. SS-Standartenführer Herbert Wachsmann (originally from the *Totenkopf* division) served as a Kampfgruppe commander. The brigade also served as a replacement pool for main-series Waffen-SS divisions decimated in the 1941 - 1942 campaigns.

9 December 1941 : Unit temporarily transferred to Wehrmacht control and participates in defensive battles around Oriol.

5 May 1943 : Cadre sent to form Estnisches SS-Freiwilligen-Brigade (precursor of the 20. Waffen-Grenadier-Division der SS [estnische Nr. 1]).

March 1944 : Remainder of unit deployed to the Agram/Cilli region (Croatia) to serve as cadre for formation of the 18. SS-Freiwilligen-Panzergrenadier-Division *Horst Wessel*.

Commanding Officers
* SS-Brigadeführer Karl Maria Demelhuber (4/24/41 - 5/25/41)
* SS-Brigadeführer Friedrich-Wilhelm Krüger (5/25/41 - 6/25/41)
* SS-Brigadeführer Richard Hermann (6/25/41 - 7/4/42)
* SS-Brigadeführer Karl von Treuenfeld (7/4/42 - 2/1/43?)

- SS-Brigadeführer August Wilhelm Trabandt (10/18/43 - 3/44)

Main Combat Units
- SS-Infanterie (mot.) Regiment 8
- SS-Infanterie (mot.) Regiment 10
- Panzerjäger-Abteilung
- Kradschützen-Kompanie
- Nachrichten-Kompanie
- Flak-Kompanie
- 1. Feldhaubitz-Batterie

Claimed Atrocities
- Zwiahel region [USSR] : 28 - 30 July 1941
- Radomyshl' [USSR] : August 1941
- Staro Konstantinov [USSR] : August 1941
- Ushomir [USSR] : September 1941
- Kamenets-Podol'skiy [USSR] : Early September 1941
- Dnepropetrovsk [USSR] : 13 October 1941 and other dates
- see also entry "1. SS-Infanterie (mot.) Brigade Operations & Atrocities in the USSR

Security Operations
- Generalgouvernement [Poland] : 20 - 24 June 1941
- Generalgouvernement [Poland] : 2 - 20 July 1941
- Zwiahel region [USSR] : 28 - 30 July 1941
- Tschernjachow-Goroschki [USSR] : 5-7 August 1941
- Owrutsch [USSR] : 21 - 26 August 1941
- Dnepr region [USSR]:23 September- 9 October 1941
- Bryansk [USSR] : 22 October - 9 November 1941
- Borissow, Minsk [USSR] : 11 August - 10 September 1942
- Rollbahn Minsk [USSR] : 10 October - 16 November 1942
- Glebokie [USSR] : 17 November - 26 November 1942
- Minsk, Naliboki-Wald [USSR] : 1 July - 10 August 1943

2. SS-Infanterie (mot.) Brigade

Organizational History

24 April 1941 : Activation of SS-Brigade (mot.) 2 ordered.

1 May 1941 : Unit formation begun in Warsaw from SS-Totenkopfstandarte 4 *Ostmark* (May 1941), SS-Totenkopfstandarte 5 (May 1941), and SS-Totenkopfstandarte 14 (July 1941) along with three unformed Latvian Schützmannschaft Bataillonen.

July - August 1941 : Unit engaged in anti-partisan operations behind Army Group North in the USSR.

13 August 1941 : SS-Totenkopfstandarte 5 disbanded.

Fall/Winter 1941 : Unit served under control of Kommandostab RFSS as needed on security duties and killing operations behind the frontlines in the USSR. Also served as a replacement pool for main-series Waffen-SS divisions decimated in the 1941 - 1942 campaigns.

30 March 1942 : Schützmannschaft-Bataillon 21 (Lettische) attached to unit.

12 May 1942 : Schützmannschaft-Bataillon 19 (Lettische) attached to unit.

Mid 1942 : A complaint was filed with the SS-Hauptamt by Colonel-General Georg Lindemann (commander of the 18th Army) listing specific instances in which members of the brigade shot POWs. Himmler defended his men's behavior in a letter to Lindemann dated 23 August 1942 [U.S. National Archives, RFSS/T-175, 109/2633404f].

23 January 1943 : Unit ordered to serve as cadre for the Lettische Legion (future 19. Waffen-Grenadier-Division der SS (lettische Nr. 2).

Other units attached to the brigade and their periods of service:

- Freiwilligen Legion Niederlande (Fall 1941 -

4/27/43)

- Freiwilligen Legion Flandern (Fall 1941 - 5/43)
- Freiwilligen Legion Norwegen (early 1942 - virtually annihilated 5/43)

Commanding Officers

- SS-Brigadeführer Karl von Treuenfeld (4/5/41 - 7/5/41)
- SS-Brigadeführer Göttfried Klingemann (7/5/41 - 1/26/43)
  [transferred to Junkerschule Tölz]
- SS-Brigadeführer Fritz von Scholz (1/26/43 - 4/20/43)
- SS-Oberführer Fritz Freitag (4/20/43 - 8/10/43)

Main Combat Units (5/26/41)

- SS-Infanterie-Regiment 4
- SS-Infanterie-Regiment 14
- Nachrichten-Kompanie
- Begleit-Bataillon *Reichsführer-SS*
- SS-Flak-Abteilung *Ost*

Claimed Atrocities

- Lublin District [Poland] : Early June 1941
- Tosno [USSR] : 15 - 23 October 1941
- see also entry "2. SS-Infanterie (mot.) Brigade Operations & Atrocities in the USSR

Security Operations

- Generalgouvernement [Poland] : 5 - 18 December 1941
- Generalgouvernement [Poland] : 19 April - 26 May 1942

SS-Totenkopfstandarten

Organizational History

29 November 1934 : Formation of Sondersturmbanne by order of Reichsführer-SS Himmler.

14 December 1934 : Units redesignated SS-Wachverbände (concentration camp guard units).

29 March 1936 : Units redesignated SS-Totenkopfverbände.

Main Combat Units

1. SS-Totenkopfstandarte *Oberbayern* : see 3. SS-Panzer-Division *Totenkopf.*

2. SS-Totenkopfstandarte *Brandenburg* : see 3. SS-Panzer-Division *Totenkopf.*

3. SS-Totenkopfstandarte *Thuringen* : see 3. SS-Panzer-Division *Totenkopf.*

4. SS-Totenkopfstandarte *Ostmark* : commander SS-Standartenführer Otto Reich; Duty Stations: Prague (5/5/40), The Hague (7/28/40); 2,931 effectives; on (5/1/41) the unit sent as cadre to the 2. SS-Infanterie (mot.) Brigade.

5. SS-Totenkopfstandarte *Dietrich Eckardt* : commander SS-Brigadeführer Franz Breithaupt; Duty Stations: Stettin (5/5/40), Oranienburg (7/28/40); 1,878 effectives; on (5/1/41) unit sent as cadre to the 2. SS-Infanterie (mot.) Brigade

6. SS-Totenkopfstandarte : commander SS-Oberführer Voss; Duty Stations: Sandefjord, Norway (5/5/40); 2,956 effectives; Summer 1940 - incorporated into SS-Kampfgruppe Nord (see 6. SS-Gebirgs-Division *Nord*)

7. SS-Totenkopfstandarte : commanders SS-Brigadeführer Richard Hermann (5/5/40), SS-Standartenführer Schneider (7/28/40), SS-Oberführer Günther Claasen (9/40 - 1/41); Duty Stations: Drammen, Norway (5/5/40); 2,771 effectives; Summer 1940 - incorporated into SS-Kampfgruppe Nord (see 6. SS-Gebirgs-Division *Nord*)

8. SS-Totenkopfstandarte : commanders SS-Oberfüh-

rer Leo von Jena (5/5/40), SS-Standartenführer Julian Scherner (7/28/40), SS-Oberführer Günther Claasen (4/41 - 9/41); Duty Stations: Cracow (5/5/40), Radom (7/28/40); 2,799 effectives; on (5/1/41) unit sent as cadre to the 1. SS-Infanterie (mot.) Brigade.

9. SS-Totenkopfstandarte : commander SS-Standartenführer Paul Nostitz; Duty Stations: Brno; 2,250 effectives; on (4/1/41) most of unit incorporated into SS-Kampfgruppe Nord (see 6. SS-Gebirgs-Division *Nord*); on (11/15/41) remaining elements used to form Sonder-Bataillon SS-Totenkopfstandarte *Prag*.

10. SS-Totenkopfstandarte : commander SS-Obersturmbannführer Karl Demme; Duty Stations: Danzig (5/5/40), Cracow (7/28/40); 2,753 effectives; on (5/1/41) unit sent as cadre to the 1. SS-Infanterie (mot.) Brigade.

11. SS-Totenkopfstandarte : commander SS-Obersturmbannführer Prof. Karl Diebitsch; Duty Stations: Radom (5/5/40), Zandvoort (7/28/40); 3,005 effectives; on (11/1/41) unit incorporated into 2. SS-Panzer-Division *Das Reich*.

12. SS-Totenkopfstandarte : commander SS-Obersturmbannführer Sacks; Duty Stations: Posen-Treskau-Litzmannstadt; 2,750 effectives; on (8/40) unit was incorporated into the 3. SS-Panzer-Division *Totenkopf*.

13. SS-Totenkopfstandarte : commander SS-Standartenführer Gottfried Klingemann; Duty Stations: Wien-Linz; 2,053 effectives; unit disbanded on (8/15/40)

14. SS-Totenkopfstandarte : commander SS-Obersturmbannführer Georg Martin; Duty Stations: Copenhagen; 2,619 effectives; 7/41 - on (5/1/41) the unit sent as cadre to the 2. SS-Infanterie (mot.) Brigade.

15. SS-Totenkopfstandarte : commander SS-Sturmbannführer Dorheit; Duty Stations: Plock-East Prussia-Allenburg; 1,679 effectives; unit disbanded on (9/1/42)

16. SS-Totenkopfstandarte : commander SS-Standartenführer Herrmann; Duty Stations: Prague; 2346 effectives; unit disbanded on (8/15/40)
SS-Totenkopfstandarte *Kirkenes* : SS-Obersturmbannführer Reitz; Duty Stations: Kirkenes, Norway; 1,014 effectives; (4/1/41) most of unit incorporated into SS-Kampfgruppe *Nord* (see 6. SS-Gebirgs-Division *Nord*); on (11/15/40) remaining elements used to form Sonderbataillon SS-Totenkopfstandarte *Prag*.

1. SS-Totenkopf-Reiterstandarte : commander SS-Standartenführer Hermann Fegelein; Duty Stations: Warsaw; 2,073 effectives; on (8/2/41) sent as cadre for SS-Kavallerie-Brigade (see 8. SS-Kavallerie-Division *Florian Geyer*)

2. SS-Totenkopf-Reiterstandarte : commander SS-Sturmbannführer Franz Magill; Duty Stations: Lublin; 1,656 effectives; on (8/2/41) sent as cadre for SS-Kavallerie-Brigade (see 8. SS-Kavallerie-Division *Florian Geyer*

Sonderbataillon, SS-Totenkopfstandarte *Prag* : commander SS-Hauptsturmführer Dr. Karl Buchegger; Duty Stations: Prague; 951 effectives; unit formed on (11/15/40) from elements of the 9. SS-Totenkopfstandarte.

Inspektorate der SS-Totenkopfstandarten : SS-Oberführer Hans Schwedler; Duty Station: Oranienburg (5/5/40), Berlin (7/28/40); 256 effectives

Waffen-SS-Bataillon-zur besondere Verwendung

Organizational and Operational History

June 1941 : Security unit (designation unknown) authorized and formed in southeastern Poland with 230 effectives from SS-Infanterie-Regiment 14 as well as a cadre from the 1. SS-Infanterie-Brigade. Initially the unit was distributed as six commando units operating out of Warsaw, Cracow, and Lublin.

4 July 1941 : Elements responsible for the execution of Polish intellectuals at Lvov.

9 July 1941 : Unit begins "cleansing operations" in Slutsk, Brest-Litovsk, Bialystok, Vilna, and Minsk.

21 - 31 July 1941 : Anti-Jewish "cleansing operations" in Lemberg (1,726 victims), Brest-Litovsk (1,280), and Bialystok (941).

27 July 1941 : Unit redesignated Sonderbataillon zur Verfügung Kommandostab Reichsführer-SS.

23 August 1941 :

Unit redesignated Waffen-SS Bataillon zur besondere Verwendung. One company officially assigned to each of three Einsatzgruppe (1. Kompanie to Einsatzgruppe A; 2. Kompanie to Einsatzgruppe B; 3. Kompanie to Einsatzgruppe C) --- this transfer had already taken place at an undetermined time earlier. As part of the various einsatzgruppen, the batallion personnel committed countless atrocities. See the *Einsatzgruppen in the USSR* entry for most of the crimes they committed. Additional service information and supporting documentation can be found in U.S. Holocaust Memorial Museum microfilm RG-48.004M (*Selected Documents from the Military Historical Institute [Prague]*, Reel 5, Fond - Bataillon der Waffen-SS z.b.V., Karton 3, 17 August 1941 - 19 January 1943).

16+ December 1941 : 3. Kompanie participated in the Drobitski Yar Massacre at Kharkov 1.

May 1942 : Elements massacred Jews in Dolhynov.

27 June 1942 : Elements massacred 4,000 Jews from the Slonim Ghetto.

28 July 1942 : Elements massacred 6,000 Jews from the Minsk Ghetto.

29 July 1942 : Elements massacred 3,000 German Jews from the Minsk Ghetto.

31 December 1942 : Bataillon strength reported as 390 effectives.

17 September 1943 : Unit disbanded; reasons unknown.

Commanding Officers
- SS-Oberführer Dr. Eberhardt Schöngarth overall CO (6/41 - 7/43)
- SS-Sturmbannführer Friedrich Dern [adjutant to Schöngarth]
- SS-Obersturmbannführer Rosenow, CO 1. Kompanie (6/21/41 - 7/29/41)
- SS-Hauptsturmführer Störtz, CO 1. Kompanie (7/29/41 - 1/19/43+)

Claimed Atrocities
- Brusilov [USSR] : August 1941
- Boskina [USSR] : 15 August 1941
- Pinsk [USSR] : 9 July 1941
  see also instances cited above

SS-Fallschirmjäger-Bataillonen

500/600

Organizational History

Fall 1943 : Activation ordered and formation begun at Chlum (Czechoslovakia). Personnel primarily Waffen-SS volunteers and disciplinary cases. Unit designated SS-Fallschirmjäger-Bataillon 500.

Mid October - November 1944 :
Unit remnants, SS-Fallschirmjäger-Ausbildungs-und Ersatz-Kompanie 500 and replacements formed into a new unit designated SS-Fallschirmjäger-Bataillon 600.

November 1944 : Incorporation of mixed replacements - reservists, convalescents, Luftwaffe and Kriegsmarine personnel.

Mid-April 1945 :
Unit decimated; rebuilt with replacements from SS-Panzergrenadier-Regiment 7 (4. SS-Polizei-Panzergrenadier-Division), miscellaneous Waffen-SS volunteers, Luftwaffe and Kriegsmarine personnel.

Commanding Officers
- SS-Sturmbannführer Herbert Gilhofer (?/43 - 4/44) transferred
- SS-Hauptsturmführer Kurt Rybka (4/44 - 6/26/44)
- SS-Hauptsturmführer Siegfried Milius (6/26/44 - 3/45)
- SS-Obersturmführer Fritz Leifheit (3/45 - ?)

Disposition
On 2 May 1945 elements of the battalion surrendered to American forces in the Wismar-Schwerin area. Two days later additional elements surrendered to the Americans near Grabow. Scattered battalion elements also surrendered to American forces in the vicinity of Hagenau.

Security Operations
- Uzice (Serbia), Tuzla (Bosnia-Herzogovina), Montenegro, Macedonia [Yugoslavia] : Early 1944
- Drvar (Bosnia) [Yugoslavia] : Operation Rösselsprung : 25 May 1944 vs. Tito's HQ
- Petrovac [Yugoslavia] : June 1944
- Operation Panzerfaust [Budapest, Hungary] : 16 October 1944

SS-Jäger-Bataillon 500

Organizational History

15 February 1942 : SS-Field Recruit Depot Bobruisk (Central Russia) established. German cadre with Volksdeutsche personnel.

15 September 1943 : Unit formed from 2. Bataillon / SS-Field Recruit Depot Bobruisk and given final designation (see above).

August 1944 : Unit attached to SS-Sonderkommando-Regiment Dirlewanger.

Commanding Officers
- SS-Standartenführer Rudolf Pannier (1944)
- SS-Sturmbannführer Armin Beilhack (6/44)

Disposition
Unit disbanded in early October 1944. Remnants transferred to SS-Panzergrenadier-Ausbildungs-und Ersatz-Bataillon 35. Later used as cadre for Kommando Stab RF-SS (continued security operations) and SS-Sturmbrigade *Wallonie*.

Security Operations
- Operation Maikafer [USSR] : 30 June 1942 - ?
- Operation Adler [USSR] : 20 July 1942 - ?
- Operation Panther [USSR] : 1942
- Operation Falcon [USSR] : 1942
- Operation Owl [USSR] : 1942
- Operation Greif [USSR] : 16 August 1942 - ?
- Operation Schneehase [USSR] : 28 January 1943 - ?
- rear area security 9th Army /Army Group Center [USSR] : 15 September 1943 - July 1944
- Warsaw Uprising [Poland] : August - September 1944

Claimed Atrocities
- Warsaw Uprising [Poland] : August 1944

SS-Jäger-Bataillon 501

Organizational History

15 February 1942 : Establishment of SS-Field-Recruit-Depot Bobruisk (Central Russia). German cadre with Volksdeutsche personnel.

15 September 1943 : Designated unit formed from 1. Bataillon / SS-Field-Recruit-Depot Bobruisk.

May 1944 : Unit disbanded; unit name transferred to 3. Bataillon / SS-Field-Recruit-Depot Bobruisk.

August 1944 : Unit attached to SS-Sonderkommando-Regiment Dirlewanger.

Commanding Officers
- SS-Sturmbannführer Hans Beyerlein (? - ?)
- SS-Sturmbannführer Rudolf Bachmann (5/44 - 10/44)

Disposition
Unit disbanded in early October 1944. Remnants transferred to SS-Panzergrenadier-Ausbildungs-und Ersatz-Bataillon 35. Later used as cadre for Kommando Stab RF-SS and SS-Sturmbrigade *Wallonie*.

Security Operations
- Operation Maikafer [USSR] : 30 June 1942 - ?
- Operation Adler [USSR] : 30 July 1942 - ?
- Operation Panther [USSR] : 1942
- Operation Falcon [USSR] : 1942
- Operation Owl [USSR] : 1942
- Operation Greif [USSR] : 16 August 1942 - ?
- Operation Schneehase [USSR] : 28 January 1943 - ?
- rear-area security 9th Army / Army Group Center [USSR] : 15 September 1943 - July 1944
- Warsaw Uprising [Poland] : August - September 1944

Claimed Atrocities
- Warsaw Uprising [Poland] : August 1944

Foreign Ministry Sonderkommando Künsberg / SS-Sonderkommando Künsberg

War crimes do not consist only of the extermination camp system characteristic of the Third Reich or the killing of POWs and civilians, they also include a wide range of cultural crimes such as the destruction of landmarks and the looting of museums and archives. As in other aspects of Nazi criminality, the Waffen-SS was also an active participant in the cultural warfare visited upon Germany's victims.

Prior to the invasion of France and the Low Countries in May 1940, German Foreign Minister Joachim von Ribbentrop organized a special civilian unit (Sonderkommando Künsberg) under the command of Freiherr Eberhard von Künsberg. The unit was small, barely one hundred men, and composed of staff, scholarly, administrative, and transport sections. It's sole purpose was to loot cultural institutions in the newly-occupied Western territories and ship their valuables back to Germany. Lists were compiled targeting major works of art in France, Belgium, and the Netherlands. The local military command authorities were kept informed of all plans since they were charged with meeting all of the Sonderkommando's transportation requirements.

The Sonderkommando began its operations on a modest scale by seizing foreign government records and precious metals in the Low Countries and northern France. Following the collapse of the Anglo-French forces, it participated in the initial wholescale looting of Parisian art galleries. Eventually, however, the unit was pushed aside by the Einsatzstab Reichsleiter Rosenberg (ERR - another looting commando, organized by Reichsleiter Alfred Rosenberg) which was accorded precedence in these matters by Hitler himself. His "collecting efforts" stymied, von Künsberg spent his time compiling acquisition lists for the contents of British repositories in preparation for the cross-Channel invasion that seemed imminent.

As summer turned into autumn it became quite apparent that the invasion of Britain had been put on a back burner. In anticipation of unspecified future operations the Sonderkommando was expanded and also underwent five weeks of rigorous military field training so that by year's end it had greatly enhanced capabilities. Meanwhile, von Künsberg, unimpressed with von Ribbentrop's lack of clout in the Parisian galleries dispute, searched about for a new sponsor.

In January 1941 von Künsberg approached Reichsführer-SS Heinrich Himmler requesting the admission of his unit into the Waffen-SS. Initially the request was turned down since it was felt that the Sonderkommando's duties were at odds with the Waffen-SS' military role. His ideological enthusiasm, however, caught Himmler's attention. In early February discussions between von Künsberg, a Foreign Ministry representative and SS-Obergruppenführer Reinhard Heydrich took place exploring the incorporation of the unit into the Waffen-SS and its use as part of an Einsatzgruppe slated to perform "special tasks" (mass executions of civilians) in the USSR. Assuming an agreement to have been reached, the Foreign Ministry submitted a written request for equipment and support services. For unknown reasons, however, this agreement was never completed and Himmler eventually saw the value of von Künsberg's original proposal.

Prior to the invasion of the USSR in June 1941 the Sonderkommando was absorbed into the Waffen-SS and von Künsberg was accorded the rank of SS-Sturmbannführer. The unit was reorganized into four independently operating companies: 2. Kompanie was attached to Heeresgruppe Nord, 3. Kompanie was attached to Heeresgruppe Mitte, and 4. Kompanie was attached to Heeresgruppe Sud. The first company (1. Kompanie) was attached to the Deutsche Afrika Korps. As of November 1942 it was still awaiting transport in Naples, Italy; it is unclear whether or not the company was ever sent to North Africa.

In practice each company would be attached to front-line Waffen-SS units and would secure anything which appeared to be of cultural value - ransacking scientific institutions, colleges, libraries, archives, palaces and historic landmarks. Once a locality had been completely cleared of combatants, "scholars" from the SS-Ahnenerbe (SS archaeological branch) would arrive to collect artifacts and other evidence of the superiority of the Germanic races. Paralleling these SS operations, the ERR also planned its standard confiscations of cultural artifacts. Although Hitler had again granted the ERR primacy in this looting (Rosenberg was now Minister of the Eastern Occupied Territories), in practice the Waffen-SS would operate unfettered in the USSR and beat out the ERR for many of the country's treasures.

In the Leningrad suburbs, 2. Kompanie made short work of the valuables stored in various Czarist palaces and pavilions. One of their first objectives was the world-renowned Amber Room in the Grand Palace-Museum of Catherine the Great at the town of Pushkin (formerly Tsarskoye Selo). Künsberg's well-trained raiders dismantled and packed away the room's priceless panels into 29 over-sized shipping crates. The crates were then sent by rail to the Königsberg Museum where the curators lost no time in unpacking and installing their "new acquisition". Also sent to Königsberg was the famous Gottorp Globe, a miniature planetarium in which twelve people could sit and contemplate the heavens depicted on the inside.

From the palace of Emperor Alexander countless pieces of ancient furniture and a library of some 7,000 French-language and 5,000 Russian-language volumes and manuscripts was packed away and shipped off to Germany. Among those books selected were numerous unique memoirs, as well as a large number of rare Greek and Roman classics. Gilded wall panels and carved artifacts, as well as intricate parquet flooring, were also dismantled and removed from the palace.

Whatever von Künsberg's men could not take with them was often deliberately destroyed. Mirrors were broken or shot-up, tapestries and hangings were torn from the walls. At Peterhof, the machinery controlling the famous cascading fountains was wrecked, and the gilded statues of Neptune and Samson were hauled off to be smelted for the war effort. Following its depredations in the Leningrad suburbs, 2. Kompanie moved on to pillage the Cathedral of Novgorod in addition to the city's cultural institutions.

In late summer of 1941 the raiders of 3. Kompanie visited their attentions on Minsk removing the cream of the city's artistic and scientific collections. By year's end the cultural treasures of Smolensk had similarly fallen prey to this company.

On the southern front 4. Kompanie was especially active. Their operations included the wholesale shipment of the Kiev medical research institute laboratories to Germany. Kiev's art museums, which had been partially evacuated by the Soviets, were stripped of their remaining works. The library of the Ukrainian Academy of Sciences was pillaged of its many unique Persian, Abyssinian, Chinese, Russian and Ukrainian books and manuscripts. Several thousand rare books were looted from the Korolenko library in Kharkov; the remaining books were simply destroyed outright by von Künsberg's men. Several hundred pictures and sculptures were removed from various Kharkov art galleries. The scientific archives of the city were also similarly stripped of anything of value. At Krasnodar the complete agricultural library was seized and shipped off to Berlin.

The Sonderkommando's heyday of cultural crimes lasted until December 1942. The exact disposition of the unit after 1942 is uncertain. It may have been disbanded to supply replacement personnel to other Waffen-SS field units. In any event, SS-Sturmbannführer von Künsberg later served with both the 1. SS-Panzer-Division *Leibstandarte Adolf Hitler* and the 8. SS-Kavallerie-Division *Florian Geyer*. His ultimate fate is unknown. Much of the material looted by his men, either disappeared into public and private collections throughout Europe or was lost during the final collapse of the Third Reich. Incredibly, the entire Amber Room vanished from the Königsberg Museum without a trace. To this day treasure hunters are pursuing leads on its long-cold trail.

Sources
(Breitman, 1991, p. 148) (Nicholas, 1994, pp. 121-126, 186, 191-193)
(Bericht über den Einsatz des Sonderkommandos AA. in Holland, Belgien, und Frankreich, 19 Dez. 1940, National Archives Record Group 238, T-1139, R 36, 1163-66; National Archives Record Group 242, T-354, R 184; National Archives Record Group 242, T-581, R 39A; National Archives Record Group 238, M-946, R 1, 109)
(Written statement of SS-Obersturmführer Dr. Norman Vörster, member 4. Kompanie / SS-Sonderkommando Künsberg, dated 10 November 1942; reproduced in Academy of Sciences, 1987, pp. 47-49)

SS-Sonderkommando 1005

SS-Sonderkommando 1005 was a special unit formed by the Germans to destroy the evidence of their mass killings in the eastern occupied territories (USSR, Poland, Yugoslavia). Under the leadership of SS-Standartenführer Paul Blobel, the unit was formed at the Chelmno death camp (near Lodz) in Poland. After much experimentation, an effective method of destroying large numbers of bodies was worked out. The bodies were removed from their burial pits and placed onto special platforms in piles of 1,200 - 1,600 bodies each. They were then sprayed with tar and gasoline and set alight. The resulting ashes and bones were sifted through special strainers in order to collect any gold (dental bridges, rings, watches, *etc.*) present. In the first five months of operation approximately 110 kilograms of gold were recovered in this manner. The ashes were then scattered over nearby fields and dug into the ground. Large bone fragments were collected separately and crushed in a bone-mill which was designed to speed up the work. As a final step, trees, grasses, shrubs, and stumps were planted to disguise the original burial and the ash disposal sites.

In order to disseminate these highly-effective clean-up techniques, the Germans established a special school at the Janov labor camp in Lvov to train Sonderkommando personnel in the art of body disposal. The same level of planning that went into the extermination of civilians was now applied to covering it up: no trace of the crimes was to be left visible. Local Sicherheitspolizei (Sipo) and Sicherheitsdienst (SD) officers, often the same ones who had committed the atrocities, led the Sonderkommando in their clean-up operations. The actual dirty work of digging up the corpses and reducing them to ash was left to work details formed of concentration camp Jews, and in some cases the local populace. Once a clean-up operation was complete, these "helpers" were killed to eliminate any potential witnesses. When the unit moved into its next operational locale, it would "recruit" a replacement workforce. Guard details from the Ordnungspolizei, Waffen-SS, and Einsatzgruppen accompanied the Sonderkommando and provided security at its work sites. Following completion of work at a site and the murder/disposal of the workers, the German personnel would celebrate with a "Kameradschaftsabend" (as per orders issued by Reichsführer-SS Himmler dated 6 January 1943). Sonderkommando personnel also received recreation breaks at the Sipo resorts in Grinizza and Zakopane. The best estimates are that the bodies of approximately one million victims of Nazi crimes were destroyed in this manner.

Organizational and Operational History

13 January 1942 : SS-Standartenführer Paul Blobel relieved as commander of Sonderkommando 4a (part of Einsatzgruppe C) due to alcoholism-related health problems.

June 1942 : Following his recuperation, SS-Standartenführer Blobel is assigned to organize and oversee the training of Sonderkommando 1005.

July 1942 : Unit formed at Lodz. Initial personnel -- 75 Jewish prisoners from Janov Labor Camp, unspecified number of SD personnel from Lvov, 80 Ordnungspolizei personnel (23rd Police Reserve Brigade). SS-Untersturmführer Walter Shallock placed in command of Sonderkommando 1005; SS-Hauptscharführer Friedrich Rauch assigned as his adjutant.

Mid - Late 1942 : Clean-up work begun at the Auschwitz, Belzec, and Sobibor deathcamps in Poland.

Early 1943 : Clean-up operations begin at the Treblinka deathcamp in Poland.

Spring 1943 : Clean-up operatons begun in Galicia (southeastern Poland).

July 1943 : Clean-up operations begun in the Ukraine. SS-Sturmbannführer Hans-Fritz Sohns now in overall command of the Sonderkommando which had been expanded into two sub-units -- Sonderkommando 1005A (CO: SS-Obersturmführer Baumann, 10 SD officers, 30 Ordnungspolizei personnel, 327 prisoners from Syretzk labor camp) and Sonderkommando 1005B (CO: SS-Hauptsturmführer Fritz Zietlow, 5 SD officers, 50 Ordnungspolizei personnel, 50 prisoners).

Summer 1943 : Clean-up operations in eastern Byelorussia delegated to an independent sonderkommando under the command of SS-Sturmbannführer Dr. Friedrich Seekel. Unit composed of 68 German personnel from Einsatzkommando 8 (Einsatzgruppe B) and 280 prisoners.

18 August - 29 September 1943 : Sonderkommando 1005A clean-up operations at Kiev (Babi Yar).

August 1943 - January 1944 : Sonderkommando 1005B clean-up operations at Kiev (Babi Yar), Dnepropetrowsk, Krivoi Rog, and Nikolayev.

September 1943 : SK1005 units formed at Vilna and Kovno. Local clean-up operations begun.

October 1943 :
SS-Hauptsturmführer Karl-Arthur Harder, deputy to SS-Standartenführer Blobel, organizes Sonderkommando 1005-Mitte for operations in western Byelorussia. Unit composed of SD officers, 30 Ordnungspolizei personnel (9th Armored Police Company), 40 Volksdeutsche SD personnel, and 100 Jewish prisoners from Minsk.
October - Middle November 1943 : Sonderkommando 1005A operations at Berdichev and Biala-Tserkov.

27 October - 15 December 1943 : Sonderkommando 1005-Mitte clean-up operations at Maly-Trostinets.

November 1943 : SS-Sturmbannführer Seekel assumes overall control of Sonderkommando 1005-Mitte.

November 1943 - January 1944 : Sonderkommando 1005A clean-up operations in Uman.

7 December 1943 : SS-Hauptsturmführer Max Krahner takes command of Sonderkommando 1005-Mitte.

16 December - 22 December 1943 : Sonderkommando 1005-Mitte clean-up operations at Molodechno.

Late 1943 - Early 1944 : An unidentified Sonderkommando unit is dispatched to Serbia for clean-up operations. Afterwards the unit is redesignated Sonderkommando zur besondere Verwendung Iitis and assigned to partisan warfare in the Alps under HSSPf Erwin Rösener.

17 January - 26 January 1944 : Sonderkommando 1005-Mitte clean-up operations at Smolevichi.

February 1944 : Sonderkommando 1005A clean-up operations at Kamenets-Podolsk.

2 February 1944 - 2 April 1944 : Sonderkommando 1005-Mitte clean-up operations in the area of Minsk.

April - May 1944 : A sub-unit of Sonderkommando 1005-Mitte (CO: SS-? Fischer, several SD officers, local Ordnungspolizei and Waffen-SS personnel, prisoners from local camp) sent to Brest-Litovsk for clean-up operations. Bulk of Sonderkommando 1005-Mitte performs clean-up operations at Pinsk.

May 1944 : SS-Hauptsturmführer Harder forms an SK1005 unit under the command of SS-Hauptsturmführer Waldemar Macholl for clean-up operations in the Bialystok District. Sonderkommando 1005A clean-up operations in Zamosc.

31 May - 24 June 1944 : Main body of Sonderkommando 1005-Mitte conducts operations at Kobryn.

June 1944 :
HSSPf Wilhelm Koppe instructs all Sipo/SD district commanders in the General Gouvernement (Poland) to form small Sonderkommando 1005 units and begin operations. Each unit received a detachment of a dozen Ordnungspolizei personnel from the 23rd Police Reserve Battalion (stationed at Rzeszow). In the eastern German provinces annexed from Poland -- Reichsgau Warteland, Graudenz and Bromberg (Reichsgau Danzig-Westpreussen), Soldau (near Allenstein), and Tauroggen (near Tilsit) -- the local HSSPf/SSPf organized Sonderkommando 1005 units for local disposal actions.

25 June - 5 July 1944 : Main body of Sonderkommando 1005-Mitte performs operations at Slonim.

15 July - 16 August 1944 : Sonderkommando 1005-Mitte units recombine; operations at Lomza.

August 1944 : Sonderkommando 1005-Mitte and Sonderkommando 1005A conduct clean-up operations at Lodz. Also, an independent Sonderkommando 1005 unit was formed from impressed Polish civilians and Waffen-SS guards. The unit disposed of the many civilians (tens of thousands) killed in the Wola District of Warsaw during the uprising by Polish nationalists.

Sources

(Spector, 1990) (Birn, 1991) (Artzt, 1974, pp. 70-72) (MacLean, 1999) (Academy of Sciences..., 1987, pp. 221-225)

Einsatzgruppen in Austria, Czechoslovakia and Poland

The Einsatzgruppen der Sicherheitspolizei (Sipo) und des Sicherheitsdienst (SD), or simply Einsatzgruppen, were motorized detachments composed of Sipo, SD, SS-Verfügungstruppe, and SS-Totenkopfverbände personnel. The latter two organizations were precursors of the Waffen-SS. Their members wore SS-Verfügungstruppe field uniforms with a distinctive black SD diamond on the left sleeve. Each Einsatzgruppe was divided into a number of Einsatzkommandos of 100 - 150 men each. All of the senior posts were occupied by SD commanders who answered personally to Reichsführer-SS Himmler. Advancing directly behind the lead elements of any German invasion force, the Einsatzgruppe were charged with performing special security operations in the occupied territories. Armed with previously prepared lists, their main duty was the "suppression of all anti-Reich and anti-German elements in rear of the fighting troops" (i.e., the murder of countless Jews, communists, aristocrats, priests, intellectuals, ethnic minorities, and homosexuals).

Austria
For the occupation of Austria in March 1938, Einsatzkommando *Osterreich* (composition unknown) was deployed under the command of SS-Standartenführer Dr. Franz Six.

Czechoslovakia
For the initial occupation of Czechoslovakia under the terms of the Munich accords, Einsatzgruppe *Dresden* (composed of five Einsatzkommandos; commanded by SS-Oberführer Heinz Jost) and Einsatzgruppe *Wien* (composed of two Einsatzkommandos and eleven smaller Kommandos; commanded by SS-Standartenführer Dr. Walter Stahlecker) were deployed into the Protectorate. On 15 March 1939, when the Germans seized the remainder of the country, they deployed three additional units : Einsatzgruppe I *Prag* (composed of four Einsatzkommandos in Budweis, Prag, Kolin, and Pardubitz), Einsatzgruppe II *Brünn* (composed of three Einsatzkommandos in Olmütz, Brünn, and Zlin), and Sonderkommando *Pilsen*.

Poland

The German deployment of Einsatzgruppen in Austria and Czechoslovakia was a mere dress rehearsal for what occurred during the invasion of Poland. On 1 September 1939, SS-Obergruppenführer Theodor Eicke informed his three SS-Totenkopfstandarten assembled outside Berlin (at Oranienburg) that they would be assisting in police and security operations behind German lines in Poland. He declared that they would have to carry out the harshest orders without hesitation. The total strength of the Einsatzgruppen deployed into Poland during the German invasion was approximately 2,700 effectives. As usual, the majority of the Einsatzgruppen commanders and officers came from the SD; the manpower was from the Sipo, Orpo and the Waffen-SS. Their operations went by the codename of Tannenberg. The Einsatzgruppe followed the main armies and entered Poland on 4 September 1939.

- Einsatzgruppe I -- CO : SS-Brigadeführer Bruno Streckenbach; composed of four Kommandos; attached to the 14th Army

- Einsatzgruppe II -- CO : SS-Obersturmbannführer Dr. Emanuel Schäfer; composed of two Kommandos including SS-Totenkopfstandarte I Oberbayern and SS-Totenkopfstandarte III Thüringen; attached to the 10th Army;

- Einsatzgruppe III -- CO : SS-Obersturmbannführer Dr. Herbert Fischer; composed of two Kommandos including SS-Totenkopfstandarte II Brandenburg; attached to the 8th Army

- Einsatzgruppe IV -- CO : SS-Brigadeführer Lothar Beutel; composed of two Kommandos; attached to the 4th Army

- Einsatzgruppe V -- CO : SS-Brigadeführer Ernst Damzog; composed of three Kommandos; attached to the 3rd Army

- Einsatzgruppe VI -- CO : SS-Oberführer Erich Naumann; composed of two Kommandos; assigned to the city and province of Posen

Some irregular units with SS and Waffen-SS associations, such as the Volksdeutsche Selbstschutz and the SS-Wachsturmbann Eimann, were also involved in the operations. In mid-September 1939, Reichsführer-SS Himmler dispatched a new unit, Einsatzgruppe zur besondere Verwendung (350 personnel under the command of SS-Obergruppenführer Udo von Woyrsch) to liquidate Poles and Jews in the Ostoberschlesien area. The unit proceeded to torch synagogues and beat and kill Jews so openly that on 22 September 1939 Field Marshal August von Mackensen insisted that they be withdrawn.

On 21 September 1939, SS-Obergruppenführer Heydrich instructed the Einsatzgruppen to start deporting Jews into the Generalgouvernement zone of Poland. Once their immediate tasks were ended, the Einsatzgruppen were converted into static outposts (Gestapo Leitstellen and SD Abschnitte). They also provided the personnel for future Einsatzgruppen. Once static, each district was under the command of a KdS (Kommandeur der Sicherheitspolizei und des SD); groups of districts were subordinate to a BdS (Befehlshaber der Sicherheitpolizei und des SD) who in turn was directly subordinate to the RSHA. The Ordnungspolizei also had a chain of command in place. The real power, however, lay with the Höhere SS und Polizeiführer (HSSPf) who covered both chains of command.

Organizational Structure, 21 September 1939

Army Group 14 :

Einsatzgruppe I	SS-Brigadeführer Bruno Streckenbach	Cieszyn
EK 1/I	SS-Sturmbannführer Dr. Ludwig Hahn	Katowice
EK 2/I	SS-Sturmbannführer Bruno Müller	Krakow
EK 3/I	SS-Sturmbannführer Alfred Hasselberg	Jaroslaw
EK 4/I	SS-Sturmbannführer Dr. Karl Friedrich Brunner	Cieszyn
Polizeigruppe 1	SS-Obergruppenführer Udo von Woyrsch	
	Polizei Bataillonen 62, 63, 81, 92, and 171	
Einsatzgruppe zbV	SS-Obergruppenführer Udo von Woyrsch	Tarnow
EK Sipo	SS-Oberführer Dr. Otto Emil Rasch	
1. TK	SS-Brigadeführer Otto Helwig	
2. TK	SS-Oberführer Hans Trummler	
EK Orpo	Oberst der Polizei Friedrich Wolfstieg	
	also Polizei-Regiment 3 and Polizei-Bataillon 1	

Army Group 10 :

Einsatzgruppe II	SS-Obersturmbannführer Dr. Emanuel Schäfer	Czestochowa
EK 1/II	SS-Obersturmbannführer Otto Sens	Czestochowa
EK 2/II	SS-Obersturmbannführer Karl-Heinz Rux	Kielce
Polizeigruppe 2	Generalmajor der Polizei Herbert Becker	
	Polizei Bataillonen 42, 71, 101, 102, and 103	

Army Group 8 :

Einsatzgruppe III	SS-Obersturmbannführer Dr. Herbert Fischer	Lodz
EK 1/III	SS-Sturmbannführer Dr. Wilhelm Scharpwinkel	Lodz
EK 2/III	SS-Sturmbannführer Dr. Fritz Liphardt	Lodz
Polizeigruppe 3	Oberstleutnant d. Pol. Hermann Franz	
	Polizei Bataillon 41, SS-TV Reiterabteilung,	
	Polizei-Regiment 4 (bataillonen 2, 3, 4, and 91)	
2. SS-Totenkopfstandarte	SS-Gruppenführer Günther Pancke	
"Brandenburg"	SS-Standartenführer Paul Nostitz	

Army Group 4 :

Einsatzgruppe IV	SS-Brigadeführer Lothar Beutel	Bialystok
EK 1/IV	SS-Sturmbannführer Dr. Helmut Bischoff	Bialystok
EK 2/IV	SS-Sturmbannführer Dr. Walter Hammer	
Polizeigruppe 5	Generalleutnant der Polizei Arthur von Mülverstedt	
	Polizei-Bataillon 1, Polizei-Reiterabteilung 5	

Army Group 3 :

Einsatzgruppe V	SS-Standartenführer Ernst Damzog	Soldau
EK 1/V	SS-Sturmbannführer Dr. Heinz Graefe	Drogusowo
EK 2/V	SS-Sturmbannführer Dr. Robert Schefe	Pultusk/Makow
EK 3/V	SS-Sturmbannführer Dr. Walter Albath	Soldau/Plonsk/ Siedlce
Polizeigruppe Eberhardt	Generalmajor der Polizei Friedrich Georg Eberhardt Polizei-Regimenten 1 and 2	

MBF Posen :

Einsatzgruppe VI	SS-Oberführer Erich Naumann	Poznan
EK 1/VI	SS-Sturmbannführer Franz Sommer	Poznan
EK 2/VI	SS-Sturmbannführer Gerhard Flesch	Poznan
Polizeigruppe 4 zbV	Generalleutnant Karl Pfeffer-Wildenbruch Polizei-Bataillon 61	

MBF Westpreussen :

Einsatzkommando 16	SS-Obersturmbannführer Dr. Rudolf Tröger	Danzig
TK Gdingen	Kriminaldirektor Friedrich Class	Gdynia
TK Bromberg	SS-Sturmbannführer Jakob Lölgen	Bydgoszcz
TK Thorn	Kriminalkommissar Hans-Joachim Leyer	Torun
SD Einsatzkommando 16	SS-Sturmbannführer Franz Röder	Bydgoszcz

The Autumn and Winter of 1939 in Poland, especially in the Generalgouvernement zone, was marked by a widespread terror and murder campaign designated the Intelligenz-Aktion. This operation was followed by the Allgemeine Befriedungs-Aktion that lasted from May - July 1940. Both of these campaigns focused on eliminating the Polish cultural and intellectual elite classes. For the most part Wehrmacht officers looked the other way with regard to these activities, even if they were disgusted by them. Colonel-General Johannes Blaskowitz, however, collected reports on SS crimes in Poland and collated them into a memorandum which he dispatched to the Wehrmacht Commander-in-Chief in the middle of November 1939. Then, in January 1940, Colonel-General Blaskowitz submitted a new list of 33 incidents complete with details. His pleas and complaints went unheeded. In May 1940 he was transferred to the Western Front.

Claimed Atrocities
- Bromberg 1
- Bromberg 2
- Ciepielow
- Ksiazki/Hohenkirch
- Nisko
- Owinsk
- Palmiry Forest
- Polish Corridor
- Rawa Mazowiecka
- Wloclawek/Leslau

Additional Atrocities

Date	Location	District	Victims	Perpetrator
9/8-15/39	Berkenek/Zbiczno	Pomorze	~ 200	Einsatzkommando
9/13/39	Bydgoszcz/Bromberg	Pomorze	~ 100	Einsatzkommando
9/24/39	Zalno	Pomorze	60	Einsatzkommando
9/28/39	Chojnice	Pomorze	40	Einsatzkommando
9/28/39	Blonie	Warszawa	~ 800	Einsatzkommando
10/8/39	Swiecie (Schwetz)	--------------	63	Selbstschutz Westpreussen (CO von Alvensleben)1
4/14/40	Jozefow	Lublin	191	Selbstschutz Westpreussen (CO von Alvensleben)
1939/40	Dabrowka	Poznan	2,500	Einsatzkommando
1939/40	Debienko	Poznan	1,700	Einsatzkommando

1 BA/Militärarchiv (Freiburg) N104/3

See also Poland - Miscellaneous Atrocities.

Sources

(Krausnick, 1981) (Höhne, 1971, pp. 336-348) (Breitman, 1991, pp. 66-71)
(Birn, 1986, p. 197) (Artzt, 1974, p. 52) (Röhr, 1989) (Wieczorek, 1968) (MacLean, 1999)

Einsatzgruppen in the USSR

BackgroundPrior to the German invasion of the USSR on 22 June 1941, Reichsführer-SS Himmler tasked SS-Obergruppenführer Reinhard Heydrich with organizing four Einsatzgruppe for deployment with the invasion force (see map of operational boundaries in *Reitlinger, 1961, p. 185*). These motorized detachments totaling 2,945 effectives were composed of Sicherheitspolizei (Sipo), Sicherheitsdienst (SD), Waffen-SS, and other personnel; they wore Waffen-SS field uniforms with the black SD diamond on the left sleeve. Advancing directly behind the lead combat elements, the Einsatzgruppe were charged with performing special security operations. Their basic orders were to round-up and execute a broad selection of individuals classed as "subversive anti-Reich elements" : Comintern officials, Communist Party officials, People's Commissars, Jews, and partisans. Additionally, no steps were to be taken to interefere with any purges that might be initiated by local anti-Jewish or anti-Communist elements in the newly occupied territories. On the contrary, these were to be secretly encouraged. As was the case previously in Poland, the term "partisan" was often a euphemism for any group slated for extermination. Thus, the "war against partisans" and "anti-partisan operations" were used by the Einsatzgruppen (and others) as convenient masks behind which their extermination program could be carried out.

A young intelligence officer could best please SS-Obergruppenführer Heydrich by volunteering for one of his Einsatzgruppen. As a consequence, the majority of Einsatzgruppen officers were recruited from the information branches of the RSHA. Some did refuse these re-assignments without suffering repurcussions, contrary to the post-war claims of Einsatzgruppe officers that they were compelled otherwise. For example, former SS-Sturmbannführer Albert Hartl of the RSHA testified at the post-war Einsatzgruppen Trial that he had refused to take command of an Einsatzkommando in the USSR and saw no deleterious effects to his career as a result (Affidavit by Albert Hartl, October 9, 1947, NO-5384). Those officers who did accept the assignment underwent three weeks of training in May 1941 at the Grenzpolizeischule Pretzsch (on the Elbe River, northeast of Leipzig) and also at nearby Düben and Bad Schmiedeberg. Upon their initial formation each Einsatzgruppe had 600 - 1,000 effectives, with the exception of Einsatzgruppe D which was somewhat smaller (approximately 470 personnel). Their strength was later augmented by large numbers of Lithuanian volunteer auxiliaries who were used in Poland, Latvia, and White Russia. By 1942, however, these auxiliaries had proven to be unreliable and were replaced by German Ordnungspolizei. During the course of the war, approximately 1,500 Waffen-SS personnel saw service with the Einsatzgruppen and 8% of Einsatzgruppe commanders saw service with the Waffen-SS.

Paralleling the establishment of the Einsatzgruppen, Reichsführer-SS Himmler established an *Einsatzstab* on 7 April 1941 in order to have a security/extermination force under his personal control. On 6 May 1942 this group was redesignated the *Kommandostab Reichsführer-SS* and placed under the command of SS-Brigadeführer Kurt Knoblauch. On 15 May, Reichsführer-SS Himmler ordered the formation of the Begleit-Bataillon *Reichsführer-SS* from several SS-Totenkopfstandarten. On 20 June 1941, these units were brigaded together with the 1. SS-Infanterie (mot.) Brigade, 2. SS-Infanterie (mot.) Brigade, SS-Kavallerie-Regiment 1, SS-Kavallerie-Regiment 2, SS Flak-Abteilung *Ost*, and SS-Freiwilligen-Regiment *Hamburg* and placed under the command of the Kommandostab *RFSS* for special operations in the USSR. (Note: the Begleit-Bataillon and Flak-Abteilung were subordinated to 2. SS-Infanterie (mot.) Brigade.)

As soon as German authority was established in the occupied territories, the Einsatzgruppen converted themselves into static outposts (as they had in Poland). Concentration camps were immediately set up for Communists in the operational areas of Einsatzgruppen B and C. The campaign of extermination against the Jews continued. Those who had survived the initial wave of mass killings were herded into ghettos organized in all of the major cities. The inhabitants were then slowly killed off during extermination actions that were disguised as "resettlement programs." From November 1941 onward, tens of thousands of

Jews from the Reich and the Generalgouvernement in Poland were shipped East to be incorporated into the ghettos and then killed by the Einsatzgruppen.

In contrast to the secrecy in which they wished to operate in the field, the Einsatzgruppen left behind a substantial official paper trail of their extermination activities. The Einsatzgruppen reports consisted of daily situation bulletins (Tätigkeitsberichte) and monthly resumes (Ereignismeldungen). This series of reports ran from June 1941 until the end of April 1942. In time the Einsatzgruppen personnel were winnowed down to a core of hardened killers. Although these men were ceaselessly indoctrinated and regarded all Jews and Communists as vermin, they often still had to be "motivated" with alcohol prior to killing operations. SS-Obergruppenführer Bach-Zelewski, who as HSSPf Russland-Mitte directed the operations of Einsatzgruppe B, suffered from severe nervous disorders, as did many of his men. In an Autumn 1941 meeting with Reichsführer-SS Himmler, SS-Obergruppenführer Bach-Zelewski claimed to have confronted him in this regard : "Look at the eyes of the men of this Kommando, how deeply shaken they are. These men are finished for the rest of their lives. What kind of followers are we training here? Either neurotics or savages!" (*Aufbau* ….)

In an effort to streamline the killing process and lessen the psychological burden on the exterminators themselves, rudimentary mobile carbon monoxide gassing vans produced by Gaubschat Farengewerke GmbH of Berlin were put into action. They were primarily used to execute women and children from hospitals, asylums, and orphanages. According to the testimony of Friedrich Pradel, the head of transport for Einsatzgruppe B, approximately twenty gas vans were delivered to the four Einsatzgruppen by 23 June 1942. The earliest gassing operations occurred at Poltava (November 1941) and at Kharkov (December 1941). Four gas vans were sent to Minsk for use against the local Jews in early Summer 1942. One was also sent to Einsatzgruppe Serbien based in Semlin, Yugoslavia. An additional 3 - 4 were sent in the second half of 1942 to Salaspils and Riga. Aside from often being defective, the gassing vans were also unpopular among the Einsatzgruppen personnel.

As of March 1942, the Einsatzgruppen had killed a minimum of 700 - 750,000 Jews in the USSR :

- Einsatzgruppe A -- 240,410
- Einsatzgruppe B -- 71,555 (134,000 as of December 1942)
- Einsatzgruppe C -- 105,988
- Einsatzgruppe D -- 91,678
- Rumanian massacres in Odessa instigated by the Einsatzgruppe -- 60,000
- Static activities of all Einsatzgruppen -- 269,264
- Activities of related and assisting agencies -- remainder

In a report on its "operational successes" Einsatzgruppe A gave the following breakdown of its victims by category : Jews (90.7%), Jews through Pogroms (2.3%), Lithuanians (2.3%), Communists (3.5%), Partisans (0.4%), Hospital Cases (0.7%), and Others (0.1%). Such figures put a proper perspective on the "anti-partisan" operations of the Einsatzgruppe. Final estimates of the death toll related to Einsatzgruppen activities in the USSR for 1941 - 1944 range from 2.5 to 4 million individuals.

Einsatzgruppe A

Einsatzgruppe A was attached to Army Group North and had as its operational area Estonia, Latvia, Lithuania and the territory between their eastern borders and the Leningrad district. Its assembly area was near Danzig. In addition to its initial complement of SD, Sipo and SS personnel, Einsatzgruppe A was strengthened with a company from Polizei-Reserve-Bataillon 9. In late July 1941, 1. Kompanie / Waffen-SS Bataillon zur besondere Verwendung (CO: SS-Obersturmführer Friedrich Störtz) with 340 effectives was received as reinforcements. As of October 1941 Einsatzgruppe A had 990 effectives, of which 34.4% were Waffen-SS personnel. A number of the anti-Jewish pogroms by the local populace that occurred in the Baltics were instigated by this Einsatzgruppe.

Commanding Officers

- SS-Brigadeführer Dr. Franz Walter Stahlecker (6/22/41 - 3/23/42) KIA
- SS-Brigadeführer Dr. Heinz Jost (3/24/42 - 9/9/42)
- SS-Oberführer Dr. Humbert Achamer-Pifrader (9/10/42 - 9/4/43)

- SS-Oberführer Friedrich Panzinger (9/4/43 - 5/6/44)
- SS-Oberführer Dr. Wilhelm Fuchs (5/6/44 - 10/44)

Sub-Units

- Sonderkommando 1a (known as KdS Estland after 12/3/41)
- SS-Obersturmbannführer Dr. Martin Sandberger (6/22/41 - Autumn 1943)
- SS-Obersturmbannführer Bernhard Baatz (10/31/43 - 10/15/44)
- Sonderkommando 1b (known as KdS Weissruthenien after 12/3/41)
- SS-Obersturmbannführer Dr. Erich Erlinger (6/22/41 - 12/3/41)
- SS-Standartenführer Dr. Eduard Strauch (12/3/41 - 6/43)
- SS-Obersturmbannführer Dr. Erich Isselhorst (6/30/43 - 10/43)
- Einsatzkommando 2 (known as KdS Lettland after 12/3/41)
- SS-Sturmbannführer Rudolf Batz (6/22/41 - 11/41)

- SS-Obersturmbannführer Dr. Eduard Strauch (11/4/41 - 12/3/41)
- SS-Sturmbannführer Dr. Rudolf Erwin Lange (12/3/41 - ?)
- Einsatzkommando 3 (known as KdS Litauen after 12/3/41)
- SS-Standartenführer Karl Jäger (6/22/41 - Autumn 1943)
- SS-Oberführer Dr. Wilhelm Fuchs (9/15/43 - 5/6/44)
- SS-Standartenführer Hans-Joachim Böhme (5/11/44 - 1/1/45)
- Einsatzkommando 1a (known as Ek 1 after Autumn 1942)
- SS-Obersturmbannführer Dr. Martin Sandberger (Mid-1942 - Autumn 1942)
- SS-Obersturmbannführer Karl Tschierschky (Autumn 1942)
- SS-Obersturmbannführer Dr. Erich Isselhorst (11/42 - 6/43)
- SS-Obersturmbannführer Bernhard Baatz (8/43 - 10/31/43)

- Einsatzkommando 1b (known as Ek 2 after March 1943)
- SS-Sturmbannfuhrer Dr. Hermann Hubig (Mid-1942 - 10/42)
- SS-Sturmbannführer Dr. Manfred Pechau (10/42 - 3/26/43)
- SS-Sturmbannführer Reinhard Breder (3/26/43 - 8/43)
- SS-Obersturmbannführer Oswald Poche (8/43 - ?)
- Einsatzkommando 1c (known as Ek 3 after November 1942)
- SS-Sturmbannführer Kurt Graaf (8/42 - 11/42)
- SS-Obersturmbannführer Karl Traut (11/42 - 5/43)

Operational Record

20 June 1941 Einsatzgruppe Stab quartered in Gumbinnen (Ostpreussen).

23 June 1941 Unit quartered in the Danzig area.

25 June 1941 SS-Brigadeführer Dr. Stahlecker and a small Vorauskommando entered Tilsit and Kaunus with advance elements of the Wehrmacht.

27 June 1941 Sonderkommando 1a (attached to the 18th Army) marched from Bad Schmiedeberg and conducted operations against towns to the NE, E, and SE of Libau. Einsatzkommando 2 located at Schaulen.

28 June 1941 SK1a located at Mitau. Sonderkommando 1b located at Kaunus.

29 June 1941 A Vortrupp of SK1a reported on the road to Riga. Other Teilkommandos reported in Schaulen and Libau.

2 July 1941 Einsatzgruppe Stab left Schaulen and headed for Riga. Gruppenchef Stahlecker (with his Vorauskommando, Teilkommandos of SK1a, and the balance of EK2) had already entered Riga with the Wehrmacht spearhead. Teilkommando of EK2 in Libau. Einsatzkommando 3 located at Kaunus.

2/10 July 1941   EGr ceased advance and concentrated on the "liberation" of Latvia and Lithuania.

3 July 1941   SK1b still located at Kaunus.

4 July 1941   EGr reported Riga as its operational location. EK3 executed 463 Jews during an action at Kaunas, Lithuania.

6 July 1941   EK3 executed 2,514 Jews at Kaunas.

7/19 July 1941   Elements of EK3 executed 227 Jews at Mariampole, Girkalinei, Wendziogala, Kauen-Fort VII, and Babtei.

8 July 1941   SK1b reported location as Dünaberg. Teilkommandos of EK2 in Mitau.

8/10 July 1941   Combined forces of EK8 and SK1b executed 8,000 Jews at Borissov. Commander of the operation is SS-Obersturmbannführer Werner Schönemann.

10 July 1941   EGr resumed advance and allocated the following operations: SK1a to Estonia (Pernau, Reval, Dorpat, and Narwa); SK1b to area south of Leningrad (Pskow, Ostrow, and Opotschka). Several days later lead elements of SK1a were in Pskow, Fellin, and Pernau; lead elements of SK1b were in Rosenow and Ostrow.

13 July/ 21 August 1941 EK3 Teilkommando executed 9,585 Jews in Dünaberg, Lithuania.

18 July 1941   EGr reported Pleskau as operational location for advance and occupation of Leningrad (never occurred). Teilkommandos of EK2 and EK3 located at Nowoselje (45 kilometers northeast of Pleskau).

21/31 July 1941   Elements of EK3 executed 1,186 Jews at Panevezys, Kedainiai, Mariampole, Agriogala, Utena, Wendziogala and Rasainiai.

July/August 1941   EGr involved in operations in the forests and swamps north and east of Pleskau.

1/9 August 1941   Elements of EK3 executed 3,017 Jews at Ukmerge, Kauen-Fort IV, Panevezys, Rasainiai, and Uteba.

9 August 1941   EK3 located at Wilna.

9/16 August 1941 EK3 executed 298 Jews at Rassainiai.

11/14 August 1941   EK3 executed 1,771 Jews at Panevezys, Alytus, and Jonava.

12 August/1 September 1941   EK3 executed 461 Jews at Wilna.

14/16 August 1941   EK3 executed 4,189 Jews at Rokiskis, Lithuania.

18 August 1941 EK3 executed 1,811 Jews at Kauen-Fort IV, Lithuania.

18/22 August 1941   EK3 executed 1,926 Jews in Kreis Rasainiai, Lithuania.

19 August 1941 EK3 executed 645 Jews at Ukmerge.

22 August 1941 EK3 executed 565 psychiatric patients, gypsies, etc. at Aglona and Dunaberg.

23 August 1941 SK1b located on front lines at Staraja Russa am Ilmensee with 16. Army. EK3 executed 7,523 Jews at Panevezys, Lithuania.

24 August 1941 EGr reported Pesje (60 kilometers southeast of Narwa) as operational location.

25 August 1941 EK3 executed 1,160 Jews at Obeliai, Lithuania.

26 August 1941 EK3 executed 6,491 Jews at Seduva, Zarasai, Kaisiadorys and Pasvalys.

27 August 1941 EK3 executed 1,649 Jews at Prienai, Dagda, Kraslawa and Joniskia.

28 August 1941 SK1a located at Reval with 18. Army. EK3 executed 2478 Jews at Kedainiai and Wilkia.

28 August/ 2 September 1941 EK3 executed 4,575 Jews at Darsuniskis, Carliava, Jonava, Petrasiunai, Jesuas, Ariogala, Jasvainai, Babtei, Wenziogala and Krakes.

29 August 1941 EK3 executed 4,566 Jews at Utena, Moletai, Rumsiskis and Ziezmariai.

31 August 1941 EK3 executed 233 Jews in the Alytus region.

1 September 1941 EK3 executed 5,090 Jews and psychiatric patients at Mariampole.

2 September 1941 EGr reported Kikerino (75 kilometers east of Narwa) as operational location. EK3 Teilkommando executed 3,700 Jews in Wilna, Lithuania.

4 September 1941 EK3 executed 929 Jews at Pravenischkis, Cekiske, Seredsius, Velinona and Zapiskis.

5 September 1941 EK3 executed 4,709 Jews at Ukmerge, Lithuania.

6 September 1941 Elements of EK3 executed 1,255 Jews during "mopping up operations" in Rasainiai and Georgenburg.

9 September 1941 EK3 executed 2,019 Jews at Alytus and Butrimonys.

9/12 September 1941 EK3 executed 3,207 Jews at Merkine, Varena, Leipalingis, Seirijai and Simnas.

12 September 1941 EK3 Teilkommando executed 3,334 Jews in Wilna.

17 September 1941 EK3 Teilkommando executed 1,271 Jews in Wilna.

20 September 1941 EK3 Teilkommando executed 403 Jews at Nemencing.

22 September 1941 EK3 Teilkommando executed 1,159 Jews at Nowo-Wilejka, Lithuania.

23/26 September 1941 Elements of EGr (with the help of local civilians) shot 4,000 Jews in the Old Jewish Cemetery and near the Christian Cemetary in Eishishok, Lithuania.

24 September 1941 EK3 Teilkommando executed 1,767 Jews at Riesa, Lithuania.

25 September 1941 EK3 Teilkommando executed 575 Jews at Jahiunai.

26 September 1941 EK3 executed 1,608 Jews at Kauen-Fort IV, Lithuania.

27 September 1941 EK3 Teilkommando executed 3,446 Jews at Eysiskiy, Lithuania.

28 September/October 1941 EK3 Teilkommando Minsk executed 3,050 Jews and Communists at Pleschnitza, 17 Bischolin, Scak, Bober and Uzda.

30 September 1941 EK3 Teilkommando executed 1,446 Jews at Trakai, Lithuania.

Late September 1941 EGr reported Meshno (50 kilometers south of Leningrad) and Riga as operational locations.

Late September 1941 Reorganization of entire EGr structure. SS-Brigadeführer Dr. Stahlecker designated Befehlshaber der Sicherheitspolizei und des SD and located offices in Riga. EGr sub-elements converted to stationary units with permanent posts. SK1a became Kommandeur der Sicherheitspolizei und des SD für den Generalbezirk Estland (location : Riga, with auxiliary postings at Narwa, Dorpat, Pernau,and Arensburg/Oesel). EK2 became KdS Lettland (location : Riga, with auxiliary postings at Scahulen and Libau). EK3 became KdS Litauen (location : Kaunus, with auxiliary posting at Wilna). SK1b became KdS Weissruthenien (location : Minsk, with auxiliary posting at Baranowicze).

2 October 1941 EK3 located at Schaulen. EK3 executed 2,236 Jews at Zagare, Lithuania.

4 October 1941 EK3 executed 1,845 Jews at Kauen-

Fort IX, Lithuania. EK3 Teilkommando executed 1,983 Jews at Wilna.

6 October 1941 EK3 Teilkommando executed 962 Jews at Semiliski.

7 October 1941 EGr reported Krasnogwardeisk (40 kilometers southwest of Leningrad) as operational location.

9 October 1941 EK3 Teilkommando executed 3,726 Jews at Svenciany, Lithuania.

16 October 1941 EK3 Teilkommando executed 1,146 Jews at Wilna.

19 October 1941 EGr kommando executed 7,620 Jews at Borissov.

21 October 1941 EK3 Teilkommando executed 2,367 Jews at Wilna.

25 October/6 November 1941 EK3 Teilkommando executed 6,655 Jews at Wilna.

29 October 1941 EK3 destroyed remnants of Kauen-Fort IX ghetto: 9,200 Jews executed.

30 October 1941 Operations in Sluzk.

3 November 1941 EK3 executed 1,535 Jews at Lazdijai, Lithuania.

7/11 November 1941 Mixed unit under the command of SS-Obersturmbannführer Hans Hermann Remmers shot 6,624 Jews in Minsk.

9 November 1941 11,034 Jews shot in Dünaberg.

15 November 1941 EK3 executed 115 Jews at Wilkowiski.

19 November 1941 EK3 Teilkommando executed 188 Jews, POWs, and Poles at Wilna

25 November 1941 EK3 executed 2,934 German Jews ("resettlers" from Berlin, München, & Frankfurt am Main) at Kauen-Fort IX.

29 November 1941 EK3 executed 2,000 German Jews ("resettlers" from Vienna and Breslau) at Kauen-Fort IX.

December 1941 27,800 Jews shot in Riga.

Mid-December 1941 2,350 Jews shot in Libau.

5 January 1942 KdS Estland expanded auxiliary postings to include Kingisepp (25 kilometers east of Narwa), Krasnoje Selo (15 kilometers southwest of Leningrad), Luga (130 kilometers southwest of Leningrad), and Pleskau. Kd S Lettland expanded auxiliary postings to include Wolmar and Dünaberg. KdS Weissruthenien reported auxiliary postings at Nowogrodek, Tschudowo (110 kilometers southeast of Leningrad), and the Cholm area.

24 March 1942 Following the death of SS-Brigadeführer Dr. Stahlecker, SS-Brigadeführer Jost is assigned as his successor and the post is redesignated as Befehlshaber der Sicherheitspolizei und des SD im Reichskommissariat Ostland.

8 April 1942 KdS Weissruthenien reported auxiliary posting at Wilejka.

September 1942 EK1a reported postings at Narwa, Kingisepp, Wolossowo (65 kilometers southwest of Leningrad), Pleskau, and Luga. EK1b reported operational location as Loknja (60 kilometers north of Welikije Luki). EK1c reported operational location as Krasnogwardeisk.

October 1942 KdS Lettland established auxiliary posting at Mitau and KdS Litauen established auxiliary posting at Ponewesch.

November 1942 EGr operational location reported as Nataljewka (45 kilometers south-southwest of Leningrad).

February 1943 EK1 reported operational location as Gatschina. EK2 reported operational location as Loknja. EK3 reported operational location as Pleskau.

2 May 1943   Operations in Sluzk led by SS-Obersturmbannführer Müller.

Einsatzgruppe B

Einsatzgruppe B was attached to Army Group Center and had as its operational area Belorussia and the Smolensk district up to the outskirts of Moscow. Its assembly area was in the province of Posen. In addition to its initial complement of SD, Sipo, and SS personnel, Einsatzgruppe B was strengthened with a company from Polizei-Reserve-Bataillon 9. In late July 1941, 2. Kompanie/Waffen-SS Bataillon zur besondere Verwendung (CO: ?) was received as reinforcements bringing total strength to 655 effectives.

Commanding Officers
- SS-Brigadeführer Arthur Nebe   (6/22/41 - 11/41)
- SS-Oberführer Erich Naumann   (11/41 - 3/20/43)
- SS-Sturmbannführer Horst-Alwin Böhme (3/12/43 - 8/28/43)
- SS-Standartenführer Dr. Erich Ehrlinger (8/28/43 - 4/44)
- SS-Standartenführer Heinrich Seetzen (4/28/44 - 8/44)
- SS-Standartenführer Horst-Alwin Böhme (8/12/44 - ?)

Sub-Units
Sonderkommando 7a
- SS-Obersturmbannführer Dr. Walter Blume (6/22/41 - 9/41)
- SS-Obersturmbannführer Eugen Karl Steimle (9/41 - 12/41)
- SS-Hauptsturmführer Karl Matschke (12/41 - 2/42)
- SS-Standartenführer Albert Rapp   (2/42 - 1/28/43)
- SS-Obersturmbannführer Helmut Looss (6/43 - 6/44)
- SS-Sturmbannführer Dr. Gerhard Bast (6/44 - 11/44)

Sonderkommando 7b
- SS-Obersturmbannführer Gunther Rausch (6/22/41 - 2/10/42)

- SS-Obersturmbannführer Adolf Ott   (3/42 - 1/43)
- SS-Obersturmbannführer Karl-Hermann Rabe (1/43 - 10/44)

Sonderkommando 7c (a.k.a. Vorkommando Moskau; joined to Sk 7a in 12/43)
- SS-Standartenführer Dr. Franz Six   (6/22/41 - 8/20/41)
- SS-Sturmbannführer Waldemar Klingelhöfer (8/21/41 - 10/41)
- SS-Obersturmbannführer Dr. Erich Körting (10/41 - 12/41)
- SS-Hauptsturmführer Wilhelm Bock   (12/41 - 6/42)
- SS-Hauptsturmführer Rudolf Schmücker (6/42 - Autumn 1942)
- SS-Obersturmbannführer Dr. Walter Blume (Autumn 1942 - 7/43)
- SS-? Wilhelm Eckhardt (7/43 - 12/43)

Einsatzkommando 8
- SS-Obersturmbannführer Dr. Otto Bradfisch (6/22/41 - 4/1/42)
- SS-Obersturmbannführer Heinz Richter (4/1/42 - 9/42)
- SS-Obersturmbannführer Dr. Erich Isselhorst (9/42 - 11/42)
- SS-Obersturmbannführer Hans-Gerhard Schindhelm (11/13/42 - 10/43)

Einsatzkommando 9
- SS-Obersturmbannführer Dr. Alfred Karl Wilhelm Filbert (6/22/41 - 10/20/41)
- SS-Obersturmbannführer Dr. Oswald Schäfer (10/20/41 - 2/42)
- SS-Obersturmbannführer Wilhelm Wiebens (2/42 - 1/43)
- SS-Obersturmbannführer Dr. Friedrich Buchardt (1/43 - 3/43)

Operational Record
23 June 1941   Egr B in Posen.

24 June 1941   Egr B quartered in Warschau.

27 June 1941   SK 7b (Minsk) attached to 4. Armee; advanced to Brest-Litovsk.

29 June 1941   EK 9 advanced from Warschau through Stadt Treuberg (Ostpreussen) towards Wilna.

30 June 1941   SK 7b marched through Kobryn and halts at Prushany. Vorkommando Moskau attached to Panzer-AOK 4.

July 1941   SK 7A marched from Minsk through Polozk and on to Witebsk. SK 7b advanced through Minsk, Borissow, and Bobruisk.

1 July 1941   EK9 entered Varena (70 kilometers southwest of Wilna). Teilkommandos sent to Grodno and Lida.

2 July 1941   EK9 entered Wilna. SK7b continued advance through Slonim and Baranowicze.

3 July 1941   Gruppenchef SS-Brigadeführer Arthur Nebe and Stab entered Wolkowysk. Elements of EK 8 and EK 9 in Krakau, Warschau, and Lublin are reassigned by order of SS-Obergruppenführer Heydrich into "Unterstützungstrupps für Weissrussland". EK8 remained in Warsaw and sent out Teilkommandos to Wolkowysk, Slonim, Baranowicze, Nowogrodek, and Borissow. Borissow Teilkommando (CO: SS-Obersturmführer Schönemann) stationed there until mid-October 1941.

3/5 July 1941   EK 9 Teilkommando originally dispatched to Grodno conducted sweep of Bielsk-Podlaski (south of Bialystok), Wolkowysk, and Slonim killing 900 Jews. Unit then rejoined main body of EK9.

4 July 1941   EK9 entered Minsk.

5 July 1941   Gruppenchef SS-Brigadeführer Arthur Nebe and Stab traveled through Slonim and entered Minsk --- for the next two weeks Minsk is the operational base for EGr B. Sonderkommandos attached for continued advance with Wehrmacht forces; Einsatzkommandos held back for cleansing operations in rear areas.

8 July 1941   321 Jews executed in Wilna.

9 July 1941   "Unterstützungstrupps" (see previous entry 7/3/41) under command of SS-Oberführer Eberhardt Schöngarth (who is also BdS Krakau at this time) and stationed at Brest-Litovsk, Pinsk, Sluzk, Bialystok, Wilna, and Minsk.

13 July 1941   Elements of Egr B shot 500 Jews and "saboteurs" near the Lithuanian border.

15 July 1941   EK8 reported new operational location as Bialystok, with a Vorauskommando in Sluzk and a Teiltrupp in Lachowicze.

17 July 1941   "Unterstützungstrupps" stationed at Lemberg, Brest-Litovsk and Bialystok with auxiliary units at Pinsk, Luck, Rowno, Kowel, Rawa-Ruska, Nowogrodek, Baranowicze, and Grodno. BdS Krakau SS-Oberführer Dr. Eberhard Schöngarth and small Stab at Lemberg.

20/24 July 1941 After leaving behind a Nachkommando in Wilna, EK9 advanced toWilejka and Molodeczno. SK 7b located at Orscha.

23 July 1941   EK8 reported operational location as Borissow-Minsk.

24 July 1941   Elements of EK8 liquidated 381 persons in Baranowicze.

August 1941   SK 7b located at Gomel and conducted clearing operations in Tschaussy, Rogatschew, Shlobin, Retschiza, Dobrush, Klinzy, and Starodub.

2 August 1941   EK9 reported Witebsk as operational location. In the following weeks, teilkommandos are dispatched on actions to Polozk (along the upper course of the Duna), Lepel (halfway between Wilejka and Witebsk), Newel, Surash (northeast of Witebsk), Janowitschi (south of Surash), and Gorodok (north of Witebsk).

5 August 1941   Gruppenchef SS-Brigadeführer Arthur Nebe and Stab reported operational location as Smolensk.

19 August 1941   "Unterstützungstrupps" incorporated into Einsatzgruppe z.b.V (under the command of SS-Oberführer Dr. Eberhard Schöngarth).

Late August 1941   SK 7a reported an operation against Jews 95 kilometers north of Newel.

1 September 1941   EK8 followed advance towards Moskau leaving behind a Nachkommando in Minsk and a Teilkommando in Orscha.

4 September 1941   SK 7a reported operational location as Welish (80 kilometers northeast of Witebsk) with Teilkommandos at Welikije Luki (130 kilometers north of Witebsk) and Toropez (75 kilometers northeast of Welikije Luki).

9 September 1941   EK8 reported operational location as Mogilew. Teilkommandos are in Borissow and Bobruisk. SK 7b located at Repki (70 kilometers south of Gomel) with a Teilkommando at Tschernigow (100 kilometers south of Gomel) and a Nachkommando at Gomel. Performed a number of actions against Jews and "party functionaries" in the Tschernigow region.

Late September 1941   EK8 reported Teilkommandos at Gomel, Gorki, Rogatschew, Klinzy, Retschiza, and Mosyr.

23 September 1941   EK9 reported that 1,025 Jews at Janowitschi and 640 Jews at Newel received "special treatment".

2 October 1941 EK8 operated in rear areas. The remainder of EGr B advanced as part of Operation Taifun (attack on Moscow). Gruppenstab and Vorkommando Moskau liquidated Jews in the Smolensk area. SK 7a with advance units liquidated "partisans and communist functionaries". SK 7b located at Klinzy and Mglin (55 kilometers northeast of Klinzy) with elements attached to AOK2 for the advance on Moskau.

7 October 1941 VK Moskau and elements of the Gruppenstab attached to AOK4 for the advance on Moscow. Reorganization ordered of the entire EGr structure (establishment of stationary SIPO and SD postings) failed to occur due to fluid situation of Army Group Center.

8 October 1941 EK9 began clearance of Witebsk Ghetto. Final report states 4,090 Jews shot.

10/11 October 1941   EK8 carried out extermination operations in the areas of Mogilew, Bobruisk, and Orscha. A Nachkommando reported at Minsk.

19 October 1941   Elements of EK8, with the help of Polizei-Regiment *Mitte*, liquidated 3,726 Jews in one operation.

21 October 1941   EK9 reported operational location as Wjasma with a Vorkommando at Gshatsk (150 kilometers from Moscow) and a Nachkommando at Witebsk. SK 7a reported operational location as Rshew (210 kilometers northwest of Moscow). SK 7b located at Orel and Brjansk.

Late October 1941   EK8 reported operational location as Mogilew with Teilkommandos at Smolensk and Gomel. Vorkommando Moskau and Gruppenstab reported operational location as Medyn (140 kilometers southwest of Moscow) with elements at Gshatsk. VKM redesignated as Sonderkommando Moskau.

November 1941   Elements of EK8, with the help of Polizei-Reserve-Bataillon 316, shot 5,281 Jews in Bobruisk during the course of one operation.

5 November 1941   EK8 reported operational location as Mogilew with Teilkommandos at Witebsk, Gomel, Orscha, and Kritschew. EK9 reported operational location as Wyasma with Teilkommandos at Gshatsk and Smolensk. SK 7a reported operational location as Kalinin (110 kilometers northeast of Rshew). SK 7b located at Brjansk and Tula.

11/12 November 1941 SK Moskau and EGr B Stab reported operational location as Malojaroslawez (100 kilometers southwest of Moscow) and elements at Moshaisk (100 kilometers from Moscow).

22 December 1941   EK8 reported operational location as Mogilew with Teilkommandos at Orscha, Gomel, Roslawl, and Brjansk. EK9 reported the execution of 207 Jews in Witebsk and 117 Jews in Wyasma. SK 7b located at Orel and Kursk.

Late December 1941   SK 7a reported operational location as Sytschewka (50 kilometers south of Rshew).

January 1942
SK 7a reported operational location as Wjasma. SK 7b located at Brjansk with Teilkommandos at Orel and Kursk.

1/9 January 1942   EK8 reported operational location as Mogilew with Teilkommandos at Orscha, Gomel, Borissow, and Bobruisk.

2 January 1942   EK9 reported operational location as Smolensk.

14 January 1942   EK9 reported operational location as Witebsk with a Teilkommando in Smolensk. During the course of the year the unit's operational location changed frequently : Newel, Polozk, Lepel, Surash, Smolensk, and Borissow.

Late February 1942   SK Moskau and EGr Stab reported operational location as Roslawl.

21 February -20 April 1942   SK 7a located at Klinzy (225 kilometers south of Smolensk).

10 April 1942   Sonderkommando Moskau no longer mentioned in reports.

May 1942   SK 7b located at Orel with Teilkommandos at Brjansk and Karatschew.

June/August 1942   SK 7a located at Sytschewka with Teilkommandos at Wjasma and Rshew.

Late August 1942   SK 7a located at Sytschewka with Teilkommandos at Olenino and Nikitje.

Autumn 1942   SK 7b located at Lokot (south-southeast of Brjansk) and Trubtschewsk (south- southwest of Brjansk).

27 November 1942
SK 7a located at Sytschewka with Teilkommandos at Wyasma, Suchinino, Andrejewskoje, Dorogobush, and Wladimirskoje.

February 1943   EK8 reported operational location as Mogilew. EK9 reported operational location as Witebsk. Sk 7a located at Orefino (15 kilometers southwest of Smolensk). SK 7b located at Orel.

Einsatzgruppe C
Einsatzgruppe C was attached to Army Group South and had as its operational area Southern and Central Ukraine. Its assembly area was near Kattowitz. In addition to its initial complement of SD, Sipo, and SS personnel, Einsatzgruppe C was strengthened with a company from Polizei-Reserve-Bataillon 9. In late July 1941, 3. kompanie / Waffen-SS Bataillon zur besondere Verwendung (CO: ?) was received as reinforcements bringing total personnel to 700 effectives. Aside from its own infamous record of atrocities, this unit also instigated Rumanian armed forces to massacre 60,000 Jews from the city of Odessa.

Commanding Officers
- SS-Oberführer Dr. Emil Otto Rasch (6/22/41 - 10/41)
- SS-Gruppenführer Dr. Max Thomas (10/41 - 8/28/43)
- SS-Sturmbannführer Horst-Alwin Böhme (9/6/43 - 3/44)

Sub-Units
Sonderkommando 4a
- SS-Standartenführer Paul Blobel (6/22/41 - 1/13/42)
- SS-Standartenführer Dr. Erwin Weinmann (1/13/42 - 7/42)
- SS-Obersturmbannführer Eugen Karl Steimle (8/42 - 1/15/43)
- SS-Sturmbannführer Theodor Christensen (1/15/43 - 12/43)

Sonderkommando 4b
- SS-Obersturmbannführer Günther Herrmann (6/22/41 - 9/41)
- SS-Obersturmbannfuhrer Fritz Braune (10/1/41 - 3/21/42)
- SS-Obersturmbannführer Dr. Walter Hänsch (3/21/42 - 7/42)
- SS-Obersturmbannführer August Meier (7/42 - 11/42)

- SS-Obersturmbannführer Friedrich Suhr (11/42 - 8/43)
- SS-Sturmbannführer Waldemar Krause (8/43 - 1/44)

Einsatzkommando 5 (disbanded in January 1942)
- SS-Oberführer Erwin Schulz (6/22/41 - 9/41)
- SS-Obersturmbannführer August Meier (9/41 - 1/42)

Einsatzkommando 6
- SS-Standartenführer Dr. Erhard Kröger (6/22/41 - 11/41)
- SS-Obersturmbannführer Robert Mohr (11/41 - 9/42)
- SS-Sturmbannführer Ernst Biberstein (9/42 - 5/43)
- SS-Obersturmbannführer Friedrich Suhr (8/43 - 11/43)

Operational Record

23 June 1941   EGr Stab left Bad Schmiedeberg and traveled through Oberschlesien and Galizien.

27 June 1941   SK 4a entered Sokal (via Krakau and Zamosc) and spent the next three days performing executions. A Vorkommando was dispatched towards Luck.

30 June 1941   SK 4b Vorausabteilung entered Lemberg. SK 4a Vorkommando in Luck carried out executions on this day and the next. Einsatzkommando 6 at Dobromil (Galizien).

1 July 1941   Stab, Einsatzkommando 5, Einsatzkommando 6, and the remainder of SK 4b arrived in Lemberg. The discovery of a large number of murdered Ukrainian nationals (work of the NKVD) in the Lemberger Sportplatz resulted in anti-Jewish operations. In the next few days approximately 7,000 Jews (and some others) were detained and shot. Afterwards, SK 4b and EK 6 continued on to Zloczow (southeast of Lemberg) and EK 5 swept through Brody and Dubno.

2 July 1941   SK 4a Vorkommando at Luck executed 1,160 Jews in retaliation for the Soviet murder of

Germans and Ukrainians (found together in a mass grave).

5 July 1941   SK 4b entered Tarnopol.

6 July 1941   SK 4a entered Rowno.

7 July 1941   SK 4a entered Zwiahel (Novograd-Volynski). A Vorkommando was dispatched to Shitomir and executed 240 "bolshevists, Jewish functionaries, spies, etc.".

14 July 1941   EGr Stab arrived in Zwiahel.

16 July 1941   SK 4b at Proskurow (100 kilometers east of Tarnopol).

18/19 July 1941 EGr Stab arrived at Shitomir. A small kommando was dispatched to Czernowitz. BdS Krakau formed eight "Unterstützungstrupps" for special duties in the rear-areas. These units are stationed at Kowel, Rowno, Luck, Lemberg, Rawa-Ruska, Przemysl, Drohobycz, and Tarnopol.

Mid-Late July 1941   SK 4b in the Winniza region.

16 July - 7 August 1941 SK 4a advanced through Baranowka, Szepetowka, Berditschew, Proskurow, and Winniza. A Vorkommando was detailed to EGr Stab in Shitomir and a Hauptkommando to Tschernjachow and Radomyschl.

Late July 1941   EK 5 in the Berditschew area.

Early August 1941   SK 4b dispatched a Teilkommado to Kirowograd. EK 6 reported operational locales as Proskurow (100 kilometers southeast of Tarnopol) and Winniza.

7 August 1941   Elements of SK 4a under the command of SS-Standartenführer Paul Blobel executed 402 Jews in the Shitomir Pferdefriedhof. A Teilkommando was sent to Wasilkow (20 kilometers southwest of Kiev). EK 6 reported operations at Korosten.

9 August 1941   EK 5 advanced to Skwira (100 kilometers southwest of Kiev).

Mid-Late August 1941 A Teilkommando of SK 4a conducted sweeps to the south and southwest of Kiev (Fastow, Belaja Zerkow,and Taraschtscha). Other Teilkommandos operated to the west and northwest of Kiev (Korosten, Iwankow, Radomyschl, and Naroditschi). EK 6 reported in the Nowo-Ukrainka region.

14 August 1941 SK 4b entered Kirowograd.

17 August 1941 EGr Stab entered Perwomaisk (on the Bug River in south Ukraine).

19 August 1941 EK 4a murdered hundreds of Jews at Belaya-Tserkov.

20 August 1941 EGr Stab reported operational locale as Nowo-Ukrainka (60 kilometers northeast of Perwomaisk). Remained there until 25 September 1941.

21 August 1941 EK 4a shot scores of young children and infants at Belaya-Tserkov.

22 August 1941 EK 5 entered Zwiahel.

Early September 1941 Teilkommandos of SK 4b entered Krementschug (on the Dnjepr) with the Wehrmacht advance elements. EK 5 performed sweeps to the west and southwest of Kiev (Ulanow, Uledowka, and Chmielnik). EK 6 reported operational location as Kriwoi Rog with a Restkommando in Winniza.

Mid-September 1941 EK 5 at Bugslaw (southeast of Kiev) with Teilkommandos at Tscherkassy and Gorodischtsche.

19 September 1941 A Vorkommando of SK 4a entered Kiev with the Wehrmacht advance elements.

21 September 1941 Vorkommando of EGr Stab arrived at Kiev.

22/23 September 1941 EK 5 performed an operation in the Uman-Belaja Zerkow region. Approximately 1,412 Jews were executed from the villages of Sokolowka, Justungrad, Wolodarka, Tychy-Chutor, Tscherepin, Shurawlinka, and Cybulow.

25 September 1941 Remainder of EGr Stab and SK4a entered Kiev. In the week following the German occupation of Kiev, numerous bombs planted by the NKVD exploded causing great damage and loss of life. A meeting between Rasch, Blobel, Jeckeln, and General Eberhard (the city kommandant) resulted in the decision to take revenge on Kiev's Jewish population. SK 4b entered Poltawa and executed 565 patients in the city hospital.

29/30 September 1941 SK 4a, EGr Stab and two kommandos from Polizei-Regiment *Süd* massacred 33,771 Jews at Babi Yar outside of Kiev. EGr Stab remained in Kiev until Summer 1942.

Early October 1941
EK5 reported operational location as Kiev.

4 October 1941 A Vorkommando of SK 4a shot 537 Jews at Perejaslaw (75 kilometers southeast of Kiev).

5 October 1941 EK 6 performed sweeps in the Dnjeprbogen area : Dnjepropetrowsk, Dnjeprodershinsk, Saporoshje, and Nikopol.

8 October 1941 SK 4a conducted operations at Jagotin (30 kilometers southeast of Kiev).

14/16 October 1941 SK 4a performed an operation at Borispol.

18 October 1941 SK 4a conducted operations at Lubny (180 kilometers southeast of Kiev).

22 October 1941 SK 4a conducted operations at Koselez (50 kilometers northeast of Kiev).

29 October 1941 SK 4a performed an operation at Oster (60 kilometers northeast of Kiev).

Late October 1941 EK 5 sent a Teilkommando to the Pogrebischtsche-Pliskov area.

Early November 1941 SK 4a performed actions at Gornostaipol (75 kilometers north of Kiev), Dymer (40 kilometers north of Kiev), and at Oster.

5 November 1941 EK 5 reported operational location as Kiev with Teilkommandos at Shitomir, Rowno, and Winniza.

6/7 November 1941 EK 5 Teilkommando at Rowno assisted Ordnungspolizei with an anti-Jewish operation in the Rowno area ordered by HSSPf z.b.V. SS-Gruppenführer Gerret Korsemann. The two day operation claimed 15,000 lives.

17 November 1941 SK 4a formed an auxiliary unit, Vorkommando Charkow, in Poltawa.

23 November 1941 SK 4b and Vorkommando Charkow began an anti-Jewish operation in Charkow.

26 November 1941 SK 4b reported operational location as Sachnowtschina. A Teilkommando from EK 5 swept villages east of the Dnjepr near Kiev. EK 6 reported operational location as Stalino. SK 4a reported operational location as Kiev.

3 December 1941 SK 4b reported operational location as Kramatorskaja. Teilkommandos were sent on sweeps through Sachnowtschina, Losowaja (130 kilometers south of Charkow), Slawjansk, Konstantinowka, and Artemowsk.

January 1942 EK 5 personnel transferred to serve at stationary KdS-Dienststellen Kiev. SK 4a continued the liquidation of Jews in Charkow (including the use of gas vans) -- estimated 10 - 20,000 victims.

12 January 1942 SK 4b reported operational location as Kramatorskaja with Teilkommandos at Shitomir, Rowno, and Winniza.

Late January 1942 SK 4a performed actions at Belgorod and Melichowo (18 kilometers northeast of Belgorod).

6 February 1942 EGr C converted to stationary Sipo/SD Dienststellen : KdS Nikolajew (SS-Sturmbannführer Dr. Spann) and KdS Charkow (SS-Sturmbannführer Dr. Kranebitter).

9 February 1942 Establishment of KdS Kiew (SS-Obersturmbannführer Dr. Erich Ehrlinger), KdS Shitomir (SS-Sturmbannführer Dr. Ratzeberger), KdS Wolhynien (SS-Obersturmbannführer Dr. Pütz), and KdS Dnjepropetrowsk (SS-Sturmbannführer Mulde).

March 1942 SK 4b reported operational location as Gorlowka.

6 March 1942 EK 6 reported the following locales as "judenfrei" as a result of Teilkommando activities: Makejewka, Gorlowka, Brjansk, Grischinew, and Andrejewka. Operational location was still Stalino.

10 April 1942 First mention of Sonderkommando Plath (CO : SS-Hauptsturmführer Karl-Julius Plath). Unit was composed of elements 7. Kompanie / SS-Infanterie-Regiment 5 and 2. Kompanie / Polizei-Reserve-Bataillon 3. Conducted operations in the Dnjepropetrowsk and Krementschug areas : Lubny, Chorol, Konotop, and Jampol.

10 April 1942 Establishment of KdS Tschernigow (SS-Sturmbannführer Christensen).

July 1942 EK 5 disbanded to supply personnel to stationary KdS-Dienststellen in Kiev and Rowno.

24 July 1942 Establishment of KdS Stalino (SS-Obersturmbannführer Dr. Erich Körting).

September 1942 EK 6 reported operational location as Rostow (until German retreat of 1943). SK 4a reported operational locale as Stalingrad (until German retreat : then Kalatsch and Kursk).

Post July 1943 SK 4a posted successively at Kursk, Konotop, Bobruisk, and Minsk. Unit then disbanded at Minsk to provide personnel for BdS Russland Mitte und Weissruthenien Dienststelle (under SS-Standartenführer Dr. Erich Ehrlinger).

Autumn 1943 SK 4b reported operational location as Rostow. This was the unit's operational location until the German retreat on the southern front in 1943.

Einsatzgruppe D

Einsatzgruppe D, comprising 600 effectives, was attached to 11. Armee and had as its area of operation

Bessarabia, the southern Ukraine, the Crimea, and Ciscaucasia. In Summer 1941 it was responsible for the massacre of Jews forcibly expelled by the Rumanian Army into the German operational zone as the Rumanians re-occupied the provinces of Bessarabia and Bukovina. At the end of March 1943 it became known as Kampfgruppe Bierkamp. As of May 1943, only Sonderkommando 10a and Einsatzkommandos 11b and 12 continued to function.

Commanding Officers

- SS-Brigadeführer Dr. Otto Ohlendorf (6/22/41 - 6/42)
- SS-Brigadeführer Walter Bierkamp (7/42 - 7/43)

Sub-Units

Sonderkommando 10a
- SS-Standartenführer Heinrich Seetzen (6/22/41 - 7/42)
- SS-Obersturmbannführer Dr. Kurt Christmann (8/1/42 - 7/43)

Sonderkommando 10b
- SS-Obersturmbannführer Alois Persterer (6/22/41 - 2/43)
- SS-Sturmbannführer Eduard Jedamzik (2/43 - 5/43)

Einsatzkommando 11a (disbanded July 1942; part attached to Ek 11b; redesignated Ek 11)
- SS-Sturmbannführer Paul J. Zapp (6/22/41 - 7/42)

Einsatzkommando 11b
- unknown (6/22/41 - 7/41)
- SS-Sturmbannführer Bruno Müller (7/41 - 10/41)
- SS-Sturmbannführer Dr. Werner Braune (10/41 - 9/42)
- SS-Untersturmführer Paul Schulz (9/42 - 2/43)

Einsatzkommando 12
- SS-Obersturmbannführer Gustav Nosske (6/22/41 - 2/42)
- SS-Standartenfuhrer Dr. Erich Müller (2/42 - 10/42)

- SS-Obersturmbannführer Günther Herrmann (10/42 - 3/43)

Operational Record

EGr D advanced into the USSR along the route Düben-Pressburg-northern Burgenland-Arad-Mühlbach-Schässburg (Siebenburgen).

4/5 July 1941   EGr D entered Piatra-Neamt (40 kilometers west of Sereth) in northern Moldau.

6/9 July 1941   SK 10b assisted Rumanian occupation forces with anti-Jewish operations in Czernowitz (3,106 Jews shot).

9 July 1941   SK 10a entered Belzy (Bessarabien) and conducted an anti-Jewish operation. A Teilkommando of SK 10b conducted operations against "Jewish intellectuals" and Communists in Chotin. EK 11 performed actions in the Ghidigeni area (25 kilometers southwest of Barlad, central Moldau).

17 July 1941   SK 11a executed 551 Jews at Kishinew.

19 July 1941   SK 11a ordered to march from Ghidigeni along the route Barlad-Vaslui-Jassy-Ungheni-Cornesti-Sanesti to join up with the LIV. Armee Korps at Redeni   (Nordbessarabien).

22 July 1941   SK 10a entered Jampol and Balta (southern Ukraine).

29 July 1941   SK 10b ordered to Czernowitz and EK 12 to Jassy.
Late July 1941   SK 10b reported at Tighina (Bendery) on the lower Dnjestr.

2 August 1941   SK 10a reported operational location as Pestschanka with a Teilkommando at Kodyma (between Jampol and Balta).

3 August 1941   SK 10b stationed to Mogilew-Podolski.
4 August 1941   SK 11a at Kishinew (68 Jews shot).

7 August 1941   EGr Stab at Olschanka (west of Jampol on the Dnjestr).

Mid-August 1941   EGr deployed along the line Balta-Perwomaisk. General unit march was to the southeast of this line. Stab located at Ananjew (50 kilometers southeast of Balta). SK 10a conducted operations at Beresowka (70 kilometers north of Odessa) and between Otschakow (on the Black Sea) and the Bug River. EK 12 located at Wosnessensk.

17/18 August 1941   SK 11a occupied Nikolajew and executed 3,500 Jews.

20 August 1941   A Vorkommando of SK 11a entered Cherson. SK 11b operated near Odessa.

Late August 1941   EGr reported a total of 27,500 Jews killed as a result of operations to date.

Early September 1941 SK 10a operated at Christoforowka (40 kilometers northeast of Nikolajew) with a Vorkommando in Berislaw (80 kilometers northeast of Kherson).

11 September 1941   SK 10a operated in the region northeast of Nikolajew.

Mid-September 1941 SK 10b finished sweeps of Ananjew, Wosnessensk (southeast of Perwomaisk), regions east of the Bug River, and in the Novaja-Odessa area that were begun in mid-August.

16/30 September 1941 SK 11a operated in the region north of Cherson and in the area of Perekop. Approximately 4,000 Jews shot.

18 September 1941   EGr operational locale was Nikolajew.

20 September 1941   EK 12 reported operational locale as Nikolajew with 2 Restkommandos in Speyer. Conducted actions in the region west of the line Melitopol-Wasiljewka-Dnjepr   bend south of Saporoshje.

September/ October 1941   SK 10a conducted actions in Berislaw, Genitschesk, Melitopol (north of the Azov Sea), and Mariupol (on the Azov Sea). SK 10b conducted actions in the the region south of the lower

Dnjepr towards the Crimea. SK 11b continued operations in the Odessa area.

30 September 1941   EGr reported 35,782 Jews and Communists killed as of this date.

October 1941   SK 10b located at Skadowsk (south of the lower Dnjepr on the Black Sea). SK 11a located at Bolschaja Majatschka.

Late October 1941   SK 10a located at Taganrog with Nachkommandos in Melitopol, Brjansk, and Mariupol.

Early November 1941   EK 12 reported operational location as Michailowka (45 kilometers north of Melitopol) with a Restkommando at Nikolajew. Later the unit reported from Stalino with a Teilkommando in Nowotscherkask (northeast of Rostov). SK 10b advanced through Kalantschak, Perekop, and Simferopol to new operational location at Feodossija on the Crimean southcoast and then deployed a Vorkommando to Kertscha and Teilkommandos to Aluschta and Sudak. SK 11a advanced through Perekop, Simferopol, Jalta with Teilkommandos sent to Bachtschissarai (between Simferopol and Sewastopol), Jewpatorija, and Sewastopol. SK 11b advanced towards Simferopol.

21 November 1941   SK 10a and EK 12 detailed to follow advance through Taganrog, Rostov, Stalino, and into the North Caucasus. SK 10b, EK 11a, and EK 11b detailed for operations in the Crimean peninsula. Stab reported operational locale as Simferopol (Crimea).

Mid-December 1941   SK 11a sent a Teilkommando to Alupka (southwest of Yalta). SK 11b reported operational location as Simferopol with Teilkommandos at Jewpatorija, Karasubasar (65 kilometers west of Feodossija),and Aluschta (30 kilometers northwest of Yalta).

December 1941/ May 1942   EK 12 operated from Federowka (20 kilometers north of Melitopol).

January 1942   SK 10b reported at Sudak and Stary-

Krym with a Teilkommando at Dshankoi (northern Crimea). SK 11a reported its operational location as Bachtschissarai with Teilkommandos at Alupka and Yalta.

Late January 1942   Auxiliary units of EK 12 were at Pologi (90 kilometers southeast of Saporoshje), Seitler (65 kilometers southeast Dshankoi on the Crimea), Sarabus (15 kilometers northwest of Simferopol),and Bijuk-Ass. SK 10b reported its operational location as Prochladny (80 kilometers southeast of Pjatigorsk) and Naltschik with Teilkommandos at Nowo-Pawlowskaja (40 kilometers southeast of Pjatigorsk), Atschikulak (140 kilometers northeast of Pjatigorsk), Mosdok (on the Terek), and Werk Akbasch.

February 1942   SK 11a sent Teilkommandos to Simeis (3 kilometers southwest of Alupka) and Kousch (22 kilometers southeast of Bachtschissarai).

20 February 1942   Auxiliary unit of EK 12 reported at Gulnj-Pole (20 kilometers north of Pologi).

Late March 1942   EGr reported that the southern half of the Crimea is "judenfrei". The total number of victims for all operations by the group was reported as 91,678.

April 1942   K 11a operated from Kokkosy (17 kilometers northwest of Yalta) with Teilkommandos at Kousch, Yalta, and Simeis.

June 1942   EK 12 reported operational location as Starobeschewo with Teilkommandos at Amwrossijewka (80 kilometers northwest of Taganrog), Uspenskaja (60 kilometers north-northwest of Taganrog), Karakubstroj (40 kilometers , and Fedorstka. SK 11a Teilkommando at Kousch   redeployed to Bachtschissarai.

July 1942   Stab reported operational locale as Taganrog. EK 12 reported operational locale as Nowotscherkask. EK 11a and EK 11b joined to form Einsatzkommando 11.

1/3 July 1942   Elements of SK 11a from Kokkosy entered Sewastopol. SK 11a disbanded to provide personnel to KdS Taurien (SS-Sturmbannführer Zapp) based in   Simferopol. Minor elements absorbed by SK 11b.

August 1942   Stab reported operational locale as Woroschilowsk (north Caucasus). SK 10a reported operational locale as Krasnodar (Kuban) with Teilkommandos at Noworossijsk, Jejsk, Anapa, Temrjuk, Warenikowskaja (35 kilometers northeast of Anapa), and Werchne-Bakanskaja (15 kilometers northwest of Noworossijisk). EK 11 reported operational locale as Maikop with Teilkommandos at Belaja Glina (50 kilometers southeast of Rostov), Kropotkin (100 kilometers north of Maikop), Armawir (west of Stavropol), Tscherkesk (90 kilometers south of Stavropol), Labinskaja (50 kilometers southwest of Armawir), and Chadyshenskaja (50 kilometers southeast of Maikop).

Late August 1942   EK 12 reported operational locale as Pjatigorsk (Caucasus) with Teilkommandos in Salsk (150 kilometers southeast of Rostov), Woroschilowsk, Kislowodsk (30 kilometers southwest of Pjatigorsk), Budennowsk (120 kilometers northeast of Pjatigorsk), and Stepnoi (60 kilometers north of Mosdok on the Terek).

October 1942   Formation of Sonderkommando Astrachan based in Elista.

February 1943   SK 10a, SK 10b, EK 11 and EK 12 were part of the general withdrawl from the Caucasus. Sent to the Pripjet Marshes for anti-partisan operations. Stab relocated to Owrutsch (100 kilometers west of the Pripjet mouth in the Dnjepr).

Sources
(Reitlinger, 1961) (Krausnik, 1981) (Aufbau [New York], 23 August 1946, pp. 1-2)
(Krausnik, 1968) (Lozowick, 1987) (Manvell, 1969) (MacLean, 1999)
(Jäger-Bericht : "Gesamtaufstellung der im Bereich des EK. 3 bis zum 1. Dez. 1941 durchgeführten Exekutionen", Zentrale Stelle des Landesjustizverwaltungen, File No. 108, Frames 27-38)
(Gesamtbericht der Einsatzgruppe A vom 16. Oktober 1941 bis 31. Januar 1942 : Zahlen der Einsatzgruppe A bis 1.2.1942 durchgeführten Exekutionen; Institut für Zeitgeschichte, München, Fb 101/35)

Höheren SS-und Polizeiführer (HSSPf)

The post of HSSPf was created on 13 November 1937 by a decree of Reichsführer-SS Heinrich Himmler in his role as Reich Minister of the Interior. The role of an individual HSSPf was to promote SS - Police integration in a designated region and to provide local political direction for both organizations. Initially the HSSPf were intended to become active during a wartime mobilization and then only to address issues of SS and police employment. Once the war had begun, however, Reichsführer-SS Himmler lost no time in augmenting their duties until the HSSPf were invested with far-reaching authority. This was especially true in the occupied territories where there existed no traditional bureaucratic structures capable of resisting such a power-grab. Since for all practical purposes the HSSPf were accountable directly to Reichsführer-SS Himmler, they functioned independently of other authorities to whom they were in theory subordinate. Thus, the HSSPf were responsible for implementing occupation policies as envisioned by the Reichsführer-SS which were often at odds with those of the German civilian and military authorities. The HSSPf were aided in their tasks by a series of lesser regional leaders under the following simplified chain of command :

- Reichsführer-SS
- HSSPf / HSSPf zbV
- Befehlshaber der Sicherheitspolizei (BdS)
- Kommandeur der Sicherheitspolizei (KdS)
- SS- und Polizeiführer (SSPf / SSPf zbV)
- Polizeigebeitsführer (Pgf)

While the coordination functions of the HSSPf position included administrative and judicial duties of a normal bureaucratic nature, the control aspect subsumed the gross atrocities that occurred at the orders of an HSSPf. The control aspect included such duties as :

1) functioning in the role of Reichskommisar zur Festigung des deutschen Volkstums (State Commissar for the Strengthening of Germandom) under which authority forced evacuations of civilians occurred,

2) anti-partisan operations in occupied territories,

3) the extermination of European Jewry, and

4) the evacuation of POW, labor, and concentration camps to avoid the inmate's rescue; these actions often went hand-in-hand with mass executions and death marchs.

An individual HSSPf could often draw on extensive manpower reserves for the various "security and cleansing" actions that they prosecuted in their operational area. For example, the number of security personnel available to the HSSPf Ukraine on 15 November 1942 was as follows :

4,228	German Schutzpolizei
15,665	Ukrainian Schutzpolizei
5,966	German Gendarmerie
55,094	Ukrainian Gendarmerie
35,000	Ukrainian Schuma battalion volunteers

This regional security apparatus was often augmented by the use of any military units available (including Waffen-SS) in the given area. For example, in Autumn 1941, the HSSPf Ukraine also had operational control of the 1. SS-Infanterie (mot.) Brigade.

In their command role for an occupied territory, the HSSPf exercised control over any Einsatzgruppen that operated in their region. Thus, they were invariably responsible at the strategic planning level for a great number of extermination actions. See the section on the Einsatzgruppen for a fuller treatment of this topic. A few examples follow :

- HSSPf Ostland (Prützmann) - 10,600 civilians killed [Ereignismeldung UdSSR, *Arad et al., 1989*]

- HSSPf Russland-Mitte (Bach)- 2,278 Jews killed in Minsk [Institute für Zeitgeschichte, München, NO 3143]; 3,726 Jews killed in Mogilev on 14 November 1941 [IfZ, München, NO 2825]

- HSSPf Ukraine (Jeckeln) -- 33,000 Jews killed in Kiev on 2 October 1941 [IfZ, München, NO 3137]; 23,600 Jews killed in Kamenez-Podolsk [report 11 September 1941 / IfZ, München, NO 3154]; 10,000 Jews killed in Dnjepropetrovsk [report 19 November 1941 / IfZ, München, NO2832]; 15,000 Jews killed in Rowno [report 7-8 November 1941 / IfZ, München, NO2827];1303 Jews killed in Berditschev [report 19 September 1941 / IfZ, München, NO3149]; 514 Jews killed in Starokonstantinov [Central State Archives CSSR 147]

In the month of August 1941 alone, approximately 44,125 civilians were killed in the operational zone of HSSPf Ukraine. The Autumn of 1941 saw the beginning of a new type of operation : the *Bandenkampfaktionen* whereby killing campaigns were carried out under the guise of anti-partisan actions. These operations were under the direct control of the regional HSSPf. For example, HSSPf Ukraine / SS-Obergruppenführer Friedrich Jeckeln's Aktion *Sumpffieber* [report 6 November 1941 / Central State Archives CSSR 392] achieved the following results: 389 bandits killed, 1,274 suspected bandits killed and 8,350 Jews executed.

As the body count climbed, concerns about security arose. Field units were instructed to use euphemisms for Jews such as *Plünderer* (looters) and *Brandstifter* (arsonists). By the end of 1941 the total number of civilians killed in all of the HSSPf areas in the USSR had reached at least one-half million. Operations continued at a pace unabated into 1942. Typical were those directed by SSPf Weissruthenien / SS-Brigadeführer Kurt von Gottberg :

- Unternehmen *Nürnberg* -- report of 26 November 1942 [IfZ, München, NO1732]; 798 bandits killed, 383 suspected bandits killed, 1,826 Jews executed, 7 gypsies executed

- Unternehmen *Hamburg* [IfZ, München NO5156] -- in the area of Slonim (Weissruthenien); December 1942 - January 1943; 2,958 Jews were executed

- Unternehmen *Altona* -- in the Kossow-Byten area (Weissruthenien); January 1943; 785 civilians executed

- Unternehmen *Hornung* [IfZ, München, NO1732] -- 8-26 February 1943; 3,300 Jews executed

SS-Brigadeführer von Gottberg followed these actions with others : Unternehmen *Zauberflöte* (17-22 April 1943), Unternehmen *Cottbus* (28 April - 21 June 1943), Ghetto-Raümung Sluzk (8 February 1943), and Ghetto-Raümung Glebokie (21 August 1943).

The time period 1940-1942 also saw the rounding up and ghettoization of those Jews still alive in German occupied territories throughout Europe and European Russia. In some cases, both small (Sluzk) and large (Riga) ghettos were liquidated on the spot through the use of firing squads and /or gas vans. Many more Jews, however, were destined to be shipped to the death camps in Poland. All of these activities occurred with the active involvement and direction of the regional HSSPf. While the orders might have come from Berlin, the HSSPf were the key personnel in each region for seeing that those orders were carried out properly. For example, the deathcamps of *Aktion Reinhardt* in the Generalgouvernement (Belzec, Sobibor, and Treblinka) were under the personal direction of SSPf Lublin / SS-Brigadeführer Odilo Globocnik.

During the later years of the war several HSSPf regions were designated as *Banden Kampfgebiete* due to the sustained level of partisan activity occurring in them. As of 21 June 1943 the regions so designated were : Oberkrain und Untersteiermark, Generalgouvernement, Bialystok (Bezirk), Russland-Mitte, Ukraine, and Kroatien. On 3 April 1944 the region Italien was added to the list.

HSSPf and SSPf Regional Listing
HSSPf Nordost (Wehrkreis I)
- SS-Gruppenführer Wilhelm Rediess (6/28/38 - 6/19/40)
- SS-Gruppenführer Jakob Sporrenburg (6/21/40 - 5/1/41)

- SS-Obergruppenführer Hans-Adolf Prütz-mann (5/1/41 - 5/8/45)
- SS-Gruppenführer George Ebrecht (6/21/41 - 12/1/44) acting deputy
- SS-Gruppenführer Hans Haltermann (7/7/44 - 1/9/45) acting deputy
- SS-Gruppenführer Otto Hellwig (1/9/45 - 5/8/45) acting deputy

SSPf Bialystok
- SS-Brigadeführer Otto Hellwig (5/21/43 - 7/15/44)

HSSPf Ostsee (Wehrkreis II)
- SS-Obergruppenführer Emil Mazuw (8/28/38 - 5/45)

HSSPf Spree (Wehrkreis III)
- SS-Obergruppenführer August Heissmeyer (9/2/39 - 5/8/45)
- SS-Brigadeführer Max Schneller (2/20/43 - 5/8/45) acting deputy

HSSPf Elbe (Wehrkreis IV)
- SS-Obergruppenführer Theodor Berkelmann (6/28/38 - 4/20/40)
- SS-Obergruppenführer Udo von Woyrsch (4/20/40 - 2/11/44)
- SS-Gruppenführer Ludolf von Alvensleben (2/11/44 - 5/8/45)

HSSPf Südwest (Wehrkreis V)
- SS-Gruppenführer Kurt Kaul (9/6/39 - 4/21/43)
- SS-Obergruppenführer Otto Hofmann (4/21/43 - 5/45)

HSSPf West (Wehrkreis VI)
- SS-Obergruppenführer Fritz Weitzel (6/11/38 - 4/20/40)
- SS-Gruppenführer Theodor Berkelmann (4/20/40 - 7/9/40)
- SS-Obergruppenführer Friedrich Jeckeln (7/12/40 - 6/29/41)
- SS-Obergruppenführer Karl Gutenberger (6/29/41 - 5/8/45)

HSSPf Süd (Wehrkreis VII)
- SS-Obergruppenführer Friedrich Karl Freiherr von Eberstein (3/12/38 - 5/45)
- SS-Brigadeführer Anton Vogler (2/1/45 - 4/45) acting deputy
- SS-Obergruppenführer Wilhelm Koppe (4/45 - 5/45)

HSSPf Südost (Wehrkreis VIII)
- SS-Gruppenführer Erich von dem Bach-Zelewski (6/28/38 - 5/20/41)
- SS-Obergruppenführer Ernst Heinrich Schmauser (5/20/41 - 2/15/45) MIA
- SS-Brigadeführer Dr. Walter Bierkamp (2/20/45 - 3/17/45) temporary
- SS-Obergruppenführer Richard Hildebrandt (3/17/45 - 5/8/45)

SSPf Kattowitz
- SS-Brigadeführer Christoph Diehm (10/44 - 1945)

HSSPf Fulda-Werra (Wehrkreis IX)
- SS-Obergruppenführer Josias Erbprinz zu Waldeck-Pyrmont (10/6/38 - 5/45)

HSSPf Nordsee (Wehrkreis X)
- SS-Gruppenführer Hans Adolf Prützmann (6/28/38 - 5/1/41)
- SS-Gruppenführer Rudolf Querner (5/1/41 - 1/30/43)
- SS-Gruppenführer Georg-Henning Graf v. Bassewitz-Behr (2/16/43 - 5/45)

HSSPf Mitte (Wehrkreis XI)
- SS-Obergruppenführer Friedrich Jeckeln (6/28/38 - 7/11/40)
- SS-Gruppenführer Günther Pancke (7/11/40 - 9/15/43)
- SS-Oberführer Wilhelm Fuchs (7/8/43 - 9/15/43) acting deputy
- SS-Obergruppenführer Hermann Höfle (9/15/43 - 10/5/44)
- SS-Obergruppenführer Rudolf Querner (10/5/44 - 5/8/45)

HSSPf Rhein-Westmark   (Wehrkreis XII)
"Rhein"
- SS-Gruppenführer Richard Hildebrandt (4/1/39 - 10/1/39)
- SS-Gruppenführer Jakob Sporrenburg (10/1/39 - 7/24/40)
- SS-Gruppenführer Erwin Rösener (7/24/40 - 11/11/41)
- SS-Obergruppenführer Theodor Berkelmann (12/10/41 - 5/21/43)

"Westmark"
- SS-Obergruppenführer Theodor Berkelmann (7/19/40 - 5/21/43)

"Rhein-Westmark"
- SS-Obergruppenführer Theodor Berkelmann (5/21/43 - 11/11/43)
- SS-Gruppenführer Jürgen Stroop (11/11/43 - 5/8/45)

HSSPf Main (Wehrkreis XIII)
- SS-Obergruppenführer Friedrich Karl Freiherr von Eberstein (3/38 - 12/17/42)
- SS-Obergruppenführer Dr. Benno Martin (12/17/42 - 5/8/45)

HSSPf Donau (Wehrkreis XVII)
- SS-Gruppenführer Dr. Ernst Kaltenbrunner (9/11/38 - 1/31/43)
- SS-Obergruppenführer Rudolf Querner (1/31/43 - 10/5/44)
- SS-Gruppenführer Walter Schimana (10/5/44 - 5/8/45)

HSSPf Alpenland (Wehrkreis XVIII)
- SS-Brigadeführer Alfred Rodenbücher (4/25/39 - 4/30/41)
- SS-Brigadeführer Dr. Gustav-Adolf Scheel (4/30/41 - 11/24/41)
- SS-Obergruppenführer Erwin Rösener (11/24/41 - 5/8/45)
- SS-Brigadeführer Erwin Schulz (5/1/44 - 5/28/44) acting deputy

SSPf Salzburg
- SS-Brigadeführer Erwin Schulz (4/45 - 5/45)

HSSPf Böhmen-Mähren
- SS-Obergruppenführer Karl-Hermann Frank (4/28/39 - 4/45)
- SS-Obergruppenführer Richard Hildebrandt (4/45 - 5/45)

HSSPf Weichsel (Wehrkreis XX)
- SS-Obergruppenführer Richard Hildebrandt (9/21/39 - 4/20/43)
- SS-Oberführer Hellmuth Willich (2/9/42 - 3/9/42) acting deputy
- SS-Gruppenführer Friedrich Katzmann (4/20/43 - 5/45)

HSSPf Warthe (Wehrkreis XXI)
- SS-Obergruppenführer Wilhelm Koppe (10/9/39 - 11/9/43)
- SS-Obergruppenführer Theodor Berkelmann (11/9/43 - 12/27/43) died
- SS-Gruppenführer Heinz Reinefarth (1/29/44 - 12/30/44)
- SS-Oberführer Friedrich Gehrhardt (8/44 - 12/30/44) acting deputy
- SS-Gruppenführer Willy Schmelcher (12/30/44 - 5/45)

HSSPf Ost
- SS-Gruppenführer Theodor Eicke (9/10/39 - 10/1/39)
- SS-Obergruppenführer Friedrich-Wilhelm Krüger (10/4/39 - 11/9/43)
- SS-Obergruppenführer Wilhelm Koppe (11/9/43 - 4/45)

SSPf Lemberg
- SS-Gruppenführer Friedrich Katzmann (4/8/41 - 4/20/43)
- SS-Standartenführer Willi Ost (4/20/43 - 7/29/43)
- SS-Brigadeführer Theobald Thier (7/29/43 - 2/25/44)
- SS-Brigadeführer Christoph Diehm (2/25/44 - 9/16/44)

SSPf Lublin
- SS-Gruppenführer Odilo Globocnik (11/39 - 8/16/43)
- SS-Gruppenführer Jakob Sporrenburg (8/16/43 - 11/25/44)

SSPf Krakau

- SS-Gruppenführer Karl Zech (11/24/39 - 10/1/40)
- SS-Oberführer Hans Schwedler (10/1/40 - 8/4/41)
- SS-Oberführer Julian Scherner (8/4/41 - 3/1/44)
- SS-Brigadeführer Theobald Thier (3/1/44 - 1/19/45)

SSPf Radom

- SS-Brigadeführer Friedrich Katzmann (11/30/39 - 8/8/41)
- SS-Brigadeführer Carl Oberg (8/8/41 - 5/12/42)
- SS-Brigadeführer Dr. Herbert Böttcher (5/12/42 - 1/16/45)

SSPf Warschau

- SS-Gruppenführer Paul Moder (11/14/39 - 8/4/41)
- SS-Oberführer Arpad Wigand (8/4/41 - 4/23/43)
- SS-Oberführer Dr. Ferdinand von Sammern-Frankenegg
  (7/22/42 - 4/19/43) acting deputy
- SS-Brigadeführer Jürgen Stroop (4/19/43 - 9/13/43)
- SS-Brigadeführer Franz Kutschera (9/25/43 - 2/1/44)
- SS-Oberführer Walter Stein (2/1/44 - 3/31/44) acting deputy
- SS-Brigadeführer Paul Otto Geibel (3/31/44 - 2/1/45)

HSSPf Nord

- SS-Obergruppenführer Friedrich Weitzel (4/20/40 - 6/19/40)
- SS-Obergruppenführer Wilhelm Rediess (6/19/40 - 5/8/45)

SSPf Nord-Norwegen

- SS-Oberführer Heinz Roch (11/21/44 - 5/45)

SSPf Mittel-Norwegen

- SS-Oberführer Richard Kaaserer (11/28/44 - 5/45)

SSPf Süd-Norwegen

- SS-Gruppenführer Jakob Sporrenburg (11/21/44 - 5/45)

HSSPf Nordwest

- SS-Obergruppenführer Hans-Albin Rauter (6/26/40 - 5/8/45)

HSSPf Ostland und Russland-Nord

- SS-Gruppenführer Hans-Adolf Prützmann (6/29/41 - 11/1/41)
- SS-Obergruppenführer Friedrich Jeckeln (1/11/41 - 5/45)
- SS-Gruppenführer Dr. Hermann Behrends (1/30/45 - 5/45) acting deputy

SSPf Estland

- SS-Brigadeführer Hinrich Möller (8/4/41 - 4/1/44)
- SS-Brigadeführer Walther Schröder (4/1/44 - 10/19/44)

SSPf Lettland

- SS-Brigadeführer Walther Schröder (8/4/41 - 10/19/44)
- SS-Oberführer Karl Schäfer (4/7/42 - 4/26/42) acting deputy
- SS-Oberführer Wilhelm Fuchs (6/42) acting deputy

SSPf Litauen

- SS-Brigadeführer Lucian Wysocki (8/11/41 - 7/2/43)
- SS-Oberführer Karl Schäfer (4/25/42 - 5/22/42) acting deputy
- SS-Brigadeführer Hermann Harm (7/2/43 - 4/8/44) SS-Brigadeführer Kurt Hintze (4/8/44 - 9/15/44)

SSPf Weissruthenien

- SS-Gruppenführer Jakob Sporrenburg (7/21/41 - 8/14/41)
- SS-Brigadeführer Carl Zenner (8/14/41 - 5/22/42)
- SS-Oberführer Karl Schäfer (5/22/42 - 7/21/42)
- SS-Brigadeführer Curt von Gottberg (7/21/42 - 9/22/43)

- SS-Brigadeführer Walter Schimana (7/21/42 - 7/15/43) acting deputy
- SS-Standartenführer Erich Ehrlinger (9/22/43 - 4/1/44)

[after 4/43 passed to command of HSSPf Russland-Mitte]

HSSPf Russland-Süd
- SS-Obergruppenführer Friedrich Jeckeln (6/23/41 - 12/11/41)
- SS-Obergruppenführer Hans Adolf Prützmann (12/11/41 - 3/18/44)

[on 10/29/43 this position was designated Höchster SS-und Polizeiführer im Reichskommissariat Ukraine und Russland-Süd, i.e. --- HöSSPf Ukraine und Russland-Süd]

SSPf Rowno
- SS-Brigadeführer Gerrett Korsemann (8/1/41 - 1/1/42)

[absorbed into SSPf Wolhynien-Brest Litovsk on 1/1/42]

SSPf Wolhynien-Brest Litovsk
- SS-Brigadeführer Waldemar Wappenhans (9/4/41 - 9/1/42)

[renamed SSPf Wolhynien-Luzk in 9/42]

SSPf Wolhynien-Luzk
- SS-Brigadeführer Wilhelm Günther (9/1/42 - 6/6/44)
- SS-Brigadeführer Ernst Hartmann (2/10/44 - 9/6/44) acting deputy

SSPf Nikolajew
- SS-Brigadeführer Fritz Tittmann (10/22/41 - 9/1/42)
- SS-Brigadeführer Waldemar Wappenhans (9/1/42 - 4/43)
- SS-Brigadeführer Paul Zimmermann (4/43 - 10/10/43)
- SS-Brigadeführer Rudolf Weiss (10/10/43 - 3/21/44) acting deputy
- SS-Gruppenführer Ludolf von Alvensleben (10/6/43 - 2/11/44)

SSPf Charkow
- SS-Brigadeführer Willy Tensfeld (8/4/41 - 5/19/43)
- SS-Oberführer Bernhard Fischer-Schweder (10/10/42 - 10/22/42) acting deputy
- SS-Gruppenführer Hans Haltermann (5/19/43 - 9/11/43)
- SS-Brigadeführer Dr. Günther Merk (9/11/43 - 10/18/43)

SSPf Dnjepropetrowsk-Krivoi Rog
- SS-Brigadeführer Georg Graf von Basse-witz-Behr (11/11/41 - 8/1/42)
- SS-Brigadeführer Hermann Harm (8/1/42 - 10/4/42)
- SS-Brigadeführer Waldemar Wappenhans (10/4/42 - 10/4/43)
- SS-Brigadeführer Karl Schäfer (10/4/43 - 11/2/43)

SSPf Kiew
- SS-Gruppenführer Hans Haltermann (10/1/41 - 5/19/43)
- SS-Gruppenführer Paul Hennicke (5/1/43 - 12/43)
- SS-Oberführer Bernhard Fischer-Schweder (10/10/42 - 10/22/42) acting deputy

SSPf Stanislav-Rostow
- SS-Brigadeführer Dr. Richard Wendler (8/4/41 - 5/27/42)
- SS-Gruppenführer Gerrett Korsemann (5/27/42 - 10/1/42)
- SS-Gruppenführer Paul Hennicke (10/1/42 - 5/1/43)
  [renamed SSPf Rostow-Awdejewka on 1/27/42]

SSPf Shitomir
- SS-Brigadeführer Otto Hellwig (10/22/41 - 5/20/43)
- SS-Brigadeführer Willy Tensfeld (4/19/43 - 5/20/43) acting deputy
- SS-Brigadeführer Willy Schmelcher (5/5/43 - 9/25/43)
- SS-Obersturmbannführer Hans Traupe (9/25/43 - 10/21/43)

- SS-Oberführer Ernst Hartmann (10/31/43 - 1/25/44)
- SS-Brigadeführer Christoph Diehm (1/25/44 - 2/25/44)

SSPf Taurien-Krim-Simferopol
- SS-Gruppenführer Ludolf von Alvensleben (11/19/41 - 10/6/43)
- SS-Oberführer Heinz Roch (3/3/43 - 12/25/43) acting deputy
- SS-Obergruppenführer Richard Hildebrandt (12/25/43 - 9/5/44) acting deputy

SSPf Stalino-Donezgebiet
- SS-Brigadeführer Hans Döring (11/19/41 - 5/19/43)
- SS-Brigadeführer Willy Tensfeld (5/19/43 - 9/4/43)
- SS-Oberführer Dr. Rudolf Heuckenkamp (8/42) acting deputy

SSPf Tschernigow
- SS-Brigadeführer Ludolf von Alvensleben (10/22/41 - 11/19/41)
- SS-Brigadeführer Willy Schmelcher (11/19/41 - 7/1/43)
- SS-Oberführer Ernst Hartmann (7/1/43 - 10/31/43)

SSPf Nord-Kaukasien
- SS-Standartenführer Karl-Heinz Bürger (8/21/42 - 10/1/42)

SSPf Awdejewka
- SS-Standartenführer Karl-Heinz Bürger (10/1/42 - 12/1/43)

SSPf Kaukasien-Kuban
- SS-Brigadeführer Konstantin Kammerhofer (8/21/42 - 11/11/42)
- SS-Brigadeführer Theobald Thier (11/14/42 - 5/3/43)

SSPf Bergvolker-Ordshonikidse
- SS-Oberführer Wilhelm Günther (5/7/42 - 8/23/42)

SSPf Aserbeidschan
- SS-Brigadeführer Konstantin Kammerhofer (11/14/42 - 4/21/43)

SSPf Kertsch-Tamanhalbinsel
- SS-Brigadeführer Theobald Thier (5/3/43 - 7/29/43)

HSSPf Schwarzes Meer
- SS-Gruppenführer Ludolf von Alvensleben (10/29/43 - 12/25/43)
- SS-Obergruppenführer Richard Hildebrandt (12/25/43 - 9/16/44)

  [post dissolved on 9/13/44 and reformed in Rumania as HSSPf Siebenbürgen]
- SS-Obergruppenführer Artur Phleps (9/16/44 - 9/18/44)

HSSPf Russland-Mitte und Weissruthenien
- SS-Obergruppenführer Erich von dem Bach-Zelewski (5/1/41 - 6/21/44)
- SS-Gruppenführer Carl Graf von Pückler-Burghaus (1/2/42 - 3/24/43) acting deputy
- SS-Gruppenführer Gerret Korsemann (3/24/43 - 7/5/43) acting deputy
- SS-Obergruppenführer Kurt von Gottberg (7/5/43 - 8/7/44) acting deputy

SSPf Bialystok
- SS-Standartenführer Werner Fromm (1/18/42 - 1/30/43)
- SS-Brigadeführer Otto Hellwig (5/20/43 - 7/18/44)
- SS-Oberführer Heinz Roch (7/18/44 - 10/22/44)

SSPf Saratow
- SS-Standartenführer Walter Schimana (9/4/41 - 11/30/41)

SSPf Pripjet
- SS-Brigadeführer Ernst Hartmann (12/18/43 - 9/6/44)

SSPf Weissruthenien [after 4/43, see above]

SSPf Mogilew
- SS-Brigadeführer Georg Graf von Bassewitz-Behr (8/1/42 - 4/20/43)

- SS-Brigadeführer Franz Kutschera (4/20/43 - 9/20/43)
- SS-Gruppenführer Hans Haltermann (9/20/43 - 7/12/44)

HSSPf Serbien, Sandschak und Montenegro
- SS-Gruppenführer August Edler von Meyszner (1/24/42 - 4/1/44)
- SS-Gruppenführer Dr. Hermann Behrends (4/1/44 - 10/44)

SSPf Sandschak
- SS-Standartenführer Karl von Krempler (9/43 - 6/21/44)
- SS-Oberführer Richard Kaaserer (6/21/44 - 11/28/44)

SSPf Montenegro
- SS-Brigadeführer Richard Fiedler (10/1/43 - 10/20/44)

SSPf Frankreich
- SS-Obergruppenführer Carl Albrecht Oberg (5/12/42 - 11/28/44)

SSPf Metz
- SS-Brigadeführer Anton Dunckern (10/1/44 - 11/18/44)

SSPf Ober-Elsass
- SS-Obersturmbannführer Friedrich Suhr (12/1/44 - 5/45)

HSSPf Kroatien
- SS-Gruppenführer Konstantin Kammerhofer (3/13/43 - 1/10/45)

Polizeigebietsführer Agram
- SS-Brigadeführer Willi Brandner (7/10/43 - 12/28/44) wounded
- SS-Oberführer Otto Reich (12/28/44 - 1/6/45)

Polizeigebietsführer Banja-Luca
- SS-Standartenführer Paul Dahm (8/2/43 - 4/20/45)

Polizeigebietsführer Essegg
- SS-Brigadeführer Dr. Ferdinand von Sammern-Frankenegg (7/15/43 - 9/20/44) KIA
- SS-Standartenführer Paul Dahm (9/20/44 - 4/20/45)

Polizeigebietsführer Knin
- SS-Oberführer Richard Kaaserer (7/27/43 - 5/20/44)

Polizeigebietsführer Sarajewo
- SS-Oberführer Werner Fromm (1/1/43 - 4/26/44)

HSSPf Griechenland
- SS-Brigadeführer Jürgen Stroop (9/8/43 - 10/4/43)
- SS-Gruppenführer Walter Schimana (10/18/43 - 9/24/44)
- SS-Brigadeführer Hermann Franz (9/24/44 - 11/18/44)

HöSSPf Italien
- SS-Obergruppenführer Karl Wolff (9/23/43 - 5/8/45)

SSPf Mittelitalien-Verona
- SS-Oberführer Karl-Heinz Bürger (12/1/43 - 5/45)

SSPf Oberitalien-West
- SS-Brigadeführer Willy Tensfeld (1/23/44 - 5/45)

SSPf Oberitalien-Mitte
- SS-Oberführer Ernst Hildebrandt (4/44 - 10/44)

SSPf Bozen
- SS-Brigadeführer Karl Brunner (9/15/43 - 5/45)

HSSPf Adriatisches Küstenland
- SS-Gruppenführer Odilo Globocnik (9/13/43 - 5/45)

SS-Polizeigebietskommandeur Quarnero
- SS-Obersturmbannführer Wilhelm Traub (10/27/44 - 1945)

SS-Polizeigebietskommandeur Istrien
- SS-Brigadeführer Erasmus Freiherr von Mals-en-Ponickau (10/27/44 - 1945)

SS-Polizeigebietskommandeur Triest
- SS-Sturmbannführer Wilhelm Michalsen (10/27/44 - 1945)

SS-Polizeigebietskommandeur Görz
- SS-Brigadeführer Karl Taus (5/1/44 - 5/45)

SS-Polizeigebietskommandeur Friaul
- SS-Standartenführer Ludolf von Alvensleben (10/27/44 - 1945)

[brother of the HSSPf with same name]

HSSPf Dänemark
- SS-Obergruppenführer Günther Pancke (10/6/43 - 5/5/45)

Polizeigebietsführer Copenhagen
- SS-Sturmbannführer Jakob Grobben (1944 - 1945)

HSSPf Albanien
- SS-Gruppenführer Josef Fitzthum (8/1/44 - 1/1/45)

HSSPf Ungarn
- SS-Obergruppenführer Otto Winkelmann (3/31/44 - 2/11/45)

HSSPf Belgien-   Nordfrankreich
- SS-Gruppenführer Richard Jungclaus (8/1/44 - 9/16/44)
- SS-Obergruppenführer Friedrich Jeckeln (9/22/44 - 1/18/45) title only
- SS-Brigadeführer Christoph Diehm (9/16/44 - 1/18/45) acting deputy

HSSPf Slowakien
- SS-Obergruppenführer Gottlob Berger (8/31/44 - 9/20/44)
- SS-Obergruppenführer Hermann Höfle (9/20/44 - 5/45)

Sources
(Birn, 1986) (Krausnick & Wilhelm, 1981) (Krausnick, 1968, pp. 213-254) (Yerger, 1997)

Individuals

Achamer-Pifrader, Dr. Humbert,
SS-Standartenführer -- CO Einsatzgruppe A / BdS Ostland (9/10/42 - 9/4/43);SD Wiesbaden; SD Stettin; killed during air raid on Linz (4/25/45)

Albath, Dr. Walter,
SS-Standartenführer -- CO Einsatzkommando 3/Einsatzgruppe V (Poland, 1939); Chef Gestapo Königsberg (1941-1943); Inspekteur Sicherheitspolizei und SD Düsseldorf (1943-1945)

Albers, Heinrich,
SS-? -- medical orderly attached to II. Bataillon / SS-Panzergrenadier-Regiment 26 / 12. SS-Panzer-Division *Hitlerjugend*; complicitous in the *Normandy* atrocities (6/7-14/44); apprehended by Allies (5/45); remanded to British authorities; tried before a British military tribunal (10/21/48); found not guilty on the grounds that defendant could not appreciate the illegality of his actions

Alvensleben, Ludolf Jakob Graf von,
SS-Gruppenführer -- Chief Adjutant, Persönlicher Stab Reichsführer-SS (11/38 - 10/39); shot one of his relatives for associating with Poles and Jews (12/39); CO Deutsche-Selbstschutz Danzig-Westpreussen: unit responsible for numerous war crimes (10/39 - 12/40); intermittently attached to Persönlicher Stab Reichsführer-SS (8/1/40 - 2/19/44); CO Deutsche-Selbstschutz Distrikt Lublin (1941); Stab HSSPf Ost (1941); SSPf Tschernigow (10/22/41 - 11/19/41); SSPf Taurien-Krim-Simferopol (11/19/41 - 10/6/43); SSPf Nikolajew (10/6/43 - 2/11/44); responsible for various war crimes in the Crimea such as the mass shooting of civilians at Simferopol (see *Zentrale Stelle des Landesjustizverwaltungen, Ludwigsburg: 213 AR-Z 43/67*); SSPf Nikolajew (10/6/43 - 2/44); HSSPf Schwarzes-Meer (10/29/43 - 12/25/43); sick leave; HSSPf Elbe (2/11/44 - 5/8/45); interned at Neuengamme POW Camp (1945); escaped to Argentina (1945); died at Santa Rosa de Calamuchita, Argentina (3/17/70)

Alvensleben, Ludolf von,
SS-Standartenführer -- SS und Polizeigebietskommandeur Friaul (10/27/44 - 1945) [identically-named brother of individual in previous listing]

Amthor, Paul,
SS-? -- SS-und Polizeigebietsführer Stalino

Andersen, Heinrich,
SS-Obersturmbannführer -- officer attached to SS-Panzergrenadier-Regiment 26 / 12. SS-Panzer-Division *Hitlerjugend*; possible complicity in the *Normandy* atrocities (6/7-17/44); KIA (4/5/45)

Augsberger, Franz,
SS-Brigadeführer -- CO 20. Waffen-Grenadier-Division der SS [estnische Nr. 1] (10/1/42 - ? and 7/1/43 - 3/17/45); KIA at Grottkau in Schlesien (3/17/45)

Aus der Fünten, Ferdinand Hugo,
SS-Hauptsturmführer -- directed the deportation of the Dutch Jews; condemned to death in Holland; sentence commuted to life imprisonment due to intervention of West German Chancellor Adenauer (1951)

Ax, Adolf,
SS-Oberführer -- various postings with 2. SS-Panzer-Division *Das Reich* (1939 - 1/42); CO SS-Panzerjäger-Ausbildungs- und Ersatzabteilung in Hilversum, Holland (4/42 - 7/42); Stab Befehlshaber der Waffen-SS Nederland (7/18/42 - 11/44); Chief of Staff, Führungsstab Ostküste (11/44 - 1/45); CO 15. Waffen-Grenadier-Division der SS [lettische Nr. 1] (1/26/45 - 2/15/45); CO 32. SS-Freiwilligen-Grenadier-Division *30. Januar* (2/17/45 - mid 3/45); Chief of Staff XVI. SS-Armeekorps (3/45 - 5/45); captured by American forces in Hochfilzen, Tirol (5/45); paroled (5/8/48)

Baatz, Bernhard,
SS-Obersturmbannführer -- RSHA Amt VID (5/42 – 6/43); CO Einsatzkommando 1/Einsatzgruppe A (8/43 - 10/31/43); CO Sonderkommando 1a-KdS Estland / Einsatzgruppe A (10/31/43 - 10/15/44); RSHA Amt IVD; captured by Soviets (1945); released and whereabouts unknown

Bachmann, Rudolf,
SS-Standartenführer -- attached to the 7. SS-Freiwilligen-Gebirgs-Division *Prinz Eugen;* complicity in the *Niksic* atrocity (5/43); CO SS-Jäger-Bataillon 501 (5/44 - 10/44); attached to 36. Waffen-Grenadier-Division

der SS: assisted in suppression of the *Warsaw Uprising* (8-10/44) and suspected of complicity in numerous atrocities

Bach-Zelewski, Erich von dem,

SS-Obergruppenführer -- HSSPf Wehrkreis VIII (6/28/38 - 5/1/41); HSSPf Russland-Mitte (5/1/41 - 6/21/44); ordered numerous killing operations in *Hauptkommissariat Baranowicze* (2/42); admitted to SS hospital at Hohenlychen due to nervous breakdown and hallucinations involving the shooting of Jews (1942); Beauftragter RFSS für den Bandenkampf / Chef der Bandenkampfverbände (10/23/42 - 11/44); directed mass murders at Riga, Minsk, and Mogilev; CO Korpsgruppe von dem Bach-Zelewski: suppression of *Warsaw Uprising* (8/44 - 10/44); CO XIV. SS-Armee-Korps (11/44 - 2/45); CO X. SS-Armee-Korps (2/45); CO Oderkorps (3/45 - 5/45); avoids post-war extradition to Poland by serving as a prosecution witness at the IMT in Nürnberg; in Allied custody until 1950; sentenced by Hauptspruchkammer München to 10 years special labor [which meant house arrest at his home in Laffenau, Franken] (3/31/51); denounced himself for mass murder (1952); re-arrested and charged with murders occurring in the 1941-42 period (1958); sentenced to three and a half years imprisonment for participation in 1934 "Night of Long Knives" purge (2/61); sentenced to life imprisonment for his role in the deaths of 6 Breslau Communists (1962); discovered furloughed from prison and resting in a private clinic at Nürnberg, reimprisoned (1971); died in München (3/8/72) *Note: last name legally changed to "von dem Bach" in November 1940. Records and sources cite both names.*

Baensch, Günther,

SS-? -- service with SS-Panzeraufklärungs-Abteilung 12/12. SS-Panzer-Division *Hitlerjugend* (1944); complicity in the *Ascq* massacre (4/1-2/44); tried and sentenced to death by French authorities (8/2-6/49); sentenced reduced to 10 years hard labor minus time served (7/14/55); paroled (1956)

Baier,

?, SS-Obersturmführer – CO 1. Batterie/SS-Flak-Abteilung 17/17. SS-Panzergrenadier-Division *Götz von Berlichingen* at time of *Maille* atrocity (8/25/44)

Bartetzko, Franz,

SS-Hauptscharführer -- Lageleiter des SS-Arbeitslager Trawniki (10/41 - Spring 1944); KIA near Kraftborn (1/31/45)

Barth, Heinz,

SS-Untersturmführer -- assigned to Reserve-Polizei-Bataillon *Kolin*; participation in *Lidice* massacre and other related actions (6/42); transferred to Waffen-SS (2/10/43); assigned to 2. SS-Panzer-Division *Das Reich* (10/19/43); participation in the *Oradour sur Glane* (6/10/44) atrocity; severely wounded in Normandy (8/44); lived openly post-war in East Germany; tried and sentenced to life imprisonment by East German authorities for participation in *Lidice* and *Oradour* atrocities (1983); released from prison due to ill-health and professed repentence (1997)

Bassewitz-Behr, George-Henning Graf von,

SS-Gruppenführer -- Chef der Kraftfahrkampftruppe im Allgemeine-SS (8/36 - 4/41); Inspektur der Kraftfahrkampftruppe im SS-Führungshauptamt (10/40 - 4/25/41); CO Panzerjägerabteilung / 6. SS-Totenkopfstandarte (5/40); service with Kommandostab RFSS (4/41 - 11/41); SSPf Dnejpropetrowsk-Krovoi Rog and SS-Standortkommandant Dnejpropetrowsk (11/11/41 - 8/1/42); SSPf Mogilew (8/1/42 - 4/20/43); Stab HSSPf Russland-Mitte (11/42 - 3/43); HSSPf Nordsee (2/16/43 - 5/8/45); brought before British military tribunal on charges of executing foreign civilian workers and KL prisoners (1947); remanded to Soviet custody; died of unspecified causes in Soviet detention (1/49)

Bast, Dr. Gerhard,

SS-Sturmbannführer -- Polizei Münster; Polizei Linz; CO Sonderkommando 7a / Einsatzgruppe B (6/44 - 11/44); killed during robbery attempt (1947)

Batz, Dr. Rudolf,

SS-Standartenführer -- CO Einsatzkommando 2/ Einsatzgruppe A (6/22/41 - 11/41); later KdS Krakau; KdS Den Haag; committed suicide while in detention awaiting trial (1961)

Baum, Otto,

SS-Oberführer -- CO 6. Kompanie / II. Bataillon / 1. SS-Panzer-Division *Leibstandarte Adolf Hitler* (9/39 - ?);

possible involvement in the *Zdunska Wola* (9/7/39), *Lodz* (9/8/39), and *Czestochowa* (10/1-2/39) atrocities; CO 7. Kompanie / II. Bataillon / 1. SS-Panzer-Division *Leibstandarte Adolf Hitler*; complicity in *Wormhoudt* atrocities (5/28/40); service with 3. SS-Panzer-Division *Totenkopf* (1941 - 1944); severely wounded (1943); CO 5. SS-Panzergrenadier-Regiment *Thule* / 3. SS-Panzer-Division *Totenkopf* (1943); CO 17. SS-Panzergrenadier-Division *Götz von Berlichingen* (6/18/44 - 7/28/44); CO 2. SS-Panzer-Division *Das Reich* (7/28/44 - 10/15/44); commander of division at time of *Bais* atrocity (8/44); CO 16. SS-Panzergrenadier-Division *Reichsführer-SS* (10/24/44 - 5/9/45)

Baumann,
?, SS-Obersturmführer -- CO Sonderkommando 1005-A (7/43 - ?)

Becher, Rolf,
SS-Sturmbannführer -- CO 4. Schwadron / SS-Totenkopf-Reiterstandarte 1 (9/39 - 11/39); CO 9. Schwadron/SS-Totenkopf-Reiterstandarte 1 (11/39 - 3/41); CO 3. platoon / Ersatz-Schwadron 3/SS-Kavallerie-Ersatzabteilung (3/41 - ?); captured by Americans (1945); employed as riding instructor

Becker, Hans,
SS-Sturmbannführer -- CO I. Bataillon / SS-Panzergrenadier-Regiment 2/1. SS-Panzer-Division *Leibstandarte Adolf Hitler* at time of the *Lago Maggiore* atrocity (9/22-24/43); KIA in Normandy (8/20/44)

Becker, Helmuth,
SS-Gruppenführer -- CO I. Bataillon / SS-Totenkopfstandarte I *Oberbayern* (1939); BdO Government General, Poland (10/25/39 - 10/31/40); CO SS-Panzergrenadier-Regiment 6/3. SS Panzer-Division *Totenkopf* (Fall 1942 - 9/43); regimental CO 16. SS-Panzergrenadier-Division *Reichsführer-SS* (9/43 - 7/13/44); CO 3. SS-Panzer-Division *Totenkopf* (7/13/44 - 5/9/45); surrendered to American forces (5/9/45); remanded to Soviet custody (5/14/45); sentenced to three concurrent 25 year sentences of hard labor (1947); accused of sabotage and executed by Soviets (2/28/53)

Becker, Herbert,
Generalmajor der Polizei --
CO Polizeigruppe 2 in Poland (1939); IdO Hamburg (11/40 - 4/42); BdO Government General, Poland (5/1/42 - 8/1/43); Generalinspektor der Schutzpolizei / Ordnungspolizei Hauptamt (8/1/43 - 5/45)

Behrends, Dr. Hermann,
SS-Gruppenführer -- Stab Volksdeutscher Mittelstelle (1941-43); active service with Waffen-SS (1943-44); HSSPf Serbien, Sandschak und Montenegro (4/1/44 - 10/44); acting HSSPf Ostland und Russland-Nord (1/30/45 - 5/45); captured by British (1945); remanded to Yugoslav custody (after 1945); sentenced to death and hung (12/4/48)

Beilhack, Armin,
SS-Sturmbannführer -- CO SS-Jäger-Bataillon 500 (6/44 - ?); attached to 36. Waffen-Grenadier-Division der SS: assisted in suppression of the *Warsaw Uprising* (8-10/44) and suspected of complicity in numerous atrocities

Bellwidt, Walther,
SS-Obersturmbannführer -- CO SS-Panzergrenadier-Ersatz-Bataillon 3 *Warschau*; assisted in suppression of the *Warsaw Ghetto Uprising* (4-5/43) and in the *Aktion Erntefest* massacres (11/3-4/43)

Berger, Gottlob,
SS-Obergruppenführer -- Stab SS-Hauptamt (1938 - 1940); Chef SS-Hauptamt (4/40 - 5/45); HSSPf Slowakien (8/31/44 - 9/20/44); tried and imprisoned (1949); paroled (1951); died (1/5/75)

Berkelmann, Theodor,
SS-Obergruppenführer -- HSSPf Elbe (6/28/38 - 4/20/40); HSSPf West (4/20/40 - 7/9/40); HSSPf Saar-Lothringen/Lothringen-Saarpfalz/Westmark (7/19/40 - 5/21/43); HSSPf Rhein (12/10/41 - 5/21/43); HSSPf Rhein-Westmark (5/21/43 - 11/11/43); HSSPf Warthe (11/9/43 - 12/27/43); died in Posen of a brain tumor (12/27/43)

Berlin, Anton,
SS-Hauptsturmführer -- CO 1. Kompanie /SS-Panzer-Regiment 12/12. SS-Panzer-Division *Hitlerjugend*;

suspected complicity in the *Normandy* atrocities (6/7-17/44); never questioned

Berschneider, Josef,
SS-Sturmbannführer -- CO 24. Waffen-Gebirgs-Division der SS *Karstjäger* (1944)

Besch, Klaus, SS-Sturmbannführer -- CO SS-Panzer-Werfer-Bataillon 1/SS-Panzergrenadier-Regiment 1/1. SS-Panzer-Division *Leibstandarte Adolf Hitler* (1944)

Best, Dr. Karl Rudolf Werner,
SS-Obergruppenführer -- Chef des Amtes I/RSHA (1939 - 1940); Kriegsverwaltungschef beim Militärbefehlshaber Frankreich (1940 - 42); HSSPf Danemark (1942 - 45); coordinated Jewish deportations (October 1943); sentenced to death at Copenhagen (1946); sentence commuted to 12 years imprisonment (7/20/49); paroled (8/29/51); tried by German authorities and found guilty of mass murder (1958); released from prison due to ill health (1972)

Bettenhauiser, Willi,
SS-Standartenführer -- CO III. Bataillon/SS-Totenkopfstandarte II *Brandenburg*; responsible for massacres at *Wloclawek* (9/22-25/39)

Beutel, Lothar,
SS-Brigadeführer -- CO Einsatzgruppe IV (Poland, 1939); ordered the execution of 500 Polish civilians at *Bydgoszcz* (9/11/39); complicity in the murder of Jews in the *Polish Corridor* (9/39); Stab Sipo Warschau (? - 10/23/39); arrested by SS for living with a Jewish woman and financial irregularities (10/23/39); demoted to rank of SS-Mann; responsible for executions in the *Palmiry Forest* (11/39 - 7/40); Abteilungsleiter in Reichsapothekenkammer (11/9/40); wounded in Hungary while serving in Waffen-SS (1944); Stab des SS-Abschnitts III Berlin (1944-1945)

Beutner, Max,
SS-Unterscharführer -- CO 2. platoon/SS-Panzerpionier-Kompanie 3/SS-Panzer-Regiment 1/1. SS-Panzer-Division *Leibstandarte Adolf Hitler*; implicated in the *Malmedy* atrocities (12/16+/44); defendant at the *Malmedy* Trial (5/16/46 - 7/11/46)

Bey, Harun-el-Raschid,
SS-Standartenführer -- real name was Wilhelm Hintersatz; a convert to Islam who saw himself as a German "Lawrence of Arabia"; CO Ostmuselmanische SS-Regiment; attached to 36. Waffen-Grenadier-Division der SS; assisted in suppression of the *Warsaw Uprising* (8-10/44) and suspected complicity in numerous atrocities

Beyerlein, Hans,
SS-Sturmbannführer -- CO SS-Jäger-Bataillon 501 (? - ?)

Beyersdorff, Friedrich,
SS-Standartenführer -- CO SS-Kampfgruppe *Beyersdorff* (sub-unit of 14. Waffen-Grenadier-Division der SS [ukrainische Nr. 1]) responsible for numerous atrocities in Poland (1943-1944); murder and deportation of Jews during the *Slovak National Uprising* (9-10/44)

Biberstein, Ernst,
SS-Sturmbannführer -- CO Einsatzkommando 6/Einsatzgruppe C (9/42 - 5/43); condemned to death during Einsatzgruppen Trial at Nürnberg (April 1948); sentence commuted to life imprisonment; released (1958)

Bierkamp, Dr. Walther,
SS-Brigadeführer -- Stab RSHA (4/39 - 2/41); IdS Düsseldorf (2/15/41 - 6/2/42); BdS Belgien-Nord Frankreich (9/41 - 4/42); CO Einsatzgruppe D (7/42 - 7/43); BdS Krakau (7/43 - 2/15/45); acting HSSPf Südost (2/20/45 - 3/17/45); BdS Südwest; killed in Hamburg or suicide (4/16/45)

Binge, Otto,
SS-Standartenführer – CO Ordnungspolizei Bataillon 22 (10/39 – 5/40); CO SS-Artillerie Regiment 4 / 4. SS-Polizei-Panzergrenadier-Division (5/10-40 – 1943); CO 17. SS-Panzergrenadier-Division *Götz von Berlichingen* (10/43 - 1/44, 6/16/44 - 6/18/44, and 8/1/44 - 8/29/44); badly wounded (8/19/44); reserve status for the remainder of the war; captured by Americans and later released; died (6/13/82)

Bischoff, Helmut,
SS-Obersturmbannführer -- CO Einsatzkommando 1/ Einsatzgruppe IV (Poland, 1939); SD Magdeburg; SD Posen

Bittrich, Wilhelm,
SS-Obergruppenführer -- CO SS-Panzergrenadier-Regiment 3 *Deutschland*/2. SS-Panzer-Division *Das Reich* (1939 - 10/13/41); CO 2. SS-Panzer-Division *Das Reich* (10/14/41 - 12/31/41); CO 8. SS-Kavallerie-Division *Florian Geyer* (5/1/42 - 11/1/42 and 2/1/43 - 2/15/43); CO 9. SS-Panzer-Division *Hohenstaufen* (2/15/43 - 6/28/44); CO II. SS-Panzer-Korps (6/29/44 - 5/8/45); captured by the Americans; remanded to French custody; tried for war crimes and acquitted (1954); died of natural causes at Wolfratshausen, Oberbayern (4/19/79)

Blobel, Paul,
SS-Standartenführer -- CO Sonderkommando 4A/Einsatzgruppe C (6/22/41 - 1/13/42, relieved of command due to alcoholism); participated in planning and execution of the infamous *Babi Yar* atrocity in which 33, 771 Jews were murdered (9/29-30/41); responsible for the murder of 21,685 Jews at *Kharkov 1* (12/14/41 - 1/42); relieved of command SK 4a due to alcohol related illness; assigned to Amt IV (Berlin); Director of exhumation activities and overall CO Sonderkommando 1005 (6/42 - Summer 1944); CO Einsatzgruppe *Iltis* operating in Carinthia (10/44); condemned to death during Einsatzgruppen Trial at Nürnberg (4/48); executed at Landsberg prison (6/7/51)

Blumberg,
?, SS-Sturmbannführer -- CO SS-Pionieresturmbann (9/39)

Blume, Dr.Walter,
SS-Standartenführer-- CO Sonderkommando 7a/Einsatzgruppe B (6/22/41 - 9/41); CO Sonderkommando 7c/Einsatzgruppe B (Fall 1942 - 7/43); KdS Griechenland; SD Düsseldorf; condemned to death during Einsatzgruppen Trial at Nürnberg (4/48); sentence commuted to life imprisonment; released (1953)

Blunck, Adolf,
SS-Obersturmführer -- attached to Einsatzgruppe C command staff (1941); CO 3. Kompanie/VII. Bataillon (Wach)/1. SS-Panzer-Division *Leibstandarte Adolf Hitler*; complicity in the *Berlin* deportations (2/27/43)

Bochmann, Georg,
SS-Oberführer -- CO SS-Panzer-Regiment 3/3. SS-Panzer-Division *Totenkopf* (7/43 - 8/28/44); CO SS-Panzer-Regiment 9/9. SS-Panzer-Division *Hohenstaufen* (8/29/44 - 1/2/45); CO 18. SS-Panzergrenadier-Division *Horst Wessel* (1/3/45 - 3/20/45, removed for insubordination); CO 17. SS-Panzergrenadier-Division *Götz von Berlichingen* (3/27/45 - 5/9/45); died of a heart attack at Offenbach (6/8/73)

Bock, Friedrich-Wilhelm,
SS-Oberführer -- service with SS-Artillerie-Regiment 4/4. SS-Polizei-Panzergrenadier-Division (1939 - 44); CO 19. Waffen-Grenadier-Division der SS [lettische Nr. 2] (3/16/44 - 4/13/44); Korpsartillerieführer II. SS-Panzer-Korps (4/44 - 7/44); CO 9. SS-Panzer-Division *Hohenstaufen* (7/29/44 - 10/10/44); possible complicity in the *Putten* atrocity (9/30/44); Korpsartillerieführer II. SS-Panzer-Korps (10/44 - ?); died in Hanover (5/6/78)

Bock, Wilhelm,
SS-Standartenführer -- CO Sonderkommando 7c/Einsatzgruppe B (12/41 - 6/42); SD Wien; SSPf Winniza

Böhme, Hans-Joachim,
SS-Standartenführer -- Preussisches Innenministerium (1937 - 10/1/38); Stab Gestapo Kiel (10/1/38 - 10/1/40); Leiter der Staatspolizeistelle Tilsit (10/1/40 - 10/43); BdS Rowno (10/43 - 10/21/43); KdS Shitomir (10/21/43 - 12/29/43); wounded and hospitalized (12/29/43 - 5/11/44); CO Einsatzkommando 3-KdS Litauen / Einsatzgruppe A (5/11/44 - 7/44); Leiter ein Panzervernichtungstrupp in Brückenkopf Memel (10/44 - 1/45); Stab Amt V / RSHA (1/45 - 3/45); BdS Stettin; Stab der 4. SS-Panzergrenadier-Division; Stab RSHA; Inspektor der SS Neustrehlitz; Division zur Strassensicherung Rostock-Lübeck; Teil der RSHA Flensburg - Schleswig/Holstein; captured by British (5/45); arrested by German authorities (8/23/56); tried before Landesgericht Ulm/Donau for crimes committed in Lithuania; sentenced to 15 years imprisonment for his role in the murder of 3,907 civilians (8/29/58); died (5/31/60)

Böhme, Horst-Alwin,
SS-Oberführer -- CO Einsatzgruppe B (3/12/43 - 8/28/43 and 8/12/44 - ?); CO Einsatzgruppe C (9/6/43 - 3/44); KdS Königsberg; BdS Prague (proposed extermination of Lidice as a reprisal for the assassination of Reinhard Heydrich)

Bothmann, Hans,
SS-Hauptsturmführer--CO Sonderkommando *Lange*: euthanasia actions against the mentally ill in East Prussia and the incorporated territories of Poland (1942); later posted to VL Kulmhof and equipped with 2 gas vans by the RSHA; CO VL Kulmhof (1942-43, 1944); unit temporarily posted to 7. SS-Freiwilligen-Gebirgs-Division *Prinz Eugen* (4/11/43 - 2/44); suicide at Heide while in British custody (4/4/46)

Böttcher, Dr. Herbert,
SS-Brigadeführer -- CO 105. SS-Standarte (8/39 - 3/41); Polizeidirektor Memel (3/40 - 10/40); Polizeipräsident Kassel (10/40 - 5/42); Stab SS-Abschnitt XXX (3/41 - 3/42); Stab RSHA (3/42 - 10/42); SSPf Radom (5/12/42 - 1/16/45); responsible for the extermination of the Jews of Ostrowiec and Czestochowa; tried and condemned to death by Polish authorities in Radom (1948); hung in Warsaw (6/12/50)

Böttcher, Karl,
SS-Hauptsturmführer -- CO SS-Panzergrenadier-Bataillon 3/SS-Panzergrenadier-Regiment 1/1. SS-Panzer-Division *Leibstandarte Adolf Hitler* (1944)

Bradfisch, Dr. Otto,
SS-Obersturmbannführer -- CO Einsatzkommando 8/Einsatzgruppe B (6/22/41 - 4/1/42); Leiter der Staatspolizeistelle Lodz (4/42 - Fall 1942); Oberbürgermeister Lodz (Fall 1942 - 1/25/43); Oberregierungsrat Lodz (1/25/43 - ?/45); In co-command during the Lodz Ghetto liquidations; KdS Potsdam (?/45 - 5/45); captured by Americans; transferred to British custody; released from custody (8/45); lived in West Germany under the assumed name of Karl Evers (1945 - 1953); investigations begun; taken into custody by West German government (4/21/58); tried by Landgericht München; sentenced to 10 years imprisonment (7/21/61); charged with murdering 70,000 Jews in Lodz before the Hannover Courts; sentenced to thirteen years imprisonment - concurrent with first sentence (9/63); sentence commuted to six years imprisonment

Brand, Dr. Ing. Hans,
SS-Standartenführer -- CO 24. Waffen-Gebirgs-Division der SS *Karstjäger* (7/42 - 1/44)

Brandner, Willi,
SS-Brigadeführer -- service with SS-Verfügungstruppe (12/39 - 8/40); service with 3. SS-Panzer-Division *Totenkopf* (8/40 - 1/41); service with 1. SS-Panzer-Division *Leibstandarte Adolf Hitler* (1/41 - 11/41); service with 2. SS-Panzer-Division *Das Reich* (11/41 - 10/42); Stab HSSPf Russland-Mitte (10/42 - 7/43); Polizeigebietsführer Agram (7/10/43 - 12/28/44) - wounded; died from wounds (12/29/44)

Brandt,
?, SS-Sturmbannführer -- CO SS-Aufklärungsabteilung (9/39)

Braune,Fritz,
SS-Obersturmbannführer -- CO Sonderkommando 4b / Einsatzgruppe C (10/1/41 - 3/21/42); RSHA Amt 1A; SD Oslo; CO Pionier-Bataillon/5. SS-Panzer-Division *Wiking* (7/44); sentenced to nine years imprisonment by Düsseldorf court (1973)

Braune, Dr. Werner,
SS-Obersturmbannführer -- CO Einsatzkommando 11b/Einsatzgruppe D (10/41 - 9/42); condemned to death during Einsatzgruppen Trial at Nürnberg (4/48); executed at Landsberg Prison (6/7/51)

Breder, Reinhard,
SS-Sturmbannführer -- CO Einsatzkommando 2/ Einsatzgruppe A (3/26/43 - 8/43); SD Düsseldorf; SD Frankfurt/Main

Breimaier, Wilhelm,
SS-Obersturmbannführer -- CO II. Bataillon/SS-Freiwilligen-Gebirgsjäger-Regiment 13/7. SS-Freiwilligen-Gebirgs-Division *Prinz Eugen*; responsible for executions at *Sinj* (11/5/43); CO SS-Panzergrenadier-Regiment 6 *Theodor Eicke*/3. SS-Panzer-Division *Totenkopf* (3/18/45 – 5/8/45)

Breithaupt, Franz,
SS-Brigadeführer -- CO 8. SS-Totenkopfstandarte (1939); CO 5. SS-Totenkopfstandarte *Dietrich Eckardt* (5/5/40); Chef Hauptamt SS-Gericht (8/16/42 - 4/29/45); killed in a car accident just before the end of the war

Bremer, Gerhard,
SS-Sturmbannführer -- service with 1. SS-Panzer-Division *Leibstandarte Adolf Hitler* (1939 - 43); CO SS-Panzeraufklärungs-Abteilung 12/SS-Panzer-Regiment 12/12. SS-Panzer-Division *Hitlerjugend* (4/43 - 5/8/45); complicity in the *Normandy* atrocities (6/7-17/44); captured by Americans; remanded to French authorities (1945); recommended for prosecution by SHAEF Standing Court of Inquiry (1945); released from custody (7/48); never investigated for crimes; retired to Spain; died at Denia las Rotas (10/29/89)

Brenner, Karl-Heinrich,
SS-Gruppenführer -- KdO Warschau; BdO Oberkrain und Südsteiermark; SSPf Bozen (1943/44); BdO Ukraine (1944); Inspektor der Ordnungspolizei (1944); CO 6. SS-Gebirgs-Division *Nord* (9/1/44 - 5/45); died of natural causes in Karlsruhe (2/14/54)

Briesemeister, Kurt,
SS-Unterscharführer -- CO Panzer 114 / SS-Panzer-Regiment 1/1. SS-Panzer-Division *Leibstandarte Adolf Hitler* (1944); implicated in the *Malmedy* atrocities (12/16+/44); defendant at the *Malmedy* Trial (5/16/46 - 7/11/46); found guilty; sentenced to death (7/16/46); sentence commuted; released from custody

Broser, Michael,
SS-Standartenführer -- CO 25. Waffen-Grenadier-Division der SS *Hunyadi* [ungarische Nr. 1] (?/45 - 5/5/45)

Brunner, Dr. Karl Friedrich,
SS-Brigadeführer -- Chef Gestapo München (4/37 - 6/40); CO Einsatzkommando 4 / Einsatzgruppe I (Poland, 1939); IdS Salzburg (6/39 - 4/44); Stab RSHA (3/41 - 5/45); SSPf Bozen (9/15/43 - 5/45); SSPf for operational area of Heeresgruppe B (4/45 - 5/45); died (12/7/80)

Buchardt, Dr. Friedrich,
SS-Obersturmbannführer -- CO Einsatzkommando 9/Einsatzgruppe B (1/43 - 3/43); SD Lodz; RSHA Amt IIIB; service with XII. SS-Korps (1944)

Buchegger, Dr. Karl,
SS-Hauptsturmführer -- CO Sonderbataillon, SS-Totenkopfstandarte *Prag* (11/15/40 - ?)

Bundschuh, Fritz,
SS-? -- medical orderly attached to II. Bataillon / SS-Panzergrenadier-Regiment 26 / 12. SS-Panzer-Division *Hitlerjugend*; complicitous in the *Normandy* atrocities (6/7-14/44); apprehended by Allies (5/45); remanded to British authorities; tried before a British military tribunal (10/21/48); found not guilty on the grounds that defendant could not appreciate the illegality of his actions

Bürger, Karl Heinz,
SS-Oberführer -- Stab SS-Junkerschule Braunschweig (11/38 - 3/40); Stab SS-Totenkopfverbände Inspectorate (3/40 - 5/40); Stab Hauptamt Dienstelle Heissmeyer (5/40 - 4/41); service with Kommandostab RFSS and SS-Ersatz-Bataillon Ost (4/41 - 11/42); SSPf Nord-Kaukasien (8/21/42 - 10/1/42); SSPf Awdejewka (10/1/42 - 12/1/43); SSPf zbV (1943); SSPf Mittelitalien-Verona (12/1/43 - 5/45); died in Karlsbad (12/2/88)

Burk, Karl,
SS-Oberführer -- CO 15. Waffen-Grenadier-Division der SS [lettische Nr. 1] (2/15/45 - 5/45)

Büss, Gustav,
SS-Hauptscharführer -- service with SS-Panzeraufklärungs-Abteilung 12/12. SS-Panzer-Division *Hitlerjugend* (1944); complicitous in the *Ascq* massacre (1/2 April 1944); sentenced to death in absentia (1949)

Butschek,
?, SS-Obersturmführer -- CO SS-Panzerartillerie-Abteilung 5/SS-Panzeraufklärungs-Bataillon 1/1. SS-Panzer-Division *Leibstandarte Adolf Hitler* (1944); implicated in the *Malmedy* atrocities (12/16+/44)

Charwat, Stephan,
SS-Hauptsturmführer -- CO 1. Schwadron/SS-Kavallerie-Regiment 2/8. SS-Kavallerie-Division *Florian Geyer* (3/21/41 - 12/41+); responsible for the massacre of 11,000 Jews at Pinsk (8/5-8/41); killed in action on 3/7/42

Christ, Friedrich,
SS-Obersturmführer -- CO SS-Panzer-Kompanie 2/ SS-Panzer-Regiment 1/1. SS-Panzer-Division *Leibstandarte Adolf Hitler*; implicated in the *Malmedy* atrocities (12/16+/44); defendant at the *Malmedy* Trial (5/16/46 - 7/11/46); found guilty; sentenced to death (7/16/46); sentence commuted; released from custody

Christensen, Theodor,
SS-Sturmbannführer
--CO Sonderkommando 4a/Einsatzgruppe C (1/15/43 - 12/43); SD Königsberg; SD Paris; RSHA Amt III

Christmann, Dr. Kurt,
SS-Obersturmbannführer -- CO Sonderkommando 10a/Einsatzgruppe D (8/1/42 - 7/43); fled to Argentina; returned to West Germany (1956); legal proceedings terminated due to defendant's incapacity to stand trial

Class, Friedrich,
Kriminaldirektor -- CO Teilkommando Gdingen (Poland, 1939)

Classen, Günther,
SS-Oberführer -- Polizeipräsident Münster (5/37 - 9/39); Polizeipräsident Warschau (9/39 - 10/41); CO 7. SS-Totenkopfstandarte (9/40 - 1/41); CO 8. SS-Totenkopfstandarte (4/41 - 9/41); Polizeipräsident Karlsruhe (4/42 - 5/45); died in a POW camp (7/22/46)

Coblenz, Manfred,
SS-Obersturmführer -- CO 2. Kompanie/SS-Panzeraufklärungs-Bataillon 1/1. SS-Panzer-Division *Leibstandarte Adolf Hitler* (1944); implicated in the *Malmedy* atrocities (12/16+/44); defendant at Malmedy Trials (5/16/46 - 7/11/46); sentenced to life imprisonment; released (1951)

Dahm, Paul,
SS-Standartenführer -- service with Waffen-SS recruiting posts in Düsseldorf and Norway (9/39 - 4/42); service with 5. SS-Panzer-Division *Wiking* (4/42 - 8/43); Polizeigebietsführer Banja-Luca (8/2/43 - 4/20/45); Polizeigebietsführer Essegg (9/20/44 - 4/20/45); died (early 1970s)

Damzog, Ernst,
SS-Brigadeführer -- CO Einsatzgruppe V (Poland, 1939); SD Posen; RSHA

Deak, Ladislaus,
Waffen-Oberführer der SS -- colonel in the Honved Army; organized and executed massacres of Serbs and Jews at *Stari Becej* (1/10-28/42); left Hungarian army for safety of Germany (4/43); joined Waffen-SS; attached to Befehlshaber der Waffen-SS Ungarn (4/44); CO Waffen-Grenadier-Regiment der SS 61/25. Waffen-Grenadier-Division der SS *Hunyadi* [ungarische Nr. 1]; last known posting as Generalinspektor XVII. Waffen-Armee-Korps der SS [ungarisches]; either killed in combat or executed by the Americans (5/3/45)

Debes, Lothar,
SS-Gruppenführer -- CO 10. SS-Panzer-Division *Frundsberg* (2/15/43 - 11/15/43); CO 6. SS-Gebirgs-Division *Nord* (1/15/44 - 5/22/44)

Degrelle, Leon,
SS-Standartenführer -- service with volunteer Walloon units on the Eastern Front (1942-44); CO 28. SS-Freiwilligen-Panzergrenadier-Division *Wallonie* (2/13/44 - 5/7/45); escaped to Norway and then Spain at war's end; tried in absentia and sentenced to death by Belgian authorities; prolific author; died (3/31/94)

Deisenhofer, Dr. Eduard,
SS-Standartenführer -- service with 3. SS-Panzer-Division *Totenkopf* (1939 - Fall 1942); Lehrgruppenkommandeur, SS-Junkerschule Tölz (Fall 1942 - 1943); Inspektor der Infanterie, SS-Führungshauptamt (1943); CO Panzergrenadier-Regiment 21 / 10. SS-Panzer-Division *Frundsberg* (1944); CO 17. SS-Panzergrenadier-Division *Götz von Berlichingen* (8/30/44 - 9/44); sent to Bucharest on recruitment drive; attached to 15. SS-Freiwilligen-Grenadier-Division [lettische Nr. 2]; captured by the Soviets in the Arnewalde area (1/31/45); missing

Deistung, ?,
SS-Untersturmführer -- CO 1. Kompanie/VII. Bataillon (Wach)/1. SS-Panzer-Division *Leibstandarte Adolf Hitler*; complicity in the *Berlin* deportations (2/27/43)

Demelhuber, Karl-Maria,
SS-Obergruppenführer-- CO SS-Standarte *Germania* (9/39 - ?); Befehlshaber der Waffen-SS *Ost* (? - 4/41); CO 1. SS-Infanterie [mot.]-Brigade (4/24/41 - 5/25/41); CO 6. SS-Gebirgs-Division *Nord* (5/25/41 - 10/41 and 4/1/42 - 5/2/42); CO Waffen-SS in the Netherlands; CO XVI. SS-Armee-Korps; died (1988)

Demme, Karl,
SS-Standartenführer -- CO 10. SS-Totenkopfstandarte (5/5/40); CO SS-Infanterie-Regiment 10/1. SS-Infanterie-Brigade (6/40-10/41)

Dern, Friedrich,
SS-Obersturmbannführer -- adjutant, Waffen-SS Bataillon zur besondere Verwendung (6/41 - 9/17/43); complicity in numerous atrocities including those at *Lvov* (7/4/41); assisted Einsatzgruppen in USSR with killing operations; responsible for massacres of Jews at Pinsk (7/41); CO 29. Freiwilligen-Grenadier-Regiment/14. SS-Freiwilligen-Grenadier-Division *Galizien* [ukrainische Nr. 1] (7/44)

Diebitsch, Prof. Karl,
SS-Oberführer -- CO 11. SS-Totenkopfstandarte (Autumn 1939 - Summer 1940+); numerous war crimes occurred under his command at *Radom* (Autumn 1939 - Summer 1940); head of Persönlicher Stab RFSS, Chefamt München (responsible for all artistic and architectual questions which might interest Himmler)

Diefenthal, Josef,
SS-Sturmbannführer -- CO SS-Panzergrenadier-Bataillon 3/SS-Panzer-Regiment 1/1. SS-Panzer-Division *Leibstandarte Adolf Hitler* (1944); implicated in the *Malmedy* atrocities (12/16+/44); defendant at the *Malmedy* Trial (5/16/46 - 7/11/46); found guilty; paroled (6/16/56); retired in seclusion to the Ardennes

Diehm, Christoph,
SS-Brigadeführer -- Polizeipräsident Gotenhafen (3/39 - 10/41); service with Wehrmacht (9/39); Polizeipräsident Saarbrücken/Metz (10/41 - 1/44); Stab HSSPf Ukraine (4/43 - 1/44); SSPf Shitomir (1/25/44 - 2/25/44); SSPf Lemberg (2/25/44 - 9/16/44); acting HSSPf Belgien-Nordfrankreich (9/16/44 - 1/18/45); Inspector of Volkssturm units, southwestern Germany (1/45 - 5/45); died in Rottenacker (2/21/60)

Diekmann, Adolf,
SS-Sturmbannführer -- signals instructor SS-Junkerschule Tölz (5/41 - 9/43); transferred to 2. SS-Panzer-Division *Das Reich* (9/12/43); CO I. Bataillon/ SS-Panzergrenadier-Regiment 4 *Der Führer*/2. SS-Panzer-Division *Das Reich*; responsible for the *Carsac-de-Carlux* (6/8/44) and *Oradour sur Glane* (6/10/44) atrocities; KIA near Noyers in Normandy (6/29/44)

Dieterichs, August,
SS-Obersturmbannführer -- CO 8. Kompanie/II. Bataillon/1. SS-Panzer-Division *Leibstandarte Adolf Hitler* (9/39 - ?); possible involvement in the *Zdunska Wola* (9/7/39), *Lodz* (9/8/39), and *Czestochowa* (10/1-2/39) atrocities; CO Kampfgruppe Dieterichs [elements of 16. SS-Panzergrenadier-Division *Reichsführer-SS*] in Italy (1943)

Dietrich, Dr. Fritz,
SS-Obersturmbannführer -- SSPf Libau (9/1/41 - 11/30/43); executed at Landsberg prison (10/22/48)

Dietrich, Josef (Sepp),
SS-Oberstgruppenführer -- Commander 1. SS-Panzer-Division *Leibstandarte Adolf Hitler* (3/17/33 - 7/43); unit commander at time of numerous atrocities in Poland (9/39), see *Warta River*; divisional commander at time of *Wormhoudt* massacre (5/28/40); accused of ordering the supposed *Gejgowa/Kherson* killings (8/41); questionable accusation of atrocity in *Rostov-na-Donu* (11/41); wrongly accused of responsibility for mass murders at *Kharkov 1* and *Kharkov 3* (12/43); accused of responsibility for atrocities at *Yefrenovka* (Spring 1943) and *Kharkov 2* (12/43); CO I. SS-Panzer-Korps (7/27/43 - 8/44); CO 5. Panzer-Armee (8/44); CO 7. Armee (9/44); CO 6. SS-Panzer-Armee (9/44 - 5/45); captured by American forces at Kufstein, Austria (5/9/45); defendant in the Malmedy Trial (5/16/46 - 7/11/46); found guilty; sentenced to life imprisonment (7/16/46); paroled (10/22/55); arrested by West German authorities (8/56); tried before Landgericht München for his role in the 1934 "Night of Long Knives" killings of Röhm and other SA leaders (5/14/57); sentenced to 18 months imprisonment for abetting a homicide; begins serving sentence (8/7/58); released from custody on grounds of ill health (2/2/59); died of natural causes (4/21/66); in the last few months of his life he worked for HIAG (ex-SS members organization)

Dietsche, Bernhard,
SS-Obersturmbannführer -- CO II. Bataillon/SS-Freiwilligen-Gebirgsjäger-Regiment 14/7. SS-Freiwilligen-Gebirgs-Division *Prinz Eugen* (1942 - 45); responsible for *Topoli* executions (11-12/42); complicity in the *Niksic* atrocity (5/43); organized and conducted massacres at *Otok Cornji, Ruda,* and *Dolac Donji* (3/28/44); died of natural causes at Pirmasens (1/28/75)

Dinse, Otto,
SS-Hauptsturmführer -- CO 14. Kompanie /SS-Panzer-Regiment 2/1. SS-Panzer-Division *Leibstandarte Adolf Hitler* at the time of the *Boves* atrocity (9/43); charged with murder by the Italian authorities (12/68); case dismissed by West German authorities (2/69)

Dirlewanger, Dr. Oskar,
SS-Oberführer -- attached to 5. SS-Totenkopfstandarte (1940); CO SS-Sonderkommando Dirlewanger [later the 36. Waffen-Grenadier-Division der SS] (9/1/40 - 11/43, wounded; and 1/44 - 2/15/45, wounded); numerous atrocities in occupied Poland (1941); assisted with the suppression of the *Warsaw Uprising* (8-10/44) and committed countless atrocities; assisted with the murder and deportation of Jews to the death camps during the suppression of the *Slovak National Uprising* (9-10/44); captured by the French in Wurttemberg at war's end; recognized by former concentration camp prisoners and beaten to death by Polish guards at French-controlled POW camp at Altshausen [Oberschwaben] (6/7/45); due to persistent rumors of his survival Staatsanwaltschaft Ravensburg exhumed his body and confirmed his death (11/12/60)

Dorheit, ?,
SS-Sturmbannführer -- CO 15. SS-Totenkopfstandarte (? - ?)

Döring, Hans,
SS-Brigadeführer -- CO SS-Abschnitt I (3/39 - 10/42); service with 1. SS-Panzer-Division *Leibstandarte Adolf Hitler* (1941); SSPf Stalino-Donezgebiet (11/19/41 - 5/19/43); service with 16. SS-Panzergrenadier-Division *Reichsführer-SS* (3/44 - 5/45); died in Nürnberg (7/2/70)

Dörner, Helmut,
SS-Standartenführer -- CO 4. SS-Polizei-Panzergrenadier-Division (8/17/44 - 8/21/44); CO SS-Panzergrenadier-Regiment 8/4. SS-Polizei-Panzergrenadier-Division; CO divisional kampfgruppe at Budapest (1945); KIA in Budapest (2/11/45)

Drescher, ?,
SS-Obersturmführer -- CO 4. Kompanie / VII. Bataillon (Wach) /1. SS-Panzer-Division *Leibstandarte Adolf Hitler*; complicity in the *Berlin* deportations (2/2/7/43)

Drescher, Walter,
SS-Scharführer -- member Nachrichten-Kompanie 8/ II. Bataillon/1. SS-Panzer-Division *Leibstandarte Adolf Hitler*; complicity in *Wormhoudt* atocities (5/28/40); KIA in USSR

Dunckern, Anton,
SS-Brigadeführer -- Chef SD Brunswick (9/39 - 3/41); BdS Lothringen-Saarpfalz and RKFDV Lothringen-Saarpfalz (7/40 - 7/44); Stab XIII. SS-Armee-Korps (7/44 - 10/44); SSPf Metz (10/1/44 - 11/18/44); captured by Americans; testified at the IMT in Nürnberg; extradited to France; tried and convicted by French authorities; paroled (1954)

Dunsch, Walter,
SS-Hauptsturmführer -- service with SS-Reiterstandarte 16 (11/36 - 11/39); CO 8. Schwadron/SS-Totenkopf-Reiterstandarte 1 (11/39 - 5/40); CO 2. Schwadron/ SS-Totenkopf-Reiterstandarte 1 (5/40 - 11/40); 2. Schwadron /III. Abteilung / SS-[Totenkopf]-Kavallerie-Regiment 1 (11/40 - 3/20/41); CO 2. Schwadron / SS-Kavallerie-Regiment 2 / 8. SS-Kavallerie-Division *Florian Geyer* (3/21/41 - 12/41); SS-Kavallerie-Ersatz-Abteilung Warschau (late 1941 - ?); Reitlehrer Remonteamt Waffen-SS Rasdolje (? - ?); Reitlehrer HSSPf Nord [Oslo] (? - ?); Schwadron CO Reit-und Fahrschule Zamosz (9/43 - 5/45); captured by British; released from custody (Spring 1946); taken into custody by West German government (12/10/62); tried by Landgericht Braunschweig; sentenced to 4 years and 6 months imprisonment (4/20/64); sentence overturned on technicalities by the 5. Strafsenat des Bundesgerichtshofs (11/17/64)

Duppel, ?,
SS-? -- CO SS-Panzer-AA-Kompanie 14 / SS-Panzer-grenadier-Regiment 2 / 1. SS-Panzer-Division *Leibstandarte Adolf Hitler* (1944)

Eberhardt, Georg,
SS-Sturmbannführer --CO Polizeigruppe Eberhardt (Poland, 1939); CO SS-Freiwilligen-Panzergrenadier-Bataillon *Narwa* / 5. SS-Panzer-Division *Wiking* (? - 7/43); KIA near Sawodskoje am Donez, USSR (7/43)

Eberstein, Friedrich Karl Freiherr von,
SS-Obergruppenführer -- Polizei Präsident München (4/37 - 10/41); HSSPf Main (3/12/38 - 12/17/42); HSSPf Süd (4/12/38-4/45); Leiter der Polizeiabteilung im Bayerischen Ministerium des Inneren (10/1/42 - 4/45); dismissed from all posts for defeatism (4/45); testified at the IMT Nürnberg regarding the Allgemeine-SS (1945); died in Bayern (2/10/79)

Ebrecht, George,
SS-Gruppenführer -- CO SS-Abchnitt XVIII (1/1/39 - 10/9/39); Selbstschutzführer Westpreussen (10/26/39 - 3/13/40); CO SS-Abschnitt XXVI (5/1/40 - 12/8/41); acting HSSPf Nordost (12/41 - 12/1/44); sick leave until war's end; settled in East Germany postwar; emigrated to West Germany; numerous legal proceedings were initiated but he was ruled incompetent to stand trial; died in Lindau, Switzerland (1/21/77)

Eckhardt, Wilhelm,
SS-? -- CO Sonderkommando 7c / Einsatzgruppe B (7/43 - 12/43)Ehlers, Ernst, SS-Obersturmbannführer -- service with Einsatzgruppe B; BdS Belgien; SD Breslau; indicted by Verwaltungsgerichtsrat Schleswig-Holstein (1980); committed suicide (10/4/80)

Ehrlinger, Dr. Erich,
SS-Oberführer -- CO of an Einsatzkommando in Prague (3/39 - 9/39); CO of a kommando of Einsatzgruppe IV, Poland (9/39 - 11/39); Stab BdS Warschau (11/39 - 3/40); Kriegsberichter, 1. SS-Panzer-Division *Leibstandarte Adolf Hitler* in the West (4/12/40 - 8/14/40); Beauftragter RFSS Norwegen (8/40 - 2/41); Stab RSHA (2/41 - 4/41); CO Sonderkommando 1b / Einsatzgruppe A (6/22/41 - 12/3/41); BdS Kiev (12/41 - 8/43); acting BdS Ukraine (9/42 - 8/43); CO Einsatzgruppe B (8/28/43 - 4/44); SSPf

Weissruthenien (9/6/43 - 4/1/44); RSHA / Inspector of Sipo and SD schools (4/44 - 5/45); arrested by West German authorities (1958); sentenced by a Karlsruhe court to 12 years imprisonment (1961); sentence appealed and verdict set aside by Federal Supreme Court (1964); proceedings discontinued by Schwurgericht Karlsruhe due to defendant's permanent disability (1969)

Eichenhain, ?,
SS-Sturmbannführer -- Stab Sipo/SD Winniza

Eicke, Theodor,
SS-Obergruppenführer -- CO KL Dachau (1933); Inspektor KL und SS-Wachverbande (1934 - 39); HSSPf Ost (9/10/39 - 10/1/39); CO 3. SS-Panzer-Division *Totenkopf* (11/14/39-7/7/41 and 9/9/41-2/26/43); divisional commander at time of the *Le Paradis* (5/27/40), *L'Arbresle* (6/19/40) and *Lentilly* (6/19/40) atrocities; KIA in USSR (2/26/43)

Eimann, Kurt,
SS-Obersturmbannführer -- CO SS-Wachsturmbann *Eimann* (7/39-1/40); responsible for numerous atrocities in Pomerania and Wartheland including the execution of 3,000 Polish psychiatric patients, see *Szpegawsk* (10/39); responsible for the murder of Jews in the *Polish Corridor* (9/39) and of Polish civilians at *Jaroszew* (10/25/39); service with II. SS-Panzer-Korps in Normandy and the Ardennes (1944-45); detained briefly after the war but released; tried by West German Government (1962); sentenced to four years imprisonment for the murders of 1,200 psychiatric patients in Pomerania (1968) [a sentence of slightly more than 1 day per victim]

Ertel, Karl-Heinz,
SS-Hauptsturmführer -- service with SS-Regiment *Germania* (1938-39); Stab SS-Junkerschule Tölz (11/39-2/40); service with SS-Regiment *Germania* (2/40-6/41); Aufstellung des Finnischen Freiwilligen Bataillonen der Waffen-SS (6/41-12/41); service with 5. SS-Panzer-Division *Wiking* (12/41 - 7/43); regimental adjutant, 23. SS-Freiwilligen-Panzergrenadier-Division *Nederland* (8/43 - 5/45); captured by the Americans in Raum Lippspringe (5/6/45); remanded to British custody (1945); remanded to Yugoslavian authorities (4/20/47);

tried and sentenced to six years hard labor for complicity in war crimes; released and returned to West Germany due to intervention of West German chancellor Adenauer (10/15/50); died in Lippstadt (1/25/93)

Fanslau, Heinz Karl,

SS-Brigadeführer – various postings SS-Hauptamt (1934 – 11/30/40); CO Supply Bataillon / 5. SS-Panzer-Division *Wiking* (12/1/40 – 9/30/41); responsible for the *Zborow* atrocity (7/9/41); returns to SS-Hauptamt (10/1/41 – 2/42); SS-WVHA (2/42 – 5/45); Chef des Amtsgruppe A / SS-WVHA (9/43 – 5/45); tried and acquitted of the *Zborow* atrocity (IMT case IV); tried before the Nuremberg Military Tribunal as part of the Pohl case (1/47 – 11/47); sentenced to 25 years imprisonment

Fassbender, Albert,

SS-Sturmbannführer -- Stab SS-Abschnitte III (? - 9/39); Stab SS-Totenkopf-Reiterstandarte 1 (9/39 - ?); CO elements SS-Kavallerie (1940 - 41); CO 6. Schwadron / SS-Kavallerie-Regiment 1 (? - ?); CO II. Abteilung / SS-[Totenkopf]-Kavallerie-Regiment 1 (11/40 - 3/20/41); CO 6. Schwadron / SS-Kavallerie-Regiment 1 / 8. SS-Kavallerie-Division *Florian Geyer* (3/21/41 - 8/1/41); CO Vorausabteilung SS-Kavallerie-Regiment 2 (8/41 - 12/41); responsible for numerous killing operations, see *SS-Kavallerie-Brigade Operations and Atrocities in the USSR*; complicity in *Pripet Marshes* massacres (1941-43); Stab SS-Truppenübungsplatz Debica (1/42 - 6/42); CO SS-Kavallerie-Regiment 3 / 8. SS-Kavallerie-Division *Florian Geyer* (6/42 - 8/42); Stab SS-Führungshauptamt (8/42 - 9/43); CO supply elements 13. Waffen-Gebirgs-Division der SS *Handschar* [kroatische Nr. 1] (9/43 - 11/44); refurbishment staff 13. Waffen-Gebirgs-Division der SS *Handschar* [kroatische Nr. 1] (12/44 - ?)

Fegelein, Hermann Otto,

SS-Gruppenführer -- member of the German Equestrian Team, Munich Olympics (1936); CO SS-Hauptreitschule München (6/16/36 - 9/39); CO SS-Totenkopf-Reiterstandarte (9/39 - 11/39); organized numerous killing operations in Poland from Fall 1939 - Spring 1940; CO SS-Totenkopf-Reiterstandarte 1 (11/39 - 11/40); CO SS-[Totenkopf]-Kavallerie-Regiment 1 (11/40 - 3/20/41); responsible for the execution of 600 Jews at Chelm, Po-

land (1/12/40); CO SS-Kavallerie-Regiment 1 (3/21/41 - 8/1/41); CO SS-Kavallerie-Brigade (8/2/41 - 5/1/42); responsible for numerous killing operations, see *SS-Kavallerie-Brigade Operations and Atrocities in the USSR*; complicity in *Pripet Marshes* massacres (1941-43); Inspektor Reit-und Fahrwesen / SS-Führungshauptamt (5/2/42 - 12/1/42); CO Kampfgruppe *Fegelein* (12/1/42 - 12/23/42, wounded); CO 8. SS-Kavallerie-Division *Florian Geyer* (4/20/43 - 11/1/43, wounded on 9/9/43); RFSS Adjutant to the Führer (1/1/44 - 4/45); married to Eva Braun's sister, Margarete (6/3/44); AWOL from the Führerbunker in Berlin (4/27/45); arrested at his Berlin home under suspicious circumstances; condemned to death for desertion by a Standgericht and executed by a Waffen-SS firing squad in the garden of the Auswärtigen Amtes, Berlin (4/29/45)

Fegelein, Waldemar,

SS-Standartenführer -- younger brother of Hermann Fegelein (see preceding entry); Stab SS-Hauptreitschule München (10/36 - 11/39); CO 1. Schwadron/1.SS-Totenkopf-Reiterstandarte (11/39 - 5/40); CO 5. Schwadron / 1. SS-Totenkopf-Reiterstandarte (5/40 - 11/40); CO 1. Schwadron/SS-[Totenkopf]-Kavallerie-Regiment 1 (11/40 - 3/20/41); CO 1. Schwadron/ SS-Kavallerie-Regiment 1 (3/21/41 - 12/41); responsible for numerous killing operations, see *SS-Kavallerie-Brigade Operations and Atrocities in the USSR*; complicity in *Pripet Marshes* massacres (1941-43); Stab SS-Führungshauptamt (12/41 - 6/43); CO SS-Kavallerie-Regiment 16 / 8. SS-Kavallerie-Division *Florian Geyer* (6/43 - 3/44); Stab SS-Führungshauptamt (4/1/44 - mid 1944); CO SS-Freiwilligen-Kavallerie-Regiment 17 / 22. SS-Freiwilligen-Kavallerie-Division *Maria Theresia* (mid 1944 - 1945); CO 37. SS-Freiwilligen-Kavallerie-Division *Lutzow* (2/20/45 - 3/45); fate unknown – some say he was KIA (3/45), murdered by the Americans (5/45), or survived the war entirely

Fehlis, Dr. Heinrich,

SS-Oberführer -- CO Einsatzkommando 1 Oslo (1940); BdS Norway (1940 - ?); committed suicide (5/45)

Feketehalmy-Czeydner, Ferenc,

SS-Obergruppenführer -- also known as Franz Zeidner; CO Hungarian V. Szegedin Army Corps (1942); organized and directed *Novi Sad* massacres (1/21-23/42); active SS duty (7/1/44 - 5/9/45); taken into custody by

American OSS (8/14/45); remanded to Hungarian custody (11/45); remanded to Yugoslav custody and held at prison in Novi Sad (1/31/46); sentenced to death for war crimes (11/4/46); executed (11/5/46)

Fellenz, Martin,
SS-Sturmbannführer -- Stab SS-und Selbstschutzführer Warschau (12/12/39 - 3/1/40); tried in Flensburg for his participation in the murder of 40,000 Jews in Poland (11/62); sentenced to 4 years imprisonment

Fendler, Lothar,
SS-Sturmbannführer -- service with Einsatzgruppe C; RSHA Amt VI; sentenced to ten years imprisonment during Einsatzgruppen Trial at Nürnberg (4/48); sentence reduced to eight years

Fick, Jakob,
SS-Standartenführer --CO 17. SS-Panzergrenadier-Division *Götz von Berlichingen* (3/24/45- 3/26/45); KIA (3/26/45)

Fiedler, Richard,
SS-Brigadeführer --CO SS-Abschnitt XVII (8/39 - 10/40); CO SS-Abschnitt XXXXIII (10/40- 8/44); service with 4. SS-Polizei-Panzergrenadier-Division (1940); service with 5. SS-Panzer-Division *Wiking* (1941 - 10/43); SSPf Montenegro (10/1/43 - 10/20/44); hospitalized until war's end; died in München (12/14/74)

Filbert, Dr. Alfred Karl Wilhelm,
SS-Obersturmbannführer -- CO SS-Infanterie-Regiment in France (5/40); CO Einsatzkommando 9 / Einsatzgruppe B (6/22/41 - 10/20/41); returned to Berlin and held under house arrest for unspecified disciplinary violations (10/41 - Fall 1943); released and detailed to Amt V / RSHA (Fall 1943 - ?); reassigned to Kriminalpolizei (? - 5/45); lived under assumed name of Dr. Selbert in Niedersachsen (1945 - 49); worked for Braunschweig-Hannoverschen Hypothekenbank under own name (1950 - 59); taken into custody by West German authorities (2/25/59); tried before Schwurgericht Berlin (5/14 - 6/22/62); sentenced to life imprisonment (6/22/62)

Fischer, ?,
SS-? -- CO sub-unit of Sonderkommando-Mitte operating at Brest-Litovsk (4-5/44)

Fischer, Dr. Herbert,
SS-Obersturmbannführer --CO Einsatzgruppe III (Poland, 9/39-10/39); complicity in massacres at *Wloclawek* (9/22-25/39) and *Bydgoszcz 2* (9/24-26/39); Landkommissar Warschau (10/39 - 1/45); responsible for establishment of the Ghetto and various Judenaktionen; extradited from West Germany (1946?); tried for his part in the liquidation of the Warsaw Ghetto; hung in Warsaw (3/8/47)

Fischer-Schweder,Bernhard,
SS-Oberführer --Stab Gestapo Breslau (8/38 - 10/40); Führer der Statliches Polizeidirektion Memel (10/40 - 6/41); Planstelle des Polizeidirektors Memel (1/41-10/22/42); CO Schutzpolizeikommando / Einsatzkommando Tilsit / Einsatzgruppe A (6/41 - 10/42); acting SSPf Charkow and SSPf Kiew (10/10/42 - 10/22/42); attached to HSSPf Russland-Süd (10/22/42 - 9/8/43); reassigned to Waffen-SS as an enlisted man due to alcoholism (9/43); service with SS-Panzergrenadier-Ausbildungs-und Ersatzbataillon 1 (11/1/43 - 1/16/45); Kompanieführer, 12. SS-Panzer-Division *Hitlerjugend* (1/16/45 - 4/11/45); wounded and captured by Americans; arrest warrant issued by German authorities (5/3/56); never located; tried *in absentia* before Landgericht Ulm/Donau for crimes committed in Lithuania; sentenced to 10 years imprisonment for his role in the murder of 526 civilians (8/29/58); died (11/28/60)

Fitzthum, Josef,
SS-Gruppenführer -- acting Polizeipräsident Wien (1938-1940); tried for embezzlement (1940); transferred to Waffen-SS (1940); service with 9. SS-Totenkopfstandarte (1940); battalion commander, 4. SS-Totenkopfstandarte (1/41 - 7/15/41); acting CO SS-Infanterie-Regiment 4 (7/15/41 - 8/15/41); acting CO I. Bataillon / SS-Infanterie-Regiment 5 (8/15/41 - 9/1/41); CO I. Bataillon / SS-Infanterie-Regiment 4 (9/41 - 4/42); CO 27. SS-Freiwilligen-Grenadier-Division *Langemarck* [flämische Nr. 1] (4/19/42 - 7/14/42); CO SS-Freiwilligen-Legion *Niederlande* (7/42 - 5/20/43); acting CO SS-Freiwilligen-Legion *Flandern* (6/20/42 - 11/15/42); Beauftragter RFSS Albanien (10/43 - 4/44); CO 21.

Waffen-Gebirgs-Division der SS *Skanderbeg* [albanische Nr. 1] (4/44 - 6/44); directed anti-Jewish actions of division, see *Albania* and *Pristina*; HSSPf Albanien (8/1/44 - 1/1/45); died in Wien-Neudorf as a result of injuries from a car accident (1/10/45)

Flanderka, Theo,
SS-? -- service with SS-Panzeraufklärungs-Abteilung 12 / 12. SS-Panzer-Division *Hitlerjugend* (1944); complicity in the *Ascq* massacre (4/1-2/44); tried and sentenced to death in absentia by French authorities (8/2-6/49)

Flesch, Gerhard,
SS-Obersturmbannführer--CO Einsatzkommando 2 / Einsatzgruppe VI (Poland, 1939); service with *Totenkopf* division in France (1940); KdS Bergen (1940); KdS Trondheim (11/11/41 – 5/8/45); responsible for the deportation of Norwegian Jews to the Auschwitz death camp (10/7/42 - 2/43), see *Norway*; tried in Norway and sentenced to death (1946); executed by firing squad (2/28/48)

Frakowiak, Heinz,
SS-? --service with SS-Panzeraufklärungs-Abteilung 12/12. SS-Panzer-Division *Hitlerjugend* (1944); complicity in the *Ascq* massacre (4/1-2/44); tried and sentenced to death in absentia by French authorities (8/2-6/49)

Frank, Karl-Hermann,
SS-Obergruppenführer -- adjutant to Sudeten Nazi leader Heinlein (1936 - 38); Staatssekretär beim Reichsprotektor (1939); HSSPf Böhmen-Mähren (4/28/39 - 4/45); Deutscher Staatsminister im Protektorat Böhmen-Mähren (8/20/43 - 5/45); responsible for the reprisals in Czechoslovakia following the assassination of SS-Obergruppenführer Reinhard Heydrich – 1,357 executions, 657 deaths in police custody, destruction of the villages of Lidice and Lezaky; in Czech custody (1945); tried and sentenced to death; hung in Prague (5/22/46)

Franz, Hermann,
SS-Brigadeführer -- Hitlerjugend Leiter (1/39 - 8/40); CO Polizeigruppe 3 (Poland, 1939); CO Polizei-Regiment Süd (7/41 - 2/42); CO Polizei-Regiment 10 (2/42 - 5/15/42); CO SS-Polizei-Gebirgsjäger-Regiment 18

(5/42 - 8/43); BdO Griechenland (11/43 - 2/45); SSPf Griechenland (9/24/44 - 11/18/44); died (2/18/60)

Freitag, Fritz,
SS-Brigadeführer -- Schutzpolizei officer attached to 14. Armee during Polish campaign (1939); Ia Kommandostab RFSS (1941); Stab 1. SS-Infanterie (mot.) Brigade (? - 10/41); Stab Ordnungspolizei Hauptamt (11/41 - ?); CO SS-Polizei-Panzergrenadier-Regiment 2/ 4. SS-Polizei-Panzergrenadier-Division; CO 8. SS-Kavallerie-Division *Florian Geyer* (2/15/43 - 4/20/43); CO 2. SS-Infanterie [mot.]-Brigade (4/20/43 - 8/10/43); CO 14. Waffen-Grenadier-Division der SS [ukrainische Nr. 1] (11/20/43 - 4/27/45); division committed numerous atrocities against Polish civilians during his command (see *14. W-G-D der SS Crimes in Poland*); atrocity committed in *Gau Steiermark* (4/26/45); committed suicide at Andra, Austria (5/10/45)

Freitag, Dr. Joachim,
SS-Sturmbannführer -- CO Einsatzkommando 15 (Balkans); RSHA; Gestapo Schneidemühl

Friedl, Gustav,
SS-Sturmbannführer -- KdS Bialystok; directed the liquidation of the Bialystok Ghetto (9/43); tried and hanged in Bialystok (1/50)

Fritsche, Karl,
SS-Obersturmbannführer -- CO replacement squadron/SS-Hauptreitschule (11/39 - ?); CO 6. Schwadron/ II. Abteilung/SS-[Totenkopf]-Kavallerie Regiment 1 (11/40 - 3/20/41); CO Pionier-Kompanie / SS-Kavallerie-Brigade (12/41+)

Fritz, Josef,
SS-Sturmbannführer -- CO 4.Schwadron /1. SS-Totenkopf-Reiterstandarte (11/39 - 5/40); CO 3. Schwadron/2. SS-Totenkopf-Reiterstandarte (5/40 - 11/40)

Fromm, Werner,
SS-Oberführer -- service with Wehrmacht (8/39 - 11/40); Stab HSSPf Ostland (9/41 - 12/41); Stab HSSPf Russland-Süd (12/41 - 1/42); SSPf Bialystok (1/18/42 - 1/30/43); Polizeigebietsführer Sarajewo (1/1/43 - 4/26/44); service with 16. SS-Panzergrenadier-Division *Reichsführer-SS* (1/45 - 5/45); died in Bielefeld (5/10/81)

Fuchs, Dr. Wilhelm,

SS-Oberführer -- CO Einsatzgruppe Serbien-KdS Belgrade (1941 - 1942); acting HSSPf Mitte (7/8/43 - 9/15/43); CO Einsatzkommando 3-KdS Litauen / Einsatzgruppe A (9/15/43 - 5/6/44); CO Einsatzgruppe A (5/6/44 - 10/44); SD Braunschweig; tried and sentenced to death (11/22/46); executed in Belgrade (3/7/47)

Fuchs, Günther,

SS-Hauptsturmführer - RSHA; Gestapo Lodz; In co-command during the Lodz Ghetto liquidations; charged before a Hannover court with the murder of 70,000 Jews (9/63)

Fürst, Werner,

SS-? -- service with SS-Panzeraufklärungs-Abteilung 12 / 12. SS-Panzer-Division *Hitlerjugend* (1944); complicity in the *Ascq* massacre (4/1-2/44); tried and sentenced to death by French authorities (8/2-6/49); sentence reduced to 10 years hard labor minus time served (7/14/55); paroled (1956)

Gehrhardt, Friedrich,

SS-Oberführer -- acting HSSPf Warthe (8/44 - 12/30/44)

Geibel, Paul Otto,

SS-Brigadeführer -- service with Gendarmerie (4/35 - 10/42); Stab Hauptamt Ordnungspolizei (11/42 - 3/44); SSPf Warschau (3/31/44 - 2/1/45); BdO Prague (2/45 - 5/45); captured by Americans in Prague and remanded to Polish custody (1945); tried by Polish authorities (1954); returned to West Germany following long prison sentence; died (11/12/66)

Geschke, Dr. Hans,

SS-Oberführer -- CO Einsatzkommando responsible for the deportation of 458,000 Hungarian Jews to the Auschwitz death camp (3/44 - 6/44); apparently committed suicide (5/45)

Gesele, Karl,

SS-Standartenführer -- CO 10. Bataillon / SS-Standarte 1 *Deutschland* (5/38 - 8/40); Stab SS-Junkerschule Tölz (8/40 - 9/41); Stab SS-Kavallerie-Brigade (9/41 - 2/43); CO 16. SS-Panzergrenadier-Division *Reichsführer-SS* (2/14/43 - 10/3/43); CO Begleit-Bataillon *RFSS* (1944); CO SS-Panzergrenadier-Regiment 35/16. SS-Panzergrenadier-Division *Reichsführer-SS* (? - late 1944); CO 37. SS-Freiwilligen-Kavallerie-Division *Lutzow* (3/45-5/45); died of natural causes in Friedrichshafen (4/8/68)

Gilhofer, Herbert,

SS-Sturmbannführer -- CO SS-Reiterstandarte 12 (12/38 - 9/39); CO SS-Fallschirmjäger-Bataillon 500 (?/43 - 4/44)

Gille, Herbert Otto,

SS-Gruppenführer -- CO SS-Artillerie-Regiment 5/5. SS-Panzer-Division *Wiking* (1941 - 1943); CO SS-Panzer-Division *Wiking* (5/1/43 - 8/6/44); CO IV. SS-Panzer-Korps (8/44 - 5/45); captured by Americans (5/45); released from detention (5/21/48); bookseller and founder of the veteran's magazine *Wiking-Ruf*; died of natural causes in Stemmen, near Hannover (12/26/66)

Glaser, Dr. Helmut,

SS-Sturmbannführer -- CO Einsatzkommando 29 (Balkans); RSHA Amt IIIA; SD Klagenfurt; SD Krakow

Globocnik, Ulrich ("Odilo"),

SS-Gruppenführer--Gauleiter of Wien (5/24/38 - 1/39); dismissed for corruption; service with *Der Fuhrer* Regiment (1939); service in Poland with the *Germania* Regiment (1939); SSPf Lublin (11/10/39 - 8/16/43); responsible for numerous killing operations in occupied eastern Poland (1941-3); directed Aktion Reinhardt extermination centers in Poland (1942-3); HSSPf Adriatisches- Küstenland (9/13/43 - 5/45); contradictory accounts of his fate: killed by partisans in Istria (5/45), took poison at Weisensee/Karnten (Karavankan Alps) to avoid capture by a British patrol (5/31/45), captured by British and committed suicide when true identity was discovered (5/31/45) or, perhaps, none of these options.

Göhrum, Kurt,

SS-Gruppenführer -- Polizeigebietsführer Berlin (1943/44)

Goltz, Heinz,

SS-Obersturmführer -- CO HQ-Kompanie /SS-Panzeraufklärungs-Bataillon 1/1. SS-Panzer-Division *Leib-*

standarte Adolf Hitler (1944); implicated in the *Malmedy* atrocities (12/16+/44); tried by Belgian authorities and sentenced to 15 years imprisonment (7/48)

Gottberg,Curt von,
SS-Obergruppenführer--Stab RuSHA (10/37 - 11/39); Stab Reichsprotektor Böhmen-Mähren (4/39 - 11/39); head of RuSHA operations with Einsatzgruppe, Poland (9/39 - 11/39); no assignment (11/39 - 7/40); Stab SS-Hauptamt (7/40 - 10/40); Chef des Erfassungsamtes im SS-Hauptamt (10/1/40 - 7/21/42); SSPf Weissruthenien (7/21/42 - 9/22/43); acting HSSPf Russland-Mitte (7/5/43 - 8/7/44); responsible for numerous killing operations in the USSR, see *Höheren SS und Polizeiführer*; CO Kampfgruppe von Gottberg, anti-partisan operations in France (6/44 - 10/44); CO XII. SS-Armee-Korps (8/44 - 10/44, taken ill); deputy commander of the Replacement Army and detailed to Wehrmacht Heeresgruppe Nordwest (1/45 - 5/45); taken into Allied custody; committed suicide at Leutzhöft in Flensburg (5/31/45)

Götze, Hans Friedemann,
SS-Standartenführer -- CO SS-Totenkopfsturmbann *Heimwehr Danzig* (1939); responsible for the Ksiazki atrocity (9/8/39); CO SS-Totenkopfsturmbann *Götze* (1940)

Graaf, Alfred,
SS-Obersturmbannführer -- CO 21. Waffen-Gebirgs-Division der SS *Skanderbeg* [albanische Nr. 1] (8/15/44 - 5/45)

Graaf, Kurt,
SS-Sturmbannführer -- CO Einsatzkommando 1c / Einsatzgruppe A (8/42 - 11/42); RSHA Amt I; SD Schwerin

Grabau, ?,
SS-Obersturmführer -- head of the Waffen-SS Garrison Administration Radom, responsible for the massacre and deportation of *Radom* Jews to death camps (8/42)

Gräfe, Dr. Heinz,
SS-Sturmbannführer -- CO Einsatzkommando 1/ Einsatzgruppe V (Poland, 1939); SD Gumbinnen; Chef RSHA Amt VIC; killed in car accident (1/25/44)

Graf, Matthias,
SS-Untersturmführer -- service with Einsatzkommando 6 in the USSR; sentenced to time already served during Einsatzgruppen Trial at Nürnberg (4/48); released

Grassy, Josef,
Waffen-Generalleutnant -- CO 13th Hungarian Honved Infantry Division; CO present at *Novi Sad* massacres (1/21-23/42); CO 25. Waffen-Grenadier-Division der SS *Hunyadi* [ungarische Nr. 1] (5/44 - ?/45); CO 26. Waffen-Grenadier-Division der SS [ungarische Nr. 2] (3/21/45 - ?/45, wounded); removed from hospital and placed in German custody; remanded to Hungarian custody (11/45); remanded to Yugoslav custody (1/31/46); sentenced to death for war crimes (11/4/46); executed (11/5/46)

Grobben, Jakob,
SS-Sturmbannführer -- Polizeigebietsführer Copenhagen (1944 - 1945)

Gührs, Erhard,
SS-Untersturmführer -- CO 13. Schützenpanzerwagenkompanie/SS-Panzer-Regiment 2/1. SS-Panzer-Division *Leibstandarte Adolf Hitler* at the time of the *Boves* atrocity (9/43); charged with murder by the Italian authorities (12/68); case dismissed by West German authorities (2/69)

Günther, Wilhelm,
SS-Brigadeführer -- IdS Stettin (10/39 - 3/41); IdS Kassel (3/41 - 9/42); SSPf Bergvolker-Ordshonikidse (5/7/42 - 8/23/42); SSPf Rowno (9/1/42 - 6/6/44); BdS Triest (5/44 - 2/45); Stab RSHA (2/45 - 5/45); died (12/31/45)

Gutenberger, Karl,
SS-Obergruppenführer -- Polizeipräsident Duisburg (5/37 - 11/39); Polizeipräsident Essen (11/39 - 6/41); HSSPf West (6/29/41 - 5/8/45); Inspektor für den passiven Widerstand / Inspektor für Spezialabwehr [Werwolf organization](11/44 - 5/45); sentenced to 12 years in prison for the execution of foreign civilian workers (1948); sentenced to 4 years imprisonment for the murder of the Aachen Oberbürgermeister (1949); other proceedings against the defendant occurred - served a total of five years in prison; died in Essen (7/8/61)

Hagetorn, ?,

SS-Stabscharführer -- member of 12. SS-Panzer-Division *Hitlerjugend* found by Canadian investigators to be complicitous in the *Normandy* atrocities (6/7-17/44); KIA

Hahn, Dr. Ludwig,

SS-Standartenführer -- CO Einsatzkommando 1 / Einsatzgruppe I (Poland, 1939); KdS Krakau (1/40); Sonderbeauftragter des RFSS Pressburg (8/14/40); Stab SS Hauptamt (9/19/40); KdS Warschau (10/20/41); commanded SD and Wehrmacht elements during suppression of the *Warsaw Ghetto Uprising* (4-5/43); directed final deportations during the Warsaw Ghetto Uprising; Regierungsdirektor Warschau (4/30/44); CO Einsatzgruppe L [Westfront] (12/16/44); Beauftragten des Chefs der SIPO und des SD beim Befehlshaber der Sperr- und Auffanglinie im Rahmen der Heeresgruppe Weichsel (1945); Stab RSHA Dresden (1945); KdS Westfalen (3/45); hid post-war; arrested (1960); released (7/61); re-arrested (12/65); released 2 years later due to poor health; put on trial by the Landgericht Hamburg and sentenced to twelve years imprisonment for killings at Warsaw's Pawiak Prison (6/73); tried and sentenced to fifteen years imprisonment for acts against Jews (7/75)

Hahn, Werner,

SS-Sturmbannführer -- CO 24. Waffen-Gebirgs-Division der SS *Karstjäger* (1944); died (7/12/82)

Haltermann, Hans Dietrich,

SS-Gruppenführer -- Stab SS-Abschnitt XIV (4/19/36 - 4/40); recalled to Wehrmacht for service in Belgrade and the Ukraine (4/20/40 - 8/41); reclaimed by SS; SSPf Kiew (10/1/41 - 5/19/43); SSPf Charkow (5/19/43 - 9/11/43); SSPf Mogilew (9/20/43 - 7/12/44); acting HSSPf Nordost (7/7/44 - 1/9/45); in charge of building defensive positions in the General Government, Poland (7/44 - 1/45); Stab SS-Personalhauptamt (1/45 - 3/15/45); Stab Polizeipräsident Bremen (3/15/45 - 5/45); died in Paderborn, West Germany (6/17/81)

Hammer, Dr. Walter,

SS-Sturmbannführer -- CO Einsatzkommando 2 / Einsatzgruppe IV (Poland, 1939); RSHA Amt VIE; SD Prague

Hampel, Desiderius,

SS-Brigadeführer -- CO IV. Bataillon/SS-Freiwilligen-Gebirgsjäger-Regiment 13/7. SS-Freiwilligen-Gebirgs-Division *Prinz Eugen* (1942 - Fall 1943); CO SS-Freiwilligen-Gebirgsjäger-Regiment 27/13. Waffen-Gebirgs-Division der SS *Handschar* [kroatische Nr. 1] (Fall 1943 - 6/44); CO 13. Waffen-Gebirgs-Division der SS *Handschar* [kroatische Nr. 1] (6/44 - 5/8/45); atrocity committed in *Gau Steiermark* (3/24-25/45); captured by British; extradition sought by Yugoslavs; escapes from POW camp and settles in Graz; died (1981)

Hänsch, Dr. Walter,

SS-Obersturmbannführer -- CO Sonderkommando 4b / Einsatzgruppe C (3/21/42 - 7/42); RSHA Amt ID; condemned to death during Einsatzgruppen Trial at Nürnberg (4/48); sentence commuted to 15 years imprisonment; released (1955)

Hansen, Christian "Cissy",

SS-Sturmbannführer -- CO Pionierzug/1. SS-Panzer-Division *Leibstandarte Adolf Hitler*; complicity in the *Torzeniec* atrocity (9/1/39); CO SS-Pionierabteilung *LAH* (Greece/USSR, 1941); fate unknown

Hansen, Max,

SS-Obersturmbannführer -- service with 1. SS-Panzer-Division *Leibstandarte Adolf Hitler* (1939 - 1945) including a stint as CO SS-Panzergrenadier-Regiment 1 (1944); died in Niebüll (3/7/90)

Hansen, Peter,

SS-Brigadeführer -- CO SS-Artillerie-Regiment (6/1/39 - 8/10//39); service with 2. SS-Panzer-Division *Das Reich* (1940 - 41); inspector of artillerie, SS-Hauptamt (Fall 1941 - ?); taken ill (? - ?); department chief of SS-Junkerschulen (? - 3/1/43); CO 15. Waffen-Grenadier-Division der SS [lettische Nr. 1] (3/26/43 - 5/43); CO 29. Waffen-Grenadier-Division der SS [italienische Nr. 1] (9/43 - 10/43); taken ill (? - ?); CO 29. Waffen-Grenadier-Division der SS [italienische Nr. 1] (12/43 - 1/45); taken ill (? - ?); Chief of Staff, XVIII. SS-Armee-Korps (1/45 - 4/45); captured by French (4/45); died (5/23/67)

Hansman, ?,

SS-Obersturmführer -- officer attached to HQ-Kompanie / SS-Panzeraufklärungs-Abteilung 12 / 12. SS-Panzer-Division *Hitlerjugend*; complicity in the *Normandy* atrocities (6/7-17/44)

Harder, Karl-Arthur,
SS-Hauptsturmführer -- deputy commander Sonderkommando 1005; CO Sonderkommando-Mitte (10/43 - 11/43); assisted with formation of sonderkommando in Bialystok District (5/44); sentenced to three years imprisonment (1962)

Harm, Hermann,
SS-Brigadeführer -- Stab SS-Oberabschnitt Nord (5/39 - 7/42); SSPf zbV attached to HSSPf Russland-Süd (7/42); SSPf Dnjepropetrowsk-Krivoi Rog (8/1/42 - 10/4/42); SSPf zbV attached to HSSPf Russland-Süd (10/42 - 7/43); SSPf Litauen (7/2/43 - 4/8/44); Stab HöSSPf Ukraine (4/44 - 11/44); acting HSSPf Alpenland (11/44 - 5/45); died in Hartenholm, West Germany (11/28/85)

Harmel, Heinz,
SS-Brigadeführer -- service with *Der Führer* Regiment in France (1940); CO SS-Panzergrenadier-Regiment 3 *Deutschland* / 2. SS-Panzer-Division *Das Reich* (12/41 - 5/44); CO 10. SS-Panzer-Division *Frundsberg* (5/1/44 - 5/8/45); possible complicity in the *Putten* atrocity (9/30/44); commander of division at the time of alleged *Horka* massacre (4/26/45); captured by British and interned for two years; died at Krefeld (9/2/00)

Harster, Wilhelm,
SS-Oberführer -- BdS Nederland (? - 1943); KdS Roma; sentenced to 12 years imprisonment by The Hague Court (1949); released (1955)

Hartmann, Erich,
SS-Sturmbannführer -- CO Einsatzkommando Luxembourg; 2. SS-Infanterie (mot.) -Brigade (1941-42); III. SS-Korps (1943)

Hartmann, Ernst,
SS-Brigadeführer -- dismissed from SS due to drunkenness (8/18/39); re-admitted to SS (10/1/39); Stab SS-Oberabschnitt Mitte (10/39 - 2/43); CO II./SS-Polizei-Regiment 2 (2/43 - 6/43); SSPf Tschernigow (7/1/43

- 10/31/43); SSPf Shitomir (9/25/43 - 10/21/43); SSPf Pripet (12/18/43 - 9/6/44); acting SSPf Rowno (2/10/44 - 9/6/44); SSPf zbV with HSSPf Nordost (9/44 - 2/3/45); KIA in Czechoslovakia (2/3/45)

Harzer, Walter,
SS-Standartenführer -- service with SS-Regiment *Deutschland* (1938 - 39); Inspektionschef und Taktiklehrer, SS-Junkerschule Braunschweig (1940); Taktiklehrer, SS-Unterführerschule Radolfzell (1940); service with 2. SS-Panzer-Division *Das Reich* (Spring 1941 - 3/43); Stab 10. SS-Panzer-Division *Frundsberg* (3/43 - 5/43); Stab 9. SS-Panzer-Division *Hohenstaufen* (5/43 - 11/44); CO 4. SS-Polizei-Panzergrenadier-Division (11/28/44 - 5/45); died in Stuttgart (5/29/82)

Hasselberg, Dr. Alfred,
SS-Sturmbannführer -- CO Einsatzkommando 3 / Einsatzgruppe I (Poland, 1939); RSHA; Gestapo Lublin

Hauck, Walter,
SS-Obersturmführer -- CO 2. (Pz. Späh.) Kompanie / SS-Panzeraufklärungs-Abteilung 12 / 12. SS-Panzer-Division *Hitlerjugend* (1944); one of the primary officers responsible for the *Ascq* massacre (1/2 April 1944); tried by French and sentenced to death (8/2-6/49), sentence reduced to life imprisonment at hard labor (7/14/55); paroled (7/57)

Hauer, ?,
SS-Untersturmführer -- CO 3. (Aufkl.) Kompanie/SS-Panzeraufklärungs-Abteilung 12/12.SS-Pazer-Division *Hitlerjugend* (1944); complicitous in the *Ascq* massacre (1/2 April 1944); never brought to trial

Hausser, Paul,
SS-Oberstgruppenführer -- main formative influence on the Waffen-SS, known as "Papa Hausser" by his men; Inspektor des SS-Verfugungstruppen (10/1/36 - 10/19/39); CO 2. SS-Panzer-Division *Das Reich* (10/19/39 - 10/14/41, wounded); divisional commander at time of the *Lahoysk* massacre (9/41); CO II. SS-Panzer-Korps (5/28/42 - 6/12/44); CO 7. Armee (6/12/44 - 1/22/45); CO Heeresgruppe Oberrhein (1/22/45 - 4/3/45); CO Heeresgruppe G (4/3/45 - 5/8/45); captured by Americans at Zell am See, Austria; main defense witness for the Waffen-SS before the International Military Tribu-

nal at Nürnberg; senior member of HIAG and author of several works on the Waffen-SS; died at Ludwigsburg (12/21/72)

Haussmann, Emil,
SS-Sturmbannführer -- service with Einsatkommando 12 in the USSR; indicted (1947); committed suicide (7/31/47)

Heilmann, Nikolaus,
SS-Brigadeführer -- Stab 4. SS-Polizei-Panzergrenadier-Division; (1940 - 44); CO 15. Waffen-Grenadier-Division der SS [lettische Nr. 1] (2/17/44 - 7/44); MIA, Eastern Front (1/4/45)

Heinrichs, ?,
SS-Untersturmführer -- CO 2. platoon / 7. Kompanie/ II.Bataillon/1.SS-Panzer-Division *Leibstandarte Adolf Hitler*; complicity in *Wormhoudt* atrocity (5/28/40); killed in action, USSR

Heissmeyer, August,
SS-Obergruppenführer -- Chef SS-Hauptamt (5/22/35 - 10/1/40); HSSPf Spree (9/2/39 - 5/8/45); Inspector of Concentration Camps and SS-Totenkopfstandarten (11/15/39 - 8/15/40); CO Kampfgruppe Heissmeyer, Berlin defense (4/45); arrested by French authorities and sentenced to 18 months imprisonment (1948); released (1949); died at Schwabisch Hall, West Germany (1/16/79)

Held, Dr. Heinrich,
SS-Sturmbannführer -- CO SS-Veterinär-Ersatz-Abteilung in *Radom*, occupied Poland; responsible for the massacre and deportation of Radom Jews to death camps (8/42)

Heldmann, Constantin von,
SS-Standartenführer -- service with SS-Artillerie-Ersatz-Abteilung (11/39 - 12/39); service with 3. SS-Panzer-Division *Totenkopf* (12/39 - 1/41); CO IV. / SS-Artillerie-Regiment 5 / 5. SS-Panzer-Division *Wiking* (1/41 - 6/41); service with SS-Artillerie-Ersatz-Regiment (6/41 - 10/41); CO SS-Gebirgsartillerie-Regiment 6 / 6. SS-Gebirgs-Division *Nord* (10/41 - 3/42); CO SS-Artillerie-Ersatz-Regiment (3/42 - 8/42); Stab Finnisches-Freiwilligen-Bataillon der Waffen-SS (8/42 - 3/44); Stab

HöSPPf Italien (3/44 - 5/45); CO 29. Waffen-Grenadier-Division der SS [italienische Nr. 1] (1/45 - 3/9/45)

Hellwig, Otto,
SS-Gruppenführer -- CO Teilkommando 1 / Einsatzgruppe zbV in southwestern Poland (8/39 - 10/39); Chef Gestapo Stettin (3/41 - 5/41); IdS Stettin (5/41 - 10/42); SSPf Shitomir (10/22/41 - 5/20/43); SSPf Bialystok (5/20/43 - 7/18/44); acting HSSPf Nordost (1/9/45 - 5/8/45); died in Hannover, West Germany (8/20/62)

Helm, Hans,
SS-? -- Stab Einsatzgruppen Serbien

Henne, August,
SS-Obersturmführer -- CO 7. Kompanie / II. Bataillon / SS-Panzergrenadier-Regiment 26 / 12. SS-Panzer-Division *Hitlerjugend*; possible complicity in the *Normandy* atrocities (6/7-17/44)

Hennecke, Hans,
SS-Untersturmführer -- CO SS-Panzer-Kompanie 1/ SS-Panzer-Bataillon 1/SS-Panzer-Regiment 1 / 1. SS-Panzer-Division *Leibstandarte Adolf Hitler* (1944); implicated in the *Malmedy* atrocities (12/16+/44); defendant at the *Malmedy* Trial (5/16/46 - 7/11/46); found guilty; sentenced to death (7/16/46); sentence commuted; released from custody

Hennicke, Paul,
SS-Gruppenführer -- Polizeipräsident Weimar (4/38 - 10/42); SSPf Stanislav-Rostow (10/1/42 - 5/1/43); SSPf Kiew (5/1/43 - 12/43); SSPf zbV with HöSSPf Ukraine (12/43 - 6/44); SS-Hauptamt (6/44 - 1/45); Inspektor Volkssturm Mitte (1/45 - 5/45); captured and tried (1949); found not guilty and released; died in Brunswick (7/25/67)

Herf, Eberhard,
SS-Brigadeführer -- CO Ordnungspolizei Minsk; BdO Ukraine (1943?); executed in Russia (1945)

Herff, Maximillian von,
SS-Obergruppenführer -- KdO Kharkov (1941 - 1942); SS Personalhauptamt (10/1/42 - 5/8/45); died of natural causes in while in British custody (9/6/45) or executed at Minsk (2/6/48)

Herrmann, Günther,
SS-Obersturmbannführer -- CO 16. SS-Totenkopf-standarte (? - ?); CO Sonderkommando 4b / Ein-satzgruppe C (6/22/41 - 9/41); CO Einsatzkommando 12/Einsatzgruppe D (10/42 - 3/43); CO Einsatzgruppe E (Balkans); sentenced to seven years imprisonment by Düsseldorf court (1973)

Hermann, Richard,
SS-Brigadeführer -- CO 7. SS-Totenkopfstandarte (? - 6/11/40); CO 6. SS-Gebirgs-Division *Nord* (6/12/40 - 5/25/41); CO 1. SS-Infanterie [mot.] Brigade (6/25/41 - 7/4/42); responsible for numerous murder actions, see *1. SS-Infanterie-Brigade Operations and Atrocities in the USSR*; responsible for massacres in the *Zwiahel region* (7/28-30/41), at *Staro-Konstantinov* (8/21/41) and at *Ush-omir* (9/17/41); assisted in the massacre of 23,600 Jews at *Kamenets-Podol'skiy* (8/29 - 9/12/41); participated in the planning and execution of the *Dnepropetrovsk* atrocity in which 32,600 Jews were murdered (10/41)

Heuckenkamp, Dr. Rudolf,
SS-Oberführer -- acting SSPf Stalino-Donezgebiet (8/42)

Heuser, Georg-Albert,
SS-Hauptsturmführer -- CO Einsatzkommando 14 in the Balkans (1941)

Hierthes, Heino,
SS-Standartenführer -- service with SS-Totenkopf-standarte 3 *Thüringen* (8/37 - 11/1/39); service with 3. SS-Panzer-Division *Totenkopf* (11/1/39 - 11/40); CO To-tenkopf-Infanterie-Ersatz-Bataillon Radolfzell (11/40 - 1/41); CO 8. SS-Totenkopfstandarte (1/10/41 - 4/9/41); CO SS-Kavallerie-Regiment 2 (4/11/41 - 8/1/41); CO SS-Infanterie-Regiment 8/1. SS-Infanterie (mot.) Bri-gade (9/41 - 1/42); CO SS-Infanterie-Ersatz-Battalion *Ost*/Kommandostab RFSS (2/42 - 10/42); responsible for numerous killing operations, see *SS-Kavallerie-Brigade Operations and Atrocities in the USSR* and *Pripet Marshes*; Stab SS Hauptamt (10/42 - 2/44); service with 20. Waffen-Grenadier-Division der SS [estnische Nr. 1] (3/44 - 5/44); Stab HSSPf Schwarzes Meer (5/44 - 9/44); CO Waffen-Grenadier-Regiment der SS 33 / 15. Waffen-Grenadier-Division der SS [lettische Nr. 1] (10/44 - 4/45); died in Soviet custody (1953)

Hildebrandt, Ernst,
SS-Brigadeführer -- Polizeipräsident Hof an der Saale (8/37 - 7/40); Polizeipräsident Dessau (7/40 - 5/45); service with Kampfgruppe Jeckeln in the USSR (6/42 - 9/42); service with SS-Gebirgsjäger-Regiment 1/7. SS-Freiwilligen-Gebirgs-Division *Prinz Eugen* (9/42 - 6/43); Stab 7. SS-Freiwilligen-Gebirgs-Division *Prinz Eugen* (6/43 - 8/43); Stab HSSPf Russland-Süd (8/43 - 4/44); SSPf Oberitalien-Mitte (4/44 - 10/44); SSPf zbV for HSSPf Südost (10/44 - 2/45); SSPf zbV for HSSPf West (2/45 - 5/45); died in Nürnberg (3/28/70)

Hildebrandt, Richard,
SS-Obergruppenführer -- HSSPf Rhein (4/1/39 - 10/1/39); HSSPf Weichsel (9/21/39 - 4/20/43); Chef RuSHA (4/20/43 - 5/8/45); HSSPf Schwarzes-Meer (12/25/43 - 9/16/44); acting SSPf Taurien-Krim-Simfer-opol (12/25/43 - 9/5/44); HSSPf Südost (3/17/45 - 5/8/45); HSSPf Böhmen-Mähren (4/45 - 5/45); sentenced at Nürnberg to 25 years imprisonment (3/10/48); re-manded to Polish custody; tried and sentenced to death (1949); hung in Bromberg (3/10/52)

Hintze, Kurt,
SS-Brigadeführer -- CO SS-Abschnitt XI (10/37 - 2/40); SS und Selbstschutz Führer, Poland (11/39 - 2/40); CO SS-Abschnitt XXXXI (2/40 - 1/41); service with 1. SS-Panzer-Division *Leibstandarte Adolf Hitler* (9/40 - 11/40); Stab RKFDV (1/41 - 10/43); Stab SS-Trup-penübungsplatz Kurmark (10/43 - 2/44); Stab HSSPf Russland-Nord (2/44 - 4/44); SSPf Litauen (4/4/44 - 9/15/44); Reichkomissar Festungsstab Oberschlesien (9/15/44 - 11/13/44); killed in Kattowitz during air raid (11/13/44)

Hoff, Otto,
SS-Hauptscharführer -- member of SS-Panzer-aufklärungs-Abteilung 2/2. SS-Panzer-Division *Das Reich*; commanded *Tulle* execution squad; tried before a French military tribunal at Bordeaux (7/5/51); sen-tenced to life imprisonment; sentence overturned on appeal; released (1953)

Höfle, Hermann,
SS-Obergruppenführer -- Selbstschutzbereichsführer Neu Sandez [Nowy Sacz] (12/10/39 - 9/1/40); posted at Zwangsarbeitslager Bug-Graben (11/1/40 - ?); attached

to staff of SSPf Lublin and staff of Aktion Reinhardt (1941 - 1943); responsible for planning and activating the deportation of 2.2 million Jews to the death camps; HSSPf Mitte (9/15/43 - 10/5/44); HSSPf Slowakien (9/20/44 - 5/45); suppressed *Slovak National Uprising* and oversaw deportations of Czechoslovakian Jews to death camps; escaped from internment camp in Austria while awaiting deportation to Poland (1947); arrested in Salzburg, Austria (1/61); committed suicide while in custody in Vienna (8/21/62)

Hofmann, Otto,

SS-Obergruppenführer -- Chef RuSHA (9/39 - 4/43); participant at the Wannsee Conference; HSSPf Südwest (4/21/43 - 5/45); sentenced at Nürnberg to 25 years imprisonment as part of the RuSHA case; released from Landsberg prison (1954); died in Bad Mergentheim (12/31/82)

Holzapfel,?,

SS-Obersturmbannführer -- CO Einsatzgruppe zbV detachment near Lvov, Poland

Huber, Hubert,

SS-Oberscharführer -- CO Panzer 624/ SS-Panzer-Regiment 1/1. SS-Panzer-Division *Leibstandarte Adolf Hitler* (1944); implicated in the *Malmedy* atrocities (12/16+/44); defendant at the *Malmedy* Trial (5/16/46 - 7/11/46); found guilty; sentenced to death (7/16/46); sentence commuted; released from custody

Hubig, Dr. Hermann,

SS-Sturmbannführer -- CO Einsatzkommando 1b / Einsatzgruppe A (mid-1942 - 10/42); RSHA Amt VIB; SD Prague; lived post-war under the alias of Helmut Haller

Isselhorst,Dr.Erich,

SS-Standartenführer -- CO Einsatzkommando 8 / Einsatzgruppe B (9/42 - 11/42); CO Einsatzkommando 1/ Einsatzgruppe A (11/42-6/43); CO Sonderkommando 1b-KdS Weissruthenien / Einsatzgruppe A (6/30/43 - 10/43); SD Strassburg; SD Stuttgart; sentenced to death by French Military Tribunal; executed (2/23/48)

Jäger, Karl,

SS-Standartenführer -- CO Einsatzkommando 3-KdS Litauen/Einsatzgruppe A (6/22/41 - Fall 1943); Chief of Police Reichenberg [Sudetenland] (late 1943); RSHA; SD Münster; arrested by West German authorities (4/59); committed suicide while in custody awaiting trial (6/22/59)

Jaskulsky, Dr. Hans,

SS-Sturmbannführer -- CO Einsatzkommando 13 (1944 Slovakian Uprising); RSHA; SD Graz

Jeckeln, Friedrich,

SS-Obergruppenführer -- HSSPf Mitte (6/28/38 - 7/11/40); CO I. Bataillon/SS-Totenkopf-Infanterie-Regiment 2/3. SS-Panzer-Division *Totenkopf* (1940); HSSPf West (7/12/40 - 6/29/41); HSSPf Russland-Süd (6/23/41 - 11/1/41); ordered the massacre of 23,600 Jews at Kamenets-Podol'skiy (8/29 - 9/12/41); participated in planning and execution of the *Babi Yar* atrocity in which 33,771 Jews were murdered (9/29-30/41); participated in the planning and execution of the *Dnepropetrovsk* atrocity in which 32,600 Jews were murdered (10/41); gave orders for the following massacres: Riga Jews (11-12/41) for a total of 17,400 deaths; Berditschev (9/41) and Rowno (11/41) massacres; HSSPf Ostland und Russland-Nord (11/1/41 - 4/45); Aktion Sumpffieber (2/42 - 3/42): 389 partisans killed, 1,274 persons executed on suspicion, 8,350 Jews liquidated; CO Kampfgruppe Jeckeln (2/17/42 - 8/13/42 and 11/11/43 - 1/14/44); CO V. SS-Freiwilligen-Gebirgs-Korps (2/17/45 - 5/45); arrested by Allies but remanded to Soviet custody; was one of six German generals, all local commanders, who were tried by a Soviet People's Court in Riga (1/26/46 - 2/3/46); hanged in the former Riga ghetto (2/3/46)

Jedamzik,Eduard,

SS-Sturmbannführer --CO Sonderkommando 10b / Einsatzgruppe D (2/43 - 5/43); RSHA AmtIII; Gestapo Plauen; Gestapo Koblenz; Gestapo Chemnitz; died during preliminary legal proceedings (1966)

Jedicke, George,

SS-Gruppenführer -- BdS Ostland

Jena, Leo von,

SS-Gruppenführer -- CO 8. SS-Totenkopfstandarte (?/39 - 5/5/40+); SS-Standortkommandant Berlin (1944)

Jöckel, Walter,
SS-Sturmbannführer -- CO 51. SS-Panzergrenadier-Brigade at time of *Troyes* atrocity (8/22-26/44); captured by Americans (8/28/44)

Jost, Dr. Heinz,
SS-Brigadeführer -- CO Einsatzgruppe *Dresden* (1939); Chef Amt IV/RSHA (1939 - 42); CO Einsatzgruppe A (3/24/42 - 9/42); service with Ostministerium, unbeknownst to Himmler (9/42 - 5/44); reduced in rank to SS-Untersturmführer and service with Waffen-SS (5/44 - 5/45); sentenced to life imprisonment during Einsatzgruppen Trial at Nürnberg (4/48); sentence commuted to 10 years imprisonment (1951); released (12/51); fined 15,000 marks by West Berlin denazification court (1959); released (1960); further legal proceedings initiated (1961); died (11/12/64)

Juels, Carl,
SS-? -- company CO with 7. SS-Freiwilligen-Gebirgs-Division *Prinz Eugen*; responsible for *Kosutica* massacre (7/12/43); tried by SS court and sentenced to eight years imprisonment

Jung, Walter,
SS-? -- service with SS-Panzeraufklärungs-Abteilung 12 / 12. SS-Panzer-Division *Hitlerjugend* (1944); complicity in the *Ascq* massacre (4/1-2/44); tried and sentenced to death by French authorities (8/2-6/49); sentenced reduced to 10 years hard labor minus time served (7/14/55); paroled (1956)

Jungclaus, Richard,
SS-Gruppenführer -- CO SS-Abschnitt IV (11/38 - 4/42); Stab SS-Junkerschule Braunschweig (1/40 - 5/40); service with 11. and 4. SS-Totenkopfstandarten (5/40 - 4/41); service with 5. SS-Panzer-Division *Wiking* (6/15/41 - 10/41); advisor to Dutch SS (9/41 - 4/42); CO Germanische Leitstelle Flandern (4/42 - 8/44); HSSPf Belgien-Nordfrankreich (8/1/44 - 9/16/44); downgraded and transferred for unauthorized retreat (9/44); service with 7. SS-Freiwilligen-Gebirgs-Division *Prinz Eugen* (late 1944 - 4/25/45); KIA at Savidovice, Yugoslavia (4/15/45)

Junker, Benno,
SS-Obersturmführer -- CO SS-Panzer-Kompanie 6/ SS-Panzer-Bataillon 1/SS-Panzer-Regiment 1/1. SS-Panzer-Division *Leibstandarte Adolf Hitler* (1944); implicated in the *Malmedy* atrocities (12/16+/44)

Jura, Karl,
SS-Oberscharführer -- service with SS-Panzeraufklärungs-Abteilung 12/12. SS-Panzer-Division *Hitlerjugend* (1944); complicity in *Ascq* massacre (4/1-2/44); KIA Normandy (6/8/44); sentenced to death in absentia (1949)

Jürgensen, Arnold,
SS-Sturmbannführer -- CO I. Abteilung/SS-Panzer-Regiment 12/12.SS-Panzer-Division *Hitlerjugend*; complicity in the *Normandy* atrocities (6/7-17/44); KIA in the Ardennes (12/44)

Kaaserer, Richard,
SS-Oberführer -- Stab SS-Abschnitt XXXII (1/39 - 12/40); Chef des Sippenamtes / RuSHA (12/40 - 12/41); Chef des Ahnentafelamt / RuSHA (12/41 - 2/42); Stab RuSHA (2/42 - 6/42); inducted into Waffen-SS and assigned to SS-Gebirgsjager-Ersatz-Bataillon *Nord* (6/20/42); CO I. Bataillon / SS-Gebirgsjäger-Regiment 2/7. SS-Freiwilligen-Gebirgs-Division *Prinz Eugen* (6/25/42 - 2/43); responsible for the massacre at *Kriva Reka* (10/13/42); transferred from *Prinz Eugen* due to his brutality towards recruits (3/43); CO SS Vehicle Replacement Battalion (3/43 - 5/43); CO SS-Panzergrenadier-Ausbildungs und Ersatz Bataillon 10 (5/43 - 7/43); Polizeigebietsführer Knin (7/27/43 - 5/20/44); Stab SS-Personal Hauptamt (5/20/44); Stab HSSPf Adriatisches Kustenland (6/21/44); SSPf Sandschak (6/21/44 - 11/28/44); SSPf Mitte-Norwegen (11/28/44 - 5/45); taken prisoner in Norway at war's end; extradited to Yugoslavia; tried and executed

Kahn, Otto,
SS-Hauptsturmführer -- attached to SS-Feldgendarmerie elements of 2. SS-Panzer-Division Das Reich and its precursor units (10/13/38 - early 1944); transferred to divisional panzergrenadier elements; CO 3. Kompanie / I. Bataillon / SS-Panzergrenadier-Regiment 4 *Der Führer* / 2. SS-Panzer-Division *Das Reich*; complicity in the *Frayssinet-le-Gelat* (5/21/44) and *Ora-*

dour sur Glane (6/10/44) atrocities; badly wounded in Normandy; posted to various reservist positions (9/44 - 2/10/45); rumored to be living post-war in Sweden under assumed identity; tried by French military tribunal at Bordeaux and sentenced to death in absentia (3/12/53); death by natural causes (4/14/77)

Kaiser, Vinzenz,

SS-Obersturmbannführer -- various commands in the 2. SS-Panzer-Division *Das Reich* (1941-45); CO SS-Panzergrenadier-Lehr-Regiment (1944 - 45); CO 17. SS-Panzergrenadier-Division *Götz von Berlichingen* (~ 3/24/45); CO SS-Panzergrenadier-Regiment 38/17. SS-Panzergrenadier-Division *Götz von Berlichingen* (4/45 - 4/19/45); MIA near Nürnberg - found wounded and then murdered by American forces

Kalischko, Ludwig,

SS-Hauptsturmführer -- CO SS-Panzerartillerie-Bataillon 1/SS-Panzer-Regiment 1/1. SS-Panzer-Division *Leibstandarte Adolf Hitler* (1944); implicated in the *Malmedy* atrocities (12/16+/44)

Kaltenbrunner, Dr. Ernst,

SS-Obergruppenführer -- HSSPf Donau (9/11/38 - 1/31/43); Reichsprotektor Böhmen-Mähren (after 1/1/43); Chef RSHA (1/43 - 5/45); fled to Tirol at war's end; captured and tried by the IMT at Nürnberg; sentenced to death (10/1/46); hung (10/16/46)

Kaminski, Bronislav,

Waffen-Brigadeführer -- CO Selbstschutz Gemeinde Lokot, USSR [nucleus for the 29. Waffen-Grenadier-Division der SS (russische Nr. 1)] (?/42 - 8/25/44); assisted in the suppression of the *Warsaw Uprising* (8/44 - 10/44) -- numerous atrocities; arrested by SS in Lodz on charges of looting; found guilty and executed (8/25/44); his death was officially attributed to a partisan ambush near Lodz

Kammerhofer, Konstantin,

SS-Gruppenführer -- CO SS-Abschnitt XXXI (3/38 - 10/42); Aufstellung flämische SS in Brüssel (6/41 - 4/42); Stab SSPf Dnjepropetrowsk (4/42 - 8/42); SSPf Kaukasien-Kuban (8/21/42 - 11/11/42); SSPf Aserbeidschan (11/14/42 - 4/21/43); HSSPf Kroatien (3/13/43 - 1/10/45); Wehrmachtsbefehlshaber Kroatien (1/10/45 - 5/45); captured by Americans (1945); remanded to Austrian cus-

tody for trial in Graz; escaped from prison; discovered in a boarding house near Oberstdorf (1958); died soon thereafter (9/29/58)

Karst, Emil,

SS-Sturmbannführer -- CO SS-Panzergrenadier-Bataillon 1/SS-Panzergrenadier-Regiment 1/1. SS-Panzer-Division *Leibstandarte Adolf Hitler* (1944); suspected complicity in *Malmedy* atrocities

Katzmann, Friedrich,

SS-Gruppenführer -- Selbstschutzführer Ostoberschlesien (9/39 - 11/1/39); SSPf Radom (11/30/39 - 8/8/41); Beauftragter des RKFDV Danzig-Westpreussen (1941 - 1942); SSPf Lemberg (4/8/41 - 4/20/43); organizer of the massacre of 400,000 Jews in Eastern Galicia; HSSPf Weichsel (4/20/43 - 5/45); assumed the alias Bruno Albrecht and vanished (1945); on the run and rumored in Egypt (1952); died in Darmstadt (9/19/57)

Kaul, Kurt,

SS-Gruppenführer -- HSSPf Südwest (9/6/39 - 4/21/43); service with SS-Artillerie-Schule Beneschau (9/22/44); CO II./SS-Artillerie-Regiment 22/22. SS-Freiwillgen-Kavallerie Division *Maria Theresia* (11/44); KIA in Budapest (12/25/44)

Kempin, Hans,

SS-Standartenführer -- CO 32. SS-Freiwilligen-Grenadier-Division *30. Januar* (mid 3/45 - 5/6/45)

Keppler, Georg,

SS-Gruppenführer -- CO SS-Panzergrenadier-Regiment 4 *Der Führer* (3/23/38 - 7/14/41); CO 3. SS-Panzer-Division *Totenkopf* (7/15/41 - 9/9/41); CO 2. SS-Panzer-Division *Das Reich* (4/1/42 - 2/15/43, taken ill); Befehlshaber der Waffen-SS Böhmen-Mähren (8/43 - 1/5/44); Befehlshaber der Waffen-SS Ungarn (4/7/44 - 6/21/44); CO I. SS-Panzer-Korps (6/21/44 - 9/18/44); CO III. [germanische] SS-Panzer-Korps (10/30/44 - 2/4/45); CO XVIII. SS-Armee-Korps (2/8/45 - 5/8/45); taken into custody by Americans (5/22/45); released from custody (4/26/48); died in Hamburg of complications from war wounds (6/16/66)

Kirchner, ?,

SS-Untersturmführer -- member of 12. SS-Panzer-Division *Hitlerjugend* found by Canadian investigators to be complicitous in the *Normandy* atrocities (6/7-17/44); fate unknown

Kleinheisterkamp, Matthias,
SS-Brigadeführer -- Stab SS-Standarte *Deutschland* (1938); service with 3. SS-Panzer-Division *Totenkopf* (1940 - 41); CO 3. SS-Panzer-Division *Totenkopf* (7/7/41 - 7/15/41); CO 2. SS-Panzer-Division *Das Reich* (1/1/42 - 4/1/42); CO 6. SS-Gebirgs-Division *Nord* (5/2/42 - 12/15/43); CO XI. SS-Panzer-Korps (Autumn 1944 - 5/2/45); committed suicide near Halbe (5/8/45)

Klingelhöfer, Oskar,
SS-Hauptsturmführer -- CO SS-Panzer-Kompanie 7/ SS-Panzer-Bataillon 1/SS-Panzer-Regiment 1/1. SS-Panzer-Division *Leibstandarte Adolf Hitler* (1944); implicated in the *Malmedy* atrocities (12/16+/44); defendant at the *Malmedy* Trial (5/16/46 - 7/11/46); found guilty; sentenced to death (7/16/46); sentence commuted; released from custody

Klingelhöfer, Waldemar,
SS-Sturmbannführer -- CO Sonderkommando 7c/ Einsatzgruppe B (8/21/41 - 10/41); RSHA Amt VI; SD Fulda-Werra; SD Kassel; condemned to death during Einsatzgruppen Trial at Nürnberg (4/48); commuted to life imprisonment (1951); paroled (1956)

Klingemann, Gottfried,
SS-Brigadeführer -- CO 13. SS-Totenkopfstandarte (? - ?); CO 2. SS-Infanterie [mot.]-Brigade (7/5/41 - 1/26/43); responsible for numerous killing operations, *see 2. SS-Infanterie-Brigade Operations & Atrocities in the USSR*; responsible for *Tosno* killings (10/15-23/41); Stab SS Junkerschule Tölz; Stab RSHA

Klingemeier, Artur,
SS-Hauptsturmführer -- CO 7. Kompanie/ II.Bataillon/1. SS-Panzer-Division *Leibstandarte Adolf Hitler* (9/12/39 - ?)

Klingenberg, Fritz,
SS-Oberführer -- Stab des Selbstschutzführer Posen-Wartheland (1939); CO Kradschützen-Bataillon/2. SS-Panzer-Division *Das Reich* (1940 - 42); Stadtkommandanten Belgrad (?/41 - ?); Lehrgruppenkomman-

deur des Verfassers, SS-Junkerschule Tölz (1942 - ?); Kommandeur der Schule für die Führerlehrgänge der germanischen Freiwilligen, SS-Junkerschule Tölz (? - 1/45); CO 17. SS-Panzergrenadier-Division *Götz von Berlichingen* (1/21/45 - 3/22/45), KIA at Herxheim-Rheinpfalz (3/22/45)

Klotz, ?,
SS-Obersturmbannführer -- CO SS-Panzergrenadier-Regiment *Schill*; assisted with the murder and deportation of Jews to the death camps during the suppression of the *Slovak National Uprising* (9/44 -10/44)

Knapp, Viktor,
SS-Standartenführer -- CO 34. SS-Grenadier-Division *Landstorm Nederland* (3/11/43 - 5/11/44)

Knittel, Gustav,
SS-Sturmbannführer -- CO SS-Panzeraufklärungs-Abteilung 1/1. SS-Panzer-Division *Leibstandarte Adolf Hitler* (1944); implicated in the *Malmedy* atrocities (12/16+/44); defendant at Malmedy Trials (5/16/46 - 7/11/46); sentenced to 15 years imprisonment; paroled (12/53); died of natural causes at Ulm (6/30/76)

Knoblauch, Kurt,
SS-Obergruppenführer -- Persönlicher Stab RFSS (9/37 - 9/30/39); service with 3. SS-Panzer-Division *Totenkopf* (10/39 - 12/40); CO 2. SS-Infanterie (mot.) Brigade (12/40 - 4/41); CO Kommandostab RFSS (4/41 - 1/43); Persönlicher Stab RFSS (2/43 - 5/45); died (12/10/52)

Knochen, Dr. Helmut,
SS-Standartenführer -- HSSPf Nord Frankreich/Belgien (1940 - 1944); sentenced to life imprisonment by British authorities at Wuppertal for the execution of captured airmen (6/46); extradited to France for a second trial (10/10/46); condemned to death by French court (1954); sentence commuted to life imprisonment (1958); paroled (1962)

Knöchlein, Fritz,
SS-Obersturmbannführer -- CO 4. Kompanie/I. Bataillon/SS-Panzergrenadier-Regiment 6 /3. SS-Panzer-Division *Totenkopf*; responsible for the *Le Paradis* massacre (5/27/40); CO SS-Flak-Abteilung 3 / 3. SS-Panzer-Division *Totenkopf* (1941 - 1/42); bataillon

CO SS-Panzergrenadier-Regiment 36/16. SS-Panzer-grenadier-Division *Reichsführer-SS* (1/42 - 4/44); CO SS-Freiwilligen-Panzergrenadier-Regiment 23 *Norge* / 11. SS-Freiwilligen-Panzergrenadier-Division *Nordland* (4/44 - ?); arrested by Allied authorities (1946); tried and convicted of all charges by British military tribunal (10/25/48); executed at Hameln (1/28/49)

Knösel, ?,
SS-Obersturmführer -- CO 2. Kompanie / VII. Bataillon (Wach) / 1. SS-Panzer *Division Leibstandarte Adolf Hitler*; complicity in the *Berlin* deportations (2/27/43)

Kohlroser, Martin,
SS-Standartenführer -- CO 34. SS-Grenadier-Division *Landstorm Nederland* (5/11/44 - 5/8/45); possible complicity in the *Putten* atrocity (9/30/44)

König, Hans,
SS-Obersturmführer -- CO 9. Kompanie / Waffen-Gebirgs-Jäger Regiment der SS 28/13. Waffen-Gebirgs-Division der SS *Handschar* [kroatisches Nr. 1]; responsible for *Jablanica* killings (10/9/44); captured by British at war's end; committed suicide to avoid extradition to Yugoslavia (1947)

Konrad, Franz,
SS-Obersturmführer -- Stab 8. SS-Kavallerie-Division *Florian Geyer* (1941 - 1942); Stab WVHA (4/30/42); Stab SSPf Lublin (4/1/43); helped liquidate the *Warsaw Ghetto* -- known as the "King of the Ghetto" (4-5/43); Stab SS-Remonteamt Fischborn-Bruck-Fusch (1/3/44); Stab SS-Oberabschnittes Alpenland (1/1/45); captured and remanded to Polish custody; condemned; hung in Warsaw (9/8/51)

Koppe, Wilhelm,
SS-Obergruppenführer -- BdS Dresden (9/36 - 10/39); HSSPf Warthe (10/9/39 - 11/9/43); responsible for setting up VL Kulmhof (Winter 1941); carried out gassings until next assignment; HSSPf Ost (11/9/43 - 4/45); organized numerous small Sonderkommando 1005 units in the General Government, Poland (6/44); HSSPf Süd (4/45 - 5/45); hid under the assumed name of "Lohmann" (post-1945); arrested in Bonn (1961); released on bail (1962); indicted by Bonn court (1964);

ruled incompetent for trial by reasons of ill health (8/65); died in Bonn (7/2/75)

Korndörfer, Rudolf,
SS-Sturmbannführer -- RSHA; SD Metz (1941); CO Einsatzkommando 11A in Croatia (1944-45)

Korsemann, Gerret,
SS-Gruppenführer -- CO police school at Fürstenfeldbruck (4/39 - late 10/39); posted to General Government, Poland (11/39 - 3/40); KdO Lublin (3/40 - 2/41); CO 14. SS-Totenkopfstandarte (1/15/41 - 4/41); Stab RSHA (4/41 - 7/42); SSPf Rowno (8/1/41 - 1/1/42); responsible for the massacre of 15,000 Jews in Rowno (11/6-7/41); Stab HSSPf Russland-Mitte (1/42 - 8/15/42); SSPf Stanislav-Rostow (5/27/42 - 10/1/42); acting HSSPf Russland-Mitte (3/24/43 - 7/5/43); demoted for unauthorized retreat and transferred to active duty in the Waffen-SS; service with 1. SS-Panzer-Division *Leibstandarte Adolf Hitler* and 3. SS-Panzer-Division *Totenkopf* (7/43 - 5/45); captured by Russians; extradited to Poland; sentenced to 18 months imprisonment (1947); released (1949); died in München (7/16/58)

Körting, Dr. Erich,
SS-Obersturmbannführer -- CO Sonderkommando 7c/Einsatzgruppe B (10/41 - 12/41); SD Dessau; legal proceedings discontinued due to defendant's permanent incapacity to stand trial

Kowatsch, Aurel,
SS-Sturmbannführer -- divisional 1c staff officer for 2. SS-Panzer-Division *Das Reich*; organized the *Tulle* executions (6/9/44); reportedly KIA in Normandy (1944); tried in absentia by French authorities (7/5/51); sentenced to death

Kraas, Hugo,
SS-Standartenführer -- service with SS-Verfügungstruppe in Poland (1939); service with 1. SS-Panzer-Division *Leibstandarte Adolf Hitler* in France and USSR (1940 - 1944); CO 12. SS-Panzer-Division *Hitlerjugend* (11/10/44 - 5/8/45); disappeared at war's end; died in Schleswig (2/20/80)

Krahner, Max,
SS-Hauptsturmführer -- RSHA; CO Sonderkomman-

do 1005-Mitte (12/7/43 - ?); service with Einsatzgruppe *Iltis* (1944)

Krämer, Fritz,
SS-Gruppenführer -- Chief of Staff, 6. SS-Panzer-Armee during the Ardennes Offensive (12/44); detained by Americans for alleged complicity in the Malmedy atrocities (6/45); defendant at the Malmedy Trial (5/16/46 - 7/11/46); found guilty; sentenced to 15 years imprisonment (7/16/46); paroled; died in Höxter (6/23/59)

Krappf, ?,
SS-? -- service with SS-Panzeraufklärungs-Abteilung 12/12. SS-Panzer-Division *Hitlerjugend* (1944); complicity in the *Ascq* massacre (4/1-2/44); never tried

Krat, M., Heneral-Khorunzhi --
CO 14. Waffen-Grenadier-Division der SS [ukrainische Nr. 1] (4/27/45 - 5/8/45)

Krause, Bernhard,
SS-Obersturmbannführer -- CO I. Bataillon/SS-Panzergrenadier-Regiment 26/12. SS-Panzer-Division *Hitlerjugend*; complicity in the *Normandy* atrocities (6/7-17/44); KIA in Muzsla, Hungary (2/19/45)

Krause, Waldemar,
SS-Sturmbannführer -- RSHA; Kripo Berlin; Kripo Saarbrücken; CO Sonderkommando 4b/ Einsatzgruppe C (8/43 - 1/44); legal proceedings terminated due to defendant's incapacity to stand trial (1976)

Krempler, Karl von,
SS-Standartenführer -- service with 7. SS-Freiwilligen-Gebirgs-Division *Prinz Eugen* (3/42 - 9/43); SSPf Sandschak (9/43 - 6/21/44); Stab 13. Waffen-Gebirgs-Division der SS *Handschar* [kroatische Nr. 1] (3/44 - 5/45)

Kremser, ?,
SS-Obersturmführer -- CO SS-Panzer-Kompanie 1/ SS-Panzer-Bataillon 1/SS-Panzer-Regiment 1/1. SS-Panzer-Division *Leibstandarte Adolf Hitler*; implicated in the *Malmedy* atrocities (12/16+/44)

Kreutz, Karl,
SS-Standartenführer -- CO Artillerieschule Jüterbog (1939); service with the 2. SS-Panzer-Division *Das Reich* (1939 - 1945); CO SS-Panzerartillerie-Regiment 2 / 2. SS-Panzer-Division *Das Reich*; CO 2. SS-Panzer-Division *Das Reich* (1/20/45 - 2/4/45 and 4/13/45 - 5/10/45); died (7/26/97)

Kreuzer, Dr. Josef,
SS-Standartenführer -- CO Einsatzgruppe G in southeastern Europe (1944); RSHA; Gestapo Köln; Kripo Hamburg; Gestapo Düsseldorf

Krieg, Paul Reinhard,
SS-Obersturmbannfuhrer -- SSPf Litauen (9/41 - ?)

Kröger, Dr. Erhard,
SS-Standartenführer -- RSHA; CO Einsatzkommando 6 / Einsatzgruppe C (6/22/41 - 11/41); SS Hauptamt; 9. SS-Panzer-Division *Hohenstaufen* (1943); sentenced to 40 months imprisonment by Tübingen court (1969)

Krüger, Friedrich Wilhelm,
SS-Obergruppenführer -- younger brother of Walter Krüger (see entry below); CO SS border units (5/36 - 10/39); Inspektor Reit-und Fahrwesen / SS-Führungshauptamt (5/38 - 10/39); HSSPf Ost (10/4/39 - 11/8/43); CO 1. SS-Infanterie [mot.]-Brigade (5/25/41 - 6/25/41); Staatssekretär für das Sicherheitswesen, Poland (4/42 - 11/43); helped plan the *Aktion Erntefest* massacres in Poland (11/3-4/43); Stab 7. SS-Freiwilligen-Gebirgs-Division *Prinz Eugen* (11/43 - 4/44); CO 6. SS-Gebirgs-Division *Nord* (5/44 - 8/23/44); CO V. SS-Freiwilligen-Gebirgs-Korps (8/26/44 - 2/15/45); committed suicide at Gundershausen, near Branau am Inn (5/10/45)

Krüger, Hans Walter,
SS-Hauptsturmführer -- company commander from 1. Bataillon/SS-Panzergrenadier-Regiment 2/1. SS-Panzer-Division *Leibstandarte Adolf Hitler*; responsible for the *Lago Maggiore* atrocity (9/22-24/43); sentenced to death by Schwurgericht Osnabrück (7/5/68); sentenced overturned by Bundesgerichtshof Berlin (4/70)

Krüger, Walter,
SS-Brigadeführer -- instructor, SS-Junkerschule Tölz

(? - 1940); Stab 4. SS-Polizei-Panzergrenadier-Division (1940 - 1941); CO 4. SS-Polizei-Panzergrenadier-Division (8/18/41 - 12/15/41); Inspektor der Infanterie / SS-Führungshauptamt; CO 2. SS-Panzer-Division *Das Reich* (4/3/43 - 11/1/43); CO VI. SS-Freiwilligen-Armee-Korps (Summer 1944 - 5/8/45); committed suicide near Lithuanian-Latvian border to avoid capture by Soviets (5/22/45)

Krukenberg, Dr. jur. Gustav,
SS-Brigadeführer -- CO 33. Waffen-Grenadier-Division der SS *Charlemagne* [französische Nr. 1] (2/45 - 4/26/45); CO 11. SS-Freiwilligen-Panzergrenadier-Division *Nordland* (4/26/45 - 5/3/45)

Kudoke, ?,
SS-Untersturmführer -- CO 1. (Pz. Späh.) Kompanie / SS-Panzeraufklärungs-Abteilung 12 / 12. SS-Panzer-Division *Hitlerjugend* (1944) complicitous in the *Ascq* massacre (1/2 April 1944); KIA Caen (6/44); never brought to trial

Kumm, Otto,
SS-Brigadeführer -- CO SS-Panzergrenadier-Regiment 4 *Der Führer* (7/12/41 - Spring 1943); Chief of Staff V. SS-Gebirgs-Korps (Summer 1943 - 2/10/44); CO 7. SS-Freiwilligen-Gebirgs-Division (2/11/44 - 1/20/45); divisional commander at the time of the following atrocities : *Blazevici, Grubisnjici, Sladovil, Smilici, Krivodol, Legatori, Otok Cornji, Ruda, Dolac Donji, Vostane, Ovrlje* (3/28/44) / *Razori* (6/9/44); questionable accusation of atrocities in the *Split - Sinj region* : *Bisko, Srijane, Gornji Dolac*, and *Putisic* (3/44); CO 1. SS-Panzer-Division *Leibstandarte Adolf Hitler* (2/6/45 - 5/8/45); captured by Americans at Hallein; founder of HIAG (post-war Waffen-SS veteran's association)

Kümmel, Paul,
SS-Hauptsturmführer -- CO 11. Schützenkompanie/ III. Bataillon/SS-Totenkopfstandarte II *Brandenburg*; complicity in massacres at *Wloclawek* (9/22-25/39)

Künsberg, Freiherr Eberhard von,
SS-Sturmbannführer -- CO SS-Reiterstandarte 15 (9/34 - 4/36); CO German Foreign Ministry Waffen-SS Bataillon zur besonderen Verwendung (5/40 - 1/43); responsible for cultural crimes in the USSR : looting museums, government buildings, etc.; service with 1. SS-Panzer-Division *Leibstandarte Adolf Hitler*; service with 8. SS-Kavallerie-Division *Florian Geyer*; died (1945)

Kutschera, Fritz,
SS-Brigadeführer -- Stab SS-Abschnitt XXX (3/38 - 6/43); SSPf Mogilew (4/20/43 - 9/20/43); SSPf Warschau (9/25/43 - 2/1/44); assassinated by Polish partisans (2/1/44)

Kutschmann, Dr. Walter,
SS-Untersturmführer -- commanded the firing squads at *Lvov* (7/4/41); escaped after the war to Argentina

Lages, Wilhelm,
SS-Sturmbannführer -- KdS Amsterdam; directed the deportation of the Dutch Jews; condemned to death (6/49); sentence commuted to life imprisonment (1952)

Lammerding, Heinz,
SS-Brigadeführer -- various postings with the 3. SS-Panzer-Division *Totenkopf* (1940 - 43); chief of staff to Chef der Bandenkampfverbände Bach-Zelewski, as such planned and conducted numerous killling operations in the USSR (1943); CO 2. SS-Panzer-Division *Das Reich* (12/9/43 - 7/26/44, wounded); commander of division at time of the *Fraysinnet-le-Gelat* (5/21/44), *Carsac-de-Carlux* (6/8/44), *Gabaudet* (6/8/44), *Tulle* (6/9/44), *Oradour sur Glane* (6/10/44), *Bagneres-de-Bigorre* (6/11/44), *Mussidan* (6/11/44), and *Dunes* (6/23/44) atrocities; questionable accusation of atrocity at *St. Germain-du-Belair* (6/44); CO 2. SS-Panzer-Division *Das Reich* (10/16/44 - 1/20/45); Chief of Staff, Army Group Vistula (1/45 - 3/45); CO 38. SS-Grenadier-Division *Nibelungen* (3/45 - 4/24/45); successfully fought extradition to France at time of the Tulle (1951) and Oradour sur Glane (1953) trials; sentenced to death in absentia by French military tribunals (1951 and 3/12/53); died of cancer at Bad Tölz (1/13/71)

Lange, ?,
SS-Obersturmführer -- battalion adjutant of III. Bataillon / SS-Totenkopfstandarte II *Brandenburg*; responsible for massacres at *Wloclawek* (9/22-25/39)

Lange, Herbert,

SS-Sturmbannführer -- CO Sonderkommando *Lange* (1939 - 1941); responsible for the murder of 1,900 psychiatric patients in *East Prussia* (5/21 - 6/8/40); similar operations eastern Germany and occupied Poland (7/40 - 11/41); unit deployed to VL Kulmhof operations (12/41); Kommandant Kulmhof; RSHA (3-4/42); SD Aachen; killed in action, Berlin (4/20/45)

Lange, Dr. Rudolf Erwin,
SS-Standartenführer -- CO Einsatzkommando 2-KdS Lettland/Einsatzgruppe A (12/3/41); BdS Latvia (1941-2); organized Riga Massacres; participant at the Wannsee Conference (1/20/42); KdS Posen; KdS Wartheland; either killed in action in Posen (2/45) or escaped from British custody (7/49)

Lange, Seppel,
SS-Hauptsturmführer -- CO 7. Kompanie/II. Bataillon/*Leibstandarte Adolf Hitler* Regiment (9/39); possible involvement in the *Zdunska Wola* (9/7/39) and *Lodz* atrocities (9/8/39); KIA (9/12/39)

Langer, Hermann,
SS-Obersturmführer -- pre-war service with SS-Totenkopfstandarte 1 *Oberbayern* at Dachau concentration camp; service with 3. SS-Panzer-Division *Totenkopf* during the French campaign (1940); suspected participant in the massacre at Le Paradis (5/27/40); CO elements of 16. SS-Panzergrenadier-Division *Reichsführer-SS* responsible for massacre at Farneta (9/2/44); lived post-war in Germany under own name; not located by Italian authorities until 2002 due to faulty information; tried in absentia by Italian military court at La Spezia (7/8/04 - 12/10/04); acquitted of charges on technical grounds

Lautenbach, Fritz,
SS-Hauptsturmführer -- CO 2. Kompanie/SS-Panzergrenadier-Regiment 7/4. SS-Polizei-Panzergrenadier-Division (6/44); responsible for the massacre of 296 civilians at *Dhistomon* (6/10/44); investigated by Wehrmacht military tribunal, punishment deferred; KIA in Greece (10/44)

Lehmann, Rudolf,
SS-Standartenführer -- service with the 1. SS-Panzer-Division *Leibstandarte Adolf Hitler* (1933 - 1945); CO 2. SS-Panzer-Division *Das Reich* (3/9/45 - 4/13/45); died in Ettlingen (9/17/83)

Leideck, ?,
SS-? -- service with SS-Panzeraufklärungs-Abteilung 12/12. SS-Panzer-Division *Hitlerjugend* (1944); complicity in the *Ascq* massacre (4/1-2/44); never tried

Leidreiter, Hans-Martin,
SS-Obersturmführer -- CO 3. Kompanie/SS-Panzeraufklärungs-Bataillon 1/1. SS-Panzer-Division *Leibstandarte Adolf Hitler* (1944); implicated in the *Malmedy* atrocities (12/16+/44);

Leifheit, Fritz,
SS-Obersturmführer -- CO SS-Fallschirmjäger-Bataillon 600 (3/45 - ?)

Leithe, Otto Ludwig,
SS-? -- involvement in *Lago Maggiore* massacres (9/22-24/43); tried by Schwurgericht Osnabrück, sentenced to death (7/5/68); case appealed to Bundesgerichtshof Berlin; defendant acquitted on the grounds that he was following merely orders and that the statute of limitations had expired (4/70)

Lenski, ?,
SS-? -- CO SS-Panzerpionier-Kompanie 15/ SS-Panzergrenadier-Regiment 1/1. SS-Panzer-Division *Leibstandarte Adolf Hitler* (1944)

Leyer, Hans-Joachim,
Kriminalkommissar --
CO Teilkommando Thorn (Poland, 1939)

Liebenau, Arno, S
S-Hauptsturmführer -- CO I. Bataillon /SS-Panzergrenadier-Regiment 39/18. SS-Panzergrenadier-Division *Horst Wessel*; possible complicity in the *Stara Cernova* atrocity (9/28/44)

Lindtner, ?,
SS-Obersturmbannführer -- CO 17. SS-Panzergrenadier-Division *Götz von Berlichingen* (1/9/45 - 1/21/45)

Lingner, Hans,
SS-Standartenführer -- CO 17. SS-Panzergrenadier-Division *Götz von Berlichingen* (11/15/44 - 1/9/45); captured

Lippert, Lucien,
SS-Sturmbannführer -- CO 28. SS-Freiwilligen-Panzergrenadier-Division *Wallonie* (? - 2/13/44), KIA

Lippert, Michael,
SS-Standartenführer -- CO SS-Freiwilligen-Standarte *Nordwest*; CO 27. SS-Freiwilligen-Grenadier-Division *Langemarck* [flämische Nr. 1] (10/1/41 - 4/18/42); CO 10. SS-Panzer-Division *Frundsberg* (2/1/43 - 2/15/43)

Liphardt, Dr. Fritz,
SS-Obersturmbannführer -- CO Einsatzkommando 2/ Einsatzgruppe III (Poland, 1939); Gestapo Stettin; Gestapo Radom; Gestapo Frankfurt/Oder

Loehr, Horst,
SS-? -- service with SS-Panzeraufklärungs-Abteilung 12/12. SS-Panzer-Division *Hitlerjugend* (1944); complicity in the *Ascq* massacre (4/1-2/44); tried and sentenced to death in absentia by French authorities (8/2-6/49)

Lölgen, Jakob,
SS-Sturmbannführer -- CO Teilkommando Bromberg (Poland, 1939)

Lombard, Gustav,
SS-Brigadeführer --CO 3. Schwadron/1. SS-Totenkopf-Reiterstandarte (11/39 - 5/40); CO 1. Schwadron / 1. SS-Totenkopf-Reiterstandarte (5/40 - 11/40); CO I. Abteilung / SS-[Totenkopf]-Kavallerie-Regiment 1 (11/40 - 3/20/41); CO Reitende Abteilung/SS-Kavallerie-Regiment 1 (3/21/41 - 8/1/41); CO SS-Kavallerie-Regiment 1/8. SS-Kavallerie-Division *Florian Geyer* (8/2/41 - 42?); responsible for numerous killing operations, see *SS-Kavallerie-Brigade Operations and Atrocities in the USSR*; complicity in *Pripet Marshes* massacres (1941 - 1943); CO 8. SS-Kavallerie-Division *Florian Geyer* (11/1/42 - 2/1/43); Stab HSSPf Russland-Mitte (9/43 - 10/43); acting CO 29. Waffen-Grenadier-Division der SS [italienische Nr. 1] (10/43 - 12/43); acting CO Kommandostab RFSS (12/43); CO Kampfgruppe HSSPf Russland-Mitte (1944); Divisionsführer Lehrgang, Kriegsakademie

Hirschberg (6 - 8/44); CO 6. SS-Gebirgs-Division *Nord* (8/23/44 - 9/1/44); CO 31. SS-Freiwilligen-Grenadier-Division (10/18/44 - 5/45); divisional commander at the time of the *Crvenka* atrocity (10/44); captured by Soviets (5/8/45), eventually released (10/10/55); died in Mühldorf, Bayern (9/18/92)

Looss, Helmut,
SS-Obersturmbannführer -- RSHA Amt VIE; RSHA Amt II; CO Sonderkommando 7a/Einsatzgruppe B (6/43 - 6/44); 16. SS-Panzergrenadier-Division *Reichsführer-SS*

Maack, Berthold,
SS-Brigadeführer -- service with 2. SS-Panzer-Division *Das Reich* (3/40 - 10/41); service with 5. SS-Panzer-Division *Wiking* (10/41 - 6/42); battalion and then regimental CO with 6. SS-Gebirgs-Division *Nord* (6/42 - 12/44); CO 26. Waffen-Grenadier-Division der SS [ungarische Nr. 2] (1/22/45 - 3/20/45); CO 20. Waffen-Grenadier-Division der SS [estnische Nr. 1] (3/20/45 - 5/8/45); died in Meran (9/26/81)

Macholl, Waldemar,
SS-Hauptsturmführer -- CO Sonderkommando 1005 unit operating in the Bialystok District (5/44 - ?)

Magill, Franz,
SS-Obersturmbannführer -- Reitlehrer SS-Führerschule Braunschweig (3/1/35 - 9/39); CO 1. Schwadron/SS-Totenkopf-Reiterstandarte (9/39 - 11/39); CO 11. Schwadron / SS-Totenkopf-Reiterstandarte 1 (11/39 - 5/40); CO SS-Totenkopf-Reiterstandarte 2 (5/40 - 11/40); CO IV. Abteilung/SS-[Totenkopf]-Kavallerie-Regiment 1 (11/40 - 3/20/41); CO SS-Kavallerie-Regiment 2 (3/21/41 - 4/10/41); CO Reitende Abteilung / SS-Kavallerie-Regiment 2 (4/11/41 - mid 9/41); CO SS-Kavallerie-Regiment 2 (mid 9/41 - 11/41); responsible for numerous killing operations, see *SS-Kavallerie-Brigade Operations and Atrocities in the USSR*; responsible for the massacre of 11,000 Jews at Pinsk (8/5-8/41); complicity in *Pripet Marshes* massacres (1941-43); Stab HSSPf Russland-Mitte (11/41 - 12/42); CO SS-Sonderbataillon *Dirlewanger* (12/42 - 2/43); responsible for several killing operations; Stab HSSPf Russland-Mitte; CO supply elements 14. Waffen-Grenadier-Division der SS [ukrainische Nr. 1] (2/43 - 5/45); captured by

British; released from custody (3/23/48); taken into custody by West German government (11/30/62); tried by Landgericht Braunschweig; sentenced to 5 years imprisonment (4/20/64); co-defendants' [Dunsch, Nenntwich, and Wegener] sentences overturned on technicalities (11/17/64)

Malsen-Ponickau, Erasmus Freiherr von,
SS-Brigadeführer -- Polizeipräsident Frankfurt an der Oder (4/38 - 5/40); Polizeipräsident Posen (6/40 - 9/43); Polizeipräsident Halle an der Saale 9/43 - 12/43); SS und Polizeigebietskommandeur Istrien (10/27/44 - 5/45); tried by Poles and served some time in prison; died (6/12/56)

Martin, Georg,
SS-Oberführer -- CO 14. SS-Totenkopfstandarte (? - ?); responsible for the murder of civilians in the *Lublin District* (6/41)

Martin, Dr. Benno,
SS-Obergruppenführer -- Polizeipräsident Nürnberg (10/36 - 12/42); HSSPf Main (12/17/42 - 5/8/45); tried by American authorities and sentenced to 3 years' imprisonment; in Allied custody until 1949; many later trials but no sentences pronounced against him; died in Germany (7/2/75)

Matschke, Karl,
SS-Hauptsturmführer -- CO Sonderkommando 7a / Einsatzgruppe B (12/41 - 2/42); Kripo Saarbrücken; Gestapo Köln

Marks, Karl,
SS-Obersturmbannführer -- CO 24. Waffen-Gebirgs-Division der SS *Karstjäger* (late Summer 1944 - late 1944)

Mazuw, Emil,
SS-Obergruppenführer -- HSSPf Ostsee (8/28/38 - 5/8/45); sentenced by Spruchkammerverfahren to 8 years imprisonment for his actions in Pommern (1948); sentenced to 8 years imprisonment for pre-war crimes against Jews and political prisoners (1953); lived in the Bundesrepublik; died (12/11/87)

Meier, August,
SS-Obersturmbannführer -- RSHA; CO Einsatz-

kommando 5/Einsatzgruppe C (9/41 - 1/42); CO Sonderkommando 4b/Einsatzgruppe C (7/42 - 11/42); SD Breslau; SD Wiesbaden; SD Limoges (1944); suicide while in custody awaiting trial

Menten, Pieter,
SS-Obersturmbannführer -- a Dutchman with Einsatzgruppe in the Lvov area

Merk, Dr. Günther,
SS-Brigadeführer -- Stab SS-Abschnitt XXV (11/39 - 12/40); Stab SS-Personalhauptamt (12/40 - 4/41); CO SS-Artillerie-Ersatz-Regiment (4/41 - 8/41); CO SS-Artillerie-Regiment 2 / 2. SS-Panzer-Division *Das Reich* (8/41 - 1/42); Stab Hauptamt Ordnungspolizei (1/42 - 9/43); SSPf Charkow (9/11/43 - 10/18/43); retired (1944); re-activated as Stab HSSPf Ost; KIA (2/20/45)

Mertsch, Gustav,
SS-Standartenführer -- CO 17. SS-Panzergrenadier-Division *Götz von Berlichingen* (9/44 - 9/44)

Meyer, Ernst,
SS-Sturmbannführer -- CO VII. Bataillon (Wach)/1. SS-Panzer-Division *Leibstandarte Adolf Hitler*; complicity in the *Berlin* deportations (2/27/43)

Meyer, Hubert,
SS-Obersturmbannführer -- CO 12. SS-Panzer-Division *Hitlerjugend* (9/7/44 - 11/9/44)

Meyer, Kurt "Panzer",
SS-Brigadeführer -- service with *LAH* in Poland (1939); CO SS-Panzeraufklärungs-Abteilung 1/1. SS-Panzer-Division *Leibstandarte Adolf Hitler* (8/40 - 7/43); alleged to have ordered the execution of 200 civilians at *Gorych* in reprisal for Soviet atrocities (7/41); CO SS-Panzergrenadier-Regiment 25/12. SS-Panzer-Division *Hitlerjugend* (7/43 - 6/15/44); complicity in *Normandy* atrocities (6/7-17/44); CO 12. SS-Panzer-Division *Hitlerjugend* (6/16/44 - 9/6/44); captured by Belgian partisans (9/6/44); remanded to American authorities (9/7/44); tried before Canadian military tribunal at Aurich (12/10/45); found guilty of assorted charges (12/27/45); sentenced to death (12/28/45); sentence commuted to life imprisonment (1/13/46); transferred to Dorchester Penitentiary, New Brunswick, Canada; transferred to

British prison at Werl, Germany (10/51); hospitalization for health problems (Summer 1952); paroled due to health problems (9/7/54); principal spokesman for HIAG (1956); author; died of heart attack at Hagen (12/23/60)

Meyszner, August Edler von,
SS-Gruppenführer -- IdO Wien (3/38 - 4/38); CO Ordnungspolizei detachment, Sudentenland (10/38 - 10/39); IdO Kassel (6/39 - 9/40); BdO Oslo (8/29/40 - 1/15/42); HSSPf Serbien, Sandschak und Montenegro (1/24/42 - 4/1/44); remanded to Yugoslav custody (post-1945); tried and condemned to death (1946); hung in Belgrade (1/24/47)

Michalsen, Wilhelm,
SS-Sturmbannführer -- SS und Polizeigebietskommandeur Triest (10/27/44 - 1945)

Milius, Karl-Heinz,
SS-Obersturmbannführer -- CO III. Bataillon / SS-Panzergrenadier-Regiment 25 / 12. SS-Panzer-Division *Hitlerjugend*; complicity in the *Normandy* atrocities (6/7-17/44); recommended for prosecution by SHAEF Standing Court of Inquiry (1945); never tried since it was erroneously believed that he was KIA in Normandy; died (5/31/90)

Milius, Siegfried,
SS-Hauptsturmführer -- CO SS-Fallschirmjäger-Bataillonen 500/600 (6/26/44 - 3/45)

Moder, Paul,
SS-Gruppenführer -- acting CO SS-Oberabschnitt Ost (11/38 - 11/39); SSPf Warschau (11/14/39 - 8/4/41); service with 3. SS-Panzer-Division *Totenkopf* (8/41 - 2/8/42); KIA in USSR (2/42)

Mohnke, Wilhelm, SS-Gruppenführer -- CO Hitler's personal bodyguard (early 1930s); service with *LSSAH* (1933 - 1945); CO 5. Kompanie/II. Bataillon/*Leibstandarte Adolf Hitler* Regiment (9/39); possible involvement in the *Zdunska Wola* (9/7/39), *Lodz* (9/8/39), and *Czestochowa* (10/1-2/39) atrocities; responsibility for *Wormhoudt* atrocities (5/28/40); CO *Leibstandarte Adolf Hitler* Ersatz Bataillon at Berlin-Lichterfelde Barracks (3/20/42 - 9/15/43); CO SS-Panzergrenadier-Regiment 26/12. SS-Panzer-Division *Hitlerjugend*; implicated in the *Normandy* atrocities (6/7-17/44); CO 1. SS-Panzer-Division *Leibstandarte Adolf Hitler* (8/20/44 - 2/6/45); divisional commander at the time of the *Tavaux-et-Pont-sericourt* (8/30/44) and *Malmedy* (12/16+/44) atrocities; CO of the Reichskanzlei [including Hitler's Bunker] in Berlin (4/22/45); captured by Soviets and sent to Strausberg POW camp (5/2/45); moved to Budirka Prison, Moscow (5/9/45); sent to Lubyanka Prison; placed on CROWCASS list of wanted war criminals (11/8/45); in Soviet custody and unavailable for Malmedy and Normandy Trials; tried for war crimes committed in the USSR and sentenced to life imprisonment at Woikowo Prison, Urals (1949); released from Soviet custody and returned to West Germany (10/10/55); immediately went into hiding; found living in Hamburg (1976); brought to attention of British Government (1988); under British pressure, West German Government opens investigation into Wormhoudt atrocities; suffers heart attack (Autumn 1988); German authorities close investigation due to "insufficient evidence" (early 1989); living in seclusion at Barsbüttel, near Hamburg

Mohr, Robert,
SS-Obersturmbannführer -- Assessor, Reichsministeriums des Innern (1937 - 10/1/39); RSHA (10/1/39 - ?); detailed to Chef der Zivilverwaltung Mittelpolen (1939); detailed to BdS Krakau (1940); Regierungsrat Krakau (9/41 - 11/41); CO Einsatzkommando 6 / Einsatzgruppe C (11/41 - mid 9/42); Leiter der Staatspolizeistelle Darmstadt (mid 9/42 - 4/1/44); Leiter der Staatspolizeistelle Magdeburg (4/1/44 - 5/45); interned by British (6/45); escaped and assumed identity Gerhard Lindzus (end 1946); arrested by West German authorities (end 5/47); escaped and assumed identity Werner Bujara (6/18/47); taken into custody by West German government (11/12/59); tried by Landgericht Wuppertal; sentenced to 8 years imprisonment (12/30/65); sentence nullified and a re-trial ordered by 2. Strafsenat des Bundesgerichtshofs (12/11/64); tried again before Landgericht Wuppertal; sentenced to 8 years imprisonment (12/13/67)

Mohrwinkel, ?,
SS-Untersturmführer -- attached to Waffen-SS depot at Lublin; responsible for the deportation of Jews from the *Lublin District* to the Majdanek death camp (Winter 1941)

Möller, Hinrich,
SS-Brigadeführer -- Polizeidirektor Flensburg (9/37 - 8/41); SSPf Estland (8/4/41 - 4/1/44); Stab Armeegruppe Weichsel (2/45 - 5/45); died in Kiel (1974)

Mühlenkamp, Johannes Rudolf,
SS-Standartenführer -- service with SS-Verfügungstruppe (1934 - 1941); CO Panzer-Aufklärungsabteilung 2 / 2. SS-Panzer-Division *Das Reich* (1941); CO SS-Panzer-Regiment 5 / 5. SS-Panzer-Division *Wiking* (1942); CO SS-Panzer-Division *Wiking* (8/6/44 - 10/9/44); CO 32. SS-Freiwilligen-Grenadier-Division *30. Januar* (?1/45 - 2/5/45); Inspektor der Panzertruppen der Waffen-SS, SS-Führungshauptamt (2/45 - 5/45?); died in Goslar (9/23/86)

Müller, ?, SS-Obersturmbannführer -- attached to Einsatzgruppe A; responsible for killing operations in Sluzk (5/2/43)

Müller, Bruno,
SS-Obersturmbannführer -- CO Einsatzkommando 2/Einsatzgruppe I (Poland, 1939); RSHA Amt IV; CO Einsatzkommando 11b/Einsatzgruppe D (7/41 - 10/41); Gestapo Stettin; Gestapo Wilhelmshaven; died of natural causes (1960)

Müller, Dr. Erich,
SS-Standartenführer -- Propaganda Ministry; RSHA Am III; CO Einsatzkommando 12/Einsatzgruppe D (2/42 - 10/42); Gestapo Berlin; escaped to Argentina after the war

Müller, Siegfried,
SS-Obersturmbannführer -- CO SS-Panzerpionier-Abteilung 12/SS-Panzer-Regiment 12/12. SS-Panzer-Division *Hitlerjugend*; complicity in the *Normandy* atrocities (6/7-17/44); recommended for prosecution by SHAEF Standing Court of Inquiry (1945); investigated but never indicted; died of natural causes (4/7/74)

Müller, Thomas,
SS-Standartenführer -- CO 9. SS-Panzer-Division *Hohenstaufen* (7/10/44 - 7/15/44); CO 17. SS-Panzergrenadier-Division *Götz von Berlichingen* (9/44 - 9/44)

Müller-John, Hermann,
SS-Sturmbannführer -- CO *Leibstandarte Adolf Hitler*

Regiment Musikzug (? - ?); ordered execution of 50 Jews at Burzeum near *Blonie*, Poland (9/18-19/39); arrested by Wehrmacht; charges dropped

Mülverstedt, Arthur,
SS-Gruppenführer -- CO Polizeigruppe 5 (Poland, 1939); CO 4. SS-Polizei-Panzergrenadier-Division (11/10/40 - 8/10/41); KIA

Munter, Heinz,
SS-? -- service with SS-Panzeraufklärungs-Abteilung 12/12. SS-Panzer-Division *Hitlerjugend* (1944); complicity in the *Ascq* massacre (4/1-2/44); tried and sentenced to death in absentia by French authorities (8/2-6/49)

Mützelfeldt, Hans-Joachim,
SS-Sturmbannführer -- CO 20. Waffen-Grenadier-Division der SS [estnische Nr. 1] (3/17/45 - 3/20/45)

Naumann, Erich,
SS-Brigadeführer -- CO Einsatzgruppe VI (Poland, 1939); CO Einsatzgruppe B (11/41- 3/20/43); directed killing operations in *Hauptkommissariat Baranowicze* (2/42); BdS Nederland; KdS Nürnberg; condemned to death during Einsatzgruppen Trial at Nürnberg (4/8/48); executed in Landsberg Prison (6/7/51)

Nebe, Artur,
SS-Gruppenführer -- Former head of Kriminalpolizei; CO Amt V/RSHA (1939); CO Einsatzgruppe B (6/22/41 - 11/41); responsible for the *Lahoysk* massacre (9/41); originator of the poison gas van concept; aided plotters planning to kill Hitler in July Bomb Plot (7/22/44); initially helped conduct investigations but then went into hiding; SS offered a 50,000 Reichsmark reward for his capture (8/44); betrayed by girlfriend and arrested by Gestapo (1/16/45); sentenced to death by a Volksgericht tribunal; said to have been executed (3/2/45); this has not been proven -- fate unknown

Nenntwich, Hans-Walter,
SS-Untersturmführer -- SS-Totenkopfverband *Brandenburg* (1938); SS-Totenkopfstandarte *Ostmark* (1939); SS-Heimwehr *Danzig* (6/39 - 10/39); attendance at SS-Junkerschule Tölz (10/39 - 1940); service with various SS-Totenkopf-Regiments in Poland (1940); SS-Regiment *Germania* (Fall 1940 - 4/41); 2.

Schwadron / SS-Kavallerie-Regiment 2 (4/41 - 12/41); SS-Kavallerie-Ersatzabteilung Warschau (12/41 - Fall 1942); SS-Kavallerie-Regiment 3 (Fall 1942 - ?) -- wounded; Genesenden Schwadron Warschau (1/43 - ?); target of SS corruption investigations; used contacts with Polish underground to flee to Sweden (4/5/43); flew to England; employed by British for German-language radio broadcasting and as a POW camp translator (1943 - 1945); returned to West Germany working for the British occupation government in Nord Rhein under the alias of Dr. Sven Joachim Nansen (11/45); West German investigations of "Nansen" blocked by the British authorities (1947); continued employment in various capacities for the British government and private firms (1947-62); identity established and taken into West German custody (7/5/63); tried by Landgericht Braunschweig; sentenced to 4 years imprisonment (4/20/64); escaped (4/22/64); sentence overturned on technicalities by the 5. Strafsenat des Bundesgerichtshofs (11/17/64)

Nieschlag, ?,
SS-Sturmbannführer – CO II. Bataillon/SS-Panzergrenadier-Regiment 38/17. SS-Panzergrenadier-Division *Götz von Berlichingen* responsible for the *Graignes* atrocity (6/12/44)

Nölle, Wilhelm,
SS-Obersturmbannführer -- CO Einsatzkommando Luxembourg; Gestapo Brünn; SD Trier; SD Marsielle

Nosske, Gustav,
SS-Obersturmbannführer -- CO Einsatzkommando 12/Einsatzgruppe D (6/22/41 - 2/42); Gestapo Frankfurt/Oder; Gestapo Aachen; SD Düsseldorf; sentenced to life imprisonment during Einsatgruppen Trial at Nürnberg (4/48); sentence reduced to 10 years imprisonment; released (1951)

Nostitz, Paul,
SS-Standartenführer -- CO SS-Totenkopfstandarte II *Brandenburg* (? - ?); directed unit's extermination operations in Poland; responsible for massacres at *Wloclawek* (9/22-25/39) and *Bydgoszcz 2* (9/24-26/39); oversaw the conversion of *Grafeneck Castle* into an extermination center (11/39); CO 9. SS-Totenkopfstan-

darte (? - ?); attached to SS-Panzergrenadier-Ersatz-Bataillon 1 (7/44); fate unknown

Oberg, Carl Albrecht,
SS-Obergruppenführer -- Polizeipräsident Zwickau (1/39 - 9/41); SSPf Radom (8/4/41 - 5/12/42); HSSPf Frankreich (5/5/42 - 11/28/44); Stab Heeresgruppe Weichsel (11/28/44 - 2/1/45); Stab SS and Police court, München (2/45 - 5/45); arrested by U.S. military police (6/45); tried and sentenced to death by a British military tribunal for executing captured airmen (1946); British sentence commuted to 20 years and prisoner remanded to French custody (10/10/46); tried and sentenced to death (10/54); commuted to life imprisonment and then to 20 years hard labor (1958); pardoned and released (11/62); lived in the Bundesrepublik; died in Flensburg (6/3/65).

Oberkamp, Carl Ritter von,
SS-Brigadeführer -- CO II. Bataillon/1. SS-Panzer-Division *Leibstandarte Adolf Hitler* at the time of the *Zdunska Wola* (9/7/39), *Lodz* (9/8/39), and *Czestochowa* (10/1-2/39) atrocities; attached to the 7. SS-Freiwilligen-Gebirgs-Division *Prinz Eugen;* complicity in the *Niksic* atrocity (5/43); CO 7. SS-Freiwilligen-Gebirgs-Division *Prinz Eugen* (7/3/43 - 2/1/44); divisional commander at time of the *Kosutica* (7/43), *Osekovo* (9/16/43), and *Sinj* (11/5/43) atrocities; CO 38. SS-Grenadier-Division *Nibelungen* (4/45 - ?); captured by Americans (1945); remanded to Yugoslav custody (1946); condemned and executed for crimes against Yugoslav civilians (1947)

Oberwurzer, Herbert von,
SS-Oberführer -- service with 6. SS-Gebirgs-Division *Nord* (? - 3/43); CO 13. Waffen-Gebirgs-Division der SS *Handschar* [kroatische Nr. 1] (3/43 - mid 1943); CO 15. Waffen-Grenadier-Division der SS [lettische Nr. 1] (7/21/44 - 1/26/45); captured by Soviets

Ohlendorf, Otto,
SS-Gruppenführer -- CO Einsatzgruppe D (6/22/41 - 6/42); Chef RSHA Amt III; condemned to death during Einsatzgruppen Trial at Nürnberg (4/10/48); hanged in Landsberg Prison (6/7/51)

Olboeter, Erich,
SS-Sturmbannführer -- CO III. Bataillon /SS-Panzergrenadier-Regiment 26/12. SS-Panzer-Division *Hitlerjugend*; complicity in the *Normandy* atrocities (6/7-17/44); died of wounds in Lazarett Charleville, Belgium (9/2/44)

Ölhafen, Otte von,
SS-Gruppenführer -- BdO Ukraine

Onken, Reinhardt,
SS-? -- service with SS-Panzeraufklärungs-Abteilung 12/12. SS-Panzer-Division *Hitlerjugend* (1944); complicity in the *Ascq* massacre (4/1-2/44); tried and sentenced to death by French authorities (8/2-6/49); sentenced reduced to 10 years hard labor minus time served (7/14/55); paroled (1956)

Ost, Willi,
SS-Standartenführer -- SSPf Lemberg (4/20/43 - 7/29/43)

Ostendorff, Werner,
SS-Gruppenführer -- Stab Panzergruppe *Kempf*, Poland (1939); Stab 2. SS-Panzer-Division *Das Reich* (1941 - 1943); Chief of Staff II. SS-Panzer-Korps (1943 - 10/20/44); CO 17. SS-Panzergrenadier-Division *Götz von Berlichingen* (10/21/44 - 11/15/44, wounded); CO 2. SS-Panzer-Division *Das Reich* (2/4/45 - 3/9/45, severely wounded in Hungary); died of wounds at hospital in Bad Aussee (5/5/45)

Ott, Adolf,
SS-Obersturmbannführer -- RSHA; CO Sonderkommando 7b / Einsatzgruppe B (3/42 - 1/43); SD München; SD Königsberg; SD Saarbrücken; condemned to death during Einsatzgruppen Trial at Nürnberg (4/48); sentenced commuted to life imprisonment; released (1958)

Painsi, Hans,
SS-? -- service with SS-Panzeraufklärungs-Abteilung 12/12. SS-Panzer-Division *Hitlerjugend* (1944); complicity in the *Ascq* massacre (4/1-2/44); tried and sentenced to death in absentia by French authorities (8/2-6/49)

Pancke, Günther,
SS-Obergruppenführer -- Chef RuSHA (9/11/38 - 7/9/40); CO SS-Totenkopfstandarte II Brandenburg (? - ?); HSSPf Mitte (7/11/40 - 9/15/43); HSSPf Dänemark (10/6/43 - 5/5/45); sentenced in Denmark to 20 years imprisonment (1948), pardoned (1953); died (8/17/73)

Pannier, Rudolf,
SS-Standartenführer -- Schutzpolizei Posen (1940 - 1941); service with 4. SS-Polizei-Panzergrenadier-Division (1941 - 6/42); Chief of Staff to Befehlshaber der Waffen-SS Nederland; Kommandeur des Rekrutendepots und des Aufstellungsstabes des 4. SS-Polizei-Panzergrenadier-Division at Truppenübungsplatz Debica (1942 - 6/43); Kommandant der Nachschubkommandantur Russland-Mitte in Bobruisk (6/43 - 4/19/44); CO SS-Jäger-Bataillon 500 (1944); CO Waffen-Grenadier-Regiment der SS 31 / 14. Waffen-Grenadier-Division der Waffen-SS [ukrainische Nr. 1] (9/44 - ?); severely wounded; captured in hospital by Soviets (5/45); released to custody of Western Allies (1948); died of natural causes (8/19/78)

Panzinger, Dr. Friedrich,
SS-Oberführer -- Chef RSHA Amt IVA; CO Einsatzgruppe A (9/4/43 - 5/6/44); SD Berlin; SD Ostland; in Soviet custody; remanded to West German custody; suicide (1959)

Paul, Arno,
SS-Hauptsturmführer -- CO 12. Schwadron/1. SS-Totenkopf-Reiterstandarte (11/39 - 5/40); CO 6. Schwadron/1. SS-Totenkopf-Reiterstandarte (5/40 - 11/40); CO 7. Schwadron/II. Abteilung/SS-[Totenkopf]-Kavallerie-Regiment 1 (11/40 - 3/20/41); CO Artillerie-Abteilung / SS-Kavallerie-Brigade (12/41+); SS-Remonteamt Rejowice (11/42 - 7/44); service with 13. Waffen-Grenadier-Division der SS *Handschar* [kroatische Nr. 1] (7/44 - 9/44); SS-Remonteamt Kischbeck

Pechau, Dr. Manfred,
SS-Sturmbannführer -- RSHA Amt IB; CO Einsatzkommando 1b/Einsatzgruppe A (10/42 - 3/26/43); SD Berlin; committed suicide (1950)

Peiper, Joachim [Jochen],
SS-Standartenführer -- Persönlicher Stab RFSS (5/38 - 5/40); active service with *LAH* in France (5/40

- 6/20/40); Persönlicher Stab RFSS (6/21/40 - 8/41); active service with 1. SS-Panzer-Division *Leibstandarte Adolf Hitler* (8/41 - 5/45); CO SS-Panzer-Regiment 2/1. SS-Panzer-Division *Leibstandarte Adolf Hitler* (? - ?); responsible for atrocities at *Boves* in northern Italy; CO Kampfgruppe Peiper [SS-Panzer-Regiment 1/ 1. SS-Panzer-Division *Leibstandarte Adolf Hitler*] during the Ardennes Offensive : charged with numerous atrocities (12/44); main defendant at the *Malmedy* Trial (5/16/46 - 7/11/46); found guilty; sentenced to death (7/16/46); sentence commuted to life imprisonment (1/31/51); life sentence reduced to 35 years' imprisonment (1954); paroled (12/22/56); West German Government pressured by Italian authorities begins investigation of the Boves atrocities (6/64); officially charged by Italian authorities (12/11/68); found innocent due to lack of criminal intent by the Landgericht Stuttgart (2/69); retired anonymously to Traves in southeastern France; exposed and received threats (1976); killed at home by unknown assailants, probably former resistance members (7/14/76)

Persterer, Alois,
SS-Obersturmbannführer -- RSHA; CO Sonderkommando 10b/Einsatzgruppe D (6/22/41 - 2/43); SD Salzburg; KIA in Austria (1945)

Petersen, Heinrich,
S-Standartenführer -- battalion commander, 3. SS-Panzer-Division *Totenkopf* (1940); CO SS-Freiwilligen-Gebirgsjäger-Regiment 13/7. SS-Freiwilligen-Gebirgs-Division *Prinz Eugen* (? - 3/19/45); CO 18. SS-Panzergrenadier-Division *Horst Wessel* (3/20/45 - 5/9/45); committed suicide in Czechoslovakia (5/9/45)

Pfeffer-Wildenbruch, Karl,
SS-Obergruppenführer -- CO Polizeigruppe 4 zbV (Poland, 1939); CO 4. SS-Polizei-Panzergrenadier-Division (10/1/39 - 11/10/40); Chef des Kolonial-Polizeiamtes, Ministerium des Innern (1941 - 43); CO VI [lettischen] SS-Freiwilligen-Armeekorps (1943); Befehlshaber der Waffen-SS Ungarn (9/44); CO IX. SS-Gebirgs-Korps (12/44 - 2/12/45, severely wounded); captured by Soviets in Budapest (2/12/45); paroled (10/9/55); died in Bielefeld (1/29/71)

Pfeifer, Friedrich, SS-Untersturmführer -- officer SS-Panzergrenadier-Bataillon 2/SS-Panzergrenadier-Regiment 1/1. SS-Panzer-Division *Leibstandarte Adolf Hitler*; implicated in the *Malmedy* atrocities (12/16+/44)

Phleps, Artur,
SS-Obergruppenführer -- former Rumanian General Staff officer; inducted into Waffen-SS (6/30/41); CO *Westland* Regiment/5. SS-Panzer-Division *Wiking* (7/5/41 - Summer 1942); Sonderauftrag des RFSS (recruitment of Serbian and Banat Volksdeutsche); CO 7. SS-Freiwilligen-Gebirgs-Division *Prinz Eugen* (3/1/42 - 6/21/43); divisional commander at the time of the following atrocities : *Goc, Biserske Livada, Zhescin, Raskoj, Ivanjica, Liga, Sancaku, Zapadne Morave, Krusevac* (Fall 1942) / *Blazevo, Topoli, Boronjina, Ravniste, Rodici, Ilinci* (Winter 1942) / *Ripac* (1/30-31/43) / *Niksic* (5/43) / *Dola* (6/7/43); CO V. SS-Freiwilligen-Gebirgs-Korps (7/4/43 - 9/44); HöSSPf Siebenburgen (9/13/44 - 9/18/44); KIA against Soviet forces at Arad, Rumania (9/21/44)

Pinsky, Zoltan von,
Waffen-Oberführer -- CO 26. Waffen-Grenadier-Division der SS [ungarische Nr. 2] (12/23/44 - 1/21/45); KIA

Pipkorn, Rudiger,
SS-Standartenführer -- CO 35. SS-Polizei-Grenadier-Division (3/45 - 4/24/45); MIA

Plänk, Willi,
SS-Sturmbannführer -- CO SS-Reiterstandarte 6 [Düsseldorf] (12/38 - 9/39); CO 1. platoon/3. Schwadron/ SS-Totenkopf-Reiterstandarte 1 (11/39 - 5/40); CO 8. Schwadron/II. Abteilung/SS-[Totenkopf]-Kavallerie-Regiment 1 (11/40 - 3/20/41); CO 7. Schwadron/ SS-Kavallerie-Regiment 1 (3/21/41 - 8/1/41); CO Radfahr-Aufklärungsabteilung/SS-Kavallerie-Brigade (12/41+); CO SS-Kavallerie-Ausbildungs-und Ersatz-Abteilung 8 *Warschau* (3/42 - 5/45); assisted in suppression of the *Warsaw Ghetto Uprising* (4-5/43)

Plath, Karl-Julius,
SS-Sturmbannführer -- RSHA Amt IVB; CO Sonderkommando Plath/Einsatzgruppe C; responsible for atrocities in the Dnjepropetrowsk and Krementschug areas (1942); KIA in USSR (7/29/43)

Poche, Oswald,
SS-Obersturmbannführer -- RSHA Amt III; CO Einsatzkommando 2/Einsatzgruppe A (8/43 - ?); SD Tromso; Gestapo Frankfurt/Main; died (1962)

Polansky, ?,
SS-? -- company commander in SS-Panzergrenadier-Regiment 26/12. SS-Panzer-Division *Hitlerjugend*; possible complicity in the *Normandy* atrocities (6/7-17/44)

Pötschke, Werner,
SS-Sturmbannführer -- service with 1. SS-Panzer-Division *Leibstandarte Adolf Hitler* (1939 - 1945); CO SS-Panzer-Abteilung 1/SS-Panzer-Regiment 1 /1. SS-Panzer-Division *Leibstandarte Adolf Hitler* (1944); implicated in the *Malmedy* atrocities (12/16+/44); severely wounded at Veszprem, Hungary (3/15/45); died of wounds (3/24/45)

Potzelt, Walter,
SS-Standartenführer -- RSHA; 1. SS-Panzer-Division *Leibstandarte Adolf Hitler* (1941); temporary CO Einsatzgruppe A (4/20/42 - 7/1/42); SD Fulda-Werra; died before post-war trial

Pradel, Friedrich,
SS-? -- head of transport for Einsatzgruppe B

Priess, Hermann,
SS-Obergruppenführer -- service with SS-Verfügungstruppe (1934 - 39); various commands in the 3. SS-Panzer-Division *Totenkopf* (1939 - 1943); CO 3. SS-Panzer-Division *Totenkopf* (10/16/43 - 7/13/44); CO XIII. SS-Armee-Korps (8/7/44 - 11/16/44); CO I. SS-Panzer-Korps during the Ardennes Offensive (10/24/44 - 5/8/45); detained by Americans for alleged complicity in the Malmedy atrocities (6/45); defendant at Malmedy trial (5/16/46 - 7/11/46); found guilty; sentenced to 20 years imprisonment (7/16/46); paroled (10/54); died in Ahrensburg (2/2/85)

Prinz, Karl-Heinz,
SS-Sturmbannführer -- CO II. Abteilung/SS-Panzer-Regiment 12/12. SS-Panzer-Division *Hitlerjugend* (6/44); complicity in the *Normandy* atrocities (6/7-17/44); killed in action at Hill 159 in Normandy (8/14/44)

Prützmann, Hans-Adolf,
SS-Obergruppenführer -- HSSPf Nordsee (6/28/38 - 5/1/41); HSSPf Nordost (5/1/41 - 5/8/45); HSSPf Ostland und Russland-Nord (6/29/41 - 11/1/41); HSSPf Russland-Süd (12/11/41 - 3/18/44); HöSSPf Ukraine (10/29/43 - 9/44); his operations in Russia resulted in the deaths of 360,000 people from 8/42 - 10/42; SS-liaison to Oberkommando der Wehrmacht (6/44 and after); Generalinspektor für den passiven Widerstand / Generalinspektor für Spezialabwehr [Head of Werwolf organization] (1/45 - 5/45); SS-liaison to the Dönitz Government (4/45 - 5/45); taken into British custody for trial; commited suicide at Lüneberg (5/21/45)

Puaud, Edgar,
Waffen-Oberführer -- CO 33. Waffen-Grenadier-Division der SS *Charlemagne* [französische Nr. 1] (9/1/44 - 2/45); severely wounded and MIA in Pommern (3/5/45)

Pückler-Burghaus, Carl Friedrich Graf von,
SS-Gruppenführer -- service with Wehrmacht as staff officer (1938 - 8/41); acting HSSPf Russland-Mitte (1/2/42 - 3/24/43); CO 15. Waffen-Grenadier-Division der SS [lettische Nr. 1] (5/43 - 2/16/44); Befehlshaber der Waffen-SS Slowakien (3/44 - 5/45); committed suicide in Pilsen (5/12/45)

Pulvermüller, Karl-Heinz,
SS-Obersturmführer -- CO SS-Panzerartillerie-Abteilung 4/SS-Panzergrenadier-Regiment 1/1. SS-Panzer-Division *Leibstandarte Adolf Hitler* (1944)

Pütz, Dr. Karl,
SS-Obersturmbannführer -- KdS Rowno (1942-3); director of the second Rowno massacre; KdS Lublin (1943); complicity in the *Aktion Erntefest* massacres (11/3-4/43); tried by the Polish authorities and executed after the war

Querner, Rudolf,
SS-Obergruppenführer -- IdO Hamburg (4/37 - 10/40); General Inspector of Gendarmerie and Schutzpolizei

/ Hauptamt Ordnungspolizei (11/40 - 4/41); HSSPf Nordsee (4/30/41 - 1/30/43); HSSPf Donau (1/31/43 - 10/5/44); HSSPf Mitte (10/5/44 - 5/8/45); taken into Allied custody; commited suicide in Magdeburg (5/27/45)

Rabe, Karl-Hermann,
SS-Obersturmbannführer -- RSHA Amt I; CO Sonderkommando 7b / Einsatzgruppe B (1/43 - 10/44); SD Krakow; legal proceedings in Hamburg courts (1978)

Radetzky, Waldemar von,
SS-Sturmbannführer -- service with Einsatzgruppe B in the USSR; sentenced to twenty years imprisonment during Einsatzgruppen Trial at Nürnberg (4/48); sentence reduced to time served and released (1951)

Raithel, Helmut,
SS-Standartenführer -- CO 23. Waffen-Gebirgs-Division der SS *Kama* [kroatische Nr. 2] (6/44 - 10/31/44)

Rapp, Albert,
SS-Standartenführer -- SS-Hauptamt Berlin (early 1939 - 9/39); Stab Einsatzgruppe VI in Poland (1939); Führer SD-Leitabschnitts Posen (1939 - 4/40); Führer SD-Leitabschnitts München (4/40 - 2/42); CO Sonderkommando 7a/Einsatzgruppe B (2/42 - 1/28/43); wounded; IdS Braunschweig (early Summer 1943 - 10/44); Hauptamt VI/RSHA Berlin (10/44 - 5/45); hid post-war under the alias of Alfred Ruppert; taken into custody by West German government (2/21/61); attempted suicide (4/17/63); tried by Landgericht Essen; sentenced to life imprisonment (3/29/65)

Rasch, Dr. Emil Otto,
SS-Brigadeführer -- KdS Prague (1939); CO Einsatzkommando Sipo / Einsatzgruppe zbV (Poland, 1939); KdS Königsberg; CO Einsatzgruppe C (6/22/41 - 10/41); participated in planning and execution of the infamous *Babi Yar* atrocity in which 33,771 Jews were murdered (9/29-30/41); RSHA; declared unfit to plead at the Einsatzgruppen Trial (2/5/48); dies in prison of Parkinson's disease (11/1/48)

Rasmussen, Johannes,
SS-? -- service with SS-Panzeraufklärungs-Abteilung 12/12. SS-Panzer-Division *Hitlerjugend* (1944); complicity in the *Ascq* massacre (4/1-2/44); tried and sentenced to death by French authorities (8/2-6/49); sentenced reduced to 10 years hard labor minus time served (7/14/55); paroled (1956)

Rauch, Friedrich,
SS-Hauptscharführer --
adjutant Sonderkommando 1005 (7/42 - 7/43)

Rausch, Gunther,
SS-Obersturmbannführer -- RSHA; CO Sonderkommando 7b/Einsatzgruppe B (6/22/41 - 2/10/42); SD Stuttgart; died during preliminary legal proceedings (1964)

Rauter, Hans-Albin,
SS-Obergruppenführer -- Stab SS-Oberabschnitt Südost (11/38 - 5/40); HSSPf Nordwest (6/26/40 - 5/8/45); seriously injured by partisan attack, on sick leave (3/45); remanded to Dutch custody (1945); tried by the Special High Court at The Hague (4/3/48); found guilty and sentenced to death; hung (3/25/49)

Reder, Walter,
SS-Sturmbannführer -- service with 3. SS-Panzer-Division *Totenkopf* (1940 - 1943); service with SS-Panzergrenadier-Ausbildungs-und Ersatz Bataillon 3 *Warschau* during the liquidation of the Waraw Ghetto (4/19 - 5/16/43); CO SS-Panzeraufklärungsabteilung 16 /16. SS-Panzergrenadier-Division *Reichsführer-SS* (1943 - 1/45); responsible for atrocities at *Farnocchia, Bardine de San Terenzo, Sant'Anna di Stazzema, Vinca di Fivizzano, Gragnola, Padule di Fucecchio, Monzone, Ponte S. Lucia, Valla*, and *Monte Sol* (8/12 - 10/5/44); CO SS-Panzergrenadier-Regiment 36/16. SS-Panzergrenadier-Division *Reichsführer-SS* (1/45 - 5/45); arrested by Americans at Salzburg (5/8/45); released to house arrest; re-interned at Glasenbach POW camp near Hallein (9/45); remanded to British custody for trials of Kesselring and Simon (9/47); remanded to Italian custody (5/13/48); tried by Italian authorities for numerous atrocities (10/ 19-30/51); found guilty and sentenced to life imprisonment (10/31/51); numerous unsuccessful appeals; transferred to Gaeta military

prison (5/16/54); expresses profound repentance in letter to people of Marzabotto (12/84); paroled after nearly 40 years (1/25/85); died in Vienna (4/26/91)

Rediess, Wilhelm,
SS-Obergruppenführer -- HSSPf Nordost (6/28/38 - 6/19/40); responsible for anti-Jewish operations in Preussen (10/39 - 11/39); HSSPf Nord (6/19/40 - 5/8/45); organized Norwegian volunteer SS units; committed suicide in Oslo (5/9/45)

Rehagel, Heinz,
SS-Untersturmführer -- CO Panzer 711/7. SS-Panzer-Kompanie/SS-Panzer-Regiment 1/1.SS-Panzer-Division *Leibstandarte Adolf Hitler* (1944); implicated in the *Malmedy* atrocities (12/16+/44); defendant at the *Malmedy* Trial (5/16/46 - 7/11/46); found guilty; sentenced to death (7/16/46); sentence commuted; released from custody

Reich, Otto,
SS-Oberführer -- CO 4. SS-Totenkopfstandarte *Ostmark* (11/38 - 12/40); CO SS-Freiwilligen-Standarte *Nordwest* (4/41 - 4/42); supply officer, North Russia (4/42 - 10/42); on leave and training; CO Ordnungspolizei Regiment, USSR (8/43 - 3/44); various Ordnungspolizei postings (3/44 - 7/44); BdO Agram (7/44 - 12/44); Polizeigebietsführer Agram (12/28/44 - 1/6/45); Stab SS-Personalhauptamt (1/45 - 5/45); died in Düsseldorf (9/20/55)

Reichenwallner, Wilhelm,
SS-Hauptsturmführer -- CO 5. Schwadron/SS-Totenkopf-Reiterstandarte 1 (11/39 - 5/40); CO 2. Schwadron / SS-Totenkopf-Reiterstandarte 2 (5/40 - 11/40); CO 4. Schwadron/III. Abteilung/SS-[Totenkopf]-Kavallerie-Regiment 1 (11/40 - 3/20/41)

Reinefarth, Heinz,
SS-Gruppenführer -- service with Einsatzkommandos I and II (1939); service with Wehrmacht (1939 - 1942); Generalinspektor der Verwaltung des Reichprotektorats Böhmen-Mähren (6/42 - 6/43); Stab Hauptamt Ordnungspolizei (6/43 - 1/44); HSSPf Warthe (1/29/44 - 12/30/44); CO Kampfgruppe Reinefarth - assisted in suppression of *Warsaw Uprising* (8/44 -11/44); CO XVIII. SS-Armee-Korps (11/44 - 2/45); Kommandant Festung Küstrin (2/1/45 - 3/2/45); CO XIV. SS-Armee-

Korps (3/45); surrendered to Americans (5/25/45); in Allied custody until 1948; lived in the Bundesrepublik; many proceedings but no sentences against defendant; ran for various political offices; served as mayor of Westerland-Sylt; died in Westerland-Sylt (5/7/79)

Reinhardt, Christian,
SS-Hauptsturmführer --
CO Vorausabteilung SS-Kavallerie-Regiment 1; responsible for numerous killing operations, see *SS-Kavallerie-Brigade Operations and Atrocities in the USSR*; complicity in *Pripet Marshes* massacres (1941 - 1943)

Reinsch, Dr. Karl,
SS-Untersturmführer -- CO Medical Detachment / SS-Totenkopf-Reiterstandarte 1 (11/39 - 5/40)

Reiter, Paul Anton,
SS-? -- commanded a company of 2. SS-Panzer-Division *Das Reich* responsible for the *Gau Niederdonau* atrocity (4/45)

Reitz, ?,
SS-Obersturmbannführer -- CO SS-Totenkopfstandarte *Kirkenes* (? - ?)

Reitzenstein, Gerd von,
SS-? -- officer attached to 12. SS-Panzer-Division *Hitlerjugend*; found by Canadian authorities to be complicitous in the *Normandy* atrocities (6/7-17/44); recommended by SHAEF Standing Court of Inquiry for prosecution (1945); fate unknown

Remmers, Hans Hermann,
SS-Obersturmbannführer -- attached to Einsatzgruppe A (11/41 - 2/42); responsible for the massacre of 6624 Jews at Minsk (11/7-11/41); SD München; sentenced to eight years imprisonment (1961); sentenced commuted to five years

Rettlinger, Karl,
SS-Sturmbannführer -- service with the 1. SS-Panzer-Division *Leibstandarte Adolf Hitler* (1933 - Summer 1944); CO SS-Panzerjäger-Bataillon 1/SS-Panzergrenadier-Regiment 1/1. SS-Panzer-Division *Leibstandarte Adolf Hitler* (Summer 1944 - 5/45); suspected complicity in *Malmedy* atrocities

Ribbentrop, Rudolf,
SS-Hauptsturmführer -- son of German foreign minister Joachim von Ribbentrop; CO 3. Kompanie/SS-Panzer-Regiment 12/12. SS-Panzer-Division *Hitlerjugend*; suspected complicity in the *Normandy* atrocities (6/7-17/44); never questioned

Richter, Heinz,
SS-Obersturmbannführer -- CO Einsatzkommando 8/ Einsatzgruppe B (4/1/42 - 9/42); SD Paris (11/42); Gestapo Wien; sentenced to seven years imprisonment by Kiel court (1969)

Richter, Hellmuth,
SS-Standartenführer -- service with SS-Totenkopfstandarten (1939); service with 5. SS-Panzer-Division *Wiking*; CO SS-Artillerie-Regiment 5/5. SS-Panzer-Division *Wiking*; CO 32. SS-Freiwilligen-Grenadier-Division *30. Januar* (2/5/45 - 2/17/45); died in Mengeringhausen (3/19/70)

Richter, Karl,
SS-Sturmbannführer -- CO SS-Panzergrenadier-Bataillon 1/SS-Panzergrenadier-Regiment 2/1. SS-Panzer-Division *Leibstandarte Adolf Hitler* (1944)

Rinner, Franz,
SS-Obersturmführer -- CO 10. Schwadron/SS-Totenkopf-Reiterstandarte 1 (11/39 - 5/40); CO 5. Schwadron/SS-Totenkopf-Reiterstandarte 2 (5/40 - 11/40)

Roch, Heinz,
SS-Oberführer -- service with 3. SS-Panzer-Division *Totenkopf* (1940); service with 1. SS-Panzer-Division *Leibstandarte Adolf Hitler* (1941); Stab HSSPf Russland-Mitte (1/42 - 3/43); acting SSPf Taurien-Krim-Simferopol (3/3/43 - 12/25/43); SS und Polizeigebietsführer Aleschki; IdS Simferopol (? - 5/43); BdS Simferopol (5/43 - 5/44); SS-Standortkommandant Simferopol (5/44); Stab HöSSPf Ukraine (5/44 - 7/44); SSPf Bialystok (7/18/44 - 10/22/44); Stab Wehrkreis I (10/44 - 11/44); SSPf Nord-Norwegen (11/21/44 - 5/45); committed suicide in Oslo (5/10/45)

Rode, Ernst,
SS-Brigadeführer -- Chief of Staff for Chef Bandenkampfverbande

Rodenbücher, Alfred,
SS-Gruppenführer -- HSSPf Alpenland (4/25/39 - 4/30/41); removed from office; transferred to service with Kriegsmarine (5/41 - 5/45); refused posting as SSPf Lettland (6/41); in British custody (1945-48); lived in the Bundesrepublik; died in Emmendingen (3/29/80)

Röder, Franz,
SS-Sturmbannführer -- CO SD Einsatzkommando 16 (Poland, 1939)

Röhwer, Friedrich,
SS-Untersturmführer -- company officer from 1. Bataillon/SS-Panzergrenadier-Regiment 2/1. SS-Panzer-Division *Leibstandarte Adolf Hitler*; complicity in the *Lago Maggiore* atrocity (9/22-24/43); sentenced to death by Schwurgericht Osnabrück (7/5/68); sentenced overturned by Bundesgerichtshof Berlin (4/70)

Rösener, Erwin,
SS-Obergruppenführer -- Stab SS-Oberabschnitt Rhein (11/38 - 6/40); HSSPf Rhein (7/24/40 - 11/11/41); HSSPf Alpenland (11/24/41 - 5/8/45); head of anti-partisan warfare staff in Laibach (10/44 - 5/45); captured by British (1945); remanded to Yugoslavian authorities (post-1945); tried and condemned to death; hung in Belgrade (9/8/46)

Rosenow, ?,
SS-Obersturmbannführer -- CO 1. Kompanie /Waffen-SS Bataillon zbV (6/21/41 - 7/29/41); responsible for numerous killing operations in the USSR

Ruge, Rudolf,
SS-Obersturmbannführer -- instructor SS-Junkerschule Tölz (? - 9/39); CO 3. Schwadron/SS-Totenkopf-Reiterstandarte (9/39 - 11/39); CO 2. Schwadron/SS-Totenkopf-Reiterstandarte 1 (11/39 - 5/40); CO 1. Schwadron/ SS-Totenkopf-Reiterstandarte 2 (5/40 - 11/40); service with 4. SS-Polizei-Panzergrenadier Division and 6. SS-Gebirgs-Division *Nord*; Stab SS-Abschnitte XXIII; CO Polizei-Reitschule Rathenow (8/42 - ?); Ordnungspolizei Cavalry Inspector

Rühl, Felix,

SS-Hauptsturmführer -- service with Sonderkommando 10 / Einsatzgruppe D in the USSR; Gestapo Augsburg; sentenced to ten years imprisonment during Einsatzgruppen Trial at Nuremberg (4/48); sentence reduced to time served and released (1949)

Rumohr, Joachim,

SS-Brigadeführer -- CO SS-Artillerie-Regiment 8/8. SS-Kavallerie-Division *Florian Geyer* (? - 4/1/44); CO 8. SS-Kavallerie-Division *Florian Geyer* (4/1/44 - 2/11/45); committed suicide in Budapest (2/13/45)

Rumpf, Erich,

SS-Obersturmführer -- CO SS-Panzerpionier-Kompanie 9/SS-Panzer-Regiment 1/1. SS-Panzer-Division *Leibstandarte Adolf Hitler* (1944); implicated in the *Malmedy* atrocities (12/16+/44); defendent at the *Malmedy* Trial (5/16/46 - 7/11/46); defendant at the *Malmedy* Trial (5/16/46 - 7/11/46); found guilty; sentenced to death (7/16/46); sentence commuted; released from custody

Rux, Karl-Heinz,

SS-Obersturmbannführer -- CO Einsatzkommando 2/Einsatzgruppe II (Poland, 1939); SD Bromberg; SD Veldes; SD Salzburg

Rybka, Kurt,

SS-Hauptsturmführer --
CO SS Fallschirmjäger-Bataillon 500 (4/44 - 6/26/44)

Sacks, ?,

SS-Obersturmbannführer -- CO 12. SS-Totenkopfstandarte (? - ?); responsible for murders at *Owinsk* (10-11/39)

Sammern-Frankenegg, Dr. Ferdinand von,

SS-Brigadeführer -- CO SS-Abschnitt IX (9/39 - 7/43); acting SSPf Warschau (7/22/42 - 4/19/43) -- responsible for the deportation of 300,000 Warsaw Jews to VL Treblinka; replaced by Stroop at the start of the *Warsaw Ghetto Uprising*; Polizeigebietsführer Essegg (7/15/43 - 9/20/44); KIA near Krasnica Luka [15 km NE of Banja Luka, Bosnia] (9/20/44)

Sandberger, Dr. Martin,

SS-Standartenführer -- Chef RSHA Amt VIB; CO Sonderkommando 1a-KdS Estland /Einsatzgruppe A (6/22/41 - Fall 1943); CO Einsatzkommando 1a/Einsatzgruppe A (mid 1942 - Fall 1942); responsible for massacre of Jews at Pskov; SD Stuttgart; BdS Nord Italien (12/1/43); condemned to death during Einsatzgruppen Trial at Nuremberg (4/48); sentence commuted to life imprisonment (1/31/51); released (5/58)

Sandig, Rudolf,

SS-Obersturmbannführer -- service with 1. SS-Panzer-Division *Leibstandarte Adolf Hitler* (1940 - 11/43); CO SS-Panzergrenadier-Regiment 2/1. SS-Panzer-Division *Leibstandarte Adolf Hitler* (11/43 - 4/45); CO of a kampfgruppe from 12. SS-Panzer-Division *Hitlerjugend* (4/45 - 5/8/45); captured by American forces near Bad Aussee (5/12/45); released (8/48)

Sauberzweig, Karl-Gustav,

SS-Gruppenführer -- CO 13. Waffen-Gebirgs-Division der SS *Handschar* [kroatische Nr. 1] (mid 1943 - 6/18/44); CO IX. Waffen-Gebirgs-Korps der SS [kroatisches] (6/19/44 - 10/31/44); dismissed and sent on sick leave (11/44 - 3/45); Corps commander, Heeresgruppe H (4/45 - 5/45); captured by British at war's end; extradition requested by Yugoslavian authorities; committed suicide hours before scheduled extradition (10/20/46)

Scapini, Hans,

SS-Hauptsturmführer -- CO II. Bataillon /SS-Panzergrenadier-Regiment 25/12. SS-Panzer-Division *Hitlerjugend*; fate unknown

Schäfer, Dr. Emanuel,

SS-Oberführer -- CO Einsatzgruppe II (Poland, 1939); responsible for numerous killing operations in Poland; responsible for the *Nisko, Ciepielow,* and *Rawa Mazowiecka* atrocities (9/39); KdS Belgrade; responsible for *Sajmiste Camp* gassings (2/42 - 5/10/42); KdS Trieste; Personalstab RFSS; in hiding post-war; identity discovered (4/51); sentenced to one year and nine months by a denazification court; charged with the gassing of 6000 Jews from Sajmiste Camp, but case postponed for further investigation (Schwurgericht Köln, 10/52); later tried and sentenced to 6 1/2 years imprisonment for the gassing of 6,280 women and children (1953)

Schäfer, Johannes,
SS-Brigadeführer -- CO SS-Abschnitt XXVI (4/38 - 5/40); CO SS and Polizei units in Danzig (6/39 - 9/39); Inspektionsführer des Selbstschutzes Ostpreussen (10/39 - 10/40); CO SS-Abschnitt XXXXIII (5/40 - 10/40); Polizeipräsident Lodz (5/4 - 10/40); service with 2. SS-Panzer-Division *Das Reich* (10/40 - 6/43); Stab 4. SS-Polizei-Panzergrenadier-Division (6/43 - 7/43); service with SS-Panzergrenadier-Ausbildung und-Ersatz-Bataillon 4. (7/43 - 5/45); died in Bielefeld (4/28/93)

Schäfer, Karl,
SS-Brigadeführer -- CO SS-Abschnitt XII (3/37 - 4/42); acting SSPf Lettland (4/7/42 - 4/26/42); acting SSPf Litauen (4/25/42 - 5/22/42); SSPf Weissruthenien (5/22/42 - 7/21/42); Stab SS-Oberabschnitt Weichsel (7/42 - 8/42); Stab HSSPf Russland-Süd (8/42 - 10/42); SSPf Dnjepropetrowsk-Krivoi Rog (10/4/43 - 11/2/43); KIA (11/2/43)

Schäfer, Dr. Oswald,
SS-Obersturmbannführer -- Gestapo München; RSHA; CO Einsatzkommando 9/Einsatzgruppe B (10/20/41 - 2/42); tried for Gestapo activities and sentenced to 2 years imprisonment, paroled soon thereafter (1951); tried again for Gestapo activities and sentenced to 1 year imprisonment, paroled again quickly (1954); acquitted by Berlin court on other charges (1966)

Schallock, Walter,
SS-Untersturmführer -- operations CO Sonderkommando 1005 (7/42 - 7/43); Polizei Stettin

Scharpwinkel, Dr. Wilhelm,
SS-Obersturmbannführer -- CO Einsatzkommando 1/Einsatzgruppe III (Poland, 1939); RSHA; Polizei Breslau; Polizei Leignitz

Scheel, Dr. Gustav-Adolf,
SS-Obergruppenführer -- IdS München (10/39 - 5/41); BdS Strassburg (7/40 - 8/41); HSSPf Alpenland (4/30/41 - 11/24/41); NSDAP Gauleiter Salzburg (11/41 - 5/45); post-war: sentenced to five years imprisonment; died in Hamburg (3/23/79)

Scheer, August,
SS-Brigadeführer -- KdO Kiev

Schefe, Dr. Robert, S
S-Obersturmbannführer -- CO Einsatzkommando 2/Einsatzgruppe V (Poland, 1939); RSHA Amt VA; SD Allenstein

Scheider, Hans,
SS-Standartenführer -- CO 6. SS-Gebirgs-Division *Nord* (10/41 - 3/30/42)

Schellong, Konrad,
SS-Obersturmbannführer -- CO 27. SS-Freiwilligen-Grenadier-Division *Langemarck* [flämische Nr. 1] (7/15/42 - 5/45)

Schenk, ?,
SS-Untersturmführer -- member of 12. SS-Panzer-Division *Hitlerjugend* found by Canadian investigators to be complicitous in the *Normandy* atrocities (6/7-17/44); fate unknown

Scherner, Julian,
SS-Oberführer -- CO Allgemeine-SS Leader's School, Dachau (10/37 - 3/40); SS-Junkerschule Tölz (4/40 - 7/40); CO 8. SS-Totenkopfstandarte (8/40 - 11/40); CO SS-Truppenübungsplatz Beneschau / SS-Standortkommandant Prague (1/41 - 8/41); SSPf Krakau (8/4/41 - 3/1/44) - oversaw murderous "resettlement" operations in his district, see *Tarnow* [Poland] (6/42 - 9/43); SSPf zbV for HSSPf Ost (11/43 - 10/44); tried for profiteering from AL Plaszow in Krakow - reduced in rank and transferred to 36. Waffen-Grenadier-Division der SS ["Dirlewanger"] (late 1944); KIA (4/28/45)

Schimana, Walter,
SS-Gruppenführer -- service with Einsatzkommandos I and II (1939); CO Gendarmerie Schule Suhl (1/40 - 11/40); CO Gendarmerie Schule Deggingen (11/40 - 9/41); SSPf Saratow (9/4/41 - 11/30/41); Stab HSSPf Russland-Mitte (11/41 - 7/42); CO Kampfgruppe 137. Infanterie-Division (12/41 - 1/42); CO of Ordnungspolizei Polizei Regiment Mitte (1/12/42 - 7/42); acting SSPf Weissruthenien and SS-Standortkommandant Minsk (7/21/42 - 7/15/43); CO 14. Waffen-Grenadier-Division der SS [ukrainische Nr.1] (7/15/43 - 11/19/43); numerous atrocities against Polish civilians during his command (see *14. W-G-D der SS Crimes in Poland*); HSSPf Griechenland (10/18/43 - 9/24/44); HSSPf Donau

(10/5/44 - 5/8/45); taken into Allied custody; committed suicide in Salzburg on eve of trial (9/12/48)

Schindhelm, Hans-Gerhard,
SS-Obersturmbannführer -- CO Einsatzkommando 8/ Einsatzgruppe B (11/13/42 - 10/43); Gestapo Krakow; SD Leipzig

Schlätel, Werner,
SS-Sturmbannführer -- service with Einsatzkommando in Czechoslovakia (1938); CO II. Kompanie/SS-Panzergrenadier-Regiment 7/4. SS-Polizei-Panzergrenadier-Division; responsible for the *Karpenisi* atrocity

Schliefenbaum, Hermann,
SS-Standartenführer -- SS-Totenkopfstandarte 2 *Brandenburg* (9/38 - ?); 3. SS-Panzer-Division *Totenkopf* (? - 8/40); CO I. Bataillon/SS-Infanterie-Regiment 8 (8/8/40 - 8/41); CO SS-Kavallerie-Regiment 2 /SS-Kavallerie-Brigade (8/1/41 - 3/42); responsible for numerous killing operations, see *SS-Kavallerie-Brigade Operations and Atrocities in the USSR*; complicity in *Pripet Marshes* massacres (1941-43); CO II. Bataillon / SS-Gebirgsjäger-Regiment 1 (5/42 - 1/43); transferred to the Wehrmacht (1/43)

Schmald, Walter, SS-Obersturmführer -- Tulle SD; complicity in the *Tulle* executions (6/9/44)

Schmauser, Ernst Heinrich,
SS-Obergruppenführer -- CO SS-Oberabschnitt Main (4/36 - 5/41); HSSPf Südost (5/20/41 - 2/15/45); CO SS-Oberabschnitt Südost (6/41 - 2/45); had jurisdiction over KL Auschwitz; captured by Soviets (2/10/45); died in Soviet custody (12/31/45)

Schmedes, Fritz,
SS-Brigadeführer -- CO 4. SS-Polizei-Panzergrenadier-Division (6/10/43 - 7/5/44 and 8/22/44 - 11/27/44); divisional commander at time of the *Ioannina* transports to Auschwitz (3/25/44) and the *Klisoura* massacre (5/5/44); relieved of command by Himmler for refusing to follow orders (11/27/44); CO 36. Waffen-Grenadier-Division der SS (2/15/45 - 4/29/45)

Schmelcher, Willy,
SS-Gruppenführer -- Polizeipräsident Saarbrücken

(3/35 - 10/42); SSPf Tscherniow (11/19/41 - 7/1/43); Polizeipräsident Metz (12/42 - 10/43); SSPf Shitomir (5/5/43 - 9/25/43); Persönlicher Stab RFSS (5/44 - 12/44); HSSPf Warthe (12/30/44 - 5/45); died in Saarbrücken (2/15/74)

Schmidhuber, August,
SS-Oberführer -- CO SS-Gebirgsjäger-Regiment 2/7. SS-Freiwilligen-Gebirgs-Division *Prinz Eugen*; responsible for atrocities in the *Kopaonik Mountains* (10/42), at *Kriva Reka* (10/13/42); *Ripac* (1/30-31/43), and *Niksic* (5/43); CO 21. Waffen-Gebirgs-Division der SS *Skanderbeg* [albanische Nr. 1] (6/44 - 8/14/44); directed anti-Jewish operations of division (6/44 - 8/44), see *Albania* and *Kukes*; CO 7. SS-Freiwilligen-Gebirgs-Division *Prinz Eugen* (1/20/45 - 5/45); tried and executed by Yugoslav authorities after the war

Schmücker, Rudolf,
SS-Hauptsturmführer --
CO Sonderkommando 7c/Einsatzgruppe B (6/42 - Fall 1942); Chef Sipo Posen

Schnabel, Dietrich,
SS-? -- orderly officer attached to SS-Panzergrenadier-Regiment 26/12. SS-Panzer-Division *Hitlerjugend*; complicitous in the *Normandy* atrocities; detained by Allies (5/45); remanded to British authorities; tried before a British military tribunal (10/21/48); found guilty and sentenced to death; executed at Hameln (1/20/49)

Schneider, ?,
SS-Standartenführer -- CO 7. SS-Totenkopfstandarte (6/12/40 - 7/28/40+)

Schnelle, Karl Herbert,
SS-Hauptsturmführer -- company officer from 1. Bataillon/SS-Panzergrenadier-Regiment 2/1. SS-Panzer-Division *Leibstandarte Adolf Hitler*; complicity in the the *Lago Maggiore* atrocity (9/22-24/43); CO SS-Panzergrenadier-Bataillon 2/SS-Panzergrenadier-Regiment 2/1. SS-Panzer-Division *Leibstandarte Adolf Hitler* (1944); sentenced to death by Schwurgericht Osnabrück (7/5/68); sentenced overturned by Bundesgerichtshof Berlin (4/70)

Schneller, Max,
SS-Gruppenführer -- Stab SS-Oberabschnitt Spree (5/34 - 4/41); acting HSSPf Spree (2/20/43 - 5/8/45); died (5/25/48)

Scholz, Fritz Elder von Raranoze von,
SS-Gruppenführer -- CO SS-Panzergrenadier-Regiment *Nordland* / 5. SS-Panzer-Division *Wiking* (12/1/40 - 1/26/43); CO 2. SS-Infanterie [mot.]-Brigade (1/26/43 - 4/20/43); CO 11. SS-Freiwilligen-Panzergrenadier-Division *Nordland* (5/1/43 - 6/28/44); died of wounds sustained at Narva (7/28/44)

Schönemann, Werner,
SS-Obersturmbannführer
-- Kriminalkommissar Gestapostelle Köln (1938 - 1940); Auswahllehrgang Sipo Pretzsch (1940); Stab RSHA (early 1941 - 6/41); attached to Einsatzgruppe A as CO Teilkommando Borrisow (6/22/41 - ?); responsible for the massacre of 8,000 Jews at Borissov (7/8-10/41); studying at Berlin University (10/41); ill and suicide attempt (1941-42); Gestapo-Leitstelle Wien (1942); Referat Wirtschaftsspionage und Industrieschutz (1942 - 9/44); Einsatzkommando 13 [Slowakei] (9/44 - 5/45); arrested by Austrian authorities (7/16/45); tried by Austrians; sentenced to 10 years imprisonment (12/22/47); paroled to West Germany (11/20/51); given amnesty by Austria (1957); legal proceedings initiated by West Germans (5/26/61); tried by Landgericht Köln; sentenced to 6 years imprisonment (5/12/64); sentence commuted to three years

Schöner, Otto,
SS-Obersturmführer -- CO 9. Schützenkompanie/III. Bataillon/SS-Totenkopfstandarte II *Brandenburg*; complicity in massacres at *Wloclawek* (9/22-25/39)

Schönfeldt, Herbert,
SS-Sturmbannführer -- CO 2. Schwadron/SS-Totenkopf-Reiterstandarte (9/39 - 11/39); CO 7. Schwadron/SS-Totenkopf-Reiterstandarte 1 (11/39 - 5/40); CO 3. Schwadron/SS-Totenkopf-Reiterstandarte 1 (5/40 - 11/40); CO III. Abteilung/SS-[Totenkopf]-Kavallerie-Regiment 1 (11/40 - 3/20/41); CO Reitende Abteilung/ SS-Kavallerie-Regiment 2 (3/21/41 - 4/10/41); CO 5. Schwadron / SS-Kavallerie-Regiment 2 (4/11/41 - 12/41+); Ordnungspolizei Hauptamt (1941); service with SS-Kavallerie-Brigade (11/41 - ?); SS WVHA

and SS Hauptamt (1942); SS-Remonteamt Cholm (? - 4/28/45, KIA)

Schöngarth, Dr. Eberhard,
SS-Brigadeführer -- Chef Gestapo Münster (3/38 - 10/39); BdS Dresden (10/39 - 1/41); BdS Krakow (1/15/41 - 6/43); heavily involved in anti-Jewish actions; CO Waffen-SS-Bataillon zur besondere Verwendung (6/41 - 7/43); responsible for the murder of Polish intellectuals at *Lvov* (7/4/41); assisted Einsatzgruppen in USSR with numerous killing operations; responsible for the massacre of Jews at Pinsk (7/41); service with 4. SS-Polizei-Panzergrenadier-Division (7/43 - 7/44); BdS Den Haag (7/44 - 5/45); acting HSSPf Nordwest (3/10/45 - 4/45); sentenced to death by British Military Court at Enschede (2/11/46); hung at Hameln (5/15/46)

Schreiber, Franz,
SS-Standartenführer -- various postings SS-Regiment *Germania* (1935 - 40+); service with 6. SS-Gebirgs-Division *Nord* (1942 - 45); CO 6. SS-Gebirgs-Division *Nord* (5/45); captured by American forces (5/45); paroled (3/25/48); died in Hamburg (2/20/76)

Schreiner, Dr. Richard,
SS-Hauptsturmführer -- second-in-command of SS-Veterinär-Ersatz-Abteilung in *Radom*, occupied Poland; responsible for the massacre and deportation of Radom Jews to death camps (8/42)

Schröder, Walther,
SS-Gruppenführer -- Polizeipräsident Lübeck (4/37 - 5/45); Stab SD Hauptamt; Stab RSHA; SSPf Lettland (4/1/41 - 10/19/44); SSPf Estland (4/1/44 - 10/19/44); miscellaneous duties in Latvia (10/44 - 1/45); died in Lübeck (11/3/73)

Schubert, Heinz-Hermann,
SS-Obersturmbannführer -- RSHA Amt IA; service with Einsatzgruppe D in the USSR (10/41 - 6/42); SD Augsburg; condemned to death during Einsatzgruppen Trial at Nürnberg (1948); sentence commuted to ten years imprisonment; released (1952)

Schuh, ?,
SS-Untersturmbannführer -- CO 23. Kompanie /IV. Bataillon/SS-Gebirgsjäger-Regiment 1/7. SS-Freiwilligen-Gebirgs-Division *Prinz Eugen*; executed civilians

along the *Jablanica-Prozor railline* and *Niksic-Avtovac railline* (8/43)

Schüldt, Hinrich,
SS-Brigadeführer -- CO SS-Totenkopf-Infanterie-Regiment 4 (12/41 - 12/42); CO SS-Kampfgruppe Schuldt (12/42 - 3/15/43); CO 19. Waffen-Grenadier-Division der SS [lettische Nr. 2] (9/5/43 - 3/15/44); KIA near Petschane, Ostrau (3/15/44)

Schultz, Oskar,
SS-? -- service with 1. SS-Panzer-Division *Leibstandarte Adolf Hitler*; involvement in *Lago Maggiore* massacres (9/22-24/43); tried by Schwurgericht Osnabrück; sentenced to death (7/5/68); case appealed to Bundesgerichtshof Berlin; defendant acquitted on the grounds that he was following merely orders and that the statute of limitations had expired (4/70)

Schulz, Erwin,
SS-Brigadeführer -- Polizeidirektor Olmütz (1939); Chef Gestapo Reichenberg (1939 - 4/40); IdS Hamburg (4/40 - 3/41); Stab RSHA (3/41 - 5/41); CO Einsatzkommando 5 / Einsatzgruppe C (6/22/41 - 10/41); CO Sipo and SD school Berlin-Charlottenburg (10/41 - 2/43); Stab RSHA (9/42 - 4/44); IdS Salzburg (4/44 - 5/45); acting HSSPf Alpenland (5/1/44 - 5/28/44); SSPf Salzburg (4/45 - 5/45); sentenced to 20 years imprisonment during Einsatzgruppen Trial at Nürnberg (4/48); sentence commuted to 15 years (1/31/51); released (1954); died in Bremen (11/11/81)

Schulz, Paul,
SS-Untersturmführer -- service with Einsatzkommandos in Poland (1939); RSHA Amt IV; CO Einsatzkommando 11b /Einsatzgruppe D (9/42 - 2/43); SD Oslo; SD Den Haag

Schulze-Kossens, Richard,
SS-Obersturmbannführer -- SS Hauptamt (4/39 – 6/8/39); assistant to German foreign minister Ribbentrop (6/39 - 4/40); service with *Leibstandarte Adolf Hitler* in the Western Campaign (4/40); badly wounded in France (7/11/40); resumes foreign ministry position (8/11/40 – 1/41); transferred back to service with *Leibstandarte Adolf Hitler* (1/41 – 10/41); becomes Hitler's ordnance officer (10/3/41 - 10/42); personal assistant to Hitler (10/42 - 12/44); last commandant of SS-Junkerschule Tölz (12/44 - 3/45); CO 38. SS-Grenadier-Division *Nibelungen* (3/45 - 4/45); died (7/3/88)

Schumann, Heinz,
SS-Hauptsturmführer -- Ohlendorf's adjutant; organized mass executions at Simferopol; sentenced to death at Nuremberg (4/48); commuted to ten years (1/51); released (1/52)

Schümers, Karl,
SS-Oberführer -- CO SS-Panzergrenadier-Regiment 7/4. SS-Polizei-Panzergrenadier-Division at the time of the *Dhistomon* massacre (6/10/44); responsible for executions in *Siatista* (1944); CO 4. SS-Polizei-Panzergrenadier-Division (7/23/44 - 8/16/44); KIA in Greece (8/16/44)

Schützek, Ernst,
SS-Sturmbannführer -- CO SS-Begleit-Bataillon *Reichsführer-SS* (5/41 - ?)

Schwedler, Hans,
SS-Brigadeführer -- instructor, SS-Junkerschule Braunschweig (11/38 - 1/40); Stab Inspektorate der SS-Totenkopfstandarten (11/39 - 1/40); instructor SS-Junkerschule Tölz (1/40 - 6/40); CO Inspektorate der SS-Totenkopfstandarten (7/40 - 10/40); SSPf Krakau (10/1/40 - 8/4/41); SS-Standortkommandant Prague (8/41 - 3/42); Stab HSSPf Russland-Süd (3/42 - 8/43); Stab SS-Führungshauptamt (8/43 - 5/45); committed suicide in Hechendorf (5/2/45)

Seekel, Dr. Friedrich,
SS-Sturmbannführer -- RSHA Amt I; CO independent Sonderkommando in Byelorussia (Summer 1943 - 11/43); CO Sonderkommando 1005-Mitte (11/43 - 12/7/43)

Seetzen, Heinrich,
SS-Standartenführer -- Sipo Kassel; SD Breslau; CO Sonderkommando 10a/Einsatzgruppe D (6/22/41 - 7/42); BdS Weissruthenien; CO Einsatzgruppe B (4/28/44 - 8/44); Gestapo Hamburg; committed suicide in Hamburg while in British custody (9/28/45)

Seibert, Willi,
SS-Standartenführer -- Chef des Amtes IIID/RSHA; Chef des Amtes IIIC/RSHA; service with Einsatzgruppe D in the USSR (5/15/41 - 5/15/42); condemned to death dur-

ing Einsatzgruppen Trial at Nuremberg (4/48); sentence commuted to 15 years imprisonment; paroled (1955)

Seiler, ?,
SS-Oberscharführer -- head of the Waffen-SS Building Directorate Radom, responsible for the massacre and deportation of *Radom* Jews to death camps (8/42)

Sens, Otto,
SS-Standartenführer -- CO Einsatzkommando 1/Einsatzgruppe II (Poland, 1939); RSHA; Gestapo Stettin

Sickel, Dr. Kurt,
SS-Sturmbannführer -- senior medical officer SS-Panzer-Regiment 1/1. SS-Panzer-Division *Leibstandarte Adolf Hitler*; implicated in the *Malmedy* atrocities (12/16+/44); defendent at Malmedy Trials (5/16/46 - 7/11/46); defendant at the *Malmedy* Trial (5/16/46 - 7/11/46); found guilty; sentenced to death (7/16/46); sentence commuted; released from custody

Siebert, ?,
SS-Untersturmführer -- CO 3. platoon/SS-Panzeraufklärungs-Kompanie 2 / SS-Panzeraufklärungs-Bataillon 1/1. SS-Panzer-Division *Leibstandarte Adolf Hitler*; implicated in the *Malmedy* atrocities (12/16+/44)

Siebken, Bernhard,
SS-Sturmbannführer -- CO II. Bataillon/SS-Panzergrenadier-Regiment 26/12. SS-Panzer-Division *Hitlerjugend*; complicity in the *Normandy* atrocities (6/7-17/44); apprehended and held in Fischbeck POW camp near Hameln (5/45); remanded to British authorities; tried before a British military tribunal (10/21/48); found guilty and sentenced to death; executed at Hameln (1/20/49)

Siegling, Hans,
SS-Obersturmbannführer -- CO 30. Waffen-Grenadier-Division der SS [russische Nr. 2] (7/44 - 2/27/45)

Sievers, Franz,
SS-Obersturmführer -- CO SS-Panzerpionier-Kompanie 3/SS-Panzer-Regiment 1/1. SS-Panzer-Division *Leibstandarte Adolf Hitler* (1944); implicated in the *Malmedy* atrocities (12/16+/44); defendant at the *Malmedy* Trial (5/16/46 - 7/11/46); found guilty; sentenced to death (7/16/46); sentence commuted; released from

custody

Silgailis, Arturs,
Waffen-Oberführer -- CO 19. Waffen-Grenadier-Division der SS [lettische Nr. 2] (5/12/44 - 5/19/44)

Simon, Max,
SS-Gruppenführer -- CO SS-Totenkopfstandarte I *Oberbayern* [later SS-Panzergrenadier-Regiment 5] (9/39 - 2/26/43); responsible for numerous killing operations; possible complicity in atrocities at *Ciepielow, Rawa Mazowiecka* and *Nisko* (9/39); CO 3. SS-Panzer-Division *Totenkopf* (2/27/43 - 10/16/43); commander of division at time of alleged *Kharkov 4* atrocity (8/43); condemned to death in absentia by Soviet authorities -- wrongly accused of responsibility for mass murders at *Kharkov 1* and *Kharkov 3* (12/43); CO 16. SS-Panzergrenadier-Division *Reichsführer-SS* (10/16/43 - 10/24/44); divisional commander at time of the atrocities at *Farneta Monastery, Farnocchia, Bardine de San Terenzo, Sant'Anna di Stazzema, Vinca di Fivizzano, Gragnola, Padule di Fucecchio, Monzone, Ponte S. Lucia, Valla*, and *Monte Sol* (8/12 - 10/5/44); CO XIII. SS-Armee-Korps (11/16/44 - 5/8/45); condemned to death by British Tribunal in Padua for war crimes in Italy; sentenced commuted to life imprisonment; paroled (1954); tried by West German court for his role in establishing Standgerichte that carried out executions (10/55); cleared of charges (10/19/55); died of natural causes at Lünen, near Dortmund with third trial pending (2/1/61)

Six, Prof. Dr. Franz Alfred,
SS-Brigadeführer -- CO Einsatzkommando *Osterreich* (1938); CO Sonderkommando 7c / Einsatzgruppe B (6/22/41 - 8/20/41); service with 2. SS-Panzer-Division *Das Reich* (1941); Chef Amt VII / RSHA; hidden and employed by U.S. intelligence services (1946-48); tried and sentenced to 20 years imprisonment during Einsatzgruppen Trial at Nuremberg (4/10/48); sentence commuted to 10 years imprisonment (1/31/51); granted clemency and released (9/30/52); returned to employment with U.S. intelligence services (10/52)

Sohns, Hans-Fritz,
SS-Obersturmbannführer -- Kreisführer Neustadt (1940); operations CO Sonderkommando 1005 (7/43 -

?); RSHA Amt IIIA; Office of Reichskommisar Ostland

Sommer, Franz,
SS-Obersturmbannführer -- CO Einsatzkommando 1/Einsatzgruppe VI (Poland, 1939); RSHA; Kripo Köln; SD Düsseldorf

Sporrenburg, Jakob,
SS-Gruppenführer -- HSSPf Rhein (10/1/39 - 7/24/40); service with SS-Brigade *Germania* in France (5/40); HSSPf Nordost (6/21/40 - 5/1/41); SSPf Weissruthenien (7/21/41 - 8/14/41); service with 2. Polizei-Regiment in USSR extermination operations; Stab Gauleiter Erich Koch (9/41 - 3/43); HSSPf Russland-Mitte (3/43 - 8/43); SSPf Lublin (8/16/43 - 11/25/44); carried out the *Aktion Erntefest* massacres (11/3-4/43); SSPf Norwegen-Süd (11/21/44 - 5/45); arrested by British (5/11/45); remanded to Polish custody (post-1945); tried in Warsaw (1950); hung in Warsaw (12/6/52)

Stadler, Sylvester,
SS-Brigadeführer -- various commands with the 2. SS-Panzer-Division *Das Reich* (1940 - 1943); CO SS-Panzergrenadier-Regiment 4 *Der Führer* /2. SS-Panzer-Division *Das Reich* (1943 - 6/28/44); complicity in the *Oradour sur Glane* atrocity (6/10/44); CO 9. SS-Panzer-Division *Hohenstaufen* (6/28/44 - 7/10/44; 7/15/44 - 7/29/44, wounded; and 10/10/44 - 5/8/45); successfully fought extradition to France at time of Oradour sur Glane Trial (1953); sentenced to death in absentia by French military tribunal (3/12/53); died (8/23/95)

Stahlecker, Dr. Franz Walter,
SS-Gruppenführer -- Chef, Amt VIA/RSHA (1938); CO Einsatzgruppe *Wien* (1939); HSSPf Böhmen-Mähren (1938-9); BdS Norwegen (5/40); CO Einsatzgruppe A (6/22/41 - 3/23/42); KIA at Krasnowardeisk (3/23/42)

Stange, Martin,
SS-Standartenführer -- CO 38. SS-Grenadier-Division *Nibelungen* (4/25/45 - 5/8/45)

Staude, ?,
SS-? -- CO SS-Panzerpionier-Kompanie 15/SS-Panzergrenadier-Regiment 2/1. SS-Panzer-Division *Leibstandarte Adolf Hitler* (1944)

Steimle, Eugen Karl,
SS-Standartenführer --CO Sonderkommando 7a/Einsatzgruppe B (9/41 - 12/41); CO Sonderkommando 4a/Einsatzgruppe C (8/42 - 1/15/43); Chef Amt VIB / RSHA; Personalstab RFSS; condemned to death during Einsatzgruppen Trial at Nürnberg (4/48); commuted to 20 years imprisonment (1951); released (1954)

Stein, Walter,
SS-Oberführer -- Stab SS-Oberabschnitt Rhein (11/38 - 8/41); Polizeipräsident Konstanz (11/38 - 3/41); Polizeipräsident Thorn (3/41 - 11/41); Stab SS-Abschnitt XI (8/41 - 10/42); Polizeipräsident Danzig-Zoppot (11/41 - 5/45); Stab RSHA (10/42 - 5/45); acting SSPf Warschau (2/1/44 - 3/31/44); Polizeipräsident Lodz (11/44 - 1/45); Stab XII. SS-Armee-Korps (1/45 - 5/45)

Steiner, Felix Martin,
SS-Obergruppenführer -- CO SS Standarte *Deutschland* (late 1936 - 12/1/40); CO SS-Panzer-Division *Wiking* (12/1/40 - 5/1/43); CO III [germanischen] SS-Panzerkorps (5/1/43 - 10/30/44, taken ill); CO 11. Panzer-Armee/ Armeegruppe Steiner (1/26/45 - 5/3/45); captured by Americans at Lüneburg (5/3/45); released from custody (4/27/48); died of natural causes (5/12/66)

Steuben, ? von, SS-Sturmbannführer -- CO II. Bataillon /SS-Gebirgsjäger-Regiment 1/7. SS-Freiwilligen-Gebirgs-Division *Prinz Eugen*; responsible for the murder of civilians at *Goc* and *Biserske Livada* (Fall 1942)

Störtz, Friedrich,
SS-Sturmbannführer -- CO 1. Kompanie/Waffen-SS Bataillon zur besondere Verwendung (7/29/41 - 1/19/43); assisted Einsatzgruppe A with numerous atrocities in the USSR; service with 20. Waffen-Grenadier-Division der SS (estnische Nr. 1).

Strathmann, Horst,
SS-Standartenführer -- CO IV. Bataillon/SS-Gebirgsjäger-Regiment 1/7. SS-Freiwilligen-Gebirgs-Division *Prinz Eugen*; ordered the execution of civilians along the *Jablanica-Prozor railline* and *Niksic-Avtovac railline* (8/43)

Strauch, Dr. Eduard,
SS-Standartenführer -- CO Einsatzkommando 2-KdS Lettland/Einsatzgruppe A (11/4/41 - 12/3/41); CO Sonderkommando 1b-KdS Weissruthenien /Ein-

satzgruppe A (12/3/41 - 6/43); SD Dortmund; KdS Wallonien (5/31/44); III SS-Panzerkorps (10/44); SD Belgium; condemned to death during Einsatzgruppen Trial at Nürnberg (4/48); execution stayed due to defendant's insanity; extradited to Belgium for a second trial as Police Commander during the Ardennes counter-offensive; sentence commuted to life imprisonment (7/19/52); died in psychiatric asylum in Uccle (9/15/55)

Streckenbach, Bruno,

SS-Gruppenführer -- Amt I/ RSHA (1935 - 9/39); CO Einsatzgruppe I in Poland (9/39 - ?); BdS General Government (11/1/39 - 1/14/41); Chef Amt I/RSHA (1941 - 42); supervised Einsatzgruppe officer's training courses at Pretzsch (5/41); CO 8. SS-Kavallerie-Division *Florian Geyer* (11/1/43 - 4/1/44); CO 19. SS Waffen-Grenadier-Division [lettische Nr. 2] (4/15/44 - 5/12/44 and 5/19/44 - 5/8/45); captured by Soviets (1945); tried and sentenced to 25 years imprisonment; released (1/10/55); charges by West Germany dropped due to the defendant's health (1973); died in Hamburg (10/28/77)

Streibel, Karl,

SS-Sturmbannführer -- CO SS-Ausbildungslager Trawniki (10/41 - Spring 1944); set free by Landgericht Hamburg (6/3/76)

Streich, Otto,

SS-Obersturmführer -- CO 10. Schützenkompanie/III. Bataillon/SS-Totenkopfstandarte II *Brandenburg*; complicity in massacres at *Wloclawek* (9/22-25/39)

Strohfahrt, ?,

SS-? -- service with SS-Panzeraufklärungs-Abteilung 12/12. SS-Panzer-Division *Hitlerjugend* (1944); complicity in the *Ascq* massacre (4/1-2/44); never tried

Strohmaier, Hubert,

SS-Brigadeführer -- captured by Soviets (1945); remanded to Yugoslav custody (1945); tried and condemned; executed (1947)

Stroop, Jürgen,

SS-Gruppenführer -- CO SS-Abschnitt XXXVIII (11/38 - 3/40); Selbstschutzführer Posen (9/39 - 10/39) - commander of 45,000 strong extrajudicial terror units responsible for numerous murders; CO SS-Abschnitt XXXXII (3/40 - 11/42); legally changed first name from "Josef" to "Jürgen" to honor his son killed in combat (5/41); company commander SS-Infanterie-Regiment 3 / 3. SS-Panzer-Division *Totenkopf* (7/41 - 9/41); transferred to Ersatzbataillon/1. SS-Panzer-Division *Liebstandarte Adolf Hitler* (9/15/41 - 10/15/41); Stab Kommandostab RFSS (10/20/41); Chief of Security, D-4 Road Project in Ukraine (11/41 - 9/42); IdS Ukraine (12/41 - 10/42); Stab SSPf Nikolajew (10/42 - 11/42) - briefly commanded SS garrisons at Kiviograd and Kherson, responsible for the liquidation of Jews in Stryg, Rawa Russkaya,Chortkov, Tarnopol, Stanislawow, and Brzeziny; SSPf Lemberg (2/43 - 4/43); SSPf Warschau (4/19/43 - 9/13/43); liquidated the *Warsaw Ghetto* (4/43 - 6/43); HSSPf Griechenland (9/8/43 - 10/4/43); HSSPf Rhein-Westmark (11/11/43 - 5/8/45); arrested (5/45); sentenced to death by American Dachau Tribunal for shooting hostages in Greece, and Allied pilots and POWs in Wehrkreis XII (3/22/47); remanded to Polish custody (5/30/47); tried in Warsaw and condemned to death (7/23/51); hung at Warsaw's Mokotow Prison (3/6/52)

Stun, Leopold,

SS-Oberscharführer -- service with HQ-Kompanie/ SS-Panzeraufklärungs-Abteilung 12/12. SS-Panzer-Division *Hitlerjugend*; complicity in Ascq atrocity (4/1-2/44); complicity in the *Normandy* atrocities (6/7-17/44); recommended for prosecution by SHAEF Standing Court of Inquiry (1945); fate unknown

Stuna, ?,

SS-? -- CO SS-Panzer-AA-Kompanie 14/SS-Panzergrenadier-Regiment 1/1. SS-Panzer-Division *Leibstandarte Adolf Hitler* (1944)

Suhr, Friedrich,

SS-Obersturmbannführer -- BdS Prague (7/39 - 5/40); Stab RSHA (5/40 - 7/41); anti-Jewish activities outside of the Reich (7/41 - 11/42); CO Sonderkommando 4b/ Einsatzgruppe C (11/42 - 8/43); CO Einsatzkommando 6/Einsatzgruppe C (8/43 - 11/43); BdS Frankreich (12/43

- 12/44); SSPf Ober-Elsass (12/1/44 - 5/45); died under mysterious circumstances at Wuppertal-Elberfeld (5/31/46)

Taus, Karl,
SS-Brigadeführer -- Stab SS-Oberabschnitt Elbe (7/38 - 6/41); Stab SSPf Lettland, SSPf Dnjepropetrowsk, SSPf Charkow (6/41 - 10/43); Stab HSSPf Russland-Süd (10/43 - 5/44); SS und Polizeigebietskommandeur Görz (5/1/44 - 5/45); died in Austria (11/19/77)

Teichmann, Ludwig,
SS-Obersturmbannführer -- RSHA; Personalstab RFSS; SD Serbien and CO Einsatzgruppe E (Balkans); complicity in *Sajmiste Camp* gassings (2/42 - 5/10/42); RuSHA; Einsatzgruppe H

Tensfeld, Willy,
SS-Brigadeführer -- Stab SS-Oberabschnitt Nordwest (1/39 - 6/42); SSPf Charkow and SS-Standortkommandant Charkow (8/4/41 - 5/19/43); SSPf Stalino-Donezgebiet (5/19/43 - 9/4/43); acting SSPf Shitomir (4/19/43 - 5/20/43); SSPf zbV to HöSSPf Italien (9/43 - 1/44); SSPf Oberitalien-West (1/23/44 - 5/45); died in Hamburg (9/2/82)

Thier, Theobald,
SS-Brigadeführer -- CO SS-Abschnitt XV (5/39 - 10/39); Stab HSSPf Danzig-Westpreussen (10/39 - 6/41); Stab SS-Oberabschnitt Weichsel (12/39 - 11/42); Stab Einsatzstab Wegener, Norway (6/41 - 12/41); Stab RSHA (1/42 - 3/42); SSPf Kaukasien-Kuban (11/14/42 - 5/3/43); SSPf Kertsch-Tamanhalbinsel (5/3/43 - 7/29/43); SSPf Lemberg (7/29/43 - 2/25/44); SSPf Krakau (3/1/44 - 1/19/45); died in Krakau (7/12/49)

Thomas, Dr. Max,
SS-Gruppenführer -- RSHA; HSSPf Nord Frankreich/Belgien (7/40 - 9/41); CO Einsatzgruppe C (10/41 - 8/28/43); HSSPf Ukraine; said either to have been killed in action (1944) or to have committed suicide (1945)

Tiemann, Ralf,
SS-Sturmbannführer -- CO 26. Waffen-Grenadier-Division der SS [ungarische Nr. 2] (? - 5/9/45)

Tittmann, Fritz,

SS-Brigadeführer -- Persönlicher Stab RFSS (4/38 - 9/41); SSPf Nikolajew (10/22/41 - 9/1/42); Stab HSSPf Russland-Süd (9/42 - 9/44); reprimanded and transferred to service in Italy (9/44 - 4/20/45); killed in Treuenbrietzen (4/20/45)

Tomhardt, Heinz,
SS-? -- CO SS-Panzergrenadier-Kompanie 11 / SS-Panzergrenadier-Bataillon 3 / SS-Panzer-Regiment 1 / 1. SS-Panzer-Division *Leibstandarte Adolf Hitler*; implicated in the *Malmedy* atrocities (12/16+/44); defendant at the *Malmedy* Trial (5/16/46 - 7/11/46); found guilty; sentenced to death (7/16/46); sentence commuted; released from custody

Trabandt, August-Wilhelm,
SS-Brigadeführer -- service with 1. SS-Panzer-Division *Leibstandarte Adolf Hitler* (1939 - 1943); CO 1. SS-Infanterie [mot.]-Brigade (10/18/43 - 3/44); responsible for numerous murder actions, see *1. SS-Infanterie-Brigade Operations and Atrocities in the USSR*; CO 18. SS-Panzergrenadier-Division *Horst Wessel* (1/25/44 - 1/3/45); CO Kampfgruppe Böhmen-Mähren (4/45 - 5/45); captured by the Soviets (5/45); released from custody (1955); died of natural causes at Ahrensburg in Holstein (5/19/68)

Traub, Wilhelm,
SS-Obersturmbannführer -- SS und Polizeigebietskommandeur Quarnero (10/27/44 - 1945)

Traupe, Hans,
SS-Obersturmbannführer -- SSPf Shitomir (9/25/43 - 10/21/43)

Traut, Karl,
SS-Obersturmbannführer -- RSHA; CO Einsatzkommando 3 / Einsatzgruppe A (11/42 - 5/43); SD Salzburg; SD Hohensalza

Treuenfeld, Karl von,
SS-Gruppenführer -- CO 2. SS-Infanterie [mot.]-Brigade (4/5/41 - 7/5/41); responsible for numerous killing operations, *see 2. SS-Infanterie-Brigade Operations & Atrocities in the USSR*; CO 1. SS-Infanterie-Brigade [mot.]-Brigade (7/4/42 - 2/1/43?); responsible for numerous murder actions, see *1. SS-Infanterie-Brigade*

Operations and Atrocities in the USSR; CO 10. SS-Panzer-Division *Frundsberg* (11/15/43 - 5/1/44); died in American custody

Tröger, Dr. Rudolf,
SS-Obersturmbannführer -- CO Einsatzkommando 16 (Poland, 1939); RSHA; SD Chemnitz; KIA with 60. Infanterie-Division in France (6/18/40)

Trummler, Dr. Hans,
SS-Oberführer -- CO Teilkommando 2/Einsatzgruppe zbV (Poland, 1939); RSHA Amt IB

Tschierschky, Karl,
SS-Standartenführer -- CO Einsatzkommando 1 (Fall 1942); Chef Amt VIC/RSHA; SD Dresden; died (1974)

Turner, Harald,
SS-Gruppenführer -- Military Administrator Serbia; ordered the shooting of Serbian Gypsies and Jews (1941); implicated in Belgrade Ghetto Massacre; sentenced to death in Belgrade (3/9/47)

Tychsen, Christian,
SS-Obersturmbannführer -- various positions with 2. SS-Panzer-Division *Das Reich* (1941 - 1944); CO 2. SS-Panzer-Division *Das Reich* (7/26/44 - 7/28/44, killed in action in Normandy)

Ullrich, Karl,
SS-Oberführer -- CO SS-Pioniere-Bataillon 3/3. SS-Panzer-Division *Totenkopf* (6/41 - Summer 1942); Korpspionierführer (Summer 1942 - 3/43); CO III. Bataillon/SS-Panzergrenadier-Regiment 5/3. SS-Panzer-Division *Totenkopf* (3/43 - 11/8/43); CO SS-Panzergrenadier-Regiment 6 *Theodor Eicke* / 3. SS-Panzer-Division *Totenkopf* (11/9/43 - 10/8/44); CO SS-Panzer-Division *Wiking* (10/9/44 - 5/8/45); atrocities committed in *Gau Steiermark* (3/45 - 4/45); captured by Americans at Radstadt (5/12/45); released from detention (9/18/48)

Unglaube, ?,
SS-? -- CO SS-Panzerpionier-Kompanie 2 / SS-Panzeraufklärungs-Bataillon 1/1. SS-Panzer-Division *Leibstandarte Adolf Hitler* (1944); implicated in the *Malmedy* atrocities (12/16+/44);

Unterkofler, ?,
SS-Hauptsturmführer -- CO SS-Panzergrenadier-Bataillon 2/SS-Panzergrenadier-Regiment 1/1. SS-Panzer-Division *Leibstandarte Adolf Hitler* (1944)

Vahl, Herbert Ernst,
SS-Oberführer -- various positions with 2. SS-Panzer-Division *Das Reich* (1941 - 1943); CO 2. SS-Panzer-Division *Das Reich* (2/15/43 - 4/3/43); CO 4. SS-Polizei-Panzergrenadier-Division (7/13/44 - 7/22/44); killed in a car accident in Greece (7/22/44)

Vogler, Anton,
SS-Brigadeführer -- Stab SS-Oberabschnitt Süd (1938 - 2/45); Standortkommandant Dachau (8/43 - 12/43); Standortkommandant München (1/44 - 7/44); acting HSSPf Süd (2/1/45 - 4/45)

Vögler, Karl-Heinz,
SS-? -- CO SS-Panzer-AA-Kompanie 10/SS-Panzer-Regiment 1/1. SS-Panzer-Division *Leibstandarte Adolf Hitler* (1944); implicated in the *Malmedy* atrocities (12/16+/44); defendant at the *Malmedy* Trial (5/16/46 - 7/11/46);

Vogt, Hans,
SS-? -- service with SS-Panzeraufklärungs-Abteilung 12/12. SS-Panzer-Division *Hitlerjugend* (1944); complicity in the *Ascq* massacre (4/1-2/44); tried and sentenced to death in absentia by French authorities (8/2-6/49)

Voigt, Werner,
SS-? -- service with SS-Panzeraufklärungs-Abteilung 12/12. SS-Panzer-Division *Hitlerjugend* (1944); complicity in the *Ascq* massacre (4/1-2/44); tried and sentenced to death by French authorities (8/2-6/49); sentence reduced to 10 years hard labor minus time served (7/14/55); paroled (1956)

Voss, ?,
SS-? -- CO SS-Schweres-Infanterie-Geschütz-Kompanie 13/SS-Panzergrenadier-Regiment 1/1. SS-Panzer-Division *Leibstandarte Adolf Hitler* (1944)

Voss, Bernhard,
SS-Brigadeführer -- Stab SS-Oberabschnitt Ost (11/38 - 8/44); CO 6. SS-Totenkopfstandarte (11/39 - 6/41);

responsible for *Ruzyn* executions (11/17/39); SS-Standortkommandant Berlin (6/41 - 10/41); CO SS-Truppenübungsplatz Beneschau (11/41 - 6/42); CO SS-Truppenübungsplatz Debica (6/42 - 9/44); Stab SS-Führungshauptamt (9/44 - 5/45); arrested by Americans (1945); questioned at Wiesbaden (6/21/45); remanded to Czech custody (1947); tried; hung in Prague (2/4/47)

Wagner, Adolf,
SS-Obersturmbannführer -- CO 24. Waffen-Gebirgs-Division der SS *Karstjäger* (late 1944 - 5/9/45)

Wägner, Erich,
SS-Obersturmführer -- CO 4. Kompanie/ SS-Panzer-aufklärungs-Bataillon 1/1. SS-Panzer-Division *Leibstandarte Adolf Hitler* (1944); implicated in the *Malmedy* atrocities (12/16+/44)

Wagner, Jürgen,
SS-Gruppenführer -- service with various SS-Standarte (1933 - 1939); various postings with the 2. SS-Panzer-Division *Das Reich* (1941 - 5/42); CO 9. SS-Panzergrenadier-Regiment *Germania*/5. SS-Panzergrenadier Division *Wiking* (5/42 - 11/43); CO 4. SS-Freiwilligen-Panzergrenadier-Brigade *Nederland*; CO IV. Bataillon / SS-Freiwilligen-Gebirgsjäger-Regiment 13 / 7. SS-Freiwilligen-Gebirgs-Division *Prinz Eugen* (? - 7/43); wrongly accused of ordering the execution of civilians along the *Jablanica-Prozor railline* and the *Niksic-Avtovac railline* (8/43); CO 23. SS-Freiwilligen-Panzergrenadier-Division *Nederland* (7/43 - 5/45); captured by the Americans (5/45); remanded to British authorities; remanded to Yugoslav custody (1945); condemned and executed by firing squad (8/47)

Waldeck-Pyrmont, Josias Erbprinz von,
SS-Obergruppenführer -- HSSPf Fulda-Werra (10/6/38 - 5/8/45); sentenced to life imprisonment at the Buchenwald Trial (1947); sentence commuted (1950); lived in the Bundesrepublik; numerous further proceedings but no sentences against the defendant; died at ancestral home, Schloss Schaumberg (11/30/67)

Waldmüller, Hans,
SS-Sturmbannführer -- CO I. Bataillon/SS-Panzer-grenadier-Regiment 25/12. SS-Panzer-Division *Hit-*

lerjugend; complicity in the *Normandy* atrocities (6/7-17/44); KIA by Belgian partisans near Basse-Bodeux (9/8/44)

Walser, Erwin,
SS-Hauptsturmführer -- CO 36. Waffen-Grenadier-Division der SS (11/43 - 1/44)

Wappenhans, Waldemar,
SS-Gruppenführer -- CO SS-Abschnitt XXXIII (11/38 - 1/42); SSPf Wolhynien-Brest Litovsk (9/4/41 - 9/1/42); SSPf Dnjepropetrowsk-Krivoi Rog (10/4/42 - 10/4/43); SSPf Nikolajew (9/1/42 - 4/43); SSPf zbV Brest-Litovsk (11/43), kampfgruppe CO (11/43 - 1/44); on reserve due to recurrent illness (3/44 - 1/45); ordered to Berlin but deserted with family (1/45); died in Hannover (12/2/67)

Wegener, Kurt,
SS-Hauptsturmführer -- SS-Totenkopfverband *Brandenburg* (4/20/38 - 8/1/40); SS-Totenkopf-Kavallerie-Regiment 1 (8/1/40 - 12/40); CO 5. Schwadron / III. Abteilung / SS-Totenkopf-Kavallerie-Regiment 1 (12/40 - 7/29/41); CO 4. Schwadron / SS-Kavallerie-Regiment 2 / SS-Kavallerie-Brigade (7/30/41 - 12/41+); complicity in massacre of 11,000 Jews at *Pinsk* (8/5-8/41); regimental commander of an unidentified SS-Kavallerie-Regiment which took part in the defense of Budapest (5/44 - 5/45); captured by Americans; released from custody (7/45); taken into custody by West German authorities (12/9/62); tried by Landgericht Braunschweig; sentenced to 5 years imprisonment (4/20/64); sentence overturned on technicalities by the 5. Strafsenat des Bundesgerichtshofs (11/17/64)

Weinmann, Dr. Erwin,
SS-Oberführer -- Chef Amt IVD /RSHA; SD Stuttgart; CO Sonderkommando 4a / Einsatzgrupppe C (1/13/42 - 7/42); BdS Bohemia (1943 - 1945); declared dead (12/49)

Weiss, ?,
SS-Sturmbannführer -- CO SS-Nachrichtensturmbann (9/39)

Weiss, Rudolf,
SS-Brigadeführer -- acting SSPf Nikolajew (10/10/43 - 3/21/44)

Weitzel, Friedrich,
SS-Obergruppenführer -- Polizeipräsident Dusseldorf (5/33 - 6/40); HSSPf West (6/11/38 - 4/20/40); HSSPf Nord (4/20/40 - 6/19/40); killed in Düsseldorf air raid (6/19/40)

Wendeleit, ?,
SS-Oberscharführer -- CO Penal Platoon /SS-Panzer-Regiment 1/1. SS-Panzer-Division *Leibstandarte Adolf Hitler* (1944); complicity in the *Malmedy* atrocities (12/16+/44)

Wendler, Dr. Richard,
SS-Brigadeführer -- Kommissar Kielce (9/39 - 6/40); Kommissar Radom (6/40 - 8/41); SSPf Stanislav-Rostow (8/4/41 - 5/27/42); Landkommissar Krakau (1/42 - 5/43); Landkommissar Lublin (6/43 - 7/44); died in Prien, Bayern (8/24/72)

Werthof, ?,
SS-? -- CO of a kommando from SS-Kavallerie-Regiment 2; responsible for the massacre of 11,000 Jews at Pinsk (8/5-8/41)

Westernhagen, Hein von,
SS-Obersturmbannführer -- CO SS-Schwere-Panzer-Bataillon 501/SS-Panzer-Regiment 1/1. SS-Panzer-Division *Leibstandarte Adolf Hitler* (1944); implicated in the *Malmedy* atrocities (12/16+/44)

Wetzlmayer, ?,
SS-Oberscharführer -- service with SS-Panzer-aufklärungs-Abteilung 12/12. SS-Panzer-Division *Hitlerjugend* (1944); complicity in the *Ascq* massacre (4/1-2/44); never tried

Wichmann, Otto,
SS-Scharführer -- member of HQ-Kompanie/SS-Panzer-Regiment 1/1. SS-Panzer-Division *Leibstandarte Adolf Hitler*; implicated in the *Malmedy* atrocities (12/16+/44); defendant at Malmedy Trials (5/16/46 - 7/11/46); found guilty; sentenced to 10 years imprisonment (7/16/46); sentence commuted; released from

custody

Wiebens, Wilhelm,
SS-Obersturmbannführer -- RSHA; CO Einsatzkommando 9/Einsatzgruppe B (2/42 - 1/43); SD Koblenz; SD Potsdam; sentenced to life imprisonment by Berlin court (1966)

Wigand, Arpad,
SS-Oberführer -- IdS Breslau (9/37 - 8/41); SSPf Warsaw (8/4/41 - 4/23/43); Stab SS-Gebirgsjäger-Regiment 13 / 7. SS-Freiwilligen-Gebirgs-Division *Prinz Eugen* (2/43 - 11/43); CO III./ SS-Gebirgsjäger-Regiment 13 / 7. SS-Freiwilligen-Gebirgs-Division *Prinz Eugen* (11/43 - 2/45); captured by British (5/45); extradited to Poland; sentenced by Poles to 15 years imprisonment; released (1956); tried in Hamburg by West German authorities and sentenced to 12 years imprisonment (1981); died in Monschau/Eifel (7/26/83)

Willich, Hellmuth,
SS-Oberführer -- acting HSSPf Weichsel (2/9/42 - 3/9/42)

Winkelmann, Otto,
SS-Obergruppenführer -- Stab Ordnungspolizei Berlin (11/37 - 11/40); Chef Kommandoamt / Hauptamt Ordnungspolizei (11/40 - 3/44); HSSPf Ungarn (3/19/44 - 2/11/45); Deputy Chief of Ordnungspolizei for southern Germany (2/45 - 5/45); testified at Nürnberg Trials against SS-Standartenfuhrer Dr. Edmund Veesenmayer [RFSS Himmler's representative to the Foreign Office]; testified at trials in Hungary against other defendants; released from Hungarian custody (1948); many proceedings but no sentences against the defendant; died in Bordesholm (9/24/77)

Winkler, Ludwig,
SS-Brigadeführer -- KdO Krakau

Wirth, ?,
SS-Oberführer -- CO 35. SS-Polizei-Grenadier-Division (? - 3/45)

Wirth, Christian,
SS-Oberführer -- Euthanasia activities at the Grafeneck, Bernburg, Brandenburg, Hadamar, and Hartheim

psychiatric clinics (1939-40); Inspector of Euthanasia Centers (1940); Euthanasia actions in western Poland (1941); CO Belzec death camp (late 1941); Inspector Einsatz Reinhardt death camps - Belzec, Sobibor, Treblinka (8/42-43); Stab HSSPf Adriatisches Küstenland (9/13/43); CO SS Task Force R in the Trieste area - extermination of Jews and others (1943 - 1944); supposedly killed by partisans while on a journey to Fiume (Istria), possibly killed by own men (5/44)

Wisch, Theodor,
SS-Brigadeführer -- service with 1. SS-Panzer-Division *Leibstandarte Adolf Hitler* (1933 - 1945); CO 1. SS-Panzer-Division *Leibstandarte Adolf Hitler* (7/43 - 8/20/44, severely wounded); divisional commander at time of the *Boves* (9/19/43) and *Lago Maggiore* (9/22-24/43) atrocities; died (1/11/95)

Wisliceny, Günther-Eberhardt,
SS-Sturmbannführer -- various postings with the 2. SS-Panzer-Division *Das Reich* (1940 - 3/44); CO SS-Panzergrenadier-Regiment 3 *Deutschland* / 2. SS-Panzer-Division *Das Reich* (3/44 - 5/8/45); questionable accusation of atrocity at *St. Germain-du-Belair* (6/44); captured by American forces (5/8/45); remanded to French custody (4/47); released from custody (7/12/51); died in Hannover (8/25/85)

Witiska, Dr. Josef,
SS-Standartenführer -- RSHA; SD Graz; SD Salzburg; CO SD Lemberg; BdS Slovakei (8/44); responsible for deportation of 9,000 Jews to the death camps; CO Einsatzgruppe H (10/10/44 - ?); responsible for the murder and deportation to the death camps of 13-14,000 Jews during the suppression of the *Slovak National Uprising* (9/44 - 10/44)

Witkowski, Sepp,
SS-Scharführer -- officer of 3. SS-Panzer-Kompanie / SS-Panzer-Bataillon 1 / SS-Panzer-Regiment 1 / 1. SS-Panzer-Division *Leibstandarte Adolf Hitler* (1944); implicated in the *Malmedy* atrocities (12/16+/44)

Witt, Fritz,
SS-Brigadeführer -- original member of *LAH* (1933 - 35); service with SS-Standarte *Deutschland* (1939 - 10/40); transferred to *LSSAH* (10/40); CO SS-Panzergrenadier-

Regiment 1/1. SS-Panzer-Division *Leibstandarte Adolf Hitler* (6/42 - 7/43); CO 12. SS-Panzer-Division *Hitlerjugend* (7/43 - 6/16/44); divisional commander at time of the *Normandy* atrocities (6/7-17/44); killed in action at Caen-Vernoix (6/16/44)

Wohlgemuth, ?,
SS-Rottenführer -- service with SS-Panzeraufklärungs-Abteilung 12/12. SS-Panzer-Division *Hitlerjugend* (1944); complicity in the *Ascq* massacre (4/1-2/44); never tried

Wolf, Hugo,
SS-Unterscharführer -- NCO attached to SS-Panzeraufklärungs-Abteilung 12/12. SS-Panzer-Division *Hitlerjugend*; complicity in the *Normandy* atrocities (6/7-17/44); recommended for prosecution by SHAEF Standing Court of Inquiry (1945); fate unknown

Wolff, Karl,
SS-Obergruppenführer -- Chef SS-Personalhauptamt (6/39 - 2/43); SS-liaison officer at Führer Hauptquatier (8/39 - 2/43); HSSPf Oberitalien West (2/43 - 9/23/43); HöSSPf Italien (9/23/43 - 5/8/45); in Allied custody through 1949; arrested by West German authorities (1962); tried and sentenced to 15 years imprisonment for role in the extermination of Italian Jews (1964); released from prison (1971); lived in the Bundesrepublik; died in Rosenheim (7/17/84)

Wolfstieg, Friedrich,
Oberst. der Polizei -- CO Einsatzkommando Orpo / Einsatzgruppe zbV (Poland, 1939)

Wolter, Wilhelm, S
S-Sturmbannführer -- SD Stettin; SD Köln; service with Einsatzkommando E in the Balkans; CO Einsatzkommando 15 in the Balkans (6/1/43 - 10/44); MIA in Rumania (10/44)

Woyrsch, Udo von,
SS-Obergruppenführer -- Persönlicher Stab RFSS (1/35 - 4/40); Polizeipräsident Gleiwitz (1939); CO Einsatzgruppe zur besonderen Verwendung (Ostoberschlesien, 9/39); CO Polizeigruppe 1 (Poland, 9/21/39 - 11/39); HSSPf Elbe (4/20/40 - 2/11/44); removed from office; in Allied custody through 1948; sentenced to 20

years imprisonment (1948); released (1952); sentenced by West German authorities to 10 years imprisonment for role in the "Night of Long Knives" [6/30/34] (1957); released (1960); further proceedings dismissed due to incompetency to stand trial (1977); died in Swabia (1/14/83)

Wronna, Fritz,
SS-? -- service with SS-Panzeraufklärungs-Abteilung 12 / 12. SS-Panzer-Division *Hitlerjugend* (1944); complicity in the *Ascq* massacre (4/1-2/44); tried and sentenced to life imprisonment by French authorities (8/2-6/49); sentenced reduced to 10 years hard labor minus time served (7/14/55); paroled (1956)

Wulf, Heinrich,
SS-Sturmbannführer -- CO SS-Panzeraufklärungs-Abteilung 2/2. SS-Panzer-Division *Das Reich*; complicity in the executions at *Tulle* (6/9/44); tried by French military tribunal (7/5/51); sentenced to 10 years hard labor; pardoned and released (5/52)

Wünnenberg, Alfred,
SS-Obergruppenführer -- Stab IdO Stuttgart (1938 - 39); CO SS-Polizeischützen-Regiment 3 / 4. SS-Polizei-Panzergrenadier-Division (1939 - 41); CO 4. SS-Polizei-Panzergrenadier-Division (12/15/41 - 6/10/43); Chef Hauptamt Ordnungspolizei (8/31/43 - 5/8/45); died in Krefeld (12/30/63)

Wünsche, Max,
SS-Obersturmbannführer -- service with *LAH* (1934 - 1944); CO SS-Panzer-Regiment 12 / 12. SS-Panzer-Division *Hitlerjugend*; investigated concerning the *Normandy* atrocities; not indicted

Wysocki, Lucian Damianus,
SS-Brigadeführer
--Polizeipräsident Oberhausen (9/37 - 11/39); Polizeipräsident Duisberg (11/39 - 8/41); SSPf Litauen (8/11/41 - 7/2/43); SSPf zbV with HSSPf Weissruthenien (7/43 - 3/44); Polizeipräsident Kassel (3/44 - 5/45); died in Rheinhausen (12/13/64)

Zapp, Paul J.,
SS-Obersturmbannführer -- RSHA; CO Einsatzkommando 11a / Einsatzgruppe D (6/22/41 - 7/42); KdS Taurien (7/1/42 - ?); sentenced to life imprisonment by Munich court (1970)

Zastrow, Hans-Viktor von,
SS-Hauptsturmführer -- CO 6. Schwadron/SS-Totenkopf-Reiterstandarte 1 (11/39 - 5/40); CO 4. Schwadron/SS-Totenkopf-Reiterstandarte 1 (5/40 - 11/40); CO 3. Schwadron/III. Abteilung/SS-[Totenkopf]-Kavallerie-Regiment 1 (11/40 - 3/20/41); CO 3. Schwadron/SS-Kavallerie-Regiment 2 (3/21/41 - 12/41+); KIA in USSR (1943)

Zech, Karl,
SS-Gruppenführer -- Polizeipräsident Krakau (9/39 - 11/15/39); SSPf Krakau (11/24/39 - 10/1/40); dismissed from the SS (3/14/44); committed suicide in Altenberg, Thüringia (4/1/44)

Zehender, August,
SS-Brigadeführer -- Stab SS-Standarte 1 *Deutschland* (11/35 - 9/39); CO Flak-Abteilung/ SS-Verfügungstruppe (9/39 - 12/40); CO I. Bataillon/SS-Totenkopfstandarte 11 (12/40 - 2/41); CO Kradschützen-Bataillon/2. SS-Panzer-Division *Das Reich* (2/41 - 6/41, wounded); CO II. Bataillon / SS-Panzergrenadier-Regiment 3 *Deutschland* /2. SS-Panzer-Division Das Reich (9/41 - ?); various commands in 8. SS-Kavallerie-Division *Florian Geyer* (1941 - 1942); CO Kampfgruppe *Zehender* (4/42 - 6/21/42); CO SS-Kavallerie-Regiment 2 / 8. SS-Kavallerie-Division *Florian Geyer* (1942 - 2/44); CO 22. SSFreiwilligen-Kavallerie-Division *Maria Theresia* (5/44 - 2/11/45); KIA in Budapest (2/11/45)

Zeidner, Franz,
SS-Obergruppenführer -- see Feketehalmy-Czeydner, Ferenc

Zenner, Carl,
SS-Brigadeführer
--Polizeipräsident Aachen (1/37 - 1/43); SSPf Weissruthenien (8/14/41 - 5/22/42); SS-Hauptamt (7/21/42 - 5/45); captured by French (5/29/45); transferred to British custody (1/6/47); tried and sentenced to 5 years imprisonment for role in "Reichskristallnacht" (6/12/47); paroled (6/13/50); tried by Landgericht Koblenz; sentenced to 15 years imprisonment (6/12/61); died in Andernach (6/16/69)

Ziegler, Joachim,
SS-Brigadeführer -- service in Poland and France (1939 - 1940); CO 11. SS-Freiwilligen-Panzergrenadier-Division *Nordland* (6/28/44 - 4/26/45); arrested on Hitler's orders due to military reverses (4/45); released following Hitler's death; either killed in action during a breakout attempt from Berlin or killed attemptimg to negotiate a truce near the Friedrichstrasse Bahnhof in Berlin (5/1/45)

Zietlow, Fritz,
SS-Hauptsturmführer -- RSHA; CO Sonderkommando 1005-B (7/43 - ?); service with Einsatzkommando H

Zimmermann, Paul,
SS-Brigadeführer -- SS representative to the Reich Four Year Plan (6/38 - 4/43); SSPf Nikolajew (4/43 - 10/10/43); SSPf zbV with HöSSPf Ukraine (10/43 - 1944); Stab HöSSPf Italien (1944 - 1945); died (5/21/80)

Zimmermann, Walter,
SS-Standartenführer -- CO 33. Waffen-Grenadier-Division der SS *Charlemagne* [französische Nr. 1] (4/26/45 - 5/45)

Zinssmeister, August,
SS-? -- service with SS-Panzeraufklärungs-Abteilung 12 / 12. SS-Panzer-Division *Hitlerjugend* (1944); complicity in the *Ascq* massacre (4/1-2/44); tried and sentenced to death by French authorities (8/2-6/49); sentenced reduced to 10 years hard labor minus time served (7/14/55); paroled (1956)

Zipfel, Gottlob,
SS-? -- company commander in SS-Panzeraufklärungs-Abteilung 1/1. SS-Panzer-Division *Leibstandarte Adolf Hitler* (1941); alleged to have massacred 200 civilians at *Gorych* (7/41)

Zwigart, Paul,
SS-Scharführer -- member of SS-Panzer-Kompanie 1/ SS-Panzer-Bataillon 1/SS-Panzer-Regiment 1/1. SS-Panzer-Division *Leibstandarte Adolf Hitler* (1944); implicated in the *Malmedy* atrocities (12/16+/44); defendant at Malmedy Trials (5/16/46 - 7/11/46); sentenced to death (1946); paroled

Individuals - Photos

Alvensleben, Ludolf Jakob Graf von,

Augsberger, Franz,

Ax, Adolf,

Bach-Zelewski, Erich von dem,

Bassewitz-Behr, George-Henning Graf von,

Baum, Otto,

Becker, Helmuth,

Becker, Herbert,

Behrends, Dr. Hermann,

Berger, Gottlob,

Berkelmann, Theodor,

Bierkamp, Dr. Walther,

Bittrich, Wilhelm,

Bochmann, Georg,

Bock, Friedrich-Wilhelm,

Böttcher, Dr. Herbert,

Brandner, Willi,

Breithaupt, Franz,

Bremer, Gerhard,

Brenner, Karl-Heinrich,

Brunner, Dr. Karl Friedrich,

Bürger, Karl Heinz,

Damzog, Ernst,

Debes, Lothar,

Degrelle, Leon,

Deisenhofer, Dr. Eduard,

Demelhuber, Karl-Maria

Diefenthal, Josef,

Diehm, Christoph,

Dietrich, Josef (Sepp),

Dietsche, Bernhard,

Dirlewanger, Dr. Oskar,

Döring, Hans,

Dörner, Helmut,

Dunckern, Anton,

Eberhardt, Georg,

Eberstein, Friedrich Karl Freiherr von,

Ebrecht, George,

Ehrlinger, Dr. Erich,

Eicke, Theodor,

Ertel, Karl-Heinz,

Fanslau, Heinz Karl,

Fegelein, Hermann Otto,

Fegelein, Waldemar,

Feketehalmy-Czeydner, Ferenc,

Fick, Jakob,

Fiedler, Richard,

Fitzthum, Josef,

Frank, Karl-Hermann,

Franz, Hermann,

Freitag, Fritz,

Geibel, Paul Otto,

Gesele, Karl,

Gille, Herbert Otto,

Globocnik, Ulrich ("Odilo"),

Göhrum, Kurt,

Gottberg, Curt von,

Grassy, Josef,

Günther, Wilhelm,

Gutenberger, Karl,

Haltermann, Hans Dietrich,

Hansen, Max,

Hansen, Peter,

Harm, Hermann,

Harmel, Heinz,

Harster, Wilhelm,

Harzer, Walter,,

Hausser, Paul,

Heilmann, Nikolaus,

Heissmeyer, August,

Hellwig, Otto,

Hennicke, Paul,

Herf, Eberhard,

Herff, Maximillian von

Hermann, Richard,

Hildebrandt, Richard,

Hintze, Kurt,

Höfle, Hermann,

Hofmann, Otto,

Jeckeln, Friedrich,

Jedicke, George,

Jena, Leo von,

Jost, Dr. Heinz,

Jungclaus, Richard,

Kaiser, Vinzenz,

Kaltenbrunner, Dr. Ernst,

Kaminski, Bronislav,

Kammerhofer, Konstantin,

Katzmann, Friedrich,

Kaul, Kurt,

Keppler, Georg,

Kirchner, ?,

Kleinheisterkamp, Matthias,

Klingemann, Gottfried,

Klingenberg, Fritz,

Knittel, Gustav,

Knoblauch, Kurt,

Knöchlein, Fritz,

Kohlroser, Martin,

Koppe, Wilhelm,

Korsemann, Gerret,

Kraas, Hugo,

Krämer, Fritz,

Krause, Bernhard,

Kreutz, Karl,

Krüger, Friedrich Wilhelm,

Krüger, Walter,

Krukenberg, Dr. jur. Gustav,

Kumm, Otto,

Kutschera, Fritz,

Lammerding, Heinz,

Lehmann, Rudolf,

Lombard, Gustav,

Maack, Berthold,

Mazuw, Emil,

Meyer, Hubert,

Milius, Siegfried,

Mohnke, Wilhelm,

Mühlenkamp, Johannes Rudolf,

Müller, Siegfried,

Müller, Thomas,

Nebe, Artur,

Ohlendorf, Otto,

Olboeter, Erich,

Ostendorff, Werner,

Pancke, Günther,

Pannier, Rudolf,

Peiper, Joachim [Jochen],

Petersen, Heinrich,

Pfeffer-Wildenbruch, Karl,

Phleps, Artur,

Pötschke, Werner,

Priess, Hermann,

Prinz, Karl-Heinz,

Prützmann,Hans-Adolf,

Puaud, Edgar,

Pückler-Burghaus, Carl Friedrich Graf von,

Querner, Rudolf,

Reinefarth, Heinz,

Rettlinger, Karl,

Ribbentrop, Rudolf,

Rösener, Erwin,

Rumohr, Joachim,

Schellong, Konrad,

Schimana, Walter,

Schmauser, Ernst Heinrich,

Schmidhuber, August,

Scholz, Fritz Elder von Raranoze von,

Schreiber, Franz,

Schüldt, Hinrich,

Schulze-Kossens, Richard,

Siebken, Bernhard,

Simon, Max,

Stadler, Sylvester,

Steiner, Felix Martin,

Streckenbach, Bruno,

Stroop, Jürgen,

Tensfeld, Willy,

Trabandt, August-Wilhelm,

Traupe, Hans,

Tychsen, Christian,

Ullrich, Karl,

Waldeck-Pyrmont, Josias Erbprinz von,

Waldmüller, Hans,

Winkelmann, Otto,

Wisliceny, Günther-Eberhardt,

Witt, Fritz,

Wolff, Karl,

Wünnenberg, Alfred,

Wünsche, Max,

Zehender, August,

Zeidner, Franz,

Ziegler, Joachim,

Dr. Eduard Strauch

Jakob Sporrenberg

Examining the Issues

Ethical and Legal Perspectives

The three major philosophical traditions concerning the ethics of war are realism, pacifism and just war theory.[1] *Realism* views war as a non-moral enterprise involving the suspension of all ethical principles and norms ("war is hell"). *Pacifism* views war as an *immoral, gross violation* of ethics, regardless of how it is prosecuted. *Just war theory*, originally formulated by Plato and then successively modified by Cicero, Aristotle, St. Ambrose and St. Augustine as a justification for wars of self-defense, identifies allowable reasons for going to war (*jus ad bellum*) and specifies proper conduct in wartime (*jus in bello*). A war is just only if it is:

1. Authorized by a legitimate authority.
2. Supported by a just cause (or good reason).
3. Motivated by a good or right intention.
4. Proportional to the offense or provocation.
5. Likely to succeed.
6. A last resort.

A combatant's actions are considered proper only if they are:

1. Proportional
(actions must do more good than harm).
2. Discriminating (attacking only combatants, as identified by their degree of war participation).

Technological innovation (nuclear, chemical, and biological) can complicate the moral analysis of war ethics since new weaponry often precludes humanitarian restraint. Despite such moral ambiguities, the three basic traditions remain unaltered. The irony, of course, is that just wars rarely succeed in being just because of the subjectivity of distinctions between justice and injustice and between defense and aggression.[2] Western societies since the days of St. Augustine have increasingly relied upon just war theory in defense of geopolitical agendas which often include unprovoked aggressive wars.

It may seem odd for a book concerned with war crimes to devote relatively little space to either the genesis of existing international agreements or the specific laws of war contained therein. The details and validity of such legislation (especially with regard to the IMT proceedings) have been debated *ad nauseum* in countless volumes by authors representing every conceivable side of the legal, moral, and ethical issues. While I have no desire to review this vast literature, clearly a minimal summary of the pertinent legislation is required for the purposes of this volume. Readers desiring a general survey of the development of war crimes legislation from ancient to modern times should consult appropriate sources.[3]

For several millennia guidelines have existed that govern the conduct of military forces during wartime, especially where the treatment of non-combatants and surrendering enemy personnel are concerned. Over the last four centuries a set of minimum rules has gained international recognition and acceptance with the aim of preventing the occurrence of battlefield excesses. It has universally been acknowledged that such acts are morally and ethically reprehensible, as well as counterproductive, since they degrade a belligerent's principles, weaken military discipline, and inevitably lead to reprisals and a stiffening of enemy resolve. In general, the laws of war stress that combatants, by taking up arms in wartime, do not cease to have moral responsibilities to one another. Illegal orders have to be disobeyed by every soldier, regardless of rank, or else the laws of war cease to have meaning.

At the start of the Second World War, Germany was a signatory nation to, and thus legally bound by, the following five agreements then governing warfare:

1) Declaration of St. Petersburg (1868) - prohibited weapons of war that cause unnecessary suffering to their victims

2) Hague Conventions concerning the Rules and Usages of Land Warfare (1899, 1907) - the first set of comprehensive laws for modern warfare; focused on eliminating unnecessary suffering (humane treatment of prisoners and wounded) and maintaining the immunity of non-combatants and non-military targets

3) Geneva Protocol (1925) - prohibited the use of poison gases and bacteriological agents

4) Pact of Paris [Kellogg-Briand Pact] (1928)
- outlawed wars of aggression

5) Geneva Conventions concerning the Amelioration of the Fate of Wounded and Sick in the Active Army (1929) - additional laws regarding the treatment of POWs and aid to wounded soldiers

It is of primary interest to note that most key principles of the preceding agreements were codified as regulations by the German Armed Forces and printed in every German soldier's paybook in a section entitled 'Ten Commandments for German Soldiers on Active Service.' Clearly, the evidence demonstrates that the Waffen-SS committed many acts during the Second World War that were immoral, inhuman, and violated both the letter and spirit of established international laws. The legal technicalities (arguments addressing venue, jurisdiction, and *ex post facto law* issues) which apologists and others use in an attempt to shield the Waffen-SS from its responsibilities have no bearing given Germany's signatory status and her armed forces official adoption of these regulations. The criminal behavior of the Axis governments throughout the war was such as to warrant new international treaties (the Geneva Conventions of 1948 and the Genocide Convention of 1949) aimed at closing loopholes and clarifying existing laws, as well as establishing previously undefined crimes. It goes without saying that widely accepted 20th Century technological changes in warfare practices (aerial and artillery bombardment) and doctrine (total war) either violate or severely strain the intent of these conventions.

Of course, questions naturally arise regarding motivational influences on the brutal behavior of German military forces, especially in the Balkans and the Soviet Union. Political indoctrination with National Socialist ideology, harsh front-line living conditions, and the brutality of the fighting itself were all important contributory factors to the barbarism displayed by German troops.4 The single most important factor in the legal realm was the issuance of criminal superior orders by the German high command (Oberkommando des Heeres [OKH] and Oberkommando der Wehrmacht [OKW]). Every government supports some level of institutional violence with claims to legitimacy that lend justification to its supporter's activities. The aim of such orders is to contradict and render ineffective previously accepted behavioral norms by sanctioning barbarism within a pseudo-legal and disciplinary framework. In practice, such orders exemplified the National Socialist Führerprinzip (leadership principle) in its purest interpretation. The recipient of an order only had to be concerned with carrying it out; the officer giving the order held all responsibility for any ramifications of the order's implementation. The front-line troops were thus absolved of any responsibility and guilt for their actions. For example, the behavior of German units serving in the Soviet Union was greatly influenced by four universally distributed sets of criminal regulations:

1) The Führer Decree (5/13/41) which established ruthless standards of behavior for German troops operating in the Soviet Union. It ordered the immediate elimination of "agitators, guerillas, saboteurs, and Jews," as well as the complete elimination of passive and active resistance.[5]

2) Einsatzgruppen directives (6/41) which provided these units with theater-wide operational independence to pursue their extermination activities.[6]

3) The Kommisarbefehl (6/6/41) which called for the immediate execution of any Red Army political commissar captured by German forces.[7]

4) The von Reichenau Order (10/10/41) which eliminated legal protections for civilians suspected of guerilla activities in occupied territories. Execution on *suspicion* of guilt and generalized collective punishment were the order of the day.[8]

Similar regulations were issued by the German high command for other theaters of war. For example, in April 1941 Field Marshall von Weichs issued operational guidelines for anti-partisan campaigns in the Balkans instructing German forces to execute all male civilians in areas of active resistance even in the absence of evidence against them. Guilt was to be assumed; innocence had to be proven. As partisan fighting in the Soviet Union and the Balkans dragged on, partisans and civilians alike were reclassified as "bandits" by official decree in August 1942 in an attempt to further justify the measures taken against civil populations. Despite the fact that these harsh guidelines proved to be counterproductive, Hitler and the OKW expanded their scope even further in January 1943 by granting combat units judicial immunity while pursuing anti-partisan operations.[9] They were ordered to use any means against the civil populace of occupied territories. Such orders served as the ultimate blank check for troops to conduct mass killings of civilians on any grounds they saw fit with the veneer of approval by superior orders. The ultimate arbiter of how these guidelines were applied was the unit commander on the ground and far too many lacked the moral fiber needed to resist the criminal influences around them.

Notes:

1. *See Fotion et al., 1995 for a discussion of these three philosophical traditions.*

2. *Niebuhr, 1994a, p. 252*

3. *See Karsten, 1978 and Jones, 1991.*

4. *See Bartov, 1986 for a detailed exploration of these influences.*

5. *IMT Document 886-PS, reproduced in Nazi Conspiracy and Aggression, 1946, vol. III, pp. 637-639.*

6. *See Arad et al., 1989 for a discussion of these directives.*

7. *See Krausnick et al., 1968 for a detailed analysis of this order and its consequences.*

8. *IMT Document UK-81, reproduced in Nazi Conspiracy and Aggression, 1946, vol. VIII, pp. 572-582.*

9. *Ziemke, 1968b, p. 113.*

Post-War Trials in Europe

Prior to the 20th century, warfare was usually viewed in terms of causes and effects with victory being the exclusive goal. The ends often justified the means and little regard, if any, was paid to broader legal, moral and ethical considerations. While certain rules and codes of conduct had evolved over the centuries in an attempt to mitigate the cruelty of armed conflict, they generally functioned as voluntary guidelines that were adhered to, or not, as fancy and circumstances dictated. The unprecedented carnage and suffering on the technologically enhanced battlefields of the First World War, however, ignited a growing international movement seeking to establish stricter legal and moral responsibilities on the behavior of both combatant nations and individuals. Needless to say, the formulation of such laws served to highlight the glaring lack of a legal apparatus that could effectively address violations of international law when they inevitably occurred. By early 1943, the four major Allied powers (France, the Soviet Union, the United Kingdom, and the United States) agreed to ignore publicly-popular calls for the summary execution of enemy leaders and their general staffs and worked toward implementing legal remedies.

United Nations War Crimes Commission and the National Tribunals

In the midst of the Second World War, as the widespread scope of Axis criminality became apparent through numerous independent reports of atrocities against civilians and prisoners of war, the Allied powers began to lay the structural and evidentiary groundwork for post-war legal actions against Axis political leaders and military personnel. On October 20, 1943 the United Nations War Crimes Commission (UNWCC) was established by representatives from seventeen member nations and immediately began to codify existing principles of international law as required for envisioned post-war tribunals that were then in the earliest planning stages. The commission's primary task was to collect and investigate evidence of Axis war crimes, and to report to the appropriate governments any *prima facie* cases. Member nations established their own national offices to assist the UNWCC in preparing formal charges against suspected war criminals, gathering substantiating evidence, locating the accused, deposing witnesses, and planning for their eventual prosecution.

For the most part, those individuals tried under the aegis of the UNWCC and the various national courts were the so-called "minor" war criminals. The majority of Waffen-SS personnel tried for war crimes fell into this category. The main courts involved in these prosecutions included U.S. Military Commissions at various locales throughout Europe, U.S. Military Government Courts in the American Zone of Occupation (Germany), British Military Courts at various locales throughout Europe, the French Permanent Military Tribunal, French Military Government Courts in the French Zone of Occupation (Germany), the Canadian Military Court (Aurich, Germany), special courts of the Netherlands, Norwegian Government Courts, the

Supreme National Tribunal of Poland, as well as military tribunals in the Soviet Union and Eastern European nations. The exact number of war crimes trials held in Europe after the war is unknown due to the sheer scale of the effort involved, the large number of defendants (many of the trials were multi-defendant proceedings), and the numerous -- occasionally conflicting -- legal authorities presiding over the cases. The best estimate of the number of trials held shows the following distribution:

USA	1,672
France	254
UK	524
Netherlands	30
USSR	10,000+
Poland	24
Norway	9
Canada	4
Austria	256
West Germany	6,487

Considering the serious nature of the crimes involved (genocide, murder, torture, starvation, *etc*.), the application of capital punishment and long-term imprisonment was not as extensive as many of the initial sentences pronounced by Western Allied courts would suggest. Most convicted war criminals eventually had their sentences substantially reduced or were pardoned entirely. According to a West German Federal Ministry of Justice study of 5,025 individuals convicted of war crimes by the Western Allies only 174 were still imprisoned in 1954. On the other hand, Soviet and Eastern European courts handed out lengthier sentences that were usually served in full. This difference was undoubtedly a result of their having borne the brunt of the Nazi's excesses. In marked contrast, West German courts proved to be the most lenient of all, especially in terms of the sentences meted out to convicted war criminals. Due to an unusually technical and legalistic judicial system, approximately 90% of the defendants in West German war crimes trials were acquitted of all charges.

International Military Tribunal (IMT) at Nuremberg

Following the establishment of the UNWCC, the Soviet Union, the United Kingdom, and the United States jointly issued the Moscow Declaration on October 30, 1943 warning Germany that it would be held accountable for its war crimes. The Soviets later used this declaration as the legal foundation for their war crimes trials of captured German personnel and Russian collaborators held at Kiev and Kharkov in December 1943. As the war ground on to its predictable conclusion throughout 1944 - 1945, the Allied powers continued the preparatory work for a post-war international tribunal. All of this activity culminated in the signing of the London Charter by the Allied powers on August 8, 1945. The charter contained provisions establishing an International Military Tribunal (IMT) and defining its jurisdiction and legal powers. The IMT was directed to prosecute "major" war criminals whose crimes were not committed against any particular nation or were not identified with any particular locality. Its provisions also allowed signatory nations to try defendants either as individuals or as members of criminal organizations. Most importantly, however, the charter held that the judgements and sentences of its courts were final, not subject to review (*i.e.*, no appeals were allowed), and could not be challenged on jurisdictional grounds. Additionally, in contrast to much of the narrowly circumscribed language of previous war crimes legislation (*e.g.*, the Hague and Geneva Conventions), the London Charter defined war crimes in the most general sense as a violation of the laws and dictates of humanity. An individual could be charged with crimes against peace, war crimes, crimes against humanity, as well as conspiracy to commit any of these acts. Article 6 of the IMT Charter stated:

The following acts, or any of them, are crimes coming within the jurisdiction of the Tribunal for which there shall be individual responsibility:

> **a)** Crimes against peace: Namely, planning, preparation, initiation or waging of a war of aggression, or a war in violation of international treaties, agreements or assurances, or participation in a common plan or conspiracy for the accomplishment of any of the foregoing:

b) War Crimes: Namely, violations of the laws or customs of war. Such violations shall include, but not be limited to, murder, ill-treatment or deportation, slave labor or for any other purpose of the civilian population of or in occupied territory, murder or ill-treatment of prisoners of war or persons on the seas, killing of hostages, plunder of public or private property, wanton destruction of cities, towns or villages, or devastation not justified by military necessity; and,

c) Crimes against humanity: Namely, murder, extermination, enslavement, deportation, and other inhumane acts committed against any civilian population, before or during the war, or persecution on political, racial or religious grounds in execution of or in connection with any crime within the jurisdiction of the Tribunal, whether or not in violation of the domestic law of the country where perpetrated. Leaders, organizers, instigators and accomplices participating in the formulation or execution of a common plan or conspiracy to commit any of the foregoing crimes are responsible for all acts performed by any persons in execution of such plan.

Such expansive, all-encompassing language resulted in bitter, protracted disputes among Allied legal counsels concerning the legality of prosecuting individuals under the charter's provisions. Forseeing other objections, Article 7 of the IMT Charter unequivocally rejected the "Act of State" defense (*i.e.*, the individual was acting as a representative of the state and thus not personally accountable for his actions), ruling that international laws were applicable to the actions of both sovereign states and individuals. Likewise, the charter rejected the "Respondeat Superior" defense (*i.e.*, the individual was only following a superior's orders and thus not personally accountable for his actions), noting that if a given order were in violation of civil or military law then both the person giving the order and the one executing it would be guilty of a crime. Procedural and evidentiary rules for the trials were also established by the Charter; many of these provisions were later incorporated into Allied Control Council Law No. 10 which served as the legal foundation for the trials of "minor" war criminals.[1]

In preparation for a post-war international tribunal the Allied powers also established war crimes investigation teams that followed behind the advancing front lines gathering documentary evidence of Axis crimes. The resulting evidence (thousands of tons) was carefully examined with only the most significant items being culled out for legal purposes. On October 18, 1945, a committee of the Chief Counsels of the four signatory nations filed a final indictment against 22 German defendants and six organizations for various crimes as defined under Article 6 of the IMT Charter. The Tribunal convened its first session on November 14, 1945 at Nuremberg and held sessions until August 31, 1946. In that time nearly 380 witnesses were questioned by the tribunal and 200,000 affidavits filed as part of the court records. In concluding its work the IMT handed down 12 death sentences, 7 prison terms of varying length, and 3 acquittals. The three defendants acquitted of all charges were later tried by West German denazification courts and found guilty of war crimes.

In addition to these sentences against individual defendants, the tribunal also declared three of the accused organizations to be "criminal organizations": the Nazi Party (NSDAP), the Geheime Staatspolizei and Sicherheitsdienst (Gestapo and SD), and the Schutzstaffel (SS). In its verdict against the SS, the tribunal was clear in its findings concerning the involvement of the Waffen-SS in criminal activities:

Definition of the SS as a "Criminal Organization"

SS units were active participants in the steps leading up to aggressive war. The Verfügungstruppe [Ed. -- precursor to the Waffen-SS] was used in the occupation of the Sudetenland, of Bohemia and Moravia, and of Memel.

The SS was even a more general participant in the commission of War Crimes and Crimes against Humanity... There is evidence that the shooting of unarmed prisoners of war was the general practice in some Waffen SS divisions... Units of the Waffen SS and Einsatzgruppen operating directly under the SS main office were used to carry out these plans [Ed. -- ethnic cleansing]. These units were also involved in the widespread murder and ill-treatment of the civilian population of occupied territories. Under the guise of combating partisan units, units of the SS exterminated Jews and people deemed politically undesirable by the SS, and their reports record the execution of enormous numbers of persons. Waffen SS divisions were responsible for many massacres and atrocities in occupied territories...

Steps were continually taken, involving the use of the Security Police and SD and even the Waffen SS, to insure that the SS had an adequate supply of concentration camp labor for its projects.

It is impossible to single out any one portion of the SS which was not involved in these criminal activities... Units of the Waffen SS were directly involved in the killing of prisoners of war and the atrocities in occupied countries. It supplied personnel for the Einsatzgruppen, and had command over the concentration camp guards after its absorption of the Totenkopf SS...

The Tribunal finds that knowledge of these criminal activities was sufficiently general to justify declaring that the SS was a criminal organization to the extent hereinafter described. It does appear that an attempt was made to keep secret some phases of its activities, but its criminal programs were so widespread, and involved slaughter on such a gigantic scale, that its criminal activities must have been widely known. It must be recognized, moreover, that the criminal activities of the SS followed quite logically from the principles on which it was organized... This mystical and fanatical belief in the superiority of the Nordic German developed into a studied contempt and even hatred of other races which led to criminal activities of the type outlined above being considered as a matter of course if not a matter of pride.

Conclusions: The SS was utilized for purposes which were criminal under the Charter involving the persecution and extermination of the Jews, brutalities and killings in concentration camps, excesses in the administration of occupied territories, the administration of the slave labor program and the mistreatment and murder of prisoners of war... In dealing with the SS the Tribunal includes all persons who had been officially accepted as members of the SS including the members of the Allgemeine SS, members of the Waffen SS, members of the SS Totenkopf Verbände, and the members of any of the different police forces who were members of the SS. The Tribunal does not include the so-called SS riding units... The Tribunal declares to be criminal within the meaning of the Charter the group composed of those persons who had been officially accepted as members of the SS as enumerated in the preceding paragraph who became or remained members of the organization with knowledge that it was being used for the commission of acts declared criminal by Article 6 of the Charter, or who were personally implicated as members of the organization in the commission of such crimes, excluding, however, those who were drafted into membership by the State in such a way as to give them no choice in the matter, and who had committed no such crimes. The basis of this finding is the participation of the organization in War Crimes and Crimes against Humanity connected with the war; this group declared criminal cannot include, therefore, persons who had ceased to belong to the organizations enumerated in the preceding paragraph prior to 1 September 1939. [2]

In accordance with this judgement the tribunal recommended that all Waffen-SS officers down to the rank of SS-Sturmbannführer be sentenced to 10 years' imprisonment and all Waffen-SS officers below that rank to 5 years' imprisonment. No general punishment for lesser-ranking personnel was specified. Thus, the vast majority of Waffen-SS veterans surviving the war were branded as war criminals complicitous in numerous atrocities perpetrated by the Nazi regime. While most Waffen-SS officers were held in custody for up to several years while war crime's accusations were sorted out, in general the IMT's imprisonment recommendations were not carried out.

U.S. War Crimes Trial Program

At the time of the Moscow Declaration the intent of the Allied powers had been to conduct a series of international tribunals judging the whole spectrum of German transgressions from major to minor war criminals. Growing political problems anticipating the Cold War and the antics of Soviet prosecutors during the IMT, however, soured the United States on the idea of further joint tribunals and caused it to pursue a policy of separate zonal (*i.e.*, occupation zone based) trials. In January 1946, President Truman directed the Judge Advocate of U.S. Forces, European Theater (later European Command) to prosecute the remaining American trials of "second-string" war criminals under the authority of IMT precedents and the recently adopted Allied Control Council Law No. 10. The aim of the program was to,

...demonstrate to the Germans the horrendous crimes Nazism had inflicted on its victims. Many U.S. officials believed that Germany's perceived preference for militarism and authoritarianism over democracy and pluralism had greatly facilitated the commission of these crimes. [3]

In general, preliminary investigations followed the previously established IMT guidelines, but there were several crucial differences. Primarily due to the adoption of looser definitions of what qualified as a war crime and what constituted membership in a criminal organization, the resulting legal net was consequently cast much wider and several thousand Germans were eventually investigated by the U.S. Army judiciary. Over the course of the next three years (October 1946 - April 1949) the Judge Advocate's office held twelve main war crimes trials at Nuremberg (Nuremberg Military Tribunal [NMT]) involving 185 defendants, as well as hundreds of other lesser proceedings. In all 3,887 individuals were investigated, of which 1,672 were later prosecuted and 1,416 were convicted. The majority of those convicted were SS concentration camp personnel, Waffen-SS personnel, "kapos" (trusties) from concentration camps, and low to mid-level Nazi party and police officials. An American military prison at Landsberg, Germany was established to hold convicted war criminals.

Few surprises came out of the twelve NMT proceedings which covered a wide array of crimes and upheld all of the basic legal principles established during the previous IMT proceedings (*e.g.*, affirmation of individual responsibility for actions and a rejection of the "superior orders" plea). The Einsatzgruppen trial (Case 9: United States vs. Otto Ohlendorf *et al.*) was

particularly important for illustrating in no uncertain terms the extensive involvement of the Waffen-SS in the Nazi extermination program carried out against Soviet Jewry from 1941 to 1944. The remaining military tribunals, many of which were held at Dachau, dealt exclusively with more traditional war crimes such as the execution of hostages and POWs. An unusual benefit that defendants received as a result of being prosecuted by American military authorities was the ability to have their conviction and sentencing appeals conducted before U.S. civilian courts, although none of these actions were ultimately successful.

What was surprising with regard to the NMT proceedings was the amount of negative press coverage that they generated back in the United States. Numerous well-respected judges objected to the tribunals as extra-legal on the grounds that they were not provided for in the U.S. Constitution. Several conservative congressmen attacked the NMT as an unwarranted abuse and accused the Truman Administration for being "soft on Communism" by its harsh post-war treatment of Germany. The Malmedy Massacre trial at Dachau attracted perhaps the most attention of all with its allegations of prosecutorial abuse and torture of defendants (see *Malmedy*). Despite the fact that a Senate panel later generally exonerated the U.S. Army's program of war crimes trials, the controversy fueled both anti-trial sentiment at home and in West Germany. All of this is not to imply, however, that there were not some problems with the conduct of the tribunals and their outcomes. In particular, many of the American legal counsels executing and reviewing the trials program were profoundly disturbed by the lack of an appellate court for procedural corrections and sentence equalization.

If the U.S. stateside reaction to the war crimes tribunals was unexpected, the West German reaction to them was predictable and disturbing. The trials were opposed by virtually every West German political party, legal body, veterans' organization, and refugee society. The strongest opposition of all to the trials came from the Roman Catholic and Evangelical (Confessing) Churches in Germany. Across the board West Germans denied collective guilt for Nazi crimes, questioned the legality of the war crimes tribunals, and sympathized with convicted war criminals as the victims of arbitrary and unwarranted Allied occupation policies. Those convicted had merely followed orders issued by their superiors and therefore should not be imprisoned. In addition to the plethora of excuses for the atrocities committed (see *Apologist's Arguments*), many West Germans actually claimed that the "mental confusion" caused by the Hitler regime was a mitigating circumstance in and of itself! In cases where the defendant's crimes were beyond any doubt, a number of West German politicians actually claimed that the war criminal was an upright citizen "who somehow ended up on the 'path of illegality'."[4] Most West Germans closed their eyes to the copious evidence of criminality and stubbornly clung to the mistaken belief that their conduct during the war had been no different from that of any other nation. By distancing themselves from the truth, they hoped to avoid confronting it altogether. The tribunals were simply an attack upon their honor and when coupled with Germany's many post-war problems (most of which were attributed to the Allied powers) it was clear that Germany was the real victim of the war. West Germans, overwhelmed by the flood of death and destruction they had unleashed upon the world, simply wanted to bury their past without confronting it, admitting guilt, or assuming responsibility for it. In fact, the West German press consciously progressed from referring to war criminals as *Kriegsverbrecher* (war criminal) to *Kriegsverurteilter* (literally, sentenced because of the war) and finally to calling them *Kriegsgefangene* (prisoners of war). Ironically, after all that had happened during the war many Germans still seemed unaware that just such an insidious redefinition process lay at the very heart of the Nazi bureaucratic and psycho-linguistic campaign to disguise and make more palatable the true nature of its crimes (*e.g.*, referring to innocent civilians as "bandits, looters, and arsonists" in order to justify their mass murder).

As early as 1947 West German opposition to the tribunals along with a number of political factors combined to shift official U.S. policy from punishing West Germany and re-educating its general public to rebuilding her as a strong democratic member of the Atlantic Alliance. These factors included the aforementioned Congressional opposition to the NMT proceedings, legal questions about procedural inadequacies and sentence equalization, constitutional considerations, the developing Cold War, the security of U.S. armed forces in West Germany, and the increasing use of clemency for war criminals in the British and French occupation zones of Germany. Accordingly, from 1946 to 1951 the U.S. Army's European Command and the U.S. High Commission established a series of clemency and sentence modification boards in hopes of addressing both German and American concerns regarding the "war crimes problem." Following the official formation of the Federal Republic of Germany in the Fall of 1949, the West German Bundestag made it one of their top priorities to campaign for individual clemency in addition to a sweeping general amnesty for all convicted war criminals regardless of the nature of their crimes. Whereas American authorities were willing to admit some mistakes were made and adjust sentences accordingly, the West Germans still believed that they were innocent of any wrong-doing. This very basic and intractable disagreement on the "war crimes problem" refused to go away. Both sides viewed it as a serious barrier on West Germany's road to rearmament, integration, and eventual sovereignty.

In response to this resistance by their erstwhile new ally, in 1951 the U.S. War Crimes Trial program entered its second phase. This phase was primarily characterized by the widespread application of executive clemency and sentence review and adjustment procedures for convicted war criminals. Despite the many horrific crimes committed by the war criminals in their custody, U.S. policymakers decided that what was morally right (to uphold and enforce the sentences meted out by tribunals) was potentially dangerous in the face of the Soviet threat to Europe. They hoped to eventually dismantle the entire program without generating public opposition to the process back home. As far as the Germans were concerned, the policy was meant to "promote the superior values of democratic society, which entitled even the perpetrators of mass murder to fair treatment."[5] The German right wing, however, was as inflexible as ever and continued to demand an immediate amnesty for all convicted war criminals. The Adenauer government showed a more moderate face and requested that West German officials be allowed to participate in the clemency and review process. In fact, the Adenauer government had essentially adopted an unspoken "clemency for rearmament" position ever since 1950 when the U.S. and United Kingdom began pressuring West Germany to rearm and help defend Europe against the burgeoning Communist menace. In the Fall of 1952 the West German press brought its own "clemency for rearmament" campaign into full swing in hopes of putting additional pressure on U.S. policy makers. American fears were confirmed when a study conducted that September found that only 10% of West Germans supported the war crimes program. With each passing month it became increasingly clear that the West Germans had been right all along in thinking that time was on their side. The campaign against the war crimes program was ultimately successful in August 1953 with the establishment of an IMPAC (Interim Mixed Parole and Clemency Board), a mixed Allied/German clemency board, in each of the three zones of occupation. In the first year of the board's operation in the U.S. Zone, 60% of the prisoners held by American authorities were released. By July 1955, American authorities had paroled 85% of the war criminals at Landsberg Prison; the last prisoner was finally released in 1958. The vocal protests of stateside veterans' organizations went unheeded. To many outside observers, the U.S. had sold out its war crimes program for the sake of political expediency. By the late 1950s, however, the United States perceived itself in a life and death struggle with the Soviet Union -- a regime generally considered to be more powerful and dangerous than Nazi Germany had been. Since West Germany was the cornerstone of Europe's defense planning, geopolitical circumstances dictated that key, albeit unpalatable, concessions be made to promote stability and cooperation in the fledgling republic. In this conflict of values between moral/legal justice and political motivation the U.S. war crimes program ultimately failed because "... it did not adequately punish convicted war criminals... [and] it did not convince the Germans that their society with its authoritarian and militaristic traditions needed reform."[6]

West German War Crimes Trials

Despite the return of jurisdictional autonomy to the West German court system in January 1950, the Adenauer government declined to establish systemic nationwide coordination for the prosecution of Nazi-era crimes. Since neither politicians nor the public had any desire for an extensive and continued dredging up of recent German criminality, the "war crimes problem" was accorded a very low societal priority. Those investigations and trials that did take place were left to the regional legal systems of the West German states. Only a small group of highly motivated and conscientious prosecutors even bothered to pursue war crimes charges through the byzantine West German judicial system. It was not until autumn 1958, following the shocking revelations at the Tilsit Einsatzgruppen Trial concerning the extent and seriousness of Nazi crimes in the East, that the West German government finally took official notice of war crimes prosecutions as a valid legal issue when it belatedly founded a much-needed central information and investigations clearinghouse (Zentrale Stelle der Landesjustizverwaltungen zur Aufklärung nationalsozialistischer Verbrechen, Ludwigsburg).

On casual inspection, the West German record of war crimes prosecutions appears impressive. From May 1945 to January 1992, slightly over 100,000 German citizens were investigated for alleged participation in war crimes. A careful examination of these investigations' results, however, shows that the entire process was little more than an exercise in impotent bureacratic paper-shuffling. All of the investigations yielded a mere 6,487 trials (6.25%) of which only 1,793 (1.73%) were for serious crimes. Of the 1,793 defendants tried for serious crimes, 974 (0.94%) were convicted. Among these serious crimes convictions, 755 (0.73%) were for genocidal activities. After various appeals and motions, only 472 (0.45%) of these convicted genocidal killers were actually sentenced to any form of punishment. The punishments meted out to those sentenced were as follows: death (1), life imprisonment (113), and imprisonment for up to 15 years (358). Of course, the lone death sentence was symbolic since the West German constitution forbade capital punishment. Individual sentences usually defied commonly accepted notions of justice and fairness. For example, in July 1961 Dr. Otto Bradfisch, former commander of Einsatzkommando 8 (a sub-unit of Einsatzgruppe B), was sentenced by a West German regional court to ten years' imprisonment for his role in the slaughter of 15,000 Jews in the Soviet Union. His sentence translated into one day of imprisonment for every four civilians murdered. The same court later sentenced a concentration camp survivor to twelve years' imprisonment for the murder of two Nazi Party members in 1945.

The difficulty in obtaining a successful war crimes prosecution and meaningful sentencing in West Germany was both the intentional and unintentional product of its baroque, legalistic judicial system. First of all, West German law allowed the normal statutes of limitation to apply to Nazi crimes, even mass genocidal activities. Thus, with each passing year fewer and fewer defendants could potentially be brought to trial. Unrealistically strict burdens of proof and intention (by most western standards) resulted in the dismissal of many cases whose evidence would otherwise have resulted in convictions. Amnesty from prosecution was often granted for those who claimed to be sick. Since a criminal case had to be tried in the state where the crime was committed and since extradition was not allowed among West German states, defendants who did not reside in the specific state where their crimes were committed could not be tried for them. Even worse was the West German legal distinction between 'murder' and 'accomplice to murder' which hinged on the principle of superior orders. Generally speaking, only those who actually ordered killings to take place were found guilty of murder. Thus, the vast majority of mass killers brought to trial were merely found guilty of the lesser charge of "accomplice to murder" and received sentences of only 3 - 15 years imprisonment. On top of all of this, the fact that the West German constitution forbade capital punishment, the extradition of its citizens to foreign countries, the use of special courts, and *ex post facto* laws meant that the efforts of prosecutors were generally hamstrung from the start and that little justice could be expected from the courts with respect to war crimes allegations. The West German government's refusal to take a lead or to provide nationwide coordination on the issue exacerbated an already problematic situation.

Given the deeply rooted resistance of West Germans to face up to the horrifying results of their enthusiastic support for Hitler's regime, it is hardly surprising that the outcome of their own house cleaning efforts fell far short of the mark. With such a dismal record, it is also no wonder that the vast majority of German war criminals remained in West Germany after the war. Fear of serious prosecution was minimal and the likelihood that such legal proceedings would result in significant punishment was vanishingly small. As de Mildt incisively noted,

> If one contrasts the enormity of National Socialist crimes with the statistical record of their post-war prosecution it is quite clear that, in this respect at least, Germany hopelessly failed in coming to terms with its past... its political representatives made no effort to equip Germany's judiciary with the appropriate means and above all the incentive to... address the problem.[7]

This failure was compounded by the fact that the United States and its Western European allies, having already undercut and dismantled the results of their own war crimes tribunals for broader geopolitical reasons, largely chose to remain silent regarding West Germany's profound shortcomings in redressings its wrongs.

Notes:

1. *Punishment of Persons Guilty of War Crimes, Crimes against Peace and Against Humanity, December 20, 1945, Official Gazette, Control Council for Germany.*
2. *International Military Tribunal, 1948/1971, vol. 1, pp. 255-273.*
3. *Buscher, 1989, p. 69.*
4. *op. cit., p. 188.*
5. *op. cit., p. 69.*
6. *op. cit., p. 159.*
7. *de Mildt, 1996, pp. 35-36.*

The Fight for Rehabilitation

The ink barely had time to dry on the IMT condemnation of the SS as a criminal organization before Allied and German legal authorities were besieged by defenders of the Waffen-SS insisting that any similarities between the two organizations were in name only, a mere accident of Himmler's unfortunate organizational structuring of his empire. Ignoring overwhelming evidence to the contrary, they argued that the Waffen-SS was a strictly honorable military organization with no connection whatsoever to the war crimes committed by other branches of the SS. Conveniently forgetful of the organization's role as National Socialism's hand-picked elite guard and "special tasks group," Waffen-SS revisionists consistently tried to reinterpret it as a fourth arm of the regular German armed forces (Wehrmacht). Despite their ceaseless efforts, this strategy of attempting to separate the Waffen-SS from both the ideological and criminal elite of the Third Reich was summarily rejected as baseless by every civil court and military tribunal before which it was argued. Historians have likewise judged the claim to be without merit since it is unequivocally contradicted by archival documentation.

Following the cessation of hostilities in Europe, the four Allied powers took all identifiable officers and NCOs of the Waffen-SS into custody. Many of these individuals remained in detention centers until 1949 despite a lack ·of specific criminal charges against them. Most were held on the basis of the IMT criminal organization ruling and its recommendation for the general imprisonment of Waffen-SS command personnel. From 1946 to 1949, several hundred members of the Waffen-SS were prosecuted and convicted on a variety of war crimes charges by post-war national tribunals. Some were even executed. As the Cold War with the Soviet Union escalated throughout the late 1940s, the Western Powers were subjected to increasing pressure from German politicians to show leniency toward convicted war criminals. Many sentences were reduced or even commuted and the parolees allowed to return home. Upon release, many former Waffen-SS men were summoned before West German de-Nazification courts. Some were again found guilty of war crimes and/or membership in a criminal organization and subjected to a variety of relatively minor civil sanctions. By 1950, however, with the war losing center-stage to the threat of Communist expansion, several leading Waffen-SS veterans decided that the time had come for a renewed attempt at removing the IMT's stigma on their honor. Among other reasons, the aura of criminality surrounding Waffen-SS veterans had caused the West German government to withhold from them the standard pension and health care benefits package that was provided to former members of the Wehrmacht.

In late 1950, the Hilfsgemeinschaft auf Gegenseitigkeit (HIAG, sometimes also referred to as the Bundesverband der Soldaten der ehemahligen Waffen-SS) was incorporated in West Germany by a number of prominent Waffen-SS veterans including Paul Hausser, Felix Steiner, Herbert Gille, Kurt Meyer, Sepp Dietrich, and Gottlob Berger. Its main objective was to lobby the West German government for the economic, historical, and legal rehabilitation of the Waffen-SS. For the most part HIAG representatives attempted to co-opt legitimate political and governmental bodies, particularly the Christian Democratic Union and the new West German armed forces (Bundeswehr), into fronting for their revisionist program. The main point brought home over and over again by HIAG lobbyists was that the Waffen-SS was a "fourth arm of the Wehrmacht" that had been unjustly stained with false war crimes accusations and an undeserved reputation for criminality. By October 1951, HIAG had 376 local branches representing 59 former Waffen-SS formations and was publishing its own newspaper, Wiking-Ruf. This was superceded in 1955 by a second newspaper, Der Freiwillige, which was edited by HIAG's Press Chief Erich Kern. Kern was, in fact, Erich Kernmayer, the former chief of the press office for the Nazi Party's gauleiters (regional leaders). Despite an earlier West German court order banning Kernmayer from publishing for the rest of his life, his activities on behalf of HIAG were not hindered in the least. Under his direction, the group's publications celebrated and exonerated the Waffen-SS for their service to the Third Reich and portrayed them as unfairly-maligned patriots. Paralleling the work of HIAG through the years were the sporadic efforts of a number of divisional-based Kameradschaften (veteran's associations). Most of their energies, however, seemed to be spent organizing festive yearly gatherings which were always controversial and picketed by leftist West German youths. HIAG's power reached its peak in the late 1950s when the organization boasted approximately 20,000 members. By that time the West German government had gone to great lengths to pacify Waffen-SS veterans without actually declaring them innocent of complicity in war crimes. By 1963, with many of its more tangible goals achieved (including a resolution of the civil rights and pension issues), HIAG membership had fallen to 6,000 and was dropping steadily. As aged veterans continued to die off and the "war crimes problem" was permanently placed on a back burner by West German society, HIAG and its activities withered away completely.

Despite the veteran's inability to directly sell the notion of their innocence to an international audience, they did give critical support to a much more effective campaign toward rehabilitating the Waffen-SS in foreign eyes. The four decades from 1950 to 1990 saw the establishment of numerous pro-SS publishing houses in West Germany including:

• Askania Verlagsgesellschaft
• Druffel Verlag (founded by Helmut Sündermann, former Nazi press chief)
• Göttinger Verlagsanstalt (founded by Leonhard Schlüter, former SS officer)
• Grabert Verlag (founded by Herbert Grabert, former SS officer)
• Holsten Verlag
• Klosterhaus Verlag
• Munin Verlag (official Waffen-SS veteran's publishing house)
• Nation Europa (founded by Arthur Ehrhardt, former SS officer/anti-partisan expert for Himmler)
• Plesse Verlag (founded by Waldemar Schütz, former SS officer)
• Podzun-Pallas Verlag
• Ring Verlag
• Schild Verlag
• K.W. Schütz Verlag (founded by Waldemar Schütz, former SS officer)
• Veritas Verlag
• Vowinckel Verlag

These publishing houses issued a number of influen-

tial revisionist memoirs and unit histories celebrating the Waffen-SS as a unique, pan-European military elite. Books such as Leon Degrelle's *Die verlorene Legion* (1952), Paul Hausser's *Waffen-SS im Einsatz* (1953) and *Soldaten wie andere auch* (1966), Ernst-Gunther Krätschmer's *Die Ritterkreuztrager der Waffen-SS* (1955), Kurt Meyer's *Grenadiere* (1957), Felix Steiner's *Die Freiwilligen der Waffen-SS* (1958) and *Die Armee der Geachteten* (1963), Peter Strassner's *Europäische Freiwillige* (1968), Friedrich Husemann's *Die guten Glaubens waren* (1971-1977), Wolf-Dietrich Heike's *Sie wollten die Freheit* (1974), Rudolf Lehmann's *Die Leibstandarte* (1977-1987), Otto Kumm's *Vorwärts Prinz Eugen* (1978), the monumental photo-album *Wenn alle Bruder schweigen* (1985), and F.G. Einer's *Treu ihrem Volk* (1987) laid the foundation for Waffen-SS revisionism giving great impetus to the movement in West Germany and abroad. Here were unabashed voices calling for a wholesale reappraisal of opinions about the actions and motives of those who had fervently supported Hitler. Waffen-SS veterans, the authors repeatedly stressed, were not accomplices to the crimes of the government they represented, but merely soldiers like any others rendering honorable service on behalf of their Fatherland.

Ironically, such obvious revisionism found fertile ground in the countries that defeated Germany, especially in the U.S. and the United Kingdom. Over the years an uncritical fascination with the Waffen-SS has developed primarily due to its status as the ideological elite of a powerful regime. An additional factor in the appeal of the Waffen-SS is its multi-nationality during the latter war years which has given rise to interpretations of the organization invoking themes of pan-European solidarity. This fascination has led numerous amateur military historians to produce a torrent of publications that seek to restore lost honor and glory to the Waffen-SS. Equally culpable are those publishing houses which exhibit a negligent attitude where the crimes of the Waffen-SS are concerned. A number of books issued by well-known publishers such as Patrick Stephens (England), Squadron/Signal (USA), Motorbooks International (Spain), Schiffer Military History (USA), and J.J. Fedorowicz (Canada) either ignore, gloss over, or apologize for Waffen-SS criminality. At one extreme are publications which openly espouse a pro-SS and pro-National Socialist in viewpoint. Even reputable researchers have been caught on the horns of the Waffen-SS revisionism controversy. The second volume of Bender and Taylor's excellent five-volume *Uniforms, Organiza-*

tion and History of the Waffen-SS (1969-1982), for example, contains a statement clarifying the authors' intentions in their first volume introduction which numerous readers interpreted as being sympathetic or biased towards the Waffen-SS.

Many examples could be cited as the current Waffen-SS literature is dominated by apologists and revisionists, but a few will have to suffice. Walther (1990), for instance, considers the Waffen-SS to be victims of circumstance and blames "bureaucrats" and the "special units" for the crimes attributed to them. Wiggers (1990) concluded that the charges against the Waffen-SS were "overblown" since the Allies supposedly allowed their emotions to interfere with judicial evenhandedness. Munoz (1991) seems to best sum up the revisionist mindset of many authors when he claims in his introduction that "The excesses of the Nazi regime forever tarnished the escutcheon of the Waffen-SS." Never mind the many crimes of the Waffen-SS itself, or the fact that they were the Nazi regime's ideological palace guard. Munoz and his like-minded compatriots woud have us believe that the Waffen-SS has been sullied by the crimes of others.

Perhaps the most problematic publications are those that combine an open admiration for the Waffen-SS and selective amnesia concerning their crimes with an otherwise informative, well-researched presentation. Such publications have a high potential to mislead unwary readers whose knowledge of the subject at hand is limited. Logusz (1997) presents a lengthy history of the 14. Waffen-Grenadier-Division der SS (ukrainische Nr. 1) that is little more than a thinly veiled rationalization and celebration of Ukrainian nationalism. He cavalierly dismisses numerous war crimes accusations and portrays the division's critics as anti-Ukrainian propagandists. Another particularly egregious recent example of revisionism is Yerger's *Riding East: The SS Cavalry Brigade in Poland and Russia* (1996). In an otherwise excrutiatingly detailed unit history scarcely a word can be found regarding the numerous atrocities committed by the brigade during its "cleansing operations" in the Soviet Union (June 1941 to December 1941). It seems highly unlikely that Yerger was unaware of these crimes since they were extensively documented and referenced during post-war trials of brigade personnel. Obviously, reporting details of the unit's cleansing actions would have resulted in a radically different image than that which the author wished to present.

Given our generally unfettered freedom of the press and a lack of laws specifically prohibiting Holocaust revisionism such as those in Canada and Europe, it is hardly surprising that the United States is home to the most extreme of Waffen-SS propagandists. For several decades now, writer/publisher Richard Landwehr has issued *Siegrunen* (an irregular, digest-size magazine devoted to extolling the virtues of the Waffen-SS) and also run Bibliophile Legion Books which has published numerous Waffen-SS unit histories. An early contributor to *National Socialist World* (a now-defunct quarterly journal issued by George Lincoln Rockwell's American Nazi Party and the World Union of National Socialists), Landwehr's work categorically denies that the Holocaust occurred, characterizes the Allied Powers as "communist and plutocratic criminals," and claims that the Waffen-SS and Nazi Germany fought the Second World War in order to preserve Western civilization. While few are familiar with his explicitly neo-Nazi writings of the late 1960s, the content and tenor of Landwehr's more recent publications make it abundantly clear to readers that they are confronted with unapologetic Nazi propaganda.

Of course, the defenders of the Waffen-SS are also keeping up with advancing technology. Several Internet websites and homepages exist which extol the virtues of German militarism and the Waffen-SS. Among the better known and certainly one of the most comprehensive sites is Jason Pipes' *German Armed Forces in World War II* site (http://www.feldgrau.com). It proudly claims to be an "apolitical military history site" whose goal is "honest, objective and impartial research" concerning military aspects of the Third Reich. Interestingly enough, the opening page of the site used to prominently feature the motto *Unsere Ehre Heisst Treue* ("Our honor is loyalty") which is a minor variation on the SS motto, *Meine Ehre Heisst Treue* ("My honor is loyalty"). The official policy of the web-site includes a ban on the posting of political messages and strict monitoring of war crimes discussions ("historical material only"). Not surprisingly, one noticeable feature of the site is its downplaying of the crimes committed by German forces in general and the Waffen-SS in particular. Honest and impartial history in this case appears to mean a willingness to promote a sanitized account of the German military.

Recent Controversies

The Historikerstreit

In 1978 the first round was fought in a controversy among West German historians that would eventually capture the public's attention and become known as the *Historikerstreit* ("historian's debate"). Hellmut Diwald, a professor of medieval history at the University of Erlangen, published a monumental popular history entitled *Geschichte der Deutschen* (*History of the Germans*). In it he argued that the German's past had been "morally disqualified" since 1945, that it was "devalued, destroyed and taken away from them." Most notable in Diwald's attempted resurrection of German history was his emphasis on the brutal expulsion of ethnic Germans from Eastern Europe at the end of the Second World War while spending a scant two pages summarizing the encyclopedic crimes of the Third Reich. Amidst furious criticism and demands that the print run of the book be destroyed, Diwald bowed to public pressure and rewrote the offending sections. Both the author and his revised book quickly dropped out of sight and the controversy was forgotten soon thereafter.

So it would have remained if not for the policies of conservative Chancellor Helmut Kohl in the early 1980s. Under the Kohl government conservative intellectuals began what became known as the *Tendenzwende* (change of tack) in which liberal accomplishments were to be denied and reversed wherever possible. Patriotic nationalism was now back in style and the Kohl government made efforts to lighten the burden of German war guilt by encouraging a positive historical consciousness. The time had come for Germans to reclaim German history for themselves. As the Bavarian Minister-President Franz Josef Strauss said in a speech before the Bundestag, Germans "should get off their knees and learn to walk tall again." Thus began the second round of the *Historikerstreit*.

The active prompting of the Kohl government led a group of conservative West German historians to resurrect and expand upon Diwald's original thesis regarding the marginalization of German history due to the events of the Second World War. Andreas Hillgruber, Ernst Nolte and others rewrote Germany's recent history in order to lift the burden of guilt imposed on the Germans and redistribute some of it onto the Allied Powers. One of their main strategies consisted of drawing comparisons between the Holocaust and a variety of other 20th Century crimes (such as the massacre of Armenians by the Turks in 1915, Stalin's mass killings in the U.S.S.R., U.S. war crimes in Vietnam, Khmer Rouge atrocities in Cambodia, *etc.*) in an attempt to blur the real differences among these events and to relativize them all. If the Holocaust and other Nazi atrocities were not unique but simply one of many modern evils, then it would be morally and historically wrong (as well as hypocritical) to single out Germany for her crimes. Nolte has been especially diligent in his attempts to marginalize the specter of Nazi crimes in the service of an uplifting German history arguing that 1) Nazi excesses were in reaction to perceived threats by world Jewry or previous Allied crimes, 2) the historiography of the Third Reich has been dominated by the "victors and victims" who are biased, 3) Nazism was a defensive reaction to a threatened Communist takeover of Germany, and 4) some Holocaust deniers should be taken seriously because they have "honorable motives" and are just searching for the "neutral truth." Nolte has also stressed that the morality of the Nazi period cannot be painted in black and white, but only in various shades of grey. The basic revisionist texts and academic responses to them, as well as excellent surveys of the debate's theoretical and methodological aspects, development, and ultimate consequences for German society, are available in the English language.[1]

The debate revolved around the validity of the conservative historian's attempt to restructure German history free of the criminal taint of Hitler's Third Reich. While it could not strictly be classified as Holocaust denial, the work of these historians created an acceptable grey zone where highly unlikely interpretations of history intermixed with the pseudohistory and misrepresentations of deniers. Rather than examine both legitimate similarities and distinctions among the various war crimes they cited and gain insight therefrom, the work of Nolte and others purposely obscured the boundaries between fact and fiction and between persecutor and victim. Most of their arguments were derived, whether consciously or not, from wartime justifications previously employed by the Nazis themselves. In the process of trying to rehabilitate the German people from their role as perpetrators of genocide, these conservative historians could not avoid denigrating Germany's victims. Their works overwhelmingly relied upon the fact that the populace did not have access to the documentation (nor in all likelihood would they make the effort to locate and read it) that undercut such highly questionable theses.

Eventually, the hollowness of the conservative historian's arguments became so transparent that the West German President entered the fray to speak out against this form of creeping revisionism. Of course, by the time the debate had played itself out in the late 1980's the reputations of Nolte and other scholars most prominently involved, as well as West German historiography in general, had suffered significant damage. Academic and public commentary outside of West Germany viewed the whole affair as a temporary, though somewhat serious, outbreak of irrationalism that the Germans seem particularly susceptible to experiencing. In West Germany itself it appears that these respected academics, by normalizing and trivializing the crimes of the Third Reich, made various aspects of far-right thinking respectable again to a much broader segment of the public.

Bitburg

The incident that best exemplified both the influence of the *Historikerstreit* and the ongoing battle over the historiography of Waffen-SS criminality was the international furor regarding the 1985 visit of U.S. President Ronald Reagan to Kolmeshöhe Military Cemetary in Bitburg, West Germany. The visit had its genesis in the June 1984 ceremonies commemorating the fortieth anniversary of the D-Day landings in Normandy, France. Despite West Germany's request to take part in the ceremonies, the principals decided that the affair was for the Allied Powers only. In September 1984, however, French President Mitterand hosted West German Chancellor Kohl at a ceremony of reconciliation at the French-German military cemetary on the Verdun battlefield. When it was announced that President Reagan would be visiting Europe in May 1985, Chancellor Kohl urged him to visit a German military cemetary and the Dachau concentration camp as a symbol of post-war reconciliation between the United States and West Germany.

From the Reagan administration's perspective, the main purpose of the visit was to rally support for the deployment of U.S. Pershing II nuclear missiles in Europe and to garner monetary pledges for its "Star Wars" space-based weapons proposal. A conciliatory move by the United States that would cast a different light on Germany's wartime crimes and lessen the resulting stain on German nationalism and patriotism, it was felt, would assuage West German sensibilities and provide the political grease necessary to move the U.S. defense initiatives forward. Accordingly, in January 1985 Reagan declined the Dachau concentration camp segment of the invitation commenting,

> I don't think we ought to focus on the past. I want to focus on the future... I want to put that history behind me.

Yet a month later, White House staffers approved a presidential visit to the Kolmeshöhe Military Cemetary in Bitburg, West Germany. On March 21st, President Reagan attempted to clarify his earlier comments regarding his decision to not visit Dachau,

> I feel very strongly that... instead of reawakening the memories... we should observe this day when, forty years ago, peace began.... [the German people] have a guilt feeling that's been imposed upon them, and I just think it's unnecessary.

How the president reconciled in his own mind the contradictions inherent in his desire to look ahead to the future while visiting a military cemetary, though not a concentration camp, was never made clear. It is probably most accurate to conclude that he was merely peddling an extremely cynical brand of *realpolitik*.

In April, amid increasingly vocal protests by American veterans and Jewish groups concerning the Bitburg visit, news reports revealed that the cemetary contained 1,887 graves -- 49 of which were of Waffen-SS personnel. Now the additional stigma of the SS was added to an already volatile mix. In fact, over the next few weeks leading up to Reagan's cemetery visit, the presence of the Waffen-SS graves became *the* symbolic crux of the whole affair. The role of the Waffen-SS in the Nazi regime and their numerous crimes were revisited by the press while a handful of defenders trotted out well-worn protestations concerning their innocence. In response to growing and unexpectedly vehement public pressure, the White House belatedly added a stop at the Bergen-Belsen concentration camp to the official trip itinerary. This change, an afterthought at best, did little to mollify detractors. The U.S. Senate registered its own disapproval of the upcoming cemetary visit by passing a resolution recommending that the president reassess his travel itinerary. The trip, however, went forward as planned though dogged by protestors every step of the way.

On the morning of May 5, President Reagan and Chancellor Kohl laid a wreath at Bergen-Belsen concentration camp. The president then gave a short speech full of abstractions which placed all responsibility and guilt for the evils committed by Germany during the Second World War squarely on the shoulders of just one man, Adolf Hitler. Hitler's supporters, in Reagan's view, were innocent and unwilling victims just like those who died at Bergen-Belsen. The leaders then went on to Bitburg where a brief wreath-laying ceremony took place. Whatever the long-term cost to his image, President Reagan had distorted history in a successful attempt at pandering to West German public and political opinion. On his end of this *quid pro quo*, Chancellor Kohl had little difficulty gaining the right-wing backing needed to allow the installation of new U.S. missiles on West German soil and in support of the "Stars Wars" proposal.

President Reagan had originally journeyed to Bitburg as a symbol of U.S./West German reconciliation in order to benefit two unrelated defense initiatives. Yet his visit became symbolic of much more than that. To some, the Bitburg visit was merely a regrettable misunderstanding that had been inflated into a *cause celebre* by misguided social activists. To many others, the visit was a reminder of the all too-human tendency to dismiss the particulars of history, to rewrite or reinterpret historical facts for political and emotional reasons, as well as to distance ourselves from past horrors by sentimentalizing them out of mind. In this regard it is significant that President Reagan chose the following quote from Anne Frank's diaries during his speech at the Bergen-Belsen camp: "In spite of everything I still believe that people are really good at heart." At best, the President would seemingly have us forget the horrors of Bergen-Belsen in favor of an almost maudlin, and ultimately mistaken, boundless optimism regarding the nature of humanity. At its worst, his choice exemplified a species of cynical opportunism that was willing to trade on the historical ignorance and flawed critical thinking of the public in service of a purely political goal. In so doing, Reagan's visit, with its motives clouded by historical denial, was a source of significant comfort to revisionists in general and Waffen-SS apologists in particular.

Waffen-SS Veterans

Since 1950 the German government under its "Social Compensation and Assistance to War Victims" law (Bundesversorgungsgesetz) had treated any veteran injured during the Second World War as a victim eligible for compensation. Early in 1996 the minority liberal Greens Party submitted a question before the Bundestag (parliament) opposing the continued payment of pensions to suspected and proven war criminals. According to German government figures, approximately 50,000 SS veterans (including an unspecified number of Waffen-SS veterans) were receiving such pensions. In most cases the pensions amounted to $560 per month, or approximately three times the reparations paid by the German government to victims of the Holocaust. While veterans qualified for benefits by simply proving a war injury, concentration camp survivors had to prove that they were interned for at least six months before being considered eligible for reparation payments.

This latest chapter in the saga of the Waffen-SS received worldwide exposure at the end of 1996 when the Reuters news service revealed that numerous Waffen-SS veterans, including suspected and convicted war criminals, were living throughout the Western world and receiving pensions from the German government. From as early as 1945 on, U.S. security and intelligence services had protected potentially useful Nazi war criminals and collaborators. They were primarily used in counter-insurgency, assassination and intelligence gathering projects.[2] Subsequent investigations revealed that in 1950 Canada accepted some 2,000 former members of the notorious 14. Waffen-

Grenadier-Division der SS (ukrainische Nr. 1) after the British government declared that each individual had been cleared of any involvement in war crimes. In fact, no such investigations had ever taken place -- British authorities at the time simply lied in order to get these detainees off their hands. Under pressure from the British government and the Ukrainian community in Canada, the Waffen-SS men were allowed to emigrate despite laws prohibiting the entry of any SS members into Canada. By 1955, former SS personnel were routinely receiving waivers to emigrate to Canada without a background check. The U.S. Justice Department's Office of Special Investigations (OSI) has estimated that 10,000 Waffen-SS veterans also entered the United States from 1950 to 1955 when the Displaced Persons Commission relaxed regulations with regard to non-Germanic SS personnel. Most of these emigrees were nationals from the Baltic States and the Ukraine whose Nazi pasts were forgiven since they were considered to be staunch anti-Communists. The most recent accounting of Waffen-SS veterans residing ouside of Germany gave the following breakdown:[3]

Australia	601
England	459
Austria	1,115
France	810
Argentina	128
Italy	152
Belgium	324
Romania	1,014
Brazil	196
Slovenia	2,380
Canada	1,882
South Africa	152
Croatia	1,010
U.S.A.	3,377

Throughout 1997, the World Jewish Congress and other organizations called on the German government to make public the names of those Waffen-SS pensioners residing in the United States so that the OSI could determine whether or not they were legal immigrants and/or wanted for war crimes. The German Labor Ministry which had responsibility for pension administration, however, insisted that a release of such information would violate Germany's strict laws on data protection. Ministry spokesmen sought to reassure critics that war criminals were not receiving pension payments since background checks had been made with various German archives concerning an applicant's wartime activities before a pension was granted. A spokesman for the Zentrale Stelle der Landesjustizverwaltungen (Germany's main investigation center on Nazi crimes) in Ludwigsburg, however, denied that pension details were ever systematically checked against records of known and suspected war criminals. It was later verified by independent investigators that several well-known war criminals were receiving pensions (e.g., Heinz Barth [Oradour-sur-Glane] and Wilhelm Mohnke [numerous, including Malmedy]). The German government eventually relented and sent the U.S. Justice Department a list of the Waffen-SS veterans living in the U.S. In November 1997 pension payments to veterans suspected of war crimes were finally cut off by the German government despite legal actions threatened by several recipients. Meanwhile, Canadian and U.S. authorities stepped up efforts to locate Waffen-SS war criminals for deportation to Germany.

Another ongoing dilemma regarding Waffen-SS veterans revolves around the emotional issue of military unit reunions. Since the early 1950s numerous Waffen-SS reunions have occurred in various towns throughout Germany. Despite often vociferous public protest, such gatherings have continued undisturbed up to the present day with the participants scrupulously abiding by Germany's stringent laws banning the display of Nazi emblems and regalia. Ironically, the most recent reunion to garner condemnation by Jewish groups did not even occur in Germany. In March 1998, approximately 500 former Latvian Waffen-SS members held a 55th anniversary reunion in the Latvian capital, Riga. The gathering was part of a two-day celebration commemorating the formation of the Latvian Legion, a German-sponsored Latvian military auxiliary that fought against the Soviets in the Second World War. A year later the Latvian Parliament declared March 16 as a national day of remembrance for Latvian soldiers. Another storm of protest erupted as the date also marked the founding of the Latvian Legion. Such protests seemingly accomplished little: the Latvian Waffen-SS veterans have marched through the streets of

Riga every year since 1998. It would not be surprising to see future reunions in other former Eastern Bloc countries (Estonia, Lithuania, Ukraine, Romania, etc.) given the number of personnel these nations supplied to the Waffen-SS.

Waffen-SS Counter-culture

One of Nazism's lasting triumphs was its masterful manipulation of imagery. Its dark pageantry continues to beguile a wide range of personality types with its creed of superiority and a life free from standard moral and ethical restraints. It is hardly surprising then that, in addition to Internet websites glorifying the Waffen-SS, there also exists a diffuse, overwhelmingly male underground Waffen-SS counter-culture in the United Kingdom and United States. It is primarily exemplified by a marked interest in, and often an open adoration of, the Waffen-SS. Thus, we have the spectacle of :

1) Retailers offering Waffen-SS divisional insignia T-shirts, expensive tailor-made replica uniforms (any rank and unit you desire), badges and other clothing items. This trend has been extended to custom-made uniforms for GI-Joe style action figures. One dealer even supplies an authentic recreation of SS-Obergruppenführer Reinhard Heydrich's uniform for those who wish to transform their GI-Joe into the "Butcher of Prague" himself.

2) World War II historical reenactment groups that specialize in portraying the Leibstandarte Adolf Hitler (1st), Das Reich (2nd), Wiking (5th), Hohenstaufen (9th), Frundsberg (10th), Hitlerjugend (12th) and Götz von Berlichingen (17th) divisions. Although denying that they glorify the Waffen-SS and National Socialism, the content and tenor of their promotional materials often seems to belie such claims. These groups are viewed with suspicion, or even considered to be pariahs, by other German-themed reenactment groups who inform interested parties that they unequivocally "don't do SS." Recently, a number of former SS reenactors have admitted they left the hobby due to the growing number and influence of neo-Nazis in their ranks.

3) The "re-establishment" of a Waffen-SS division as represented by the Bosnian government's 6,000-man strong *Handzar* division formed in 1993 out of Bosnian, Albanian and Afghani Muslims. The unit stresses connections to its precursor (13. Waffen-Gebirgs-Division der SS *Handschar* [kroatische Nr. 1]) and has quickly earned a reputation of brutality toward non-Muslim civilians.

4) The glut of Waffen-SS related items in the worlds of scale-modeling and wargaming. Their representation in these fields is clearly out of all proportion to both their actual presence and scale of military contributions during the Second World War.

5) The growing popularity among military history buffs of collecting authentic Waffen-SS insignia, uniforms, autographs, souvenirs and other memorabilia.

6) The wholesale adoption of the Waffen-SS by a broad spectrum of the American and European extreme right as **the** elite military force of the white race. For example, the last three years in Budapest has seen an annual commemorative march and wreath-laying by thousands of uniformed European neo-nazis, skinheads, and racial nationalists in honor of the Waffen-SS men who died defending the city against the Soviets in 1945.

Perhaps concern over these trends is overblown or misplaced. Certainly, with regard to the worlds of scale modeling, wargaming and memorabilia collecting, the line between a person merely being titillated by a fearsome reputation and actually feeling psychically drawn to the same is an uncertain one. It is feared by some observers, however, that such developments are all serious indications of the seemingly inevitable attraction that evil holds for a significant portion of humanity. That the Waffen-SS, despite its record of atrocities and association with Hitler's regime, can still generate such fascination should certainly give us considerable pause for thought.

Notes:
1. *Augstein et al., 1987; Evans, 1989; Maier, 1988.*
2. *Lee, 1997; Simpson, 1988.*
3. *"Outrage....", 1997.*

Excuses for War Crimes

The process of systematically examining and refuting the claims of Waffen-SS defenders requires that their multi-faceted arguments be carefully separated and analyzed in a somewhat artificially reductive manner. Many revisionist statements overlap or parallel one another; among some no clear boundary can be established. When a defense strategy revolves around invoking as many competing explanations as possible, even to the point of contradicting and undercutting their own thesis (see Theile [1997] as a prime example), the benefits of rational examination can seem doubtful. Nevertheless, even the most absurd propaganda should not go uncorrected or else the reliability of the historical database will become increasingly compromised. Whether an author is simply naive, uninformed, or driven by unscrupulous motives, their efforts are much the same: to dust off the same tired excuses in a futile attempt to dispel the sinister face of the Waffen-SS.

Charney has developed an extremely useful "template for denial of a known genocide" which neatly summarizes the twelve statements that comprise the backbone of Holocaust denial.[1] It is equally applicable to the strategies pursued by Waffen-SS apologists.

1) Do not acknowledge the genocide.

2) Direct denials should not be attributed to goverment or high leaders, only to functionaries and anonymous spokesmen.

3) Deny the facts of the genocide by transforming them into other kinds of events.

4) Picture the perpetrators and perhaps others as victims, and if at all possible charge the victims with being perpetrators, or at the least make them less victims than the others.

5) Not only deny outright the claims of genocide, but proceed to advance counterclaims that the victims received good treatment.

6) Insist for as long as possible that the full data are not available, or that facts of the alleged genocide are forgeries and hoaxes, and that further research is needed and/or that new research disproves the claims of the genocide.

7) Question the statistics so that the number of dead victims is far smaller than usually stated.

8) Move from the facts of the genocide to some kind of relativism that mitigates the horror of the events.

9)Describe the victims as strangers -- physically and/or emotionally different from the familiar or dominant ethnicity, so that it will not be natural to identify with the victims.

10)Describe the victims as unattractive, problematic,if possible cruel or dangerous people, and rationalize the deaths as an inevitable logical consequence given the nature of the people and their history.

11)Distance the event -- it all happened so long ago, there is a new generation of the (perpetrator) people today, why not let wounds heal?

12) Justify not antagonizing the successor people to those who committed the genocide by the real politik of today.

As is apparent from their writings, Waffen-SS defenders have adopted this basic structure for their own needs to such an extent that their arguments can accurately be characterized as a sub-set of mainstream Holocaust denial. They are especially prone to employ statements 1, 3, 4, 6, 7, 8, 9, and 10 in their attempts to revise history. The explanations which follow all clearly fall within the bounds of Charney's denial template.

Superior Orders and Fear of Retribution

One of the primary defenses claimed by virtually all suspected war criminals, regardless of time period, is that they were merely simple soldiers following the orders of their immediate superiors ("Respondeat Superior" defense) or enacting governmental policies ("Act of State" defense). It was not their place to determine whether any particular request of them was criminal in nature or intent. Thus, all of the moral and legal culpability for their actions lay with either their immediate commanding officer or some other official higher up in the organizational structure. As noted previously, the IMT and virtually all subsequent post-war tribunals -- on the basis of prior international agreements explicit on this point -- vigorously rejected such arguments stressing that the responsibility for war crimes lay equally among those who issue illegal orders and those who carry them out. Soldiers are not expected to behave like automatons and it is a widespread fallacy that they are required to mindlessly obey all of their superior officer's orders.

Often the auxiliary defense that the individual followed an illegal order out of fear of retribution is also offered. The "fear of retribution" defense was especially popular among Waffen-SS defendants despite the fact that no historical evidence supports such a claim. Evidence indicates that while the SS usually dealt arbitrarily and harshly with others, it displayed a tendency towards leniency for its own personnel, who were after all ideological equals. In fact, there is no evidence of any proceedings against Waffen-SS personnel who refused to follow orders involving the commission of war crimes. Such claims are self-serving, post-war inventions that seek to capitalize on the generally accurate and widely-accepted image of the Third Reich as a brutal regime. For example, at the post-war Einsatzgruppen Trial several former unit commanders claimed that they had unwillingly accepted their assignments out of a fear for their lives. Original documentation and testimony of witnesses before the NMT, however, indicated that when the leadership positions of the Einsatzgruppen were being filled all potential candidates were informed that participation was strictly voluntary. Many officers accepted the postings that were offered to curry favor with their immediate superiors. Several individuals who could not overcome their moral qualms about leading an extermination unit declined to participate and did not suffer any negative consequences in either their personal or professional lives.

Buchheim has carefully studied the various alternatives that SS personnel had available to them with regard to "mandatory orders."[2] He pointed out that orders did not need to be openly refused in order to be rendered ineffective. Rather, SS personnel could pursue one of three options: plead mental, moral or physical incapability; raise practical objections to continually delay the execution of the order (the 'Yes - but' method); or quietly evade the order. The main obstacle to all of these methods of resistance lay in the fact that by joining the SS, or any other National Socialist formation, individuals had "freely given their ideological assent and so placed themselves under a degree of compulsion." In fact, the SS heirarchy recognized that by the very fact of their voluntary commitment to the organization, SS personnel were making themselves available for ideological tasks that lay outside the bounds of an average citizen's required duties to the state (*i.e.*, extermination actions). Complicating the situation even further was the fact that previous orders carried out by individuals without resistance made them increasingly liable to receive orders they might wish to evade in the future. For after participating in questionable activities, it became increasingly difficult to extricate oneself from the situation yet correspondingly easier to rationalize and justify such actions. Thus, Waffen-SS personnel were largely in a trap of their own making whose compliance mechanisms were social pressure and the demand for ideological steadfastness. To refuse an order did not place one's life at risk, but instead might jeopardize one's standing in the ideological community.

Immoral Equivalence -- "No One Has Clean Hands"

Perhaps the oldest rationalization of all for committing atrocities is the claim that every nation's armed forces are equally guilty of such acts during wartime. This is paralleled by the often cited adage that what *everyone* does is acceptable and excusable behavior. Lipstadt has termed such a defense to be that of "immoral equivalences -- everybody did something wrong and all should be equally punished... there is no moral distinction between combatants."[3] Thus, Waffen-SS apologists point to a wide-ranging spectrum of Western Allied and Soviet war crimes to support their contention of immoral equivalence: the Allied strategic-bombing offensives, post-war population transfers in central and eastern Europe, the brutality of Soviet occupation forces in eastern Germany, the murder of Waffen-SS troopers by Allied and Soviet forces, as well as the atomic bombings of Hiroshima and Nagasaki. Extreme propagandists, such as Landwehr (1985), go even further and categorically state that the wartime record of the Waffen-SS was cleaner than that of its enemies. Such a defense and the principal question it raises -- *Who's behavior was worse?* -- compels us to establish comparisons among putative war crimes. Are some acts more brutal and more criminal than others? Is there any substantive difference between killing hundreds, thousands, tens of thousands, or millions of innocent civilians? How do the records of the Western Allied and Soviet armies in this regard compare with those of the German Wehrmacht, and the Waffen-SS in particular?

Clearly, those whose moral and ethical senses have not been impaired can agree in principle that some acts are more brutal than others and some motivations may be more criminal than others. Contrition about our own failings, however, should not be allowed to obliterate moral distinctions. International law has consistently ruled that the commission of a crime by one party in a conflict does not exonerate a second party for the same crime, even if carried out in revenge. Thus, the defense of immoral equivalence is legally hollow at its core. It does not aim to clarify the genesis, nature, and consequences of atrocity, but merely distorts real phenomenological differences that exist among activities spanning a continuum stretching from individual killings to genocide. Ultimately, such distortions are employed by revisionists to mitigate unique aspects of Nazi criminality, making it appear to be another variant in the long history of "normal" wartime excesses. Yet there are few modern equivalents for some of the crimes committed by the Third Reich (*e.g.*, Khmer Rouge genocide in Cambodia, 1970s).

Despite claims to the contrary, documentary evidence from the Second World War also makes it clear that there were substantial differences between the Western Allies and the Germans respecting the scale, frequency, duration, premeditation, organizational planning, and, perhaps most importantly, intent of the war crimes committed by each side. The infrequent crimes committed by Western Allied forces (with the significant exception of their strategic air operations) are dwarfed by the monumental scale of the excesses visited by the Germans upon their European neighbors. There is no doubt that many units of the Waffen-SS willingly took part in a variety of these excesses. That these profound differences between the major combatants is even questioned in light of the evidence attests to the intellectual dishonesty and cynical agenda of many revisionists. Additionally, there is only limited parallelism between acts of warfare with military objectives such as aerial bombardment and the premeditated killing of civilians unrelated to the pursuit of military objectives. Whatever our moral reservations may be concerning the Allied strategic air offensive (and they should be considerable), its goal was to destroy Germany's war machine and ostensibly not to punish her people. Similarly, the Allied saturation bombing of German defenses around the city of Caen during the Normandy campaign that resulted in thousands of French civilian deaths was fundamentally different in nature than the reprisal actions of the Waffen-SS at Oradour-sur-Glane. The atomic bombings of Hiroshima and Nagasaki, while indefensible, criminal acts tainted by racial and political overtones in the view of many, were still not the phenomenological equivalents of Nazi genocidal activities in Europe. The crucial difference, unpalatable though it may be, is that:

> Bombing deaths are buffered by the all-important factor of distance. They represent an impersonal act of war in which specific deaths are unintended... Execution of civilians is, on the other hand, a highly personal act of psychotic irrationality that openly refutes the humanity of the victims. So what is the difference? Ultimately, the difference is distance. [4]

There are a number of known instances where Western Allied ground troops murdered significant numbers of unarmed opponents (*e.g.*, in Sicily, Normandy, and the Ardennes). One of the worst atrocities by Allied ground troops in Europe was committed against the Waffen-SS itself. On 29 April 1945 more than 520

Waffen-SS troopers were executed in and around Dachau concentration camp by members of 3rd Battalion / 157th Infantry Regiment / U.S. 45th Infantry Division (battalion CO: Lt. Col. Felix Sparks). The sad irony was that the SS troopers had been brought in only a day or two earlier so that the concentration camp guards could escape into the countryside. Most of these recent combat veterans were wounded and had to be rousted out of their hospital beds prior to being murdered by the Americans. [5] Even in the Pacific Theater fighting with its subtext of racial hatred, the higher rate of Allied criminality still did not approach that of the Axis forces. By comparison, the combat behavior of the Wehrmacht[6] and the Waffen-SS was notable for its brutality and consistent pattern of intentional violation of war crimes agreements to which Germany was a signatory nation.

As far as the Eastern Front is concerned, both German and Soviet armed forces ignored the accepted conventions of warfare from the very outbreak of hostilities. There is no doubt again, however, that the overwhelmingly greater share of guilt rests with the Germans. In their conduct of an ideological war of extermination and projected future population resettlement, the Germans massacred millions of civilians and laid waste to whole regions of the Soviet Union as a matter of official policy. Given such extreme barbarism on the part of the invading German forces, it was sadly inevitable that the Soviets responded in kind, both in defending their homeland and during their advance into eastern Germany. Those apologists who invoke the specter of Soviet atrocities in eastern Germany would do well to remember that these crimes were but a shadow of the horrors that Germany visited upon the Soviet Union. Nonetheless, as was true with the Western Allies, the Soviet's motivation was not to exterminate their enemy, but rather to defeat and punish them. The Soviet's crimes, perhaps, are an explicable, though unacceptable, byproduct of their suffering. As noted previously, international conventions do not consider revenge to be an extenuating circumstance in the commission of war crimes.

War is Hell

Even more fundamental than the idea of immoral equivalence is the defense that, given the nature of warfare, it is incredibly naive to expect combat troops to respect the high-minded principles of various international conventions. These commonly accepted laws are simply irrelevant to the conduct of warfare. War itself is inherently evil and to assign blame for specific incidents is morally and ethically suspect. In fact, the very concepts of "war crime" and "war crimes trials" are thoroughly invalid, nonsensical, and contradictory. While there is a consensus on what constitutes acceptable behavior for military personnel, this cannot reasonably be compared to peacetime standards of conduct. While the immoral equivalence defense argues that we should not draw distinctions regarding the behavior of individuals in wartime, this argument posits that such distinctions do not exist. Thus, all aspects of combat behavior, however extreme, are inescapable and eternal manifestations of warfare. Additionally, in wartime extenuating circumstances are the order of the day and critics who are not veterans have no basis for their opinions:

> That the war on the Eastern Front was brutalising there is no doubt and one cannot but help repeat Max Wünsche's comment that no one who had not fought on it could have any conception what it was like. Those who wish to moralise on it are on weak ground if they have no personal experience of it. [7]

If the opinions of those who have not "walked the walk" are invalid, then ultimately only the Waffen-SS troopers are in a position to judge their own actions.

All of these contentions are patently false, self-serving, as well as morally and spiritually corrosive. They represent the worst sort of intellectual abdication which holds that, "It has always been like this, always will be like this."[8] Such circular rationalizations exist solely to promote ethical vacuums wherein men are transformed into murderers by their willingness to sacrifice everything for a cause. All societies, in an effort to promote their safety and stability, have invariably chosen to carefully restrict the activities of their members through the establishment and enforcement of innumerable codes, laws, and proscriptions. The very relevance of such regulations decreases as they are flouted with impunity or officially circumvented by governmental authorities. The existence of internationally-accepted conventions regulating armed conflicts between states indicates that societies have recognized the need to strictly limit military operations to those actions deemed essential to warfare. Atrocities of the sort detailed in this volume have never been considered essential conduct. The fact that international laws may be flawed, ignored, or only imperfectly enforced testifies not to their inherent impraticality, but rather to the flawed nature of humanity itself. The rules of war are a thin line of rationality attempting to hold at bay cthonic forces that threaten to overwhelm both the individual and the nation-state alike. The notion that those of us who (thankfully) have not been thrust into the crucible of war have no grounds on which to moralize about wartime behaviors seems, at first glance, a fair criticism. But only at first glance, for the kinds of atrocities considered here are clearly horrific criminal activities *independent* of one's own life experience or any specific context. There can never be an extenuating circumstance, excuse or explanation for crowding women and children into a church and blowing it up as Waffen-SS personnel did on a number of occasions. To concede this point would be giving our tacit approval to the most heinous of activities. For if we are able to rationalize or relativize the massacre of innocents, is there anything which we will not accept? Judging from their wartime behavior, a significant portion of the Waffen-SS had reached just such a spiritual nadir where all was permitted and nothing forbidden.

War Crimes Trials as "Victor's Justice"

Another common defense offered by Waffen-SS defenders of every persuasion is the argument that post-war tribunals, the IMT and NMT in particular, were no more than cynical, legally-baseless exercises in "victor's justice." Solely as a result of losing the war, Germany and her people were tried and punished for assorted crimes as defined by her conquerors. Numerous volumes have been written on the injustice of the Allied war crimes tribunals. It is also usually argued that no state has the right to try an enemy national for the violation of *ex post facto* laws (literally "after the fact": laws non-existant at the time of the purported crime's occurrence). If any investigations and trials are deemed necessary,

they should be carried out by neutral third parties or by the restored authorities of the defeated nation itself.

The basis of the "victor's justice" argument is rooted in two fallacious notions: 1) that the necessary trials would be held if the defendant nation prevailed in the conflict, and 2) that the crimes of an individual nation should not be subject to censure since all nations commit atrocities. The first point is an obvious attempt to distract our attention from the real issues involved. Obviously, if the Allied powers had not won the Second World War there would have been no prosecution of Axis war criminals. An unbowed and victorious Nazi regime certainly would not have tried any of its personnel for their role in state-sponsored crimes. In fact, Germany's previous failure to prosecute its WWI war criminals emphasizes this very point. The second notion is merely a recapitulation of the specious idea that there existed an "immoral equivalence" between the conduct of the Allied and Axis forces (see previous section). The real question being dodged by revisionists is whether or not Germany's actions during the war merited the judgment they received.

Whether the Allied powers had the legal right to hold war crimes trials is besides the point considering the scope and nature of German criminality. The legal foundation of the IMT and other tribunals was certainly not *ex post facto*, but rather firmly established in numerous long standing traditions, international conventions, military directives, and national criminal codes. Critics of the trials allege that they significantly lowered normal civil legal standards with regards to rules of evidence and the imposition of death sentences. Generally speaking, no evidence was excluded (including hearsay) if it was thought to have a bearing on the proceedings. Unlike civil trials, a unanimous decision was not required for the defendant to be executed on a capital charge. Despite these and other less weighty criticisms, experience has shown that the Allied tribunals were the only reasonable mechanism for dealing with the war crimes problem given the prevailing circumstances in post-war Europe.

Many revisionists have declared that the Germans should have been given the exclusive responsibility to "clean their own house" after the war. As previously demonstrated, however, the record of the West German courts when afforded the opportunity to prosecute war crimes cases was anything but impressive. As critics have noted,

> The country's legal system is complicated and legal matters are conducted with an unusual adherence to the letter of the law..... the West Germans have consistently failed to convict the most barbarous war criminals, even when the evidence against them, by the legal standards of any other civilized nation, was overwhelming. They have also persistently failed to prosecute suspected war criminals on the grounds of insufficient documentary and other evidence, even when such evidence could be made readily available to them. And they have persistently failed to take action against war criminals deported from other countries... [9]

Complicating matters even further was West Germany's constitutional ban on the deportation of its citizens previously convicted of war crimes by the country's courts. When coupled with the demonstrated leniency of the West German judicial system, it resulted in allowing most war criminals to escape with a minor rebuke for their murderous activities. Here lie the roots of the collective guilt imposed on Germans for the crimes of the Nazi era. Instead of properly judging and casting out the perpetrators of these crimes, the Germans ignored, forgave, and then finally reintegrated them back into their communities in the first decade following war's end.

"Neutral" History

Another strategy common to apologists is to passionately call for a "neutral" approach to history so that all "historical falsehoods" may be uncovered and suitably discredited. While certainly reasonable sounding enough, in practice this tactic results in the creation of an artificially relativized playing field. Even though there may exist a preponderance of evidence in favor of a particular conclusion, rational examination is set aside in favor of a post-modern deconstructionist dialectic wherein all sides of an argument are accorded equal and unchanging weight. The apologists's arguments, however, are invariably accorded a *more equal*

weight in a fashion recalling the Orwellian dictum that "all pigs are equal, it's just that some are more equal than others." Among Waffen-SS apologists this tactic finds concrete expression in the frequent practice of citing the writings of former Waffen-SS commanders such as Paul Hausser, Georg Keppler, Felix Steiner, and Otto Weidinger as "neutral" sources, while the testimony of surviving victims and actual documentation of crimes is denigrated as being hostile or biased. Yerger exemplified this approach in the acknowledgements section of a recent publication,

> Otto Weidinger taught me to be an objective and neutral historian void of political opinion. He was my confidant, friend and the person I've admired most in my lifetime so his inspiration will never be forgotten. [10]

After such a glowing tribute to a former Waffen-SS divisional commander implicated in a number of war crimes, does the author seriously expect us to believe that he can function as anything but an apologist for, and promoter of, the Waffen-SS and its ideals?

Like many former Waffen-SS members, most current revisionists prefer to write documentary studies professing historical objectivity rather than honestly acknowledging and wrestling with the conflicts of interest inherent in their work. For example, Blandford (1995) excoriates a whole host of unnamed researchers for not doing impartial research on the Waffen-SS, yet it is apparent from the thin substance and shoddy argumentation of his work that, far from being a neutral expert, he is merely the latest apologist to come along. The contrast between the methods of historical examination and those of revisionism could not be clearer,

> The historian does not create, the historian uncovers. The validity of a historical interpretation is determined by how well it accounts for the facts. Though the historian's role is to act as a neutral observer   trying to follow the facts, there is increasing recognition that the historian brings to this enterprise his or   her own values and biases. Consequently there is no such thing as value-free

history. However, even the historian with a particular bias is dramatically different from the proponents of these pseudoreasoned ideologies [*Ed. -- revisionists*]. The latter freely shape or create information to buttress their convictions and reject as implausible any evidence that counters them. They use the language of scientific inquiry, but theirs is a purely ideological enterprise. [11]

As noted in the preceding quote, another method universally employed by revisionists to arrive at their "neutral" history is to reject any documentation that does not support their preconceived notions. Yerger (1996) is a prime example. His history of the SS-Kavallerie-Brigade, while fabulously detailed with regard to the unit's formation, structure and leadership, lacks any information concerning the unit's well-documented and extensive record of atrocities during operations in the USSR. The author appears to be relying on the fact that the average reader will not have the requisite knowledge of the subject to realize that he is presenting a highly sanitized and misleading account of the brigade's history.

Denying and Obfuscating Evidence

While the previously-examined "neutral" history defense is primarily based on the unfair weighting of evidence and an ignorance of evidence (whether active or passive), this tactic of apologists functions exclusively through the violent distortion and/or denial of evidence on an as-needed basis. If an incident cannot be dismissed entirely out of hand, then the facts surrounding it can be twisted to cast doubt on the veracity of the atrocity claim. Truth is combined with lies, half-truths, and fictional embellishments in a mixture designed to confuse the unwary and leave them with an erroneous impression of the actual events. Documentary evidence and oral testimony unfavorable to or impugning the Waffen-SS are quickly dismissed as frauds and falsehoods. Most revisionists, to varying degrees, employ such methodology when examining Waffen-SS criminality. Blandford (1995) and Theile (1997), for example, spare no effort in their attempts to undercut well-documented atrocities such as those that occurred at Boves, Klisoura, Lahoysk, Le Paradis, Malmedy, Monte Sol, Oradour-sur-Glane, and Tulle.

As previously noted, Waffen-SS defenders rely on the fact that most readers have neither the time nor the resources to determine if they have been presented with "edited" information. An excessive amount of time and resources should not be wasted, however, in responding to contentions based upon a denial of the historical record. Such arguments quickly develop a closed-loop nature as the revisionist switches their focus or denies and distorts additional evidence in order to refashion their case anew. In such instances, it is the very speciousness of the arguments, rather than the arguments themselves, that requires a response.[12]

Our Actions Were Legal / The Victims Deserved It

If it is possible to single out one particular argument of Waffen-SS defenders as the most cynical and repugnant this is assuredly it. When in doubt, blame the victims of a crime. The Waffen-SS is innocent of any criminality since its victims were actually subversives, spies, saboteurs, criminals, or unfortunates caught up in the conduct of internationally legal reprisals.

> The glorious fight of the partisans was nothing more than mean common murder. The intellectual originators of partisan war were the real criminals. They acted against all humanity and appealed to the lowest of instincts... Without the perfidious actions of the 'brave' partisans there would have been no cause for 'war crimes trials'. [13]

Of course, if the Germans had not invaded neighboring countries then partisan activities would have been unnecessary. Additionally, even partisan forces were technically supposed to be afforded various protections contained in both the Hague Convention (Article I) and Wehrmacht regulations.

In the revisionist texts I have examined, this "pass the blame" defense has frequently been used as a justification for the slaughter of civilian non-combatants deemed expendable by either the occupation authorities or the individual units themselves. Ironically, this rationale is almost always applied *ex post facto* to incidents for which no other explanation exists. Since the documented facts of these cases don't support the revisionists' claims (*e.g.*, the *Dhistomon* and *Oradour-*

sur-Glane atrocities), unsubstantiated "testimonial evidence" is invariably created as needed to vindicate the Waffen-SS. Thus, we are treated to fantastic tales of rural villages literally bursting with concealed ammunition caches and fanatic partisans. In such circumstances the beleaguered Waffen-SS troopers are invariably compelled by their enemies to execute every inhabitant down to the last bedridden invalid and unweaned child.

Guilt by Association

Many Waffen-SS defenders feel that critics have overstated their case against the organization as a result of intense prejudice against it. Rather than accepting the Waffen-SS for what it was (another branch of the German Armed forces), critics have unfairly stigmatized these soldiers with the same loathing reserved for Nazism in general. This is a grave disservice to men who bravely served their country and had no part in the numerous crimes of the Third Reich.

> The final tragedy of the Waffen-SS is that, in the name of the anti-Communist crusade, hundreds of thousands of Germans and foreign volunteers, most of them decent men, unwittingly helped to sustain a regime that killed six million Jews and millions of other peoples. They paid for the crimes of the criminals by forever being linked to the concentration camp spectre, even though most of them fought on the front lines and never committed any war crimes. Guilt by association was the verdict handed down at Nuremberg. It is not up to this author to judge the fairness or unfairness of that. [14]

Despite his statement to the contrary, Munoz obviously feels that the Nuremberg condemnation of the Waffen-SS was unfair. Yet, as has been previously demonstrated in numerous criminal trials as well as the present publication, the Waffen-SS was an integral part of the Third Reich and committed hundreds of atrocities, both of its own accord and as part of state-sanctioned genocidal operations (see Appendix D). In fact, only nine (18%) of the major Waffen-SS units under consideration in this volume

appear to have a clean record with respect to war crimes. The historical record is clear on the guilt of the Waffen-SS to everyone but its defenders. This is not guilt by association, but as a direct result of their actions. Since a significant portion of Waffen-SS activities were criminal and were undertaken by a sizable portion of its membership it is fair to apply such a characterization to the organization in its entirety. There is, however, a separate burden of guilt by association that the Waffen-SS does and indeed should bear. After all, as the military and ideological elite of the Third Reich they fought for the duration of the war in active and informed support of one of the most criminal governments in recent history. How could there not be levied a justified guilt by association on those individuals who voluntarily became both the symbolic and physical embodiment of National Socialism's principles in action?

Collective Guilt

In some ways the arguments of "collective guilt" and "guilt by association" are two sides of the same coin. To many of its defenders, the Waffen-SS has been unfairly judged complicitous in the crimes of the Third Reich. In this section, however, I examine more specific theories of collective guilt and the illogical, misleading boundary-drawing that is often performed in order to exempt the Waffen-SS from a criminal classification. Revisionists offer three basic arguments: 1) the Waffen-SS was a fourth arm of the Wehrmacht only incidentally linked to the SS and its extermination apparatus; 2) the Waffen-SS was composed of numerous entities, each of which must be judged separately; and 3) atrocities were only committed by those Waffen-SS units having predominantly Volksdeutsche and/or non-Germanic elements.

The idea that the Waffen-SS was a fourth branch of the Wehrmacht and not really part of the SS after all is a very popular argument among revisionists. They attribute the evil reputation of the Waffen-SS to Himmler's unfortunate organizational scheme which conveys a supposedly misleading view of the SS power structure. Their aim is to permanently detach the Waffen-SS from its sinister organizational home (which included the concentration camp administration) and graft it onto the "innocent" Wehrmacht. Such an attempt is ironic given the Wehrmacht's own extensive record of war crimes.[6] The assertion that the Waffen-SS was not really a part of the SS is ludicrous. As Wegner has noted,

> ... the history of the Waffen-SS cannot be considered isolated from the history of the SS as a whole, which in its turn is inseparable from the story of national socialism. The political and ideological closeness of the Waffen-SS to national socialism was the precondition of its very existence... [15]

If the Waffen-SS cannot be successfully detached from the SS in general, then some revisionists will settle for disavowing any links between the Waffen-SS and the concentration camp system administered by the SS-WVHA. As usual, such claims conveniently ignore the copius evidence that explicitly demonstrates just such a linkage.[16] It is critical to note that SS organizational boundaries appearing to separate various sub-units were in practice extremely porous. During 1939-1940, for instance, fourteen SS-Totenkopfstandarten were used for repressive occupation duties that included the execution and/or deportation of innocent civilians throughout German-occupied territories. These regiments were later incorporated into the Waffen-SS during one of its many periods of expansion. There was also a continuous exchange of personnel between the Waffen-SS and the concentration camp system which fell under its administration. For example, by 1944 the Auschwitz extermination camp had transferred all of its personnel fit for front-line duty to Waffen-SS combat units.[17] From March 1942 through April 1945, approximately 45,000 Waffen-SS personnel served tours of duty at various concentration camps.[18] Nine of the twenty-eight original commanders of SS-Sonderkommandos detailed to "Einsatz Reinhardt", the extermination of Jews in the East, were Waffen-SS officers.[19] An especially grisly link is that between the Waffen-SS and the looted belongings of those exterminated at the Nazi death camps in Poland. A number of memos exist detailing shipments of looted razors, watches, and fountain pens being sent to specific front-line Waffen-SS units.[20] Furs confiscated from

murdered Jews were sent to SS clothing factories for refurbishment and use in Waffen-SS winter clothing. The distinction that is often drawn by revisionists between the Waffen-SS and the Einsatzgruppen is also a false one since virtually all of the "special action" units contained cadres of Waffen-SS personnel at the time of their formation and subsequently received wayward Waffen-SS men posted to them as a disciplinary measure. Finally, 45% of Waffen-SS divisions incorporated substantial numbers of personnel from known criminal units at some point in their existence, primarily at the time of their formation (see Appendix D). Despite these extensive inter-relations, propagandists such as Theile (1997) maintain that the Waffen-SS remained essentially uncontaminated despite having to take personnel from other SS entities.

In an attempt to rejuvenate the reputations of what are considered to be the "classic" Waffen-SS divisions (1. SS-Panzer-Division *Leibstandarte Adolf Hitler*, 2. SS-Panzer-Division *Das Reich*, 3. SS-Panzer-Division *Totenkopf*, 5. SS-Panzer-Division *Wiking*, 8. SS-Kavallerie-Division *Florian Geyer*, 9. SS-Panzer-Division *Hohenstaufen*, 10. SS-Panzer-Division *Frundsberg*, and 12. SS-Panzer-Division *Hitlerjugend*), revisionists often insist upon separating the Waffen-SS itself into several supposedly distinct entities. This is generally an attempt to compartmentalize those units of the Waffen-SS that are widely known to have particularly bad records with regard to atrocities. Williamson (1994), for example, suggests the following false distinctions: 1) Totenkopfstandarten, 2) "classic" divisions, 3) foreign volunteers, and 4) home front and rear-area units. Theile (1997) argues for an even more complex separation stating that the Totenkopfstandarten, SS-Polizei, and Einsatzgruppen were completely unrelated to the Waffen-SS. Such distinctions are contradicted by German documentary records and are merely convenient latter-day fictions. Having established such erroneous and unfounded distinctions, however, revisionists then proceed to vindicate the "classic" divisions at the expense of the bulk of the Waffen-SS. Interestingly enough, however, while the "classic" divisions comprise only 16% of the units under consideration in this present study, they committed 36% of the known atrocities (see Appendix D).

Occasionally, a revisionist will acknowledge Waffen-SS atrocities and attempt to shift the blame for them onto units containing a high percentage of Volksdeutsche (ethnic Germans from outside the Reich) or non-German personnel. That some of these "less germanic" units (*e.g.*, 7. SS-Freiwilligen-Gebirgs-Division *Prinz Eugen*) had horrendous records with regard to atrocities is not in dispute. It should be noted, however, that nearly all of these units had exclusively Reichsdeutsche (native German) command staffs and heavily Reichsdeutsche officer cadres. Additionally, as demonstrated throughout the present volume, the combat records of the primarily Reichsdeutsche-composed divisions are replete with crimes. The Reichsdeutsche 8. SS-Kavallerie-Division *Florian Geyer*, for example, clearly exceeded all other Waffen-SS divisions in the commission of atrocities. In fact, Reichsdeutsche Waffen-SS units committed 72% of the known atrocities while Volksdeutsche and foreign units accounted for the remaining 28% (see Appendix D). Clearly, the argument to reassign war crimes guilt onto certain ethnic, racial or national sub-sets of the Waffen-SS is an untenable one.

War Crimes Charges are Communist Propaganda

As an argument of last resort invariably employed by propagandists, this defense would have us discount all testimony, documentation, *etc.* sourced from certain Eastern European nations (Czechoslovakia, Hungary, Poland, Yugoslavia, and the Soviet Union). This is a very convenient defense since it was in these same countries that the Waffen-SS perpetrated the majority of its crimes. There is no defensible reason, however, to *a priori* disregard or view with suspicion evidence related to German war crimes available in eastern archives. In most instances the documents are German originals captured at war's end. The lengths to which some Waffen-SS propagandists will go is best illustrated by Theile's (1997) long-winded, tendentious presentation which summarily dismisses all "Communist evidence" of atrocities committed by the Waffen-SS as untrustworthy by definition. In a later argument employing the immoral equivalence defense,

however, the same author accepts without question North Korean and North Vietnamese claims of war crimes committed by American forces. Theile appears oblivious to the fact that his multi-layered defense of the Waffen-SS contains such a glaring internal contradiction. In an unusually candid passage of his memoirs Kurt Meyer, an unrepentant National Socialist and former Waffen-SS divisional commander, dismissed such disingenuous hand-waving,

> It would be silly to reject all the events with which we are charged by our former enemies as propaganda inventions... crimes happened. It is irrelevant to discuss the number of victims, the facts are incriminating enough. [21]

Despite such admonitions, propagandists continue to play the Communism card. Logusz (1997), for example, has promised to reveal in a future publication how "certain nations benefitted (or continue to benefit)" from war crimes allegations against the 14. Waffen-Grenadier-Division der SS (ukrainische Nr. 1) which was stationed exclusively on the Eastern Front during the war. The tenor of his writings seems to indicate that either the Poles, Jews or Communists (or perhaps all of them) will be blamed for the rash of "false" accusations against the division.

Notes:

1. *Charney, 1991, vol. 2, pp. 13-15.*
2. *In: Krausnick, 1968, pp. 305-396.*
3. *Lipstadt, 1993, p. 90.*
4. *Grossman, 1995, p. 106.*
5. *Buechner, 1986.*
6. *For a partial accounting of war crimes committed by the German Wehrmacht see Bartov, 1986; Central Commission, 1946-47; Cooper 1979; Datner, 1962; Hondros, 1983; IMT, 1948/1971; Mazower, 1993; Rossino, 1997; UNWCC, 1947-49; and Wiley, 1996.*
7. *Messenger, 1988, p. 211.*
8. *Levi, 1986, p. 144.*
9. *Sayer and Botting, 1989, p. 349.*
10. *Yerger, 1996, p. 4.*

11. *Lipstadt, 1993, pp. 25-26.*

12. *op. cit., p. 28.*

13. *Meyer, 1994, pp. 173-174.*

14. *Munoz, 1991, p. 302.*

15. *Wegner, 1990, pp. 360-361.*

16. *MacLean, 1999a.*

17. *Gutman and Berenbaum, 1994, pp. 283-284.*

18 *International Military Tribunal, 1948/1971, vol. 35, Documents D-745, D-746, D-747 and D-750.*

19. *Beförderungsliste für Angehörige der SS-Sonderkommandos 'Einsatz Reinhard' aus Befehl des RF-SS, reproduced in Sauer, 1977, pp. 63-64.*

20. *Komitee der, 1960, pp. 128-132.*

21. *Meyer, 1994, p. 230.*

Psychosocial Perspectives

The Psychology of Atrocity

Despite what we have been led to believe by political leaders and the media, numerous studies have shown that the combat performance of soldiers is usually not motivated by fear, hatred of the enemy, or ideological indoctrination. As Grossman (1995) noted, the primary motivational factors are group pressures and processes involving 1) regard for their comrades, 2) respect for their leaders, 3) concern for their own reputation with both, and 4) an urge to contribute to the success of the group. In his study of a German police battalion Browning (1992b) concluded that participation in extermination operations was determined by peer pressure, maintenance of a masculine self-image, individual careerism, need for conformity, and models of obedience. As trite as it may sound, an examination of human group dynamics and their psychological underpinnings is absolutely essential for a broader understanding of a soldier's behavior during wartime.

Atrocities by combat troops are often thought of as a problem of bygone times. The lengthy record of war crimes committed during the 20th century against both enemy combatants and subjugated populations, however, shows such a characterization to be mere wishful thinking. The seemingly clear demarcations between killing an armed, resisting opponent, a surrendering opponent, and an unarmed civilian can become blurred under the stress of combat. Perhaps the most important action of the combat soldier is to be able to identify his victims as legitimate and sanctioned enemy combatants. Such "after the kill" rationalizations provide critical psychic shielding between the soldier and the deadly results of his actions. The first step in this process is to "figure out" why the target deserved to be killed. If the target of his actions, however, is a civilian or some other individual who is not a significant or potential threat then the soldier is faced with the difficult process of rationalizing a murder. This is especially true since the advent of widespread guerilla warfare as a concomitant part of hostilities.

If we wish to understand war crimes, and perhaps even lessen their future occurrence, then we must recognize the factors that influence the commission of atrocities. Staub (1989) examined the origins of genocide and other expressions of group violence and identified a phenomenology consistent across racial, ethnic and temporal boundaries.

This genocidal tendency is characterized by:

Compartmentalization of functions
Euphemistic language
Culture of obedience / Authoritarianism
Ingroup-Outgroup differentiation / Devaluation of outgroups
Persistent aggressiveness
Individual submission to group needs
Participatory learning
Stepwise progression along a continuum of destruction

To this listing we should add the observations of Charney (1982) concerning the devaluation of human experience, the pursuit of power over others, the absence of control mechanisms for managing escalatory spirals, and the application of excessive force in conflict resolution.

A number of other factors have been identified that can have a cumulative effect: predisposition as a result of military training and ideological instruction, combat theater conditions and the recent loss of friends, cultural/ethnic distance between killer and victim (especially significant in ideological and colonial warfare), character and personality traits of those involved, and the perceived frustration or failure of conventional military efforts. Group absolution, or the inferred assumption of total responsibility by a commanding officer, also plays a powerful role in motivating soldiers to commit and rationalize atrocities. The 20th Century's unique contribution to influencing the occurrence of atrocities is the increased bureaucratization of killing that has become a routine character of modern warfare with its efficient mass-produced death. In addition to complicating the issue of personal responsibility, modern bureacracies grant individual absolution upon compliant "organization men" who commit homicide on behalf of the state.

Often overlooked in the rush to comprehend atrocities are three benefits gained by those military forces committing such crimes: 1) terrorism, 2) self-empowerment, and 3) self-radicalization. The most frequently cited benefit is that of terrorism or the ability to cow one's opponent and reduce their likelihood of offering effective resistance. The experience of numerous occupation authorities since the First World War, however, indicates that this benefit is a fleeting one at best. Often the commission of an atrocity has the exact opposite effect and serves to stiffen resistance and rekindle the flames of a feeble cause. The very act of killing in cold blood affirms the killer's superiority and can serve to restore self-confidence among wavering soldiers. More importantly, when a soldier participates in an atrocity they have "burned their bridges" with this radical behavior. Any opportunity they may have had to reconcile with the enemy is now no longer possible. The conduct of German and Soviet soldiers on the Eastern Front during the Second World War is a prime example of this self-radicalization effect.

It is truly disturbing that the previously mentioned mechanisms of social compliance are so powerful that only rarely do individuals have the moral fiber necessary to overcome group pressure, superior orders, and the instinct for self-preservation. All of us would certainly like to believe that we would not commit murder, but who among us can be absolutely certain that he would refuse to follow orders or try to defend the defenseless? Of course, none of this excuses the guilt of those who commit atrocities. While totalitarian states can exert tremendous pressure on an individual, such pressure is not irresistible. Experience tells us that making the proper moral or ethical decision is never easy, but it is the one unchanging standard to which human heritage and traditions hold us.

Mystical Thinking, Authoritarianism and Ideological Totalism

It is clear from an examination of human societies that various forms of mystical thinking have traditionally exerted, and continue to exert, a profound degree of influence on the educated and uneducated alike. Despite the social advances of the past five centuries, much human thought continues to be driven by highly irrational and anti-intellectual forces that are seemingly impervious to controls such as scientific skepticism and critical thinking. Mystical thinking has an obvious kinship with dreaming, in that both rely upon storylines full of fantastic elements and suspensions of ordinary reality, yet still can invoke deeply subjective feelings of meaning and relevance. The paradox of mystical thinking is that while giving the appearance of delving deeply into the essence of things its reliance on unreal concepts means that its analysis is superficial. By appearing to explore profound depths, however, mysticism provides an illusory sense of well-being and oneness with greater forces. Mysticism's great power lies in its ability to stop thinking. Human preference for mysticism is evident in the reactionary precursors which provided much of the ideological and psychic underpinnings of National Socialism. Mosse (1975), in particular, has convincingly demonstrated how 19th Century nationalism helped to strengthen the foundation on which the racist ideas of National Socialism were later constructed. According to Hatheway (1992), National Socialism also drew upon ideals of perfectionism inherent in Western culture to actualize physical and spiritual links between Germany and its purported Aryan predecessors. It will be seen that a concern with myths, symbols, and fantasies forms an especially critical component in the development of authoritarian and reactionary ideologies.

The controversial Austrian psychiatrist Wilhelm Reich was the first to explore the mass psychological basis for fascism in general, and Nazism in particular. He observed that the forces of political reaction derived most of their vitality from sexual repression, regimented compulsory education, and the traditional authoritarian family structure. The family structure took on an additional measure of importance since it was also the main pedagogic source of mystical and nationalistic sentiments. These associations were clearly recognized by the early National Socialists themselves who made the authoritarian family the core of their cultural politics with endless calls for the safeguarding of Germanic land, culture, and tradition. Such a narcissistic and xenophobic cultural framework was absolutely imperative since authoritarian societies can only replicate themselves in the individual through the mediation of the authoritarian family. Reich concluded that "patriarchal family attitudes and a mystical frame of mind are the basic psychological elements of fascism and imperialistic nationalism in the masses."[1]

Through the adoption of the National Socialist "leadership principle" (Führerprinzip) in which the leader exercises total authority, Hitler freed the German people from all responsibility for their fate and actions. Incapable of conceiving of themselves as part of a non-authoritarian, self-regulatory society, the majority of Germans subserviently waited for the all-powerful Führer to direct their lives. Irrational theories concerning racial purity and struggle also went hand in hand with National Socialism's reliance on traditionally repressive authoritarian social structures. The Aryan was considered to be pure and asexual; the Near Eastern was denigrated as sexual, dirty, and consequently, demonic. National Socialism thus transferred physical sensuality to an "inferior race" which was then constantly demonized as a prelude to the brutal forces that would be unleashed against it.

In the process of formulating and adopting any ideology man reshapes his psychic core with the same processes characteristic of the beliefs in question. Thus, the formation of an irrational ideology will invariably make man's psychic core itself irrational. Political parties merely orient themselves to the perceived structure of the masses whether it is rational or not. National Socialism was primarily characterized by mystical thinking, unorthodox faith, an obsession with abstract ethical ideals, and a belief in the divine predestination of the leader. The origin of each of these features can be traced back to more fundamental layers of the Western authoritarian tradition. Reich recognized that it was this elementary, or irrational, nature of National Socialism that rendered it immune to the reasoned argumentation of its opponents. Hitler himself repeatedly stressed that one could only get at the masses with feelings and beliefs (mysticism).

Unlike many of his contemporaries in the burgeoning field of psychoanalysis, Reich recognized that psychological problems were the synergistic result of mind, body, and social field effects. Whenever the forces of psychological and sexual repression affect entire nations to the extent that an individual's ability to experience natural, self-regulatory lives is suppressed or completely eliminated, the dammed up energies inevitably give rise to unhealthy secondary drives, biopathic disfunctioning (neurotic and physical pathologies), and an eventual societal illness termed the "emotional plague."[2] Such an outbreak is characterized by mysticism, a striving for control and authority, moralism, sadism, authoritarian bureaucracy, idealization of war, nationalism, race hatred, criminal anti-sociality, and a masochistic tolerance for all of the preceeding behaviors. Individuals affected by the emotional plague can be recognized by their relentless pursuit of life-destructive social activities. They cannot tolerate and seek to destroy all that is different, since its very existence serves as a provocation and threatens to undermine their psychic core. Their thinking, distorted by concepts originating from irrational and mystical emotions, is circular in that it merely functions to confirm and legitimize erroneous conclusions. Plague individuals "give the impression of rationality without being rational."[3] The degree of violence exhibited by plague individuals and societies mirrors the severity of their own repressive psychic armoring and concomitant biopathic disfunctioning. As Reich noted, the emotional plague "manifests itself essentially in social living... Periodically [it] takes on the dimensions of a pandemic, in the form of a gigantic breakthrough of sadism and criminality..."[4]

From this viewpoint, most political behavior is symptomatic of the profoundly irrational nature of the emotional plague. For Reich, the ascendency of National Socialism in Germany was proof of his ideas concerning the emotional plague afflicting mankind. This plague in varying degrees of severity is all around us, though unrecognized by most people. Proactive measures are rarely taken against its more obvious early manifestations. The problem is usually only addressed at the pandemic stage[5] and then the standard solution invokes the very behaviors -- violence and repression -- that gave rise to the plague in the first place. In this manner, emotional plagues develop into self-sustaining, as well as self-referential and insulated, societal illnesses of the most intractable sort. While we may disagree with the utility of Reich's view of the emotional plague as a diagnosable illness, we certainly cannot ignore its usefulness as a metaphor for the eternal problems of evil and human cruelty.

Goodrick-Clarke (1992) has authored the most profound and unappreciated study of the occult roots and mystical content of National Socialist ideology. He presents a socio-historical account of the lives, doctrines, and activities of the Ariosophists, a racist and nationalistic occult fraternity active in Germany and Austria prior to the First World War. Although a diminutive organization exercising little obvious influence, its abstruse ideas and apocalyptic visions clearly anticipated the political doctrines and institutions of the Third Reich. From the best available evidence it seems certain that Hitler and a number of other high-ranking Nazi leaders were thoroughly versed in the reactionary and millenarian writings of the Ariosophist philosopher, Jörg Lanz von Liebenfels. The lineage of the early Nazi Party itself is convincingly traced back to two occult organizations, the Thule Gesellschaft and the Germanenorden, both of which also drew heavy inspiration from Ariosophy. Well into the 1930s, two Ariosophist philosophers were closely cooperating with Reichsführer-SS Heinrich Himmler on various SS-sponsored prehistory and ideology projects.

An examination of Ariosophy's fantastic teleological content is clearly necessary for any study of the Third Reich and its ideological/philosophical grounding. The doctrines of the Ariosophists that were directly coopted by National Socialism include the conscious creation of a racially elite population, the extermination of lesser beings, and the establishment of a prosperous Germanic New World Order. Lanz's specific recommendation for the disposal of perceived racial inferiors emerged as actual and contemplated Nazi practices: enslavement and use as beasts of burden, deportation to Madagascar, and incineration as a sacrifice to God. As Goodrick-Clarke noted, "the psychopathology of the Nazi holocaust and the subjugation of non-Aryans in the East were presaged by Lanz's grim speculations."[6] These Ariosophist fantasies ultimately found concrete expression in the nightmare world created by Nazi Germany with its "wretched slave cities where the Jewish demons were immolated as a burnt sacrifice, or holocaust."[7] Of course, the powerful emotional and psychological appeal of the Ariosophist vision in post-World War I Germany and Austria is at least clinically understandable since it relieved universal feelings of anxiety, defeat, and demoralization. National Socialism was pitted against the forces of darkness and decay: a Jewish conspiracy was threatening to destroy the Fatherland. Only the total destruction of the Jews and their allies could save Germany by allowing it to enter a millenarian promised land of a perfect, racially pure Thousand-Year Reich. In this great cosmic battle terrible deeds would be required of all Germans, but especially of the country's ideological elite.

Numerous correspondences have also been drawn between the Nazi Party and the Freikorps, a conglomeration of paramilitary units that battled Communist uprisings throughout post-World War I Germany.[8] The Freikorps functioned as a testing ground for proto-Nazi thinking and contributed immeasurably to the growth and eventual success of National Socialism by later supplying the hardened cadre of Hitler's stormtroopers. Theweleit (1987, 1989) has provided concrete evidence supporting Reich's theoretical observations regarding the origins of fascism and its grounding in biological and psychological processes gone horribly awry. In an examination of Freikorps' diaries and fictional literature of the inter-war years, Theweleit has successfully mapped the political culture from which National Socialism slowly emerged and developed. In reconstructing the mystical content of the Freikorp's authoritarian imagination, he demonstrated that their complete repudiation of the female body (with subsequent sublimation of "female" traits such as weakness, fear, and guilt into repressive psychic armoring) developed into a psychic compulsion equating masculinity with hardness, self-denial, and destruction. The parallels between this development and the National Socialist self-image, especially as expressed in the SS ideals (see below), could not be clearer. With the application of repetitive and dehumanizing conditioning regimes such undesirable characteristics are then projected outward onto perceived enemies. The Freikorps men did not employ screen imagery but openly enthused about their desire to exterminate their enemies. In a similar manner Nazi propaganda was ultimately truthful. It was a future truth largely consisting of horrific predictions for which Hitler's minions were prepared to change the world so that they might prove accurate.

Lifton coined the term *ideological totalism* to designate the synergistic meeting point of extreme ideologies with equally extreme individual characteristics.[9] It is usually sweeping messianic ideologies that are eventually "totalized" by their adherents. Although his work dealt exclusively with thought reform and brainwashing in Communist China, his principles and ideas clearly illuminate authoritarian mindsets in general. Lifton identified eight features common to all totalistic environments:

1) Milieu Control : The complete control of human communication by the totalistic environment with the ultimate penetration being the control of the individual's inner dialogue. Since the totalistic ideology is omniscient, any individual doubts need to be dispelled or transformed into the "truth." Exposure to milieu control leads to an erosion of the boundaries between self and the outside world with a concomitant loss in the individual's ability to accurately judge his environment.

2) Mystical Manipulation : Extensive personal manipulation aimed to provoke specific behavioral and emotional patterns in such a manner that they appear to spontaneously arise from the environment.

3) Demand for Purity : The polarization of the world into the absolutely pure and good (the totalistic ideology itself) and the impure and evil (all else). This demand for purity invariably includes a call for the destruction of all impurities. Since the totalist world is pure, any perceived ills must have their sources in outside influences. Individuals who succumb to the demand for purity lose their ability to properly balance the complexities of human morality.

4) Cult of Confession : It is demanded that adherents confess to transgressions they have not committed. This is simply another reminder of the totalistic environment's complete ownership of individuals and their minds. The private retention of anything is a *de facto* crime.

5) Sacred Science : The ideology of the totalistic environment is equated with the absolute truth and is considered to be the "ultimate moral vision for the ordering of human existence." Dogma, as well as its bearers, is not to be questioned, but revered. It ignores ordinary logic at the same time it claims to be the absolute truth. Adherents often derive much comfort and security from the intense feeling of truth that results from this fusion of mystical and rational thinking.

6) Linguistic Modification : Since language is yet

another human product, it too is controlled by the totalistic environment. It is manipulated and twisted in whatever fashion the ideology requires. Ideology is not analyzed; it is simply a set of approved cliches. For the individual, linguistic modification is one more source of intellectual constriction that leads to psychological atrophy and even states of profound dissociation.

7) Doctrine over Person : As with language and thought, the totalistic environment also requires the subordination of life experience to its "sacred" ideological claims. An individual's actual experiences and identity are discarded, edited, or re-interpreted so as to comply with dogma. The human is modified to reaffirm the myth; abstract ideas such as service to the nation-state are accorded a higher value than human life.

8) Dispensing of Existence : As an outgrowth of its demand for purity and claim to be the one true path in life, totalistic environments erect boundaries between those who have a right to exist (adherents) and those who don't (all others - "non-people"). Non-people are often disposed of as readily as heretical thoughts.

The greater the degree to which an environment can be described by the preceding factors, the greater its resemblance to a system of ideological totalism. The result is the creation of an entirely self-contained ideological environment exhibiting extreme personal closure, censorship, and a degree of hostility toward outsiders that usually leads to dangerous group excesses. The driving force behind the totalization of an ideology is its adherents' need for an omnipotent philosophical system which addresses ultimately unsolvable mystical and psychosocial needs.

Merton's (1976) observations on totalitarianism and the *mass man* complements the work of Reich and Lifton. The mass man, having lost his sense of limitation, weakness, and fallibility, renounces personal responsibility, avoids decision-making and allows himself to drift with the crowd. Mass men are quickly transformed into fanatics who refuse to acknowledge the humanity of their fellow man. The cause or movement is placed above individuals and everything is sacri-

ficed on behalf of the movement's interests. Mass men will "go to any extreme, stop at no crime, intoxicated as they are by the slogans that give them a pseudo-religious sense of transcending their own limitations... There are crimes which no one would commit as an individual which he willingly and bravely commits when acting in the name of his society, because he has been convinced that evil is entirely different when its done for the common good."[10] The consequences of man's renunciation of moral responsibility and acceptance of the mass movement are exemplified by the horrific atrocities of the 20th century.

Zukier, on the other hand, has argued that the inclusion of biological, cultural, and psychosocial factors in the assessment of wartime behavior "implies a dilution of moral responsibility for even the most horrendous crimes."[11] By including the influence of social coercion and similar constraints, for example, an individual's actions are said to be *a priori* drained of their intentionality. Zukier also criticizes the "weakness of will" defense as being typically propounded by those sympathetic to perpetrators of crime. He also entirely discounts the existence of an "authoritarian personality" (as defined by rigid adherence to conventional values, strict submission to authority, obsession with power and toughness) and calls for a more differentiated interactional approach to the psychological dimensions of genocide. It is unclear on what basis Zukier makes these sweeping criticisms. The inclusion of environmental factors merely helps us to grasp the "how could", but does not answer the ultimate "why", of atrocities. Barring a debilitating psychological disorder, each individual still retains free will and the responsibility for his actions despite any underlying biological, cultural, and psychological influences. Of course, one can retain rationality, act lawfully, be well-intentioned and still pursue choices that are morally and ethically wrong.

Notes:
1. Reich, 1933/1970, p. 131.
2. Reich, 1949, p. 248.
3. Reich, 1933/1970, pp. 255-256.
4. Reich, 1949, p. 248.
5. Reich's pandemic stage of the emotional plague corresponds with theologian Reinhold Niebuhr's ideas regarding entire nations becoming psychopathic. Evidence of Nazi

psychopathology (assessed in non-Reichian terms), however, has proven to be elusive.

6. *Goodrick-Clarke, 1992, p. 97.*

7. *op. cit., p. 203.*

8. *For a general history of the Freikorps movement, see Waite,1969 and Jones, 1987.*

9. *Lifton, 1961.*

10. *Merton, 1976, pp. 132-135, 139.*

11. *Zukier, 1997, p. 196.*

National Socialist Ideology and Vocabulary

The horror of totalitarian excesses stems in part from the fact that they are completely unintelligible to outsiders whose psyches have not been molded by the requisite ideology.[1] On first examination it would appear self-evident that the Waffen-SS was simply part of a larger society in which virulently anti-rational and criminal philosophies had taken hold, obliterating the ethical and moral sensibilities of its citizens. There is no evidence, however, that individuals under the influence of National Socialism and its worldview either rejected or inverted all established norms and values. Rather, they accepted an ideology, fictitious to all but its adherents, that Germany had arrived at an unprecedented historical and political crossroads requiring the suspension of accepted moral and ethical standards *in certain areas of activity for a limited duration*. Thus, many otherwise decent individuals, who in normal circumstances would never have entertained committing a crime, were able to rationalize their participation in horrendous atrocities solely on the basis of National Socialist ideology.

In Himmler's view, the Waffen-SS was to be a political and military elite at the forefront of the National Socialist movement. As such, it was part of the larger 'SS-Orden' he envisioned as "an elite organization, linked by self-imposed laws and rituals, unswervingly ministering to an ideal which represented absolute truth."[2] The explicit goal of SS ideology was to disengage its members from everyday life and to wholly reintegrate them into the Orden. SS authority was justified by self-imposed norms established without respect to either a legitimate government or any specific legal precedents. Additionally, SS ideology completely lacked any control mechanisms with

which to restrain its inherently totalistic inclinations. The SS were truly a law unto themselves. This is not to imply, however, that they did not want to exist on a seemingly legitimate basis. Through the accumulation of self-created historical myths, the production of enemy stereotypes, and the ideologically warranted policies of expansion and genocide, the SS sought to create anew just such a legitimate grounding to secure its long-term survival. This combination of a totalistic authoritarian worldview and a belief in racial superiority with its implicit dehumanization of others inevitably led to the murderous contempt which the SS lavished on its perceived enemies.

In theory, if the Waffen-SS was to function as a political and military elite then ideological indoctrination and military training should have been accorded approximately equal weight. Such was the practice early on.

It eventually became clear to Himmler and his generals, however, that such a balance was incompatible with the timely creation of an effective military formation. Accordingly, ideological instruction was slowly reined in and finally reduced to a minimum. Under the increasing pressure of war-time demands, such instruction was routinely decentralized and delegated down to the level of troop commanders. This change was not unwelcome since, as Wegner indicated: "Such efforts coincided with the commander's desires to use ideological indoctrination principally as an instrument to fanaticize the soldier, to maintain and enforce his readiness to fight and resist the enemy."[3] Many Waffen-SS veterans claim that they did not take ideological instruction seriously and discount its impact on the average soldier. In view of the amount of time that was devoted to such instruction (especially among pre-1943 Waffen-SS personnel), however, there is little doubt that the majority of Waffen-SS personnel were well informed concerning the basic tenets of National Socialism, accepted them, and that these ideas influenced their subsequent combat behavior. This is particularly true of Waffen-SS officers and non-commissioned officers who were exposed to a more systematic program of ideological, military, and political training at the many Waffen-SS schools. As an outgrowth of National Socialism, SS ideology focused on several themes that resonated throughout the movement: hardness and cameraderie; loyalty, duty, honor, and obedience; modesty and decency; achievement; and racial struggle.

Hardness and Cameraderie:

The Waffen-SS were taught that their basic attitude must be that of a fighter for fighting's sake. They were to be hard and impervious to all weakness or emotion. As soldiers they were to be "as swift as greyhounds and hard as Krupp steel," as a popular saying went. Sayer and Botting noted that,

> The SS concept of härte ("hardness") meant toughness in adverse situations, recklessness under fire, fearlessness in the face of death, ruthlessness in the execution of orders, total dedication to victory in battle. Härte also meant contempt for the enemy, callousness toward prisoners, brutality towards all who stood in their way. [4]

The SS attitudes of toughness and self-mastery were the functional antitheses of charity, mercy, and humility. Hardness and cameraderie were two sides of the same coin. Hardness was reserved for enemies and those who did not belong to the Orden. Such enemies were rarely viewed as individuals, usually they were viewed in a generalized and absolute fashion that robbed them of their humanity. Cameraderie was extended to those who belonged to the Orden and often functioned as a screen to purposely obscure illegal and immoral actions (not unlike the self-protective "blue wall" found among modern law enforcement organizations). It could also function, however, as an "instrument of reciprocal ideological control and indoctrination" -- i.e., social pressure of the most extreme variety.[5]

Loyalty, Duty, Honor and Obedience:

For the most part, SS ideology displayed the signs of mental totalitarianism in its treatment of loyalty, duty, honor, and obedience as functional synonyms. All loyalty was directed exclusively to the person of Adolf Hitler in his dual role as political leader and physical embodiment of the Reich. All freedom of choice and conscience were lost before the unrestricted power of state mandates. Orders were to be blindly obeyed.

For the soldiers of most nations, one's sense of duty involves the satisfaction of an individually-motivated ethical contract with the state. Among the Waffen-SS, however, this often abstract sense was replaced by a concrete, fanatical compulsion to fulfill SS codes of loyalty, whatever the cost. Such a situation naturally invested leaders with a great deal of influence regarding the conduct of their troops. It is clear that those Waffen-SS commanders who ordered, encouraged, or condoned misbehavior by their troops laid the groundwork for the commission of large-scale atrocities. Such leadership was common enough for terror and socially-sanctioned criminal behavior to become emblematic of the entire Waffen-SS.

Modesty and Decency:

As Himmler personally sought to demonstrate through his ascetic lifestyle, modesty implied an actively-practiced disregard for one's personal needs in favor of the state's total claim on an individual. Decency was similarly a characteristic subsumed by ideological demands and had little to do with one's behavior toward others, but rather reflected one's ability to carry out required duties in a controlled and reserved manner. The decent SS man was expected to exterminate his racial enemy without exhibiting untoward emotional or behavioral displays. Thus, it was necessary to erect a psychological firewall between one's conduct in everyday life and one's activities on behalf of the state. The warrior archetype that is turned on by training and participation in warfare must be turned off when the "soldier" becomes a "citizen" again.

Achievement:

The rigidly pragmatic view of their men as fighters for fighting's sake inevitably led the Waffen-SS to stress its corollary: achievement for achievement's sake. The ability to achieve was all-important -- the cost involved was often unimportant. Tasks were to be carried out to perfection without worrying about their purpose, justification, or the methodology employed. Such an ideal, in combination with their constant deployment to critical hotspots throughout the war accounts for the disproportionately high mortality rates in front-line Waffen-SS units (especially among officers and NCOs).

Racial Struggle:

The National Socialist theory of a timeless racial struggle confronting Germany found its most concrete expressions in the party's core ideological literature such as Hitler's *Mein Kampf*, Walter Darre's *Um Blut und Boden*, and Alfred Rosenberg's *Der Mythus des 20. Jahrhunderts*. From such sources were developed the countless pamphlets, books, and curricula that dominated the German social and intellectual landscapes during the Nazi era. Himmler, in his role as guardian of the Germanic blood, constantly reiterated this theme of inevitable racial struggle in his speeches to Waffen-SS personnel. Germany's victims were invariably portrayed as being either "subhumans" trying to pollute the Aryan gene pool or as ideological enemies resisting the sacred truths revealed in Nazi ideology and bent on destroying Western civilization. Such pernicious indoctrination in due time bore the fruit that Himmler wished since it has long been recognized that soldiers find it easier to kill a dehumanized opponent than one whom they consider to be their equal. The result was an unparalleled brutalization of warfare by Waffen-SS units free of guilt or remorse for their actions.

All of the preceding concepts are perhaps best illustrated in the following excerpt from Himmler's infamous speech to a gathering of upper-level SS leaders at Posen (Poland) on October 4, 1943:

> I want to also mention a very difficult subject... before you, with complete candor. It should be discussed amongst us, yet nevertheless, we will never speak about it in public...
>
> I am talking about the evacuation of the Jews, the extermination of the Jewish people. It is one of those things that is easily said. 'The Jewish people is being exterminated,' every Party member will tell you, 'perfectly clear, it's part of our plans, we're eliminating the Jews, exterminating them, a small matter.' And then along they all come, all the 80 million upright Germans, and each one has his decent Jew. They say: all the others are swine, but here is a first-class Jew. And... none of them has seen it, has endured it. Most of you will know what it means when 100 bodies lie together, when 500 are there or when there are 1000. And... to have seen this through and -- with the exception of human weakness -- to have remained de-

cent, has made us hard and is a page of glory never mentioned and never to be mentioned. Because we know how difficult things would be, if today in every city during the bomb attacks, the burdens of war and the privations, we still had Jews as secret saboteurs, agitators, and instigators. We would probably be at the same stage as 16/17 [1916/1917], if the Jews still resided in the body of the German people.

> We have taken away the riches that they had, and... I have given a strict order, which Obergruppenführer Pohl has carried out, we have delivered these riches to the Reich, to the State. We have taken nothing from them for ourselves. A few, who have offended against this, will be judged in accordance with an order, that I gave at the beginning: he who takes even one Mark of this is a dead man. A number of SS men have offended against this order. They are very few, and they will be dead men WITHOUT MERCY! We have the moral right, we had the duty to our people to do it, to kill this people who would kill us. We, however, do not have the right to enrich ourselves with even one fur, with one Mark, with one cigarette, with one watch, with anything that we do not have. Because we don't want, at the end of all this, to get sick and die from the same bacillus that we have exterminated. I have never seen it happen that even one... bit of putrefaction comes in contact with us, or takes root in us. On the contrary, where it might try to take root, we will burn it out together. But altogether we can say: We have carried out this most difficult task for the love of our people. And we have suffered no defect within us, in our soul, or in our character. [6]

National Socialist ideology and the aforementioned SS 'ideals' were aided by the highly euphemistic official vocabulary of the Third Reich which served as a psychological shield protecting state representatives from the brutality and criminality of their actions. Innocent civilians were *shot in flight, liquidated, gotten rid of, rendered harmless, taken care of, done away with*, and *subjected to special treatment*. Such coded, sanitized language purged actions of their political, moral and ethical consequences and also legitimized ideologically motivated activities for the troops and commanders required to carry them out. By obscuring and falsifying the reality of mass murder, language salved the consciences and lessened the sense of guilt experienced by those participating in extermination actions. As National Socialism illustrated all too well, language when employed as a carrier and formative agent of ideology can both represent perceptions of reality, as well as constitute them. The victims of Nazism were linguistically dehumanized (*e.g.*, continual references to Jews and Slavs as vermin, traitors, and sub-humans), classed as "outsiders," and then placed beyond the limit of the societal and moral universe of obligation which governs our behavior toward others.[7] Once individuals were defined as being outside of this protective circle, the same dehumanizing language then functioned to demand and justify their extermination as a self-defense measure by the in-group. Mazower noted that such euphemisms,

> also helped resolve the ultimate paradox which lay at the heart of Nazi ideology, between the regime's self-image as guarantor of legality, and its desire to wipe out any opposition through untrammelled violence. Crude and appalling brutality... could be dressed up in the vocabulary of... military justice and public security. [8]

Once this critical linguistic distancing had taken place, many individuals willingly gave in to those dark motive forces lying dormant within us all and which ultimately proved to be the powerful well-springs of National Socialist ideology. The power to define had become the power to destroy. [9]

Unfortunately, the rhetorical language of extermination employed by the Nazis to describe their crimes cannot be dismissed as a mere historical aberration. Such Orwellian vocabulary, along with the falsification of memory and negation of reality that it promotes, has its roots in the writings of early Roman historians and thrives today in the bureaucratic constructs, corporate promotions, and managerial policies intrinsic to post-1945 militarism. For example, during the Vietnam War American programs for eliminating Communist political cadres were known by the jargon of "rooting out the infrastructure." This war also gave us the terms "body count" and "collateral damage." When the term "search and destroy" was perceived to have become a linguistic liability, it was replaced with "sweep and clear"; the nature of the operation

was unchanged. Particularly disturbing is the realm of "nukespeak" where bland euphemisms are routinely employed to rationalize and render acceptable the nuclear annihilation of millions of people (*e.g.*, 'countervalue' = destroying a city). Instead of learning any lessons from previous instances of euphemistic corruption, mankind appears to be improving upon its misuse. This euphemism-driven negation of memory is exploited by all societies to promote an intergenerational tendency to romanticize war. Only by actively working to hide the horror and destruction of past wars can we effectively recruit the soldiers that will fight in future wars.

Notes:
1. *Canovan, 1974, pp. 17-18.*
2. *Wegner, 1990, p. 11.*
3. *op. cit., p. 220.*
4. *Sayer and Botting, 1989, p. 18.*
5. *Wegner, 1990, p. 19.*
6. *Himmler, Heinrich. Speech of the Reichsführer-SS at the SS-Gruppenführer Meeting in Posen, 4 October 1943.* U.S.
   National Archives document 242.256, reel 2 of 3, audio recording. [see also Nuremberg Document No. 1919-PS]. (Text used is a transcription/translation from the audio recording by Stephane Bruchfeld, Gordon McFee and Dr. Ulrich Rössler for the Nizkor Project.)
7. *Charney, 1991, vol. 2, p. 386.*
8. *Mazower, 1993, p. 191.*
9. *Wilson, 1987, p. 119.*

The Illusion of Nazi Psychopathology

Since the end of the Second World War and the shocking revelation of the true extent of Nazi crimes, we have been trying to comprehend the seemingly incomprehensible. What led a nation as cultured as Germany to such depths of inhumanity? What kind of men could bring themselves to commit such long-term campaigns of mass murder? These questions -- perhaps the questions of paramount importance for mankind -- have yet to be answered satisfactorily. Inexplicably, some social theorists have advanced the view that any impartial, objective examination of Nazi motivations would grant them undeserved respectability and is unwarranted due to the immense suffering they inflicted upon others. Such mistaken views are a recipe for the repetition of the very behaviors that these theorists abhor.

The standard explanation of these crimes based on power political models was deemed unsuitable due to the unique qualities of the Nazi genocidal campaign. Initial explanations offered by numerous observers included psychological theories invoking authoritarian personality complexes[1] and collective ethnic guilt. A homogeneous "Nazi type" existed which was invariably characterized as anomalous, evil, demonic, fascistic, German, ideological, and psychopathic. It was a comforting, if false, stereotype for several reasons. Such an identification and delineation meant that Nazism and its abberations were restricted to the German people and, thus, had little or no relationship to the vast majority of mankind. Concluding that the Nazis were evil or demonic placed their motives outside the realm of recognized and accepted human desires. In essence, the Nazis were inhuman; seemingly normal people such as ourselves would never engage in similarly amoral, destructive behaviors. As a theory of Nazi criminality, however, invoking genetic differentiation or psychopathology are inherently self-defeating. If the Nazis were truly inhuman or mentally ill, then they are absolved of all normal standards of moral culpability for their actions and should have been sent to hospitals for treatment, not the gallows.[2] Such essentialist theories that only fanatic, sick or evil people commit such crimes explain nothing, yet serve as the perfect alibi for monstrous behavior. Ironically, the Nazis themselves employed similar types of essentialist demonization of those groups they had targeted for destruction.

Doubts about genetic, demonic, and pathological interpretations of the Nazis first began to surface in the 1960s as social theorists explored the normalcy issue in light of the Adolf Eichmann trial. Eichmann, a high-level functionary in the Nazi extermination bureaucracy, was shown to be a non-descript, amoral everyman bureaucrat -- a far cry from the sadistic Nazi stereotype. Despite the desire of many to simply write off the Nazis (and by extension the entire German people) as abnormal, the proof for such a conclusion was wholly lacking. Perhaps the Nazis, especially those who took part in the extermination operations, were

not the "pathological demons of a diseased Germany" after all, but actually more or less ordinary men.[3] In a controversial and groundbreaking thesis, Arendt (1958, 1964) concluded that the vast majority of Nazis were simply banal, morally indifferent individuals lacking any specific ideological hatred toward their victims. They were stultifyingly ordinary people who were merely doing their duty because it was easier to act than to think under a totalitarian regime. Anyone placed in such circumstances is capable of perpetrating evils that they would never have considered in "normal" life. Arendt found Adolf Eichmann (an SS overseer of the Holocaust machinery) to be "terribly and terrifyingly" normal. This was a most unwelcome conclusion. As Merton observed,

> One of the most disturbing facts that came out in the Eichmann trial was that a psychiatrist examined him and pronounced him perfectly sane. I do not doubt it at all, and that is precisely why I find it disturbing. If all the Nazis had been psychotics, as some of their leaders probably were, their appalling cruelty would have been in some sense easier to understand. [4]

The inescapable conclusion was that one need not be either mentally ill or an ideological fanatic in order to derive some degree of satisfaction from the annihilation of millions of people. This morally indifferent personality structure was not limited to Eichmann; it surfaced time and again in trials of other former Nazis. The massive and still-growing *Justiz und NS-Verbrechen* series of Rüter-Ehlerman *et al.* (1968-1981) and its finding aid (Rüter and deMildt, 1998) are undoubtedly the most overlooked evidential resources regarding the normalcy of Nazi war criminals. Volumes 1 - 33 cover West German war crimes trials from 1946 - 1970; future volumes in the series will cover trials from 1970 – present day. They have also issued a series of six volumes covering East German war crimes trials. In case after case the perpetrators are shown to be average men. De Mildt has speculated that this evidence has been neglected precisely because those with a more traditionalist perspective on the evils of Nazi Germany find its message that mass murderers are ordinary people like you and me "too unpalatable to digest."[5] Of course, this in no way excuses their deeds or minimizes the threat posed by war criminals.

If anything, such a perspective draws into sharp focus the fragility of the moral and ethical barriers we've erected between ourselves and the behavior of others.

Lifton's research (1961, 1986) on mind-control techniques utilized in China and the psychology of medical doctors intimately involved in the Nazi euthanasia and extermination programs clearly demonstrated that ordinary people were quite willing to commit "unthinkable" crimes under the proper circumstances. We can be seduced or beguiled into doing evil "when we find ourselves in a social setting where the immediate circumstances dominate our entire field of moral vision."[6] Theweleit (1987, 1989), after conducting in-depth studies of German right-wing literature of the inter-war period, proposed that the fascist when killing is not doing "something else" or some screen activity as has often been claimed, but rather exactly what he wants to do. Similarly, acts of terror do not necessarily arise from some invented psychopathology but from irreducible human desires and from ordinary human behaviors. In a comprehensive review on the topic Megargee stressed that,

> Although a variety of functional and organic disturbances can lead to aggression and violent behavior, most violence is committed by people suffering from no diagnosable impairment. Even if we exclude legal, socially condoned forms of violence such as warfare, we find criminal violence is often performed by normal people for rational motives. [7]

Browning's (1992) study of a German reserve police battalion and its participation in the Holocaust seemingly hammered yet another nail into the coffin of Nazi psychopathology. In agreement with Arendt and others, he concluded that psychopathology simply is not a required precursor for atrocity. Virtually anyone can be placed within a context in which they will most likely engage in violent behavior. Contributory factors include cultural influences on child-rearing, the behavior of the one's peers, the behavior of potential victims, the accessibility of weapons, and the occurrence of opportunities to engage in violence. Despite what we may wish to believe, ordinary men will often perform horrendous acts for operationally rational reasons in societies where traditional standards of law and morality have been set aside in favor of state-sponsored violence.

In a review of contemporary historiography, Zillmer et al. (1995) concluded on the basis of "vast and solid evidential foundations" that the concept of Nazi psychopathology was entirely without merit. That same year, however, Goldhagen (1995) attempted to reopen the debate with his presentation of an essentialist political-cultural argument rejecting both universalizing psychoanalytical approaches and the effects of increasing barbarization of warfare in modern times as abstract and ahistorical concepts that fail to explain anything. Goldhagen's work touched off an extraordinary international debate of multiple dimensions (historiography, media influences, political identity, etc.). The author proposed that Nazi crimes, specifically the extermination of European Jewry, stemmed exclusively from a particular strain of anti-Semitism unique to the German people and their culture ('eliminationist anti-Semitism') that demanded the destruction of Jews in Germany. This cultural tendency was simply awaiting the right leaders and circumstances in order to reach its long-awaited fulfilment. Complicating the situation was the book's tone which was seen as a calculated attack on numerous senior Holocaust scholars (e.g., Browning, Hilberg). While describing his own work as the "unassailable truth," Goldhagen habitually dismissed out of hand the works of the most learned and respected historians.

Goldhagen's thesis immediately drew extensive, and in many cases vitriolic, criticism from fellow academics.[8] It was apparent that Goldhagen had misinterpreted historical data in support of a simplistic, misleading, poorly-argued, and untenable thesis. He was attacked for selectively reinterpreting historical data, making sweeping conclusions without employing a comparative framework to prove his contentions, presenting a work loaded down with serious internal contradictions, quoting documents out of context, and ignoring contradictory evidence. Rather than allowing the source materials to drive his theorizing, Goldhagen twisted the data to fit his preconceived notions. Neusner (1997) has characterized the work as "propaganda masquerading as serious scholarship." Goldhagen was accused of "catering to those who want simplistic answers to difficult questions, to those who seek the security of prejudices."[9] Most critiques were concerned with Goldhagen's rejection of a multicausal approach for complex historical events, as well as his denial that all humans have the potential for evil, destructive behaviors. Zukier (1997), for example, has discounted all monocausal, undifferentiated essentialist explanations (including Goldhagen's) as implausible and appealed for a more differentiated interactional approach to the psychological dimensions of genocide. As de Mildt so aptly observed,

> Dismissing them [Nazis] as 'satanic evil-doers' or blinded fanatics may well satisfy important emotional demands, but it brings us no further in our efforts to make any sense of the catastrophe and learn something from it. On the contrary, by converting the criminal actors of the story into demon-like lunatics, we distance ourselves from them in a radical fashion, assuming them to belong to a different species. [10]

Quite the opposite, the historical record clearly demonstrates that Goldhagen's "eliminationist" sentiments have appeared in all societies. In many cases these sentiments have been acted on with murderous results. Equally problematic was Goldhagen's conclusion that post-war West German culture was so vastly different from that of Nazi Germany (due to American re-education programs!) as to make a repeat of Nazism highly unlikely. Goldhagen didn't bother to explain how this could be true given Germany's abysmal post-war record of war crimes prosecutions. Despite this critical reception by his academic peers, Goldhagen's thesis was welcomed with open arms by a supportive news media since it effectively played to the most universal of all stereotypes: that of 'the other as different' (in this instance, Nazis not being quite human like the rest of us). As Ash (1997) observed, Goldhagen's text was quickly elevated to canonical status and the negative reactions of most academics were attributed to an unwillingness to face the truth. For the most part, media outlets did little but spread the nationalistic and moralistic stereotypes at the core of his work. Unsurprisingly, his critics soon found themselves the target of censorship attempts, *ad hominem* attacks, and legal threats for presuming to question the new wisdom. Most disturbing of all was the gap between academia and the public that readily accepted Goldhagen's thesis. It was almost as if all of the research into human behavior and the nature of evil since the 1960s had

never happened... the Nazis/Germans were a unique specimen of inhuman bogeymen after all. Historians had completely failed to establish a meaningful dialogue with the public and would need to learn to deal effectively with the media in the future. Of even more concern was the fact that the public had shown itself so willing "to suspend not their critical capacities but their very power of reasoned judgment" in their easy acceptance of Goldhagen's spurious thesis.[11]

Despite a complete lack of merit and its exclusion from serious scholarly inquiries, Goldhagen's thesis is still very much alive and worrying to the consciences of historians and social scientists alike. The myth of Nazi psychopathology will undoubtedly be with us for some to come, if for no other reason than the false consolation it offers concerning our own normality. As this affair has illustrated, many people need a simple binary view of the world in which to segregate evil and locate the "murderous potential of modernity itself somewhere far away from the good old USA."[12] The situation was no different in Germany where Goldhagen's reception was similar to that in the United States (strong academic criticism coupled with popular acclaim). The idea that "we" would never engage in such murderous acts is certainly a more comfortable prospect than confronting Primo Levi's "grey band" that radiates out from regimes based on terror and obsequiousness, engulfing all but the morally exceptional in a tide of self-serving apathy and malignant indifference to others.

Notes:
1. *Adorno et al., 1950.*
2. *de Mildt, 1996.*
3. *Zillmer et al., 1995, p. 176.*
4. *Merton, 1964a, p. 45.*
5. *de Mildt, 1996, p. 13.*
6. *Katz, 1993, p. 6.*
7. *Megargee, 1984, p. 523.*
8. *The primary critiques of Goldhagen's thesis are Ash, 1997; Finkelstein and Birn, 1998; Littell (ed.), 1997; Hilberg, 1997; and Neusner, 1997.*
9. *Finkelstein and Birn, 1998, p. 148.*
10. *de Mildt, 1996, p. 14.*
11. *Neusner, 1997.*
12. *Ash, 1997, p. 405.*

Conclusions

By now, I hope that it is clear to readers that the Waffen-SS was fully deserving of the judgment and punishment meted out by post-war tribunals. The evidence presented in support of this conclusion has been five-fold:

1) Waffen-SS units, of their own accord, committed hundreds of atrocities against civilians, battlefield opponents, and POWs during military campaigns on all fronts to which they were deployed (e.g., Monte Sol).

2) Waffen-SS units took part in numerous state-sponsored genocidal operations (*e.g.*, Babi Yar).

3) The Waffen-SS utilized personnel with known criminal backgrounds during the formation and reinforcement of nearly half of its divisions (see *Unit Histories* and Appendix D).

4) Waffen-SS units assisted in a wide variety of state-sponsored cultural crimes while stationed in occupied territories (*e.g.*, looting of art collections).

5) The Waffen-SS was an integral part of the National Socialist state and functioned as its elite guard. A such, it bears a measure of responsibility for any crimes of the regime that it fought so hard to preserve.

Defenders of the Waffen-SS naturally try to raise doubts concerning the evidentiary basis of such a damning conclusion. It is hardly surprising, however, that the evidence for war crimes is often incomplete and usually less than ideal given the inherently chaotic nature of wartime conditions. While perhaps not unique when viewed against the broader canvas of world history, the Waffen-SS record of atrocities certainly resides at the extreme end of the behavioral spectrum. Numerous contributory psychosocial factors in combination with the all too human propensity for violence seem to have made such expressions of criminality relatively common among German elite forces during the Second World War. While every Waffen-SS member was not directly involved in the commission of war crimes, for the most part they all voluntarily served as the ultimate protectors of a violent, expansionist, racial-nationalist government that precipitated humanity's most destructive war to date. For this reason alone, the Waffen-SS *in its entirety* merits condemnation.

Yet, as noted earlier, an examination of the historical record leads to the inescapable conclusion that such atrocities or their kin have always been a part of warfare. Modern atrocities are not anomalous breaks with historical tradition, but have numerous parallels and precedents. Few countries have proven to be immune to outbreaks of violence stemming from intolerance, economic difficulties, power-lust, racism, nationalism, or political fanaticism.[1] While all military organizations inherently possess the capacity to authorize the commission of war crimes, certain situations serve to heighten this potential by first moving soldiers toward and then across the threshold of criminality. It is often felt that comparative studies of atrocities run the risk of blurring distinctions, trivializing specific events, and sacrificing rational understanding on the altar of moral disapproval. As Evans has noted, however,

> The act of historical comparison does not involve an equation of two or more events, or a blurring of distinctions between them; on the contrary, it means isolating what they have in common in order to find out how they differ. [2]

In truth, our continued failure to confront the misconduct of combat troops (regardless of nationality) ensures that the specter of atrocity remains undispelled, lurking in the shadows of future military operations.

From 1798 to 1993 the United States used its armed forces abroad a total of 234 instances in situations of conflict or potential conflict.[3] Numerous war crimes have been committed by U.S. armed forces from the American Revolution through the Vietnam War.[4] One of the more recent but little-known crimes was the murderous "pacification" operations of U.S. forces during the Phillippine-American War (1899 - 1902). Following the defeat of Spain in the Spanish-American War (1898), President McKinley brushed aside Filipino pleas for independence and occupied the country. Guerilla warfare quickly broke out and American commanders found themselves fighting an elusive and frustrating enemy. Under the banner of "Benevolent Assimilation," 70,000 U.S. soldiers brought massacres, concentration camps, the water-cure torture, scorched earth policies, rape, racial hatred, and free-fire zones to bear on the spirited but under-equipped Filipino resistance. In the war's most infamous incident, U.S. Brigadier General Jacob Smith ordered the 6th Separate Brigade to turn the province of Samar into a howling wilderness in response to an earlier ambush of American forces.

> I want no prisoners. I wish you to kill and burn, and the more you kill and butn the better you will please me. I want all persons killed who are capable of bearing arms in actual hostilities against the United States. 5

Smith set the minimum age limit at ten. Over the next five months, U.S. Marines would kill some 40,000 Fillipinos. At the same time, U.S. General Franklin Bell conducted a scorched-earth campaign in Batangas Province that resulted in the mass extermination of civilians. In two and one-half years (1899 - 1902), America's pursuit of "benevolent assimilation" resulted in the deaths of an estimated 500,000 Filipino's in what historian's have dubbed America's first Vietnam. Despite public outrage over these crimes, only a handful of American military personnel received minor reprimands for their behavior. The war was soon forgotten, one of its few legacies being the racial epithet "gook" (a corruption of *goo-goos*, an American term of contempt for Filipinos).

The Pacific conflict between the United States and Japan displayed many similarities with the horrific fighting between the Germans and Soviets on the Eastern Front. In both theaters, the order of the day was war without mercy with racial and ideological hatred fueling atrocities on all sides. Japanese troops displayed savage behavior toward civilian populations throughout Southeast Asia with torture, bayonetting and beheading common punitive measures. They also murdered civilians wholesale during retreats (e.g., 100,000 residents of Manila massacred by Japanese troops in February/March 1945). Japanese treatment of prisoners of war was no better. While only 4% of Allied POWs in German custody died during the war, 27% of those in Japanese custody died. Several thousand Allied POWs died in Manchuria as a result of medical and biological weapons experimentation by the infamous Unit 731. While the behavior of U.S. forces was generally more restrained, atrocities were still committed to a disheartening degree. As Jones observed,

> What kind of war do civilians suppose we fought, anyway? We shot prisoners in cold blood, wiped out hospitals, strafed lifeboats, killed or mistreated enemy civilians, finished off the enemy wounded, tossed the dying into a hole with the dead, and in the Pacific boiled the flesh off enemy skulls to make table ornaments for sweethearts, or carved their bones into letter openers. We topped off our saturation bombing and burning of enemy civilians by dropping atomic bombs on two nearly defenseless cities, thereby setting an all-time record for instantaneous mass slaughter... We fought a dishonorable war, because morality had a low priority in battle. 6

While accounts of Japanese atrocities were widely reported in the U.S., little was heard concerning American excesses. The U.S. military was particularly diligent at confiscating preserved enemy body parts that were mailed or carried home by GIs.

The Vietnam War was a rare instance where the general public had to confront the all too real face of war. As Anderson observed, "The thought that Americans themselves (apart from some stereotyped villains) could be evil simply didn't exist for most Americans."[7] Americans' willful historical ignorance was clearly demonstrated by their reaction to a number of war crimes committed in Vietnam, particularly the firing of Cam Ne village (August 1965) and the My Lai and My Khe massacres (March 1968).[8] In some ways, the circumstances leading up to these unprovoked massacres of civilians were a replay of the events that influenced Waffen-SS units to commit similar atrocities in the Soviet Union and the Balkans. Clearly though, American policymakers and military leaders had not learned the requisite lessons from Nazi Germany's conspicuous anti-partisan failures on the Eastern Front during the Second World War. The nature of American operations in Vietnam, especially those policies and weapons which failed to differentiate between combatants and non-combatants ("free-fire" and "free-bomb" zones, saturation bombing, assassination programs, search and destroy operations, forcible removal of civilian populations, "mere gook rule" body counts [if it's dead and it's Vietnamese, it's VC], cluster bombs, napalm, white phosphorus, etc.), set the stage for the normalization of atrocity and called into question the very legality of the war's overall conduct. At the field command level, inept and unscrupulous officers were often responsible for many otherwise preventable atrocities committed against Vietnamese civilians by U.S. forces ostensibly on a mission of "winning hearts and minds."

Despite their most cherished beliefs about themselves, many American soldiers in Vietnam did not question orders that directed them to raze villages and exterminate non-combatants in suspected Viet Cong-controlled or infiltrated areas. Additionally, the failure of the military justice system to fairly punish its own war criminals, as well as domestic political intereference with trials, showed the conscience of America's leadership to be gravely flawed. Sadly, the lessons of massacres such as that at My Lai are only slowly being taken to heart by our military personnel. Despite a renewed emphasis on the laws of war at the staff and command schools, an initial random sample survey of several hundred U.S. military and civilian officials at the Pentagon indicated that, contrary to long-established protections for all non-combatants, many of those polled did not believe enemy civilians should be treated the same as friendly civilians.[9] More recent studies and the performance of Coalition Forces during the first Gulf War, however, appear to show tentative indications that the message may finally be sinking in.[10]

On the homefront, atrocities during the Vietnam War posed an irreconcilable contradiction that was intolerable for the American general public.[11] When presented with the choice of either sheltering themselves in naiveté or having their myths concerning U.S. national character undermined, the overwhelming majority of Americans -- like the Germans before them -- chose a psychologically easy retreat into ignorance and denial. Rather than confront the complexities and moral ambiguities of the war, most Americans chose to wrap the historical record in the flag. American moral superiority remained firmly grounded; atrocities were only committed by uncivilized foreigners ("Our boys would never do something like that."). A recent My Lai massacre poll indicated that only 35% of Americans felt that the officer in charge on the ground, Lt. William Calley, should have been prosecuted for his actions.[12] An even lower number of those polled (32%) felt that American officers should be tried for war crimes they may have committed and a mere 45% thought it had been right to try Nazis for their crimes. Most disturbing of all was the fact that 67% of Americans polled said that they would have shot the villagers of My Lai if ordered to do so. Equally as distressing was the hero's welcome that Lt. Calley received from an assortment of political and veterans' organizations; atrocity clearly had its admirers in the United States. In relying on blindness to assuage its conscience, America failed to confront its guilt or to examine the amoral criminality that the war revealed in many of its soldiers. Most Americans are still incapable of reappraising their cherished historical and cultural assumptions in light of the Vietnam War. The poll cited above and others indicate that Americans experience serious cognitive and motivational obstacles when it comes to challenging authority figures. We are living in a society that has absorbed without fundamental self-examination or confrontation first Hiroshima, then My Lai, and finally revelations that our military and intelligence communities protected and utilized Japanese scientists responsible for killing thousands of Allied POWs in gruesome biological warfare experiments.[13]

While Germany must not be excused for rejecting and minimizing its horrific recent past, it must be recognized that denial is a universal and time-worn human psychological defense mechanism. Arendt (1968) has coined the term "inner emigration" for this phenomenon of withdrawing into an interior realm where seemingly unendurable realities cease to exist. World history and public life are sanitized and reshaped along desired lines. The crimes of the past are expunged; horror is reduced to sentimentality. The public of every nation prefers to ignore the dark corners and disquieting truths of their history focusing instead on the transgressions of others and mythologizing the realities of war. Denial and apologism are unkillable, anti-intellectual movements whose power is derived from our resistance to face the truth about the horrible nature and consequences of our actions during wartime. When left unchallenged and unrefuted, they continually feed off our moral reserve eventually leaving behind empty husks in place of our souls. The choice we are faced with is either pursuing a road of painful introspection and candor or a quick, easy path of dissociation that disturbs no sensibilities. Unfortunately, humans are all too ingenious at finding ways to exculpate themselves or rationalize their actions. We wish to attenuate and relativize the horrors of war, especially those for which we are personally responsible. We would rather think better of ourselves and dare not leave our protective societal cocoons constructed of a surreal mixture of military nostalgia and idealized carnage. We all want to be "the good man." It is against our nature to accept that those like us are capable of such horrific acts against other human beings. We resist all evidence that ordinary, seemingly upstanding men will commit cold-blooded murder given the proper circumstances. Such hopeful naiveté allows atrocities to continue unabated while the discomfited quickly look away. As Charney noted, if we were to take a true appraisal of the human condition,

> ... we would likely be burned up - destroyed - for having looked at the unbearably ugly side of the countenance of God as it were, i.e., the terribly tortured realities of suffering and premature death that are the fates of millions of us. 14

We tend to forget that from 1939 to 1948 what passed for "Western Civilization" in Europe at the time completely broke down and nearly disappeared from the world stage. Many find comfort in the mistaken notion that the rise of Nazism was the result of factors somehow unique to the German people, their culture, and the times. Such a conclusion represents the most dangerous sort of historical ignorance and intellectual myopia. Fascism represents "a particularly vivid refutation of the democratic view of human nature"15 which posits that people, even those possessing self-interests, are basically harmless. Instead, there is increasing evidence,

> "that beneath the liberal surface of respectable intellectual people there is a dark underside that can very easily flame up into fascist fury in times of stress and anxiety."16

At their most fundamental level, Fascism and National Socialism were particularly effective forms of nationalism. Germany under Adolf Hitler is an especially illuminating case study in the fragility of traditional moral and ethical codes when juxtaposed against raw self-interest. Despite centuries of the supposedly moderating influences of Christianity, there still lurks just below the surface of Western man a primeval barbarism that continually threatens to reassert itself, especially when backed by well-organized force and seemingly sanctified by law and doctrine. This is the great danger of fanaticism: an outpouring of intolerance, hate and violence from the crippled nature of the man who is afraid of being fully human.

In an essential way, technological and primitive societies differ little from each other: they both invoke rituals to rationalize their insatiable addictions to sadism and masochism. While we have not advanced ethically as far from our barbaric ancestors as we would like to believe, we have unfortunately developed the technological tools to butcher our enemies on a scale unimaginable in earlier

times. Warfare has become an increasingly dirty affair; the traditional distinctions between legitimate killing and war crimes have been blurred by the use of aerial attacks, artillery bombardment, and guerilla warfare. In this century we have witnessed the phenomenon of "man-made mass death" reach global proportions simply because the technological means have finally become available.[17] The never-ending modernization of combat (greater firepower and accuracy; expanding kill zones), the restructuring of military training to actively dehumanize the enemy (turning them into video targets), the increasingly slick marketing of the military, and the erosion of ethical restraints in general society all lead down a descending spiral into atrocity. The recent Persian Gulf conflicts may be structurally prophetic of future engagements: the standoff destruction of an enemy rendered faceless by technology with its horrible toll of random "collateral damage" (civilian deaths) followed by ground-based mopping-up operations so brief that traditional atrocities are completely lacking, or at least rare. In such scenarios, the disproportionate number of civilian deaths is inevitably rationalized as an unavoidable aspect of the conflict that the enemy brought upon itself.

As war has grown more mechanical and impersonal the imposition of elaborate barriers and distances between combatants has resulted in a marked lessening of certain natural scruples of humanity. This was made explicit by the atomic bombings of Hiroshima and Nagasaki which, in addition to forever destroying America's moral credibility, demonstrated that humanity had entered a new age where civilians could unilaterally be declared legitimate targets. Our drift into acceptance of total war was codified with the U.S. Army's expansion of the legitimate scope of strategic bombing in the 1956 revisions of the *Law of Land Warfare* so as to permit easy justification of unrestricted bombing of civilian targets in the future. The recent imbroglio concerning the Smithsonian Institution's proposed Enola Gay exhibition put in stark relief America's hypocrisy and inability to acknowledge the questionable morality of its actions. Despite the fact that technological developments have now reached the point where no political goal can justify the destructive potential of the weapons we possess, we continue to be so enamoured of authoritarianism as to be ruled by and obey those who threaten us with nuclear annihilation.[18] Lifton and Markusen (1990) have identified a number of parallels between the Nazi genocidal and modern nuclear mentality. These include: the brutalizing power of technology, anticommunist totalism, mystification and ideology, bureaucratic language, dissociation, and illusion. In such dire circumstances it is vital for modern societies to develop the self-discipline needed to restrain their military activities.

Having long ago accepted the contradictions and false justifications inherent to the Augustinian "just war" concept, Western society has proceeded down a slippery slope of rationalization and pseudo-ethical handwaving. Even more disturbing is the realization that modern military activities are increasingly being accorded a separate moral realm of their own, a realm in which the only imperative is often to follow orders. Many of our political and military leaders speak of the harsh realities of the world in a manner that abets and encourages brutality. Obedience has become perverted and is increasingly invoked as the license to destroy others dictated solely by the whims and fancies of recognized authority figures.[19] Yet we also have the duty to disobey.[20] Three fundamental orientations can be taken towards authority: rules, roles, and values. Only an orientation based on values will avoid the commission of atrocities. All of us must break the habit of unquestioning obedience based on an adherence to rules or the fulfillment of an accepted role. Modern societies have created a combat milieu wherein acts of common decency towards an opponent are increasingly rare because they are simply beyond the feeble character-strength of the average soldier. We submissively accept the violence of our time without attempting to overcome it. We have been subsumed by the social organizations around us and have surrendered our individuality and freedom before a smothering wave of conformity and passivity.[21] However, "our society shouldn't be structured, ought not to be structured, so that only the extraordinary few can conduct themselves in a moral fashion."[22]

Contrary to accepted wisdom, studies indicate that an individual's religious affiliation appears to have little influence on the capacity to observe the laws of war.[23] This observation is clearly illustrated by the Holocaust in Europe during World War II. The 800,000 or so Jews saved by conscientious Christians is dwarfed by the numbers of those killed by hatred and indifference. For each person who intervened, scores stood idly by or looked the other way. As Niebuhr observed, it is not unusual for Christians "to act differently as private individuals and as members of large groups."[24] For nearly two millenia Western churches have preached the *imitatio Christi* (in fact, war was repudiated by Christians until the time Constantine), but to actually conduct one's life as Jesus taught is to risk being considered a madman by the world at large. There is a gulf "between the openly proclaimed word and its authenticity, between the confession and political action in the name of humaness."[25] It is usually objected that it may be a greater evil not to resist tyranny. As Bonhoeffer observed however,

> The Christian ideal of non-resistance to evil is invariably viewed as impracticable given the evil nature of the world we live in. Yet Jesus preached that it was for this very reason that we must not be of this world and that the precept of non-resistance must be put into practice. [26]

We have forgotten what it would be like to act out of faith. We have passively accepted a false faith, which is no more than conventional opinion and culture, and come to think of it as our religion. We no longer practice virtue because it is not expedient. Our true selves have become mired in contingent and arbitrary factors which are accorded undue consideration.[27] As Merton lamented,

> It does not even seem to enter our minds that there might be some incongruity in praying to the God of peace... and at the same time planning to annihilate... millions of civilians and soldiers, men, women, and children without discrimination... [28]

The vicissitudes of modern power struggles dictate that morality may be cast aside at any moment as useless baggage. We can either discard our values altogether and act in a purely ruthless manner or shore up our conscience and cleave to those moral laws we know to be just.[29] In order to stand any chance of becoming more fully human, we must unshackle ourselves from the dominant political and social illusions of our time.

The Reichian metaphor of an emotional plague afflicting all of humanity seems to hit closest to home. Is mankind capable of waking up from its perpetual sleep and taking responsibility for its actions? Or are we so trapped by our psychological armoring that we will continue to robotically follow our leaders right into a final nuclear or biological mass suicide? Interestingly enough, Merton (1961, 1964b, 1968) diagnosed Western societal illness in a fashion strikingly similar to Reich's conception of the emotional plague. He wrote deploringly of the "false mysticism of the Mass Society" captivating men alienated from their true selves and dead to their personal needs. Once free and reasonable men, they have become dissociated and transformed into the pliant instruments of the power politician. They are no longer individuals with independent consciences but have become personae (masks) who submit and conform to the mass society around them fearing that dissent would expose them to ostracism. They are no longer in touch with their own capacity to express and transcend hostility. Each must now fight against an internal totalitarianism -- an individualistic, hidden tendency toward fascist or totalist sentiments. Failing to win this battle, they are transformed into patriotic, dutiful citizens who practice the greatest evil with ritual solemnity as if it were somehow noble, intelligent and important.

Clearly, we must either pay the immediate price of our beliefs or risk burning to ash our hopes and dreams for the future. Atrocities demand painful self-examination, for if we continue to calmly accept the unrestricted murder of non-combatants -- women, children, the mentally and physically handicapped, prisoners, the elderly -- then there is ultimately nothing that we will not learn to accept. In this regard, the much-maligned Nuremberg Trials and the later enumerated Nuremberg Principles (see Appendix C) have given citizens a critical set of legal arguments to place as a buffer between themselves and the criminal solicitations of their own government. Beyond trying to shelter ourselves in the protection of such well-meaning documents, we must learn to admit our violent propensities without ever acquiescing to them. A knowledge of atrocities will help us cast off our hubris and learn to see ourselves as members of a worldwide struggle to overcome mass slaughter and to ensure the continuity of human life.[30] We must learn to hate the true root causes of war: the injustice, tyranny, greed, and disorder in our own souls.

Notes:

1. Levi, 1986, pp. 199-200.
2. Evans, 1989, pp. 85-91.
3. Collier, 1993.
4. Karsten, 1978.
5. Order reproduced in Galang, 1997.
6. Jones, 1956, pp. 48-53.
7. Anderson, 1998, p. 14.
8. On March 16, 1968 elements of Task Force Barker massacred over 400 Vietnamese civilians at the village of My Lai. The My Khe massacre (100 civilians executed) occurred at the same time and was also perpetrated by elements of Task Force Barker. See Peers, 1970; Bilton and Sims, 1992.
9. Karsten, 1978, p. 90.
10. Anderson, 1998, p. 165.
11. Falk et al., 1971, p. 462.
12. Poll reported in Kelman and Hamilton, 1989.
13. Falk et al., 1971, pp. 25-26; Powell, 1981; Harris, 1995
14. Charney, 1991, vol. 2, p. 19.
15. Niebuhr, 1972, p. 24.
16. Wilson, 1987, p. 4.
17. Wyschogrod, 1985; Totten et al., 1995
18. Arendt, 1969, p. 3.
19. Chittister, 1992, p. 96.
20. Kelman and Hamilton, 1989.
21. Kelley, 1974, p. 176.
22. Bilton and Sims, 1992, p. 374.
23. Karsten, 1978, p. 130.
24. Bainton, 1960, p. 216.
25. Bethge, 1975, pp. 119-120.
26. Bonhoeffer, in Kelly and Nelson, 1995, pp. 317-318.
27. Niebuhr, 1949a, p. 252.
28. Merton, 1961, p. 120.
29. Merton, 1964b, p. 156.
30. Lifton, in Anderson, 1998, p. 25.

Kiev 1946: The execution of German War criminals, most of them are from the Waffen SS.

Smolensk 1946: The execution of German war criminals. Among them are Waffen SS soldiers.

Appendices

Appendix A: Table of Corresponding Ranks

Schutzstaffel (SS)	German Army (until 5/45)	U.S. Army [British Army, where different]
Reichsführer	Generalfeldmarschall	General of the Army [Field Marshal]
Oberstgruppenführer	Generaloberst	no equivalent
Obergruppenführer	General	General
Gruppenführer	Generalleutnant	Lieutenant-General
Brigadeführer	Generalmajor	Major-General
Oberführer	Oberst	Brigadier-General
Standartenführer	Oberst	Colonel
Obersturmbannführer	Oberstleutnant	Lieutenant-Colonel
Sturmbannführer	Major	Major
Hauptsturmführer	Hauptmann	Captain
Obersturmführer	Oberleutnant	First Lieutenant
Untersturmführer	Leutnant	Second Lieutenant
Sturmscharführer	Stabsfeldwebel	Sergeant-Major [Regimental Sergeant-Major]
Stabsscharführer	Hauptfeldwebel	Sergeant-Major
Hauptscharführer	Oberfeldwebel	Master-Sergeant [Sergeant-Major]
Oberscharführer	Feldwebel	Technical-Sergeant [Quartermaster-Sergeant]
Scharführer	Unterfeldwebel	Staff Sergeant
Unterscharführer	Unteroffizier	Sergeant
Rottenführer	Gefreiter	Corporal
Sturmmann	Oberschütze	Private 1st Class [Lance-Corporal]
SS-Mann	Schütze	Private

Appendix B: Glossary

Abschnitt	district
Abteilung	section or detachment
Allgemeine-SS	General SS
Amt	office or branch
Arbeitslager (AL)	labor camp
Armee	army
Artillerie	artillery
Aufklärung	reconnaissance
Ausbildungs und Ersatz Bataillon	training and replacement battalion
Bataillon	battalion
Beauftragter	representative or commissioner
Befehlshaber	senior commander
Befehlshaber der Ordnungspolizei (BdO)	senior commander of the Order Police
Befehlshaber der Sicherheitspolizei und Sicherheitsdienst (BdS)	senior commander of the Security Police and the Security Service
Chef	chief
Dienststelle	headquarters, administrative office or depot
Einheit	unit
Einsatzgruppe (EG)	operational group or task force
Einsatzkommando (EK)	task force commando (subset of Einsatzgruppe)
Einsatzstab	operational staff
Ersatz	replacement
Feldpolizei	field police (military police)
Freiwilliger	volunteer
Führer	leader
Führungstab	leadership staff
Fuss-Standarten	General SS infantry regiments
Gau	area/region
Gauleiter	area leader
Gebirgs	mountain
Geheime Feldpolizei (GFP)	Secret Field Police (military police)
Geheime Staatspolizei (Gestapo)	Secret State Police
Gendarmerie	Rural Police
Gericht	court of law, tribunal
Grenadier	infantry
Grenzpolizei	Frontier Police
Gruppe	group
Hauptamt	main office
Heer	army
Heeresgruppe	army group
HIAG	Waffen-SS veteran's organization
Hitlerjugend (HJ)	Hitler Youth
Höchste SS und Polizeiführer (HöSSPf)	Supreme SS and Police Leader
Höhere SS und Polizeiführer (HSSPf)	Higher SS and Police Leader

Infanterie	infantry
Inspektor	inspector
Inspektor der Ordnungspolizei (IdO)	inspector of the Ordnungspolizei
Inspektor der Sicherheitspolizei und Sicherheitsdienst (IdS)	inspector of the Security Police and Security Service
Jäger	hunter
Judenaktion	Jewish action (execution, rounding up, or both)
Judenfrei	Jew-free
Junkerschule	officer cadet training school
Kampfgruppe	battle group
Kommandoamt der Waffen-SS	Waffen-SS operational headquarters
Kommandostab	field command staff
Konzentrationslager (KZ)	concentration camp
Korps	corps
Kreis	province
Kriegsberichter	war correspondent
Kriegsmarine	navy
Kriminalpolizei (Kripo)	Criminal Police
Lager	camp
Landgericht	provincial court
Leiter	leader or commander
Leitstelle	regional Gestapo/Kripo headquarters
Luftwaffe	air force
Militärbefehlshaber (MBF)	military governor
Nachrichten	intelligence or signals/communications
Nationalsozialistische Kraftfahr-Korps (NSKK)	National Socialist Motor Corps
Oberabschnitt	main district
Oberkommando	High Command
Oberkommando des Heeres	German Army High Command
Oberkommando Wehrmacht	German Military High Command
Ordnungspolizei (Orpo)	Order Police
Organization Todt (OT)	state construction organization
Panzer	armoured
Panzergrenadier	armoured infantry
Persönlicher Stab Reichsführer-SS	Himmler's personal staff
Pioniere	engineers/sappers
Polizei	police
Polizeidirektor	police director
Polizeigebietsführer (Pgf)	police area commander
Polizeipräsident	police president
Polizeiregiment	police regiment
Reichsarbeitsdienst	National Labor Service
Reichsführer-SS (RFSS)	Reich Leader of the SS
Reichsführung-SS	SS High Command
Reichskommisar für die Festigung des Deutschen Volkstums (RKFDV)	Reich Commissioner for the Strengthening of German Nationhood
Reichssicherheitshauptamt (RSHA)	Reich Central Security Main Office

Reiter	mounted/cavalry
Reiterstandarten	General SS cavalry regiments
Reitlehrer	riding instructor
Remonteamt	cavalry remount center
säuberungsaktion	cleansing action
Schule	school
Schutzmannschaft	Auxiliary Police
Schutzpolizei (Schupo)	Protection Police
Schutzstaffel (SS)	protection detachment
Selbstschutz	Self-Protection Police (Volksdeutsche militia)
Sicherheitsdienst (SD)	Security Service
Sicherheitshauptamt (SD-Haupamt)	Central Security Office
Sicherheitspolizei (Sipo)	Security Police
Sonderbehandlung	"special treatment", euphemism for execution
Sonderkommando	special detachment
SS-Führungshauptamt (SS-FHA)	SS Main Operational Office
SS-Gerichtsamt	SS Legal Office
SS-Hauptamt	SS Main Office
SS-Personalhauptamt	SS Personnel Main Office
SS-Rasse und Siedlungshauptamt (RuSHA)	SS Race and Resettlment Main Office
SS-Totenkopfstandarten (SSTK)	Death's Head Regiments, became part of W-SS
SS-Totenkopfverbände (SSTV)	Death's Head units, became part of W-SS
SS und Polizeiführer (SSPf)	SS and Police Leader
SS und Polizeigebietskommandeur	SS and Police area commander
SS-Wirtschafts- und	SS Economic and
Verwaltungs-Hauptamt (WVHA)	Administrative Main Office
Stab	staff
Standarte	regiment
Standortkommandant	garrison commander
Stelle	post
Stellvertreter	deputy or representative
Sturmbann	battalion
Technische Nothilfe	Technical Emergency Corps
Teilkommando (TK)	sub-unit
Truppenübungsplatz	troop training area
Verfügungstruppe (VT)	Special Purpose Troops, forerunner of the Waffen-SS
Vernichtungslager (VL)	extermination camp
Vlaamse Wacht	Dutch paramilitary colloborationist group
Volksdeutsche	ethnic Germans
Volksdeutsche Mittelstelle (Vomi)	Ethnic German Assistance Office
Volkssturm	Home Guard
Waffen-SS (W-SS)	Armed SS
Wehrkreis	military district
Wehrmacht	armed forces
zur besonderer Verwendung (zbV)	special purpose

Appendix C: The Nuremberg Principles (1946)

Principles of International Law Recognized in the
Charter of the Nuremberg Tribunal and in the
Judgment of the Tribunal

As formulated by the International Law Commission, June - July 1950

Principle I

Any person who commits an act which constitutes a crime under international law is responsible therefor and liable to punishment.

Principle II

The fact that internal law does not impose a penalty for an act which constitutes a crime under international law does not relieve the person who committed the act from responsibility under international law.

Principle III

The fact that a person who committed an act which constitutes a crime under international law acted as Head of State or responsible government official does not relieve him from responsibility under international law.

Principle IV

The fact that a person acted pursuant to order of his Government or of a superior does not relieve him from responsibility under international law, provided a moral choice was in fact possible to him.

Principle V

Any person charged with a crime under international law has the right to a fair trial on the facts and law.

Principle VI

The crimes hereinafter set out are punishable as crimes under international law:

a. Crimes against peace:
> **(i)** Planning, preparation, initiation or waging of a war of aggression or a war in violation of international treaties, agreements or assurances;
> **(ii)** Participation in a common plan or conspiracy for the accomplishment of any of the acts mentioned under (i).

b. War crimes:
Violations of the laws or customs of war which include, but are not limited to, murder, ill-treatment or deportation to slave-labour or for any other purpose of civilian population of or in occupied territory, murder or ill-treat-

ment of prisoners of war or persons on the seas, killing of hostages, plunder of public or private property, wanton destruction of cities, towns, or villages, or devastation not justified by military necessity.

c. Crimes against humanity:

Murder, extermination, enslavement, deportation and other inhuman acts done against any civilian population, or persecutions on political, racial or religious grounds, when such acts are done or such persecutions are carried on in execution of or in connexion with any crime against peace or any war crime.

Principle VII

Complicity in the commission of a crime against peace, a war crime, or a crime against humanity as set forth in Principle VI is a crime under international law.

Appendix D: Atrocity Statistics

Unit	Active Service	Atrocities
1. SS-Panzer-Division *Leibstandarte Adolf Hitler*	1939 - 1945	27
2. SS-Panzer-Division *Das Reich*	1939 - 1945	29*
3. SS-Panzer-Division *Totenkopf*	1939 - 1945	18*
4. SS-Polizei-Panzergrenadier-Division	1939 - 1945	8
5. SS-Panzer-Division *Wiking*	1940 - 1945	7*
6. SS-Gebirgs-Division *Nord*	1940 - 1945	1*
7. SS-Frewilligen-Gebirgs-Division *Prinz Eugen*	1942 - 1945	42+*
8. SS-Kavallerie-Division *Florian Geyer*	1941 - 1945	30+
9. SS-Panzer-Division *Hohenstaufen*	1943 - 1945	5
10. SS-Panzer-Division *Frundsberg*	1943 - 1945	0
11. SS-Freiwilligen-Panzergrenadier-Division *Nordland*	1943 - 1945	1
12. SS-Panzer-Division *Hitlerjugend*	1943 - 1945	7
13. Waffen-Gebirgs-Division der SS *Handschar* (kroat. 1)	1943 - 1945	6+
14. Waffen-Grenadier-Division der SS (ukrainische 1)	1943 - 1945	27+*
15. Waffen-Grenadier-Division der SS (lettische 1)	1943 - 1945	0*
16. SS-Panzergrenadier-Division *Reichsführer-SS*	1943 - 1945	9
17. SS-Panzergrenadier-Division *Götz von Berlichingen*	1943 - 1945	4
18. SS-Freiwilligen-Panzergrenadier-Division *Horst Wessel*	1944 - 1945	2*
19. Waffen-Grenadier-Division der SS (lettische 2)	1943 - 1945	0*
20. Waffen-Grenadier-Division der SS (estnische 1)	1942 - 1945	0*
21. Waffen-Gebirgs-Division der SS *Skanderbeg* (alban. 1)	1944 - 1945	3
22. SS-Freiwilligen-Kavallerie-Division *Maria Theresia*	1944 - 1945	1
23. Waffen-Gebirgs-Division der SS *Kama* (kroatische 2)	1944	1*
23. SS-Freiwilligen-Panzergrenadier-Division *Nederland*	1943 - 1945	1+
24. Waffen-Gebirgs-Division der SS *Karstjäger*	1942 - 1945	0
25. Waffen-Grenadier-Division der SS *Hunyadi* (ungar. 1)	1944 - 1945	2*
26. Waffen-Grenadier-Division der SS (ungarische 2)	1944 - 1945	2*
27. SS-Freiwilligen-Grenadier-Division *Langemarck* (fläm. 1)	1943 - 1945	0
28. SS-Freiwilligen-Panzergrenadier-Division *Wallonie*	1943 - 1945	0
29. Waffen-Grenadier-Division der SS (russ. 1) ["Kaminski"]	1943 - 1944	2+*
29. Waffen-Grenadier-Division der SS (italienische 1)	1944 - 1945	1+
30. Waffen-Grenadier-Division der SS (russische 2)	1944 - 1945	0*
31. SS-Freiwilligen-Grenadier-Division	1944 - 1945	1
32. SS-Freiwilligen-Grenadier-Division *30. Januar*	1945	0
33. Waffen-Grenadier-Division der SS *Charlemagne* (fränz 1)	1944 - 1945	0
34. SS-Grenadier-Division Landstorm *Nederland*	1944 - 1945	2*
35. SS-Polizei-Grenadier-Division	1945	0*
36. Waffen-Grenadier-Division der SS ["Dirlewanger"]	1940 - 1945	24*
37. SS-Freiwilligen-Kavallerie-Division *Lutzow*	1945	0
38. SS-Grenadier-Division *Nibelungen*	1945	0
1. SS-Infanterie (mot.)-Brigade	1941 - 1945	60+

Sources

Academy of Sciences of the Ukrainian SSR, Institute of State and Law (1987). *Nazi Crimes in Ukraine*. Kiev: Naukova Dumka Publishers.

Adorno, Theodore; Frenkel-Brunswik, E.; Levinson, D.J. and Sanford, R.N. (1950). *The Authoritarian Personality*. New York: Harper & Row.

Ailsby, Christopher (1997). *SS: Roll of Infamy*. Osceola, WI: Motorbooks International.

Ainsztein, Reuben (1974). *Jewish Resistance in Nazi Occupied Eastern Europe*. New York: Barnes and Noble Books.

Ainsztein, Reuben (1979). *The Warsaw Ghetto Revolt*. New York: Holocaust Library.

Aitken, Leslie (1977). *Massacre on the Road to Dunkirk: Wormhoudt 1940*. London: William Kimber.

Allen, Charles R. (1985). *Nazi War Criminals in America: Facts... Action, The Basic Handbook*. New York: Highgate House.

Anderson, David L. (1998). *Facing My Lai: Moving Beyond the Massacre*. Lawrence, KS: University Press of Kansas.

Angolia, John R. and Schlicht, Adolf (1997). *Uniforms and Traditions of the Luftwaffe* [2 volumes]. San Jose, CA: R.J. Bender Publishing.

Anonymous (1944). *The Trial in the Case of the Atrocities Committed by the German Fascist Invaders in the City of Kharkov and in the Kharkov region, December 15 - 18, 1943*. Moscow: Foreign Languages Publishing House.

Arad, Yitzhak (1982). *Ghetto in Flames: The Struggle and Destruction of the Jews in Vilna in the Holocaust*. New York: Holocaust Library.

Arad, Yitzhak (1987). *Belzec, Sobibor, Treblinka: The Operation Reinhard Death Camps*. Bloomington: Indiana University Press.

Arad, Yitzhak; Krakowski, Shmuel and Spector, Shmuel (1989). *The Einsatzgruppen Reports: Selections from the Dispatches of the Nazi Death Squads' Campaign against the Jews in Occupied Territories of the Soviet Union, July 1941 - January 1943*. New York: Holocaust Library.

Arendt, Hannah (1958). *The Origins of Totalinarianism*. New York: Meridian Books.

Arendt, Hannah (1964). *Eichmann in Jerusalem: A Report on the Banality of Evil*. New York: Penguin Books.

Arendt, Hannah (1968). *Men in Dark Times*. New York: Harcourt, Brace & World, Inc.

Arendt, Hannah (1969). *On Violence*. New York: Harcourt, Brace & World, Inc.

"Army to Present posthumous Awards in Dallas Ceremony", III Corps and Fort Hood News Release, dated 13 March 1998.

Artzt, Heinz (1974). *Mörder in Uniform: Organisationen, die zu Vollstreckern nationalsozialistischer Verbrechen wurden*. München: Kindler Verlag.

Aschenauer, Rudolf (1978). *Der Fall Reder: ein Pladoyer fur Recht und Wahrheit*. Berg am See: Kurt Vowinckel Verlag.

Aschenauer, Rudolf (1982). *Krieg ohne Grenzen: Die Partisankampf gegen Deutschland 1939-45*. Leoni am Starnberger See: Druffel Verlag.

Ash, M.G. (1997). "American and German perspectives on the Goldhagen debate: history, identity, and the media". *Holocaust and Genocide Studies*, vol. 11, no. 3, pp. 396 - 411.

Auerbach, Hellmuth (1962). "Die Einheit Dirlewanger," *Vierteljahrshefte für Zeitgeschichte*, band 10, heft 3, Juli, pp. 250-263.

Augstein, Rudolf et al. (1987). *'Historikerstreit': Die Dokumentation der Kontroverse um die Einzigartigkeit der nationalsozialistischen Judenvernichtung*. München: R. Piper.

Aziz, Phillipe and Fretard, Dominique (1974). *Les Criminels de Guerre*. Paris: Denoel.

Baade, Fritz et.al. [eds.](1965). *Unsere Ehre Heisst Treue: Kriegstagebuch des Kommandostabes Reichsführer-SS, Tätigkeitsberichte der 1. und 2. SS-Inf.-Brigade, der 1. SS-Kav.-Brigade und von Sonderkommandos der SS*. Wien: Europa Verlag.

Baglioni, Astorre (1975). *La Certosa dello Spirito Santo: la sanguinosa tragedia della Certosa di Lucca (settembre 1944) vissuta e narrate da un testimone e superstite*. Pitigliano: Azienda tipolitografica.

Bainton, Roland H. (1960). *Christian Attitudes toward War and Peace: A Historical Survey and Critical Re-evaluation*. Nashville, TN: Abingdon Press.

Baker, James T. (1971). *Thomas Merton, social critic*. Lexington, KY: Univesity Press of Kentucky.

Bartov, Omar (1986). *The Eastern Front, 1941-5, German Troops and the Barbarisation of Warfare*. New York: St. Martin's Press.

Bartov, Omar (1997). *Industrial Killing: World War I, The Holocaust, and Representation*. Paper presented at the 16th Annual Conference on the Holocaust, Millersville University, Millersville, PA, 12 pp.

Bauserman, John M. (1995). *The Malmedy Massacre*. Shippensburg, PA: White Mane Publishing Co.

Bayer, Hanns (1982). *Kavallerie Divisionen der Waffen-SS im Bild*. Osnabrück: Munin Verlag.

Beau, Georges and Gaubusseau, Leopold (1969). *R.5. : les S.S. en Limousin, Perigord, Quercy*. Paris: Presses de la Cite.

Bender, David L. and Leone, Bruno (1983). *War and Human Nature: Opposing Viewpoints*. St. Paul, MN: Greenhaven Press.

Bender, Roger J. and Taylor, Hugh P. (1969 - 1982). *Uniforms, Organization and History of the Waffen-SS* [5 volumes]. Mountain View, CA: R.J. Bender Publishing Co.

Bertic, Ivan (1987). *Veliki Geografski Atlas Jugoslavije*. Zagreb : SNL.

Bethge, Eberhard (1975). *Bonhoeffer: Exile and Martyr*. New York: Seabury Press.

Bilton, Michael and Sim, Kevin (1992). *Four Hours in My Lai*. New York: Penguin Books.

Birn, Ruth B. (1986). *Die Höheren SS- und Polizeiführer: Himmlers Vetreter im Reich und in den besetzten Gebieten*. Düsseldorf: Droste Verlag.

Birn, Ruth B. (1991). "Austrian Higher SS and Police Leaders and their participation in the Holocaust in the Balkans," *Holocaust and Genocide Studies*, vol. 6, no. 4, pp. 351-372.

Blandford, Edmund L. (1995). *Hitler's Second Army : the Waffen-SS*. London: Motorbooks International.

Bradley, John (1972). *Lidice: sacrificial village*. New York: Ballantine Books.

Braham, Randolph L. (1977). *The Hungarian Labor Service System, 1939 - 1945*. Boulder, CO: East European Quarterly (East European Monographs #31).

Braham, Randolph L. [ed.] (1983). *Contemporary Views on the Holocaust*. Boston: Kluwer-Nijhoff.

Breitman, Richard (1991). *The Architect of Genocide: Himmler and the Final Solution*. New York: Alfred A. Knopf, Inc.

Brode, Patrick (1997). *Casual Slaughters and Accidental Judgments: Canadian War Crimes Prosecutions, 1944 - 1948*. Toronto: University of Toronto Press.

Browning, Christopher R. (1992a). *The Path to Genocide: Essays on Launching the Final Solution*. New York: Cambridge University Press.

Browning, Christopher R. (1992b). *Ordinary Men: Reserve Police Battalion 101 and the Final Solution in Poland*. New York: HarperCollins Publishers.

Bruce, George L. (1972). *The Warsaw Uprising, 1 August - 2 October 1944*. London: Rupert Hart-Davis.

Büchler, Yehoshua (1986). "Kommandostab Reichsführer-SS: Himmler's Personal Murder Brigades in 1941," *Holocaust and Genocide Studies*, vol. 1, no. 1, pp. 11-25.

Buechner, Howard A. (1986). *Dachau: The Hour of the Avenger*. Metairie, LA: Thunderbird Press.

Bundesverband der Soldaten der ehemaligen Waffen-SS (1985). *Wenn alle Bruder schweigen*. Osnabrück: Munin Verlag.

Burleigh, Michael (1994). *Death and Deliverance: Euthanasia in Germany, 1900-1945*. Cambridge: Cambridge University Press.

Butler, Rupert (2002). *SS-Wiking: The History of the Fifth SS Division, 1941-45*. Havertown, PA: Casemate.

Buscher, Frank M. (1989). *The U.S. War Crimes Trial Program in Germany, 1946-1955* (Contributions in Military Studies, Number 86). New York: Greenwood Press.

Canovan, Margaret (1974). *The Political Thought of Hannah Arendt*. New York: Harcourt Brace Jovanovich.

Carnier, P.A. (1982). *Lo Sterminio Mancato*. Roma: Mursia.

Central Commission for Investigation of German Crimes in Poland (1946-7). *German Crimes in Poland* [3 volumes]. Warsaw: Tloczono w Drukarni sW Wojciecha Pod Zarzadem Panstwowym w Poznaniu.

Central Zydowska Komisja Historyczna w Polsce (1946). *Dokumenty i Materialy do Dziejow Okupacji Niemieckiej w Polsce* [3 volumes]. Warszawa: Wydawnictwa Centralnej Zydowskiej Komisji Historycznej.

Central Registry of War Criminals and Security Suspects [CROWCASS] (1946 - 1948). *Detention List* [11 volumes]. Berlin: U.S. Army, Allied Control Authority.

Central Registry of War Criminals and Security Suspects [CROWCASS] (1947). *Consolidated Wanted Lists* [2 volumes]. Berlin: U.S. Army, Allied Control Authority.

Charney, Israel W. (1982). *How can we commit the unthinkable? - Genocide: the Human Cancer*. Boulder, CO: Westview Press.

Charney, Israel W. [ed.] (1991). *Genocide: a critical bibliographic review* [2 volumes]. New York: Facts on File Publishers.

Chittister, Joan (1990), *Wisdom Distilled from the Daily: Living the Rule of St. Benedict Today*. San Francisco: HarperCollins Publishers.

Chittister, Joan (1992), *The Rule of St. Benedict: Insights for the Ages*. NewYork: Crossroad Publishing.

Ciechanowski, Jan M. (1974). *The Warsaw Uprising of 1944*. Cambridge: Cambridge University Press.

Coates, John M. (1973). *Schoolbooks and Krags: The United States Army in the Philippines, 1899-1903*. Westport, CT: Greenwood Press.

Collier, Ellen C. (1993). *Instances of Use of United States Forces Abroad, 1798-1993*. Washington, DC: Library of Congress, Congressional Research Service, Foreign Affairs & National Defense Division.

Cooper, Matthew (1979). *The Nazi War against Soviet Partisans, 1941-1944*. New York: Stein & Day Publishers.

Creel, George (1944). *War Criminals and Punishment*. New York: Robert M. Mc Bride & Co.

Cunliffe, Marcus (1956). *History of the Royal Warwickshire Regiment, 1919-1955*. London: William Clowes.

Cuppens, Gerd (1989). *Massacre á Malmedy? - Ardennes, 17 decembre 1944 - le Kampfgruppe Peiper dans les Ardennes*. Bayeux: Editions Heimdal.

Cyz-Ziesche, Jan (1975). *Die Kämpfe um die Befreiung der Lausitz während der grossen Schlacht um Berlin 1945*. Bautzen: VEB Domowina Verlag.

Czechoslovak Republic (1942). *German massacres in occupied Czechoslovakia following the attack on Reinhard Heydrich*. London: Czechoslovak Ministry of Foreign Affairs, Department of Information.

Czechoslovak Republic (1945). *German Crimes against Czechoslovakia: Official Reports*. London.

Datner, Szymon (1962). "Crimes Committed by the Wehrmacht during the September Campaign and the Period of Military Government (1 Sept. 1939 - 25 Oct. 1939)," *Polish Western Affairs* 3 (2), pp. 294-338.

Datner, Szymon, Gumkowski, Janusz, and Leszczynski, Kazimierz (1962). *Genocide 1939-1945*. Warszawa: Wydawnictwo Zachodnie.

Datner, Szymon (1964). *Crimes Against POWs*. Warszawa: Zachodnia Agencja Prasowa.

Dawidowicz, Lucy S. (1976). *The War against the Jews, 1933-1945*. New York: Bantam Books.

Degrelle, Leon (1952). *Die verlorene Legion*. Stuttgart: Veritas Verlag.

Degrelle, Leon (1985). *Campaign in Russia: The Waffen SS on the Eastern Front*. Costa Mesa, CA: Institute for Historical Review.

de Keizer, Madelon (1996). "The Skeleton in the Closet: The Memory of Putte, 1/2 October 1944," *History and Memory*, vol. 7, no. 2, pp. 70-99.

Delaforce, Patrick (1994). *Churchill's Desert Rats : from Normandy to Berlin with the 7th Armoured Division*. Dover, NH: Alan Sutton Publishing Ltd.

Deschner, Gunther (1972). *Warsaw Rising*. New York: Ballantine Books.

Deutsch, Harold C. (1968). *The Conspiracy against Hitler in the Twilight War*. Minneapolis: University of Minnesota Press.

de Zayas, Alfred M. (1990). *The Wehrmacht War Crimes Bureau, 1939-1945*. Lincoln: University of Nebraska Press.

Dicks, Henry V. (1972). *Licensed Mass Murder: A Socio-psychological study of some SS killers*. London: Chatto-Heinemann for Sussex University Press.

Dordevic, Bozidar et. al. (1960). *Imenik Mesta -- pregled svih mesta, opstina i srezova u jugoslaviji sa postama i teritorijalno nadleznim sudovima i javnim tuziostvima*. Beograd: Izdanje "Sluzbenog Lista FNRJ".

Dower, J.W. (1986). *War without Mercy: Race and Power in the Pacific War*. New York: Pantheon Books.

Drechsler, Robert H. (1978). *Walter Reder, der Gefangene von Gaeta*. Wien: R.H. Drechsler.

Drozdiak, William (1997). "Nazi SS Veterans Receive Pensions for War Injuries", *The Washington Post*, Thursday, May 8, page A20.

Duprat, Francois (1973). *Les Campagnes de la Waffen-SS*. Paris: Les Sept couleurs.

Ecer, Bohuslav (1944). *The Lessons of the Kharkov Trial*. London: Russia Today Society.

Einer, F.G. (1987). *Treu ihrem Volk: Des Selbstverständnis der Soldaten der Waffen-SS*. Osnabrück: Munin Verlag.

Evans, Richard J. (1989). *In Hitler's Shadow: West German Historians and the Attempt to Escape from the Nazi Past*. New York: Pantheon Books.

Falk, Richard A.; Kolko, Gabriel and Lifton, Robert J. (1971). *Crimes of War: a legal, political-documentary, and psychological inquiry into the responsibility of leaders, citizens, and soldiers for criminal acts in wars*. New York: Random House.

Farmer, Sarah (1999). *Martyred Village: Commemorating the 1944 Massacre at Oradour-sur-Glane*. Berkeley, CA: University of California Press.

Feneyvesi, Charles (1998). "Latvia: Former Members of Waffen SS Face New Scrutiny", Radio Free Europe/Radio Liberty Inc.,

press release dated 2 April.

Finkelstein, Norman G. and Birn, Ruth B. (1998). *A Nation on Trial: the Goldhagen Thesis and Historical Truth*. New York: Henry Holt and Company.

Fotion, Nicholas; Lachs, John and Massell, Mike (1995). *War, Terrorism, and Violence* (Morality in Our Age audio cassette series). Nashville, TN: Knowledge Products.

Fouche, Jean-Jacques (2005). *Massacre at Oradour, France 1944: Coming to Grips with Terror*. DeKalb, IL: Northern Illinois University Press.

Fried, Morton; Harris, Martin and Murphy, Robert [eds.] (1968). *War: the Anthropology of Armed Conflict and Aggression*. Garden City, NY: American Museum of Natural History, Natural History Press.

Friedlander, Henry (1997). "The Judiciary and Nazi Crimes in Postwar Germany", *Simon Wiesenthal Center Annual 1* [on-line at http://motlc.wiesenthal.com/resources/books/annual1/chap02.html].

Friedman, Tuviah [ed.] (1992). *The SS and Gestapo Criminals in Radom, 1939-1945*. Haifa, Israel: Institute of Documentation in Israel for the Investigation of Nazi War Crimes.

Friedman, Tuviah [ed.] (1993). *Die sechs SS- und Polizeiführer in Warschau von November 1939 bis Januar 1945: Dokumentensammlung*. Haifa, Israel: Institute of Documentation in Israel for the Investigation of Nazi War Crimes.

Gac, Stanislaw (1962). *Udzial 2. Armii Wojska Polskiego w Operacji Praskiej*. Warszawa: Wydawnictwo Ministerstwa Obrony Narodowej.

Galang, Reynaldo S. (1997). *The Burning of Samar*. Bakbakan International.

Germany [Territory under Allied Occupation, 1945 - U.S. Zone] (1949 - 1953). *Trials of War Criminals before the Nuremberg Military Tribunals under Control Council Law No. 10, Nuremberg, October 1946 - April 1949* ["Green series", 15 volumes]. Washington, DC: U.S. Government Printing Office.

Glishishch, Dr. Ventseslav (1970). *Terror and Crimes Committed by Nazi Germany in Serbia 1941-1944*. Belgrade: Izdavachko Preduzeshche "Rad".

Goldhagen, Daniel J. (1996). *Hitler's Willing Executioners: Ordinary Germans and the Holocaust*. New York: Alfred A. Knopf.

Goodrick-Clarke, Nicholaus (1992). *The Occult Roots of Nazism : Secret Aryan Cults and Their Influence on Nazi Ideology - The Ariosophists of Austria and Germany, 1890-1935*. New York: New York University Press.

Grabitz, Helge and Scheffler, Wolfgang (1988). *Letzte Spuren: Ghetto Warschau, SS-Arbeitslager Trawniki, Aktion Erntefest*. Berlin: Edition Hentrich.

Greil, Lothar (1958). *Die Wahrheit über Malmedy*. Munchen-Lochhausen: Schild Verlag.

Greil, Lothar (1959). *Die Luge von Marzabotto: ein Dokumentarbericht uber den Fall Major Reder*. Munchen-Lochhausen: Schild Verlag.

Greil, Lothar (1977). *Oberst der Waffen-SS Joachim Peiper und der Malmedy-Prozess*. Munchen-Lochhausen: Schild Verlag.

Greil, Lothar (1977). *Marzabotto: Begriff eines infamen Weltbetruges*. Perg: F. Strasser.

Greil, Lothar (1992). *Drei Kapitel Zeitgeschichte*. Coburg: Nation Europa Verlag.

Greece, Hellenikon Ethnikon Grapheion Enklematon Polemou [Office National Hellenique des criminels de Guerre] (1946). *Les Atrocites des Quatre Envahisseurs de la Grece: Allemands, Italiens, Bulgares, Albanais*. Athens.

Groen, Koos and Van Maanen, Willem G. (1977). *Putten op de Veluwe: Het spoor terug naar de tragedie van 1944*. Zutphen: De Walburg Pers.

Grossman, Lt. Col. David A. (1995). *On Killing: The Psychological Cost of Learning to Kill in War and Society*. Boston: Little, Brown and Company.

Gumkowski, Janusz and Leszczynski, Kazimierz (1961). *Poland under Nazi Occupation*. Warszawa: Polonia Publishing House.

Gutman, Israel [ed.] (1990). *Encyclopedia of the Holocaust* [4 volumes]. New York: MacMillan Publishing Company.

Gutman, Yisrael and Berenbaum, Michael [eds.] (1994). *Anatomy of the Auschwitz Death Camp*. Bloomington: Indiana University Press.

Haberbusch, Kuno (1997). "Germany Pays Billions to Nazi War Criminals: Nazi war criminals officially termed victims", NDR/Panorama press release dated 30 January.

Harris, Sheldon H (1995). *Factories of Death: Japanese Biological Warfare 1932-45 and the American Cover-Up*. New York: Routledge Publishing.

Hartman, Geoffrey [ed.] (1986). *Bitburg in Moral and Political Perspective*. Bloomington: Indiana University Press.

Hastings, Max (1981). *Das Reich: The March of the 2nd SS Panzer Division through France*. New York: Holt, Rinehart & Winston.

Hatheway, Joseph G. (1992). *The Ideological Origins of the Pursuit of Perfection within the Nazi SS*. Ph.D. thesis, University of Wisconsin at Madison.

Hausser, Paul (1953). *Waffen-SS im Einsatz*. Gottingen: Plesse Verlag.

Hausser, Paul (1966). *Soldaten wie andere auch: Der Weg der Waffen-SS*. Osnabrück: Munin Verlag.

Headland, Ronald (1992). *Messages of Murder: A Study of the Reports of the Einsatzgruppen of the Security Police and the Security Service, 1941-1943*. Rutherford, NJ: Fairleigh Dickinson Univ. Press.

Heike, Wolf-Dietrich (1974). *Sie wollten die Freiheit: Die Geschichte der Ukrainischen Division, 1943-1945*. Dorheim: Podzun Verlag.

Held, Walter (1978). *Verbände und Truppen der deutschen Wehrmacht und Waffen-SS im Zweiten Weltkrieg: Eine Bibliographie der deutschsprachigen Nachkriegsliteratur*. Osnabrück: Biblio Verlag.

Hilberg, Raul (1985). *The Destruction of the European Jews* [3 volumes]. New York: Holmes & Meier.

Hilberg, Raul (1997). "Le Phenomenon Goldhagen". *Les Temps Modernes*, no. 592, Feb.-Mar., pp. 1-10.

Höhne, Heinz (1971). *The Order of the Death's Head*. New York: Ballantine Books.

Hondros, John L. (1983). *Occupation and Resistance: The Greek Agony, 1941-1944*. NewYork: Pella Publishing Co.

Höss, Rudolf (1992). *Death Dealer: The Memoirs of the SS Kommandant at Auschwitz*. Buffalo, NY: Prometheus Books.

Husemann, Friedrich (1971 - 1977). *Die guten Glaubens waren: Geschichte der SS-Polizei-Division* [3 volumes]. Osnabrück: Munin Verlag.

Infield, Glenn B. (1990). *Secrets of the SS*. New York: Jove Books.

International Military Tribunal, Nuremberg (1948/1971). *Trial of the Major War Criminals before the International Military Tribunal, Nuremberg, 14 November 1945 - 1 October 1946* [42 volumes]. New York: AMS Press.

International Military Tribunal (1949). *Trials of War Criminals Before the Nuremberg Military Tribunals under Control Council Law No. 10*, Vol. IV, Washington, DC: U.S. Government Printing Office.

Jansen, Christian and Weckbecker, Arno (1992). *Der "Volksdeutsche Selbstschutz" in Polen 1939/40*. München: R. Oldenbourg Verlag, Schriftenreihe der Vierteljahrshefte für Zeitgeschichte Band 64.

Jolly, Cyril [ed.] (1956). *The Vengeance of Private Pooley*. London: Heinemann Ltd.

Jones, Dorothy V. (1991). *Code of Peace: Ethics and Security in the World of the Warlord States*. Chicago: University of Chicago Press.

Jones, Edgar L. (1956). "One War is Enough", *Atlantic Monthly*, February, pp. 48-53.

Jones, Nigel H. (1987). *Hitler's Heralds: The Story of the Freikorps, 1918 - 1923*. New York: Dorset Press.

Judt, Tony [ed.] (1989). *Resistance and Revolution in Mediterranean Europe, 1939-1948*. London: Routledge.

Jurado, Carlos C. and Lyles, Kevin (1983). *Foreign Volunteers of the Wehrmacht 1941-1945*. London: Osprey Publishing.

Jurado, Carlos C. and Hannon, Paul (1985). Resistance Warfare 1940-1945. London: Osprey Publishing.

Kaczmarek, Kazimierz (1978). *Druga Armia Wojska Polskiego*. Warszawa: Wydawnictwo Ministerstwa Obrony Narodowej.

Karsten, Peter (1978). *Law, Soldiers, and Combat* (Contributions in Legal Studies, Number 3). Westport, CT: Greenwood Publishing Group.

Katz, Fred E. (1993). *Ordinary People and Extraordinary Evil: A Report on the Beguilings of Evil*. Albany, NY: State University Press of New York.

Kavanaugh, Kevin P. (1996). "An Ethical Analysis of a Massacre and a Trial" (graduate paper downloaded from Internet).

Keegan, John (1970). *Waffen SS - the Asphalt Soldiers*. New York: Ballantine Books.

Kelley, Frederic J. (1974). *Man before God: Thomas Merton on Social Responsibility*. Garden City, NY: Doubleday and Company.

Kelly, Geffrey B. and Nelson, F. Burton [eds.] (1995). *A Testament to Freedom: the Essential Writings of Dietrich Bonhoeffer*. San Francisco: HarperCollins Publishers.

Kelman, Herbert C. and Hamilton, V. Lee (1989). *Crimes of Obedience*. New Haven, CT: Yale University Press.

Kennedy, R.M. (1954). *German Anti-Guerilla Operations in the Balkans, 1941-1944*. Washington, DC: Department of the Army.

Kern, Erich (1948). *Der Grosse Rausch: Russlandfeldzug 1941-1945*. Zurich: Thomas Verlag.

Kladov, Ignatii F. et. al. (1944). *The People's Verdict: A Full Report of the Proceedings at the Krasnodar (July 1943) and Kharkov (December 1943) German Atrocity Trials*. London: Hutchinson.

Klausch, Hans-Peter (1993). *Antifaschisten in SS-Uniform: Schicksal und Widerstand der deutschen politischen KZ-Häftlinge, Zuchthaus- und Wehrmachtgefangenen in der SS-Sonderformation Dirlewanger*. Bremen: Edition Temmen.

Klee, Ernst, Dressen, Willi, and Riess, Volker [eds.] (1991). *"The Good Old Days": The Holocaust as seen by its Perpetrators and Bystanders*. New York: The Free Press.

Klietmann, Dr. Kurt-Georg (1965). *Die Waffen-SS: eine Dokumentation*. Osnabrück: Verlag "Der Freiwillige".

Kmiecik, Edward (1972). *Berlinska Victoria*. Warszawa: Wydawnictwo "Ruch".

Koehl, Robert L. (1983). *The Black Corps: The Structure and Power Struggles of the Nazi SS*. Madison, WI: University of Wisconsin Press.

Kogon, Eugen; Langbein, Hermann and Rückerl, Adalbert [eds.] (1993*). Nazi Mass Murder : A Documentary History of the Use of Poison Gas*. New Haven, CT: Yale University Press.

Komitee der Antifaschistischen Widerstandskämpfer in der Deutschen Demokratischen Republik (1960). *SS im Einsatz: Eine Dokumentation über die Verbrechen der SS*. Berlin: Kongress Verlag.

Korman, Aleksander (1990). *Nieukarane zbrodnie SS-Galizien z lat 1943-1945: Chodaczow Wielki, Huta Pieniacka, Podkamie'n, Wicy'n i inne miejscowo'sci*. London: Kolo Lwowian.

Kosicki, Jerzy and Koslowski, Waclaw (1955*). Bibliografia Pismiennictwa Polskiego zu lata 1944-1953 O Hitlerowskich Zbrodniach Wojennych*. Warszawa: Wydawnictwo Prawnicze.

Krätschmer, Ernst-Gunther (1982). *Die Ritterkreuztrager der Waffen-SS*. Preussisch Oldendorf: Verlag K. W. Schütz.

Krausnick, Helmut et.al. (1968). *Anatomy of the SS State*. New York: Walker & Co.

Krausnick, Helmut and Wilhelm, Hans-Heinrich (1981). *Die Truppe des Weltanschauungskrieges: Die Einsatzgruppen der Sicherheitspolizei und des SD, 1938-1942*. Stuttgart: Deutsche Verlags-Anstalt.

Kruuse, Jens (1969). *Oradour-sur-Glane*. Paris: Fayard.

Kumm, Otto (1978). *Vorwärts Prinz Eugen: Geschichte der 7.SS-Freiwilligen-Division "Prinz Eugen"*. Osnabrück: Munin Verlag.

Kunz, Wolfgang (1967). *Der Fall Marzabotto: Analyse eine Kriegsverbrecherprozesses*. Würzburg: Holzner-Verlag.

Kurzman, Dan (1976). *The Bravest Battle: The 28 days of the Warsaw Ghetto Uprising*. Los Angeles: Pinnacle Books.

Landwehr, Richard (1985). *Fighting for Freedom: The Ukrainian Volunteer Division of the Waffen-SS*. Silver Spring, MD: Bibliophile Legion Books.

Landwehr, Richard (1987). *Italian Volunteers of the Waffen-SS*. Glendale, OR: Siegrunen.

Landwehr, Richard (1988). *Hungarian Volunteers of the Waffen-SS*. Brookings, OR: Bibliophile Legion Books.

Landwehr, Richard (1989). *Charlemagne's Legionnaires: French Volunteers of the Waffen-SS, 1943-1945*. Silver Spring, MD: Bibliophile Legion Books.

Lappas, Takes (1945). *He sphage tou Distomo*. Athens.

Lappin, Eleonore (2004). *Die Rolle der Waffen-SS beim Zwangsarbeitseinsatz Ungarischer Juden im Gau Steiermark und bei den Todesmärschen ins KZ Mauthausen (1944/45)*. In: Dokumentationsarchiv des österreichischen Widerstandes, Jahrbuch 2004, Wien, pp. 77-112.

Large, David C. (1987). "Reckoning with the past: the HIAG of the Waffen-SS and the politics of rehabilitation in the Bonn Republic, 1950-1961," *Journal of Modern History*, vol. 59, March, pp. 79-113.

Lauterbach, Richard E. (1945). "How the Russians try Nazi Criminals: Kharkov Trial," *Harper's Magazine*, vol. 190, June, pp. 658-664.

Lazzero, Ricciotti (1982). *Le SS Italiane*. Milano: Rizzoli.

Lee, Martin A. (1997). *The Beast Reawakens*. Boston: Little, Brown and Co.

Lehmann, Rudolf (1977 - 1987). *Die Liebstandarte* [5 volumes]. Osnabrück: Munin Verlag.

Lepre, George (1997). *Himmler's Bosnian Division: The Waffen-SS Handschar Division 1943-1945*. Atglen, PA: Schiffer Military History.

Leszczynski, Kasimierz [ed.] (1963). *Fall 9: Das Urteil im SS-Einsatzgruppenprozess, gefällt am 10. April 1948 in Nürnberg von Militärgerichtshof II der Vereinigten Staaten von Amerika*. Berlin: Rütten und Loenig.

Levi, Primo (1986). *The Drowned and the Saved*. New York: Summit Books.

Lewis, John R. (1979). *Uncertain Judgement: A Bibliography of War Crimes Trials*. Santa Barbara, CA: ABC-Clio.

Lewis, Rand C. (1990). *Right-wing Extremism in West Germany, 1945-1989: A Nazi Legacy*. Ph.D. Thesis, University of Idaho.

Lifton, Robert J. (1961). *Thought Reform and the Psychology of Totalism: a study of "brainwashing" in China*. New York: W.W. Norton & Co.

Lifton, Robert J. (1986). *The Nazi Doctors: Medical Killing and the Psychology of Genocide*. London: MacMillan Publishing.

Lifton, Robert J. and Markusen, Eric (1990). *The Genocidal Metality: Nazi Holocaust and Nuclear Threat*. New York: Basic Books.

Linenthal, Edward T. and Engelhardt, Tom [eds.] (1996). *History Wars: the Enola Gay and Other Battles for the American Past*. New York: Henry Holt & Co.

Lippman, Matthew (1995). *War Crimes: American Prosecutions of Nazi Military Officers*. *Tuoro International Law Review*, vol. 6, no. 1, p. 263 - 374.

Lipstadt, Deborah (1993). *Denying the Holocaust: The Growing Assault on Truth and Memory*. New York: The Free Press.

Littell, Franklin H. [ed.] (1997). *Hyping the Holocaust: Scholars answer Goldhagen*. Merion Westfield Press International.

Littlejohn, David (1972). *The Patriotic Traitors: A History of Collaboration in German-occupied Europe 1940-1945*. London: Heinemann.

Logusz, Michael O. (1997). *Galicia Division: The Waffen-SS 14th Grenadier Division 1943-1945*. Atglen, PA: Schiffer Military History.

Long, Wellington (1968). *The New Nazis of Germany*. Philadelphia, PA: Chilton Book Company.

Lovecraft, Howard P. (1976). *Selected Letters 1934-1937*. Sauk City, WI: Arkham House Publishers.

Löwenthal, Dr. Zdenko (1957). *Savez jevrejskih opstina Jugoslavije*. Belgrade: Federation of Jewish Communities of the Federative People's Republic of Yugoslavia.

Lozowick, Yaacov (1987). "Rollbahn Mord: The Early Activities of Einsatzgruppe C," *Holocaust and Genocide Studies*, vol. 2, no. 2, pp. 221-241.

Luczak, Czeslaw (1968). "Aktion Warschau: plunder of Polish property by Heinz Reinefarth's detachments in Warsaw during the Uprising," *Polish Western Affairs* 9(1), pp. 163-166.

Lukas, Richard C. (1990). *Forgotten Holocaust: The Poles under German Occupation 1939 - 1944*. New York: Hippocrene Books.

Luther, Craig W.H. (1987). *Blood and Honor: The History of the 12th SS Panzer Division "Hitler Youth", 1943-1945*. San Jose, CA: R. J. Bender Publishing.

MacDonald, B.J.S. (1954). *The Trial of Kurt Meyer*. Toronto: Clarke, Irwin & Company, Ltd.

Mackness, Robin (1988). *Massacre at Oradour*. New York: Random House.

MacLean, French (1998). *The Cruel Hunters: SS-Sonderkommando Dirlewanger, Hitler's most notorious anti-partisan unit*. Atglen, PA: Schiffer Military History.

MacLean, French (1999a). *The Camp Men: the SS Officers who ran the Nazi Concentration Camp System*. Atglen, PA: Schiffer Military History.

MacLean, French (1999b). *The Field Men: the SS Officers who led the Einsatzkommandos - the Nazi Mobile Killing Units*. Atglen, PA: Schiffer Publishing.

Madeja, W. Victor (1985). *German Army Order of Battle: Field Army and Officer Corps, 1939-1945*. Allentown, PA: Game Publishing Company.

Madeja, W. Victor (1990). *Russo-German War: Balkans (November 1940 - November 1944)*. Allentown, PA: Valor Publishing.

Madeja, W. Victor (1992). *Hitler's Elite Guard - between Fascism and Genocide*. Allentown, PA: Valor Publishing.

Maier, Charles S. (1988). *The Unmasterable Past: History, Holocaust, and German National Identity*. Cambridge, MA: Harvard University Press.

Majewski, Ryszard (1977). *Waffen SS: Mity i rzeczywistosc*. Wroclaw: Zaklad Narodowy Imienia Ossolinskich Wydawnictwo.

Manvell, Roger (1969). *SS and Gestapo - rule by terror*. New York: Ballantine Books.

Margolian, Howard (1998). *Conduct Unbecoming: the Story of the Murder of Canadian Prisoners of War in Normandy*. Toronto: University of Toronto Press.

Massara, Enrico (1984). *Antologia dell'antifascismo e della Resistenza novarese: uomini ed episodi della lotta di liberazione*. Milan: n.p.

Mayda, Giuseppe (1978). *Ebrei sotto Salo: La persecuzione antisemita 1943-1945*. Milan: Feltrinelli Editore.

Mazower, Mark (1993). *Inside Hitler's Greece: The Experience of Occupation, 1941-1944*. New Haven, CT: Yale University Press.

Megargee, E.A. (1984). "Aggression and Violence". In: Adams, H.E. and Sutker, P.B. [eds.], *Comprehensive Handbook of Psychopathology*, New York: Plenum Publishing, pp. 523 - 548.

Merton, Thomas (1961). *New Seeds of Contemplation*. New York: New Directions Publishing Corporation.

Merton, Thomas (1964a). *Raids on the Unspeakable*. New York: New Directions Publishing Corporation.

Merton, Thomas (1964b). *Seeds of Destruction* (4th printing). New York: Farrar, Straus & Giroux.

Merton, Thomas (1968). *Faith and Violence: Christian Teaching and Christian Practice*. Notre Dame, IN: University of Notre Dame Press.

Merton, Thomas (1976). *Disputed Questions*. New York: Farrar, Strauss and Giroux.

Messenger, Charles (1988). *Hitler's Gladiator: The Life and Times of Oberstgruppenfuhrer and Panzergeneral-Oberst der Waffen-SS Sepp Dietrich*. London: Brassey's Defense Publishers.

Meyer, Brün [ed.] (1987). *Dienstaltersliste der Waffen-SS: SS-Obergruppenführer bis SS-Hauptsturmführer, Stand vom 1. Juli 1944*. Osnabrück: Biblio Verlag.

Meyer, Hubert (1982). *Kriegsgeschichte der 12. SS-Panzerdivision "Hitlerjugend"* [2 volumes]. Osnabrück: Munin Verlag.

Meyer, Kurt (1994). *Grenadiers*. Winnipeg, Canada: J.J. Fedorowicz Publishing.

Milazzo, Matteo J. (1975). *The Chetnik Movement and the Yugoslav Resistance*. Baltimore, MD: Johns Hopkins University Press.

de Mildt, Dick (1996). *In the Name of the People: Perpetrators of Genocide in the Reflection of their Post-war Prosecution in West Germany - the 'Euthanasia' and 'Aktion Reinhard' Trial Cases*. The Hague: Martinus Nijhoff Publishers.

Miller, Stuart C. (1982). *"Benevolent Assimilation": The American Conquest of the Philippines, 1899-1903*. New Haven, CT: Yale University Press.

Militärbefehlshaber in Frankreich - Ia/MilGeo Wehrmacht (1943). *Ortschaftsverzeichnis Frankreich mit übersichtskarte*. Paris.

Militärgeographische Angaben uber das Europäische Russland: Mappe B - Die Baltischen Länder [Estland, Lettland, Litauen] (1941). Berlin: Generalstab des Heeres, Abteilung fur Kriegskarten und Vermessungswesen.

Militärgeographische Angaben uber das Europäische Russland: Mappe C - Gebiet Leningrad (1941). Berlin: Generalstab des Heeres, Abteilung fur Kriegskarten und Vermessungswesen.

Militärgeographische Angaben uber das Europäische Russland: Mappe E - Weissrussland (1941). Berlin: Generalstab des Heeres, Abteilung fur Kriegskarten und Vermessungswesen.

Militärgeographische Angaben uber das Europäische Russland: Mappe F - Ukraine mit Moldaurepublik und Krim (1941). Berlin: Generalstab des Heeres, Abteilung fur Kriegskarten und Vermessungswesen.

Militärgeographische Angaben uber das Europäische Russland: Mappe G - Zentral Russland [ohne Moskau] (1941). Berlin: Generalstab des Heeres, Abteilung fur Kriegskarten und Vermessungswesen.

Militärgeographische Beschreibung von Frankreich - Teile 1, 2 & 4 - (1940). Berlin: Generalstab des Heeres, Abteilung fur Kriegskarten und Vermessungswesen.

Militärgeographische Beschreibung von Griechenland (1941). Berlin: Generalstab des Heeres, Abteilung fur Kriegskarten und Vermessungswesen.

Militärgeographische Beschreibung von Jugoslawien (1940). Berlin: Generalstab des Heeres, Abteilung fur Kriegskarten und Vermessungswesen.

Militärgeographische Beschreibung von Polen (1939). Berlin: Generalstab des Heeres, 9 Abteilung.

Militärgeographischer Uberblick über Belgien und angrenzende Gebiete, 2. Auflage (1940). Berlin: Generalstab des Heeres, Abteilung fur Kriegskarten und Vermessungswesen.

Militärgeographischer Uberblick über die Niederlande (1939). Berlin: Generalstab des Heeres, Abteilung fur Kriegskarten und Vermessungswesen.

Mocq, Jean-Marie (1984). *Ascq, 1er Avril 1944: La longue marche du souvenir.* Dunkerque: Editions des Beffrois.

Mocq, Jean-Marie (1994). *La 12. SS Panzer-Division: massacre Ascq, cite martyre.* Bayeux: Editions Heimdal.

Moczarski, Kazimierz (1981). *Conversations with an Executioner.* Englewood Cliffs, NJ: Prentice-Hall.

Mosse, George L. (1975). *The Nationalization of the Masses.* New York: Meridian Press.

Mouret, G. (1958). *Oradour: le crime, le proces.* Paris: Plon.

Munoz, Antonio J. (1991). *Forgotten Legions: Obscure Combat Formations of the Waffen-SS.* Boulder, CO: Paladin Press.

Munoz, Antonio J. (1999). *The Iron Fist Division: A Combat History of the 17. SS Panzergrenadier Division "Goetz von Berlichingen", 1943-1945.* Bayside, NY: Axis Europa.

Musmanno, Michael A. (1961). *The Eichmann Kommandos.* Philadelphia: Macrae Smith.

Musso, Fernand (1980). *Apres le raz de maree: temoignage du prefet de Correze sur le massacre de Maille.* Treillieres: Pierre Gauthier Editeur.

Nationalrat der Nationalen Front des Demokratischen Deutschland (1965). *Braunbuch: Kriegs- und Naziverbrecher in der Bundesrepublik.* Berlin: Staatsverlag der DDR.

Nelson, Gail H. (1972). *The Molding of Personality: SS Indoctrination and Training Techniques.* M.A. thesis, University of Colorado at Boulder.

Neumann, Inge S. (1951). *European War Crimes Trials: A Bibliography.* Westport, CT: Greenwood Press Publishers.

Neusner, Jacob (1997). *Hype, Hysteria and Hate the Hun: the latest pseudo-scholarship from Harvard.* Article posted on the Jewish Communication Newstand (http://www.jcn18.com).

Nicholas, Lynn H. (1994). *The Rape of Europa: The Fate of Europe's Treasures in the Third Reich and the Second World War.* New York: Alfred A. Knopf.

Niebuhr, Reinhold (1949a). *The Nature and Destiny of Man: A Christian Interpretation.* New York: Charles Scribner's Sons.

Niebuhr, Reinhold (1949b). *Faith and History: A Comparison of Christian and Modern Views of History.* New York: Charles Scribner's Sons.

Niebuhr, Reinhold (1972). *The Children of Light and the Children of Darkness: A Vindication of Democracy and a Critique of its Traditional Defense.* New York: Charles Scribner's Sons.

Olsen, Jack (1968). *Silence on Monte Sole.* New York: G.P. Putnam's Sons.

Ortner, Christian S. (1986). *Marzabotto: the crimes of Walter Reder - SS-Sturmbannfuhrer.* Wien: Dokumentationsarchiv des österreichischen Widerstandes.

"Outrage over SS Pensions," *Response,* vol. 18, nos. 1/2, Spring-Summer, 1997.

Pallud, Jean-Paul (1984). *Battle of the Bulge: Then and Now.* London: Battle of Britain International Ltd.

Pallud, Jean-Paul (1987). *Ardennes 1944: Peiper and Skorzeny.* London: Osprey Publishing Ltd.

Pauchou, Guy (1945). *Oradour-sur-Glane: Vision d'epouvante.* Limoges: Charles Lavauzelle et Cie.

Payon, Abbe Andre (1945). *Un Village martyr, Maille: recit du massacre du 25 aout 1944.* Tours: Arrault et Cie.

Peers, William R. (1970). *Report of the Department of the Army Review of the Preliminary Investigation into the My Lai Incident* [4 volumes]. Washington, DC: U.S. Government Printing Office.

Perrigault, Jean-Claude and Meister, Rolf (2004). *Götz von Berlichingen*, Volume 1. Bayeux: Editions Heimdal.

Philippine-American War Centennial Initiative (1998). *Chronology of Events Leading to the Philippine-American War.* Internet document formerly available at www.phil-am-war.org.

Philippine-American War Centennial Initiative (1998). *Parallels to the Vietnam War - America's 'First Vietnam': A Forgotten Experience.* Internet document available at www.phil-am-war.org.

Phillips, Raymond [ed.] (1949). *Trial of Josef Kramer and forty-four others (the Belsen Trial).* London: W. Hodge Publishers.

Planheft Italien (1943). Berlin: Generalstab des Heeres, Abteilung fur Kriegskarten und Vermessungswesen.

Powell, John W. (1981). "A hidden chapter in history", *Bulletin of the Atomic Scientists,* October, pp. 43-52.

Poznanski, Stanislaw [ed.] (1963). *Struggle, Death, Memory, 1939-1945*. Warsaw: Council for the Preservation of the Monuments of Struggle and Martyrdom.

Presser, Jacob (1969). *The Destruction of the Dutch Jews*. New York: E.P. Dutton and Co., Inc.

Preradovich, Nikolaus von (1980). *Osterreichs Höhere SS-Führer*. Berg am See: Kurt Vowinckel Verlag.

Quarrie, Bruce (1986). *Hitler's Samurai: The Waffen-SS in action*. Wellingborough: Patrick Stephens.

Quarrie, Bruce (1987). *Hitler's Teutonic Knights: SS Panzers in action*. Wellingborough: Patrick Stephens Ltd.

Rahner, Karl and Vorgrimler, Herbert (1985). *Dictionary of Theology, 2nd Edition*. New York: Crossroad Publishing Company.

Ready, J. Lee (1987). *The Forgotten Axis: Germany's Partners and Foreign Volunteers in WWII*. Jefferson, NC: MacFarland and Co., Inc.

Reck-Malleczewen, Friedrich (1947). *Tagebuch eines Verzweifelten*. Lorch/Wurttemberg: Burger.

Rees, Philip (1991). *Biographical Dictionary of the Extreme Right Since 1890*. New York: Simon and Schuster.

Reich, Wilhelm (1949). *Character Analysis*. New York: Orgone Institute Press.

Reich, Wilhelm (1933/1970). *The Mass Psychology of Fascism*. New York: Farrar, Straus & Giroux.

Reitlinger, Gerald (1957). *The SS: Alibi of a Nation, 1922-1945*. New York: Viking Press.

Reitlinger, Gerald (1961). *The Final Solution: the Attempt to Exterminate the Jews of Europe, 1939-1945*. New York: A.S. Barnes & Co.

Reynolds, Michael (1995). *The Devil's Adjutant: Jochen Peiper, Panzer Leader*. New York: Sarpedon.

Roeder, George H. (1993). *The Censored War: American Visual Experience During World War Two*. New Haven, CT: Yale University Press.

Röhr, Werner; Heckert, Elke; Gottberg, Bernd; Wenzel, Jutta and Grünthal, Heide-Marie, (1989). *Die faschistische Okkupationspolitik in Polen (1939-1945)*. Berlin: VEB Deutscher Verlag der Wissenschaften.

Rosenbaum, Alan S. (1993). *Prosecuting Nazi War Criminals*. Boulder, CO: Westview Press.

Rossino, A.B. (1997). "Destructive impulses: German soldiers and the conquest of Poland". *Holocaust and Genocide Studies*, vol. 11, no. 3, pp. 351 - 365.

Rostowski, Dieter (1980). "SS-Verbrechen an Verwundeten der 2. Polnischen Armee Ende 1945," *Militärgeschichte* 19 (4), pp. 454-457.

Royaume de Belgique, Ministere de la Justice, Commission des Crimes de Guerre (1948). *Les Crimes de Guerre commis pendant la contre-offensive de von Runstedt dans les Ardennes, Decembre 1944 - Janvier 1945*. Liege: Georges Thone.

Rückerl, Adalbert (1980). *The Investigation of Nazi Crimes, 1945-1978*. Hamden, CT: Archon Books.

Russell, Edward F.L. (1954/1970). *The Scourge of the Swastika -- A Short History of Nazi War Crimes*. London: Cassell and Company/Corgi Books.

Rüter, C.F. and de Mildt, D.W. (1998). *Die westdeutschen Strafverfahren wegen nationalsozialistischer Tötungsverbrechen 1945-1997:*
Eine systematische Verfahrensbeschreibung mit Karten und Registern. Amsterdam: APA Holland University Press.

Rüter-Ehlermann, A.L.; Rüter, C.F.; Fuchs, H.H. and Sangel-Grande, I. [eds.] (1968-1981). *Justiz und NS-Verbrechen : Sammlung deutscher Strafurteile wegen Nationalsozialistischer Tötungsverbrechen 1945 - 1966* [22 volumes]. Amsterdam, The Netherlands: University Press Amsterdam.

Sabrin, B.F. [ed.] (1991). *Alliance for Murder: The Nazi-Ukrainian Nationalist Partnership in Genocide*. New York: Sarpedon Publishers.

Sauer, Karl (1977). *Die Verbrechen der Waffen-SS: Eine Dokumentation Herausgegeben im Auftrag des Präsidiums der VVN-Bund der Antifaschisten*. Frankfurt/Main: Röderberg Verlag.

Sayer, Ian and Botting, Douglas (1989). *Hitler's Last General --- The Case Against Wilhelm Mohnke*. London: Bantam Press.

Schott, Joseph L. (1964). *The Ordeal of Samar*. Indianapolis, IN: Bobbs-Merrill Publishing.

Schreiber, Gerhard (1996). *Deutsche Kriegsverbrechen in Italien - Täter, Opfer. Strafverfolgung*. München: C.H. Beck Verlag.

Schröder, Gerhard [ed.] (1979). *Die SS - Ein 4. Wehrmachtsteil?* München: Pressedienst Demokratische Initiative.

Schulze-Kossens, Richard (1982). *Militärischer Führernachwuchs der Waffen-SS: die Junkerschulen*. Osnabrück: Munin Verlag.

Sereny, Gitta (1974). *Into that Darkness: from mercy killing to mass murder*. London: Andre Deutsch.

Shermer, Michael (1994). "Proving the Holocaust: The refutation of revisionism and the restoration of history", Skeptic, vol. 2, no. 4, pp. 32-57.

Siegrunen magazine (edited by Richard Landwehr), Whole Numbers 42, 53, 54, and 57.

Simpson, Christopher (1988). *Blowback: America's Recruitment of Nazis and its Effects on the Cold War.* New York: Collier Books.

Soviet Government Statement on Nazi Atrocities (1946). London: Hutchinson.

Spector, Shmuel (1990). "Aktion 1005 -- Effacing the Murder of Millions," *Holocaust and Genocide Studies*, vol. 5, no. 2, pp. 157-173.

Staub, Ervin (1989). *The roots of evil: the origins of genocide and other group violence.* Cambridge: Cambridge University Press.

Stein, George H. (1966). *The Waffen SS - Hitler's Elite Guard at War, 1939-1945.* Ithaca, NY: Cornell University Press.

Steiner, Felix (1958). *Die Freiwilligen der Waffen-SS: Idee und Opfergang.* Gottingen: Plesse Verlag.

Steiner, Felix (1963). *Die Armee der Geachteten.* Gottingen: Plesse Verlag.

Stern, Robert C. (1978). *SS Armor: A Pictorial History of the Armored Formations of the Waffen-SS.* Warren, MI: Squadron/Signal Publications.

Stöber, Hans (1966). *Die Eiserne Faust: Bildband und Chronik der 17. SS-Panzergrenadier Division "Götz von Berlichingen".* Neckargemünd: Kurt Vowinckel Verlag.

Strassner, Peter (1968). *Europäische Freiwillige: Die Geschichte der 5. SS-Panzer-Division "Wiking".* Osnabrück: Munin-Verlag, GmbH.

Stroop, Jürgen (1979). *The Stroop Report: The Jewish Quarter of Warsaw is No More!* New York: Pantheon Books.

Sydnor, Charles W. (1973). "The history of the SS-Totenkopfdivision and the post-war mythology of the Waffen-SS," *Central European History*, VI, pp. 339 - 362.

Sydnor, Charles W. (1977). *Soldiers of Destruction: The SS Death's Head Division, 1933-1945.* Princeton, NJ: Princeton University Press.

Taege, Herbert (1981). *Wo ist Kain? - Enthüllungen und Dokumente zum Komplex Tulle + Oradour.* Lindhorst: Askania Verlag.

Taege, Herbert (1985). *Wo ist Abel? - weitere Enthüllungen und Dokumente zum Komplex Tulle + Oradour.* Lindhorst: Askania Verlag.

Tanaka, Yuki (1998). *Hidden Horrors: Japanese War Crimes in WWII.* Boulder, CO: Westview Press.

Tesher, Ellie (1997). "How Nazi War Criminals Got into Canada". *The Toronto Star* [Wednesday, November 12]

Tessin, George. (1979-1988). *Verbande and Truppen der Deutschen Wehrmacht und Waffen SS im Zweiten Weltkrieg 1939-1945* [15 volumes]. Osnabrück: Biblio Verlag.

The SS (1988). Alexandria, VA: Time-Life Books.

Theweleit, Klaus (1987). *Male Fantasies, volume 1: women, floods, bodies, history.* Minneapolis: University of Minnesota Press.

Theweleit, Klaus (1989). *Male Fantasies, volume 2: male bodies - psychoanalyzing the white terror.* Minneapolis: University of Minnesota Press.

Thiele, Karl H. (1996). *Beyond "Monsters" and "Clowns" - The Combat SS, De-Mythologizing Five Decades of German Elite Formations.* Lanham, MD: University Press of America, Inc.

Thomas, Nigel; Abbott, Peter and Chappell, Mike (1983). *Partisan Warfare 1941-1945.* London: Osprey Publishing Ltd.

Tiemann, Ralf (1993). *Der Malmedyprozess.* Coburg: K.W. Schütz Verlag.

Totten, S.; Parsons, W.S. and Charney, I.W. [eds.] (1995). *Genocide in the Twentieth Century: Critical Essays and Eyewitness Accounts.* New York: Garland Publishing.

Tutorow, Norman E. [ed.] (1986). *War Crimes, War Criminals, and War Crimes Trials: An annotated bibliography and Sourcebook.* New York: Greenwood Press.

United Nations War Crimes Commission (1944-1947). *Charges by the European and United States Governments against German, Italian and Japanese War Criminals* [41 volumes]. London: HMPO.

United Nations War Crimes Commission (1944-1948). *List of War Criminals* [60 volumes]. London: UNWCC.

United Nations War Crimes Commission (1947-1949). *Law Reports of Trials of War Criminals, selected and prepared by the UNWCC*

[15 volumes]. London: HMPO.

United States Board on Geographical Names (1944). *Gazetteer to maps of France, Belgium and Holland.* Washington, DC: U.S. Army Corps of Engineers (Army Map Service).

United States Board on Geographical Names (1954). *Gazetteer to AMS 1:50,000 Maps of Yugoslavia.* Washington, DC: U.S. Army Corps of Engineers (Army Map Service).

United States Board on Geographical Names (1955). *Gazetteer to AMS 1:25,000 Maps of Czechoslovakia.* Washington, DC: U.S. Army Corps of Engineers (Army Map Service).

United States Board on Geographical Names (1955). *Gazetteer -- Poland [2 volumes].* Washington, DC: U.S. Army Corps of Engineers (Army Map Service).

United States Board on Geographical Names (1956). *Gazetteer #23 -- Italy and Associated Areas.* Washington, DC: U.S. Army Corps of Engineers (Army Map Service).

United States Board on Geographical Names (1960). *Gazetteer -- Greece.* Washington, DC: Central Intelligence Agency.

United States Board on Geographical Names (1970). *Gazetteer #42 -- U.S.S.R.* [7 volumes]. Washington, DC: U.S. Government Printing Office.

United States Board on Geographical Names (1983). *Gazetteer of Yugoslavia, 2nd Edition* [2 volumes]. Washington, DC: U.S. Defense Mapping Agency.

United States Board on Geographical Names (1993). *Gazetteer of Hungary.* Washington, DC: U.S. Defense Mapping Agency.

United States Congress, Senate (1949). *Malmedy Massacre Investigation: Hearings before a Subcommittee of the Committee on Armed Services, U.S. Senate, Pursuant to Senate Resolution 42, 81st Congress, 1st Session.* Washington, DC: U.S. Government Printing Office.

United States Holocaust Memorial Museum (1994). *Genocide in Yugoslavia during the Holocaust.*

U.S. Office of United States Chief Counsel for Prosecution of Axis Criminality [Barrett, Roger W. and Jackson, William E. (eds.)] (1947). *Nazi Conspiracy and Aggression* [10 volumes]. Washington, DC: U.S. Government Printing Office.

Valland, Rose (1961). *Le Front de l'art.* Paris: Plon.

van der Heide, Albert (1994). "Nearly all of Putten's captives perished in labour camps," *Windmill Herald,* no. 766, October 23.

van Garsse, Dr. Yvan (1970). *Hungarian literature on War Crimes and Crimes against Humanity: Documentation on genocide, crimes against peace, crimes against humanity and war crimes.* Sint Niklaas Waas: Information Retrieval System.

Veale, F.J.P. (1968). *Advance to barbarism: the development of total warfare from Serajevo to Hiroshima.* London: Mitre.

von Krannhals, Hans (1964). *Die Warschauer Aufstand 1944.* Frankfurt/Main: Bernard und Graefe Verlag für Wehrwesen.

Vukcevich, Bosko S. (1990). *Diverse Forces in Yugoslavia, 1941-1945.* Los Angeles: Authors Unlimited.

Waite, Robert G.L. (1969). *Vanguard of Nazism: the Free Corps movement in postwar Germany, 1918 - 1923.* New York: W.W. Norton & Company, Inc.

Walther, Herbert (1990). *The Waffen SS: a pictorial documentation.* West Chester, PA: Schiffer Publications Ltd.

Wegner, Bernd (1990). *The Waffen SS.* London: Basil Blackwell.

Weidinger, Otto (1984). *Tulle and Oradour: a Franco-German Tragedy.* city?: publisher?

Weiner, Jan G. (1969). *The Assassination of Heydrich.* New York: Grossman Publishers.

Weingartner, James J. (1974). *Hitler's Guard: The Story of the Leibstandarte SS Adolf Hitler, 1933 - 1945.* Nashville, TN: Battery Press Inc.

Weingartner, James J. (1979). *Crossroads of Death: The Story of the Malmedy Massacre and Trial.* Berkeley, CA: University of California Press.

Weliczker, Leon (1946). *Brygada Smierci (Sonderkommando 1005) Pamietnik.* Lodz: Wydawnnictwa Centralnej Zydowskiej Komisji Historycznej przy Centralnym Komitecie Zydow Polskich, nr. 8.

Whistine, Bob (1998). "World War II veteran killed in action receives posthumous Purple Heart". Army News Service, press release dated 20 April.